▼ 作者简介

慧立（615—？），唐代僧，永徽元年敕任大慈恩寺翻经大德，后任太原寺主。彦悰，唐代僧，籍贯，生卒年均不详，贞观末年就学于玄奘大师之门，识量聪敏，博通群经，善属文章，长于著述，颇为同侪推重。著有《大唐京师寺录传》十卷等。

▼ 译者简介

王欣，世界史专业博士，现任教于西安电子科技大学外国语学院，硕士生导师；西北大学玄奘研究院特聘研究员。长期从事英美文学、跨文化比较及翻译研究。

大唐大慈恩寺三藏法师传

（汉英对照）

［唐］慧立　撰　彦悰　笺
王欣　译

陕西师范大学出版总社　西安

佛子，菩萨摩诃萨，有十种求法。何等为十？所谓直心求法，无有谄诳故。精进求法，远离懈漫故。一向求法，不惜身命故。为断一切众生烦恼求法，不为名利恭敬故。为饶益自他一切众生求法，不但自利故。为入智慧求法，不乐文字故。为出生死求法，不贪世乐故。为度众生求法，发菩提心故。为断一切众生疑求法，令无犹豫故。为满足佛法求法，不乐余乘故。是为十。若诸菩萨安住此法，则得不由他教一切佛法大智慧。

——《大方广佛华严经·卷第五十八·离世间品第三十八之六》

Great enlightening beings have ten kinds of quest for truth: quest for truth with a straightforward mind, being free from dishonesty; diligent quest for truth, being free from laziness; wholly devoted quest for truth, not begrudging their lives; quest for truth to destroy all sentient beings' afflictions, not doing it for fame, profit, or respect; quest for truth to benefit self and others, all sentient beings, not just helping themselves; quest for truth to enter knowledge and wisdom, not taking pleasure in literature; quest for truth to leave birth and death, not craving worldly pleasures; quest for truth to liberate sentient beings, engendering the determination for enlightenment; quest for truth to resolve the doubts of all sentient beings, to free them from vacillation; quest for truth to fulfill buddhahood, not being inclined to lesser aims. Based on these ten, enlightening beings can attain great knowledge of all elements of buddhahood without being instructed by another.

Chapter 38 Detachment from the World in The Flower Ornament Scripture

The following is a brief description of the *A Biography of the Tripitaka Master of the Great Ci'en Monastery of the Great Tang Dynasty*《大唐大慈恩寺三藏法师传》kept in the East Asian Library at Princeton University and the Shaanxi Provincial Library.

According to *Pulinsidun Daxue Tushuguan Cang Zhongwen Shanben Shumu* 《普林斯顿大学图书馆藏中文善本书目》(*Catalogue of the Chinese Rare Books in the Princeton University Library*), the *Qisha Canon* 碛砂藏 was engraved in Yanshengyuan of Pingjiang Prefecture 平江府碛砂延圣院 in the period of Song and Yuan dynasties (ca. 1231–1322). This collection totals 5,359 volumes. The format of binding is sutra binding. The collection is incomplete, with 1,479 titles, 6,014 *juan*, in 561 *han*(函， cases). It is a mixture of different editions, and hand-copied manuscripts. The frame is 25 centimeters high, with 6 columns in each half page and 17 characters in each column. The frame is single-lined.[1]

---

1 *Pulinsidun Daxue Tushuguan Cang Zhongwen Shanben Shumu*《普林斯顿大学图书馆藏中文善本书目》(*Catalogue of the Chinese Rare Books in the Princeton University Library*), Beijing: National Library of China Publishing House, 2017, volume 2, p.730.

A Biography of the Tripitaka Master of the Great Ci'en Monastery of the Great Tang Dynasty, in the *Qisha Canon* (1231 – 1322), engraved in the Yuan Dynasty, the East Asian Library, Princeton University. The East Asian Library keeps an almost complete set of Qisha Canon, totaling 1479 works, in 6014 fascicules. The front and back covers are made of beautiful silk brocade. They are well preserved. They are hand-written copies. The cataloging word in *Qianziwen*《千字文》(*A Thousand Word Reader*) is "you 右."
Courtesy of Professor Long Darui.

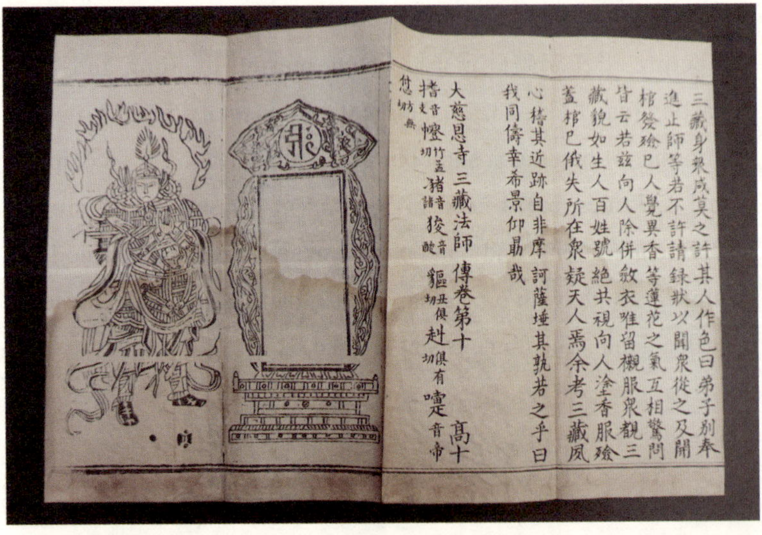

Woodcut illustration of image of Skanda (Weituo) on the last page to protect and preserve the teachings, of *A Biography of the Tripitaka Master of the Great Ci'en Monastery of the Great Tang Dynasty,* in the *Qisha Canon* , Princeton University Library. Courtesy of Professor Long Darui.

The *Qisha Canon* is the only collection preserved in Shaanxi Provincial Library which was printed in the period of the Song and Yuan dynasties (ca. 1231–1322). The Canon was engraved in the course of 91 years, crossing two dynasties. It totals 591 *han* (函, cases) and 6362 *juan*, compiling 1521 Buddhist scriptures from the Jin to Song dynasties (ca.266–1279). Among them, the complete sets of 5594 *juan* are currently preserved in Shaanxi Provincial Library.

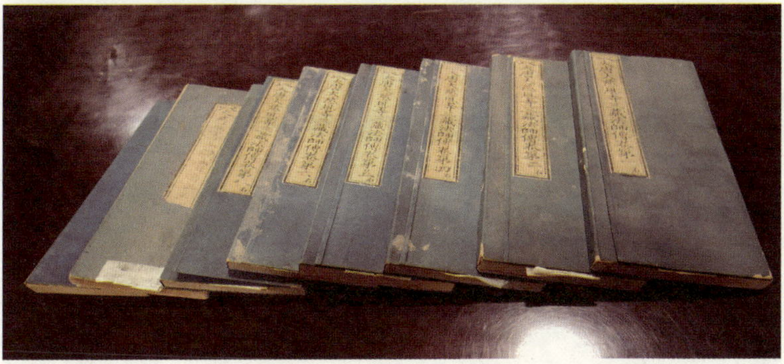

A Biography of the Tripitaka Master of the Great Ci'en Monastery of the Great Tang Dynasty, in the *Qisha Canon,* indigo paper as the cover, also cataloging word "you 右." The third and seventh fascicles have been lost. Courtesy of Shaanxi Provincial Library.

At the beginning of each *han*函, there is a frontispiece of woodcut illustration of Shakyamuni's preachings.

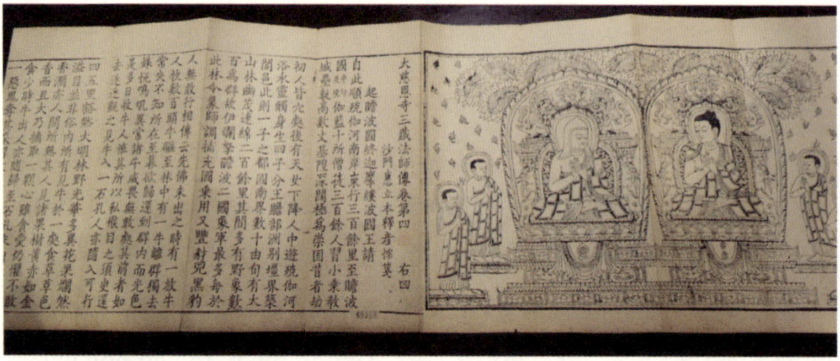

Frontispiece of woodcut illustration of the fourth fascicle of *A Biography of the Tripitaka Master of the Great Ci'en Monastery of the Great Tang Dynasty,* the *Qisha Canon,* courtesy of Shaanxi Provincial Library.

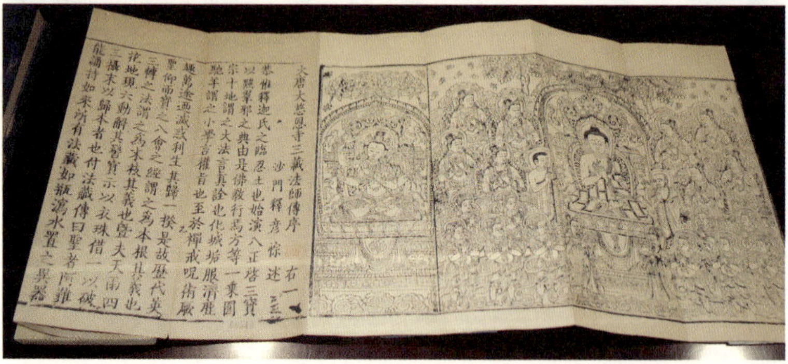

Frontispiece of woodcut illustration of the preface to *A Biography of the Tripitaka Master of the Great Ci'en Monastery of the Great Tang Dynasty,* the *Qisha Canon,* courtesy of Shaanxi Provincial Library.

前　言

中国世界史学界有一种被称作文明交往史观的理论，这种史观通过对人类古今历史现象和历史演进机制的综合考察，使我们发现文明交往广泛存在于各民族、各国家、各地域之间，也存在于同一地域内各地区、各领域、各阶层、各文化体系之间，进而认识到这种存在对一个地区、一个国家乃至整个人类社会众多历史现象和总体进程具有重要意义，由此得出结论：文明交往既是人类历史的核心，也是人类历史基本框架的支撑；既是人类历史发展的永恒动力，也是人类历史变革和社会进步的标尺；既是历史发展走向的主导因素，也是人类未来的希望所在。文明交往作为人类从古到今最基本的实践活动，是剖析人类历史内涵、理解人类历史动因、把握人类历史轨迹、展望人类未来趋势的一把金钥匙。

人类历史大约二百万年，人类文明史大约五千年。纵观这五千年的人类文明史可发现，人类的文明大致可划分为物质文明、制度文明和精神文明三大类型。在精神文明之中，既有理性领域的世俗精神文明，也有超越理性的神圣精神文明。自雅思贝尔斯所说的轴心时代之后，人类的精神文明逐渐形成印度婆罗门教文明、中国儒释道三教文明、欧洲基督教文明和以中东地区为主的伊斯兰教文明的四大文明区域，直到今天这四大文明区域依然是全球多元文明布局与交往框架的基本支撑。在这种文明格局与交往框架的形成过程中，无数的文化使者行走在不同文明区域之间，以其独特的付出为不同文明之间的交往做出了巨大的贡献。正是因为他们的努力，人类不同文明之间交往的大门才是敞开的，人类不同文明才得以保持交流互鉴、不断进步并呈日益会通的态势。玄奘，就是这种伟大的文化使者之一。

玄奘是中国唐代初期的一位僧人，其最辉煌的业绩：一是赴印取经，历时 17 年，沿丝绸之路走过 110 多个国家，所述经历形成《大唐西域记》，涉及 130 多个国家；二是回国后主持佛经翻译，历时 19 年，共译出印度佛教经典 1335 卷，超出四大译经家中其他三家所译经典之总和；三是在译经规制、政治支持、派系会通等方面为佛教经典在中国的生存与传播开辟了可靠的路径。对于取经和译经这两大业绩，我们可以分别从丝绸之路和中华文化这两个大的文化坐标来定位，从而得出两个基本结论：第一，玄奘是丝绸之路人类文明交往的杰出代表；第二，有组织成规模的佛经翻译活动，使玄奘成为是中华传统文化体系的主要塑造者之一。

今天我们回望丝绸之路的历史，那些穿梭其中的富商们已难知其名，尽管在历史上，商贸以及由此推动的物质文明交往曾经占据丝绸之路的主流；那些怀揣皇帝敕令沿丝绸之路远走他国的使节们很多消散在历史的烟尘中，尽管因为他们的努力而搭建了不同国家之间政治交往的纽带；那些沿丝绸之路远征的将士们也褪去了当初的威风，走下了历史的舞台；但像玄奘大师这样的文化使者，在当时的丝绸之路上是最清贫的一族，因为他们信仰的虔诚、信念的坚定、精神的崇高以及对人类精神文明传播的巨大影响而永远载入史册。纵观丝绸之路的历史，从精神文明交往的角度看，祆教、佛教、摩尼教、景教、伊斯兰教、犹太教，包括印度的婆罗门教和耆那教等，都是通过丝绸之路传入中国的。借助丝绸之路，希腊文化传播到西亚、中亚和南亚部分地区，印度婆罗门教传入中亚和东南亚地区，但历时最久、规模最大、影响最深的宗教文化传播还是佛教从印度向中国的传播。从两汉到两宋，在长达1000年的历史长河中，有史可考的至少有900多位僧人往来于丝绸之路，在唐中期时，已翻译了7000多卷经书，谱写出丝绸之路文明交往史最辉煌的一页。玄奘以其十七载的丝路跋涉，取得佛教典籍657部，途中既能勤奋学习、广泛交流，也能深入考察、翔实记录，堪称丝绸之路佛教传播伟业的第一代表。

佛教向中国的传播，不但是丝绸之路人类文明交往史上最灿烂的篇章，也是中华传统文化不断丰富的主要推动力量。中华文化源远流长，号称上下五千年，并以其强烈的个性而自成体系，影响整个东亚世界，也因此形成超强的文化自信，但从未停止吸收外来文化，其中最重要的有两次，一次是印度佛教文化的输入，一次是西方文化的输入，这两次文化输入都影响了中华文化的结构，丰富了中华文化的内涵，也因此而涵养了中华民族的精神，完善了中华传统文化的体系。佛教输入前，中国文化经历了从春秋战国时期的百家争鸣，到秦汉时期相继出现的法家独尊、道家独尊和儒家独尊的过程；但到汉末前后，一家独尊的文化格局在中国仍然难以维系。佛教正是在这个时候进入中国。从思想内涵来看，无论是百家争鸣，还是一家独尊，中国的先哲们似乎主要在关注人的社会性，致力于人与人之间关系的处理，尤其是儒、法、墨、兵、纵横诸家，甚至包括崇尚自然、批判社会的道家，应对社会问题的倾向均十分鲜明。文化的单向与单薄十分明显。从汉魏到唐宋，在长达1000年的历史上，舍身求法者不绝于途，印度佛典源源不断地输入中国，这些经典以其对精神世界的关注、对命运的反思、对救度的承担、对宇宙时空的探索、对人性及其终极归宿的全新解读，而散发着前所未有的魅力，势不可挡地挤入曾经百家争鸣的中国文化舞台。中国文化在筛选和融合中，逐渐形成儒佛道三家并立互补的文化新格局。佛教文化的嵌入对中华文化结构的丰富是无数高僧大德不懈努力的结果，尤其是经典的翻译、宗派的创立、不同思想的融会、政教关系的和谐等。在这些方面，玄奘都做出了重大的贡献，堪称中国特色的佛教文化的主要塑造者和中华传统文化格局的主要建构者。

在古代，玄奘取经走出国门，在100多个国家进行各种考察与交流，不但在这些国家留下自己的足迹，也带回那些国家的资讯，成为那个时代走得最远和扬名于最多国家的中国人，特别是在印度，玄奘通过与高僧、国王以及其他各界人士的交往而获得极高的声誉。此后，玄奘在丝绸之路沿线各国不同程度地保持着自己的知名度，尤其是近代以来，随着印度佛教考古事业以及中亚各国古代历史研究的发展，玄奘《大唐西域记》的作用越来越不可替代，玄奘的贡献也因此不断为人们所传颂。与此同时，西方世界也在接触东方的过程中开始了解佛教文化及佛教文化的历史，自然也对玄奘产生了浓厚的兴趣，尤其是随着东方学在西方世界的兴起，《大唐西域记》和《大唐大慈恩寺三藏法师传》（以下简称《慈恩传》）逐渐引起西方世界的关注。

有关玄奘事迹的历史记述分散于游记、僧传、经录、碑刻等多种文献之中，其中最系统全面的当属《慈恩传》。然而，西方对玄奘的了解首先是从《大唐西域记》开始的，相比之下，《慈恩传》的翻译和研究显得比较薄弱。据本书英译者王欣女士研究，《慈恩传》的西文翻译和研究总体上落后于《大唐西域记》，最早出现在欧洲的《慈恩传》译本是1853年由法国学者M·斯坦拉·儒莲翻译的《慧立、彦（悰）的〈玄奘传〉及其629—645年旅行》。从英译本的情况来看，目前相关的只有三本：第一本是比尔（Samuel Beal, 1825—1889）于1911年出版的《玄奘的一生》（*The Life of Hiuen-Tsiang*），仅对《慈恩传》前五卷进行了编译；另外两个英译本都出自李荣熙先生（1916—1997）：一是1959年中国佛教协会为纪念玄奘法师逝世一千三百周年组织翻译的，英文题目是 *The Life of Hsuan Tsang*，此译本从第六卷到第十卷并未按照原文全部翻译，略去了很多诏书、奏表和信件等；二是1995出版的 *A Biography of the Tripitaka Master of the Great Ci'en Monastery of the Great Tang Dynasty*，这本显然是在前一本的基础之上修改润色的全译本，因而就译文的质量而言，也是当时最好的。

翻译活动从来都不只停留在语言学意义上，它更是一种在跨文化背景下的文化学意义上的语言转换。译本的形成除了受到译者自身诠释及翻译能力的制约外，也受到时代背景、文化环境的影响。对《慈恩传》这样的中华古籍外译而言，译者不仅需要广泛研读和借鉴前人对古代文献的翻译和注释，更需要熟悉学术界相关的新研究成果，最大限度地领会和传递典籍的内容和意义。《慈恩传》的完整英语翻译至今已过近三十年，随着有关唐代佛教研究、中印佛教交往、丝绸之路沿线佛教考古，尤其是玄奘研究的进展，《慈恩传》中的很多史实记述、佛教名相以及情境描写和措辞意涵等都可进一步得到理解和认识。也就是说，学术研究发展到今天这样的高度，我们可以更加准确也更加深刻地解读一千多年前的《慈恩传》中很多语句真义，特别是那些模糊、含蓄、多义的源于古汉语固有特征的词句。不仅如此，那些因信仰的神圣性而呈现的具体宗教体验性描写也可有进一步的解读和体现。翻译往往见仁见智，可以说，现在已经到了必须重新翻译《慈恩传》的时候了，复译《慈恩传》是有必要的，也是不可或缺的。

王欣女士主要从事英语语言及英语文学研究，特别专注于语言学视野下的中西方文化交流问题。她于2005—2009年在西北大学世界史专业世界宗教文化方向攻读博士学位，在此期间，她对印度文化尤其是印度佛教文化有比较系统的学习，对印度佛教向中国的传播以及由此开启的中印古代文化交往关系也有很多思考。她又以此为基础结合自己的教学科研工作，将研究的视角从古代中印佛教文化交往转向现代中美佛教文化交往，实现了时间上的古今贯通和空间上的印度、中国、美国的三级飞跃。这种时空转换中的佛教文化交往进程本质上是佛教起源与外传地、佛教扎根与壮大地、佛教拓展与初兴地之间不同社会生活和不同文化精神的彼此呼应，必须具有广博的学术视野和深厚的知识积累才可以完成对这种文化交往变迁的深刻理解和准确描述。王欣女士以严谨而认真的态度和专注而勤勉的精神对待这一学术问题，高质量地完成了这一学术视域下的具体研究任务，圆满完成了全部博士学业。对我来说，过去的研究领域基本聚焦于古代中印之间的佛教交往，正是因为她的学术兴趣和勇敢的探索，带动我拓宽学术视野，将古代佛教的跨文化交往问题推进到现代中西文化交往的新视域之下，由此得以发现不同时代的佛教跨文化传播的不同内涵以及由此所展现的不同问题。

近年来王欣女士对玄奘相关事迹的历史记述及玄奘在西

方世界的传播情况产生了浓厚的兴趣。通过这次的翻译工作，她试图将沟通古代中印佛教交往关系的玄奘再次推介给西方社会，以完整重译《慈恩传》的方式回应佛教从印度到中国再到西方世界的时空跨越。我相信，在这一学术视野下的翻译工作一定不会只是一种纯语言学的介入过程，而是有深刻理论基础的跨时空、跨文化的佛教历史资讯的现代传播，其中所包含的对历史记述的解读以及对佛教文化心理的把握，都不再是一个简单的语言转换与措辞拿捏问题，而是中印古代佛教关系及其相关问题在现代西方文化背景下的精准传达问题。

据我所知，王欣女士对《慈恩传》的翻译下了苦功，除了前期的积累外，她为此专门对玄奘的相关历史文献进行了广泛的收集和系统的研究，并对学术界的相关研究进行了全面的梳理和理解，对西方学术界的玄奘研究尤其是玄奘历史文献的翻译历程和存在问题做了探析，而具体的翻译过程也充满了想象不到的困惑，层出不穷的问题以拦路虎的方式向她不断地提出挑战，她以坚韧顽强的意志，一个一个地攻克难关，经过多年的努力，终于完成了全部书稿的翻译。回想这一历程，其中的艰辛或许只有她本人才能深切地感受到，付出的心血也都浸润于逝去的时光里。在此书正式出版之际，我要向王欣表示祝贺，更要向她表达我的赞佩。她的志向与坚忍，她的清净与专注，连同她的严谨与认真，都印在了这部译作的字里行间，最终呈现出来的这部作品，既是一部古代汉语文献的当代英译，也是一部见证理论基础与考证功力的学术成果，更是一种蕴含着纯洁而炙热的学术情怀的精神产品。我相信，真挚而富有情怀的人是富裕的，也是快乐的。只有他们才与玄奘大师的品格相应，也才有资格整理玄奘的历史遗产并将其传向文明世界。

李利安

2022年8月12日于香港大学佛教研究中心

Foreword

In China's academia of World History Studies, there is a historical perspective on the exchange of civilizations, which, based on a comprehensive investigation of historical phenomena and of the mankind evolution mechanisms, holds that exchanges not only widely exist among various ethnic groups, countries, and regions, but among different places, academic fields, social strata, and even cultural systems within the same region. And the exchange of civilizations is of great significance to a region or a country, causing many historical events that have had a significant impact on the overall process of human society. Therefore, we could conclude that the exchanges among civilizations are the mainstream of human history, constructing the framework of human progress, providing an eternal driving force for human progress and producing a yardstick by which to judge historical transformations and social progress. Exchanges have been a dominant factor in the development of history, and will continue to open up more choices for the future mankind. All in all, as the most fundamental activity of humanity, civilization exchanges provide us a golden key to examine history, help us identify the driving forces of history, explore its trajectory, and even predict its orientation.

The history of humanity is approximately two million years, and the history of human civilization is approximately five thousand years. Throughout the five-thousand-year history, human civilization can be roughly divided into three types — material civilization, institutional civilization and spiritual civilization. The spiritual civilization includes the secular spiritual civilization in the rational field and the sacred spiritual civilization that transcends rationality. Since the Axial Era termed by Karl Theodor Jaspers (1883—1969), the spiritual civilization of mankind has gradually taken shape in four regions, namely the Brāhmaṇical civilization in India, tri-civilization (Confucianism, Buddhism and Taoism) in China, Christian civilization in Europe, and Islamic civilization in Middle East. Even in today's world, these four spiritual traditions continue to consolidate the global multi-civilization configuration and create communication frameworks.Looking back at the history, we could see there used to be countless cultural messengers who travelled across the continents to dialogue with different civilizations and learn from each other. Thanks to their efforts, the door to exchanges has hitherto opened, mutual understanding deepened and an alliance for progress formulated. Among these cultural messengers, Xuanzang (602-664) was one of the most outstanding.

Xuanzang was a monk in the early Tang Dynasty of China. He has made many brilliant achievements, and here we just mention a few of them. Firstly, he took a 17-year pilgrimage to collect Buddhist scriptures in India, and visited more than 110 countries along the

Silk Road. His travelling experience was recorded in a book entitled *Datang xiyu ji* (the *Buddhist Records of the Western Regions of the Tang Dynasty* or *Great Tang Records on the Western Regions*), in which he wrote of more than 130 countries; Secondly, after returning to China, he presided over a massive translation project sponsored by Tang Court to render Buddhist canon into Chinese. During 19 years of hard work, he translated 1335 volumes of Buddhist texts, exceeding the sum of the scriptures translated by the other three famous translators (Kumārajīva, Paramārtha, and Amoghavajra). Thirdly, he paved a reliable path for the dissemination of Buddhism in China by establishing Chinese translation regulations, utilizing governmental support for dharma transmission, and promoting the sectarian communication. In short, to evaluate his achievements, we'd better locate him in the long history of the Silk Road and Chinese culture. It is my keenly felt conviction that Xuanzang was an eminent representative on the Silk Road who accelerated civilization exchanges and made a great contribution to the formation of the China's cultural framework.

Today, however, when we step into the history, it is difficult for us to know the names of the wealthy merchants who once traveled back and forth on the Silk Road, even though they invigorated transportation and material exchange. Along with them dissipated in the dust were also the names of those once-powerful envoys who traveled along the ancient Road bearing imperial edicts to forge political ties between various nations. Besides, soldiers who used to march along the Silk Road valiantly, also walked down the stage of history with their burning heroism. Besides, soldiers who used to march along the Silk Road bravely also walked down the stage of history with their burning heroism. On the contrary, Xuanzang and other cultural messengers, lack of resources but possessing firm beliefs and lofty spirits, have exerted a tremendous influence on the dissemination of human spiritual civilization, and thus, they have been and will forever be recorded in the annals of history by historians.

Throughout the history of spiritual and cultural exchanges on the Silk Road, Zoroastrianism, Buddhism, Manichaeism, Nestorianism, Islam, Judaism, even Indian Brahmanism and Jainism, also other religions have entered China. Greek culture spread into some areas of West Asia, Central Asia and South Asia. Indian Brahmanism was introduced into Central Asia and Southeast Asia. Relatively speaking, the longest, largest and most influential religious and cultural propagation was Buddhism, which was introduced from India into China. According to the statistics, during over one thousand years from the Han Dynasty (202BCE-220 CE) to the Song Dynasty (960-1279 CE), there were at least 900 monks traversed the Silk Road, and by the middle of the Tang Dynasty (618-907 CE), there had been more than 7,000 volumes of Buddhist texts translated into Chinese. What a glorious page written on the history of Silk Road! It is on this very route that Xuanzang studied diligently, communicated extensively, conducted in-depth investigations and thereafter, recorded his experience accurately. After seventeen-year journey, he finally obtained as many as 657 Buddhist texts, undoubtedly known as the most important figure in the dissemination of Buddhism along the Silk Road.

The introduction of Buddhism into China is the most brilliant chapter in the history of civilization exchanges along the Silk Road, also it is the main driving force in forming the basic system of Chinese traditional culture. As we know, Chinese culture boasts a rich and illustrious history spanning 5,000 years, renowned as one of the four major civilizations of the world, and with unique features, it has exerted far-reaching influences on East Asia. Though it has occasionally exhibited a sense of over-confidence, Chinese culture has never ceased to absorb foreign influences throughout its lengthy history. Two of the most significant absorptions are Indian Buddhist culture and Western culture. These two cultural inputs have restructured the traditional Chinese culture, changed its connotation, and rebuilt the ethos of Chinese people, thus laid the basic pattern for modern China. Before the introduction of Buddhism, China had gone through the Contention of a Hundred Schools of Thought in the Spring and Autumn period and the Warring States period, and witnessed the alternating dominance of Legalism, Taoism and Confucianism in the Qin and Han dynasties. Such an ideological disunification had not been changed until the end of the Han Dynasty when Buddhism entered China.

In China's ideological history, neither the juxtaposition of "hundred schools" nor "the pre-eminence of a single school" could run counter to the following law: Chinese thinkers were mainly concerned with the social nature of human beings, and they devoted themselves to the human relations and human affairs, just as what we see in Confucianism, Legalism, Mohism, Strategic or Diplomatic School, and even in Taoism. There is no exception. Taoism, for example. though being considered to advocate naturalism and immortality, still exhibits a clear inclination in solving social problems. Generally speaking, Chinese ancient culture used to be one-way and single-faceted, which eventually was totally changed by the introduction of Buddhism. During more than a thousand years from the Han and Wei dynasties to the Tang and Song dynasties, there were a large number of monks who risked their lives to seek Buddhist teachings in alien lands and brought back a lot of Buddhist texts. These texts embraced a peculiar concern for the spiritual needs of people, revealed the fate of human beings, undertook the mission of salvation, explored time and space, interpreted human nature, and designated the ultimate destination to humanity in a very fresh way. As a new ideology, Buddhist teachings began to radiate irresistible charm and finally stepped on the China's cultural stage. Thus, a new cultural pattern was gradually established—the complementary coexistence of Confucianism, Taoism and Buddhism. The reorganization of the Chinese cultural structure was finalized only after the indigenization of Buddhism, a process facilitated by the tireless efforts of numerous eminent monks and scholars. These luminaries translated scriptures, established sects, synthesized diverse ideas, and harmonized the relationship between politics and religion. Among them, Xuanzang stands out for his significant contributions. He is worthy of the titles of the great shaper of Buddhist culture with Chinese characteristics and of the important constructor of Chinese traditional culture.

Xuanzang went abroad to study and conducted investigations and exchanges in more than 100 countries. He not only left footprints in these lands, but also brought back China information about them, which made him the first Chinese of his time who traveled the farthest and won the greatest reputation abroad. Particularly in India, Xuanzang distinguished himself when contacting eminent monks, kings and people from all walks of life. Actually, Xuanzang has also maintained his popularity to varying degrees in the countries along the Silk Road. In modern times, Xuanzang's contribution has been widely recognized, whose *Datang xiyu ji* has been regarded to be indispensable to the archaeology in India and Central Asia. The Western world, as we know, began to heed Buddhist culture and history during its contact with the East, and especially with the rise of Orientalism, it has gradually developed a strong interest in Xuanzang, then into its view coming the *Da tang xiyu ji* and *Datang da ci'en si sanzang fashi zhuan* (*Biography of the Tripiṭaka Dharma Master of the Great Ci'en Monastery of the Great Tang Dynasty*, hereinafter, referred to as the *Biography of Ci'en* or *Ci'en zhuan*).

The historical records on Xuanzang could be found in various literature, including travel notes, monk biography, scriptural catalogue (*jinglu*), inscriptions and so on, among which the most systematic and comprehensive is the *Biography of Ci'en* (*Ci'en zhuan*). However, it was the *Datang xiyu ji* rather than *Ci'en zhuan* that made Xuanzang known in the Western world, so the translation and research of the latter are relatively weak. According to Mrs. Wang Xin, the translation and research of the *Ci'en zhuan* have lagged behind those of the *Datang xiyu ji*. The earliest translated version of *Ci'en zhuan* was a French one made by Stanislas Julien, entitled the Histoire de la vie de Hiouen-Thsang et de ses voyages dans l'Inde,depuis l'an 629 jusqu'en 645, par Hoei-li et Yen-thsong: Suivie de documents et d'eclaircissements geographiques tirés de la relation originale de Hiouen Thsang, published in Paris by Imprimerie imperiale in 1853. Now, there are three English versions available:

(1) Hwui Li. The Life of Hiuen-Tsiang. Translated by Samuel Beal. London: Kegan Paul, Trübner and Co.Ltd, 1911. Reprint New Delhi: Munshiram Manoharlal, 1973.

(2) Hui-li. The Life of Hsuan Tsang. Translated by Li Yongshi. Beijing: Chinese Buddhist Association, 1959.

(3) Sramana Huili and Shi Yancong. A Biography of the Tripitaka Master of the Great Ci'en Monastery of the Great Tang Dynasty. Translated by Li Rongxi. Berkeley, California: Numata Center for Buddhist Translation and Research, 1995.

In version (1) by Samuel Beal (1825-1889), only the first five fascicles of the *Ci'en zhuan* have been translated, while the remaining five fascicles were condensed into one ending chapter. Both versions (2) and (3) are from the same translator Li Rongxi (1916-1997). Version (2) was produced in 1959 to commemorate the 1300 anniversary of the death of Xuanzang under the sponsorship of the Chinese Buddhist Association, in which the fascicles 6 to 10 of the original text were not fully translated, for Mr. Li omitted many edicts, memorials and letters. Version (3) is an unabridged one which was improved on version (2) and was of high quality at the time.

Translation has never been confined to the field of linguistics, rather, it is a kind of culturological conversion. The production of translated works is not only constrained by the translator's own comprehension and language abilities, but also influenced by the historical and cultural environment in which he is. To render such an ancient Chinese book as the *Ci'en zhuan* into other languages, a translator needs to extensively study the available inter-and intra-translations as well as the annotations made by ancient and contemporary scholars, and to acquaint himself/herself with the latest researches on Xuanzang, so as to thoroughly comprehend the classic and then translate it as faithfully as possible. Nearly 30 years have passed since the unabridged English version of the *Ci'en zhuan* by Li Rongxi was published. Over the past decades, new researches on specialized fields such as the Buddhism of the Tang Dynasty, Sino-Indian Buddhist exchanges, and Silk Road Buddhist archaeology in general, and the studies on Xuanzang in particular, have required us to renew our interpretation of some historical facts, Buddhist terms, biographical descriptions and wordings in the *Ci'en zhuan*. In other words, contemporary academic studies have reached a high level that enable us to be more accurate in catching the true meaning of many sentences heavily laden with suggestive, implicit and polysemous expressions, usually the typical features of the ancient classic composed more than a thousand years ago. Besides, in the *Ci'en zhuan*, accounts of religious experiences of Xuanzang embracing his devout faith also requires further interpretation. In a word, translation is often a matter of subjectiveness. It is necessary and inevitable to re-translate the *Ci'en zhuan*.

Mrs. Wang engages in English literature and translation studies, meanwhile showing a particular interest in the cultural exchanges between China and the West. From 2005 to 2009, she pursued a doctoral degree in World History at Northwestern University, mainly focusing on world religions and cultures.In those years, she conducted systematic research on Indian culture, especially Indian Buddhism and its dissemination in China, as well as ancient Sino-Indian cultural contact and diffusion. Furthermore, she expanded her research scope from the ancient Sino-Indian Buddhist cultural exchange to the modern Sino-American one, striding across the temporal chasm from ancient to modern times, and clearing away the spatial obstacles to leap from India to China and ultimately to the United States. Essentially, this time-and-space transformation of Buddhist culture is a kind of communication made by peoples of different social and spiritual ethos in different places where Buddhism originated and where it grew, where it rooted and where it prospered, and where it spread and where it sprouted. So, only with a broad academic vision and intense knowledge could a researcher profoundly understand and accurately depict these cultural transformations. Mrs. Wang approached her academic interest with a rigorous and serious attitude, dedicating herself to it and ultimately completing her doctoral studies with high appraisal. As for me, my past research primarily focused on Buddhist communication between China and India in ancient times. It was her academic interest and courageous exploration that helped me broaden my academic horizon to advance from Sino-Indian relation in ancient times to the cultural exchanges of Buddhism between China and the West in modern times. This new perspective promises to uncover the diverse meanings and complexities of cross-cultural Buddhist exchanges across different eras, while addressing the challenges that accompany such interactions.

In recent years, Mrs. Wang has developed a strong interest in the historical documents about Xuanzang and their dissemination in the western world. Through the unabridged translation of *Ci'en zhuan*, she tried to reintroduce Xuanzang to the West. From an academic perspective, her translation is guaranteed by a profound theoretical foundation, for it goes beyond language itself and touches upon a modern dissemination of Buddhist historical information across the time, space, and culture, in which the interpretation of historical literature and the cultural psychology of Buddhism is no longer dealt with as a matter of linguistic conversion and wordings, but a matter of how to accurately decode the historical relationship between Chinese and Indian Buddhism and other relevant issues in the modern western culture.

As far as I know, Mrs. Wang has made painstaking efforts in translating the *Ci' en zhuan.* Based on her academic accumulation, she extensively collected and systematically studied the historical literature related to Xuanzang. In addition, she sorted through relevant studies in the western academic circles, and examined the available English versions as well as their existing problems. Nevertheless, once she embarked on the translation process, she was challenged by various difficulties. With her tenacious will, she tackled knotty problems one by one. Now her endeavors have been immersed in bygone days, and after so many years of hard work, she finally completed her translation. Looking back, perhaps only she herself could tell the hardships. I would like to congratulate Mrs. Wang and express my admiration on the occasion of publication. Her ambition and tenacity, her purity and concentration, also her preciseness and seriousness have found the final expression in every line of this English version. The work presented here not only serves as a contemporary English translation of ancient Chinese literature, but also represents an academic accomplishment that attests to the translator's solid theoretical foundation and her proficiency in conducting textual research. Above all, it is a spiritual product with pure academic passion. I believe that people of sincerity and sentiment are always self-contained and happy. If not the equal of the character of Master Xuanzang, they are still worthy to sit in his company. Only they are qualified to sort out his historical legacy, and only they are authorized to pass it on to the modern world.

Li Li'an

On August 12, 2022, at the Centre of B uddhist Studies, HKU.

Translator's Foreword

This is an English translation work of the *Datang Da Ci'ensi Sanzang Fashi Zhuan* (*Biography of the Tripiṭaka Dharma Master of the Great Ci'en Monastery of the Great Tang Dynasty*, hereinafter referred to as the *Biography of Ci'en or Ci'en Zhuan*) written by Shi Huili and Shi Yancong, two disciples of Xuanzang, in the seventh century, a formative period for the Weishi or Faxiang School in China that is the Yogācāra School of Mahāyāna Buddhism in India. It is a companion volume to the *Datang Xiyu Ji* (*Records of the Western Regions of the Great Tang Dynasty*) compiled in 646 by Bianji, a disciple of Xuanzang, through the master's dictation. The popularity of Xuanzang is attested by the fact that *Datang xiyu ji* and *Ci'en Zhuan* remain in print, and translations are still read and studied by experts in archaeology and religious studies around the world. Started in 2020, an inter-disciplinary humanities project, The Xuanzang Trail project, led by Professor Deeg and BDHS executive director Dr Bijoy Choudhury was carried through, which is aimed to transform understanding of early medieval Buddhism by identifying the places and sites made famous in the writings and travels of Xuanzang.

The Tang Dynasty witnessed the prime time of Chinese Buddhism, with the Faxiang sect being one of the most influential ones. Its nominal founder was Xuanzang, whose life experiences, truly unique among Buddhist pilgrimages, were accounted in *Ci'en zhuan*. This is a ten-fascicle classic work. The first five fascicles are a travelogue recording his great pilgrimage along the Silk Road to India, while the remaining five depict his activities after returning to China. It is a book establishing a rich network of historical, textual, geographical, archaeological, anthropological, religious, narrative, and literary connections, so it is international, transhistorical, and transcultural. No modern discussion on Xuanzang or relevant topics would be complete without referencing it. Indeed, this biography is every bit informative and indispensable, as everyone has believed, to orientalists, historians, Buddhists, geographers, archaeologists, travelers, and geopoliticians, to mention a few. I have to say it has another value as well—its sheer literary excellence.

In the introduction to the *Shorter Columbia Anthology of Traditional Chinese Literature*, Victor H. Mair wrote, "Much of the finest literature in China was written in the form of biography; strictly in terms of sheer literary merit, biography deserves to occupy a prominent position in any anthology of Chinese literature. Furthermore, a large proportion of Chinese history—both official and unofficial—was written in the form of biography."[1] *Ci'en Zhuan* is

1 The *Shorter Columbia Anthology of Traditional Chinese Literature* , Victor H. Mair edited. Columbia University Press. 2000.

one of such great biographies. It is regarded as the most systematic exposition of a Buddhist's life ever composed, being unmatched in its content and masterful narrative structure. The book shows Xuanzang in a favorable light, with some descriptive accounts crossing the borderline between fact and fiction, so attracting readers with different, even opposing, cultural backgrounds, and even the readers who are not interested in Buddhism at all.

Due consideration for its esthetic merit and genuine emotional appeal is deserved. This biography was written in Classical Chinese (also called Literary Chinese or Literary Sinitic) and Buddhist Hybrid Sinitic, excellent in its aesthetic value of language—a quintessence of classical Chinese. To be sure, the implicitness of the succinct classical written language is esthetically pleasing, but this makes it difficult for modern readers, even for Chinese people, to understand it. In this seventh-century biography, there are so many letters, petitions and memorials to the throne, and imperial edicts, which are the most sophisticated, mannered, and abstruse kinds of texts—the typical writing style or genre of Chinese literati-officials in ancient times. The challenges of "translating" petitions or memorials are immense. Such writings often have regular lines arranged in couplets, each line matching in length and reinforcing a particular theme. This parallel prose has tight restrictions in metrical, tonal, and thematic terms, called *pianwen. Pianwen* couplets are aligned and parallel, showing a pleasing symmetry, so it is regarded as an art form in Chinese literature, the most sophisticated examples of belles-lettres. As the Chinese couplet form is more tightly restrained than that in English, so in most cases, the English versions of them lose much beauty in language form. In this regard, the English version may fail in the immediate physical vitality of sight and sound of Chinese Characters. However, even if the translation is not as beautiful as the original text, it still can reveal a great deal about the power of original words. So, I hope the new English version will win appreciation from readers both at home and abroad. I also long for their support and suggestions so that it may live up to the expectations of the reading public.

It is an exciting but knotty job to do. During my translation, I always asked myself: What style of translation should I strive for, accuracy or felicity? I have tried to answer this question expediently. I try to produce readable English from complex archaic Chinese by being relatively consistent in my choices of terms while remaining flexible enough to allow context to determine alternate readings of a word. I have tried to preserve as much of its style as possible and present this text as it is—an early seventh-century Chinese genteel and solemn text while presenting it in contemporary English. The text, indeed, demands that the readers open themselves to a distant expression style. I have to point out that this text is challenging to read in Chinese, and I haven't therefore attached to making it more familiar to English readers who are culturally or temporally alien, while I hope I have not made the text any more difficult in English than in Chinese.

Turning Chinese classics into foreign languages has been no easy task. The Chinese and English languages simply are not designed for each other. Finding words or phrases in one language with a similar semantic range to those in the other is often nearly impossible, let alone the suggestiveness of classical Chinese is always open to interpretation. I apologize again for any vagueness in my translation. Something is inevitably lost when I try to render classical Chinese into English. May the day come soon when other translators, much better at belles-lettres, will bring out a new translation.

Typical features of this new translation

Firstly, this is a Chinese-English edition.

This new version is intended to open up the Chinese classic to modern readers, invoke interest in the text, and advance the scholarship in the field; therefore, here we have the Chinese-English edition with you. It has been adapted to fit the needs of readers interested in Chinese culture and language, who want to get accurate information from the original text alongside the translated version for some scholarly purpose, and who are inclined to render Chinese Classics into English. Moreover, with due allowance for mistranslation, the English version may still be helpful for those who cannot read the original. Although it presents formidable problems in translation and interpretation, I still would be most gratified if readers who do not have any academic affliction became acquainted with and learned to appreciate Chinese literature through this book. If this translation can point something out to help even a few people learn more about Xuanzang and the Tang Dynasty, the efforts to produce it will have been most worthwhile. If this translation is helpful in the evolution of Buddhist studies in the West, the steps to create it will have been worthwhile.

Secondly, it is heavily annotated, and all notes are consulted from authentic sources.

Although it is said that too bulky, overly detailed notes and commentaries would distract readers from the pleasure of reading, it seems impossible to devise this translation that can stand on its own as literary text in English without elaborate notes when the original Chinese text is characterized by heavy use of uncommon words and allusions to literary, religious or historical events. As mentioned above, the English version was originally intended as a general reference for Western scholars, but in order to make it readable to more ordinary readers, copious notes and explanations have to be provided,so that it is now as heavily annotated as the ordinary readers might typically expect of this type of book.

Footnotes are of two main types, providing background information necessary for understanding the passage in question. Both Chinese and Indian philosophical, logical, and religious terms pose unique difficulties, for they might not be widely known by readers not conversant with Buddhist philosophy. Although it is not good to require a reader of contemporary English to learn a new language to read the translation, technical terms in Buddhism, typically Sanskrit terms, are often used with explanations given as complete as possible in the notes. Also, I have found it necessary to include more Chinese historical explanatory materials than is usual in the footnotes, being aware that the general readers are not fully conversant with all the idiomaticity of the source culture and language. The Western readers, I predict, will find this text difficult going to some degree, but it is hard to make them not be bothered with a glossary for a lot of background in Buddhist learning, and Chinese culture is a prerequisite.

Conventions used in this new version

As to the original of the classic that the present translation is made, the edition that is in wide circulation has been chosen—the edition published by Zhonghua Publishing House with punctuation marks, which is from Jinling Sutra Publishing House's edition. To be convenient for readers to read, the simplified characters and punctuation marks of the new system are used in printing. Necessary annotations are made. The names of persons and places and special terms are spelt according to the Chinese Phenetic Alphabet, except for the accepted transliterations. Titles of books are rendered by both transliteration and free translation. Brackets are employed to distinguish one from the other. Chinese characters are provided at the first occurrence in the footnotes in each chapter and may reoccur later for easy reference.

In the course of translating, especially in solving some knotty problems of understanding classical Chinese, I took the authority to the writings of the erudite scholars, some of which are mentioned in the selected bibliography, though not an exhaustive list of studies available, at the end of the book. The journal articles on Xuanzang published by scholars in China and abroad are too numerous to enlist, so a bibliography of them is impossible to make.

Diacritics for Sanskrit words are provided. The translation is primarily directed to the readers with some scholarly purposes, so when Sanskrit appears in Roman characters instead of the Devanāgarī script, diacritics are used to help the readers pronounce words correctly. However, the romanization system for Standard Mandarin Chinese also includes four diacritics denoting tones, which should be used to spell Chinese names and comments in this translation, but I am afraid that the mere sight of all those squiggles and dots may make readers fall into a kind of confusion, so *pinyin* without tone marks is adopted, except for the ü sound.

Acknowledgements

One day in April of 2015, I received an invitation from Shaan'xi Normal University General Publishing House and then embarked on the translation of this Chinese Classic. I have long wanted to translate a vital book relevant to Chinese Buddhism into English. But I knew how incompetent I was in translating such a complex text since neither my relevant knowledge nor my linguistic attainment qualified me for the work. I hesitated until I consulted Mr. Long Darui(龙达瑞), a professor in the Department of Religious Studies at the university of the West ,a scholar dedicated to the study of Yongle Northern Canon,and now a chief editor of international Chinese Buddhist Canon Research Newsletter,a professional information exchange platform for the study of Chinese Buddhist canons .He knew my misgivings but still insisted that the new translation be done if I follow the original text without deviation, and if I could supply rich annotations to locate the text in a rich cultural and historical context. For this reason, I accepted this assignment with enthusiasm. My translation ended up in 2022 with the proofreading work completed by Mr. Long. It took me nearly seven years to work on and off, and the result of my attempt is now put before the readers. My desire is now fulfilled. My happiness is beyond measure.

So, I begin by thanking Prof. Long Darui for his support and assistance during the initial and final stages of this translation. He gave me invaluable assistance in understanding some troubling classical passages. Especially, his careful proofreading provided pertinent suggestions about the Sanskrit equivalents to Chinese terms. The clarity of his explanations, his concern for Buddhist scholarship, and his effort put into improving this book has inspired me constantly.

I also wish to record my thanks to the late translators Samuel Beal (1825–1889) and Li Rongxi (Li Yung-his李荣熙1916–1997). Beal made a groundbreaking contribution to the relevant studies of Master Xuanzang and Li provided a faithful and expressive translated work for English readership. I have learned a great deal from their translations. I particularly note my gratitude to Mr. Li Rongxi whose translation provided me with glossaries of Sanskrit terms so that I might, as far as it is possible, make my translation authentic and authoritative. Besides their English versions, I also took several Chinese books as a reference. This new version has absorbed or used the findings achieved by contemporary Chinese researchers, especially the intra-translations of the book from ancient to modern Chinese. I am grateful for permission to quote from their valuable annotations and commentaries. I thank other erudite scholars (some, not all, are mentioned in the selected bibliography at the end of the book.) for their research and writings.

I owe an enormous debt of gratitude to Prof. Li Li'an（李利安）, dean of Xuanzang Research Institute at the Northwest University in China. He not only introduced me to the world of Buddhist scholarship when I was a doctoral student at Northwest University but also has been and will be an unwavering source of support and wisdom in my life and academic career. My debts to him are significant.

What's more, other good teachers and helpful friends, especially

Prof. Li Haibo（李海波） and Prof. Wang Xuemei（王雪梅）of Xuanzang Research Institute, and Prof. Wang Bangwei （王邦维）of Peking University were very kindly to encourage me to undertake the project and reassured me of its value when I felt discouraged. Words cannot convey my heartfelt gratitude to them. Besides them, I also want to thank Prof. Jing Sanlong（荆三隆）of Xidian University, Dr. Jing Tianxing（景天星）of Shaanxi Academy of Social Sciences, Dr. Gao Yongshun（高永顺）of Baoji University of Arts and Sciences, Dr. Yu Hengwei（宇恒伟）of Zunyi Medical University and Prof. Wang Zhaomin（王赵民）of China Xuanzang Research Center. As established experts either in the study of Buddhism or in classical Chinese, they patiently and repeatedly answered my questions concerning Buddhist doctrines and classical Chinese, whose helpful suggestions I gratefully acknowledge here. I am particularly appreciative of my students Liu Ya'ning （刘亚宁）and Zheng Biao（郑彪）who helped me in solving some problems of computer software and the Internet. There are still many other people who have helped me in one way or another; however, only a few of them I can mention here. I want to pay my gratitude for their inspiration and support, for this translation could not have been completed without them.

I would like to express my appreciation to all those who have done so much to give my book its present form, in particular Ms. Chenliu Dongxue（陈柳冬雪）and the editorial staff, especially Wang Hongkai（王红凯）of Shaan'xi Normal University General Publishing House, who have shown extraordinary patience and skill in helping to prepare this volume for publication.

I wish to register my thanks to the School of Foreign Languages at Xidian University, for it provided the perfect environment in which I worked on this translation and my teaching. I wish to thank *en masse* all my colleagues with whom I worked together for so many years, and I am grateful to them for their continuing help with my life and work. Especially Kenya Pressley, thank her for her valuable suggestion on my English.

I dedicate the translation to my parents. I owe enormous gratitude to my dear father and mother, who graciously allowed me to be absent from so many happy family reunions and work on this project. I wish to express my deepest gratitude.

There are so many people who have supported this work in many ways. My debts to them are more outstanding than I can ever hope to repay. Reflecting on that, I genuinely understand the truth that all things are dependently arising, coexistent, interwoven, and interrelated, so there is the tremendous debt each of us owes to many others.

Finally, although I have made the scrutiny into this translation, it will have the inevitable errors and faults. I apologize for all of my mistakes. I hope that readers will kindly point them out to me. Criticisms and suggestions will be gratefully received and used to improve any future editions.

WANG Xin

August 12, 2022

TABLE OF CONTENTS

A Preface to the Biography of the Tripiṭaka Dharma Master of the Great Ci'en Monastery of the Great Tang Dynasty

Preface by the Respectful Śramaṇa Shi Yancong (r.ca.648–688) on the Fifteenth Day of the third Month in the Fourth Year of *Chuigong* (688)

Not until the Śākyamuni Buddha came to the Land of Endurance[1] was the Eightfold Nobel Path[2] demonstrated and the Triple Gem[3] revealed to banish the texts of varied heretical schools; thereafter, the teachings of Buddha have been circulating broad and wide. The Vaipulya[4] teachings of the Ekayāna[5] and the Ten Stages of the Perfect Truth[6] have been esteemed as the Great Dharma for expounding the ultimate truth[7]; whereas parables of the phantom city[8], of the filthily ragged clothes[9], and of the deer and goat carts[10] are analogies to various expedient methods, thus being called the lesser learning. Dhyāna[11], vinaya[12], dhāraṇī[13] and myriad others, though displaying varied ways of self-cultivation, lead to the same destination, that is, to eliminate illusions as well as to benefit sentient beings, hence being worshiped and treasured by the wise and sagacious of successive generations. The (Avataṃsaka) Sūtra[14] to eight assemblies has been valued as the genuine root of all teachings, while the Four Noble Truths unfolded by three turnings of the dharma wheel[15] has been cherished as branches sprouting subsidiary doctrines. Metaphors such as the rain of four kinds of celestial flowers[16], the six earth-shakings[17], the jewel removed from topknot and the gem revealed from the robe[18], are employed to trace the offshoots back to root or gather the "three vehicles"[19] into One Vehicle (Ekayāna).

It was recorded in the *Fufazang Zhuan* (Recor*d of the Causes of Transmitting the Dharma Piṭaka*[20]) that the venerable Ānanda, with a memory soaking up the teachings of the Buddha like a bottle receiving the water poured from the other, was able to recite and uphold all the Dharma Piṭaka of the Tathāgata[21]— the skillfully-expedient and well-timed teachings taught by the World-Honored One during his forty-nine-year preaching time. When the Ajitavatī River[22] dried up and Śāla trees[23] withered, the Buddha attained His Nirvāṇa, and along with that, His abstruse teachings were also consigned to oblivion. At the cremation ritual, seeing the coffin was to be closed in which the corpse of Buddha elaborately wrapped in cotton shroud, our grand master Kāśyapa[24] grieved bitterly at the loss of the Buddha valuable as the eyes of Celestial and Human beings. Afraid there might be no salvation to sentient beings hereafter, he convened the holy disciples of the Buddha to recollect the subtle teachings they had learned. Together, they examined their experiences to fix down the methods of Dhyāna, and used Gāthā[25] to teach Vinaya; based on the discourses of the Upadeśa[26] they analyzed the conceptions of non-existence[27] and existence, thereby debunked the heresies of annihilation or permanence; they practiced the self-cultivation as the fundamental cause for the Buddhahood. Their endeavors not only set a model for the people of this age but exemplify the Way for the future generations. Because of them, Buddhist followers have adhered to the true teachings of the Buddha.

Later, reckoned by a man with an aureole of a sun appeared in the dream, the Emperor Ming of Han dispatched Wang [Zun] and Qin [Jing][28] as envoys to the Western Regions to seek the teachings of the Buddha. At the invitation, Kāśyapa-Mātṅga[29] and Dharmaratna came to China to propagate the dharma, usually translating the scriptures late into night. Hitherto, the glowing names of other foreign masters with supernatural power, such as Buddhasiṁha[30] and Guṇabhadra[31], spread far and wide and beyond, while the abstruse texts written on palm leaves in tendril-like scripts were exquisitely translated and introduced into this mundane land of China.

So profound and esoteric are the Buddhist theories that scholars racked their brains but still lost in the noumenal and the phenomenal; of such obscurity and inconceivability are the discourses that the debaters often failed to tell right from wrong. What was more, it had been a long time since the demise of the holy Buddha and the teachings transmitted into this land were inevitably in abundant defects, so disputes among various interpretations of the teachings sprouted out, contradictory to each other just like many carriages racing on varied roads, which are dashing ahead into different direction.

A bow was hung[32] on the door, auspiciously notifying the Master was born, which is also a very demonstration of how *being* was generated from *non-being*. Sincere as Mañjuśrī[33], he decided to pursue the Way at a very young age. Having perceived that there is no boat in the sea of desires to the yonder shore and there is a land of enlightenment for the divine consciousness to dwell in, he broke the shackles of the mundane life by having his hair shaved off (to be a monk) and earnestly devoted himself to the study of the twofold emptiness[34]. Galloping off on horse, or taking swift chariot, he ranged across the nation for thousands of miles to learn the Buddha's teachings from the erudite ones. Consequently, he found that many misinterpretations were brought about by many a miswritten word of the texts passed down from the ancient saints, and even more suspicions and doubts were merely provoked by erroneous doctrines circulated by former scholars. Then he thought to himself that when the music was performed under a tree, there must be sounds of bells and chime stones, and so the true texts of Buddha must be found in Wutianzhu[35] for He once preached there. Making a firm resolution to seek the truth, he was totally preoccupied by eagerness; eventually, ignoring hardships, he trod on the rough places as if on the flat ground. Defying death, he took countless risks to cross the Cong River[36]; for seeking a single word of the Buddha, he visited the Āmravana Garden[37]. He scaled the Vulture Peak[38] and reached the Monkey Pond[39] to pay homage to the holy sites, often marveling at the sight of wonders; he looked for the bequeathed Dharma among the moth-eaten books in Deer Park[40] and other sacred cities. Toiled through the cold and hot weathers with four seasons rotating by, during seventeen years he traveled in and heard of more than one hundred thirty countries, where he glorified our Emperor's majestic brilliance and held the authoritative aliens in shock and awe; where he subdued the arrogant heretical scholars and towered above his fellow disciples in knowledge; and where he won the obeisance from reputable kings and kept company with outstanding scholars. Indeed, it is hard to meet for thousands of years a man of such lofty demeanor and integrity like him. So unequal is our Master!

From those countries, the Master obtained the Tripiṭaka[41] of the Greater and Lesser Vehicles[42] and Sanskrit texts as well, totally six hundred fifty seven that were carried back by massive elephants and postal steeds. Thanks to the blessing of heaven, he came through all kinds of the atrocious weathers, and by relying on the influential power of our Emperor, he turned various perils and hardships into safeties and advantages. In the nineteenth year of Zhenguan (645) he returned to the capital Chang'an. Upon his arrival, the clerics and laypeople awaiting him crammed thickly and nosily in both the inner and outer cities. What a grand occasion it was! Then Son of Heaven[43]granted him with an audience and received him with a warm hospitality. After that, an imperial decree was issued ordering the relevant government departments to inaugurate the enterprise of translation for the sake of him. From that time on, the Master was highly honored, which, however, I could hardly mention in more details. Some other issues, such as under his influence, the nobles and high-ranking officials' abandonment of their secular life in pursuit of the right Way, compliments from compatriots and foreigners on his preaching trip, even his return to the ultimate truth, just as the flame died out when the fuel was exhausted, and the like, were all narrated in this biography.

Originally, the biography consisted of five fascicles and it was written by Śramaṇa Huili (615–?)[44] who formerly resided at Western Monastery of Weiguo[45]. His secular family name was Zhao. He was a descendant of Gongliu of Binzhou, and the son of [Zhao] Yi who was Personal Chronicler to the Emperor and Assistant Judicial Inspector of the Sui Dynasty (581–618). He was erudite with the knowledge of both Confucianism and Buddhism, and especially adept in writing. His eloquence was always on wings and gifted thoughts gushing over like overflowing spring. With a decorous manner, he minced no words in face of force and power; for the just cause, he never hesitated to go through fire or water. Witnessing the words and deeds of Tripiṭaka Master Xuanzang, he perceived that the deeper he probed into the recesses of the Master's character and knowledge, the more unfathomable the Master became. And he was so impressed with the Master's appearance and demeanor that he marveled at the fact that the Master seemed to be higher and further in spiritual plane no matter how hard he tried to explore him. He thus recorded the life stories of the Master, with the purpose to pass them down to the subsequent generations. After many revisions, the final draft of the biography was made. However, for fear that some of the merits and practices of the Master might have been left out, he hid it in an underground chamber for the future supplement; since then, no one had ever heard of it any more. Later, he came down with a serious illness, and when his time came to the last moment, he asked his disciples to dig the manuscript out. The moment it was taken out, he passed away, at which his disciples were grief-stricken, wailing and sobbing bitterly. Afterwards, for whatsoever reasons, the biography had fallen apart, with its segments scattering about in various places. It had taken me several years to search and purchase, and recently I have brought them altogether to its complete form.

When I was asked to write a preface to it and was urged to recompile it in the proper order, I declined, because I felt it beyond my ability to do so. Later I, however, changed my mind when someone encouraged me by saying, "On the one hand, it seems inappropriate to put any matter concerning the Buddha Dharma in the hands of laymen; on the other hand, it is a meritorious thing for you to do. How could you refuse it so insistently?" So with a shame and some hesitation, I reconsidered it for a time. At long last, feeling abashed at my incompetence, sobbing with a heavy lump in my throat, I spread out paper and took up my writing brush. Consequently, I supplemented some annotations to the original text and extended the book into ten fascicles. What I have done is just like mixing the dogs and goats into the herd of tigers and leopards, or juxtaposing the pieces of tiles and stones with the heaps of jades and jasper. I sincerely hope the readers of posterity will not sneer at it.

The fifteenth day of the third month in the fourth year of Chuigong (688)

ANNOTATION

1 Land of Endurance or the sahā world (sahā-loka-dhātu), refers to this world which is regarded as a place where the living beings have power of great tolerance to suffering, also be called the world system of endurance.

2 Eightfold Noble Path: (1) right view; (2) right thought; (3) right speech; (4) right action; (5) right livelihood; (6) right effort; (7) right mindfulness; (8) right concentration.

3 Triple Gem or Three Jewels: (1) the Buddha, the unsurpassed perfectly enlightened teacher; (2) the Dharma, His teachings; (3) the Saṅgha, the Buddhist community.

4 Vaipulya: extensive (broad) Mahāyāna, a number of important Mahāyāna works, including the *Lotus Sūtra*, *Aṣṭasāhasrikā prajñāpāramitā*, and *Laṅkāvatāra sūtra* and so on.

5 Ekayāna: the One Vehicle, also called the Buddhayāna (Buddha Vehicle); the Mahayāna (q.v) doctrine which contains the final and complete Buddha Dharma and not merely a part, or a preliminary stage, as in the Hīnayāna. It is often identified with the teaching of the Lotus Sūtra.

6 Ten Stages of the Perfect Truth refers to the Ten Stages of Bodhisattvahood: (1) the stage of joy, in which one experiences the joy of entering on the path to Buddhahood; (2) the stage of stainlessness, in which one is liberated from all possible defilements; (3) the stage of bright radiance, the stage of further enlightenment; (4) the stage of blazing fire; (5) the stage that is difficult to conquer, in which one masters final difficulties; (6) the stage of presence, the open way of wisdom above definitions of impurity and purity; (7) the stage of reaching afar in which one gets above ideas of self in order to save others; (8) the stage of imperturbability; (9) the stage of subtle wisdom, in which one possesses the finest discriminatory wisdom, knowing where and how to save beings, and the ten powers; (10) the stage of the Dharma-cloud, in which

one attains to the fertilizing power of the Dharma-cloud. These stages of Bodhisattva practice could make Bodhisattva progress from initial aspiration to the highest station in the bodhisattva's path, which are described in the Ten Stages Sūtra, or Daśabhūmika Sūtra of the Avataṃsaka Sūtra (alternatively, the Mahāvaipulya Buddhāvataṃsaka Sūtra). This Sūtra gives details on the ten stages (bhūmis) of development a bodhisattva must undergo to attain supreme enlightenment. The Ten Stages are also depicted in the *Laṅkāvatāra Sūtra* and the *Śūraṅgama Sūtra*. Actually, the Ten Stages of the Perfect Truth here should stand for the *Buddhavatamsaka-mahavaipulya Sūtra*, also called the *Flower Adornment Sūtra* or the *Garland Sūtra*, *Avataṃsaka-sūtra*, in Chinese《大方广佛华严经》.Three translations have been made: (1) by Buddhabhadra, who arrived in China A.D. 406, in 60 juan; (2) by Śikṣānanda, about A.D. 700, in 80 juan; (3) by Prajñā about A.D. 800, in 40 juan.

7 "真荃" in the source text refers to the ultimate truth of Buddhism indicated by the skillful expedients, such as "荃", means basket-trap, coming from a passage in the twenty-sixth chapter of the *Zhuangzi*, which reads: "A basket-trap is for catching fish, but when one has got the fish, one need think no more about the basket. A foot-trap is for catching hares; but when one has got the hare, one need think no more about the trap. Words are for holding ideas, but when one has got the idea, one need no longer think about the words." A Short History of Chinese Philosophy, page 12. Or Selected Philosophical Writings of Fung Yu-lan, Beijing: Foreign Language Press, 1991, pp.205-206.

8 There are seven parables in the *Lotus Sūtra* (*Saddharma Puṇḍarīka Sūtra*, literally "*Sūtra on the White Lotus of the Sublime Dharma*"): (1) The Burning House (Chapter 3 Parable of Three carts and Burning house); (2) The Lost Heir (Chapter 4 Parable of the Wealthy Man and His Poor Son); (3) The Plants (Chapter 5 Parable of Three kinds of Medicinal Herbs); (4) The Phantom City (Chapter 7 Parable of Phantom City and Treasure Land); (5)

The Concealed Gem (Chapter 8 Bestowal of Prophecy to the Five Hundred Monks); (6) The Topknot Jewel or the Jewels in the Robe (the Concealed Gem) (Chapter 14 Peaceful Practices); (7) The Physician's Sons (Chapter 16 Parable of Skilled Physician and His Sick Children)." In the Chapter 7, "the Phantom City" tells a story about a group of people who are led by a knowledgeable guide through a wilderness to a place where they will find great treasure. After some time, the group becomes weary and disheartened and wish to turn back. The guide tells them that, just a short distance ahead, there is a city where they can lodge and refresh themselves. They enter the city, and, when they feel better, the city vanishes. The guide explains that he created it by magic in order to satisfy their needs. The treasure, he says, is near, and if they make one more effort, they will find it. Indeed, the guide is the Buddha; the group of people are disciples; the phantom city is Buddhism; and the treasure is the Buddha Nature.

9 In the Chapter 4 of the *Lotus Sūtra*, "Understanding and Belief," there is a story about a lost heir: A boy leaves home and wanders from place to place, taking odd jobs to support himself. At age fifty, he enters a big city and sees a millionaire who is in fact this poor man's father. The son does not recognize his father, but the father recognizes his son and sends men to capture him into a luxurious mansion. The son is terrified, and the father orders him released, subsequently sending other men who, abandoning force, entice him to accept the job of cleaning the latrines in his father's house, a work that the son finds appropriate to his low sense of self-worth. Occasionally, the father disguises himself and works alongside his son. He frequently sends servants to encourage him and gradually promotes him to chief steward. On his deathbed the father reveals that his faithful servant is in fact his true son and bequeaths to him all his estate. It is explained that the Buddha is the father; the son is a disciple; wandering in poverty is living in samsara; the menial jobs are the teachings and practices of Buddhism; and the inheritance is the Buddha Nature.

10 In the Chapter 3 of the Lotus Sūtra, "the parable of Burning House," the Buddha teaches a parable in which a father uses the promise of various toy carts— bullock-carts, goat-carts, and deer-carts— to get his children out of a burning house. Once they are outside, he gives them all one large cart to travel in instead. This symbolizes how the Buddha uses the Three Vehicles: Śrāvakayāna, Pratyekabuddhayāna and Bodhisattvayāna, as skillful means to liberate all beings – even though there is only one vehicle. The many "skillful" or "expedient" means and the "three vehicles (yāna)" are revealed to all be part of the One Vehicle (Ekayāna), which is also Samyaksambuddhahood.

11 Dhyāna: the practice of meditation.

12 Vinaya: the precepts, the disciplinary rules.

13 Dhāraṇī: an incantation.

14 Refers to the *Huayan Sūtra*, or the *Avataṃsaka Sūtra* (alternatively, the *Mahāvaipulya Buddhāvataṃsaka Sūtra*), which is one of the most influential Mahāyāna Sūtras of East Asian Buddhism. The title is rendered in English also as the *Flower Garland Sūtra*, *Flower Adornment Sūtra*, or *Flower Ornament Scripture*. The discourses in the sutra are delivered to eight different audiences or "assemblies" in seven locations such as Bodh Gaya and the Tusita Heaven.

15 The Three Turnings of the Dharma Wheel refers to the three times the Buddha expounding the teachings of the Four Noble Truths. During the first turning for indication, the Buddha reveals, "This is suffering; this is accumulation of afflictions; this is cessation of suffering; this is the path." During the second turning for persuasion, He advises, "This is the suffering you should know; this is the accumulation of afflictions you should destroy; this is the cessation of suffering you should achieve; this is the path you should take." During the third turning for confirmation, He testifies, "This is the suffering I have known; this is the accumulation of afflictions I have destroyed; this is the cessation of suffering I have achieved; this is the path I have completed."

16 They are large and small māndarāva (曼陀罗花) which are red blooms of the coral tree, as well as large and small mañjūṣaka (曼殊沙花) which are white blooms of an herbaceous plant.

17 Also, the six earthquakes, or earth-shakings, of which there are three different categories. (1)Those at the Buddha's conception, birth, enlightenment, first preaching, when Māra besought him to live, and at his nirvāṇa; some omit the fifth and after "birth" add "leaving home." (2) The six different kinds of shaking of the chiliocosm, or universe, when the Buddha entered into the samādhi of joyful wandering, see *Dapin bore jing* (*Pañcaviṃśatisāhasrikā Prajñāpāramitā Sūtra* 《大品般若经》), i. e. east rose and west sank, west rose and east sank, north rose and south sank, south sank and north rose, middle rose and borders sank, and borders rose and middle sank. (3). Another group is shaking, rising, waving, reverberating, roaring, arousing, the first three referring to motion, the last three to sounds; see the above; which in later translations gives shaking, rising, reverberating, beating, roaring, crackling.

18 In the *Lotus Sūtra*, both the parables of "The Topknot Jewel" in Chapter 14 Peaceful Practices and "The jewels in the robe" or "The Concealed Gem" in Chapter 8 Bestowal of Prophecy to the Five Hundred Monks, are alluded to the precious Buddha Dharma. In the parable of the Topknot Jewel, a mighty king gives lavish gifts of all kinds to his victorious soldiers, holding back only his topknot jewel. At length, however, after their repeated victories, he gives his topknot jewel to the entire army. The king, then, is the Buddha; the soldiers are disciples. The Concealed Gem tells a story that a poor man visits a rich friend, gets drunk, and passes out. The rich man, who leaves on business, gives this poor friend a priceless gem, which he sews into the lining of his friend's clothes. After the rich man leaves, the poor man resumes his life as a vagrant, unaware of the treasure he received during his blackout. Later, he meets the rich man again, who shows him where the gem is concealed, and

the poor man realizes his wealth. In the story, the rich man is the Buddha; the poor man is a sattva, drunk with the passions; and the jewel is the truth about the Buddha Nature.

19 Vehicles are the means to take living beings across from suffering to nirvāṇa. Three vehicles: the three paths to enlightenment: (1) the Śrāvaka-vehicle, or Śrāvakayāna or the Hearer vehicle: A path that meets the goals of an arhat who achieves liberation after listening to the teachings of a samyaksambuddha (fully enlightened buddha).(2) the Pratyekabuddha-vehicle or Pratyekabuddhayāna: the pratyekabuddha achieves liberation, but does not teach other beings. Pratyekabuddhas do not depend on a teacher and can discover the Dharma even if they do not encounter a buddha. They are sometimes said to remain silent and solitary.(3) the Bodhisattva-vehicle or Bodhisattvayāna: the bodhisattva attains liberation and wishes to benefit as many beings as possible. A bodhisattva who has accomplished this goal is called a samyaksambuddha. A samyaksambuddha can establish the Dharma and lead disciples to enlightenment

20 *Or Accounts of the Causes and Conditions of the Transmission of the Dharma Treasury* (*Fufazang Yinyuan Zhuan*《付法藏因缘传》) is the work explaining the handing down of Śākyamuni's teaching by Mahākāśyapa and the elders, twenty-four in number; tr. in the Yuan Dynasty (1271—1368) in six juan.

21 Tathāgata : a title of the Buddha, also Thus-come, Thus-gone, or Suchness, means absolute truth, or ultimate reality; the content of wisdom-insight into things, just as they are, i.e., empty and dependently co-arisen.

22 Ajitavatī: also known as Airavatī, Ajiravatī, or Achiravatī. A river flowing through Kushinagara in India, where Shakyamuni Buddha entered nirvāṇa. The river is generally believed to be identical with the Hiraṇyavatī River, which is where Shakyamuni died in a grove of śāla trees near its west bank.

23 It was said that in Kuśinagar, by Ajitavatī River, between two śāla trees, the

Buddha attained parinirvāṇa on the fifteenth day of the second month of the year 483 BC, where the final sermon of the 80-year-old Buddha was imparted to his followers that surrounded him.

24 Mahākāśyapa (摩诃迦叶or Kāśyapa)was one of the principal disciples of Gautama Buddha. Mahākāśyapa assumed the leadership of the Sangha after the death of the Buddha, presiding over the First Buddhist Council. He is considered to be the first patriarch in a number of Mahāyāna School dharma lineages.

25 Gāthā: a stanza, works in poetic form. "song" or "verse." Gāthā belongs to one of nine divisions of Sūtras, and is an important Buddhist style.

26 Upadeśa: discussions of doctrine—sometimes esoteric doctrine—often in question-and-answer form. The term has also been used for Abhidhamma (scholastic section of the canon), for philosophical treatises, for Tantric works, and for commentaries.

27 Or the noumenal and the phenomenal.

28 Wang Zun 王尊, a general of the Eastern Han Dynasty (25–220). Qin Jing秦景, a scholar-official of the Eastern Han Dynasty. One night, Emperor Ming (r. 58–75) of the Han Dynasty dreamed a golden deity flying into his palace. On the morning, he consulted his ministers about the dream and was told by Fu Yi傅毅, one of his ministers, that the golden deity must be the Buddha. Thus, he dispatched 12 envoys abroad to learn more about the Buddha and the Dharma. Among them, there were Wang Zun and Qin Jing. The envoys returned with the *Sūtra in Forty-two Chapters* (*Sishi'er Zhang Jing* 《四十二章经》), which was later translated into Chinese by Kāśyapa-Mātnga and Dharmaratna.

29 Jiayemoteng 迦叶摩腾, or Kāśyapa-Mātaṇga: was an Indian Buddhist monk who is traditionally believed to have first introduced Buddhism into China in the 1st century CE. According to popular accounts of Chinese Buddhism, Emperor Ming of Han (28–75) dreamt of a golden deity interpreted as the

Buddha and sent a delegation to India. They returned circa 67 CE with the monks Kāśyapa-Mātaṇga and Dharmaratna (or 竺法兰Zhu Falan), and white horses carrying Buddhist texts and images. The emperor established White Horse Temple in the Han capital Luoyang, where the two supposedly first translated the *Sūtra of Forty-two Chapters into Chinese.*

30 Or Fotucheng佛图澄 (or竺佛图澄ca. 232–348) , was a Buddhist monk and missionary from Kucha. He is also called Buddhasiṁha佛陀僧诃. He studied in Kashmir and came to Luoyang in 310 AD. He was good at the mantric arts and active in the spread of Buddhism in China.

31 Guṇabhadra 求那跋陀罗(tr. 德賢Dexian 394–468), was a monk of Mahāyāna Buddhism from Magadha, India. He is a follower of the Mahīśāsakā in Kapiśā and a brāhmaṇa of Central India, tr. He travelled to China by sea in 435. He was treated as honored guest by Emperor Wen of Liu Song (407–453), the ruler of South China at the time. In China, he translated the *Laṅkāvatāra Sūtra*, the *Saṃyuktāgama* and some seventy-eight works into Chinese.

32 As a custom in ancient China, hanging a bow on the door symbolizes the birth of a boy into the family.

33 One of Mañjuśrī's epithets is miaode (妙德, meaning "wonderful virtue") .

34 Emptiness (śūnyata): the absence of permanent essence in things. The twofold emptiness has various interpretations, among which the most popular is pudgalanairātmya (non-substantiality of the self) and dharma-nairātmya (non-substantiality of the dharmas).

35 Wutianzhu (五天竺, literally the five realms of India), also Five Indias, refers to five geographical regions in India known to the Chinese in ancient times: Central, Eastern, Western, Northern, and Southern India. Tianzhu is the historical East Asian name for India, which comes from the Chinese transliteration of the Persian Hindu, which is itself derived from the Sanskrit Sindhu, the native name of the Indus River. Tianzhu is just one of several Chinese transliterations, others are Sindhu, Tiandu, Hindu, and so forth.

36 Refers to the northern flow of the Hotan River (和田河, also spelt ancient Khotan River于阗河) which merges with the Yarkand River and flows eastward into Lop Nor. The Yarkand River in southern Xinjiang today was called the Congling River (葱岭河or Cong River 葱河) in records from the Western Han Dynasty to the Southern and Northern Dynasties (206 BC–589CE).

37 Āmrapālī is the name of the mango groves, which Āmrapālī, a celebrated royal courtesan of the republic of Vaishali (located in present-day Bihar) in ancient India around 500 BC, donated to the Buddhist order and wherein the Buddha preached some famous Sūtras.

38 The Vulture Peak, also Gṛdhrakūṭa Mountain or Gádhrakúta, was the Buddha's favorite retreat in Rājagṛha and the scene for many of his discourses. It is in Rajgir, Bihar, India.

39 Near the garden of Amrapali, in the city of Vaisali, where the Buddha once preached.

40 The Deer Park, Mṛgadāva of Vārāṇasī, also referred to as Isipatana, a favorite resort of Śākyamuni where the Buddha delivered his first sermon. The modern Sarnath near Benares.

41 Tripiṭaka (three baskets): the Buddhist canon.

42 Lesser Vehicle, refers to Hīnayāna Buddhism.

43 The Emperor Taizong (太宗, r. 626–649) of the Tang Dynasty previously was Prince of Qin, and his personal name was Li Shimin. He was the second emperor of the Tang Dynasty of China, ruling from 626 to 649. He is traditionally regarded as a co-founder of the dynasty for his role in encouraging Li Yuan 李渊 (r. 618–626), his father, to rebel against the Sui Dynasty in Jinyang in 617. Taizong subsequently played a pivotal role in defeating several of the dynasty's most dangerous opponents and solidifying its rule over China.

44 Huili (615–?): is a native of modern Tianshui, in Gansu Province. His ancestor was promoted to take an official position in Xinping (新平, later

called Binzhou 豳州 or 邠州, modern Binxian 彬县) of Shaanxi Province. He became a monk at 15 years old at Zhaoren Temple in Binzhou (豳州昭仁寺). In 605, he participated in the translation center of Xuanzang at Da Ci'en Monastery. Later he served as rector of Ximing Monastery (西明寺), and then abbot of Taiyuan Temple (太原寺) in Chang'an.

45 Or Weiguo xi si, situated in Chang'an.

Fascicle I

Beginning from the Birth of Xuanzang in Goushi and Ending with His Arrival in Gaochang

Xuanzang was the dharma-name (ordination name) of the Master. His family was the nobility with surname Chen[1] in Chenliu Prefecture[2]. He was a descendant of [Chen] Zhonggong[3], Magistrate of Taiqiu prefecture[4] of the Han Dynasty (206 BC–220 AD.). His great grandfather was [Chen] Qin, Governor of Shangdang region[5] of the Later Wei Dynasty (386–535). His grandfather [Chen] Kang was a distinguished scholar who was a professor of the National Academy[6] at the court of Qi (550–577) and lived upon the revenue of Zhounan[7] where descendants of the family took their residence hereafter. The Master was born in Goushi[8]. His father [Chen] Hui was a man of elegant nature and high morality, well-versed in Confucian classics from an early age. Being eight *chi* in height, with handsome eyebrows and bright eyes, Hui was disposed to dress himself in a loose garment with a broad girdler as a Confucian scholar usually did. As a gentleman of composed and simple nature, he sought neither political promotion nor prestige, hence was often likened to Guo Youdao[9] by the people of his time. Disgusting with the decay and fall of the Sui Dynasty (581–618), he retired and devoted himself to the study of the ancient classics. He was repeatedly offered with the official honor of *xiaolian*[10] by the prefecture authorities and even summoned by the Emperor to take up the position of judicial inspector, but he declined all of them on the excuse of bad health, because of which, he was esteemed and praised by some far-sighted contemporaries. Among his four sons, the Master was the youngest.

The Master was outstanding in morality and endowments, also exceptionally perspicacious when he was still a child. At eight years old, once his father taught him *Xiao jing* (the *Classic on Filial Piety*) face to face at a small table, and when he heard that Zengzi stood up from his mat to show his respect to Confucius when listening to his teacher's discourse[11], the Master arranged his dress and suddenly stood up. Being asked for the reason, the boy replied, "Zengzi rose from mat to show his reverence to the teacher for his instructions. How can I sit still and listen to the earnest teachings from my father?" On hearing this, the father was delighted, foreseeing that his son would make some achievement in the future. The father, then, gathered his clansmen, shared them with this incident, and thus received congratulatory remark, "You have a prodigy like Yang Wu[12]." We can see how precocious the Master was. Later, the Master gained a thorough knowledge of various abstruse classics. Preferring only ancient texts and admiring the worthy, he never read any books of no literary value or of no propriety, nor did he ever learn from anyone who was not the sagacious scholar. Young as the Master was, he never mixed with the children of his own age nor set his foot at the marketplace. Even if there were the noises of drums and bells in thoroughfares, or din of performances and songs in lanes, or throngs rolling like clouds in front of his chamber, never did he go outside to see the sight. Besides, at a very young age, the Master already knew how to treat his parents with a kind and pleasant countenance, amiable and scrupulous in filial manner.

Ven. Changjie[13], second elder brother of the Master, became a monk earlier and was then living in Jingtu Monastery[14] at the Eastern Capital[15]. When he perceived that the Master was qualified to be a receiver of the Dharma, he brought him to the temple and taught him Buddhist scriptures. Shortly afterwards, here came an imperial edict to the effect that fourteen persons were to be ordained as monks in Luoyang. At the time, however, there were several hundred candidates with intimate knowledge of Buddhism. Not old enough, the Master even was not permitted to be a candidate. One day the Master stood at the gateway to the government office, Zheng Shanguo (572–629), Lord of Justice in charge of the issue, a man good at judging people's talents, saw him and felt quite curious. Then he asked the lad, "Whose family do you come from?" The Master told him his family clan.

"Do you want to be ordained?" asked Zheng.

"Yes," replied the Master, "but since I haven't studied scriptures for long enough time and my knowledge is shallow, I am not supposed to be a candidate for the election."

Hearing this, Zheng Shanguo continued to demand, "Why do you want to be a monk?"

"To inherit the Tathāgata's teachings, to glorify the bequeathed Dharma in the present." the Master replied.

Appreciating his ambition and impressed with his appearance and manner, Zheng generously granted him a special admission. He told his official colleagues, "It is easy for one to recite Buddhist texts but hard to have such a noble quality. Now the lad has been admitted, no doubt he will grow into a brilliant monk of Śākya family, but what a pity it is when I think that neither Your Excellences nor I shall live long enough to see the day he is soaring high above the clouds and sprinkling down Sweet Dew (amṛta) to the world. Moreover, I don't think we should miss a scion of a distinguished family."

Considering what happened in the later days, the words of the Lord Zheng proved true.

Having become a monk, the Master dwelt with his brother in Jingtu Monastery. At that time, there was a Ven. Jing[16] lecturing on the *Mahāparinirvāṇa Sūtra* at the monastery, from whom the Master learned. Being overwhelmed by a strong zeal for study, the Master held the *Sūtra* in his hands all day and night, even forgetting to eat and sleep. With much more interest, he also studied the *Mahāyānasaṅgraha Śāstra*[17] under the instruction of Ven. Yan[18]. Showing great learning capacity, he was able to grasp the gist of any Buddhist text at the first reading and digested it thoroughly at the second time. Greatly amazed at his extraordinary talent, the fellow monks invited him to mount the pulpit to repeat what he had learned. The Masters never failed — he was capable of making a concise and complete elucidation of what he had heard from the preaching of his teachers; thereupon, he became well-known for his refined sermons.

He was then only thirteen years old.

Afterwards, Sui Court[19] lost its power and the whole nation fell into a great chaos: the capital city became the liar of despots cruel as [Xia] Jie[20] and the den of insurgents recalcitrant as [Dao] Zhi[21]; the region between the Yellow River and the Luo River was turned into the haunt of the wicked and evil; the propriety and laws were exterminated and the Buddhist communities destroyed; and human bones and corpses were heaped up in the midst of thoroughfares and the cooking smoke no longer spotted. Alas! Even the riots brought up by the usurpation of Wang [Mang][22] and Dong [Zhuo][23], or the confusion caused by the aggression of Liu [Yuan][24] and Shi [Le][25], were no horrible than massacre and calamity at that time. Young as he was, the Master knew how to adapt himself to the circumstances. He said to his brother, "Here is our hometown, but now violence and disorder are visited upon it so severely that we could not continue to stay here and wait for death. I have heard that Emperor of Tang[26] mustered his troops from Jinyang[27] and occupied Chang'an, and our fellow countrymen are all flocking to him like children to their parents. I want to go there with you too." His brother consented. They arrived at Chang'an in the first year of Wude (618).

As a newly-established dynasty, Tang government gave priority to the matters concerning armaments, and so the military art of Sun [Wu][28] and Wu [Qi][29] were urgently explored to the exclusion of all else; as a result, there were no preaching gatherings held in the capital Chang'an to propagate Confucianism or Buddhism, which made the Master despondent. Formerly, Emperor Yang of the Sui Dynasty constructed four monasteries in the Eastern Capital to beckon eminent monks throughout the empire to come and reside in. Those who were summoned were monks with peculiar knowledge in certain topics of Buddhism, thus in the four monasteries gathered many distinguished Buddhist scholars, among them [Hui]jing, [Zhi]tuo, [Dao]ji and [Bao]xian[30] being the most renowned. During the late years of Sui, the national tumult called a halt to the supplies to the monasteries, forcing most scholar monks to remove to Mian and Shu regions[31], where Buddhist intellectual centers thus came into being. The Master said to his elder brother, "Don't waste our time here since there is no more dharma activities to attend. Why not go to Shu to further our Buddhist studies?" Then they crossed the Ziwu Valley[32] and arrived at Hanchuan[33], where they ran across two Buddhist masters Kong and Jing, both being the great virtuous teachers. At such an unexpected encounter, all of them were overwhelmed by intermingled feelings of grief and joy. Staying there, the Master and his elder brother studied under them for more than a month; after that, they proceeded together to Chengdu[34].

Since a large number of the venerable Buddhist scholars assembled in Chengdu, there were a lot of gatherings held to propagate the Dharma extensively. The Master attended the lectures on the *Mahāyānasaṅgraha Śāstra* and the *Abhidharmasamuccaya Śāstra* delivered by [Dao]ji and [Bao]xian, also the *pitan*[35] *of Kātyāyana* by [Dao]zhen[36]. Without wasting a minute in laxity, he studied diligently and earnestly for two to three years, and finally became well-versed in doctrines of various Buddhist schools. At the time, the region of Shu was the only place where people could live peacefully in abundance despite severe famine and riot rampant the country, and therefore it was full of monks from the rest parts of the nation. The listeners attending lectures often amounted to several hundred on average. Surpassing other monks in intelligence and talent, the Master won his name in the regions of Wu[37], Shu, Jing and Chu[38]. Because of his erudition and personality, he was idolized by his contemporaries who often likened him to Li (Ying)[39] or Guo (Tai)[40] in the ancient times.

The Master's elder brother was then living in the Konghui Monastery at Chengdu. Being like his father, he was also well-built, refined, and vivacious. He was fond of both Buddhist and Confucian teachings. Apart from delivering lectures on Buddhist texts, such as the *Mahāparinirvāṇa Sūtra*, the *Mahāyānasaṅgraha Śāstra* and the *Abhidharmasamuccaya Śāstra,* he was also quite learned in traditional Chinese classics, such as the *Shangshu Kongshi Zhuan*[41], especially erudite in the *Laozi*[42] and *Zhuangzi*[43]; therefore, he was respected by the Shu people, particularly appreciated, and thought highly of by the local governors, such as Wei Yunqi (?–626) and Dou Gui (?–630). As regards his eloquence, literary ability, refined manners, worldly wisdom and his expedients in moralizing the people, he was indeed no inferior to his younger brother, but the Master outshone his elder brother in other aspects as follows: his distinguished demeanor and pure personality, his long journey to pursue the profound and abstruse truth, his great and extensive ambition, his determination of carrying on the tasks of the sagacious forebears, his revitalization of what had been degenerating, his refutation and abolition of the evil customs, his unabated willpower after experiencing disturbances, and his moral integrity preserved in the presence of the sovereigns. In a word, the two brothers lived purely in obedience to the monastic rules, they enjoyed high prestige for the nobility of character, even Lushan Brothers[44] could not do better.

In the fifth year of Wude (622), when the Master was twenty years old, he was fully ordained in Chengdu. During his summer retreat, he learned the Vinaya rules — the five classifications and seven groups of the Vinaya[45], which he studied once for all. After having completed the study of all scriptures and commentaries available in the region of Yi[46], he planned to go to the capital Chang'an to further his study and dispel his doubts. But forbidden by law and disapproved by his elder brother, the Master had to follow some merchants to sail down the Three Gorges[47] secretly, and floating along the Yangzi River[48], he arrived at the Tianhuang Monastery in Jingzhou[49]. Having heard of his name for a long time, the monks and laity were so honored with his unexpected presence that they jumped at the chance to invite him to preach the Dharma. Then the Master delivered the lectures on the *Mahāyānasaṅgraha Śāstra*as well as the *Abhidharmasamuccaya Śāstra*, each text for three times from summer to winter. At the time, Prince of Hanyang[50], a relative of the royal family, was the governor of Jingzhou, who was a man of great virtue. Delighted at the Master's arrival, he went to pay homage the Master. On the first day at the Master's preaching assembly, the topic of the sermon was hardly revealed when the Prince came to attend as audience, leading his subordinate officers, monks and laity who were all well-versed in some particular school of Buddhism. During the preaching, questions and inquiries came up one after another from the listeners, to which the Master gave clear answers and explanations convincingly. With satisfaction, all listeners acquired a deep understanding of what the Master had taught, some of whom even could not help shedding tears in thankful excitement. Eulogizing the Master in highest terms, the Prince, in addition, offered him with various gifts piling up like a hillock, but the Master didn't take any of them.

After the Master finished his preaching activities, he traveled northward to look for some more virtuous teachers. At Xiangzhou[51], he visited the venerable teacher [Hui]xiu[52], inquired about some difficult problems and had his doubts solved. Then he went to Zhaozhou[53] to visit the venerable teacher [Dao]shen[54] and from him learned the *Satyaśāsana Śāstra.* After that, he went to Chang'an and stayed in Dajue Monastery[55], where he learned the *Abhidharmakośa Śāstra* from the venerable teacher [Dao]yue[56]. The Master grasped the essentials of all these texts by the first hearing and memorized them once for all. Even the erudite seniors could do no better. Besides, whenever coming to a profound doctrine that was beyond the understanding of other learners, he was alone capable of developing a thorough comprehension of it and revealing its hidden and subtle meanings. This happened to more than one doctrine.

At the time, there were two teachers of great virtue in Chang'an, [Fa]chang[57] and [Seng]bian[58], who were well-learned in the Two Vehicles[59] and the Three Studies[60]. As the leading Dharma teachers of the capital, they were followed by disciples, both monks and laity. Their reputation for erudition was known throughout the country and far abroad, so the people eager to be their disciples flocked to them as the clouds gathering in the sky. They preached on doctrines of various

Buddhist scriptures, especially on the *Mahāyānasaṅgraha Śāstra*. The Master had already achieved his fame in Wu and Shu regions, and after he arrived at Chang'an, he resumed his study with them and quickly grasped the deepest truth of what they preached. Impressed with him, they spared no effort in their compliments, "You are a winged steed among the descendants of Śākyamuni. Because of you, the sun of wisdom will illumine once again, but we, in our dotage, may not be able to see that day. What a pity it is!." Henceforward, the fellow disciples looked up to the Master with veneration and his renown was then well-established in the capital.

Having paid visits to various teachers, the Master acquainted himself with varied theories, but after a close examination, he found that these theories failed to elucidate the Buddhist teachings completely for each of them was misled by the biased view held by a particular school. But when he checked the holy scriptures for verification and rectification, he still felt at a loss because the differences only lay in the clarity or vagueness of the words rather than in theories. Thus, he resolved to make a journey to the West to inquire about his own curiosities and bring back the *Saptadaśabhūmi Śāstra,* which is now called the *Yogācārabhūmi Śāstra,* and to remove the doubts of others as well. Once he said to other monks, "In the past, there were the outstanding monks like Faxian[61] and Zhiyan[62] who pursued the Buddha Dharma for the purpose of guiding and benefiting the sentient beings. Why should such meritorious deeds be obliterated today and why should their noble character be lost without a successor? A great man must follow suit!" Afterwards, the Master, together with several monks, submitted a petition to the court pleading for a journey to the West, but which was declined by an imperial decree. Other companions withdrew, with the Master alone braving on.

Having determined to take a solitary journey and to face up the hardships and dangers on the Western road, he deliberately tested and tempered his willpower by taking various self-inflicted cultivation without flinching. Also he went to a Buddhist pagoda to make known his aspiration and asked for the divine protection to ensure there would be no hindrance on his journeys forth and back. Formerly, when the Master was born, his mother dreamed that he was going westward in a white robe[63]. In the dream, the mother asked, "You are my son. Where are you going?" and got the reply, "I'm going to seek the Dharma." Obviously, it was a portent indicting the Master's future journey to the West.

In the autumn, the eighth month of the third year of Zhenguan (629)[64], before the Master was about to start his journey, he prayed again for a good omen. Then one night he dreamed that in the middle of the great sea there was the Mount Sumeru[65] which was made of four precious substances[66], appearing solemnly high and beautiful. He wanted to scale the mountain but could not approach it because there was no boat or raft available to cross the roaring waves. Dauntlessly, he decided to walk into the sea. When such a thought came up, suddenly underneath his foot stepping forward, a stone lotus cropped up from the water to support him, but disappeared instantly when he paused to look at it. In a moment, he arrived at the foot of the mountain, but could not climb up it for it was precipitously steep. The moment he tried to leap, he was carried by a soughing whirlwind up to the top of the mountain. There he stood and looked around, obtaining a clear vision of everything without obstacles. In delight he woke up, and so decided to set out on his journey. At the time the Master was twenty-six years old.

In the capital there was a monk, named Xiaoda, coming from Qinzhou[67], who had been studying the *Mahāparinirvāṇa Sūtra*. After he finished his learning, he left for home. The Master then followed him to Qinzhou, where the Master stayed for one night and made acquaintance with a man from Lanzhou[68], and so with this man he came to Lanzhou. After spending one night in Lanzhou, he came cross a native of Liangzhou[69] who was driving some official horses back home, and the Master went to Liangzhou with him. He stayed there for more than one month, and during his sojourn, at the request of the local monks and laity, he delivered the lectures on the *Mahāparinirvāṇa Sūtra*, the *Mahāyānasaṅgraha Śāstra* and the *Mahāprajñāpāramitā Sūtra*.

Liangzhou, encircled by the western tribes, was a city of vital importance to the Hexi region[70], also a link of various countries situated to the west of the Pamirs[71], and so the coming and going of the merchants had never stopped. On the day when the Master began to preach the Dharma, many merchants came to offer the jewelry gifts, who swore obeisance to him by touching their foreheads on the ground in admiration. After they returned to their countries, besides highly praising the Master, they also told their rulers and superiors that the Master wanted to go to the West to search for the ultimate truth in the Brahminic countries. Hearing the news, in delight, the city authorities in the Western Regions[72] set about preparing for the coming of the Master. On the conclusion day of the preaching assembly, abundant treasures, jewelries, gold and silver coins, and horses of good breed were presented as offerings, but of which the Master only remained the half for buying lamps to worship the Buddha and distributed the rest among other monasteries.

At that time, the regime of the Tang Dynasty was newly established and the borders were so often threatened by the invasion of neighboring tribes that an edict was issued prohibiting the common people to go to the Western Regions. Li Daliang, then Governor of Liangzhou, adhered to this strict edict rigorously. He felt worried when he heard the report that a monk from Chang'an intended to go to the countries in the West for the unknown purpose. Liang summoned the Master to him to inquire about his purpose. After the Master told him that his intention was to seek for the Buddha Dharma, Liang ordered him to go back to the capital.

There was a venerable teacher named Huiwei, a man of great intelligence and wisdom, who was the head of the Buddhist communities in the region of Hexi. He appreciated the Master's eloquence and knowledge, and on hearing the ambition of the Master, he rejoiced at it. Secretly, he sent his two disciples, Huilin and Daozheng, to escort the Master westward. Together, however, they dared not to proceed overtly, then concealed themselves by day and marched by night. They reached Guazhou[73], where the prefecture governor Dugu Da felt greatly delighted at the arrival of the Master and provided him with abundant provisions. The Master inquired about the way to the West and got the answer as follows: going forward from here to the north fifty odd *li*, you will come to the Hulu

River[74] which is broad in the lower course and narrow in the upper. It is impossible for you to ferry across it for it is turbulent and deep. At the river's upper reaches is Yumen Pass[75], the only way to the Western Regions. It is the route you must choose! Northwest to the Pass are five watchtowers with garrisons, one hundred *li* apart from each other, with barren and arid lands in between. Beyond those five watchtowers is Moheyan Desert[76] that is in the territory of Yiwu[77].

On hearing this, the Master became worried and deplored; what's worse, his horse had died. Not knowing what to do, he pondered over the journey in silence for more than a month.

During his sojourn, here came a search warrant from Liangzhou, saying that there was a monk named Xuanzang trying to enter the region of the western tribes, and that prefectures and counties along the route must take every precaution for his arrest. Li Chang, prefect of Guazhou, who was a devoted Buddhist, suspected that the Master was the wanted man. So, he revealed the search warrant to the Master in confidence and asked him, "Reverend teacher, you are not the wanted man in the warrant, are you?" With some hesitation, the Master didn't reply. Chang said, "You must tell me the truth. If you are the wanted man, I would help you to cope with it." Then the Master told him he was. Extolling the extraordinary ambition of the Master, Chang said, "Now that you could pursue your ideal, why can not I destroy the warrant for you?" By saying this, Chang tore it up in front of the Master and urged him to set out as soon as possible. The Master, however, became more and more frustratingly lost. He had two monk companions; one was Daozheng, who had already gone to Dunhuang, and the other was Huilin, who, though hung back to company the Master, was known to be incapable of taking an arduous journey; therefore, the Master asked Huilin to go back home too. After that, the Master bought himself a horse, but still worried that there was no guide. Then he went to pay homage to the image of Bodhisattva Maitreya[78] in the monastery where he lodged, and prayed for a man who could guide him to pass the watchtowers. At that night, a man of *hu* tribe[79], named Damo [meaning "dharma"], had a dream in which he saw the Master sitting on a lotus flower going westward. He was amazed by the dream, and so in the next morning, he came on to report it, at which the Master was delighted, regarding it as an auspicious omen for his westbound journey. But he said to Damo, "A dream is nothing but an illusion, not worthy of serious consideration." Then the Master entered the shrine hall to pray. Shortly, a man of *hu* tribe entered the hall to pay homage to the image of the Buddha. He walked around the Master for two or three times in worship. When the Master demanded his name, he answered, "My family name is Shi, private name Pantuo," and then begged the Master to confer the Buddhist precepts on him. Having received the conferment of the Five Precepts[80], he was much pleased and left. Very soon, he came back again with some cakes and fruits as offerings. Trusting this *hu* man who was bright and strong, humble and earnest, the Master made his intention of going to the West known to him. And the Master was overjoyed when the *hu* man forthwith promised to escort him to pass the five watchtowers and made an appointment with him to meet the next evening. Again, the Master bought some clothes and a horse, and waited for his coming. On the next evening when the dusk nearly fell, the Master went into the bushes. Before long, the *hu* man was coming, followed by a senior *hu* man riding on an aged lean horse reddish in hue. Seeing this, the Master became disheartened.

The young man said, "This old chap knows the route to the West very well. He has traveled back and forth to Yiwu for more than thirty times. I've brought him here for you to consult with." Then the old *hu* told the Master, "The westbound road is long and dangerous, blocked by the River of Drift Sand, and no one can avoid being inflicted by demons and hot winds. Even if travelling in a large group, there are still ones losing their lives or going astray. How could you, reverend teacher, go by yourself? Please think twice. Don't trifle with your life." The Master replied, "I, a humble monk, for the sake of the great Dharma, have made up my mind to go to the West. I would not return to the East before I reach the Brahminic countries. I would not regret it even if I lose my life on the way." The senior *hu* said, "If you, reverend teacher, insist on going, you'd better ride my horse. Knowing the route, this steady stager has traveled to and from Yiwu for fifteen times, by contrast, your horse is too young to cope with such a long journey." His words reminded the Master of an incident happening in Chang'an before:

After the Master set up his mind to go to the West, he consulted a fortune-teller named He Hongda about the journey, who was said to be capable to make accurate predictions through reciting the mantra or playing the art of divination. Then he told the Master, "You will be able to go. I see that you are to ride an old lean reddish horse with an iron piece in front of the varnished saddle."

Now, looking at the horse of the old *hu*, lean, reddish, especially with an iron piece in front of the varnished saddle, which was the same as the description of the sorcerer, the Master felt rest assured. Then he changed his horse for that of the old *hu*. Quite pleased, the old *hu* made obeisance and bade farewell to the Master.

Having packed the outfit, the Master set out on his journey with the young *hu* the very night. At about the third watch[81], they reached a river and saw Yumen Pass[82] at a distance. Walking up along the river 10 odd *li* to the pass, they came to a place where the river banks were more than one *zhang*[83] apart, thick with scrubby phoenix trees. The young *hu* cut down the tree branches to make a bridge, spread the grass on it, paved it with sand, and drove the horses on. They crossed the river, and only on the other shore did the Master breathe again. The Master unsaddled his horse and took a rest at a place fifty paces away from the *hu*. Having spread their quits to sleep, the *hu* man, however, crept up, drew his knife, walked slowly towards the Master, but at about ten paces away from the Master, he turned back. Although not knowing the *hu*'s intention, the Master suspected he brewed an evil idea; so, he sat up to chant scriptures and invoke the name of Bodhisattva Avalokiteśvara mindfully. Seeing this, the *hu* man had to lie down to take a sleep. When it was nearly daybreak, the Master woke him up to fetch some water to wash and cook. After the breakfast, the moment they were about to resume their journey, the *hu* man suggested, "Our journey ahead will be long and dangerous, no grass and no water. Only at the foot of five watchtowers could we find water, and we must steal it at night, but if we are discovered for once, we shall be dead men. So, in order to keep our lives, we'd better turn back." The Master steadfastly dismissed it. The *hu* man had to proceed reluctantly. After a while, he suddenly unsheathed his knife and drew the bow, ordering the Master to walk in front of him, but was refused by the Master again. After walking for several *li*, the *hu* man stopped and said, "I, your disciple, can't go further on, because I have a big family to support and I also don't want to violate the national law." Hearing those words and knowing his intention, the Master asked him to go back.

"Since you will not be able to reach your destination," said the *hu* man, "what should I do if you turn me in when you get caught?"

The Master swore, "I will not turn you in even if my body is cut into pieces."

Hearing this deep-sworn vow, the *hu* gave up his bad intent. Out of gratitude, the Master gave him a horse in return, and bade farewell to him.

Henceforward, the Master traveled alone in the desert, advancing ahead by observing the trails marked by bones, horse dung and the like. In a flash, before his eyes, appeared several hundred military troops scattering all over the desert, moving or stopping now and then. He also saw soldiers donning fur and felt uniforms, on camels or horses, with their flags and banners fluttering, spears shinning; in every blink, they changed in shapes and appearances. All those sights were clear at a distance but became obscure when coming close to him. Initially the Master thought they might be bandits, but as he approached to them, they soon vanished, which made him realize that they actually were demons and spirits. Meanwhile, he heard a voice in the air, saying "Have no fear! Have no fear!" On hearing this, he composed himself. Moving forward more than eighty *li*, he came to the first watchtower. Afraid of being discovered by the guard, the

Master hid himself in a sandy ditch and stayed there until the night fell. Stealthily, the Master went to the water pool at the western foot of the watchtower to drink and wash. When he was about to fill his leather bag with water, here came an arrow, whizzing by, which nearly hit his knee, and a moment later, another arrow came. Realizing that he had been spotted, the Master said in a loud voice, "I am a monk from the capital! Don't shoot at me!" Then leading the horse, he came to the tower. The men in the tower opened the door and went out. Seeing that he truly was a monk, they ushered him to the captain Wang Xiang. Xiang ordered others to light the torch and took a close look at the Master; then he said, "He doesn't look like a monk of our Hexi region, certainly he is coming from the capital." Again, he inquired of the Master's purpose of traveling.

The Master said, "Has the captain ever heard from the men of Liangzhou that there is a monk named Xuanzang who intends to go to Brahminic countries to seek the Dharma?"

The captain answered, "Yes. But I've heard Master Xuanzang already went back. How come you've arrived here?"

Then the Master took from the luggage his petition to the Emperor, on which there was his name. Xiang was convinced, he kindly told the Master, "I'm afraid the teacher will not be able to reach the destination because the route to the West is long and perilous. Now I do not want to punish you, and as I am a native of Dunhuang, so I wish to send you there, for there is a venerable monk, named Zhangjiao, who is a man showing reverence to the worthy and virtuous. I'm sure he would be happy when he meets you. Please head to Dunhuang."

The Master replied, "I was born in Luoyang, and from a young age, I have cherished an aspiration for the Buddhist Path. I used to study under the venerable teachers of the two capitals[83] and the monk scholars in Wu and Shu, all of them possessing considerable expertise in certain school of Buddhism. After I had mastered their knowledge, I was flattered as one of the contemporary prominent teachers for the elucidation of Buddhist doctrines. If I want to benefit myself and establish my fame, why don't I remain in these places? Comparing with these masters, what do you think of the master at Dunhuang, inferior or superior? In fact, what I felt regretful was that the Buddhist scriptures were incomplete and the doctrines ambiguous, so I made a pledge to risk my life to seek the bequeathed Dharma from the West, disregard of whatsoever hardships and dangers I might meet on my road. Now you, an almsgiver[84], instead of encouraging me, persuaded me to shrink from my commission, could such a deed serve as the due cause for relieving us from the worldly sufferings and attaining nirvāṇa? If you are to detain me, I'm at your disposal, ready to receive any punishment, but I shall not move a single step eastward to betray my original mind."

On hearing this, Xiang was greatly touched and said, "Today it is my great honor to meet the teacher. How dare I not support you? After an exhausted trek, why don't you take a rest first? Tomorrow morning, I will see you off by myself and show you the proper route."

Then the bedding was spread out for the Master to take a rest. In the next morning, after the breakfast, Xiang ordered his men to prepare the water and parched-wheat cakes for the journey, then he sent the Master off in person.

After walking together for more than ten *li*, he said, "Master, you can walk along this road straight up to the fourth watchtower. The captain in charge is a kindhearted man and he is of my family origin. His name is Bolong with the surname Wang. When you arrive, you can tell him that it is me who show you the way there." With those words, tears in eyes, he made obeisance to the Master and bade farewell.

At night, the Master arrived at the fourth watchtower. Lest he should be detained, he planned to fetch some water secretly and resume his journey unknowingly, but hardly had him got down to the pool when an arrow flew nearby. He had to announce his identity aloud and went up to the tower. Then the guard in the tower came down and ushered him inside. The official in charge interrogated him. The Master replied, "I came here on my way to India. The captain Wang Xiang of the first watchtower sent me on this way." On hearing this, in delight, Bolong put up him for the night. At the departure, he gave the Master a larger water bag and some more barley for the horse, and told him, "You needn't go to the fifth watchtower, for the man there was rude and rash. I'm afraid if seeing you he would brew evil intention. From this place, walking one hundred *li* or so is the Wild Horse Pool, Where you can get water."

Proceeding forward, the Master entered the Moheyan Desert, also called the River of Drift Sand in ancient times, stretching more than eight hundred *li*, no birds flying above and no animals roaming below, with neither grass nor water. Trudging along, nothing could be espied but the Master and his shadow. All he did was the ceaseless invocation of the name of Bodhisattva Avalokiteśvara or the recitation of the *Prajñāpāramitāhṛdaya Sūtra*[85]. Formerly in Shu region, he once met a ragged man with skin ulcer, very filthy and stingy. Showing compassion, the Master took the man to the temple and gave him money to buy clothes and food. Out of gratitude, the patient taught the Master the *Prajñāpāramitāhṛdaya Sūtra* face to face. Thereafter, the Master often recited it. Now in the desert, from time to time he was surrounded by devils of various shapes and kinds; at the beginning he recited the name of Bodhisattva Avalokiteśvara, which was effective but still could not dispel all of them, and so he chanted the *Prajñāpāramitāhṛdaya Sūtra* instead, and in an instant the words came out of his mouth, the devils were dismissed all at once. Therefore, he began to resort to this Sūtra for rescue when he fell into any danger.

After having moved on for more than one hundred *li,* he lost his way to the Wild Horse Pool. When he took the water bag down the horse back to drink, so heavy the bag was that he dropped it accidentally and the water was spilt all over. What's worse, he could not discern the directions, for the roads wound their ways intricately. So, he resolved to return eastward to the fourth watchtower, but after going back for ten odd *li,* he thought to himself, "Formerly, I took a vow that no matter what happened on the road I would never take a single step back to the East before I reached India. And now why am I going back? I would go westward to die rather than turn eastward to live!" Thinking so, he reined back his horse and proceeded toward the northwest, meanwhile invoking the name of Bodhisattva Avalokiteśvara attentively. Looking around, what he saw was merely the vast desert, no sign of inhabitant and no so much as a bird. At night, the spirits and devils raised the fire torches glittering like stars in the sky, while in the daytime, the lurid wind rolled the sands up high and sprinkled them down like a shower. However, he wasn't least frightened by what he encountered, but nevertheless, because of the lack of water, soon he was consumed with thirst, and hardly moved on. For four nights and five days, his throat had not been moistened even by a single drop. His mouth and stomach became parched. He was about to faint and could not even move one step forward. Now he had to lie down on the sand but still revoked the name of Bodhisattva Avalokiteśvara in heart ceaselessly despite being exhaustedly dehydrated. The Master prayed to the Bodhisattva by saying, "I have taken this journey neither for revenues nor for a good name, but for the supreme Right Dharma. Reverentially I believe that the Bodhisattva, full of the compassion and mercy, has taken up the responsibility to save all living beings from sufferings. Now, I'm suffering. Don't you know?" Then, he kept his mind on praying without intermission. At midnight on the fifth day, suddenly being touched by a gust of cool breeze, he felt chilly as if he was bathing in the ice-cold water. Forthwith, his eyes became bright again and the horse was also able to stand up. Now that the strength had been renewed, he took a nap for a while. He dreamed that a giant deity, several *zhang* in height, holding a halberd and a flag, reproached him, "Why are you lying here? Why don't you plunge ahead?" Shocked, the Master was awakened and resumed his journey. After pressing on for ten odd *li*, the horse suddenly veered on a road branched off, no matter how hard the Master pulled on the rein, he failed to get it back. Then a few *li* farther on, he caught sight of a grassland of several *mu*.

He dismounted and grazed his horse to its content. Then the Master was about to return but saw a pool ten paces away from the grassland, with the water crystal and sweet, clear as the mirror. The Master led the horse down to drink their fill. Their vitality restored, and they felt refreshed again. The pool and the grassland could not have been here before; presumably, they should be the merciful display of the supernatural power of the Bodhisattva as a response to the Master's sincere prayer. Indeed, it was only one of such miraculous cases showing how the Master's sincerity was in communion with the divine beings. He remained there for one day. In the next morning, having replenished the water and packed some grass, he started out again. Proceeding for another two days, finally he got out of the desert and arrived at Yiwu. During his journey, the hardships and perils of this sort were numerous, and it is hard for me to relate them all in detail.

The Master was to reside in a temple of Yiwu, where there lived three Chinese monks, among whom a senior one, before dressing himself properly, run out with bare feet, to welcome the Master. Bearing the Master in arms he could not refrain himself from wailing piteously, "Never have I expected I should meet someone from my motherland!" Those words also made the Master shed tears with him. Shortly after the other *hu* monks and the king came to pay homage to the Master. The king invited him to the palace and entertained him with all kinds of offerings.

In Yiwu, there was an envoy dispatched by Qu Wentai (? –640)[86], king of Gaochang[87]. He was about to return to his country and met the Master by chance before his departure. When he came back to

Gaochang, he reported the case to the king. On hearing this, the king immediately dispatched another envoy to Yiwu and requested the king there to send the Master to him. At the same time, he prepared tens of the good breed steeds and ordered several high-ranking officials to arrange the board and lodging along the road for the Master's coming. The Master had remained in Yiwu for more than ten days before the arrival of the envoy who, with sincerity and hospitality, delivered the intention of Qu Wentai and sent out the invitation. Originally, the Master had planned to resume his journey by the way passing the Khan Futu City[88], now that he was invited by the king, he had no choice but hit the road in the southern desert. After six days, at sunset he arrived at Baili City[89] in Gaochang. The Master intended to stay over, but was dissuaded by the envoy and the officers from the city, who urged him by saying, "For the royal city is near us, please keep moving on. Fine horses are available to you, and don't worry, your reddish horse will come on afterwards."

Thus, at midnight, he reached the royal city. The gatekeeper had already made a report to the king, then the gate was opened, and in came the Master. There the king, surrounded by his attendants with bright torches, came forth from his palace to meet the Master. Ushering the Master into an inner court and having him seated behind a precious curtain in a storeyed pavilion, the king made obeisance to him and asked about his journey. "From the moment hearing your name, we have been so delighted that we have lost our mood for eating and sleeping. Calculating the distance, we reckoned you would arrive here tonight; so, together with our family, we have been awake awaiting you meanwhile wholeheartedly reciting the Buddhist scriptures." said the king. A moment later, the consorts, together with several tens of maids entered to pay homage to the Master. Not until it was near daybreak after a long talk with the Master did the king feel tired, then he had to retire to his palace, leaving several eunuches to attend to the Master.

In the next early morning, before the Master got up, the king, together with his consorts and other subordinates, had already been at the door of the Master's chamber to pay their morning regards. "I, your disciple," said the king, "when thinking of the dangers in your journey crossing the desert, am overwhelmed by the great wonder that you have come here all by yourself." With those praises, a tide of emotion surging through the king, he could not refrain himself from shedding tears. Then the breakfast was served, and after that, the Buddhist scriptures were chanted. The king ushered the Master to a monastery situated by the side of the palace and asked him to live there, ordering some eunuches to be on guard. There at the monastery was a Dharma teacher named Tuan, who used to study in Chang'an, and was well-learned in Dharmalakshana[90], so he had been held in high esteem by the king. At the king's command, he visited the Master to make a short interview. Then the king left. Shortly after, another royal teacher over eighty years old, came to live with the Master, with the purpose to persuade him not to go to the West, and without doubt, his suggestion was rejected by the Master.

Having remained there for more than ten days, the Master thought it was time for him to leave, so he came up to the king to bide farewell. The king asked, "I have already ordered my royal teacher to enquire about your plan and asked him to urge you to stay here.

What's your decision?"

The Master replied, "Surely it is a great favor conferred from your Majesty by asking me to stay here. I'm afraid I can not accept it for it betrays my original aspiration."

The king continued to persuade the Master by saying, "The late king and we have been to your great nation in the past. Together with the Sui Emperor, we visited the eastern and western capitals[91], as well as the regions of Yan, Dai, Fen, and Jin[92]. Although having met a lot of eminent monks, we have never developed any adoration for them. The moment we heard your name, we experienced so much pleasure in our body and heart that we could not help but dance for joy. We made up our mind to let you stay here when you arrived, and so you could receive our offerings in the rest of your life. If you grant my wish, we promise to issue an order to let our people be your followers and attend your Dharma lectures. Now in our country, the monks, though not so large in number, are still no less than several thousand. We will ask them to pick up scriptures to be your listeners. We sincerely wish you to reconsider our request and accept our humble invitation. We hope you will give up your plan to go westward."

Again, the Master declined the invitation. He proclaimed, "I, a humble monk, do not deserve such a generosity of Your Majesty. The purpose of my journey is not to receive offerings. What makes me worried is that in my native land we fail to obtain the complete scriptures to reach the true Dharma tenets, many doubts thus can not be solved. For this reason, I determin to risk a journey to the West to seek the genuine teachings unavailable to my country, so that the sweet dew of vaipulya[93] teachings will sprinkle outside the

Kapilavastu[94] and the subtle words on truth can spread to the Eastern country! As time goes by, my will of Sadāprarudita[95] to inquire after the Way and my aspiration of Sudhana[96] to learn from beneficial friends and teachers have become ever stronger. How can I give up halfway? I hope your Majesty will take back your invitation, no need to concern my personal welfare."

The king said, "We, out of great adoration for the Master, are determined to stay you here to receive our offerings. Even if the Pamir Range were moved, our determination would not be changed. We beseech you to trust our stubborn sincerity, never to fall into suspicion of it."

The Master stated again, "Your Majesty keeps telling me your earnestness; what's the need of it? I know your heart. Xuangzang has come here on the westbound way to seek for Buddha Dharma , so how is it possible for me to give up halfway before obtaining it? That is why I declined your offer. Please show me understanding and sympathy. It is owing to the great merits cultivated in your past existences that Your Majesty has ascended the throne. Not only do the people rely on you for their well-being, but Buddha Dharma also depends on you for its prosperity. You are supposed to assist in the dissemination of the Buddhist teachings, so how can you set obstacles to it?"

"We dare not set obstacles." replied the king, "Because there is no teacher available in our country, we ask you to stay here to give guidance to the ignorant and the deluded."Still the Master didn't consent to stay. Then a furious look flashed across the king's face. He rolled up the sleeves and shouted, "If we have had an arrangement on you, how can you go your own way? Stay here or be sent back to your country! Think twice! You should know better to take our advice."

"I've been here for seeking the Great Dharma. Now that I am encountering the hindrance set up by your Majesty, I might leave my bones and flesh here," proclaimed the Master, "but my consciousness and spirit would not be detained." With those words, he choked with sobs and could not speak more.

The king didn't change his mind, on the contrary, he issued an order to increase offerings to the Master. Every day at mealtime, the king carried the tray in his hands to serve the Master, but since he was detained and forced to run counter to his original aspiration, the Master decided to refuse the meal, hoping such behavior could affect the king into changing his mind. Then sitting upright still, the Master hadn't taken even a sip of soup or water for three days. On the fourth day, the breath of the Master gradually became feeble, which made the king feel guilty and very fearful. At last, he bowed down to the Master in apology and pleaded him, "You can resume your journey to the West as you want. Please eat some food now."

Fearing that the king's concession might be made on an impulse, the Master asked him to swear to the sun. The king said, "If we need to do so, why don't we strengthen our friendship before a Buddha image?"

Then they went to the monastery together to worship the Buddha. And under the witness of Queen Mother Zhang, the king and the Master there took an oath to become sworn brothers.

The king said, "We'll give you permission to seek Dharma as you wish, but on your return journey, please take a three-year residence in our country to receive offerings. When you attain Buddhahood in the future, as your kin, we wish to become your protector and patron just as what Presenajit and Bimbisāra[97] did before. Well, please stay for another month to preach the *Prajñāpāramitā Sūtra of the Benevolent King*, and at the same time we will have the clothes for your journey made."

The Master consented to all these arrangements, which made the Queen Mother much delighted too; in addition, she next expressed her wish to bind family relations to the Master, expecting that he would help the royal family members to ferry across the sea of suffering in samsara and attain nirvāṇa in the end. Not until all these things had been done did the Master begin to eat some food. He was resolute and staunch as such.

Two days later, the king set up a massive tent for the Master to preach in, large enough to hold more than three hundred people to listen to the sermon. There were different seating arrangements for the Queen Mother and others below her in rank, including the king, the royal teacher, and the ministers. Every time before the sermon, the king would carry a censer by himself and usher the Master into the tent. When the Master was about to ascend the Dharma seat, the king knelt to serve as a stool for him to step on. Such a rite was performed every day.

On the conclusion day, four men were ordained to be Śrāmaṇeras[98] to attend to the Master. Also, thirty suits of religious garments were made for him; besides, considering the cold weather in Western Regions, the face-covers, gloves, boots, socks, stockings and other items were also prepared for him. What's more, one hundred taels of gold, thirty thousand silver coins, as well as five hundred rolls of silk and satin were provided, sufficient for a 20-year back-and-forth journey. Thirty horses and twenty-five labor men were assigned to the Master. Huanxin, a palace attendant and royal secretary, was ordered to escort the Master to Yehu khan's[99] residence. Then, the king wrote twenty-four letters to Qiuci[100] and other twenty-three countries along the route, with a roll of brocade as a sign of credence attached to each letter. Particularly, five hundred rolls of brocade and satin as well as two cartloads of fruits and other foods were prepared as gifts for Yehu Khan, together with a letter which reads, "Master Xuanzang is our younger brother who wants to seek Dharma in Brahminic countries. we supplicate you to take care of him just as what you have done to us. And please show kindness to give orders to the other nations in the West to require them to escort the Master out of their territories by corvée horses stage by stage."

When the Master saw the arrival of the Śrāmaṇeras, credentials, silk and satin, he was greatly touched by the king's generous farewell gifts and then wrote a letter to extend his gratitude:

> I have heard that only by taking a boat could a man ferry across rivers and seas, and only by the words of the sages the confused and ignorant thus be educated. Bearing the loving compassion as deep as a mother's love to her single son, Tathāgata was born into this impure world; and with sun-like wisdom of the Three Insights[101], He threw the light on darkness and obscurity. His compassion has been hovering over the formless realm and His teachings have been pouring down on the Three Thousand Worlds.

Having finished granting the benefit and peace to the sentient beings, He abandoned the nirmāṇakāya[102] and returned to the ultimate truth. More than six hundred years have already passed since his bequeathed teachings came to the East, during this span of time, Kāśyapa-Mātaṅga and Kang Senghui[103] glorified the Dharma in the regions of Wu and Luo[104] while Lokakṣema[105] and Kumārajīva[106] magnified it by their translation in districts of Qin and Liang[107], all of whom not only had kept the enigmatic flavor of the doctrines well-reserved, but also carried forward the great enterprise to propagate the Dharma. However, because those guest translators were from the distant alien lands, they often failed to put themselves right about some phonetic notations and expressions (of Chinese); in addition, since it was remote from the times of Buddha, distortions and misunderstandings cropped up inevitably, causing the unique flavor of the teachings bequeathed at the twin Śāla trees[108] by Buddha to split apart upon topics, such as whether the Buddha-nature is something inherently possessed by a man at the beginning or is about to be possessed upon one's attainment of Buddhahood. Consequently, this dispute made the undividable truth of Mahāyāna[109] divide into the Southern and Northern schools[110], from which the argumentation and contentions thus arose throughout the country. This situation has been lasting for several hundred years without getting any better.

I, Xuanzang, am fortunate to have built up good causes

in my previous lives, and as an effect in present life I entered the monastic order at a young age. Having ranged across the country for nearly twenty years, I have learned a lot from the eminent and worthy scholars as well as the beneficial friends, acquainting myself with scriptures and commentaries of both the Mahāyāna and Hīnayāna Schools. However, when I held the scriptures in my hands, I often deliberated on some ambiguities but felt disappointed at the explanations. On tiptoe, I earnestly looked in the direction of the Jetavana Garden[111] ; with admiration, I greatly desired for the distant Vulture Peak. I dreamed to make a pilgrimage there to settle all my doubts. Although I knew that neither could the sky be seen through a thin pipe nor the sea be measured with a gourd ladle, I still did not dare to give up my sincerity for seeking the truth; therefore, having made a simple and brief preparation, I set forth on my westbound road. Time elapsed quickly, now I have arrived at Yiwu.

Humbly I believe that Heaven and Earth have bestowed honesty and amiability on Your Majesty, and the limpid material forces of the *yin* and *yang*[112] have been balanced in your temperament. Since you were crowned as the sovereign, you have nurtured the people as your own offspring. In the east you are on intimate terms with the grand nation and in the west you respect the customs of the various tribes, so the lands of Loulan[113] and Yuezhi[114] and the countries of Cheshi[115] and Langwang[116] are all being enveloped in your deep benevolence and profound virtues. You have valued the worthy and talented, held on to what's wholesome and compassionate. Being constantly friendly to the visitors coming from afar, you condescended to receive me with hospitality. No sooner had I arrived than you favored me with deep kindness, and after I settled, you earnestly enjoined me to propagate the Dharma. I'm indebted to you for making me your sworn brother and for showing me so much brotherly care. You have written letters to more than twenty countries in the Western Regions, and thoughtfully, with warm and enthusiastic words you asked of them to send me out of their domains stage by stage. Moreover, taking pity on my solitary figure on the road westward, having mercy on my desolate journey, you issued the decree to have four men ordained as Śrāmaṇeras to be my companions. What's more, you provided me with more than fifty articles of religious garments, black silk hats, fur blanket, boots, socks and stockings; also presented me with rolls of silk and satin as well as gold and silver money, and so on. Indeed, what you have given me is sufficient for a two-decade journey forth and back. Moved by these favors on me meanwhile ashamed of my own insignificance, I lost my words but make obeisance to you in gratitude. I think that the water of the Jiao River[117] can not be compared with your kindness in depth, and that the mountains on Pamir Plateau fail to match your munificence in weight. From now on, I will no longer be bothered by the dangers of climbing mountains or crossing rivers; I am sure it will be around the corner that I could pay my homage to the Heavenly Ladder[118] and the Bodhi Tree[119]. When I succeed, to whom shall I owe my achievement? No one but Your Majesty!

I shall visit various teachers and receive the right Dharma. When I come back, I shall translate the scriptures and widely propagate the teachings at home. As a result, the forest of perverse doctrines would be demolished and the far-fetched interpretations of heretics be eradicated; what has been unknown to the Image Period[120] would be supplemented and the essential doctrines of Buddha be laid down. I will return all merits made by me, no matter how trivial it might be, to you as a repayment for your exceptional kindness. Now, because it is a long way ahead to go, I'm afraid I can't tarry longer. I'm going to leave tomorrow, for which I feel very sorrowful. Effusive in gratitude, I am writing this letter to Your Presence.

The king replied, "Since you have become our sworn brother, whatever belonging to this country is our common property. Why then give us so many thanks?"

On the departure day, the king, together with monks, ministers and commoners, went out of the capital to see the Master off as far as they could go in the western suburbs. Holding the Master in arms, the king wailed bitterly, which made the monks and laity also deeply depressed. The voices of bidding farewell were resounding around the suburbs. After ordering the consorts and others to go back, the king, together with some eminent monks and attendants, each riding a horse, escorted the Master for another several tens of *li*. Henceforth, the kings and nobility of other countries along the road also treated the Master with the similar courtesy and propriety.

From here proceeding westward, the Master passed the cities of Wuban[121] and Dujin[122], then entered the country of Agni[123] which was wrongly called Wuqi in olden times.

ANNOTATION

1 His personal name was Yi (祎).

2 Chenliu is situated in modern Henan 河南 Province, covering a large area around modern Kaifeng 开封.

3 Zhonggong is the courtesy name of Chen Shi 陈寔(104–187). Recorded in the *Bibliography of Chen Shi* in the *History of Eastern Han* (*Houhan Shu-Chenshi Zhuan*《后汉书·陈寔传》), a story goes: One year in the Eastern Han Dynasty, there was a serious famine in Henan. One night, a thief sneaked into Chen Shi's house and hid himself on the beam. When Chen Shi was aware of this, he got out of bed without haste, called his children and grandchildren to his room and said in a stern voice, "One must always restrain and encourage oneself no matter under what circumstances. Bad men were not born bad. It is only because they don't restrain themselves that they develop bad habits and turn bad gradually. That gentleman on the beam is just a case in point." Much ashamed upon hearing this, the thief hiding on the beam promptly jumped down to the ground, kowtowed and begged for forgiveness. Chen Shi enlightened him by saying, "Judging from your appearance, you don't look like a bad man. Perhaps you are driven by poverty to steal. But you should carefully examine yourself and turn over a new leaf." Then he immediately asked someone to bring two bolts of white silk to give the thief as a present. The thief kowtowed and thanked him repeatedly. Since then, very few thefts occurred in this locality. Later on, this story became a famous allusion of moralization in China.

4 Taiqiu is situated in the north-west of the modern Yongcheng 永城 County of Henan Province.

5 Shangdang region is present-day Changzhi 长治, Shanxi 山西 Province.

6 National Academy, or Guozijian 国子监, also called the School of the Sons of State, Imperial Academy, and so forth, was the highest institution of learning

in China's traditional educational system after the Sui Dynasty.(581–618)

7 The south of present Luoyang 洛阳 which was the capital of the Zhou Dynasty, the western area of Henan Province.

8 Xuanzang was born in Chenhe陈河 village of Goushi 缑氏town in the south of the modern Yanshi 偃师 County, near present-day Luoyang, Henan Province.

9 Guo Tai 郭泰 (128–169) was an eminent Confucian scholar of the Eastern Han, whose courtesy name was Linzong 林宗, and often addressed by people at that time as Mr. Youdao (meaning possessing virtue), a native of Jiexiu介休 in Shanxi 山西 Province. He refused to be an official of the government because of its corruption and degeneration, and lived a life as a teacher to moralize people and thus had a thousand students.

10 Distinguished Person of Filial Piety and Honesty.

11 Zengzi曾子(505–435), one of Confucius' disciples, is famous for his filial piety. Zengzi stood up from his mat to show his respect to Confucius when he was listening to his teacher's discourse, which was recorded in the *Xiaojing* (*Classic of the Filial Piety*《孝经》).

12 Yang Wu 扬乌, a son of Yang Xiong扬雄 (53 BC–18CE), was a prodigy during the Western Han, and at a very young age he contributed to his father's composition of the *Taixuan Jing* (*Classic of the Profound Theory*《太玄经》).

13 Changjie is the Buddhist name of Xuanzang's second brother Chen Su 陈素.

14 Or Pure Land Monastery. Pure Land: the name of the Buddha Amitabha's land.

15 Refers to Luoyang 洛阳, Henan Province.

16 Huijing 慧景.

17 This *Śāstra* was particularly popular in the Southern and Northern dynasties (420–589), serving as the fundamental text of the Sect of Shelun 摄论学派, later also as the basic text of the School of Faxiang 法相宗. Among the 13 domestic teachers from whom Ven. Xuanzang learned from, eight were monk

scholars of the Sect of Shelun.

18 Huiyan 慧严, a disciple of Ven. Zhikuang 智旷, who was a disciple of Zhendi 真谛 (Paramārtha, 449–569).

19 The Sui Dynasty (581–618) was relatively short. The eventual fall of the Sui Dynasty was due to the massive conscription of labor and allocation of resources for the grand projects, such as the Grand Canal, also to the many losses caused by the failed military campaigns against Goguryeo. It was after these defeats and losses that the country was left in ruins and rebels soon took control of the government. Emperor Yang of Sui 隋炀帝 (r. 605–618) had gone South after the capital being threatened by various rebel groups and was killed by his advisors (Yuwen Clan). Meanwhile, in the North, the aristocrat Li Yuan (566–635) held an uprising, and ended up ascending the throne to become Emperor Gaozu of Tang.

20 King Jie 桀(r.1589–1559 BC) was the last ruler of the Xia Dynasty (c.2070–c.1600 BCE). He is traditionally regarded as a tyrant who brought about the collapse of the dynasty.

21 Dao Zhi 盗跖(Robber Zhi), a slave rebel leader of the Spring and Autumn period (722–481 BC). Jie and Zhi are used to refer to persons of atrocious cruelty.

22 Wang Mang 王莽 (c. 45 BC –23 CE), courtesy name Jujun 巨君, was a Han Dynasty official who seized the throne from the Liu family and founded the Xin Dynasty, ruling 9–23 AD. The Han Dynasty was restored after his overthrow, and his rule marks the separation between the Western Han Dynasty (before Xin) and Eastern Han Dynasty (after Xin).

23 Dong Zhuo 董卓 (?–192), courtesy name Zhongying 仲颖 , was a military general and warlord who lived in the late Eastern Han Dynasty. He seized control of the capital Luoyang in 189 when it was in a state of turmoil following the death of Emperor Ling汉灵帝 (r. 168–189) and a clash between the eunuch faction and some court officials led by General-in-Chief He Jin

何进(?–189). Dong Zhuo subsequently deposed Emperor Shao and instated Emperor Xian. Dong Zhuo rose to power in the Han imperial court and ruled the nation with tyranny and cruelty for a brief period of time. The following year, a coalition of regional officials and warlords launched a punitive campaign against him, forcing him to move the capital to Chang'an. Dong Zhuo was assassinated in 192 by his subordinate Lü Bu吕布(?–199) as part of a plot orchestrated by Interior Minister Wang Yun王允 (137–192).

24 Liu Yuan 刘元(?–310), courtesy name Yuanhai 元海, Emperor Guangwen of Han Zhao 汉赵光文帝 (r.304–310) , the founding emperor of the Xiongnu state Han Zhao in 304.

25 Shi Le 石勒 (274–333), courtesy name Shilong世龙, Emperor Ming of Zhao, was the founding emperor of the Later Zhao (319–351).

26 Refers to Li Yuan 李渊 (566–635).

27 Modern Taiyuan太原in Shanxi Province.

28 Sun Wu孙武 (ca.545–470 BC), also Sunzi 孙子, was a Chinese general, military strategist, and philosopher who lived in the Spring and Autumn period of ancient China. Sunzi is traditionally credited as the author of *The Art of War*, a widely influential work of military strategy.

29 Wu Qi吴起 (440–381 BC) was a Chinese military leader, Legalist philosopher, and politician in the Warring States period (403–222 BC). His military treatise, the *Wuzi*《吴子》, is included as one of the *Seven Military Classics.* It is said there were two books on the art of war by Wu Qi, but one was lost, hence leaving the *Wuzi* as the only existing book carrying Wu Qi's military thoughts.

30 Huijing 慧景, Zhituo 智脱, Daoji 道基 and Baoxian 宝暹.

31 Mian: Mianzhou, today the region east to Mianyang 绵阳, Sichuan Province. Shu: Shujun, modern Chengdu 成都 and its surrounding region. Sichuan 四川 Province .

32 Ziwu Valley is in Qinling Mountains 秦岭, going south from Chang'an and turned west at its southern junction with the main road to Hanzhong 汉中, south

of Shaanxi.

33 Present Nanzheng 南郑 county in Shannxi Province.

34 Present Chengdu 成都, Sichuan Province.

35 Might refer to *Apitan Jing ba jiandu lun*《阿毗昙经八犍度论》, *Jiazhanyan apitan* 迦旃延阿毗昙, translated by Saṃghadeva 僧伽提婆and Zhu Fonian 竺佛念 in 383 CE. From 657–660, Xuanzang served up another translation of this text: *Abhidharmajñānaprasthāna Śāstra* (*Apidama fazhi lun*《阿毗达摩发智论》). However, *pitan* would have to be something else.

36 Alternative, 道振.

37 Today the region including the north of Jiangsu 江苏 Province and the east of Zhejiang 浙江 Province.

38 Jing and Chu: present Hubei 湖北 Province.

39 Li Ying 李膺(110–169) or Li Yuanli 元礼was a lineal descendant of Li Er 李耳(commonly thought to be Laozi's real name). Li Ying was one of the foremost Confucian scholars of the Eastern Han, and a governor of Henan Commandery. He was involved in a Partisan Prohibitions case and was killed in the second case (169). He was regarded as a moral model in his time, thus won a deep respect from the people.

40 Guo Tai 郭泰(128–169), also named Guo Youdao 郭有道, an eminent Confucian scholar in the Eastern Han Dynasty.

41 *Shangshu* (*Book of History*《尚书》), is one of the Chinese ancient *Five Classics*. It is a collection of orations made by rulers and important ministers from mythical times to the middle of the Western Zhou period, and some other texts. The *Shangshu* consists of five parts. The first and shortest one is the *Tangshu* (*Book of Tang*); the second one the *Yushu* (*Book of Yu*《禹书》); the third one is called *Xiashu* (*Book of the Xia Dynasty*《夏书》), which is followed by the *Shangshu* (*Book of the Shang Dynasty*《商书》), and finally the *Zhoushu* (*Book of the Zhou Dynasty*《周书》). The Old Text *Shangshu*: According to tradition, the local ruler Prince Gong of Lu demolished a

building of the Kong family complex in the process of enlarging his palace, and some ancient texts were discovered hidden in a wall, including *Shangshu*. They had apparently been hidden there in order to escape the book burning of the First Emperor of Qin 秦始皇(259–210 BC). This version of *Shangshu* contained 16 more chapters than the one transmitted by Fu Sheng. As the hidden texts were written in the ancient seal script, this newly discovered version is called "Ancient Script" or "Old Text" *Shangshu*, whereas Fu Sheng's version is called the "Modern Script" or "New Text." Kong Anguo 孔安国(ca. 156–ca. 74BC) compiled and wrote a commentary to the Old Text, thus called *Shangshu Kongshi Zhuan* (literally *Kong's Commentary of Shangshu*《尚书孔氏传》).

42 Laozi《老子》, or Daodejing《道德经》, is a Chinese classic text. The text's true authorship and date of composition or compilation are still debated.

43 *Zhuangzi*《庄子》is an ancient Chinese text from the late Warring States Period (476–221BC) which contains stories and anecdotes that exemplify the carefree nature of the ideal Daoist sage.

44 Two brothers of Lushan refer to Huiyuan慧远 (334–416) and Huichi慧持 (337–412), who lived in Donglin Monastery at Lushan Mountain in Jiangxi 江西 Province. Huiyuan is regarded as the founder of the Pure Land School of China. He and his brother Huichi organized the White Lotus Society with 123 monks and laymen.

45 The five classifications of the Vinaya: Pārājika, Pratimokṣa, pāyattika, pratideśanīya, duskrta. Seven groups of the Vinaya: Pārājika, Pratimokṣa, sthūlātyaya, pratideśanīya, and duskrta that is further divided into Evil Action and Evil Speaking.

46 Roughly Sichuan in general.

47 Three adjacent gorges along the middle reaches of the Yangtze River, in the hinterland of China.

48 Refers to the lowest 435 km (270 mi) of the Yangtze River between Nanjing

and Shanghai.

49 Tianhuang Monastery is in modern Jiangling江陵, Hubei 湖北 Province.

50 Li Xiang 李瓖, a brother of Li Xiaogong李孝恭(591–640).

51 Present Anyang 安阳, Henan Province.

52 Huixiu 慧休.

53 Present Zhaoxian county 赵县 in Hebei Province.

54 Daoshen 道深.

55 Or Great Enlightenment Monastery.

56 Daoyue道岳.

57 Fachang 法常(567–645).

58 Sengbian僧辩(468–624).

59 Hīnayāna and Mahāyāna teachings.

60 Three Studies or Three Vehicles of Learning: discipline, meditation and wisdom

61 Faxian 法显(337–c. 422) was a monk-scholar who travelled by foot from China to India, visiting many sacred Buddhist sites in what are now Xinjiang Uygur Autonomous Region, Pakistan, India, Nepal, Bangladesh and Sri Lanka between 399–412 to acquire Buddhist texts. His journey is described in his important travelogue, *A Record of Buddhist Kingdoms* (*Foguo Ji*《佛国记》).

62 Zhiyan 智严 was a monk of the Eastern Jin Dynasty (317–420). According to fascicle 2 of *Chu sanzang jiji*《出三藏记集》and fascicle 3 of *Gaoseng zhuan*《高僧传》(*Biographies of Eminent Monks*), he was born in Liangzhou 凉州, Gansu 甘肃. He became a monk at the age of twenty. He traveled westward with Baoyun and others, and visited India to acquire Buddhist texts between the Jin (316–420) and Song (420–479) dynasties.

63 The white robe represents the typical clothing of the laity. It might indicate that Xuanzang would set out on his journey in secrecy by disguising himself to be a laity.

64 The date is also said to be the first year of Zhenguan of the reign of Emperor Taizong, i.e. 626, which is more reliable.

65 Sumeru: according to Buddhist cosmology, Mt. Meru lies in "the middle of the Earth." The world-mountain of Sumeru is an immense, strangely shaped peak which arises in the center of the world, and around which the sun and the moon revolve. Its base rests in a vast ocean, and it is surrounded by several rings of lesser mountain ranges and oceans. The three worlds listed below are all located on, or around Sumeru: the Trāyastriṃśadevas live on its peak, the Cāturmahārājikakāyikadevas live on its slopes, and the Asuras live in the ocean at its base. Sumeru and its surrounding oceans and mountains are the home not just of deities, but also vast assemblies of beings of popular mythology who only rarely intrude on the human world.

66 Gold, silver, Vaidurya, and crystal.

67 Present Tianshui 天水 in Gansu 甘肃 Province.

68 Present capital of Gansu Province.

69 Present Wuwei 武威 county in Gansu province, located at the eastern end of Hexi corridor. Hexi Corridor or Gansu Corridor is the historical route in Gansu province. As part of the Northern Silk Road running northwest from the bank of the Yellow River, it was the most important route from North China to the Tarim Basin and Central Asia. The corridor is a string of oases along the northern edge of the Tibetan Plateau.

70 Hexi region refers to the region west to the Yellow River in Qinghai 青海 and Gansu Provinces, including the Hexi Corridor and Huangshui valley.

71 The Pamir Mountains, or the Pamirs, also called Congling in Chinese, are a mountain range in Central Asia at the junction of the Himālayas with the Tian Shan, Karakoram, Kunlun, Hindu Kush, Suleman and Hindu Raj ranges.

72 According to Chinese geographical nomenclature, the term Xiyu西域, meaning "Western Regions," in ancient times referred rather loosely to places further west to China at the time. It covered a vast area west of Yumen Pass 玉门关, including

what is now China's Xinjiang Uygur Autonomous Region and areas along the ancient Silk Routes. Cities were built in these oasis in the Taklamakan desert and areas further to the west in Central Asia.

73 The old site of Guazhou is situated in the southeast of Anxi 安西 County in Gansu Province.

74 Also called the Shule River疏勒河, in northwest Gansu Province, which flows generally westwards through the Tibetan Plateau and the desert regions of northwestern China.

75 The old site is located at an area northwest to Suoyang city 锁阳 (called Guazhou 瓜州 in the Tang Dynasty) in modern Guazhou prefecture (formerly Anxi 安西), Gansu province.

76 Moheyan Desert or Moheyan Gobi refers to a vast desert between Lop Nur or Lop Nor and Yumen Pass, now also called Hashun Gobi in Xinjiang Uygur Autonomous Region. Lop Nur is a former salt lake, now largely dried-up.

77 Modern Hami Prefecture 哈密 in Xinjiang Uygur Autonomous Region.

78 The future Buddha, now in the Tusita heaven.

79 The word "胡" was applied to Non-Chinese people, especially tribal nomads living in the north, northwest, and northeast of China.

80 Also Panchashila or five shilas, refers to the first five of the 10 commandments: (1) to refrain from taking life, or be against killing; (2) to refrain from taking that which is not given, or from stealing; (3) to refrain from misusing of the senses, or from adultery; (4) to refrain from telling lies; (5) to refrain from self-toxication with drink and drugs.

81 The third watch is about 23:00 pm to 01:00 am.

82 Yumen Pass, or Jade Gate or Pass of the Jade Gate, is the name of a pass of the Great Wall located west of Dunhuang in today's Gansu Province of China.

83 Luoyang and Chang'an.

84 Dānapati in Sanskrit, means a patron, or a donor.

85 Also the *Heart Sūtra*.

86 From the mid-5th century until the mid-7th century, there existed four independent statelets in the narrow Turpan basin. These were controlled by the Kan clan, Zhang clan, Ma clan, and Qu clan. Qu family was originated from Gansu. Jincheng commandery金城 (present Lanzhou), district of Yuzhong 榆中. However, fearing Tang expansion, Qu Wentai later formed an alliance with the Western Turks and rebelled against Tang suzerainty. Emperor Taizong sent an army led by General Hou Junji 侯君集(?–643) against the kingdom in 640, and Qu Wentai apparently died of shock at the news of the approaching army. Gaochang was annexed by the Tang Dynasty and turned into a sub-prefecture of Xizhou 西州, and the seat of government of Anxi 安西.

87 Modern Turpan, also known as Turfan or Tulufan, is a prefecture-level city located in the east of Xinjiang Uygur Autonomous Region.

88 Refers to Beiting Protectorate in the Tang Dynasty created in 702 to control the Beiting region north of Gaochang. It was later known as Beshbalik and became one of the capitals of the Uygur Khaganate and then the Kingdom of Qocho. Present ancient city of Hubaozi 护堡子古城 in Jimsar County 吉木萨尔县, Changji Hui Autonomous Prefecture, Xinjiang Uygur Autonomous Region, China.

89 Present Shanshan 鄯善 located at the north-eastern end of the Taklamakan Desert near the great, but now mostly dry, salt lake known as Lop Nur. It was previously known as Loulan Kingdom or Kroran.

90 All things are of the same nature but differ in form.

91 Eastern capital refers to Luoyang and western capital Chang'an.

92 Yan, Dai, Fen, and Jin, refer in general to Hebei and Shanxi Provinces.

93 Vaipulya means broad, vast, extensive, so it is used to refer to the *Mahāyāna Sūtras*, including the *Lotus Sūtra*, *Aṣṭasāhasrikā-prajñāpāramitā*, and *Laṅkāvatāra-sūtra* and so on.

94 The birth place of Buddha, 迦毗罗卫城 in Chinese.

95 Sadāprarudita or Sadāvilāpa, literally meaning "ever weeping", is a Bodhisattva, famous for his quest for Prajñāpāramitā, "to see and hear the Tathāgatas", whose stories can be found in various Buddhist *prajñāpāramitā sūtras*.

96 A Buddhist disciple mentioned in the *Huayan Sūtra*, or the *Avataṃsaka Sūtra*, who visited or studied under fifty-three teachers in order to find the ultimate truth.

97 Both of Presenajit and Bimbisāra were Indian Kings of the sixth century BC. They are contemporaries of the Buddha, and the patrons of Buddhism.

98 According to the monastic discipline, a man under the age of 20 cannot be ordained as bhiksu, but can be ordained as a Śrāmaṇera. The female counterpart of the Śrāmaṇera is Śrāmaṇerīs.

99 Tong Yabghu Qaghan 统叶护可汗(r. 618–628 or 630) (also known as T'ung Yabghu, Ton Yabghu, Tong Yabghu Khagan, Tun Yabghu, was khagan of the Western Turkic Khaganate from 618 to 628 AD. Tong Yabghu's reign is generally regarded as the zenith of the Western Göktürk Khaganate. His clan was syncretized Buddhist and native folk religion. Some scholars believe the khagan described by Xuanzang was his son Si Yabghu, rather than Tong Yabghu. The Turkic people in the west gave the highest title to the Tang Emperor Taizong 唐太宗 as their absolute ruler: "Tian Kehan 天可汗", heavenly ruler, Tengri Khagan.

100 Or Kucha or Kuche, was an ancient Buddhist kingdom located on the branch of the Silk Road that ran along the northern edge of the Taklamakan Desert in the Tarim Basin and south of the Muzat River. The area lies in present-day Aksu Prefecture, Xinjiang, China Uygur Autonomous Region.

101 Or Trividyā, or the three clear conceptions: (1) Anitya, all is impermanent, impermanence of all existence; (2) Duhkha, misery as the lot of all beings, all beings are sorrowful; (3) Anatman, all is devoid of a self. In the case of the saint, it includes knowledge of future incarnation, of the past

incarnation, and of the present incarnation: (1) insight into the previous births of self and others; (2) insight into future births; (3) insight into present sufferings so as to overcome all passions and realize nirvāṇa.

102 Here the nirmāṇakāya simply means the physical body of Buddha.

103 Kang Senghui 康僧会(fl. 247–280) was a Buddhist monk and translator during the Three Kingdoms period. He was born in Jiaozhi (modern-day northern Vietnam). He is regarded as the first Vietnamese patriarch of Zen Buddhism in Vietnam. Kang contributed to the diffusion and translation of Buddhist Sūtras into the Chinese.

104 Including South Jiangsu province, north Zhejiang province and Luoyang in Henan province.

105 Zhiloujiachen支娄迦谶 (fl. c. 168–189) whose Indian name is generally reconstructed as Lokakṣema (Lokarakṣa or Lokakṣin) and who was of Yuezhi 月氏 ancestry, is regarded as the earliest of the translator-monks. Lokakshema went to Luoyang in the late years of Emperor Heng (r. 146–167) of Eastern Han Dynasty and translated many Mahāyāna scriptures into Chinese.

106 Kumārajīva鸠摩罗什(344–413) was a Buddhist monk, scholar, and translator from the Kingdom of Kucha. He first studied teachings of the Sarvastivadin schools, later studied under Buddhasvāmin, and finally became an adherent of Mahāyāna, studying the Mādhyamaka doctrine of Nāgārjuna. Kumārajīva settled in Chang'an during the Sixteen Kingdoms era. He is mostly remembered for his prolific translation he carried out during his later life.

107 Shannxi and Gansu provinces.

108 According to the Mahāyāna *Mahāparinirvāṇa Sūtra*, the Buddha made his journey to Kushinagar, at the age of 80, entered nirvāṇa there by lying down on his right side in the auspicious position on a couch between twin Śāla trees and wherein he was cremated. "一味之旨", the unique flavor of

teachings, implies the universality of the teachings of Buddha, One, or the same flavour, kind or character, i.e. the Buddha's teaching; single taste.

109 Mahāyāna ("Great/Greater Vehicle"): the teaching on the attainment of enlightenment or Buddhahood; the seeker of enlightenment is the Bodhisattva.

110 Bodhiruci 菩提流支 and Ratnamati 勒那摩提 (5th–6th centuries) from central India jointly translated from Sanskrit into Chinese *A Treatise on the Sūtra of the Ten Grounds* (*Daśa-bhūmika-sūtra-śāstra*), written by Vasubandhu (世亲, c. 320–80). Then Bodhiruci' s students in northern China established the Ground Treatise School (Dilun Zong 地论宗), and Ratnamati's students in southern China established their school with the same name. Although both paths of this school were founded on Vasubandhu's treatise, they differed in their views of the nature of ālaya consciousness (ālayavijñāna). The northern path viewed ālaya consciousness as an impure consciousness and upheld dependent arising of dharmas from ālaya consciousness, while the southern path viewed ālaya consciousness as one's inherent pure mind, one's Tathāgata store (Tathāgata-garbha), and upheld dependent arising of dharmas from dharma nature (dharmatā), which is true suchness. Then the northern path merged into the Samgraha School (Shelun Zong 摄论宗). The southern path stood as the orthodox Ground Treatise School for some time, and then merged into the Huayan School. Paramārtha 真谛 (499–569) translated from Sanskrit into Chinese many treatises, among which the most significant are Vasubandhu's *A Commentary on the Treasury of the Abhidharma* (*Abhidharma-kośa-bhāṣya*), and the *Mahāyāna-saṁgraha-bhāṣya*, etc, on which the Abhidharma School (Pitan Zong毗昙宗) was founded; and Asaṅga's无著(c. 310–90) *A Treatise on Adopting the Mahāyāna* (*Mahāyāna-saṁparigraha-śāstra*) on which the Parigraha Treatise School was founded. Then in the Tang Dynasty, the Abhidharma School merged into the Kośa School (Jushe Zong俱舍宗),

founded on the Chinese version of Vasubandhu's *A Treatise on the Treasury of the Abhidharma* (*Abhidharma-kośa-śāstra*), translated from Sanskrit by Xuanzang; the Parigraha Treatise School merged into the Dharma-Appearance School (Faxiang Zong法相宗), also called the Consciousness-Only School.

111 Or Jetavanavihāra: a park in Savatthi, India. When the Buddha accepted Anathapindika's invitation to visit Savatthi, Anathapindika was seeking a suitable place for the Buddhas residence, discovered this park belonging to Jetakumara. Anathapindika decided to buy the garden by covering Jetavana with pieces of gold laid side by side. However, Jeta, inspired by Anathapindikas earnestness, asked to be allowed to give this spot. Anathapindika agreed and Jeta erected there a gateway, with a room over it. Anathapindika built in the grounds dwelling rooms, retiring rooms, store rooms and service halls, halls with fireplaces, closets, cloisters, halls for exercise, wells, bathrooms, ponds, open and roofed sheds, and so forth. It is said that Anathapindika paid eighteen crores for the purchase of the site, all of which Jeta spent in the construction of the gateway gifted by him.

112 *Yin* and *yang*: two primal forces, negativity and positivity. Also Sun and Moon.

113 Loulan, also called Kroràn or Kroraina, was an ancient kingdom based around an important oasis city along the Silk Road already known in the 2nd century BC on the northeastern edge of the Lop Desert. The term Loulan is the Chinese transcription of the native name Kroràn and is used to refer to the city near Lop Nur as well as the kingdom. The kingdom was renamed Shanshan after its king was assassinated by an envoy of the Han Dynasty in 77 BC; however, the town at the northwestern corner of the brackish desert lake Lop Nur retained the name of Loulan. The ruins of Loulan are near the now-desiccated Lop Nur in the Bayingolin Mongol Autonomous Prefecture, Xinjiang Uygur Autonomous Region, and they are

now completely surrounded by desert.

114 Yuezhi is an ancient country located in an arid grassland area in the western part of the modern Chinese province of Gansu, during the 1st millennium BC. After a major defeat by the Xiongnu (Huns), during the 2nd century BC, the Yuezhi split into two groups: the Greater Yuezhi and the Lesser Yuezhi.

115 Cheshi is roughly modern Changji Hui Autonomous Prefecture, Xinjiang Uygur Autonomous Region.

116 Langwang, a place of Xiongnu (Huns). Xiongnu was a dominant power on the steppes of north-east Central Asia, centred on an area known later as Mongolia. The Xiongnu were also active in areas now part of Siberia, Inner Mongolia, Gansu Province and Xinjiang Uygur Autonomous Region.

117 Jiao River refers to the river around the Jiaohe which is a natural fortress located atop a steep cliff on a leaf-shaped plateau between two deep river valleys. Its ruins are a Chinese archaeological site found in the Yarnaz Valley, 10 km west of the city of Turpan in Xinjiang Uygur Autonomous Region.

118 Refers to the three precious stairways of the country of Kapitha in Central India. In the past, by descending those stairways, the Buddha returned to Jambudvīpa after delivering sermons on Dharma to Mahāmāyā in Trayastriṃśa Heaven.

119 The Bodhi Tree, also known as Bo (from the Sinhalese Bo) and "peepal tree" in Nepal and Bhutan, was a large and very old Sacred Fig tree (Ficus religiosa) located in Bodh Gaya (about 100 km from Patna in the Indian state of Bihar), under which Siddhartha Gautama is said to have achieved enlightenment, or Bodhi.

120 Buddhism is supposed to exist for three periods, i.e., three ages of the Dharma. After these three ages the Dharma of Śākyamuni Buddha will end: (1) The true Dharma age or the Right Dharma Period, lasted 500 to 1,000 years after His passing. During this age, there were teachings, carrying out

of the teachings, and attaining of fruits. (2) The Dharma-likeness age or the Resemblance Period or Image Period, lasted 500 to 1,000 years. During this age, there were teachings and carrying out of the teachings, but no attaining of fruits. (3) The Dharma-ending age or the Final Period will last 10,000 years. During this age, the teachings will gradually vanish, and there will be neither carrying out of the teachings nor attaining of fruits. Because people will no longer be receptive, the Dharma will be gone for a long time until the advent of the next Buddha. In the *Sūtra of the Bodhisattva in Mother's Womb*, fascicle 2, the Buddha prophesies that, after 56 koṭi and 70 million years, which means 630 million years (if a koṭi is 10 million), Maitreya Bodhisattva will descend from Tuṣita Heaven and become the next Buddha, bringing the Dharma to a renewed world.

121 Present Bugantai County, Hami and Turpan, Xinjiang Uygur Autonomous Region.

122 Present Toksun County, Xinjiang Uygur Autonomous Region.

123 Situated at modern Yanqi County in Xiangjiang Uygur Autonomous Region.

Fascicle II

Beginning with the Country of Agni and Ending with the Country of Kanyākubja

Proceeding westward, the Master came to a fountain named A-fu-shi (Fountain of the Teacher) in the country of Agni. The fountain was on a sandy cliff to the south of the road. The cliff was several *zhang* in height, with the water spurting out half-way up it. According to a legend, in the olden times here came a company of several hundred travelling merchants, and among them was a monk who didn't carry any provisions and relied on others for travel costs. Running out of the water on their road, when they arrived here, they were at the end of their tether. The merchants got together to discuss how to solve this predicament, and one of them complained, "This monk is a follower of Buddha, and that is why we have given him alms and allowed him to travel through a thousand *li* without carrying any necessities. Now we are suffering but he doesn't give a damn care. Why not tell him the plight at hand?" They then did so, and got the reply from the monk, "If you want water, you should pay homage to the Buddha, take the threefold refuge[1] and receive the Five Commandments[2]. After that, I will climb the cliff and make the water for you." Since the merchants were eager to find a way out of the plight, they had to follow the monk's words. After they took the Precepts, the monk enjoined them by saying, "When I climb up the cliff, you should shout 'A-fu-shi, give us water' and then tell me how much you want." The merchants shouted as they were told, and instantly, the water flowed down abundantly, which made them very delighted and grateful. As they realized that the monk hadn't come back, they climbed up the cliff to have a look and saw he had already passed away. The merchants, young and old, overwhelmed by grief, were wailing sadly. Following the custom of the Western Regions, they cremated him, and piled up bricks and stones into a stūpa[3] at the very spot where he sat into nirvāṇa. The stūpa was still in existence and the water had never ceased its flowing. According to the number of travelers, the water flowed down either in trickle or flood, or merely oozed down when there was no wayfarer. The Master and his companions stayed overnight beside the fountain.

Then the Master set out the next morning and came to the Silver Mountain[4]. The mountain was high and large, rich in silver, which was a source of silver currency of the Western countries. To the west of the mountain, he encountered a gang of bandits. They left when given the valuables. Then he reached the river bank where the imperial city was situated. He stopped and spent the night there. Among his fellow travelers, there were tens of *hu* merchants who stealthily set off at midnight in the hope of doing business before others, but ahead going for more than ten *li,* they came upon robbers and were totally killed.

When the Master and others came to the spot, what they saw were the corpses, with no properties remained. At the scene, everyone felt sad and signed grievously.

Moving on gradually, the Master saw the capital in the distance. The king of Agni, together with his administers, came out to meet and ushered them into the city to receive offerings. But because Agni was once invaded and harassed by Gaochang in the past, the king, with hatred, was reluctant to give the horses to the Master. Thus, the Master and others stayed up for one night and then left.

Crossing a river ahead, and proceeding westward on the plain for several hundred *li,* he entered the domain of Kucha (in olden times wrongly called Qiuci) . When he came close to the royal capital, the king led his subjects, as well as the virtuous monk Mokṣagupta, and others, coming out to receive him. Outside the eastern gate to the city, several thousand monks had already set up canopies and tents to camp themselves. They also had statues installed and the music played. When the Master arrived, the virtuous monks rose to greet him. When they took their seats again, a monk walked up holding a tray of fresh flowers and presented it to the Master. Taking the tray, the Master went up to the Buddha statue, scattered the flowers and offered his worship. After that, he took his seat below Mokṣagupta; then the Master was presented with flowers again, and next with grape juice that was offered by local temples. He accepted grape juice from the first temple, and did so in order from the others until it was late that day. At last, the monks dispersed.

There were several tens of monks from Gaochang, who had received their ordination in Kucha, residing in a separate monastery located in the southeast of the city. Since they knew that the Master was coming from their hometown, they invited him to spend the first night at their temple. The Master accepted the invitation. Then the king and other monks returned to their places. On the following day, the king invited the Master to his palace and entertained him with an abundant feast including the three kinds of pure meat,[5] which the Master refused to take. Seeing the king was greatly curious about it, the Master explained, "Eating meat is permitted by the doctrines of the Gradual Teaching[6], but is prohibited by the Great Vehicle that I follow." Then he took some other foodstuffs. After the meal, the Master went to a monastery named Āścarya (meaning "extraordinary") in the northwest of the city, where Mokṣagupta resided.

Mokṣagupta was thought to be astute, well-versed in Buddhist doctrines, and thus, won a regional fame as the greatest teacher. He had once travelled and learned in India for more than twenty years, gaining an extensive knowledge of Buddhist scriptures, especially being good at Śabdavidyā[7]. Revered by the king and the people in the country, he was honorably entitled "the Unparalleled." On seeing the Master's coming, he greeted him in an ordinary way as if he was receiving a common guest, not showing the due respect to a monk erudite in Dharma.

He said to the Master, "In this country we have the *Saṃyuktābhidharmahṛdaya Śāstra,* the *Abhidharmakośa Śāstra*, the *Vibhāṣā Śāstra*, and others. They are enough for you to study. I don't think you need to take hardships to make a journey to the west."

The Master asked him, "Do you have the *Yogācārabhūmi Śāstra*? "

Mokṣagupta answered, "Why did you inquire about such a heretical book? The true disciples of the Buddha don't study it."

At first, the Master bore a deep veneration for him, but at hearing those words, he disdained him as a speck of dust. Then, the Master retorted, "Both the *Abhidharmakośa Śāstra* and the *Vibhāṣā Śāstra* have been available in my country, but it is a pity that they are crude in theory and shallow in explanation. They are not of supreme teachings. That is why I have come here. I want to learn the Mahāyāna *Yogācārabhūmi Śāstra*. And it is a book composed by the future Buddhisattva Maitreya; how could you call it a heretical work? Aren't you afraid of falling into bottomless hell, are you?" Mokṣagupta responded, "Not knowing about the *Vibhāṣā Śāstra* or the other works, how could you say they are not profound in theory?"

The Master asked back, "Do you, the teacher, understand them?"

"Yes, I comprehensively understand all of them." was the answer.

Then the Master asked him some questions related to the beginning passage of the *Abhidharmakośa Śāstra,* Mokṣagupta, however, made mistakes whenever he opened his mouth to answer. What's worse, under the further questionings of the Master, his countenance began to change, at last, he had to say, "Why not ask me some questions about the rest parts?" But, being inquired of about another passage, he still failed to elaborate on it; once more, he excused himself by saying "It is not a passage of the *Abhidharmakośa Śāstra.*" At the time, Zhiyue (Jñānacandra), uncle of the king, a monk familiar with Buddhist scriptures and commentaries, was sitting beside them, who opened the *Abhidharmakośa Śāstra* and pointed out the same passage. Mokṣagupta felt greatly abashed and pleaded for himself, "I'm too senile to remember clearly." However, when the Master asked him about other Śāstras, he still failed to give a correct elucidation.

At the time, the snowy route through the Ice Mountains[8] was not yet open, and the Master had to remain in the country for another more than sixty days. He often looked eagerly into the distance. From time to time the Master went to Mokṣagupta to have a talk. When he saw the Master was coming, Mokṣagupta either stood up to greet or evaded him, no longer dared to squat in his chair. Privately, Mokṣagupta told the others, "It is not easy to answer the questions put forward by this Chinese monk. If he arrives in India, there will be no young peer equal to him." In such a way he thought highly and felt awesome of the Master. On the departure day, the king provided the Master with porters, also camels and horses. Accompanied by laity and monks of the whole city, the king saw the Master off.

From here moving westward for two days, the Master met more than two thousand Turkish cavalry bandits who fought against each other for the uneven distribution. And quickly they dispersed and vanished in the distance.

Walking for six hundred *li*, crossing a small desert, the Master and others arrived at Bālukā[9] (known as Gumo in olden times), where they stayed over for one night. Walking northwest for three hundred *li*, they crossed another small desert and came to the Ice Mountains, the northern part of the Pamir Range. The Ice Mountains were precipitous, towering high, which were covered by the enormously thick ice and snow accumulated since the formation of the world, with icicles not melting even in springs and summers. The cold air mingling with dirt was frozen into mist, rising high to touch the clouds, stretching out as far as eye could see, losing itself in the dazzling white. The falling-down ice peaks lying across the road were either as high as a hundred *chi* or wide as several *zhang*, rendering mountain defiles rugged and rough, difficult for people to climb. What's worse, the blowing blasts and flying snowflakes made the Master and others shivering all over despite their double boots and heavy fur coats. When it was time for meal and rest, there was no single place dry to stay, and so they had to cook by hanging the pot and sleep on the ice. It took seven days for them to get out of the mountain. Three to four out of every ten died of hunger and cold, while death rates of bulls and horses exceeded this number.

Coming out of the mountain, they reached a lake called Clean Pool[10]. (In contrast to the Ice Mountains, it had never frozen, hence the name Hot Sea that doesn't unnecessarily denote the waters were warm.) It was fourteen or fifteen hundred *li* in circumference, long from east to west and narrow from south to north. The water expanse stretched widely, and the choppy waves could rise several *zhang* tall, even with no gale at all. Walking along the lake toward the northwest for more than 500 *li,* the Master reached a city called Sūyāb[11], where he met Turkish Yehu Khan who was out there for a hunting expedition with his gorgeous army and horses. The Khan was clad in a green satin robe, and his hair was exposed, hanging behind his back, with this forehead wrapped by a white silk turban one *zhang* or so in length. Surrounding him were over two hundred high-ranking officials, all in brocade robes, wearing plaited hair. Their soldiers were in fur, pelt or woolen coats, with spears, banners or bows in their hands. Camels as well as horses were large in herds, scattering everywhere and immeasurable. The Khan rejoiced at meeting the Master and said, "I am leaving for a short while and will come back in two or three days. You teacher could go to my official residence." Then he ordered Dharmaja, one of his attendant officials, to escort the Master and accommodate him there.

After three days, the Khan returned. The Master was then ushered in a big tent where the Khan stayed, which was decorated with dazzling golden flowers. In front of the Khan, in two long rows of mats were sitting the high-ranking officials in exquisite brocade garments, while behind the Khan were standing armed safeguards. A spectacular view! As a lord of felt tent, the Khan looked so dignified and magnificent. When the Master was about thirty paces away from the tent, the Khan went out to salute him and greeted him through an interpreter. Then they took their seats inside the tent. Because the Turkish people worshiped fire and believed that the wood contained the element of fire, they never used wooden benches but laid out the double-layer mattresses to sit in. The Master was seated in an iron folding chair with a soft cushion on. After a while, the ambassadors from China and Gaochang were ushered inside to present the State Credentials and other authenticating objects. Seeing them, the Khan was very pleased, and he invited the ambassadors to take their seats too. Then with the wine served and music played, the Khan, together with his ministers as well as the ambassadors, enjoyed the fine wine, while the Master was entertained with grape juice. Toasting each other with various drinking vessels, big mugs, goblets or bowls, the guests enthusiastically urged each other to drink to satiety; the music played on ethnic musical instruments was resounding through the room, which, despite being alien and crude, was quite enjoyable to the ear and eye, also pleasing to the mind too. In a moment, the foods, such as the cooked fish, lamb, veal and the like, were heaped up abundantly in front of the guests, while the Master was served separately with the pure food, including pancakes, rice, butter, milk, sugar, honey, grapes, and so forth. After the meal, grape juice was presented again, and the Master was invited to preach the Dharma. Taking this chance to admonish them, the Master spoke upon the doctrines such as the Ten Good Deeds[12], the compassion to the living creatures and the emancipation through pāramitās[13]. Joining their hands up to the foreheads, the listeners prostrated, delightedly accepting the teachings with faith.

Thus, the Master stayed for several days. Then the Khan detained him by saying, "You needn't go to the country of Indica (India), for its weather is always hot. The climate of the tenth month there is the same as here of the fifth month. Judging by your appearance, I'm afraid you might soon wilt in the hot weather. Also, naked and swarthy, the people there are not decorous, not worth seeing."

The Master replied, "My purpose of going there is nothing else but to follow the trace of the sages and acquire the Dharma."

The Khan issued an order to summon someone from his army who could speak Chinese and other dialects along the route. Finally, a young man was found, who had expertise in Chinese for he once had spent a few years in Chang'an. The Khan immediately appointed him as an official translator to escort the Master to the country of Kapiśā[14], and asked him to write State Credentials to recommend the Master to the countries along the route. Besides, the Khan presented the Master with a religious garment made of red damask silk, as well as other fifty bolts of fine silk. After that, the Khan and his ministers saw the Master off for more than ten *li*.

Proceeding westward for over four hundred *li*, the Master came to a place named Qianquan[15], meaning thousand springs, several hundred odd *li* in circumstance, with many pools scattering, and densely covered by trees of rare species. Being sepulchral, moist and cool, it was the summer resort of the Khan. From here going one hundred fifty *li* westward he came to the city of Taras[16]; then going southwestward for two hundred *li* he reached the city of White Water[17]; farther advancing southwest for two hundred *li* he came to the city of Gongyu[18]; going southward from here for fifty *li* he reached the country of Nujakath [19]; and then advancing westward for two hundred *li* he came to the country of Shash[20] (known as the Stone City), on the west border of this country being the Yaxartes River[21]. Advancing to the west for more than one thousand *li* he reached the country of Sutṛṣṇa[22], which bordered on the Yaxartes in the east. The Yaxartes River had its source in the northern plateau of the Pamir Range and flowed in a north-westerly direction. Again going northwest, he entered a big desert with neither water nor grass, where he had to make an arduous march by following the remains of the animals and humans.

After five hundred odd *li*, he reached the country of Samarkand[23] (known as the Kingdom of Kang), where the king and the people didn't believe in Buddhism, instead, they worshiped the fire. There were two temples but with no monks in. If there were guest monks to reside in, the *hu* people would set fire to dispel them. At the beginning when the Master arrived, the king treated him with a light attitude. In the night staying here, the Master preached about the Buddhist doctrines to the king, including the law of causality of human and heavenly beings, merits of lauding the Buddha, and benefits as well as blessings accrued by worshiping the Buddha so on and so forth. After hearing those teachings, the king became delighted and forthwith eager to observe the Precepts. From that time on, he treated the Master with hospitality. Once, when the Master's two young disciples went to the temple to pay homage, several *hu* men drove them out with the fire. Then two śrāmaṇeras returned and reported the case to the king. Upon hearing it, the king issued an order to arrest the arsonists. After the culprits were caught, the king gathered the people to witness the penalty of having their hands cut off. Unwilling to see their body to be mutilated, and intending to guide the evil people to the path of kindness, the Master begged the king to mitigate their torture. At last, the king had them whipped heavily as a substitute punishment, and drove them out of the capital. Seeing this, the commoners and the senior officials, almost to a man, became pious and eager to convert to Buddhism. Then a great meeting was held to ordain people to be monks who took up the residence in those two temples. To a great degree, this case manifested that the Master had the ability to rectify the perverse view and enlighten the obscure and vulgar. And it was his way for things wherever he went.

Going westward for more than three hundred *li*, he reached the country of Kuṣāṇika[24]; farther west for more than two hundred *li,* he reached the country of Kharghan[25] (known as the Dong'an Country); going farther west for four hundred *li*, he reached the country of Bukhārā[26] (known as the Zhong'an Country); going farther west for over one hundred *li,* he reached the country of Vadi[27] (known as the Xi'an Country); going farther west for five hundred *li*, he reached the country of Horiṣmīka[28], which bordered on the Oxus[29] in the east; going farther southwest for over three hundred *li* he reached the country of Kuśāna[30] (known as Shi Country); and going southwest for another two hundred *li* he entered the mountainous region[31] where the paths were long and dangerous, only passable to one person, without vegetation nor water. Walking for more than three hundred *li* in the mountains, he came to the Iron Gate[32]. These narrow and steep precipices were rich in iron ore, and on cliff there was a cast-iron door, iron bells hanging from the door leaves, hence the name Iron Gate. This was the frontier fortress of the Turks. Going out of the Gate, he reached the country of Tukhāra[33] (wrongly called Tuhuoluo in olden times).

From there going for several hundred *li,* after crossing the Oxus River, he came to the country of Ghūr[34], where Tardu Shad[35] resided, who was the eldest son of Yehu Khan, and the husband of the younger sister of the king of Gaochang. The Gaochang king had already sent a letter to him in advance. When the Master arrived, the princess Khatun[36], the younger sister of the Gaochang king, had already passed away. Tardu Shad was ill at the time, however, when he heard the coming of the Master from Gaochang, he, holding the letter, could not refrain himself from sobbing with his family members. Then he arranged an audience with the Master. He said,

"On seeing the teacher, my eyes become bright again. Would you please stay here to take a rest for some time? If you'd like to, we will escort you to the Brahminic countries in person." At the same time, an Indian monk entered and invoked the mantra to cure Shad, which gradually alleviated his illness. The Khatun, the new queen of the Shad, was a young woman. Abetted by the former queen's son, she murdered Tardu Shad, her husband, with poison. Because the son of the Princess of Gaochang was under age, Tagin, the son of the former queen, usurped the throne to be the new Shad and then married his stepmother. Delayed by the funeral services, the Master had to remain here for over one month.

There was a Śramaṇa named Dharmasaṃgha, who used to study in India and so was hailed as the greatest Dharma Teacher by the people in the area west to the Pamir Range. None of the monks in Kashgar[37] or Khotan[38] ever ventured to discuss or debate with him on Dharma. Wanting to know the depth of Dharmasaṃgha's knowledge of Buddhism, the Master sent someone first to ask how many scriptures and commentaries he had mastered. Upon hearing the inquiry, the disciples of Dharmasaṃgha were irritated, while Dharmasaṃgha smiled and said, "I have mastered all of them. You can ask me whatever questions as you like." Knowing that he had not studied the Mahāyāna Buddhism, the Master put forward questions on several sects of the *Hīnayāna Vibhāṣā Śāstra*. However, Dharmasaṃgha failed to answer them properly. Finally he apologized and submitted, and his disciples felt abashed. From then on, whenever he met the Master, he turned to be delighted and wherever he went, he complimented him by saying that he was inferior to the Master in learning.

Now that the new Shad came to the throne, the Master paid him a visit and asked for a guide as well as corvée horses for the southbound journey to the Brahminic countries. The Shad said, "The country of Balkh[39] is our vassal. It borders on the Oxus in the north and is also called the Small Rājagṛha. There are a lot of holy sites. we suggest the Master take time to visit them. After that, you could return to take horses to go to the south." At the time, there were tens of monks from Balkh who had come to mourn the death of the late Shad and to congratulate the ascendancy of the new Shad. The Master visited them and told them his intention. They said, "Why not follow us? We have a good route. You need not come back here otherwise you will take a vain roundabout." Following their advice, the Master bad farewell to the Shad, and taking the horses, he resumed his journey with the monks.

When the Master arrived in the country of Balkh, he saw that both the capital city and its outskirts were spacious, with fertile fields stretching expansively. What a good place! There were over one hundred monasteries[40] accommodating more than three thousand monks of the Hīnayāna Buddhism. Situated in the southwest outside the city, the Navasaṃghārāma Monastery (meaning "new monastery") was adorned gorgeously. A bathing jar used by the Buddha, with the capacity of more than one *dou*, was kept in the Buddha Hall at the monastery; there was also a Buddha tooth of the one inch long and eight or nine *fen* broad, yellowish white in hue, which often gave out auspicious light; besides, a Buddha's broom was preserved there, which was made of kuśa grass, more than three *chi* in length, and seven *cun* in perimeter, with a handle inlaid with various precious gems. Those three objects would be exhibited on the fast days for the worship of monks and laity, and would issue the divine light as the response to their high sincerity. To the north of the monastery, there was a stūpa, more than two hundred *chi* in height. To the southwest of the monastery there was an abode for self-cultivation built long time ago, where the men who had attained the four grades of saintship[41] by practicing the self-cultivation could be seen incessantly in the past generations. After entering nirvāṇa, those saints were recorded by the inscriptions of the stūpas. Standing there one after another, those stūpas numbered over several hundred. Proceeding for fifty *li* northwest to the city, the Master arrived in the city of Trapuṣa, forty *li* north to which was the city of Bhallika, where there were two stūpas, three *zhang* in height. In the past, when the Buddha attained enlightenment, he accepted the fried wheat flour and honey offered by two elders[42], and for the first time, he preached to them about the Five Commandments and the Ten Good Deeds. Being asked for something for adoration, the Tathāgata gave them some of his hair and snail parings, also taught them the ritual procedures of the stūpa's construction. The two elders took the holy relics and returned to their native land to establish the sacred shrines (caitya)[43] that were the very ones seen here. Over seventy *li* to the west of the city there was another stūpa, over two *zhang* high, built in the age of Kāśyapa Buddha in the far distant past.

At the Navasaṃghārāma there was a Hīnayāna Tripiṭaka teacher from the country of Ṭakka[44], named Prajñākara (known as Huixing, meaning "wisdom-nature"). For he heard that there were a lot of holy sites in Balkh, he had come here to pay his homage. Young and candid, he was a person of intelligence and profound learning. He was specialized in the Nine Sections of the Hīnayāna Buddhism[45], and well versed in the Four Āgamas[46]. Well known throughout India, he was good at the elucidation on the Buddhist theories, with a particular mastery of the Hīnayāna Abhidharma[47] doctrines, including the *Kātyāyana's Abhidharmaprakaraṇaśāsaṇa Śāstra*, the *Abhidharmakośa Śāstra*, the *Jñānaprasthānaṣaṭpādābhidharma*[48], the *Abhidharmasamuccaya Śāstra*, and so forth. Upon hearing that the Master had come from afar to seek the Dharma, he was very delighted to meet him. When the master inquired of him on his doubts and curiosities about the scriptures such as the *Abhidharmakośa Śāstra* and the *Vibhāṣā Śāstr*a, he gave the answers very proficiently. Thus, the Master had stayed for more than one month learning the *Vibhāṣā Śāstra* after him. In the monastery lived two other Hīnayāna Tripiṭaka teachers, Dharmapriya (known as Fa'ai, meaning "affection for the Dharma") and Dharmākara (known as Faxing, meaning "nature of the Dharma"), who were also revered by the local people. When they saw that the Master had a bright and intelligent presence, they too greatly adored him.

To the southwest of Balkh were the countries of Zumathān and Gūzgānān[49]. When the kings of these countries knew the Master's coming from a distant country, they sent their senior officials to invite him to visit their countries to receive offerings, which was declined by the Master. But when the envoys consistently extended the invitation, the Master accepted it, which made the kings overjoyed. They presented the Master with gold, treasures, as well as food and drink;

however, when the Master returned he didn't take any of them.

Going south from Balkh, in company with the Dharma teacher Prajñākara, the Master entered the country of Gaz[50]. Then they came into the Great Snow Mountains[51] in the southeast, and forging ahead for six hundred *li*, they went out of the domain of Tukhāra and reached the country of Bāmīyān[52] in the snow mountains, which was more than two thousand *li* from east to west. The mountain paths were even much more dangerous and difficult to travel than those of glacier and desert. The clouds had been frozen into hydrometeors and the snowflakes have been flying wildly from day to night obscuring the sunshine; particularly worse in some spots, the narrow path was broken by perpetual snows several tens of feet thick. No wonder Song Yu[53] once wrote of the difficulties on the westbound road as "Lofty icy peaks are rising high, while feathery snows are blowing far." True it is! Alas! If it had not been for the sake of living beings, why should the Master have risked his precious life to trudge over such a difficult road to seek the supreme Right Dharma? In the past, when Wang Zun was climbing up the Nine Zigzag Slope[54], he claimed, "I am a loyal minister of Han Imperial House"; likewise, now when the Master was scaling the Snow Mountains, he was a veritable offspring of the Tathāgata.

Trudging on like this, the Master arrived at the capital of Bāmīyān, where there were about a dozen monasteries with several thousand monks, who were adherents of the Hīnayāna Lokottaravāda school. The king of Bāmīyān went out of the city to receive the Master and invited him to his palace to take the offerings. After spending several days in the palace, the Master left. There were two learned monks, Āryadāsa (known as Shengshi, meaning "holy servant") and Āryasena (known as Shengjun, meaning "holy army"), who had a profound knowledge of the doctrines of the Dharmalakṣaṇa school. Upon seeing the Master, they marveled that in a country distant as China there could come such a brilliant monk. Showing lavish hospitality, they guided him to pay homage to all the local holy places. At the foot of a mountain southeast to the capital, there was a standing rock statue of Śakyamuni Buddha, one hundred and fifty *chi* in height, to the east of which was a monastery. To the east of this monastery there was a standing brass statue of Śakyamuni Buddha one hundred *chi* tall. In the monastery there was a reclining statue of Śakyamuni Buddha attaining nirvāṇa, one thousand odd *chi* in length, solemnly and exquisitely decorated. From here going southeast for over two hundred odd *li*, out of the Great Snow Mountains, the Master came to a small river. There was a monastery where a tooth of the Buddha was preserved, together with a tooth of a Pratyekabuddha who lived at the beginning of the present kalpa[55], five inches long and less than four inches wide; there also was a tooth of a Gold Wheel King[56], three inches long and two inches wide. Besides them, there was an iron alms bowl used by Śāṇakavāsa[57](wrongly called as Śaṇavāsa in olden times) with a capacity of eight or nine *sheng,* and his saṃghāṭi[58] robe was in deep red. This robe had been worn by Śāṇakavāsa for five hundred lives in both his corporal form and the intermediate state of existence[59]. He was always born with this robe on, and later the robe was turned into kāṣāya (when he was ordained as a monk). The more stories about him are narrated in the other book[60].

After fifteen days, the Master went out of Bāmīyān. Encountering a snowstorm, he had lost his way for two days before he came to a small sandy hill and a hunter showed him the right way. Then climbing over the Black Mountain[61], he entered the domain of Kapiśā[62], which was a country of more than four thousand *li* in perimeter, with its back against the Snow Mountains in the South. The king was of the kṣatriya caste[63], majestic in looking and skillful at the statecraft, and under his control there were about a dozen kingdoms around. When the Master was approaching the capital, the king, together with monks, went out of the city to receive him. Within the city, there were over one hundred monasteries. The monks were contending with one another for inviting the Master to sojourn in their monasteries. There was a Hīnayāna monastery named Śālāka which was said had been built by a son of one emperor of the Han Dynasty when he once stayed here as a hostage. One monk from this monastery said to the Master, "Our monastery was constructed by a prince of a Han emperor, since you have come from that country, why don't you to stay at our monastery first?" Seeing that he was sincere and hospitable, in addition, considering that the Dharma teacher Prajñākara was an adherent of the Hīnayāna school and not willing to live in any Mahāyāna monastery, the Master accepted the invitation to take his sojourn there.

When the hostage prince built this monastery, he had a large amount of treasure buried under the feet of a Devarāja statue at the south side of the eastern door of the monastery, which was intended to cover the future repair expenses of the monastery. Showing their gratitude, the monks had the portraits of the hostage prince painted everywhere on the walls of the monastery. In order to perpetuate the meritorious deeds of the hostage prince, on every conclusion day of retreat[64], the monks always recited scriptures and preached the Buddhist teachings. This tradition had been passed down from one generation to another ceaselessly till the present. Later a wicked king, greedy and cruel, wanted to seize the treasure of the monks. At that moment the men were to dig at the feet of the deity statue on the king's order, the earth shook greatly, and the parrot image on the head top of the statue fluttered its wings and blared in alarm, which frightened the king and his army men down to the ground, losing consciousness. Full of fear, they had to give up. When the Wheel Sign[65] atop the stūpa was in dilapidation, monks attempted to take the treasure out for its reconstruction, but the earth quaked and bellowed again; consequently, no one dared to come close to it. Now the Master was here. So, they came together and told him the past incidents; and then following the Master, they came to the site. At the spot, the Master burnt the incenses and prayed by saying, "Formerly, you hostage prince hid the treasure for the performance of meritorious deeds. Now it is a high time to unearth it for the proper use. Please examine our mind to see whether it is pure from evil thoughts, and surely it is! Please relieve your awesome power a little bit and grant us your kind permission. If so, (Xuan)Zang will supervise the men on my own to unearth the treasure, measure the exact weight and hand the appropriate amount over to the monks in charge of renovation. I will require them to make repairs according to convention, not allowing any waste. May the spirit of deity condescend to examine our intention and show us the sympathy." After these words, he asked men to dig the earth. Then the work was done peacefully without any disturbance. Seven or eight *chi* underneath the earth, a big bronze vessel was discovered that held several hundred catties of gold and tens of pearls. The congregation rejoiced and developed the admiration for the Master heartily.

Then the Master resided in this monastery for the summer retreat. The king of this country thought little of the arts but attached great importance to the Mahāyāna Buddhism, preferring to attend preaching and recitation activities. So he invited the Master and the Tripiṭaka teacher Prajñākara to convene a Dharma assembly at a Mahāyāna monastery. There were a Tripiṭaka teacher named Manojñaghoṣa (known as Ruyisheng, meaning "voice-at-will"), and a monk of the Sarvāstivāda school named Āryavarman (known as Shengzhou, meaning "holy amor"), and a monk of the Mahīśāsaka school named Guṇabhadra (known as Dexian, meaning "virtuous sage"), all of whom were the leading monks at that monastery. But, lacking a comprehensive knowledge, they were adherents of either the Great or the Small Vehicle, and limited to a certain theory, their views were biased and incomplete. By contrast, only the Master had got a thorough knowledge of various teachings, able to answer various questions in accordance with the related convictions of different schools, which made the congregation utterly convinced and submitted in appreciation. This Dharma assembly went thus on for five days. With pleasure, the king presented the Master with five bolts of pure brocade and gave the other monks different offerings. When the retreat at Śālāka finished, the teacher Prajñākara was summoned again by the king of Tukhāra and had to go back. Thus, the Master bade farewell to Prajñākara.

Proceeding eastward for more than six hundred *li,* crossing the Black Ridge[66], the Master entered the territory of North India. He arrived in the country of Lampāka[67], which was over one thousand *li* in circumference and had ten monasteries with Mahāyāna monks. After staying there for three days, the Master went southward to a small hill, in which there was a stūpa, the very spot where the Buddha once stood when he came here from the south. Later, out of affection and respect, people erected this stūpa for commemoration. The extensive area from here to the north was all called mleccha[68] (meaning "barbarian land"). When the Tathāgata wanted to admonish the local people by his teachings, he came here in the air instead of treading on the ground, for if he walked, the earth would shake.

Advancing to the south for more than twenty *li*, going down the hill, and crossing the river, the Master arrived in the country of Nagarahāra[69] (in the domain of North India). Southeast to the capital city about two *li* at a distance, there was a stūpa, more than three hundred *chi* in height, which was built by King Aśoka[70]. This was the place where the Śākya Bodhisattva[71] spread his deerskin garment and his hair over the muddy earth to receive Dīpaṃkara Buddha in the second asaṃkhyeya kalpa and where he obtained a prediction about his future Buddhahood. Although having experienced the kalpa Destruction[72], this site remained intact and would permanently exist, and Heavenly beings often scattered flowers over it as offerings. No sooner had the Master arrived than he paid homage to it and walked around the stūpa to show his respects. When the Master was doing so, a senior monk standing nearby told him about the history of the stūpa.

Curiously, the Master asked him, "It was in the second asaṃkhyeya kalpa that the Bodhisattva spread his hair over the ground, and since then, there were numerous kalpas between the second and third asaṃkhyeya kalpa. During each kalpa, the world experienced countless cycles of the creation and destruction, even Mount Sumeru was burnt to ashes in the period of conflagration. How could this site alone have remained intact?"

The senior monk answered, "When the world was destroyed, this site was also perished with it; whereas when the world came into being, the site appeared again as what it once was at the original place, just like, say, Mount Sumeru, which was demolished but would be recreated again. So why the holy site alone might not exist? Take this as an explanation, and don't bother to doubt any longer." It really was the pertinent reply.

Over ten *li* to the southwest was a stūpa built on the spot where the Buddha once purchased flowers[73].

Then going farther southeast for more than ten *li* and climbing over a sandy ridge, the Master came to a city where the parietal bone of the Buddha[74] was preserved. There was a storeyed pavilion in the city, and on its second storey, there was a small-sized pagoda decorated with seven different kinds of jewels[75], which kept the parietal bone of the Tathāgata. In a precious chest, the bone was one *chi* and two *cun*[76] in perimeter, yellowish white in hue, and the hair pores on its surface clearly discernible. Anyone who wanted to get predictions about his fortune should grind some incense into powder, wrap the powder with a piece of white silk, and press it on the top of the bone. Then by reading the impression left on it, he would know whether it was auspicious or ominous in the future. After so doing, what the Master had obtained was a print in the shape of a Bodhi tree. Of the two accompanying Śrāmaṇeras, the older one got a print resembling a Buddha image, the younger one a lotus image. In admiration, the brahminic bone-keeper snapped his fingers and threw flowers towards the Master. He said, "What the teacher has obtained is very rare. It clearly indicates that you are qualified to attain Bodhi in future."

Also, there was a stūpa which kept a piece of skull of the Buddha in the shape of a lotus leaf, and a Buddha's eye relic as large as a crab apple which so glared that its light often darted outside the chest, and a garment of the Buddha's saṃghāṭi robe made by exquisite cotton cambric, and a Khakkara[77] of the Buddha with pewter rings and a sandalwood handle. To all of them the Master paid his homage and showed his condolences and respects. After presenting some offerings including fifty gold coins, one thousand silver coins, four gorgeous silk pennants, two bolts of brocade, and two suits of Buddhist vestment, the Master scattered flowers of various kinds, prostrated himself in worship again, and left.

He heard that twenty odd *li* to the southwest of the city of Dīpaṃkara there was a cave residence for the Dragon[78] King Gopāla. In the former time, the Tathāgata left his shadow inside the cave after he subdued this dragon, which the Master wanted to pay homage to. But the road to the cave was desolate and blocked, often infested with bandits. Over the past two or three years, the people who had been there to see the shadow, in most cases, failed to see anything; thus, rarely anyone visited it now. The Master intended to go there to worship, but the envoys escorting him from Kapiśā wanted to go back earlier, unwilling to detain any longer. They tried to persuade the Master not to go, but the master said to them, "It is hard to meet the shadow of the true body of the Tathāgata even in a hundred million kalpas. Now that I have come here, why should I not go there to pay my worship? You'd better move on slowly, (Xuan) Zang will come up with you soon."

Then the Master went alone to the city of Dīpaṃkara. He entered a monastery to ask the way and look for someone to be his guide, but no one was willing to go with him. Later, he met a kid who said to him, "The manor of the monastery is not far from here. I could show you there." So following the kid, the Master went to the manor to stay over. There he met an old man who knew the location of the cave. Led by him, the Master set out. After proceeding for several *li*, they encountered five bandits who came up to them with swords drawn out. Forthwith, the Master took off his hat and revealed his Buddhist vestment to them.

The bandits asked, "Where are you going, teacher?"

The Master answered, "I am going to pay my homage to the Buddha's shadow."

The bandits said, "Haven't you ever heard there are bandits around?"

The Master replied, "Bandits are no other than human beings. With the purpose of worshiping the Buddha, (Xuan) Zang has never been frightened by savage beasts on the road, let along dānapati, you are humans."

Hearing those words, the bandits decided to go with him to show their worship to the shadow too.

They arrived at the cave, which was in the eastern steep of a ravine, with the door opening to the west. When peeping inside, nothing could be seen but darkness.

The old man told the Master, "Teacher can go straight in, walk for about fifty paces till you touch the eastern wall, look to the due east, and the shadow is there." Then the Master entered the cave, walked ahead about fifty paces and actually touched the eastern wall. Following the advice, he stopped there and paid his worship wholeheartedly. First, he prostrated himself for more than one hundred times but saw nothing at all, which he blamed on himself, self-reproaching for hinderances accumulated in the past existences. He wailed in remorse. Then, he sincerely recited the stanzas in praise of the Buddha from the *Śrīmālādevīsiṃhanāda Sūtra* and other scriptures. After he prostrated himself again for another one hundred times or so, and extolled the virtues of the Buddha simultaneously, he saw there on the eastern wall a bright light the size of an alms bowl, but suddenly, it disappeared. With a mixed feeling of grief and joy, he continued to worship. Again, a bright light as large as a tray appeared and then went out, which evoked more affection and adoration in the Master's heart. He swore that he would not leave until he saw the shadow of the world-honored One. Then he made two hundred prostrations and more. Suddenly the cave lighted up, and the shadow of the Tathāgata appeared clearly on the wall, as if the gold mountain turned visible at the moment the clouds and mists dissipated. The wonderful and subtle features of the Buddha appeared lustrously divine, which the Master gazed up with the heartfelt admiration, losing himself in an indescribable rapture. Both the Buddha's body and cassock[79] was of reddish yellow and the figure above the knees was very clear and luminous, whereas the part below the lotus seat looked a little dim and vague. Shadows of the Bodhisattvas as well as the holy monks standing on the left and right sides of the Buddha, and behind his back, were also discernible. Seeing the shadow, the Master ordered the six men outside the cave to bring in a torch to light incense, but when the fire was brought in, the Buddha's shadow disappeared in an instant. Hurriedly, the Master asked them to put out the fire, and prayed again, thus the shadow reappeared. Among those six men, five did see the shadow, but one saw nothing at all. The shadows had lasted for half a meal's time, keeping clearly visible. After they paid homage, chanted acclaims, scattered flowers around and offered incenses, the shadows faded away. Then they came out. The brāhmaṇa, who guided the Master there, was delighted, exclaiming over such an unprecedented case. He said, "If it had not been for the teacher's great sincerity and the strong will-power, the sight could not have been seen." Outside the cave, there were a lot of holy sites, stories of which are told in the other book[80]. Together they returned. The five bandits destroyed their weapons, received the Buddhist commandments, and then left.

Then the Master rejoined other companions. Going southeast for five hundred odd *li* in mountains, he came to the country of Gandhāra[81] (in olden times wrongly called Jiantuowei, in the domain of North India). It bordered on the Indus[82] in the east, with the capital called Puruṣapura[83]. There had been a lot of sagacious and virtuous men, who were famous for writing some śāstras in ancient times, including Nārāyaṇadeva, Bodhisattva Asaṅga, Bodhisattva Vasubandhu[84], Dharmatrāta, Manoratha, and the venerable Pārśva, and all of them were born in this country. There once had a precious altar in the northeast of the royal city for keeping the Buddha's alms bowl. Later, this alms bowl was passed around neighboring countries for worship and at present was kept in the country of Vārāṇasī[85].

About eight or nine *li* southeast to the capital, there was a *pippala*[86] tree, over one hundred *chi* in height. The four Past Buddhas[87] used to sit under the tree. At present, there were statues of the four Tathāgatas. Nine hundred and ninety-six future Buddhas would also come and sit here. Beside the tree, there was a stūpa constructed by King Kaniṣka, which was four hundred *chi* tall. The base of the stūpa was one and a half *li* in circumference and one hundred fifty *chi* in height. On the top of the stūpa was a twenty-five-layer Diamond Wheel Sign, which contained one *hu* of relic bones of the Tathāgata. About one hundred paces southwest to this big stūpa, there was a white stone Buddha statue one *zhang* and eight *chi* in height, facing the north, displaying miraculous signs from time to time. Frequently it was seen circumambulating the big stūpa at night.

Over a hundred *li* to the northeast of the monastery built by King Kaniṣka, the Master crossed a great river[88] and reached the city of Puṣkalāvatī[89]. In the east of the city there was a stūpa constructed by King Aśoka, the very place where the four Past Buddhas once preached the Dharma. Four or five *li* to the north of the city, at another monastery there was a stūpa, more than two hundred *zhang* high, which was also built by King Aśoka, on the very site where Sakyamuni Buddha practiced the Bodhisattva Way by plucking out his eyeballs and gave them away to others as alms, when he was the lord of this country in his one thousand births and glad to perform almsgiving. In the neighborhood, holy sites of the kind were large in number, all of which were visited and worshiped by the Master. To show his devotion, he offered the gold, silver, silk, satin and garments given by the king of Gaochang to the great stūpas and large monasteries he visited. After doing so, he departed.

He reached the city of Uḍakhāṇḍa[90], and then proceeded to the north for more than six hundred *li,* climbing mountains and crossing rivers, and at last entered the country of Udyāna[91](meaning "garden," which once was a garden of King Aśoka in olden times. Formerly was wrongly called Wuzhang). In the past, there were fourteen hundred monasteries on both banks of the river of Śubhavastu[92], housing eighteen thousand monks, but at present the monasteries were in the dilapidation and the monks declined greatly in number. The disciplinary rules of the Sangha[93] were handed down along the lines of five schools, namely, (1) the Dharmagupta, (2) the Mahīśāsaka, (3) the Kāśyapīya, (4) the Sarvāstivāda, and (5) the Mahāsāṃghika. The king of this country lived in the city of Maṅgala[94] most of the time that was prosperous and densely populated. Four or five *li* to the east of the city, there was a great stūpa, often manifesting magic and auspicious signs. The stūpa was situated in the place where the Buddha cultivated himself as Kṣānti Ṛṣi[95] in one of his previous lives and was dismembered by King Kali (meaning "combat," formerly known as Geli by mistake). Two hundred fifty *li* to the northeast of the city, the Master entered a great mountain, and reached the Apalāla Dragon Spring, the source of the Swat River[96] . The river was flowing toward the southwest. Under the biting cold weather, it was frozen even in springs and summers. When the night fell, snowflakes of five colors began to fly, dancing madly in the air like various flowers mingled in confusion. More than thirty *li* southwest to the Dragon Spring, there was a Buddha's footprint in a boulder on the northern bank of the river, which was left by the Buddha after he had subdued the dragon king Apalāla at a former time. The footprint changed its size correspondingly to the different merit and will of the people when they measured it. More than thirty *li* down the river, there was a rock on which the Tathāgata washed his vestment. Impressed in the rock, the marks of strips on his Kāṣāya were still distinctly visible. Proceeding over four hundred *li* to the south of the city, the Master came to Hiḍḍa Mountain. This was the place where the Tathāgata jumped down from a tree to make a bodily sacrifice to a yakṣa in order to show his gratitude for hearing a half *ji* from him (*ji* formerly was an abbreviation of the Sanskrit word, or *jituo*, the mispronunciation of the Sanskrit. The correct reading is gāthā, and in the Tang Dynasty, also is referred to as stanza, metrical hymns, or chants, consisting of thirty-two syllables)[97].

Fifty *li* to the west of the city of Maṅgala, there was a great river. The Master crossed it and came to Rohitaka (meaning "red") Stūpa that was over ten *zhang* in height. Built by King Aśoka, it was the site where the Tathāgata was born as the King Maitrībala in one of his previous lives and pricked his body to feed five yakṣas (formerly called *yecha* by mistake). Proceeding more than thirty *li* to the northeast of the city, he reached the Adbhuta (meaning "miraculous") stone stūpa, thirty *chi* in height. In former times, the

Buddha preached the Dharma to both human and heavenly beings at this place, and after the Buddha had passed away, the stūpa cropped up from earth spontaneously. To the west of the stūpa, crossing a river and proceeding three or four *li*, the Master came to a *vihāra*[98] where a statue of Bodhisattva Avalokiteśvara was enshrined, being divinely efficacious. (The name of this Bodhisattva is a compound word: Avalokita and Īśvara, the former meaning "observe" and the latter "the being of sovereign freedom." Formerly it was wrongly translated as Illumination World Voice, or Observing the Voice of the World, or Observing World Voice Sovereign Freedom Being.)

The master heard that to the northeast of the city, after scaling the mountains, crossing a gully, going upstream along the Śītā River[99], and continuously proceeding for more than one thousand *li*, one could reach the Darada Valley[100] where the capital of Udyāna was. However, the way to it was so perilous that one had to climb up with the rope chains and walk on the suspension bridge. It was also said that in the valley, next to a great monastery, there was a dignified wooden sculpture of Bodhisattva Maitreya, golden, and more than one hundred *chi* in height. It was made by the Arahat Madhyāntika (wrongly called Motiandi in olden times), who by displaying his miraculous power, ascended the craftsman up into the Tuṣita Heaven[101] (wrongly known as Doushuaituo in olden times) to see the wonderfully refined visage of Maitreya. And it was not until the craftsman went there and back three times in this way that he finally finished the statue.

From the city of Uḍakhāṇḍa moving onward to the south, the Master crossed the Indus River which was three or four *li* broad, with torrents extremely clear and rapid, haunted by venomous dragons and cruel beasts. If a man crossed the river with some Indian precious gems, rare flowers or relic bones, his boat would be overturned. After crossing this river, the Master came to the country of Takṣaśilā[102] (in the domain of North India). There was a stūpa located about twelve or thirteen *li* to the north of the capital city. Built by King Aśoka, the stūpa often radiated the divine light, for it was the place where the Tathāgata, when he was a great king named Candraprabha (meaning "moonlight") in one of his previous lives, was practicing the Way of Bodhisattva by cutting off his head for one thousand times in order to pursue the Supreme Wisdom. Beside the stūpa, there was a monastery where Kumāralāta (known as Tongshou), a teacher of the Sautrāntika School, composed his many śāstras. Form here going seven hundred *li* to the southeast, there was the country of Siṃhapura[103] (in the domain of North India). The Master crossed the Indus River at the northern territory of the country of Takṣaśilā. Proceeding to the southeast for over two hundred *li* he passed the Great Stone Gate, where in the far distant past, Prince Mahāsattva gave up his body to feed a starving tigress and her seven cubs. At that time the soil had been stained red by the blood of the prince, and now it was still in deep red, so was the color of the vegetation here.

And again, proceeding southeast in the mountainous area for over five hundred *li*, the Master reached the country of Urasā[104]. He continued to proceed southeast, scaled the precipitous passes, crossed an iron bridge, and after covering more than one thousand *li* came to the country of Kaśmīra[105] (wrongly known as Jibin in olden times). Bordering on a great river[106] in the west, its capital[107] had over one hundred monasteries with more than five thousand monks.

There were four stūpas, impressive and splendorous, which were built by King Aśoka, each of them preserving one *sheng* of relic bones of the Tathāgata or so. When the Master was about to enter the territory of Kaśmīra, he first came to Stone Gate, the western gate of the country. The king sent his maternal uncle to receive him with horses and carriages. After entering Stone Gate, the Master visited the monasteries and stayed over at one of them with the name of Huśkara. At that night, many a monk in the monastery had a dream in which a deity admonished them by saying "This guest monk has come from Mahāchina. He is highly motivated to study Buddhist scriptures in India, to pay homage to the holy sites, and to learn from eminent teachers about what he hasn't heard. Since he has come here for the Dharma, numerous good deities escort and protect him. Now here he is! So much merit accrues to you that you are admired by such a monk coming from a distant land. You should win his respect and praise by applying yourselves with greater diligence than ever to recite scriptures and do meditation. How could you be so lazy and murky in sleep?" By hearing those words, the monks were startled to wake up widely. Forthwith, they rose to walk or sit in meditation and chant scriptures till the day broke. Then, they gathered around the Master and told him what had happened to them at night. From then on, the congregation bore much more respect.

After staying there for a few days, the Master resumed his journey, proceeding close to the royal city. About one *yojana*[108] away from the city, he reached Dharmaśāla (known as Fushe, meaning "the residence of happiness," which was constructed by the king to accommodate the travelers and the needy people). The king, leading his ministers and monks of the city, came to Fushe to welcome the Master, with the total entourage over one thousand people. The roads were crammed with flying banners and covered a forest of canopies; the air was perfumed with flowers and incense. No sooner had the Master arrived than the king greeted him with hospitality. He paid tribute to the Master and scattered numerous flowers over him. After that, he invited the Master to mount an elephant and follow him into the city. In the capital city, he lodged the Master at Jayendra Monastery (which was built by the maternal uncle of the king). On the following day, the king invited the Master, together with several tens of the great virtuous monks, including Saṃghakīrti and others, to go to the palace to receive religious offerings. After the meal, the king requested the Master to preach the Dharma and asked the other monks to argue with him or consulted him on some questions. The king himself stood by, watching this occasion, and feeling highly pleased. Considering that the Master had come from afar and there were no written books available to him to study, the king ordered a score of scribes to transcribe the scriptures and commentaries for the Master. Moreover, he gave the Master five persons as his attendants. Also, he issued an order that the accommodations of the Master be covered by public expenditure.

The Dharma teacher Saṃghakīrti was a person of noble character, who had observed religious precepts scrupulously and chastely; and being a man of high thinking, he learned broadly and obtained a complete knowledge of Buddhism. He wasn't proud of his own talent and intelligence, but showed much respect to the virtuous and erudite scholars. He treated the Master as the distinguished guest and entertained him in hospitality, being considerate of his needs. The Master wholeheartedly consulted him on Buddha Dharma day and night without feeling tired, and further asked him to expound various śāstras. At the time, Saṃghakīrti was approaching seventy years old, so his physical strength went weaker; yet delighted at meeting such a monk of tremendous promise as the Master, he went all out to preach the dharma and elucidate the doctrines. By noon, he delivered the sermon on the *Abhidharmakośa Śāstra*; in the afternoon, he lectured on the *Nyāyānusāra Śāstra*; in the first part of night, he preached the *Hetuvidyā* and *Şabdavidyā*. Scholars in the locality gathered around him to study. From Saṃghakīrti, the Master gained a thorough comprehension of the abstruseness of the Buddhist theory and reached its very kernel, thus, he was appreciated and praised by the teacher to the utmost. Saṃghakīrti once said to others, "This Chinese monk has an extraordinary intelligence. No one in this congregation can match him. His wisdom and virtue make him qualified to be a successor of Vasubandu and his half-brother, Asanga. But it is a pity that he was born in such a distant country and hasn't received the bequeathed teachings of the saints and sages earlier."

Among the congregation there were two Mahāyāna scholar monks: Viśuddhasiṃha (known as Jinshizi, meaning "pure lion") and Jinabandhu (known as Zuishengqin, meaning "victorious kinsman"); two Sarvāstivāda scholar monks: Sugatamitra (known as Rulaiyou, meaning "Tathāgata's friend") and Vasumitra (known as Shiyou, meaning "friend of the world"); and two Mahāsāṃghika scholar monks: Sūryadeva (known as Ritian, meaning "sun-god") and Jinatrāta (known as Zuishengjiu, meaning "victorious protector").

Prior to the Master, they had come to this country to study. They were steadfast in the Buddhist Path and talented in understanding, even not good enough to be compared with Saṃghakīrti, at least they were much better than other monks. On seeing that the Master was highly praised by their great Dharma teacher, none of them begrudged any effort to refute and interrogate him, but the Master answered all the questions put forward by them without ambiguities and hesitation, which at last made those eminent monks ashamed, knowing to humble themselves before the Master.

Formerly, this country was a lake possessed by a dragon. In the fiftieth year after the Nirvāṇa of the Buddha, the dragon king was converted by Arhat[109] Madhyāntika, a disciple of Ānanda, and so presented the lake as an offering, on which five hundred monasteries had been constructed hereafter. Then the saints and sages were invited to reside there to receive the offerings of the dragon. Later, in the four hundredth year after the Buddha's Nirvāṇa, King Kaniṣka invited 499 monks who were well-versed in the Tripiṭaka and proficient in Pañca-vidyā[110], plus the Venerable Vasumitra, a total of 500 distinguished and saintly monks, to congregate here to recite and collect the Buddhist Tripiṭaka. Firstly, they compiled the *Upadeśa Śāstra* (formerly known as the *Youbotishe* by mistake) in 100,000 gāthā[111] for the exposition of the Sūtra Piṭaka (formerly known as the *Xiuduoluo* by mistake); next, the *Vinayavibhāsā Śāstra* in 100,000 gāthā for the Vinaya Piṭaka (formerly known as the *Pinaye* by mistake), and thirdly, the *Abhidharmavibhāṣa Śāstra* in 100,000 gāthā for the *Abhidharma* Piṭaka (formerly known as the *Apitan* by mistake). Totally there were 300,000 gāthā and 960,000 syllables.[112] The king had the red copper tempered into the flat and thin plates to incise the *śāstras* on, then sealed them in stone chests. Having had the big stūpa constructed to preserve the stone chests, he ordered *yakṣas* to guard it. Owing to the endeavor of the king, the profound doctrines have thus been known to the world till the present time. The Master spent two full years here studying all kinds of scriptures as well as commentaries, also trekked to various holy sites to pay his homage. After that, he left.

Crossing a mountain stream in the southwest, and going for seven hundred *li*, he reached the country of Parṇotsa[113]. From here proceeding southward for over four hundred *li*, he came to the country of Rājapura[114] (in the domain of North India). Then proceeding to the southeast for more than seven hundred *li*, down the mountain and across the river[115], the Master arrived in the country of Ṭakka (in the domain of North India). It was such a remote and desolate place from Lampāka that the people lived here were crude and uncultured, also their costumes and languages slightly different from the rest of India. Leaving Rājapura, after walking for two days, the Master crossed the Candrabāgā (known as Yuefen, meaning "moon division") River[116], and reached the city of Jayapura, where he stayed over in a heretical temple outside the western gate to the city, and at the time there were more than twenty priests in the temple. The day after the following day, he entered the city of Śākala[117], where there was a monastery with more than one hundred monks. At this monastery, in former times, Vasubandhu Bodhisattva composed the *Paramārthasatya Śāstra*. Beside the monastery, there was a stūpa, two hundred *chi* in height, where the four Past Buddhas once preached the Dharma, and now the footprints left during their walking meditation still could be seen.

From here out of the city of Nārasiṃha, he entered the big palāśa[118] woods in the east, where he was encountered by a band of about fifty brigands, who robbed the Master and his companions of all their clothes and property. Then, brandishing knives, the brigands drove them to a dried-up pond with the intention to slay them all. The pond was covered with lush thorny bushes and wild climbing plants. Through the bushes, a Śrāmaṇera, one of the Master's companions, saw there was a water drain at the southern bank of the pond, large enough for a man to pass through. He told the Master secretly, then they slipped away through the drain. After running to the southeast for about two or three *li,* they met a brāhmaṇa tilling the field, to whom they told what had happened. Falling in consternation at the news, the brāhmaṇa unbridled his bull and handed it over to the Master; then he blew the conch, beat the drum, and summoned more than eighty men from the village. Carrying weapons in their hands, they swiftly headed for the place where the brigands were. Upon seeing them, the brigands scattered away into the woods. The Master went to the pond to set his companions free, and distributed clothes among them. Supporting each other, they sought shelter in the nearby village. The Master smiled, not showing any grief or sorrow; in contrast, the others were weeping sadly.

One of them asked the Master, "All our clothes and property have been deprived by robbers, now nothing is left, save our lives, which must be the toughest and the most dangerous moment in life. When recollecting what happened in the woods, we feel very miserable. Why are you cheerful and smiling, not sad as we are?"

The Master answered, "Life is the greatest prize to a living creature. Now that our lives have been spared, what else to worry about? A secular book in my country says, 'The greatest treasure between Earth and Heaven is life', and here we are alive, so the Greatest Treasure isn't lost. It is no need for us to worry about the rest, or to be stingy with something of no importance like clothes and property."

Hearing those words, the other travelers were greatly touched and convinced. From it, we can see that the Master's magnanimity truly resembles an unbounded stretch of water, capable to keep calm and clear under disturbances.

On the following day, the Master arrived in a big city at the eastern frontier of the country of Ṭakka. There was a large mango grove on the northern side of the road in the western city, where lived a seven-hundred-year-old brāhmaṇa, tall and robust. Observed face to face, he looked like a man about thirty years old. With a comprehensive knowledge, he was not only proficient in the *Mūlamadhyamakakārikā, Catuḥśataka* and others, but also well-versed in the Vedas[119] and other books. He had two attendants, and both were over one hundred years old. When the Master came over to visit him, he was delighted, receiving the Master with hospitality. After knowing that the Master had encountered the brigands, he sent one of his attendants to take his order to the Buddhist devotees in the city and asked them to prepare the food for the Master. There were several thousand households in the city, of whom only a small portion believed in Buddhism, whereas the rest were heretical believers. When the Master was in the country of Kaśmīra, his prestige had already been known locally and far afield, so he had been well-known to various countries, even here. The messenger sent by the brāhmaṇa walked around the city and announced, "Here comes that Chinese monk. He was robbed by brigands nearby and lost all his garments. It befits you all to know that this is the right time to perform meritorious deeds." Impressed with the Master's merits and virtues, those with heretical faith changed their minds. There were more than three hundred local prestigious people coming over to the Master, each of them carrying a piece of cotton cambric, and food and drinks. Having piled the lavish offerings up in front of the Master, they knelt to worship and extend greetings to him. Then the Master chanted incantation, bestowed them blessings and delivered sermons to them on convictions of causality as well as retribution. As a result, the hearers resolved to seek the Buddhi Way by forsaking heresy and returning to truth. Satisfactorily, they smiled into each other's face, danced in delight, and then left for home. The senior brāhmaṇa exclaimed over the rarity of such an event. Thereafter, the Master distributed the rolls of cotton cambric among his fellow travelers. After each of them obtaining a portion enough for several suits, there were still some left, so the Master offered five bolts to the senior brāhmaṇa. Then the Master remained there for a month and learned the *Sūtraśata Śāstra* and the *Śataśāstravaipulya* from him. This senior brāhmaṇa once was a disciple of Nāgārjuna[120] and received the teachings face to face from Nāgārjuna, which made his elucidation quite clear and accurate.

From here proceeding to the east for five hundred *li,* the Master reached the country of Cīnabhukti[121]. Then he came to Toṣasana Monastery. There lived a virtuous monk named

Vinītaprabha (meaning "light of subjugation," who was a prince of North India), being elegant in presence and proficient at the Tripiṭaka. He had composed the *Exposition of the Pañcaskandha Śāstra* and the *Exposition of the* Vidyāmātrasiddhitridaśakārikā Śāstra. Then the Master stayed with him for fourteen months and learned from him the *Abhidharmasamudāyavyākhyā Śāstra*, the *Abhidharmaprakaraṇaśāsaṇa Śāstra*, the *Nyāyadvāratāraka Śāstra*, and so forth.

To the southeast of the big city, moving onward for more than fifty *li*, the Master reached Tamasāvana (meaning "dark woods") Monastery, with more than three hundred monks of the Sarvāstivāda school. It was the very place where a thousand buddhas of this present kalpa[122] would preach the Dharma to the congregation of the human as well as Heavenly beings. In the three hundredth year after the Nirvāṇa of Śākyamuni Tathāgata, a *Śāstra* teacher named Kātyāyana (formerly known as Jiazhanyan by mistake) wrote the *Abhidharmajñānaprasthāna Śāstra* here.

From here going to the northeast for forty or fifty *li*, the Master reached the country of Jālaṃdhara[123] (in North India). He went to Nageradhana Monastery, where there was a virtuous monk named Candravarman (meaning "moon armor"). For he had an intimate knowledge of the Tripiṭaka, the Master remained there for more than four months to study the *Vibhāṣāprakaraṇapāda Śāstra* with him.

From here he climbed over high mountains and proceeded northeast for more than seven hundred *li* to reach the country of Kulūta[124](in the domain of North India). From Kulūta going southward for more than seven hundred *li*, scaling mountains and crossing rivers, he reached the country of Śatadru[125](in the domain of North India). From here advancing to the southwest for more than eight hundred *li*, he reached the country of Pāriyātra (in the domain of Central India). From here going eastward for more than five hundred *li*, he reached the country of Mathurā[126](in the domain of Central India). Many relic stūpas of the holy disciples of Śākya Tathāgata were still in existence, including the stūpas of Śāriputra (formerly known as Shelizi or Shelifu by mistake), Maudgalaputra (erroneously known as Mujianlian in olden times), Pūrṇamaitrāyaṇīputra (meaning "full compassion son"; formerly known as Miduoluonizi, being an erroneous abbreviation), Upāli, Ānanda, Rāhula (formerly known as Luohouluo or Luoyun by mistake), and Mañjuśrī (meaning "wonderfully auspicious"; in olden times erroneously known as Rushou, Wenshushili, or Manshushili or translated as Wonderful Virtue), and so forth. Every year on festival days, monks came here to make separate offerings according to their different doctrinal inheritance: the Abhidharma monks made offerings to Śāriputra; monks who practiced meditation made offerings to Maudgalaputra; monks who recited scriptures made offerings to Full Compassion Son; monks who studied the Vinaya made offerings Upāli; the bhikṣuṇīs[127] made offerings to Ānanda; monks who hadn't received full ordination made offerings to Rāhula; and the Mahāyāna monks made offerings to various Bodhisattvas. About five or six *li* to the east of the city, the Master came to a mountain monastery built by the venerable Upagupta[128] (known as Jinhu, meaning "near protection"), in which the hair and snail parings of the Buddha were preserved. In the northern cliff beside the monastery, there was a stone cave, more than twenty *chi* high and thirty *chi* wide, the floor of which was covered with numerous small tally sticks four odd *cun*[129] long. The venerable Jinhu dropped one tally stick as a record every time a married couple attained Arhatship together after hearing his sermons on Dharma. If only one member of the couple attained the fruition of Arhatship or the couple attained other kind of fruition, he merely gave the confirmation but never made a record by dropping the stick.

From here walking over five hundred *li*, the Master came to the country of Sthāneśvara[130] (in Central India); then proceeding to the east for more than four hundred *li,* he reached the country of Śrughna[131] (in Central India), bordering on the Ganges in the east and backing onto a great mountain, with the Yanunā River[132] flowing through its central part; to the east of the river, proceeding for more than eight hundred *li,* the Master reached the source of the Ganges[133], about three or four *li* broad, flowing southeast into the sea where the estuary was more than ten *li* wide. Carrying the fine sands down, the water tasted refreshing and sweet, which was depicted as "auspicious water" by the local secular books. A prevailing superstition went that to take a bath in the river could eliminate sins, to drink the water or rinse with it could eradicate the misfortunes and calamities, and even to be into it could make a person ascend to Heavens to enjoy permanent happiness. Although these heretical statements were groundless, the ignorant men and women often flocked to the riverside; and not until Deva Bodhisattva[134] debunked the falsehood and revealed the truth to them did the custom come to an end completely. In the country, there was a virtuous monk named Jayagupta, who was well-versed in the Tripiṭaka, so the

Master spent a winter plus a half spring attending his lectures on the *Sautrāntikavibhāṣā Śāstra*.

Then crossing the Ganges to its eastern bank, the Master reached the country of Matipura[135], whose king was of the śūdra caste[136]. There were about a dozen monasteries with over eight hundred monks who studied the Hīnayāna teachings of the Sarvāstivāda school. About four or five *li* to the south of the big city, there was a small monastery with more than fifty monks, where in the past, the Śāstra master Guṇaprabha (known as Deguang, meaning "virtue Light") lived and composed the *Tittvasatya Śāstra* and others, totally more than one hundred treatises. This Śāstra master, a native of the country of Parvata[137], originally studied the Mahāyāna teachings; but later, he retrogressed to learn the Hīnayāna. At the time, Arhat Devasena (known as Tianjun, meaning "heaven army") often went up to the Tuṣita Heaven. Virtue Light wished to visit Maitreya to resolve his doubts and ambiguities, so he asked Tianjun to display divine power to bring him to the Heavenly palace. But when he saw Maitreya, he merely bowed slightly with no more proper salutations, and said, "I am a fully-ordained monk, while you, Maitreya, are showing yourself as a layman in Heaven, so it is not proper for me to pay homage to you." Subsequently, he went to and back from the Tuṣita Heaven for three times, but never saluted Maitreya in the proper way. Since he was arrogant and supercilious, his doubts remained unsettled all the time.

Three or four *li* to the south of Guṇaprabha's monastery was a monastery where the Śāstra master Saṃghabhadra passed away. Now there were more than two hundred monks of the Hīnayāna school.

The Śāstra master was a native of Kaśmīra, erudite and very talented, well-versed in the *Vibhāṣā Śāstra* of the Sarvāstivāda school. At his time, another intelligent and learned master was Vasubandhu Bodhisattva, who formerly refuted Vibhāṣā teachers' doctrines by composing the *Abhidharmakośa Śāstra*. For its profound theories and literary grace, this Śāstra was acclaimed and admired by Buddhists in the Western Regions, and even was taught and studied by the spirits and deities. After reading the Śāstra, Saṃghabhadra became indignant. Then he spent twelve years in deliberation and finally composed the *Kośakarakā Śāstra* in twenty-five thousand stanzas with eight hundred thousand syllables. When he finished the treatise, he wished to have a debate with Vasubandhu face to face, but passed away before fulfilling this desire. Later, Vasubandhu read this treatise and praised Saṃghabhadra, saying that he was a man of perspicacity, and that his faculty of thinking was above all other Vibhāṣā teachers. In addition, he suggested that it be entitled the *Nyāyānusāra Śāstra* since the treatise accorded closely with his own teachings, thus, the new name was settled. After the death of Saṃghabhadra, a stūpa was built in the mango grove, which was still existing.

Beside the grove, there was a big stūpa built at the very place where the Śāstra teacher Vimalamitra (known as Wugoucheng, meaning "pure friend") passed away. The Śāstra teacher was a native of Kaśmīra, and became a monk in the Sarvāstivāda school. Having traveled in five parts of India and studied the Tripiṭaka thoroughly, he intended to return to his homeland. On his way back, he passed by the stūpa of Saṃghabhadra, for feeling a pity for the early demise of Saṃghabhadra before his treatise being widely propagated,

Vimalamitra took a vow to compose another treatise to refute the Mahāyāna doctrines and demolish the fame of Vasubandhu so as to make the teachings of the Śāstra teacher Saṃghabhadra pass down through the generations forever. No sooner had those words come out of his mouth than he went into insanity. Five tongues grew out of his mouth and blood was seeping out from all over his body. When he realized that all these agonies were caused by his incorrect views, he became remorseful, so he wrote a letter to admonish his companions not to slander the Mahāyāna doctrines. Hardly had he finished writing this letter when he died. On the spot of his death, the earth sank into a pit.

In that country, there was a virtuous monk named Mitrasena, who was ninety years old and a disciple of the Śāstra teacher Guṇaprabha. For Mitrasena had an intimate knowledge of the Tripiṭaka, the Master spent a half spring and the following summer staying with him to study the *Tattvasandeśa Śāstra* (known as the *Tittvasatya Śāstra* in twenty-five thousand stanzas, which was composed by Guṇaprabha), the *Anujñāprasthāna Śāstra*, and others.

From here going northward for more than three hundred *li,* the Master reached the country of Brahmapura[138] (in Central India). Again going southeast for over four hundred *li*, he reached the country of Ahicchattra[139] (in Central India). Again, going southward for over two hundred *li*, after crossing Ganges, he came to the country of Vilaśāṇa[140] (in Central India) in the southwest. Again, going eastward for over two hundred *li,* he reached the country of Kapitha[141] (in Central India). More than twenty *li* to the east of the city, there was a great monastery, and in the courtyard of it, there were three stairways made of precious substances, standing from south to north in a row slopping down from east to west. In the far distant past, descending those stairways, the Buddha returned to Jambudvīpa[142] after he had delivered his dharma sermons to Mahāmāyā in Trayastriṃśa Heaven[143]. The middle stairway was made of gold, the left one of crystal and the right one of silver. When the Tathāgata set out from the Hall of Good Dharma, he walked down the stairway in the middle, with Mahābrahmā holding a white whisk down the silver stairway on the right and Indra holding a jeweled canopy down the crystal one on the left. Simultaneously, hundreds and thousands of the heavenly beings and the great Bodhisattvas also accompanied the Buddha going down the stairways. Several hundred years before, the stairs were still visible, but they gradually vanished, being no longer in existence. Later, the stairways were reconstructed by a king to show his adoration to the Buddha. The new ones were built of bricks and stones, however, in the original architectural style. As high as seventy *chi*, the stairways were also decorated with a variety of precious substances, on top of which sat a *vihāra* to enshrine a stone statue of the Buddha that was flanked by the statues of Mahābrahmā on the left and of Indra on the right. By imitating the previous architectural style, the past scene was vividly reproduced. Beside it, there was a stone column, seven *zhang* in height, which was erected by King Aśoka. Next to it, there was a stone terrace fifty paces long and seven *chi* high, where the Buddha walked up and down in meditation in former times.

From here proceeding for two hundred *li*, the Master reached the country of Kanyākubja[144] (known as the city of Qunü, meaning "the city of hunchbacked maiden," in Central India), four thousand *li* in perimeter. Bordering on the Ganges in the west, its capital city, over twenty *li* long and five or six *li* broad, had more than one hundred monasteries with over ten thousand monks adhering to both the Mahāyāna and Hīnayāna schools. The king of the country was of the *vaiṣya* caste[145], with the name of Harṣavardhana (known as Xizeng, meaning "joy-increasing"), whose father was named Prabhākaravardhana (known as Zuozeng, meaning "deed-increasing"), and whose elder brother, Rājyavardhana (known as Wangzeng, meaning "kingdom-increasing"). During the reign of Xizeng, he practiced the benevolent governance, thus won compliments from his people. At the time, in the country of Karṇasuvarṇa[146] in East India, there was a king named Śaśāṅka (known as Ri, meaning "sun"). Out of jealousy, he hated Rājyavardhana for his brilliance and regarded him as a dangerous neighbor, so he framed Rājyavardhana up and murdered him. The chief minister Vāṇi (known as Mingliao, meaning "understanding") and his colleagues felt pity for the people who had lost their lord, and enthroned the king's younger brother Śīlāditya[147](known as Jieri, meaning "sun of morality") as the successor to the royal lineage. With the majestic appearance and refined manner, the king Śīlāditya, a man of a broad vision, was very intelligent and resourceful. His virtue could rouse much resonance from Heaven and Earth, and his integrity touched the mortals and deities. He revenged the murder of his elder brother, thereafter put India under his bright reign. Wherever his prestige had reached, his edification had spread as well, overwhelming the people by his virtue. Neighboring countries were on good terms with each other and masses were living in security. Later, having disbanded the army and putting the weapons on shelf, he began to launch the meritorious undertakings by prohibiting the slaughter of animals within his domain and preventing his people from eating meat. In addition, he had monasteries built on the holy relic sites where monks were given the offerings annually, usually twenty-one days at a time. He also held the Great Equal Assembly every five years, at which all property in the national storehouse was given away as alms. Because of his meritorious deeds, he could be compared with Sudāna[148].

There was a stūpa in the northwest of the city, two hundred *chi* high. Six or seven *li* to the southeast of the city, on the southern bank of the Ganges was also stūpa two hundred *chi* in height. Both were built by Aśoka on the preaching sites of the Buddha. The Master entered this country, lived at the Bhadra Vihāra for three months. Under the tutelage of Tripiṭaka-master Viryasena, he finished his study of the Buddhadāsa's *Vibhāṣā Śāstra* and the Sūryavarman's *Vibhāṣā Śāstra*.

ANNOTATION

1 Also Triśaraṇa. One becomes a Buddhist by taking refuge, for protection and guidance, in the Three Jewels: the Buddha, the Dharma, and the Saṅgha.

2 Also Five Precepts. See note 80 of Fascicle I.

3 Stūpa: a tope, or pagoda, a reliquary.

4 The Kumush Mountain.

5 The three kinds of pure meat refer to the meat that a Buddhist monastic may consume when he or she has not seen a creature killed, hasn't heard of its being killed, and has no doubt that it is killed for him or her.

6 Buddha's teachings are divided into the "gradual" and "sudden" teachings, the former beginning with the Hīnayāna and proceeding to the Mahāyāna, while the latter immediately starting with Mahāyāna.

7 Śabdavidyā: grammar and composition; one of the Five Sciences (q.v.).

8 Bedel Pass is a mountain pass in the Tianshan mountain range between Kyrgyzstan and China's Xinjiang Uygur Autonomous Region. It has an elevation of 4,284 metres (14,055 ft). The pass linked China to Barskon, a settlement on the southern shore of lake Issyk-kul. Historically, the Bedel Pass served as a Silk Road trade route between China and Central Asia. On the Chinese side, the Bedel Beacon Tower is located on the foothills along the path. It was built during the Han Dynasty as part of the Han Great Wall. The beacon was reused and renovated during the Tang Dynasty. During the Sui and Tang dynasties, the pass was the main trade route linking Tarim Basin and Western Turks in Central Asia. It is commonly known as *bingdaban* 冰达坂 in China.

9 It was known during the Han Dynasty as the kingdom of Gumo 姑墨, in the region of Aksu 阿克苏 and present Wensu County 温宿县 in Xinjiang Uygur Autonomous Region.

10 Also called the Hot Sea, today the Issyk-Kul Lake, an endorheic lake in the northern Tianshan mountains in eastern Kyrgyzstan. It is the tenth largest lake in the world by volume (though not in surface area), and the second largest saline lake after the Caspian Sea. Issyk-Kul means "warm lake" in the Kyrgyz language; although it is surrounded by snow-capped peaks, it never freezes.

11 Also known as Ordukent (modern-day Ak-Beshim), was an ancient Silk Road city located some 50 km east from Bishkek, and 8 km southwest

from Tokmok(Tokmak), in the Chui River valley, present-day Kyrgyzstan.

12 Or the Ten Meritorous Actions, or the Ten Forms of Good Actions for layman, or Ten Wholesomeness, or the non-commision of ten evils: (1) No killing; (2) No stealing; (3) No adultery; (4) No lying; (5) No slandering; (6) No harsh speech; (7) No idle talks; (8) No greed; (9) No hatred; (10) No perverse views. It is essential for the rebirth in Devá realm.

13 Pāramitā: spiritual perfection. In Mahāyāna Buddhism, the Prajñapāramitā sūtras, the *Lotus Sūtra* and a large number of other texts list the six spiritual perfections: (1) Dāna pāramitā: generosity, giving of oneself; (2)Śīla pāramitā: virtue, morality, discipline, proper conduct; (3)Kṣānti pāramitā: patience, tolerance, forbearance, acceptance, endurance; (4)Vīrya pāramitā: energy, diligence, vigor, effort; (5)Dhyāna pāramitā: one-pointed concentration, contemplation; (6)Prajñā pāramitā: wisdom, insight.

14 Ancient Kapiśā refers to the present-day Bagram town of Parwan Province in the Shomali Plain of Afghanistan, which is 60 km north of the capital Kabul.

15 Also Pingyu (屏聿 Bingyul), at the northern foot of the Kyrgyz Mountains.

16 Taraz (Aulieata) is located in the south of Kazakhstan.

17 Isfidjab (Sairam or Sayram), Isbījāb in turkish, and situated east of Taras in Kazakhstan.

18 Also called "the city of springs", Kūyu in Turkish, meaning "well" or "spring", which covers the branch of the Chirchik River and the region of the Angren River.

19 Nujikath or Nūjkath, situated at Tashkent in Uzbekistan.

20 Modern Binkath, 50 kilometers to the west of the city of Tashkent, Uzbekistan.

21 The Yaxartes River originates in the Tianshan Mountains in Kyrgyzstan and eastern Uzbekistan and flows for 2,212 kilometres (1,374 *mi*) west and north-west through Uzbekistan and southern Kazakhstan to the northern remnants of the Aral Sea.

22 Modern Ura-tepe, an ancient city in Turkestan between Kojend and Samarcand.

23 Sāma-gama in Sanskrit, its ancient site is situated at Afrasiab (Afrosiyob), in northern Samarkand, Uzbekistan.

24 The ancient site is located at present Peishimbe, about 100 kilometers northwest to Samarkand, alternatively Samarqand or Samarcand which is a city in modern-day Uzbekistan and is one of the oldest inhabited cities in Central Asia. Prospering from its location on the Silk Road between China and the Mediterranean, at times Samarkand was one of the greatest cities of Central Asia.

25 Kharghan is situated in the northeast of Bukhārā (Bukhara), one of the cities of Uzbekistan.

26 Be supposed to be the present city of Bukhara.

27 Present Betik, situated to southwest to the city of Bukhara.

28 Present Kara-kalpak in Uzbekistan, is situated at the lower reaches of the Amo River.

29 The Amu Darya, also called the Amu or Amo River, and historically known by its Latin name Oxus, is a major river in Central Asia. It is formed by the junction of the Vakhsh and Panj rivers, in the Tigrovaya Balka Nature Reserve on the border between Tajikistan and Afghanistan, and flows from there north-westwards into the southern remnants of the Aral Sea. In ancient times, the river was regarded as the boundary between Greater Iran and Turan.

30 Modern Stalinabad, the capital and largest city of Tajikistan.

31 The Master entered the region of today Badakhshan, which is primarily bordered by Gorno-Badakhshan Autonomous Province and Khatlon Province in Tajikistan to the north and east. In the east of the province a long spur called the Wakhan Corridor extends above northern Pakistan's Chitral and Northern Areas to a border with China. The province has a total area of

44,059 square kilometres (17,011 sq *mi*), most of which is occupied by the Hindu Kush and Pamir mountain ranges.

32 It is situated ninety kilometers south of Shahrisabz in Uzbekistan, which once was the southern boundary of Western Turkic Khaganate.

33 Present region between the Hindu kush Mountains of northern Afghanistan and the upper reaches of the Amu River.

34 Or the kingdom of Huo, modern Kunduz Province, in Afghanistan, located in the northern part of the country next to Tajikistan.

35 Shad being an official title.

36 Khatun is a female title of nobility and alternative to male "khan" prominently used in the First Turkic Empire and in the subsequent Mongol Empire. It is equivalent to "queen" or "empress" approximately.

37 Modern Kashi (Kashgar) Prefecture in the Xinjiang Uygur Autonomous Region.

38 The Kingdom of Khotan was an ancient Iranic Saka Buddhist kingdom located on the branch of the Silk Road that ran along the southern edge of the Taklamakan Desert in the Tarim Basin. The ancient capital was originally sited to the west of modern-day Hotan 和田 at Yotkan. From the Han Dynasty until at least the Tang Dynasty it was known in Chinese as Yutian 于阗.

39 Modern Balkh in northern Afghanistan.

40 A Buddhist temple or monastery, or a monastery with its garden or grove, called 僧伽蓝摩in Chinese, abbreviated as伽蓝, which is transliterated from Sanskrit word: saṅghārāma. For the rest of the book, the term伽蓝 is all translated as "monastery."

41 The four *phala*, i.e. fruitations: Srota-apanna (stream-enterer/ stream winner); Sakrd-agamin (once-returner); Anagami (never-returner/ non-returner); Arhat.

42 Two merchants of the town of Ukkala, by name Trapuṣa and Bhallika.

43 The caitya or cetiya, "reminders" or "memorials", are objects and places used

by Theravada Buddhists to remember Gautama Buddha, traditionally divided into four categories: (1) śarīraka, pieces of the body; (2) paribhogaka, things he used; (3) udeśaka, reminders. A fourth category; (4) dhammaka, was added later to remind monks that the true memory of Gautama Buddha can be found in his teachings.

44 This country is lying between the Bibas in the east and the Indus in the west, thus including the western part of Punjab in Pakistan.

45 Nine of the Hīnayāna 12 classes of Sūtras, that is, all except the Vaipulya, Vyākaraṇa, and the Udāṇa.

Nine sections of the Hīnayāna Sūtras: (1) Sūtras, the Buddha's sermons; (2) geyas, metric pieces; (3) Vyākaraṇas, prophecies; (4) gāthās, stanzas, chants and poems; (5) udānas, impromptu or unsolicited addresses; (6) ityuktas or itivṛttakas, narratives; (7) jātakas, stories of former lives of the Buddha; (8) vaipulyas, expanded Sūtras; (9) adbhutadharmas, miracles.

46 The Four Āgamas are: (1)Dīrghāgama; (2)Madhyamāgama; (3)Saṃyuktāgama; (4)Ekottarāgama.

47 Abhidharma: the section of the Buddhist canon containing philosophical commentaries.

48 Jñānaprasthānaṣaṭpādābhidharma: Saṅgītiparyāya, Dharmaskandha, Prajñāpti, Dhātukāya, Vijñānakāya, Prakaraṇapāda, Jñānaprasthāna.

49 These small two kingdoms were situated to the south of Shibirghan.

50 Present Darrah Gaz in Afghanistan.

51 The Hindu Kush is an 800-kilometre-long (500 *mi*) mountain range that stretches near the Afghan-Pakistan border, from central Afghanistan to northern Pakistan. It forms the western section of the Hindu Kush Himalayan Region. It divides the valley of the Amu Darya (the ancient Oxus) to the north from the Indus River valley to the south. The Hindu Kush range has numerous high snow-capped peaks, with the highest point in the Hindu Kush being Tirich Mir or Terichmir at 7,708 metres (25,289 ft) in the Chitral

District of Khyber Pakhtunkhwa, Pakistan. To the north, near its northeastern end, the Hindu Kush buttresses the Pamir Mountains near the point where the borders of China, Pakistan and Afghanistan meet, after which it runs southwest through Pakistan and into Afghanistan near their border. The eastern end of the Hindu Kush in the north merges with the Karakoram Range. Its southern end connects with the Spin Ghar Range near the Kabul River.

52 Bamyan Province in central Afghanistan.

53 Song Yu宋玉 (ca.298–222 BC) was a disciple of Qu Yuan 屈原(340–278 BC), the poet of the kingdom Chu. The passage was quoted from his metrical prose the *Consolation of Souls* (*Zhaohun*招魂).

54 Or Jiuzheban slope. It is a hill of nine windings, situated among the Qionglai Mountain 邛崃山 in Sichuan Province which runs in the general north-south direction, and is located mostly within the Ngawa Tibetan and Qiang Autonomous Prefecture, in the north-central part of the province.

55 Kalpa is a Sanskrit word meaning an aeon, or a relatively long period of time (by human calculation) in Hindu and Buddhist cosmology. Generally, a kalpa is a period of time between the creation and recreation of a world or universe. Shakyamuni Buddha is said to have practiced self-cultivation for three great asaṃkhyeya kalpas before becoming a Buddha. Asaṃkhyeya means "incalculable" for Buddha Śākyamuni, and the first asaṃkhyeya goes from the ancient Buddha Śākyamuni to the Buddha Ratnaśikhin. From that time on, the Bodhisattva was free of all female births. The second asaṃkhyeya goes from the Buddha Ratnaśikhin to the Buddha Dīpaṃkara. That was when the Bodhisattva offered seven blue lotus blossoms (nīlotpala) to the Buddha Dīpaṃkara, laid out his garment of antelope skin (ajinavāsa) and spread out his hair (keśa) to cover the mud (kardama). On that occasion, the Buddha Dīpaṃkara made the prediction: "Later you will be Buddha under the name Śākyamuni." The third asaṃkhyeya goes from the Buddha Dīpaṃkara to

the Buddha Vipaśyin. After these three asaṃkhyeyakalpas, the Bodhisattva accomplishes the actions producing the thirty-two marks.

56 Wheel-Turning King (cakravartīrāja): a ruler, the wheels of whose chariot roll everywhere unimpeded. The wheel (cakra), one of the seven precious things he owns, comes in four ranks: iron, copper, silver, and gold. The iron wheel king rules one continent, the south; the copper wheel king rules two, east and south; the silver wheel king rules three: east, west, and south; the gold wheel king rules all four continents. A Buddha, the universal Dharma King, turns the Dharma wheel, giving teachings to sentient beings.

57 Śāṇakavāsa was the son of a merchant of Rājagṛha. At the persuasion of Ānanda, he entered the Order and later became well learned in Tripiṭaka.

58 Saṃghāti: a double layers robe of Bhikkhus or Bhikkhunis used as an outer cloak for various occasions. It comes over the upper robe (uttarāsaṅga), and the undergarment (antarvāsa). In representations of the Buddha, the saṃghāti is usually the most visible garment, with the undergarment or uttarāsaṅga protruding at the bottom. It is quite similar in shape to the Greek himation, and its shape and folds have been treated in Greek style in the Greco-Buddhist art of Gandhāra.

Kāṣāya, or cassock, is a general term referring to the robes of fully ordained Buddhist monks and nuns, named after a brown or saffron dye. In Sanskrit and Pali, these robes are also given the more general term cīvara, the robes without regard to color. Original kāṣāya were constructed of discarded fabric. These were stitched together to form three rectangular pieces of cloth, which were then fitted over the body in a specific manner. The three main pieces of cloth are the antarvāsa, the uttarāsaṅga, and the saṃghāti. Together they form the "triple robe," or ticīvara.

Antarvāsa (Antaravāsaka): the antarvāsa is the inner robe covering the lower body. It is the undergarment that flows underneath the other layers of clothing. It has a large top, and almost entirely covers the torso. In representations of the Buddha, the bottom of the antarvāsa usually protrudes, and appears in the rough shape of a triangle. This garment is essentially a skirt, which was common enough as ancient menswear. When needed, its height could be adjusted so it did not hang as low as the ankles.

Uttarāsaṅga: a robe covering the upper body. It comes over the undergarment, or antarvāsa. In representations of the Buddha, the uttarāsaṅga rarely appears as the uppermost garment, since it is often covered by the outer robe, or saṃghāti.

59 Also called Antrabhara or Antara-bhara, an intermediate state of existence between death and reincarnation.

60 Refers to the *Great Tang Records on the Western Regions* (*Datang Xiyu Ji* 《大唐西域记》). Detailed record is in the first fascicle of it.

61 The Black Mountain denotes the Hindu Kush, the parts of the Great Snow mountains which are not covered by perpetual snow.

62 Kāfiristān or Kāfirstān, is a historical region that covered present-day Nuristan Province in Afghanistan and its surroundings. This historic region lies on, and mainly comprises, the basins of the rivers Alingar, Pech (Kamah), Landai Sin and Kunar, and the intervening mountain ranges. It is bounded by the main range of the Hindu Kush on the north, Pakistan's Chitral District to the east, the Kunar Valley in the south and the Alishang River in t he west.

63 It is one of the four social orders of the Hindu society. Traditionally, the kshatriya constituted the ruling and military elite. Their role was to protect society by fighting in wartime and governing in peacetime. Historically Kshatriyas are the royal and top caste in social order until the Muslim occupation of India. Apart from the four varṇas, brahmins (brāhmaṇa), kṣatra (kṣatriya, Kshatriya), vaiṣya (Vaishya) and śūdra (Sudra), there are also several other castes that sprang from their intermixing.

64 A retreat during the three months of the Indian rainy season, and also, say

some, in the depth of winter. Also it is called tranquil dwelling, varṣā, varṣās, or varṣāvasāna. During the rains it was difficult to move without injuring insect life. But the object was for study and meditation. The two annual periods are sometimes called 坐夏 and 坐腊 sitting or resting for the summer and for the end of the year.

65 The Wheel Sign is the most outstanding characteristic of the steeple of Buddhist pogodas, which refers to the discs around the pole of the steeple, also called golden basins or dew basins, or *xianglun* 相轮 in Chinese (meaning wheel or disc), a symbol of honor or respect for the Buddha. Generally, the bigger the pagoda, the more and bigger the discs.

66 Hindu Kush Mountains.

67 Modern Laghman, one of the 34 provinces of Afghanistan, is in the eastern part of the country. In some historical texts the name is written as "Lamghan" or as "Lamghanat." Near the source of the Kabul River.

68 The lands are also known as Mlecchadeśa. Mleccha (and its equivalent milakkha) are usually translated as foreigner or barbarian.

69 Modern Jalalabad.

70 Aśoka, who died in 232 BC, was an Indian emperor of the Maurya Dynasty, ruling almost all of the Indian subcontinent from c. 268 to 232 BC.

71 Later Śākyamuni Buddha.

72 Or the Kalpa of Destruction: the period of time between the creation and the recreation of the world.

73 The Buddha was said to have bought some flowers to offer to the Dīpaṃkara Buddha in one of his previous lives.

74 It is supposed to be in the modern Hidda, situated about five miles south of Jalalabad.

75 The seven jewels include: (1) suvarṇa (gold); (2) rūpya (silver); (3) vaiḍūrya (aquamarine); (4) sphaṭika (crystal); (5) musāragalva (conch shell or white coral); (6) lohita-muktikā (ruby); and (7) aśmagarbha (emerald). Its various

sources alter this list slightly. Sometimes pearl, coral and amber are included in place of crystal and ruby, and vaiḍūrya is matched with lapis lazuli, and aśmagarbha with diamond. Also, vaiḍūrya means beryl; abhraroha means lapis lazuli; aśmagarbha means emerald; vajra means diamond. Contexts of vaiḍūrya mentioned in Buddhist sūtras indicate that it should be a pale blue variety of beryl, i.e., aquamarine, not lapis lazuli, an opaque deep blue stone.

76 One *chi* and two *cun* is about fifteen inches.

77 A religious staff, or a monk's staff, with metal rings for shaking to announce one's presence or to expel demons.

78 Or *nāga*.

79 Or Kāṣāya in Sanskrit, a monk's robe.

80 Refers to the *Great Tang Records on the Western Regionss* (*Datang Xiyu Ji* 《大唐西域记》).

81 Modern Charsadda, in the Khyber Pakhtunkhwa Province of Pakistan. Its ruins are located on the banks of Swat River, near its junction with Kabul River. Pushkalavati was the capital of ancient kingdom Gandhara from the 6th century BC, until it became an Achaemenid regional capital in the 2nd century CE.

82 Or locally called Sindhu River: one of the longest rivers in Asia. Originating in the Tibetan Plateau in the vicinity of Lake Manasarovar, the river runs a course through the Ladakh region of Jammu and Kashmir, towards the Gilgit-Baltistan region of Pakistan and the Hindukush ranges, and then flows in a southerly direction along the entire length of Pakistan to merge into the Arabian Sea near the port city of Karachi in Sindh. It is the longest river and national river of Pakistan.

83 Modern Peshawar, located on the banks of Swat River.

84 Vasubandhu 世亲 (fl. 4th to 5th century AD) was an influential Buddhist monk and scholar from Gandhara. Vasubandhu is one of the most influential thinkers in the Indian Buddhist philosophical tradition. Vasubandhu

wrote on the Abhidharma from the perspectives of the Sarvastivada and Sautrāntika schools. Along with his half-brother Asanga 无著, he was also one of the main founders of the Yogacara school after his conversion to Mahāyāna Buddhism. Vasubandhu's *Abhidharmakośakārikā* (*Commentary on the Treasury of the Abhidharma*) is widely used in Tibetan and East Asian Buddhism as the major source for non-Mahāyāna Abhidharma philosophy. Apart from this, he wrote several commentaries, works on logic, argumentation and devotional poetry.

85 Benares.

86 Long pepper.

87 Or called The Four Buddhas of Antiquity: According to the Theravada tradition, these four Buddhas are from the current kalpa, with the current Buddha, Gotama, being the fourth. They are Kakusandha, 俱留孙佛 (the first Buddha of the current bhadrakalpa); Koṇāgamana 拘那含佛(the second Buddha of the current bhadrakalpa); Kassapa 迦叶波佛(the third Buddha of the current bhadrakalpa); and Gautama (the fourth and present Buddha of the current bhadrakalpa).

88 The Indus River.

89 It was situated at the north of present Peshawar.

90 Modern Und at the north of Attock.

91 It was situated in the present Svat Valley.

92 Śubhavastu is the Swat River, a tributary of the Indus River.

93 Sangha: the Buddhist Order.

94 The capital of Udyāna, the modern Manglaur, a village at the foot of one of the north-west spurs of the Dosirri Mountain between Swat and Boner.

95 A deity of tolerance.

96 The name Swat is derived from an old Sanskrit term, Śubhavastu.

97 Refers to a story told in Chapter Twenty-two On Pure Actions (b) of *The Mahāyāna Mahāparinirvāṇa Sūtra* (Translated into English by Kosho

Yamamoto, 1973 from Dharmakshema's Chinese version.). The story goes that Shakrodevanamindra transformed himself into a rākṣasa (flesh-eating demon) and came down to the Himālayas. He first spoke half of a gāthā from the Buddhas of days past: "All things change. This is the law of birth and death." In order to hear the second half, Bodhisattva-mahasattva sacrificed his life. The second half said by rākṣasa is: "When birth and death are done away with, Quietude is bliss." http://lirs.ru/do/Mahapari nirvāṇa Sutra, Yamamoto, Page, 2007.pdf

98 Vihāra: a hall, a monastery.

99 Śītā is the ancient Sanskrit name for the Tarim River, an endorheic river in Xinjiang Uygur Autonomous Region, China. It is the principal river of the Tarim Basin, a desert region of Central Asia between the Tian Shan and Kunlun Mountains. The river historically terminated at Lop Nur, but today reaches no further than Taitema Lake before drying out.

100 Modern Dārel, on the west bank of the Indus River.

101 The fourth of the six heavens in the desire world.

102 Modern Rawalpindi (Rāwalpiṇḍī), a city in Punjab, located on the Pothohar Plateau in Pakistan.

103 Kalabagh in Pakistan. It is located on the western bank of Indus River. It is the site of the proposed Kalabagh Dam. It is also famous for its red hills of the salt range.

104 Modern Hazara, a region comprising several districts in the eastern part of the Khyber Pakhtunkhwa province in Pakistan.

105 Kashmir.

106 The Jhelum River is a river of northwestern India and eastern Pakistan. It is the westernmost of the five rivers of Punjab, and passes through Jhelum District. It is a tributary of the Chenab River.

107 Srinagar, lies in the Kashmir Valley on the banks of the Jhelum River, a tributary of the Indus, and Dal and Anchar lakes. It is the largest city and the

summer capital of the Indian state of Jammu and Kashmir.

108 *Yojana*: in point of Indian measurements, originally it was regarded as a day's march for an army. The old accounts say it is equal to 40 *li*; according to the common reckoning in India it is 30 *li*, but in the Buddhist texts the *yojana* is only 16 *li*. In the subdivision of distances, a *yojana* is equal to eight krośas; a krośa is the distance that the lowing of a cow can be heard. So, one *yojana* may refer to one day's journey in an ox cart.

109 *Arhat*: a perfect saint who has freed himself from the bonds of samsara by eliminating all passions and desires.

110 Refers to the five sciences of ancient India, means Śāstras of great importance: the first is called Śabdavidyā (sheng ming, 声明), that is, the elucidation of sounds, whose treatise explains and illustrates the agreement (concordance) of words, and provides an index for derivatives. The second vidyā is called Śilpasthānaridyā (gongqiao ming, 工巧明); it treats of the arts, mechanics, the calendar, and so forth. The third is called Chikitsāvidyā (yifang ming, 医方明) , meaning the medicinal treatise, which embraces formulate for protection, secret charms (the use of) medicinal stones, acupuncture, and mug-wort.

The fourth vidyā is called Hetuvidyā (yin ming, 因明), dealing with the science of logic, dialectics.

The fifth vidyā is called Adhyātmavidyā (nei ming, 内明), meaning the science of "the interior", e.g. Buddhist philosophy.

111 Or *ślokas*, refers roughly to *gāthā*, which has a count of thirty-two syllables.

112 Or 9,600,000 words according to the *Record of the Western Regions*.

113 Modern Punch, Kashmir.

114 Modern Rājapuri.

115 The Chenab River, a major river of India and Pakistan, forms in the upper Himālayas in the Lahaul and Spiti district of Himachal Pradesh, India, and flows through the Kishtwar district of Jammu region in Jammu and Kashmir

into the plains of the Punjab, Pakistan.

116 The Chenab River.

117 Modern Sialkot, a city in Punjab, Pakistan.

118 Perhaps Butea monosperma, a species of Butea native to tropical and sub-tropical parts of the Indian Subcontinent and Southeast Asia. It is a small-sized dry-season deciduous tree. Common names include flame-of-the-forest, palash and bastard teak.

119 Vedas: Hindu scriptures.

120 Ācārya Nāgārjuna 龙树 (c. 150–250), is widely considered one of the most important Mahāyāna philosophers. Along with his disciple Āryadeva, he is considered to be the founder of the Madhyamaka school of Mahāyāna Buddhism. Nāgārjuna is also credited with developing the philosophy of the *Prajñāpāramitā* Sūtras (*Perfection of Wisdom Sūtras*) and, in some sources, the story also goes that in his meditation, he saw the *Śūraṅgama Sūtra* and the *Mahāvaipulya Sūtra of Buddha Adornment* in the nāga (dragon) palace and memorized these texts.

121 The capital of this country is supposed to be the present Patti, an old city and a municipal council of the Tarn Taran district in the Majha region of Indian state of Punjab, located 45 km from Amritsar.

122 Also Bhadrakalpa: the Good Aeon or Auspicious aeon, in which a thousand Buddhas are to appear. The five most important Buddhas of the present kalpa are: Kakusandha (the first Buddha of the bhadrakalpa), Koṇāgamana (the second Buddha of the bhadrakalpa), Kassapa (the third Buddha of the bhadrakalpa), Gautama (the fourth and present Buddha of the bhadrakalpa), and Maitreya (the fifth and future Buddha of the bhadrakalpa).

123 Modern Jalandhar, a city in the Doaba region of the northwestern Indian state of Punjab.

124 Modern Sultanpur. The kingdom of Kulūta was situated in the upper Beas valley which is also known as the Kullu valley.

125 The Sutlej valley. The Sutlej River is the longest of the five rivers that flow through the historic crossroads region of Punjab in northern India and Pakistan.

126 It was situated in the Jumna Valley.

127 A Buddhist nun.

128 It is considered that the site of this monastery was that of the Idgah or Katra of the present Muttra.

129 Four inches.

130 It means "the country of freedom", because of its fertile land and rich residents. The capital city is in taneshar, Punjab, India.

131 It was situated to the north of the present Rohtak in the Indian state of Haryana.

132 Modern Jumna River, the longest tributary of Ganges.

133 This is supposed to be Haridwar, the place where the Ganges emerges from the Sivalik Mountain into the plains.

134 Deva Bodhisattva: Āryadeva (3rd century CE), was a disciple of Nāgārjuna and author of several important Mahāyāna Madhyamaka Buddhist texts.

135 It is identified with Madawar, a large town in western Rohilkhand, near Bijnor.

136 It is the lowest rank of the four varṇas.

137 Parvata is now Harappa in Panjab, the old riverbed of the Ravi River, about 25 kilometers from Montgomery.

138 It is supposed to be in the districts of Garhwal and Kumaon.

139 This country occupied the eastern part of Rohikhand.

140 The capital of this country has been identified with the great mound of ruins called Atranjikhera which is situated on the west bank of the Kali River (or Kalinadi, a river flowing through Karwar, Uttara Kannada district of Karnataka state in India), four miles to the south of Karsana, and eight miles to the north of Eyta, on the Grand Trunk Road.

141 It was located at a Samkasya (the present Samkisa) village 40 kilometers to the west of the city of Farrukhabad, a city in the state of Uttar Pradesh in northern India.

142 It is one of the four continents, situated to the south of Mt. Sumeru. Its shape is trapezoidal or resembling the shape of an axe-head. It is the human world in which we live.

143 The thirty-three gods who live on the top of Mt. Sumeru in the second heaven of the desire world.

144 Modern Kanauj, a city, administrative headquarters and a municipal board or Nagar Palika Parishad in Kannauj district in the Indian state of Uttar Pradesh.

145 vaiṣya caste is one of the four basic orders (Varṇa s or castes) of the Hindu social order in Nepal and India. Hindu religious texts assigned vaiṣya to traditional roles in agriculture and cattle-rearing but over time they came to be landowners, traders and money-lenders. Therefore, making it their responsibility to provide sustenance for those of higher class, since they were of lower class. Apart from the four varṇas, Brahmin, kṣatra, vaiṣya and śūdra, there are also several other castes that sprang from their intermixing.

146 Modern Murshidabad in Bangladesh.

147 After Harṣavardhana succeeded to the throne in 606, he was known as Śīlāditya, the king of the Puṣyabhūti Dynasty, ruling parts of Northern India during 6th and 7th centuries. The Dynasty reached its zenith under its last ruler Harsha-Vardhana. At the height of Harsha's power, his Empire covered much of North and Northwestern India, extended East till Kamarupa, and South until Narmada River; and eventually made Kannauj (in present Uttar Pradesh state) his capital, and ruled till 647 CE.

148 Sudāna was an elder of Śrāvastī and a patron of the Buddha. He bought the Jetavana garden from Prince Jeta and offered it to the Buddha.

Fascicle III

Beginning with the Country of Ayodhyā and Ending with the Country of Īraṇaparvata

From here proceeding to the southeast for more than six hundred *li*, crossing the Ganges, and then to the south, the Master reached the country of Ayodhyā[1](in Central India), where there were more than one hundred monasteries with several thousand monks, learning both Mahāyāna and Hīnayāna teachings. In the great city, there was an old monastery, the very place where Vasubandhu Bodhisattva (meaning "world kinsman," formerly transliterated as Posoupandou; translated as Celestial Kinsman by mistake) composed his treatises on Mahāyāna and Hīnayāna teachings and delivered Dharma discourse to the congregations. Four or five *li* northwest to the city, on the bank of the Ganges River was a stūpa constructed by King Aśoka, over two hundred *chi* high, was situated at a great monastery, where the Buddha preached the Dharma for three months at a former time. Beside the stūpa, there was the site where the four Past Buddhas once practiced religious circumambulation.

Five or six *li* to the southwest of the city, there was an old monastery where Bodhisattva Asaṅga delivered his sermons. At night, the Bodhisattva ascended to the Tuṣita Heaven to hear the *Yogācārabhūmi Śāstra*, the *Mahāyānasūtrālaṃkāra Śāstra* and the *Madhyāntavibhāga Śāstra* from Bodhisattva Maitreya. In the daytime, he descended from Heaven and preached the Dharma to the people. Asaṅga, also known as Wuzhu[2], was a native of Gandhāra and was born into this world one thousand years after the Nirvāṇa of the Buddha. He became a monk of the Mahīśāsaka school but later converted to Mahāyāna teachings. His younger brother Vasubandu Bodhisattva was a monk of the Sarvāstivāda school at first, but later turned to Mahāyāna teachings. Both had extraordinary intellectual endowments and noble character. Gifted with literary ability, they composed many treatises to elucidate the Mahāyāna doctrines, and thus were revered as the greatest Buddhist masters of India. Many famous masterpieces written by them, including the *Mahāyānasaṅgraha Śāstra*, the *Prakaraṇāryavācā Śāstra,* the *Abhidharmasamudāya Prakaraṇa Śāstra*, the *Vijñaptimātratāsiddhi Śāstra*, the *Abhidharmakośa Śāstra*, and so forth.

After worshiping the holy sites in Ayodhyā, the Master, together with more than eighty people, sailed down the Ganges River eastward in a boat, heading for the country of Hayamukha[3]. Sailing ahead for over one hundred *li,* they came to a place where aśoka woods was densely flourished on both banks of the river. There were about a dozen boatloads of pirates hiding themselves among the woods on each bank; suddenly, altogether rowing against the current, they came out toward the boat the Master and others aboard. The passengers were so frightened that some of them even jumped into the river. The pirates derived the boat to the bank, ordered the passengers to take off their clothes, and started rifling through for the jewels and other valuables. Those pirates were believers in Goddess Durgā[4]. In every autumn, they would find a man of good appearance to kill as immolation and offer his blood and flesh to the Goddess for blessings. Seeing that the Master was strong and handsome, they thought he was a right man.

Exchanging eye contact in pleasure, they said, "We have intended to find a sacrifice to our deity, but as the time is running out, we still could not find one. Now that this śramaṇa is graceful in bearing and handsome in looking, is it auspicious if we kill him as a sacrifice, isn't it?"

The Master responded, "I dare not begrudge to sacrifice a flesh body defective and dirty as mine to your deity, but I have come here over such a long distance with the purposes of paying homage to Buddha Images, visiting Gṛdhrakūṭa Mountain[5], and seeking for genuine scriptures bequeathed by the Buddha, so I don't think it would be auspicious if you alms-givers kill me before I realize my dream."

At this juncture, other passengers on the boat were also begging for the mercy on the Master, and even some of them were willing to substitute the Master, but the pirates didn't consent.

The head of the pirates, then, asked his men to fetch some water, clear a patch of field off the weeds in the flowery bushes to set up an altar there, and cover the altar with clay mixed by the water and soil. After that, drawing out knives, two men forced the Master to step on the altar. When they brandished their knives at the Master, there was not a slightest fear on his face, which made the pirates astonished and bewildered. Knowing the death would not be avoided, the Master said to the pirates, "Please give me a few minutes without disturbance, for I want to settle my mind in calmness and die with pleasure." Then the Master concentrated his mind on the image of Maitreya in Tuṣta palace, and simultaneously, took the following vows, "I wish to be born in Tuṣta palace to serve and worship Maitreya. I wish to hear the wonderful Dharma of the *Yogācārabhūmi Śāstra* to achieve the supernatural powers induced from supreme wisdom. After that, I wish to return to this world again to admonish the pirates in front of me, making them practice self-cultivation and abandon unwholesome actions. Also, I wish to promulgate the Dharma widely so as to benefit and pacify all sentient beings." After making obeisance to the buddhas in ten directions and rectifying his mind, the Master sat down in meditation and concentrated on Maitreya without any distracting thoughts. Then in his vision, he scaled the Mount Sumeru and ascended above the first, the second and the third Heavens successively. He saw the Tuṣta Palace where the Bodhisattva Maitreya was sitting on a Precious Terrace decorated with valuable substances, surrounded by Heavenly beings. At such a moment, physically and mentally, the Master was so delighted that he forgot that he was on the altar besieged by pirates, while his companions wailed pitifully. A minute later, gusts of black wind began to blow from different directions, breaking trees and rolling up sand, throwing waves high and turning ships upside down. In great panic, the pirates asked the companions of the Master, "Where does this śramaṇa come from?

What is his name?" and got the reply, "He is the very monk who has come from China for seeking the Dharma. If you kill him, you will commit an enormous sin. Look at the wind and surge. The deity must be in indignation. You should repent right away." With fear, one after another, the pirates knelt to apologize and beg for forgiveness. They bowed their heads before the feet of the Master in obeisance and took refuge in the Three Jewels, but the Master wasn't aware what had happened until a pirate touched him with a hand, then he opened his eyes and asked, "Is it already the time?" The pirate replied, "We don't dare to harm the teacher. May you accept our penitence." The Master granted them absolution; furthermore, he told them that sins, such as killing, stealing, and worshiping the heretic deities, would lead people to the unceasing suffering in Avīci Hell[6] in the future. At last, he admonished them not to use such a lifetime ephemeral as a lightning or a morning dew to sow the seed of pain lasting for Asaṃkhyeya kalpa.

Hearing this, the pirates kowtowed again with gratitude and said, "Being driven by distorted and delusive views, we have done what shouldn't have been done and served the deities we shouldn't have served. If it were not for the teacher's merit and virtue which have aroused the response from the divine beings, how could we have the chance to hear your instructions and admonition? From now on, we shall stop our trade. You teacher may be our witness." Thus, persuading one another, they gathered their weapons and threw them into the river. After returning the property and clothes they had grabbed, they received the Five Commandments from the Master. Thereupon, the turbulence on the river also gradually calmed down.

Delightedly, the pirates prostrated in homage and bid farewell to the Master. With veneration, the fellow travelers were marveled at the Master's capability of correcting people's mistakes and assisting them to turn over a new leaf. Upon hearing this incident, the people far and near, without exception, showed their admiration at such a miracle—changing the danger into safety. If it had not been for the Master's sincerity and eagerness of seeking the Dharma, how could it have happened?

From here proceeding eastward for more than three hundred *li*, crossing the Ganges River, the Master reached the country of Ayamukha[7] (in Central India) in the north. From here, going southeast for more than seven hundred *li,* crossing the Ganges to the south, on the northern bank of Jumna River, he reached the country of Prayāga[8](in Central India). In the woods of *campaka* flower in the southwest of the capital city, there was a stūpa built by the King Aśoka, where the Buddha subdued heretics at a former time. Beside it, there was a monastery where the Deva Bodhisattva composed the *Vaipulyaśata Śāstra* to refute the Hīnayāna school and other heretics.

To the east of the capital city there was a confluence of two rivers, to the west of which there was a tableland about fourteen or fifteen *li* in perimeter, for being flat and regular in shape, from ancient times, which had been the place where the kings and aristocrats practiced the charity, hence the name the Great Alms Ground. King Śīlāditya inherited this tradition. Having accumulated the wealth for five years, he distributed all of it during seventy-five days as offerings to the Triple Gem and as alms to orphans and the poor.

From here going southwest, the Master entered a large forest where ferocious bests and wild elephants often haunted. Proceeding for over five hundred *li*, he reached the country of Kauśāmbī[9] (formerly known as Jushanmi by mistake, in Central India), with about a dozen monasteries and over three hundred monks. In the old palace, there was a large vihāra, more than sixty *chi* in height, enshrining a Buddha statue carved out of sandalwood with a stone canopy over it. The statue was constructed by King Udayana (meaning "issuing affection," formerly called as Youtianwang by mistake). In former times, the Tathāgata spent a summer preaching the Dharma to his mother in the Trayastriṃśa Heaven; during the course of it, King Udayana, in admiration, was eager to see the Buddha, so he asked Maudgalyāyana to bring a skilled craftsman to Heaven to observe the visage and the manner of the Buddha. When the craftsman returned, he carved this facsimile statue from a piece of red sandalwood. It was this statue that went up to receive the World-honored One when he descended from Heaven after his sermon.

There was an old mansion in the south of the city and formerly, it was the old residence of the Elder Ghoṣila (formerly known as Qushiluo by mistake). Not far from the south of the city, there was an old monastery that used to be the Elder's garden, in which a stūpa built by King Aśoka was more than two hundred *chi* tall. Farther in the southeast there was a storeyed pavilion where Vasubandu composed the *Vijñānamātrata Śāstra.* Again in the east, in a mango grove were the remains of the site where the Asaṅga Buddhisattva composed the *Prakaraṇāryavācā Śāstra*.

Proceeding eastward for over five hundred *li*, the Master reached the country of Viṣaka[10]. There were more than twenty monasteries with about three thousand monks of the Saṃmitīya school of Hīnayāna Buddhism. In the southeast by the left side of the road was a large monastery where in former times the Arhat Devaśaman composed the *Vijñānakāyapāda Śāstra* to elucidate the doctrine of non-self and non-others, but at the same time, the Arhat Gopa composed the *Treaties on the Essential Realities of the Holy Teaching* to advocate the existence of self and others, thus a fierce debate arose because of their different views. It was also the place where the Dharmapāla Bodhisattva, in a seven-day debate, subjugated one hundred *śāstra* teachers of the Hīnayāna school. Beside it, there was a place where the Buddha had preached the Dharma for six years. There stood a tree over seventy *chi* tall. At a former time, the Buddha threw away a twig here after he cleaned his teeth with it. Having taken the root, the twig grew into this luxuriant tree. Some heretics often came here to cut the tree, but no sooner had it been cut down than it grew up again and thrived as before. It never failed.

From here going northeast for more than five hundred *li*, the Master reached the country of Śrāvastī[11] (formerly known as Shewei by mistake), over six thousand *li* in perimeter. There were several hundred monasteries with several thousand monks of Saṃmitīya school. This was the capital of the country where King Prasenajit (known as Shengjun, meaning "victorious army," formerly called Bosini by mistake) lived when the Buddha was alive. There were remains of the palace of the king, and not far from here in the east, there was a stūpa built on the remains of a preaching hall constructed by King Prasenajit for the Buddha. There was another stūpa where the vihāra of the Buddha's aunt, Bhikṣuṇī Prajāpatī (meaning "mistress of creatures," formerly known as Boshebiti by mistake), was once situated. Again to the east, there was a stūpa on the old residence of Sudatta (meaning "delighted in giving," formerly known as Xuda by mistake). Beside the residence, there was a large stūpa where Aṇgulimāla (wrongly called Yangjumoluo in olden times) forsook his evil views and deeds.

Five or six *li* south to the city, there was the Jetavana Wood (meaning "glorious speech wood," formerly known as Qituo by mistake), which was the garden of Anāthapiṇḍika. It used to be a monastery in the past, but was in dilapidation at present. On both sides of the eastern gate were stone pillars set up by King Aśoka, more than seventy *chi* in height. All rooms were in ruins except a brick room with a golden statue enshrined in. At a former time, the Buddha ascended into Heaven to preach the Dharma to his mother, which won the admiration of King Prasenajit who, after knowing King Udayana had carved the sandalwood into the image of the Buddha, followed suit by having golden statue of Buddha made. Behind the monastery, not far away was the place where a heretical brāhmaṇa killed a woman and slandered the Buddha for the crime. East to the monastery about one hundred paces there was a big and deep hole in the ground where Devadatta fell into the hell alive when he attempted to poison the Buddha. To the south there was another big pit where bhikṣu[12] Kokālika fell into the hell alive when he defamed the Buddha. More than eight hundred paces south to the pit, it was the spot where the brāhmaṇa woman Ciñcā fell into the hell alive for smearing the Buddha. The depth of three pits was unfathomable.

More than seventy paces east of the monastery, there was a

vihāra, spacious and high, enshrining a Buddha statue facing the east. It was the place where the Tathāgata had a debate with the heretics in former times. Again, to the east, there was a shrine of Devá[13], as large as the vihāra aforementioned. With the moving of the sun, the shadow of the Devá shrine could not reach the monastery whereas the shadow of monastery often overcast the shrine. Farther to the east for three or four *li*, there was a stūpa where Śāriputra carried a debate with heretics. Over sixty *li* away in the northwest to the big city, there was an ancient city, belonging to Buddha Kāśyapa's father, and at the time the longevity of human beings were twenty thousand years in Bhadrakalpa[14]. In the south of the city, there was a place where the Buddha met his father for the first time after he had attained enlightenment. In the north of the city, there was a stūpa housing the relics of the whole body of Buddha Kāśyapa. Both stūpas were constructed by King Aśoka.

Proceeding to the southeast for more than eight hundred *li*, the Master reached the country of Kapilavastu[15] (formerly known as the country of Jiapiluowei), more than four thousand *li* in perimeter, with its capital city more than ten *li* in perimeter, both of which were in dilapidation. The walls of the palace city, however, fifteen *li* in perimeter and constructed with bricks, was indeed very solid. Inside the palace, there were remains of the main palace hall of King Śuddhodana, on which a temple had been built for the enshrinement of his statue. To the north, there was a sacrificial hall to Lady Māyā, on which a temple was built with her statue enshrined in. Beside it, there was a memorial temple indicating the place where the spirit of Bodhisattva Śākya descended into his mother's womb, and a statue of the birth of the Bodhisattva was worshiped inside. According to the Sthaviravāda, the Bodhisattva descended into his mother's womb at the night of the thirtieth day of Uttarāṣāḍha month, which was corresponding to the fifteenth day of the fifth month of Chinese calendar, whereas other schools believed it was on the twenty-third day of that month, corresponding to the eighth day of the fifth month of Chinese calendar. There was a stūpa in the northeast where the immortal Ṛṣi Asita once read the physiognomy of the prince. On the left and right sides of the city, there were several sites where the prince and other young men of Śākya clan once jousted, where the prince went over the city wall on a horse, and where he stopped halfway of sightseeing to turn back to his palace with a strong sense of the world-weariness after he caught sight of the old, the sick, the dead and the *Śramaṇa* at the four entrances of the city.

From here to the east, he walked for more than five hundred *li* in a forest, and reached the country of Rāmagrāma (in Central India), which was sparsely populated. To the east of the old city, there was a brick stūpa, over one hundred *chi* tall. In the former time, after the Nirvāṇa of the Tathāgata, the king of this country obtained a share of the relics which he brought back and constructed this stūpa to preserve them. The stūpa often emitted a bright light. Next to it, there was Dragon pond. Frequently, the dragon transformed into a human being and circumambulated the stūpa to practice self-cultivation. Also, wild elephants often held flowers to make offerings to the stūpa. Not far from here, there was a monastery, the abbot of which was a śramaṇera[16]. According to a legend, once there was a śramaṇera who summoned other monks to pay homage to the stūpa. When they came here, they saw that many wild elephants were worshipping the stūpa, busy with collecting the flowers to place them in front of the stūpa, removing the weeds with their tusks and spraying water with trunks to clean the site. This sight touched the monks so much that the śramaṇera volunteered to give up his chance of taking the Great Precepts to be a fully ordained bhikṣu, instead, was willing to remain alone here to offer his service. He said to others, "even animals, like elephants, know to worship the stūpa by offering flowers, sprinkling water, and doing cleaning, how could we human beings, especially adherents of the Buddha, have the heart to leave the stūpa deserted and neglected without doing any services?" Then he parted company with other monks and stayed here alone. He built houses, dredged a pond, grew flowers and planted fruit trees, kept working tirelessly through the summers and winters. Hearing about his deeds, peoples of the neighboring countries collectively raised the money and treasures to construct a monastery here, and invited this *śramaṇera* to be an abbot to manage the monastic affairs. Since then, the tradition of inviting a *śramaṇera* to be the abbot of this monastery had been passed down.

Proceeding for over one hundred *li* in the large woods to the east of the Śramaṇera monastery, the Master came to a stūpa built by King Aśoka. It was the first place the prince Śākyamuni arrived after he came out of the royal city. Here he put off his precious clothes, took off his royal crown, untied pears from his hair bun, and had them taken back to the palace by Chandaka (formerly known as Che'ni by mistake). There was also another stūpa marking the place where the prince shaved off his hair.

Out of the forest, the Master came to the country of Kuśinagara[17], which was in an extremely desolate and isolated condition. In the northeast corner of the city, there was a stūpa constructed by King Aśoka on site of the old residence of Cunda (formerly known as Chuntuo by mistake). Inside the yard was a well that was dug by Cunda when he was preparing offerings for the Buddha, and its waters still very clear.

Three or four *li* to the northwest of the city, the Master crossed Ajitavatī River (meaning "invincible river," erroneously called the Alibati River in olden times). Not far from the river, the Master came to a Śāla Grove. A Śāla tree looked like an oak tree, except for the bark of the former was more greenish and leaves more bleached, looking very glossy. Four pairs of trees were in the same height, among which the Tathāgata attained the nirvāṇa. A giant brick temple was built here, enshrining the declining statue of the Buddha in Nirvāṇa, with his head toward the north. By the side of the temple, there was a great stūpa as high as over two hundred *chi*, constructed by King Aśoka who also erected a stone column to record the event of the Buddha's Nirvāṇa but failed to inscribe its exact date. According to the traditional saying, the Buddha had lived in the world for eighty years, and attained nirvāṇa on the fifteenth day of the second half of the month Vaiśākha[18], corresponding to the fifteenth day of the second month of the Chinese calendar. While the Sarvāstivāda school believed the date should be in the second half of the month Kārttika[19], corresponding to the eighth day of the ninth month of the Chinese calendar. Regarding the time which had passed since the Buddha's Nirvāṇa, some supposed it was twelve hundred years, or fifteen hundred years, while others believed more than nine hundred years but less than one thousand years. There were also other stūpas constructed to commemorate the important events concerning the Buddha's Nirvāṇa, including the Tathāgata sitting in a golden coffin and preaching the Dharma to his mother, extending his arm and inquiring Ānanda, showing his feet to Kāśyapa, being cremated with scented wood, distributing the relics among eight kings, so on and so forth.

From here going for over five hundred *li* again in a large forest, the Master reached the country of Vārāṇasī[20], more than four thousand *li* in perimeter. Bordering on the Ganges in the west, its capital city was more than ten *li* long and five to six *li* broad. There were more than thirty monasteries housing over two thousand monks, who were adherents of the Hīnayāna Sarvāstivāda school.

After crossing a river in Vārāṇasī, the Master went for more than ten *li* to the northeast and reached the monastery at the Deer Park[21], where terraces and pavilions towered to the clouds and long corridors linked to one another on four sides. There were fifteen hundred monks adhering to the Hīnayāna Saṃmitīya school. In a large yard, there was a temple hall more than one hundred *chi* in height, with a stone stairway and over one hundred tiers of brick niches carved with the golden images of the Buddha in intaglio. Inside the temple, there was a life-size brass statue of the Tathāgata in the posture of preaching the Dharma. To the southeast of the temple, there was a stone stūpa built by King Aśoka, more than one hundred *chi* in height. In front of the stūpa, there was a stone column, more than seventy *chi* tall, indicating that it was the very place where the Buddha turned the

Wheel of the Dharma[22] for the first time. Beside it, there was a site where Bodhisattva Maitreya (meaning "compassionate one," formerly called Mile by mistake) received a prediction that he would become a Buddha in the future. Again, to its west, there was a stūpa erected at the place where the Buddha, being the Bodhisattva Prabhāpāla in one of his previous lives in Bhadrakalpa when the life span of human beings was twenty thousand years, received a predictive assurance on his future Buddhahood from the Buddha Kāśyapa.

To the south of the site where Śākyamuni Buddha received his prediction, there was the platform which was the place, where four Past Buddhas did the walking meditation in former times. It was piled up by bluestones, more than fifty paces long and seven *chi* high, on which stood their statues.

To the west of the Deer Park, there were a bathing pool of the Tathāgata and a pond for cleaning his alms bowl and a pond for washing clothes, all of which were guarded by divine dragons from being contaminated by people's touch. Beside the pool was a stūpa marking the place where the Buddha, born as a six-tusk white elephant in one of his previous lives, practiced the Bodhisattva Way by giving his tusks as alms to a hunter. There was a stūpa marking the place where the Buddha, born as a bird, met a monkey and a white elephant at a banyan tree and made a promise that they would take turn by age to edify the people. Also, there was another stūpa marking the place where, being a Deer King, the Buddha enlightened the five disciples, including Kauṇḍinya and the others.

From here proceeding eastward along the Ganges for more than three hundred *li*, the Master reached the country of Yuddhapati[23].

To the southeast from here, crossing the Ganges and going for one hundred forty or one hundred fifty *li,* he came to the country of Vaiśāli[24](formerly known as Pisheli by mistake), which was over five thousand *li* in perimeter, and covered by fertile soil producing plentiful mangoes and plantains. Its capital city was in ruins and sparsely populated, with the remaining city foundation sixty or seventy *li* in perimeter. Five or six *li* to the northwest of the palace city, there was a monastery, and beside it, a stūpa stood at the place where the Buddha preached the *Vimalakīrti nirdeśa Sūtra*. Again, three or four *li* to the northeast, there was a stūpa erected at the former residence of Vimalakīrti[25], which often manifested miraculous signs. Not far from here there was a chamber piled up by stones, the very place where Wugoucheng[26] made a discourse on the Dharma by deliberately showing the illness. Beside it, there were the old residences of Ratnākāra and of the Āmrapālī. Three or four *li* farther to the north was a stūpa marking the place where the celestial and human beings were standing and staring at the Buddha when he started to take his way to the country of Kuśinagara to enter Parinirvāṇa. Farther to the west, there was the place where the Buddha gave a last look at Vaiśāli. Then to the south, there was a place where Āmrapālī offered her garden to the Buddha. Also, there was the place where the Buddha consented to enter nirvāṇa at the request of King Māra.

In the southern domain of Vaiśāli, more than one hundred *li* away from the Ganges, the Master reached the city of Śvetapura[27], where he obtained the *Bodhisattvapiṭaka Sūtra.* Again he crossed the Ganges in the south, and arrived in the country of Magadha[28](formerly known as Mojiatuo by mistake), more than five thousand *li* in perimeter. People in this country attached importance to knowledge and moral people, which is a custom. There were more than fifty monasteries with over ten thousand monks, majority of whom were adherents of the Mahāyāna Buddhism. To the south of the river, there was an old city, more than seventy *li* in perimeter, which was in ruins but a crenellated wall of the city remained. This city was called Kusumapura (meaning "palace city of fragrant flowers") in olden times when the human lifespan was incalculably long, for the palace was abounded with flowers, hence the name of the city. Later, when the lifespan of the people was reduced to several thousand years, the city's name was then changed to be Pāṭaliputra[29] (formerly known as Xilianfuyi by mistake), a name taken after the Pāṭali tree.

In the first one hundredth year after the Nirvāṇa of Buddha, King Aśoka (meaning "the king without worries," formerly called King Ayuwang by mistake), a great grandson of King Bimbisāra (meaning "stone shadow"), moved his capital from Rājagṛha to this city. At present, only the foundation of the original city remained, together with two or three monasteries survived out of several hundred monasteries once in the past. To the north of the old palace, bordering on the Ganges, there was a small city with more than one thousand households. To the south of the palace was a stone pillar which had been erected by King Aśoka at the place where he built the replica Hell. During the sojourn of seven days, the Master visited and worshiped the holy sites in this small city. To the south of the Hell, there was a stūpa which was one of eighty-four thousand stūpas. The stūpa was built by craftsmen on the order of King Aśoka, and it preserved one *dou* of the Tathāgata's relics bones, which often sent forth a miraculous light. Next to the stupa, there was a Vihāra keeping a stone slab that the Tathāgata once stepped on. On it, there were two discernible footprints, each eight inches long and six inches wide. There were signs of the Thousand-spoke Wheel in both soles and also patterns of swastika, vase, fish and others on the tips of ten toes, which were all distinctively visible. When the Tathāgata was going to enter nirvāṇa, he left Vaiśāli and came to stand on a big square boulder on the southern bank of the river, and turning to Ānanda, and said, "This is the last time I take a look at the Diamond Seat and Rājagṛha. I will leave my footprints here."

To the north of the Vihāra, there was a stone column more than thirty *chi* high, recording that King Aśoka offered Jambudvīpa to the Triple Gem for three times and thrice redeemed it with precious gems and jewels. To the southeast of the old city was the old base of the Kukkuṭārāma monastery (meaning "pheasant garden")[30]. Built by King Aśoka, it was the place where the king convened one thousand monks and granted them four kinds of offerings[31]. All these holy sites the Master visited and paid his homage to during his seven-day sojourn.

Further going southwest for six or seven *yojanas,* the Master reached Telāḍhaka Monastery where a few tens of Tripiṭaka masters lived. Upon hearing the arrival of the Master, they all went out to receive him in a friendly way and ushered him into the monastery. From here going southward for more than one hundred *li*, he came to the Bodhi tree enclosed by a brick wall. Extremely high and solid, the wall was long from east to west and narrow from south to north. Its front gate faced the Nairañjanā River in the east, its south gate connected to a big Flower Pond, its west gate held a strategic place on a dangerous hillside, and its north gate led to a large monastery. Within the wall, there were many holy sites, such as Vihāras and stūpas, adjoining to one another, all of which had been successively constructed by kings, administers, and wealthy Elders, as a way to show their admiration for and eulogies to the Buddha. At the center, there was a Diamond Throne which arose with the creation of the earth at the beginning of the Bhadrakalpa, and which was right in the middle of the world systems of the trichiliocosm[32]. Made of diamond, the Throne stretched down to the golden section at the bottom[33] of the earth and up to the earth's surface. The perimeter of it was more than one hundred paces. It was called Diamond Throne because diamond was strong and indestructible and able to destroy all other things. The throne was situated on the Diamond Wheel, so when the Buddha was to attain his enlightenment he came here, because if he hadn't, the earth would never stop quaking; in addition, if the throne had not been made of diamond, there would have been no suitable place to trigger the Diamond Samādhi[34]. At present, anyone who wished to subdue Māras[35] and attain enlightenment must reside here, because if he resided in other places, the ground would collapse to one side. Therefore, one thousand buddhas of Bhadrakalpa would come here. In brief, it was the due place for people to attain Buddhahood, hence the name Place of Enlightenment[36]. Even when the world tilted and quaked, only this Diamond Seat would not move at all.

In the past one or two hundred years, due to their lack of blessings, people had been to the Bodhi tree but they could not see the Diamond Seat. After the Nirvāṇa of the Buddha, the kings of various countries collectively set up two statues of Bodhisattva Avalokiteśvara which were facing the east and demarcating the northern and southern territories. It was said when the bodies of Bodhisattvas sunk into the earth and became invisible, the Buddhist teachings would vanish from the world. Now the southern statue of Bodhisattva had already sunk down to the chest. The Bodhi tree was a *pippala* tree, when the Buddha was living in the world, it used to be as high as several hundred *chi*; but later, because it was frequently cut down by rapacious kings, at present it was only more than five *zhang* in height. In the far distant past, just sitting beneath it, the Buddha had obtained the supreme full and equal Enlightenment[37], thus it was also called the Bodhi tree. The tree trunk was yellowish white; and its branches and leaves were smoothly green, didn't wither in autumn and winter. On the anniversary day of the Buddha's Nirvāṇa, the leaves fell by themselves but in the next morning, they looked like the night before. Each year on this day, the kings and ministers assembled at the tree to water and clean it with the milk, also light lamps and scatter flowers around it; they even collected the fallen leaves before they retired.

On his arrival, the Master paid homage to the Bodhi tree as well as the statue of the Buddha made by Bodhisattva Maitreya to commemorate the moment when the Buddha attained Buddhahood. After worshiping them with great sincerity, the Master prostrated himself in depression, and said to himself remorsefully, "I don't know where I was in the process of transmigrations when the Buddha attained His enlightenment, but now in this Image-period I've come here at the long last. How terrible my karmic obstacles are!" With those words, his eyes were filled with tears in sadness. Coincidentally, it was the time when the monks dispersed from the summer resort, so about thousands of them gathered here to see the sight. On seeing what was happening, none of them could check from sobbing bitterly. Within a neighborhood of one *yojana*, holy sites abounded, and the Master spent eight or nine days to pay his homage to all of them.

On the tenth day, the congregation of Nālandā[38] dispatched four great virtuous monks to receive the Master, and proceeding together for seven *yojanas*, they came to a manor belonging to the monastery, which was the birthplace of the venerable Maudgalyāyana. Soon after the Master had the meal at the manor, more than two hundred monks followed by over one thousand almsgivers, holding banners, canopies, flowers and incenses, came to welcome him. Lauded and surrounded by them, the Master entered the Nālandā Mahāvihāra. No sooner had he arrived than all the monks assembled, and the Master greeted them all. By the side of the abbot, a special seat had been set ready for the Master, and after he sat down, other disciples took their seats too. After they sat down, the deacon[39] was asked to strike a *ghanta*[40] to announce that the Master would reside in the monastery and that he would be provided with the religious utensils and instruments same as the rest monks. Then twenty men with solemn presence, neither too young nor too old, having a mastery of scriptures and precepts, were assigned to lead the Master to meet the Right Dharma Store, the venerable Śilabhadra. (The *Biography*[41] recorded he was one hundred and six years old; the *Brief Obituary*[42] recorded he was one hundred sixty years old.)

Out of veneration, monks never addressed him by his name, and instead, they called him Right Dharma Store. Then following them, the Master went to pay a visit to him. Meeting Right Dharma Store, the Master formally acknowledged him as his personal tutor, and in order to show his utmost veneration, he followed the local rituals to draw near to Right Dharma Store with knees and elbows, pressed his head against his feet and kissed them; after so doing he extended his greeting and eulogies. When the greetings were completed, Right Dharma Store enjoined his attendants to spread out seats and invited the Master and other monks to sit down.

After they had taken their seats, Right Dharma Store asked the Master where he came from. The Master answered, "I have come from China, and wish to learn the *Yogācārabhūmi Śāstra* under your instruction." Upon hearing those words, the venerable Śilabhadra began to weep. He asked his disciple Buddhabhadra (meaning "enlightened sage"), his nephew, to come up to him. Buddhabhadra was over seventy years old, being eloquent and well-versed in scriptures as well as commentaries. Dharma Store said to his nephew, "Please tell the present congregation about the cause for my illness that I took three years ago." Hearing the words, Buddhabhadra began to sob, and then wiping his tears, he related the story which happened in the past, saying, "Years ago, the venerable Upādhyāya[43] suffered from gout. Every time it broke out, his four limbs became spastic and hurt like being burnt by fire or stabbed by a knife. The disease had attacked him from time to time for more than twenty years. Three years ago, the pain became even more aggravated, so he abhorred his physical body and wanted to renounce it by restraining from food. One night, he dreamed of three celestial beings (according to the *Brief Obituary*, he dreamed of a golden deva), one golden, another lapis lazuli, and the third silver. They had proper features, refined demeanor, and wore filmy and bright garments. They came up and asked Upādhyāya, 'You want to renounce your physical body, don't you? Scriptures say that there are sufferings to our corporeal body, but never allow us to detest and reject it. In one of your previous lives, as a king, you made a lot of disturbances to the people, which incurs the present retribution. Now, you should make a self-examination on the wrong deeds you have done before, sincerely repent them, bear the present sufferings at ease and work hard to elucidate the scriptures and commentaries. Only by doing so will your disease clear up by itself. Otherwise, even if you detest your body, you will not put an end to your suffering.' On hearing those words, Upādhyāya sincerely made obeisance to them. Then the golden figure, pointing at the bluish figure, told Upādhyāya, 'Do you recognize him? He is Bodhisattva Avalokiteśvara.' Then he pointed at the silvery figure and said, 'This is Bodhisattva Maitreya.' Then Upādhyāya worshiped Maitreya and asked, 'Śilabhadra has constantly expected to be reborn in your palace, but I wonder if I will? ' Maitreya replied, 'After you spread the right Dharma far and wide, you will be reborn in my palace.' The golden figure introduced himself by saying, 'I am Mañjuśri. We saw you wanted to renounce your physical body, but it is futile to do so for you won't get any ensuing benefits by doing so. That is why we have come here to persuade you to give up your wrong view. You should follow our words to glorify and propagate the right Dharma, such as the *Yogācārabhūmi Śāstra* and the others, to the people who are still in ignorance, then you will regain your health. You need not worry about your illness. In the future, there will come a Chinese monk eager to learn the great Dharma under your guidance. You should wait for him and teach him.' On hearing these words, he paid tribute to them again and announced, 'I will follow your instructions.' As soon as he finished his words, the bodhisattvas disappeared. Since then, the pain of Upādhyāya has gradually eased." Hearing this, all monks were surprised at its rarity.

Having heard it, the Master could not help developing a mixed feeling of delight and sadness. Again, he made obeisance and extended his gratitude by saying, "If what you have said is true, I will go all out to study and practice. May you, the honored one, show me compassion, accept me as your disciple and instruct me!" The Dharma Store asked, "How many years have you spent on the way?" The Master replied, "Three years." Exactly, the time accorded closely with that of the dream. Showing the affection between a teacher and a student, Dharma Store unreservedly gave him various instructions and explanations, which made the Master very delighted.

After the talk, the Master left. He was lodged on the fourth floor of the multiple-storeyed mansion of Buddhabhadra in the King Bālāditya Courtyard. After a seven-day entertainment, he was relodged in the main chamber north of the house of Bodhisattva Dharmapāla, offered with even more daily sustenance provision, including one hundred twenty betel nuts, twenty areca nuts, twenty nutmegs, one tael of borneol incense, and one *sheng* of the Rice Provided to the Superior Man[44]. With each grain larger than a black bean, this non-glutinous rice was much tastier than any other rice when cooked. It was produced only in the country of Magadha, not available in other places, so it was specially supplied to the king, the learned scholars and the virtuous ones, hence the name the Rice Provided to the Superior Man. Three *dou* of oil was also supplied per month; butter, milk and others were sufficiently provided according to the everyday need; and a servant (or it was said to be four servants) and a brāhmaṇa were assigned at his service. What's more, he was exempted from all monastic duties. He was also privileged to travel in the elephant-driven carriage. Plus the Master, totally ten persons out of the ten thousand host and guest monks of Nālandā Mahāvihāra were furnished with such a provision. (Previously the monastery had made a stipulation which set the quota of the monks who were well-versed in the Three Tripitaka to be ten. There had been one vacancy left, so when the Master came, because of his prestige, he was invited to take it.) Wherever the Master went, he was treated with such utmost courtesy.

Nālandā Mahāvihāra meant the monastery of Untiring Almsgiving. According to a story told by the aged and prestigious, in the mango grove south to the monastery there was a pond, in which a dragon dwelt whose name was Nālandā, and for the monastery was built by the side of the pond, hence the name Nālandā Mahāvihāra. It was also said, in former times, when the Tathāgata was practicing the Bodhisattva Way, he was a king of a great kingdom, and established his capital in this place where he, out of sympathy, often distributed money, clothes, or food to the solitary and the poor. To commemorate his kindness, this spot was thus called the Untiring Almsgiving. At the very beginning, it was a garden belonging to the Elderly Āmra, and later, it was purchased by five hundred merchants with a koṭi[45] gold coins, who then gave it to the Buddha as offering. Subsequently, the

Buddha had preached the Dharma here for three months here, which made most of the merchants attain sainthood. After the Nirvāṇa of the Buddha, out of the veneration, the ancestral king of this country, Śakrāditya (meaning "Indra sun") had a temple built as a memorial to the Buddha. After he passed away, his son King Buddhagupta (meaning "enlightened secret") inherited his grand undertaking and had another temple built to the south of the first one. Again, his son King Tathāgata (meaning "thus come") had another temple built to the east, whose son King Bālāditya (meaning "young sun") also had another constructed to the northeast. Later when seeing a holy monk from China coming to receive his offerings, King Bālāditya was so delighted that he renounced his throne to live a monastic life. His son (meaning "diamond") succeeded to the throne, and had another temple constructed in the north; later, next to it, a prince of Central India had another temple built.

Six kings had the six temples constructed successively, and at a later time, bricks were piled up to enclose all of them into a monastery with only one entrance. The monastery consisted of eight courtyards each with a separate gate. Within the monastery, the sights were spectacular: terraces were beautifully decorated, scattering all over like stars in the sky; impressive buildings rose high like hills; temple halls towered in misty clouds; palaces hovered over the clouds; fresh breezes and gauzy mists were blowing in and out from the windows and doors; the sun and the moon shone above the eaves alternately day and night. Moreover, meandering through the compounds were crystal-clear brooks with blooming cyan lotuses and buds of water lilies. The flowers of sandalwood trees were flourishing brightly inside the monastery and the mango trees outside growing prosperously. Within each yard, the buildings for monk were four storeys, with the ridgepoles and beams stretching like the flying dragons or the overhanging rainbows in the sky. The green beam-supporters well matched the red pillars. The frontal posts were engraved with exquisite designs and lattices decorated with hollowed-out work. The plinths were made of jade and even the front boards of the eaves were elegantly inscribed with literary verses. The ridges stood up to the bright sky and the colored silk pendants hung down from the rafters. There were thousands of monasteries in India, no one but it was unsurpassable in its magnificence and holiness!

Monk disciples, including both hosts and guests, often amounted to ten thousand, who studied the Mahāyāna teachings as well as the doctrines of Eighteen Sects of Hīnayāna[46], together with secular classics, such as Vedas, and others. They also learned the knowledge of logic, grammar, medicine, and divination. The monks who had a profound understanding of twenty scriptures and commentaries amounted to one thousand and more, and those who had mastered thirty were over five hundred; however, those who were well-versed in fifty, including the Master, were merely ten persons. It was the venerable Śilabhadra alone who had a complete knowledge of all the Buddhist texts. In addition, his gracious virtue and advanced age made him esteemed as the greatest master of India. There were more than one hundred teaching halls holding lectures every day. Begrudging to waste a split second, disciples here studied very diligently. As a residential place for the virtuous people, the monastery was well-disciplined, very solemn and dignified. During over seven hundred years since the monastery was established, there had not been even a single monk who transgressed the monastic rules, so, to show appreciation and respect, the king offered more than one hundred villages as the manor for the sustenance of the monastery. Each village had two hundred households who provided several hundred *shi* of non-glutinous rice, butter, and milk every day, so that the monks could be supplied sufficiently in four necessities, no need to have a slight worry about where to get them. Thanks to the efforts of almsgivers, the congregation had achieved accomplishments in pursuing the Way.

After the Master dwelled in Nālandā Mahāvihāra, he went to the city of Rājagṛha to worship the holy sites. The old city of Rājagṛha, which was also called the city of Kuśāgrapura (meaning "palace city of good cogon grass"), was situated in the center of the country of Magadha. In ancient times, the kings usually lived here. For it produced good fragrant cogon grass, hence the name of the city. Encircled by precipitously high mountains, the city had a small path leading to the west and a main gate in the north. It was long from east to west and narrow from south to north, having the perimeter of more than one hundred and fifty *li*. Within it, there was a smaller city with its foundation over thirty *li* in perimeter. Groves of sandalwood trees were found everywhere, budding, and blossoming incessantly during four seasons, with leaves golden in hue.

Outside the north gate of the palace city, there was a stūpa, marking the place where Devadatta and King Ajātaśatru set loose the intoxicated elephant named Protector of Wealth[47] to injure the Buddha. To the northeast of it, there was another stūpa where

Śāriputra attained sainthood upon hearing the Dharma teachings from the bhikṣu Aśvajit. Not far away in the north, there was a big deep pitfall, where Śrigupta (meaning "unsurpassable secret"), having been incited by the evil heretics, attempted to injure the Buddha with a fire pit and a bowl of poisoned rice. Farther in the southeast to the fire pit, at a bend of a hill-city, there was a stūpa, marking the place where the great physician Jivaka (formerly called Qipo by mistake) once built the preaching hall for the Buddha. By the side of it, the old residence of Jivaka was still there.

Going northeast for fourteen or fifteen *li* away from the palace city, the Master reached Gṛdhrakūṭa Mountain (meaning "vulture peak," also "vulture terrace," formerly known as Qidujue Mountain by mistake), which linked to the ranges of mountains in the north. A ridge of it humped up extremely high, looked like a vulture atop the peak or terrace, hence the name. Here the springs were crystal clear, the rocks grotesque in shape, and trees luxuriantly dense. When the Tathāgata was living in the world, he often dwelt in this mountain to preach the *Saddharmapuṇḍ arīka Sūtra*, the *Mahāprajñāpāramitā Sūtra* and numerous other scriptures.

From the north gate of the hill-city, moving on for more than one *li* to the north, the Master reached the Karaṇḍa Bamboo Grove in which there was a brick chamber. In the past, the Tathāgata lived here and laid down the disciplinary rules. The original owner of this grove was Karaṇḍa. At first, he gave this grove to some heretics; later, after meeting the Buddha and hearing the profound Dharma, he regretted not having offered it to the Tathāgata. At the time, the Earth God, knowing his intention, helped him to frighten the heretics out of the grove by creating various calamities and strange phenomena. Then the Earth God commanded the heretics by saying, "You should get out of the garden right away because Karaṇḍa wishes to offer it to the Buddha." So, the heretics had to leave but in a fury. The Elderly Karaṇḍa was thus delighted, and having a Vihāra constructed, he went to invite the Buddha to live in. The Buddha accepted the invitation. To the east of the Bamboo Grove was a stūpa built by King Ajātaśatru (meaning "the king of hatred before birth," formerly called Asheshi by mistake). After the Nirvāṇa of the Tathāgata, the kings divided the relics, and King Ajātaśatru carried his share, returned to build this stūpa for the enshrinement. Later, King Aśoka made his resolution to construct the stūpas in other places, so he opened this stūpa and took out some relics. Now only a small portion was left which still emitted a magic light frequently.

In the southwest to the Bamboo Grove for five or six *li* odd, there was another bamboo grove at the foot of a hill. In the grove there was a large stone chamber, where the venerable Mahākāśyapa and nine hundred ninety-nine great *arhats* once assembled to collect the Tripiṭaka after the Tathāgata's Nirvāṇa. On the assembly day, because too many saints and monks flocked here, Kāśyapa had to claim, "Only those who could swear that they have already had a mastery of Three Insights[48] and six supernatural powers[49], and completely upheld the Dharma piṭaka of the Tathāgata without a slight erroneous and perverse view, are permitted to remain here. And the rest of you could disperse as you like." Thus, the number of monks was reduced to nine hundred ninety-nine. As Ānanda was still at the learning stage, so Kāśyapa said to him, "Your defilements have not been eliminated.

Don't contaminate the purified people here." Being ashamed, Ānanda had to leave, but on that very night, he earnestly did self-cultivation to eliminate the āsrava of the Three Realms[50], and subsequently attained the Arhatship.

Then he came back and knocked at the door. Kāśyapa asked him, "Have you liberated yourself from the bonds[51]?"

"Yes!" replied by Ānanda.

Then Kāśyapa said, "If you have already liberated from the bonds of transmigration, I'm not bothered to open the door for you, because you are supposed to be able to come in at your will."

Then, Ānanda entered the chamber through a crack in the door and prostrated himself at the feet of Kāśyapa. Kāśyapa held his hands and told him, "In order to make you annihilate all defilements to attain sainthood, I drove you away. I want you to know my intention and not bear me any grudge."

Ānanda said, "If I developed a hatred, how can I be said as one free from defilements?"

After making obeisance to extend the gratitude again, he took the seat in the assembly. At the time, it happened to be on the fifteenth day at the summer retreat.

Kāśyapa said to Ānanda, "The Tathāgata often praised you as the supreme hearer and upholder of all the dharmas, so why don't you ascend to a high seat and recite the Sūtra Piṭaka, that is, the scriptures?"

Accepting the invitation, Ānanda rose from his seat, paid homage in the direction of the mountain where the Tathāgata attained his Nirvāṇa, and ascended to a high seat to recite the

Sūtras; simultaneously, other monks wrote down what they heard. After that, Upāli was invited to recite Vinaya Piṭaka, namely, all the commandments and precepts. In succession, Kāśyapa recited Abhidharma Piṭaka, namely, all the commentaries and expositions. During this two-to-three-month retreat, the Tripiṭaka had been collected, and by recording it on palm leaves, the Tripiṭaka, thereafter, was made possible to spread widely. When this meritorious undertaking was accomplished, those holy monks looked at each other and said, "What we have done is aimed to requite the gracious kindness of the Buddha. Because of His powerful assistance, we have gotten this chance to collect the Tripiṭaka and learn the Buddha Dharma ." As Mahākāśyapa was a sthavira[52] among the monks, this congregation was called the Sthavira School.

Farther to the west from here about twenty *li* was a stūpa built by King Aśoka, which marked the place where monks of Mahīśāsaka School assembled. At this place there congregated several thousand monks, some of whom were still learning[53] and others had completed their learning[54], also there were those who hadn't participated in the congregation of Mahākāśyapa. They said to one another, "When the Tathāgata was living, we were all learning under Him. Now after the Nirvāṇa of the Worldly Honored One, we have been driven out of the assembly. Why can't we collect the Dharma Piṭaka to requite the kindness of the Buddha?" Then they collected the Sūtra *Piṭaka*, the *Vinaya Piṭaka*, the *Abhidharma Piṭaka*, the *Miscellaneous Piṭaka*, and the *Dhāraṇi Piṭaka*, totally five *Piṭakas.* Since the participators were composed of ordinary learners and saints, the congregation was known as the Mahīśāsaka School[55].

Farther going northeast for three or four *li*, the Master came to the city of Rājagṛha (meaning "city of king's residence"). The outer city wall had already worn out, while the inner wall was still majestic. The perimeter of the city was more than twenty *li* and one gate opened on each side of it. Formerly, when King Bimbisāra was living in the Palace of Good Cogon Grass, the city was densely populated with a forest of houses, which, however, incurred the fire for several times; therefore, a strict edict was issued that anyone who caused a fire imprudently would be exiled to the Forest of Coldness—the dire place for keeping the corpses of the country. Soon after, the imperial palace caught a sudden fire. The king reproved himself by saying, "As the lord of the people, if I violate the law but escape penalty, the punishment will not be meted out to my subjects." So, he ordered his crown prince to reign and voluntarily moved into the Forest of Coldness. At the time, when the king of Vaiśāli heard that King Bimbisāra was residing in the wild field outside the palace, he intended to rally his forcing troops to commence an attack. Knowing the news, a watchman made a report to the king, so this city was constructed for defense. Since King Bimbisāra formerly lived here, hence the name—City of King's Residence, also called New City. Later, King Ajātaśatru succeeded to the Throne and took it as his capital. During the reign of King Aśoka, he offered this city to brāhmaṇas and moved his capital to Pāṭaliputra. At present, there were no inhabitants other than a thousand more brāhmaṇa households. In the southwest corner of the palace city, there was a stūpa marking the old residence of the Elderly Jyotiṣka (meaning "luminary," formerly known as Shutiqie by mistake), beside it was the place where Rāhula (the Buddha's son) was converted by the Buddha.

To the northwest of the Nālandā Mahāvihāra was a great Vihāra, more than three hundred *chi* in height, which was built by King Bālāditya, looking very majestic and beautiful, enshrining a statue of Buddha the same as the one enshrined under the Bodhi tree. To the northeast of this Vihāra, there was a stūpa built on the spot where the Tathāgata made his seven-day discourse on the Dharma. To the northwest was the site where the four Past Buddhas once sat in meditative absorption. To the south was a brass Vihāra constructed by King Śilāditya, which was still under construction at the time, but after carefully examining its blueprint, the height of which was supposed to be more than ten *zhang*. About more than two hundred paces farther to the east of the city, there was a brass standing-statue of the Buddha, more than eighty *chi* high, which was sheltered by a multi-layer pavilion with the storeys as many as six, built by King Pūrṇavarman in olden times. Going eastward for several *li,* the Master came to a stūpa, where King Bimbisāra, together with hundreds and thousands of his people once received the Buddha when he was on his way to Rājagṛha after attaining the Way.

Farther proceeding eastward for more than thirty *li*, the Master reached a stūpa standing in front of a monastery on the eastern peak of Indraśailaguhā Mountain[56], named Haṃsa (meaning "wild goose") stūpa. In former times, the monks of this monastery were adhering to the gradual teachings of Hīnayāna School so they were permitted to eat three kinds of pure meat[57]. One day the monk in charge of the food was at his wit's end because he found nowhere to purchase the meat, and when a group of wild geese were flying by, he looked up at them and jokingly said, "Today, I haven't got enough food to sustain the other monks. It seems that the Mahāsattva[58] should know better (to make sacrifice) at this proper time." When he finished those words, the leading goose flew back as a response, soared high above the clouds, folded its wings, dropped to the ground, and died. On seeing this, feeling ashamed and fearful, this Bhikṣu returned to tell the incident to other monks. All the hearers were astonished. Signing and sobbing at the dead wild goose, they said to one another, "It must be a Bodhisattva. How dare the mortals like us eat it? In order to prevent them from committing the unwholesome karmas[59], the Tathāgata has set his teachings skillfully for the people at different levels, but his skill-in-means words for the learners at the primary stage have always been mistakenly taken by us as the ultimate truth. It is because we have been attaching to the stupidities without correcting our views and deeds that we have committed such a sinful harm today. From now on, we shall adhere to the teachings of the Mahāyāna School and give up eating three kinds of pure meat forever." Thereafter, a pagoda was built to bury the dead goose with an commendatory inscription recording its benevolent sacrifice, to make sure its virtuous deed could be passed down to the posterity forever. That was the cause for the construction of this stūpa.

After the Master had visited and worshiped all such holy sites, he came back to Nālandā Mahāvihāra. Then he requested the Dharma teacher Śilabhadra to expound the *Yogācārabhūmi Śāstra.* Apart from the Master, there were other several thousand disciples attending the lectures. Hardly had the subject been exposed when a brāhmaṇa outside the congregation began to wail and laugh, at the same time, murmuring something. So, a man was dispatched to inquire of him for the reason. In reply, the brāhmaṇa said, "I am a native of East India. Once a time I took a vow before the statue of Bodhisattva Avalokiteśvara at Potalaka Mountain that I would become a king. The Bodhisattva appeared and reproached me by saying, 'Don't make such a low vow. In the future, in some year and month and day, the Dharma teacher Śilabhadra in Nālandā Mahāvihāra will expound the *Yogācārabhūmi Śāstra* for a Chinese monk. You should go there to listen to it. Because of hearing the Dharma, you would encounter the Buddha in the future. What is the use, then, of becoming a king?' Now I see that this Chinese monk has come here and the teacher is delineating the Sūtra for him, which accorded closely with the prediction I got in the past. That is why I felt both sad and happy." Hearing those words, the Dharma teacher Śilabhadra allowed him to attend lectures. Having spent fifteen months elaborating on the Sūtra thoroughly, the Ven. Śilabhadra enjoined a man to escort this brāhmaṇa to King Bālāditya, who then bestowed the brāhmaṇa with three villages.

At the monastery, the Master listened to the *Yogācārabhūmi Śāstra* three times; the *Nyāyānusāra Śāstra*, the *Prakaraṇāryavācā Śāstra*, and the *Abhidharmasamudāya Prakaraṇa* once; the *Hetuvidyā*, the *Ṣabdavidyā*, the *Samuccayapramāṇa Śāstra* twice; also the *Mūlamadhyamakakārikā* and the *Catuḥśataka* three times. As to the *Abhidharmakośa Śāstra*, the *Vibhāṣā Śāstra*, the *Jñānaprasthānaṣaṭpādābhidharma* and others, he had already studied them in Kaśmīra and other countries, now he merely read them again to have his doubts resolved. Besides the aforementioned books, he also studied the Brāhmaṇical texts.

There was an ancient Hindu text named *Jilun* (*Analytical Exposition of Grammar*) which could not be traced back to its origin or its author. At the very beginning of each Kalpa, it was the Brahmā[60] who preached the book first and transmitted it to celestial beings, thus the book was also called Brāhmaṇical book. Being a very voluminous one, it consisted of one million stanzas, which was translated as the *Pijialuolun* in olden times; but this transliteration was erroneous, and it should be corrected as *Vyākaraṇa*, meaning "analytical exposition of grammar," for it gave a full grammatical analysis of Sanskrit language which could be used to explain the dharmas. In the far distant past, when the Kalpa was newly formed, Brahmā firstly preached one million stanzas; subsequently, at the formation of the Kalpa of Existence, Indra[61] reduced it to one hundred thousand stanzas; still later, the immortal Ṛṣi Pāṇini, a brāhmaṇa of Śālātura city of Gandhāra in North India, abridged it further to eight thousand stanzas, which was the extant book prevailing in India. Recently, a brāhmaṇa of South India had shortened it to two thousand and five hundred stanzas for the king, which became quite popular in remote and uncivilized countries, but had never been studied by the erudite scholars of India. It was also the fundamental text of the phonological writing in the Western Regions. There were also auxiliary works functioning to explain the specific subject: one was called the *Concise Analytical Exposition of Grammar* in a thousand stanzas; one dealt with the roots of words in three hundred stanzas. Besides, two books are on inflections. one entitled the *Maṇṭhaka* in three thousand stanzas, and the other *Uṇādi* in twenty-five hundred stanzas which showed the distinctions between roots and inflections of words. There was another book named the *Aṣṭadhātu Śāstra* in eight hundred stanzas, briefly coping with the compound words.

Based on two verb paradigms, all above books classified the grammatical voices into active one and passive one. One was the paradigm of *tiṇanta*, with eighteen verbal inflections; the other was the paradigm of *subanta,* with twenty-four nominal inflections. The *tiṇanta* paradigm was usually used in elegant writing, and rarely used in ordinary writing. The twenty-four nominal inflections were used in all writing styles. The eighteen verbal inflections of *tiṇanta* paradigm were classified into two categories, one was the *parasmai*, and the other was the *ātmane,* with nine inflections each, so in total eighteen inflections. Of the first nine inflections, there were three for the subject of a statement, three for the narrative in the third person and three for the narrative in the first person. There were three morphological changes in each of the three groups: the singular, the dual and the plural. Both *parasmai* and *ātmane* were inflected similarly, but for differing in voice, they were separated into nine inflections for each. In the *parasmai* voice, there were positive and negative statements. With regards the positive statement, there were in three numbers: *bhavati* (one thing exists), *bhavatas* (two things exist) and *bhavanti* (many things exist). In the second person, there were three ways: *bhavasi* (thou does exist), *bhavathas* (thou two exist), and *bhavaths* (you all exist). In the first person, there were three ways: *bhavāmi* (I exist), *bhavāvas* (we two exist) and *bhavāmas* (we all exist). For the nine verb forms of the *ātmane* voice, what was needed was to add the suffix *vyati* to the above endings. The rest were the same as above.

These rules had been set to express the subtlety of the language and avoid ambiguity, also to show the elegance in expression. The twenty-four inflections of the *subanta* consisted of eight principal cases, each of which contained three forms: the singular, the dual and the plural, thus totally twenty-four inflections. Further to each reflection, there were three genders: the masculine, the feminine and the neuter. The so-called eight principal cases were as follows: the first was the nominative, indicating the subject; the second was the accusative, indicating what was acted upon; the third was the instrumental, denoting the doer or the instrument with which something was done; the fourth was the dative, indicating for whom the a thing was done; the fifth was the ablative, indicating the cause of something; the sixth was the genitive, signifying the possessor of something; the seventh was the locative, showing the location where something was done; the eighth was the vocative, for addressing or calling a thing. Taking the word "man" of the masculine gender for example, the eight principal cases could be explained. The Indian word for "man" being *puruṣa*, thus we have:

1. *puruṣas, puruṣau, puruṣās* for the nominative case.
2. *puruṣam, puruṣau, puruṣān* for the accusative case.
3. *puruṣeṇa, puruṣābhyām, puruṣavya[sic] or puruṣais* for the instrumental case.
4. *puruṣāya, puruṣābhyām, puruṣebhyas* for the dative case.
5. *puruṣāt, puruṣābhyām, puruṣebhyas* for the ablative case.
6. *puruṣasya, puruṣābhyām[sic], puruṣāṇām* for the genitive case.
7. *puruṣe, puruṣayos, puruṣeṣu* for the locative case.
8. *hi[sic] puruṣa, hi puruṣau, hi puruṣās* for the vocative case.[62]

It was difficult to make an explanation of all the endings of the words here, so taking the above several examples, the other declensions may be understood. Indeed, the Master was proficient in this language and even could use it with more elegance and exquisiteness. He had spent five years making a profound study of the teachings of various schools as well as Sanskrit books.

From here the Master resumed his journey again to the country of Īraṇaparvata[63], and on his way, he came by a monastery named Kapotaka. Two or three *li* to the south of this monastery was a solitary hill of highly erect peaks, thick with bushes, rich in limpid springs and ponds, and the air here permeated with the fragrance of flowers, which had been a holy place replete with temples known for manifesting miraculous and uncanny signs. In the central Vihāra, there was a sandalwood statue of Bodhisattva Avalokiteśvara, which was extremely sublime and awesomely inspiring. Frequently, several tens of people, for seven days or a fortnight, refraining from food and drink, prayed for the fulfillment of their wishes. If bearing the wholehearted sincerity, people would behold the Bodhisattva of stately features and majestic appearance, illuminating brightly and coming out of the sandalwood statue to console them and grant them their wishes. Over the past years, there had been a lot of people who saw such vision time and again. For this reason, the ever-increasing devotees came to worship it. In order to protect the holy image from being carelessly smeared by the frequent visits of the people, the temple-keepers had the wooden railings erected around the statue seven steps away in the four directions. When a man was coming to pay homage, he had to worship outside the railings and could not get near to the statue. So, the incenses and flowers had to be flung to the statue from a distance. When the flower garlands rested in the hands or hung upon the arms of the Bodhisattva's statue, he would take it as an auspicious omen indicating that his wishes could be fulfilled.

The Master intended to go there to consult oracles, so he bought all kinds of flowers and strung them into garlands, and came to the statue. Having shown obeisance and lauded it in utmost sincerity, he knelt down before the Bodhisattva and made three wishes, saying, "First, if I could safely return to my homeland without calamities after I complete my studies here, may a garland rest in your hands; second, I have been cultivating my merits and wisdom in order to ascend to Tuṣita Palace to attend the Bodhisattava Maitreya. If my ideal would be achieved, may a garland hang on your arms; third, according to some holy teachings, among living beings there is a kind of people who does not have the Buddha-nature[64]. Now I am wondering whether I have it or not. May a garland hang on your neck if I have the Buddha nature and can attain Buddhahood through spiritual cultivation." After saying so, he flung the flower garlands to the statue from a distance, all the garlands fell exactly on the very places as what he had expected. Now his wishes had been fulfilled, he was in great pleasure. On seeing this, not only the people worshiping beside him but also the Vihāra keepers flipped the fingers, kissed his feet, and exclaimed over the rarity of the case. They said to the Master, "In the future if you attain Buddhahood, wish you to recall what happened today and awaken us first."

Continuing to move on from here, the Master reached the country of Īraṇaparvata which had ten monasteries and more than four thousand monks, majority of them studying Hīnayāna teachings of Sarvāstivāda school. Recently, a king of a neighboring country abolished the monarch and offered the capital city to the Sangha. Thereafter, two monasteries had been constructed in the city center, each of them housing one thousand monks. There were two great virtuous monks, one named Tathāgatagupta (meaning "Tathāgata secret"), the other Kṣāntisiṃha (meaning "forbearance of lion"), both of whom were well-versed in the teachings of the Sarvāstivāda school. The Master had stayed there with them for a year to learn the *Vibhāṣā Śāstra,* the *Nyāyānusāra Śāstra*, and other texts.

There was a stūpa in the south of the capital city, where the Buddha formerly had preached the Dharma for three months for Heavenly beings, beside which were relic sites of the four Past Buddhas. The west frontier of the country was bordering on the Ganges. The southern border of the country reached a small solitary hill, where the Buddha subdued Yakṣa Vakula during his three-month retreat. On the surface of a boulder at the foot of southeastern cliff of the hill, there was a sitting print left by the Buddha, which recessed into the rock for more than one inch, and was five feet two inches in length, four feet one inch in breadth. Also, there was a depression left by the Buddha's Kuṇḍikā (a bathing jag, in olden times transliterated as *junchi* by mistake). The depression was more than one inch in depth, in the shape of octagon. In a wild forest on the southern border of the country, there were many elephants haunting, strong and tall.

ANNOTATION

1 Present Oudh, also Kingdom of Oudh, or Awadh State, was a princely state in the Awadh region of North India until annexation by the British in 1856. Oudh, the now obsolete but once official English-language name of the state, also written historically as Oude, derived from the name of Ayodhyā(which is a city located in Faizabad district of Uttar Pradesh, India). It shares municipal corporation with its neighboring twin town of Faizabad. The city is identified with the legendary city of Ayodhyā, and as such, is the birthplace of Rāma and setting of the epic Rāmāyana. The accuracy of this identification is central to the Ayodhyā dispute: modern scholars variously believe that the present-day Ayodhyā is the same as the legendary Ayodhyā, or that the legendary city is a mythical place that came to be identified with the present-day Ayodhya only during the Gupta period around the 4th–5th century CE. The present-day city is identified as the location of Saketa, which was an important city of the Kosala mahajanapada in the first millennium BC, and later served as its capital.

2 Asaṅga无著 (Wuzhu, meaning No Attachment. fl. 4th century C.E.) was a major exponent of the Yogacara tradition in India, also called Vijñānavāda. Traditionally, he and his half-brother Vasubandhu are regarded as the founders of this school. The two half-brothers were also major exponents of Abhidharma teachings.

3 Situated at the northwest of Allahabad in the Indian state of Uttar Pradesh.

4 Durgā is a principal and popular form of Hindu goddess. She is the warrior goddess, whose mythology centers around combating evils and demonic forces that threaten peace, prosperity and dharma of the good. Durgā is depicted in the Hindu pantheon as a goddess riding a lion or tiger, with many arms each carrying a weapon, often defeating the mythical buffalo demon. She appears in Indian texts as the wife of god Shiva, as another form

of Parvati or mother goddess. She is a central deity in Śāktaṃ tradition of Hinduism.

5 Gṛdhrakūṭa Mountain or Gádhrakúta, the Vulture Peak.

6 Avīci: the hell of uninterrupted suffering.

7 An ancient kingdom in Central India, where Buddhadāsa composed the *Abhidharmamahāvibhāṣā Śāstra*.

8 Present Allahabad.

9 Or Kaushambi, was an important city in ancient India. It was the capital of the Vatsa kingdom, one of the sixteen kingdoms. It was one of the greatest cities in India from the late Vedic period until the end of Maurya Empire with occupation continuing until the Gupta Empire. It was located on the Yamuna River about 56 kilometres (35 *mi*) southwest of its confluence with the Ganges at Prayaga (modern Prayagraj).

10 It was situated on the northern bank of the Gumit River, a tributary of the Ganges, to the north of Lucknow.

11 The old site of this country is said to be in the Sahet-Mahet district to the northwest of Patna, however according to other investigation, maybe in the district of Khajura in Nepal.

12 A bhikṣu is an ordained male monastic (monk) in Buddhism. Female monastics (nun) are called bhikṣuṇī.

13 Devá means "heavenly, divine, anything of excellence", and is also one of the terms for a deity in Hinduism. Devás along with Asuras, Yakshas (nature spirits) and Rākṣasas (ghosts, ogres) are part of Indian mythology, and Devás feature in one of many cosmological theories in Hinduism. In Buddhism, a Devá is one of many different types of non-human beings who share the characteristics of being more powerful, longer-lived, and, in general, living more contentedly than the average human being. An inhabitant of Heavenly realms, which is characterized by long life, joyous surroundings, and blissful states of mind. In the Buddhist tradition, these states are understood to be

impermanent, not eternal.

14 The present kalpa is called the Bhadrakalpa (Auspicious aeon).

15 In the southern part of Nepal.

16 A person under the age of 20 cannot be ordained as a bhikkhu or bhikkhuni but can be ordained as a śrāmaṇera or śrāmaṇērī.

17 Also known as Kusinagar, Kusinara, Kasia and Kasia Bazar, is a pilgrimage town and a Notified Area Council in the Kushinagar district of the Indian state of Uttar Pradesh, 52 km east of Gorakhpur city. It is an important Buddhist pilgrimage site, where Buddhists believe Gautama Buddha attained Parinirvāṇa after his death.

18 Vaisakha is a month of the Hindu calendar that corresponds to April/May in the Gregorian Calendar. In Indian national calendar, Vaisakha is the second month of the year.

19 Kārttika is a month in Hindu calendar, that typically overlaps October and November.

20 Benares, is a city on the banks of the Ganges in the Uttar Pradesh state of North India, 320 kilometres (200 *mi*) south-east of the state capital, Lucknow, and 121 kilometres (75 *mi*) east of Allahabad.

21 See note 40 of Preface.

22 In Buddhism, the Dharma Chakra is widely used to represent the Buddha's Dharma (Buddha's teaching and the universal moral order), Gautama Buddha himself and the walking of the path to enlightenment. The symbol is also connected to the Four Noble Truths, the Noble Eightfold Path and Dependent Origination. The Three Turnings of the Wheel (of Dharma) is an attempt to categorize the content, philosophical view, and practical application of the whole array of Buddhist sūtrayāna teachings. Sūtrayāna encompasses the teachings of both Hīnayāna and Mahāyāna, is known as the "Causal Vehicle", because the path is followed in order to establish the cause for attaining enlightenment.

23 It is identified with the modern Gharipur, a city and municipal corporation in the state of Uttar Pradesh, India.

24 Modern Bihar, which covered most of the Himalayan Gangetic region of present-day Bihar. Gautama Buddha delivered his last sermon at Vaishali and announced his Pari nirvāṇa there. Vaishali is also renowned as the home of Amrapali, a great courtesan who appears in many folktales as well as in Buddhist literature. Amrapali became a disciple of Gautama Buddha.

25 Vimalakīrti is the central figure in the *Vimalakīrti Sūtra*, which presents him as the ideal Mahāyāna Buddhist upāsaka ("lay practitioner"). There is no mention of him in Buddhist texts until after Nāgārjuna (1st century BC to 2nd century CE) revived Mahāyāna Buddhism in India.

26 Vimalakīrti .

27 Also "White City".

28 Ancient kingdom of India, situated in what is now west-central Bihar state, in northeastern India.

29 Modern Patna, the capital and largest city of the state of Bihar in India.

30 Kukkuṭārāma was a Buddhist monastery in Pāṭaliputra (adjacent to modern-day Patna) in Eastern India, which is famous as the location of various "Discourses at the Kukkuṭārāma Monastery", and for the eponymous "*Kukkuṭārāma Sūtra*".

31 Or the Four requisites or necessities refers to the offerings needed by a monk or nun, usually including: (1) food and drink; (2) clothing; (3) bedding and; (4) medicine.

32 Or the three-thousand-great-thousand system of worlds (trichiliocosm), Sanskrit: tri-sahasra-mahā-sahasra-loka-dhātu, a great chiliocosm 三千界, 三千世界. Mt. Sumeru and its seven surrounding continents, eight seas and ring of iron mountains form one small world; 1, 000 of these form a small chiliocosm 小千世界; 1, 000 of these small chiliocosms form a medium chiliocosm 中千世界; a thousand of these form a great chiliocosm 大千世界,

which thus consists of 1, 000, 000, 000 small worlds. The 三千 indicates the above three kinds of thousands, therefore 三千大千世界 is the same as 大千世界, which is one Buddha-world.

33 According to the Buddhist cosmology, the foundations of the world system are depicted in the following way: All of the structures of Earth, Sumeru and the rest, extend downward to a depth of 80,000 *yojanas* below sea level – the same as the height of Sumeru above sea level. Below this is a layer of "golden earth", a substance compact and firm enough to support the weight of Sumeru. It is 320,000 *yojanas* in depth and so extends to 400,000 *yojanas* below sea level. The layer of golden earth in turn rests upon a layer of water, which is 8,000,000 *yojanas* in depth, going down to 8,400,000 *yojanas* below sea level. Below the layer of water is a "circle of wind", which is 16,000,000 *yojanas* in depth and also much broader in extent, supporting 1,000 different worlds upon it.

34 Also Vajrasamadhi, the meditation of the last stage of the Bodhisattva, attained after all remains of illusion have been cut off.

35 Māra(s): demon; the devil.

36 Or bodhimaṇḍa in Sanskrit, meaning the bodhi place or platform.

37 Sanskrit equivalent: anuttarasamyaksaṃbodhi; literally unsurpassed complete perfect Enlightenment. This term may distinguish the enlightenment of an Arhat from the complete enlightenment of a Buddha.

38 Nālandā, a famous monastery (Mahāvihāra) seven miles north of Rājagṛha, built by the king Śakrāditya. Nālandā means "Unwearying benefactor", a title attributed to the nāga which dwelt in the lake Āmra there.

39 A Buddhist deacon, or the Director of Duties (*weina*维那in Chinese and karmadāna in Sanskrit), is an assigner of duties in a monastery, who directs the monks, usually the second most senior member of a monastery, so also translated as a duty-distributor.

40 Bell.

41 The *Biography of the Tripiṭaka Dharma Master of the Great Ci'en Monastery of the Great Tang Dynasty.*

42 Refers to The *Brief Obituary for the Tripiṭaka Dharma Master Xuanzang of the Great Tang Dynasty* (*Datang Gu Sanzang Xuanzang Fashi Xingzhuang* 《大唐故三藏玄奘法师行状》) composed by Mingxiang冥详.

43 Upādhyāya: a teacher/ a preceptor; related to the generic Chinese term for a monk.

44 Mahāśāli rice.

45 Koṭi: an extremely large number, usually ten million, sometimes one million.

46 Eighteen Sects of Hīnayāna: One hundred years after the Buddha's Nirvāṇa, a schism occurred in the Buddhist order resulting in the formation of two schools: Mahāsāṃghika and Sthaviravādin schools. At the time of 200 years after the Buddha's nirvāṇa, the Mahāsāṃghika School was subdivided into eight sects: 1. Ekavyavaharikāḥ; 2. Lokottaravadinaḥ; 3. Kaukkuṭikaḥ (Gokulika); 4. Bahuśrutīyaḥ; 5. Prajñātivādinah; 6. Jetavaniyāḥ (Caityasailah); 7. Avaraśailaḥ, 8. Uttaraśailāḥ. At the beginning of the third century after the Buddha's nirvāṇa, Sthaviravādin School was divided into the Haimavatāḥ and Sarvāstivāda/ Sarvāstivādaḥ schools. The Sarvāstivādaḥ School again gave rise to nine schools: 1. Vatsiputriyaḥ (developed from Sarvāstivādaḥ); 2. Dharmottariyaḥ (developed from Vatsiputriyaḥ); 3. Bhadrayaniyāḥ (developed from Vatsiputriyaḥ); 4. Sammatiyāḥ (developed from Vatsiputriyaḥ); 5. Sannagarikaḥ (developed from Vatsiputriyaḥ); 6. Mahiśāsakaḥ; 7. Dharmaguptaḥ (developed from Mahiśāsakaḥ); 8. Kasyapiyaḥ (developed from Sarvāstivādaḥ); 9. Sautrāntika (developed from Sarvāstivādaḥ).

47 Dhanapāla.

48 Trividyā, or Three Insights. See note 101 of Fascicle I.

49 Six supernatural powers: 1. supernatural vision; 2. supernatural hearing; 3. the power to know others' thoughts; 4. the power to know the past lives

of oneself and others; 5. the power to perform miracles, such as appearing anywhere at will; 6. the power totally to eradicate defilements.

50 Āsrava ("influx") refers to the influence of body and mind causing the generation of Karma, such as passions, or desires, which extends transmigration in the Three Realms: 1. the desire realm, which is the sphere of sensuous desire, of sex and food; 2. the form realm or the realm of pure matter, which is above the desire world and comprises part of heaven; 3. the formless realm or the immaterial realm, which is the sphere of pure spirit.

51 The bond of transmigration, 结in Chinese. There are categories of three, five, and nine bonds; e.g. false views, the passions, etc. means to tie up, bind men to mortality. For example, the nine bonds are love, hate, pride, ignorance, (wrong)views, possessions (or grasping), doubt, envy, meanness (or selfishness).

52 Sthavira: the elder of monks. Sthavira School: the School of the Elders.

53 Also termed as Śaikṣa in Sanskrit: in Hīnayāna those in the first three stages of training as arhats, the fourth and last stage being aśaikṣa who are beyond the need of further teaching or study (see the following note). There are eighteen grades of śaikṣa; actively involved in applied practices.

54 Also termed as Aśaikṣa in Sanskrit: those who have attained arhatship; no longer learning, beyond study, the state of arhatship, the fourth of the śrāvaka stages; the preceding three stages requiring study; there are nine grades of arhats who have completed their course of learning; no more applied practice.

55 Mahīśāsaka School: the School of Majority.

56 Indraśailaguhā Mountain is in Bihar. Indrasālaguhā, means "Indra's rock cave" or "Cave of the Indrasāla tree". Buddhaghosa explained that the cave was between two mountains and an indasāla tree grew at its entrance. When the Buddha was in this cave, Sakka (Indra) came to ask him a series of questions that are recorded in the Sakkapañhasutta. The Chinese pilgrims who visited this cave found fragments of the Sakkapañhasutta engraved on

the rock. The visit of Indra has been represented on the monuments at Bārhut, at Sāncī; at Bodhgayā; at Gandhāra; at Mathurā.

57 See note 5 of Fascicle Ⅱ.

58 Mahāsattva ("great being"): a Bodhisattva with great wisdom and compassion.

59 Karma is defined as the latent effects of the wholesome and unwholesome actions taken by sentient beings in prior reincarnation.

60 Or Mahabrahmā, the great heavenly king Brahmā.

61 Indra or Shakra is one of the principal gods of Hinduism, a principal deity of the Rig Veda. In the Rig Veda, Indra is depicted as the most powerful god. However, in latter texts, his importance has been considerably diminished. He is no longer all-powerful, instead he is subject to the overlordship of the supreme trinity of Shiva, Vishnu and Brahmā. According to Buddhist cosmology, Indra resides in the Heaven of the Thirty-Three, which is one of the six heavens of the desire realm. In the Buddhist scriptures he is also sometimes presented as a Dharma protector.

62 The present translation, about 527 words from "Based on" to "the vocative case", is mainly quoted from the corresponding section in the English version of Li Rongxi. (Sramana Huili and Shi Yancong. *A Biography of the Tripitaka Master of the Great Ci'en Monastery of the Great Tang Dynasty*. Translated by Li Rongxi. Berkeley,California: Numata Center for Buddhist Translation and Research, 1995. P.102–104).

63 This country is identified with the modern district of Monghyr(or Munger district), one of the thirty-eight districts of Bihar state in eastern India.

64 Buddha-nature refers to several related terms, most notably tathāgatagarbha and buddhadhātu, simply meaning the seed of Buddhahood or enlightenment. It indeed involves in various strands of Buddhist thought. In the *Tathāgatagarbha sūtras*, icchantikas 一阐提 is one who has no interest in the path to Awakening, or one whose good roots are completely covered. The *Mahāyāna Mahāparinirvāṇa Sūtra* translated by Faxian 法显(337–c.

422), indicates that the icchantika has so totally severed all his/her roots of goodness that he/she can never attain Liberation and nirvāṇa. The full-length Dharmakṣema (385–433 CE) version of the *Mahāyāna Mahāparinirvāṇa Sūtra*, in contrast, insists that even the icchantika can eventually find release into nirvāṇa, since no phenomenon is fixed (including this type of allegedly deluded person) and that change for the better and best is always a possibility. Other scriptures (such as the *Laṅkāvatāra Sūtra*) indicate that the icchantikas will be saved through the liberational power of the Buddha, who, it is claimed, will never abandon any being. After the death of Xuanzang, his disciple Kuiji 窥基 (632–682), the true founder of the Faxiang school of Chinese Buddhism, reaffirmed the Yogācāra's view about three distinct (and unequal) religious careers and its corollary that some beings, the icchantikas, were inherently incapable of any religious development and were thus forever barred from liberation, which indeed was particularly unacceptable to Kuiji's contemporaries. As a result, in spite of its early prominence, the Faxiang School soon experienced a rapid decline in China.

Fascicle IV

Beginning with the Country of Campā and Ending with the Invitation of the King of Kāmarūpa

Proceeding for more than three hundred *li* eastward along the southern bank of Ganges, the Master came to the country of Campā[1] (in the domain of Central India). There were about a dozen monasteries containing over two hundred monks who studied the teachings of the Hīnayāna School. The city wall was constructed of bricks, rising several *zhang* in height. The moat and wall base of the city were deep and wide, making the city indestructibly solid. In ancient times, at the beginning of the Kalpa, human beings were living in caves, a goddess descended to the human world. When she took a bath in the Ganges, the water spirit touched her body and impregnated her, thus she gave birth to four sons who later grew up to be kings reigning over Jambudvīpa. Each of them demarcated his national boundaries and had cities and villages constructed. This city was the capital of one of the sons' countries. Dozens of *yojanas* away from the southern boundary of the country, there was a huge mountain forest, sepulchral and dense, stretching for more than two hundred *li.* There were a large number of wild elephants living there, with hundreds in each herd. Therefore, both Iraṇaparvata and Campā had the largest elephant troops. Frequently elephant trainers were sent to this forest to catch elephants and tame them for transportation and heavy labor. Since the forest was replete with jackals, rhinoceroses, and black leopards, nobody dared to travel in it.

According to a legend, a long time ago, before the birth of the Buddha, there was a cowherd. He often drove several hundred cows and bulls into the forest. One of the cows frequently left for some place unknown to anyone, but came back at the nightfall. What's more, every time the cow came back, it was enveloped in an aura, looking high in spirits. When it mooed, its voice is particularly loud and clear, which made other cows feel awed and dare not walk in front of it. This situation happened repeatedly for several days. Out of curiosity, the cowherd waited for a chance to trace the cow. One day, after feeding on the grass for a while, the cow went away again, and the cowherd followed it quietly. The cow entered a hole in a rock, so did he. After four or five *li,* the cowherd suddenly came into the full glare of an open space. Under the dazzling light, he saw that woods and fields were full of bizarre flowers and fruits, which was a scene not seen in the secular world. Then he saw the cow gorging on the grass so fragrant and moist that could not be seen in the mortal world. Looking up, the man saw trees bearing the golden fruits, sweet-smelling and large, from which he picked one off. Although he liked the fruit so much, he dared not eat it. After a while, the man followed the cow and was about to go out through the rock; however, the moment the man stuck out his foot, a demon suddenly appeared and seized the fruit away, not allowed him to take it out. Later, after the cowherd came back, he told a famous doctor the appearance of the fruit and asked him what it was. The doctor told him that the fruit was inedible, but suggested he bring one out next time. On the following day, once again he entered the hole with the cow. Then, he picked a fruit and hid it inside his cloth, intending to carry it back secretly. When the demon found it, it managed to snatch the fruit by force. In a hurry, the man put the fruit into his mouth, so the demon grabbed his throat, which made the man accidentally swallow the fruit. No sooner than the fruit went down into his stomach, the man's body became bigger and bigger. His head had already come out of the hole but his body was stuck inside, so he could not go back home. Later, his family came here to look for him, and when they saw him deformed, they fell into a panic. The herdsman, however, was still able to speak at that time, so he told them what had happened to him. Quickly his family returned home and gathered many more strong men. Together, they tried to drag him out but could not move him even a little. Having heard of the story, the king came to see the man in person. To avoid future trouble, the king ordered more people to dig and drag him out, but their efforts were also in vain. Over time, the man was the man was gradually changed into a stone, but still in the shape of a human body. Finally, when another king perceived that the human-shape stone had been formed because of the immortal fruit taken by a man, he spoke to his attending ministers, "Since the man has been transformed by the effect of the drug, his body itself must be drugs. Although looks like a stone, the body indeed is the divine thing.

So why not send some men there to hammer and chisel some stone pieces off?" Then, under the king's command, the minister went there with many craftsmen. But, having vigorously chiseled and hammered for ten days, they still failed to get a single piece. The rocky figure was existing now.

From here going westward for more than four hundred *li*, the Master arrived in the country of Kajuṅghira[2] (in the domain of Central India) to worship the holy sites. There were six or seven monasteries with more than three hundred monks. Crossing the Ganges to the east of Kajuṅghira, and proceeding for over six hundred *li*, he reached the country of Puṇḍravardhana [3](in the domain of South India) to seek and worship holy sites. There were more than twenty monasteries with over three thousand monks who studied both Mahāyāna and Hīnayāna teachings. More than twenty *li* to the west of the city, there was a monastery and seven hundred monks were living here in grand terraces and pavilions. Beside it was a stūpa, built by King Aśoka on the spot where the Tathāgata had formerly preached the Dharma for three months. A bright light was frequently emanated from the stūpa. There were also the traces left by the four Past Buddhas when they did the walking meditation, close to which was a monastery enshrining an image of Bodhisattva Avalokiteśvara. And if one prayed to this image with the utmost sincerity, all his wishes would be fulfilled.

From here going to the southeast for more than nine hundred *li,* the Master came to the country of Karṇasuvarṇa[4] (within the domain of East India). There were about a dozen monasteries with over three hundred monks, all of whom were the adherents of the Hīnayāna Saṃmitīya school[5]. There were also three other monasteries where the monks were not allowed to drink milk or yogurt, a tradition subject to the bequeathed teachings of Devadatta. By the side of the great city, there was a monastery named Raktamṛttikā (meaning "red mud"). In the past, before the introduction of Buddhism into this country, a *Śramaṇa* from South India once travelled here and refuted the perverse views of a heretic who usually wore a metal sheet over his belly[6], and subdued him. In order to commemorate this event, the king had this monastery constructed. Nearby, there was a stūpa built by King Aśoka on the spot where the Buddha had preached the Dharma for seven days.

From here to the southeast, the Master reached the country of Samataṭa[7](in the domain of East India), bordering on the sea, with harmonious and pleasant climate. There were more than thirty monasteries inhabited by over two thousand monks, studying the doctrines of the Sthavira school. There were variegated heretical worshipers. And Deva temples also large in number. Not far away from the city was a stūpa built by King Aśoka on the spot where the Buddha had preached the Dharma to beings in both celestial and earthly realms for seven days. Not far from here, there was another monastery enshrining a blue jade statue of Buddha, eight *chi* high, with refined features and majestic countenance, which frequently expired the natural fragrance to permeate the courtyard and often issued forth the auspicious light of five colors, soaring up high and illumining the sky. Without exception, people who heard about or witnessed those miraculous signs would develop the aspiration for seeking the Bodhi way.

Again, to the northeast, there was the country of Śrīkṣetra[8] in a valley by the seaside; again, to the southeast, there was the country of Kāmalāṇkā[9] by the bay; again, to the east, there was the country of Dvārapatī[10]; again, to the east, there was the country of Īraṇapura[11]; further to the east, there was the country of Mahācampā[12] (meaning "city of woods"); and then to the west, there was the country of Yamanadvīpa[13]. All the six countries mentioned above were either hidden in deep mountains or separated by vast seas. Although the Master had not entered the domains of them, he was well-informed about their ethos and mores.

From Samataṭa proceeding to the west for nine hundred *li*, he reached the country of Tāmralipti[14] (in the domain of East India), which was near the sea. There were about a dozen monasteries with over one thousand monks. By the side of the city was a stūpa built by King Aśoka, more than two hundred *chi* in height, beside it were the traces left by the four Past Buddhas when they formerly did walking meditation.

At the time, the Master heard that in the sea, there was a country called Siṃhala[15] (meaning "lion catcher") which had scholars well-versed in the Tripiṭaka of the Sthavira school and the *Yogācārabhūmi Śāstra*, and that to get there, one had to sail in the sea for about seven hundred *yojanas*. When the Master was to take his voyage to that country, he met a monk from South India who suggested him by saying, "There are too many calamities caused by Yakṣas, tempests or angry billows in the sea, and it seems not practical to go to the Lion Catcher kingdom by sea. So, why not start off from the southeast cape of South India and spend three days by water to get there? Although you still must scale mountains and cross rivers, you needn't face other dangers. And on the way, you could also visit holy sites in Uḍra[16] and other countries."

Following his advice, the Master then left for Uḍra (in the domain of East India) in the southwest. There were more than one hundred monasteries with over ten thousand monks who studied the Mahāyāna teachings. Also, there were Deva temples and heretical worshipers of various kinds. Indeed, the orthodox and the heterodox were living in juxtapositions. There were about a dozen stūpas, all of which were constructed by King Aśoka, showing the divine signs from time to time. Bordering on the sea in the southeast of the country was the city of Caritra[17] (meaning "start going"), which was a stopover for the travelers from the distant places. The city was situated twenty thousand *li* away from the country of Siṃhala. The lights rays were issued forth from the precious gem and pearls atop a Buddha-teeth relic stūpa inside the city, dazzling like the stars and candles in the sky. In quiet and cloudless nights, it could be seen from far off.

To the southwest, proceeding in a great forest for more than one thousand and two hundred *li*, the Master reached the country of Koṅgoda[18](East India). Farther to the southwest, walking in a great desolate forest for fourteen hundred or fifteen hundred *li,* he came to the country of Kaliṅga[19] (in the domain of South India). There were about a dozen monasteries with more than five hundred monks who studied the dharma of the Sthavira school. Previously, the country was densely populated, but one day, an immortal of five supernatural powers[20] came here, and for some reason, he felt offended and angrily cast an evil spell to kill all the local people, including both the young and old. Later on, people from other places gradually moved here, but nevertheless it was still sparsely inhabited.

From here proceeding to the northwest for more than one thousand and eight hundred *li*, he came to the country of South Kosala[21] (in the domain of Central India). The king was a Kṣatriya by caste, holding Buddhism in veneration and valuing scholarships. There were one hundred monasteries with ten thousand monks. Variegated heretics and Deva temples were also densely distributed. Not far from the city was an ancient monastery; nearby, there was a stūpa built by King Aśoka on the spot where the Tathāgata displayed his great divine power to subdue the heretics in the past. Nāgārjuna Bodhisattva, later, resided in this monastery. At the time, the King named Śātavāha (meaning "right guidance"), out of the veneration, made abundant offerings to Nāgārjuna and protected him cautiously. Formerly, Deva Bodhisattva came here from the country of Lion Catcher to launch a discussion and debate with Nāgārjuna, at the residence of Nāgārjuna, he asked the gate keeper to announce the guest, and the gate keeper did it for him. Having long heard of the guest's name, Nāgārjuna filled a bowl with water and asked his disciple to take it out to Deva. Deva simply threw a needle into the bowl without saying anything, which the disciple carried back to Nāgārjuna. On seeing it, Nāgārjuna was greatly pleased and extolled, "The bowl of water is analogized to my virtue, into which he threw a needle, implying he was capable of exhausting my knowledge. It is worthwhile to discuss profound teachings and the Way with such a man. Obviously, he is the right man to whom I will transmit my lamp of wisdom." Thus, he asked his disciple to usher Deva in. Having taken the seats, they exchanged remarks to and fro. Both were ecstatic about this encounter just as the fish found the water. Nāgārjuna said, "I am senile, so it is in your hands, not mine, that the duty rests to glorify the Sun of wisdom." Rising from his seat, Deva prostrated himself before the feet of Nāgārjuna and said, "Although I am not intelligent, I still venture to follow your kind indoctrination." In this country, there was a brāhmaṇa who was adept at Hetuvidyā[22], so the Master remained with him to study the *Samuccayapramāṇa Śāstra* for a few months.

From here proceeding southeast in a great forest in the south of this country for more than nine hundred *li*, the Master reached Andhra[23] (in the domain of South India). By the capital city was a large monastery, loftily constructed and decorated with beautiful engravings, looking solemnly splendid. In front of it, there was a stūpa, several hundred *chi* in height, built by Arhat Ācāra (meaning "action"). There was a solitary hill in the southwest, more than twenty *li* away from this Arhat's monastery. In the hill was another stūpa, built at the place where Dignāga (meaning "bestowing") Bodhisattva[24] once composed the *Hetuvidyā* .

From here going southward for more than one thousand *li*, the Master arrived in the country of Dhānakaṭaka[25](in the domain of South India). In the hill, there was Pūrvaśaila (meaning "eastern hill") Monastery to the east of the city, and to the west was Avaraśaila (meaning "western hill") Monastery, both of which were built for the Buddha by the king of this country in the ancient times. In the picturesque scenery of woods and springs, the monasteries exceeded other imposing mansions in architectural styles. They were also under the protection of the deities, and visited or inhabited by the saints and the worthy men. Within a thousand years after the Buddha's Nirvāṇa, every year one thousand ordinary monks gathered here to take a summer retreat, and when the retreat was concluded, all of them attained Arhartship and flew away in the air. After the first thousand years, commoners as well as saints began to live here. Over the past one hundred years or so, the spirits of mountain had changed their temperament and disturbed the travelers too often; for this reason, no one dared to come here again. Thereafter, the two monasteries were deserted and became desolate, empty of monks. Not far from the city in the south, there was a high rocky mountain, where Śāstrin[26] Bhāvaviveka (meaning "clear discernment") lived in Asura's [27] palace waiting for the Bodhisattva Maitreya's attainment of Buddhahood; at that time, he would consult the Bodhisattva to solve his doubts.

The Master met two monks in this country, one named Subhūti, the other Sūrya, and both were well-versed in the Tripiṭaka of the Mahāsāṃghika school. Thus, the Master had stayed with them for several months to study the *Mūlābhidharma Śāstra* and other treatises, and they, in turn, learned various treatises of Mahāyāna school from the Master. Thereafter, sharing a common goal, they went on a pilgrimage to various holy places.

From here going westward for more than one thousand *li*, the Master reached the country of Colya[28](in the domain of South India). To the southeast of the capital city was a stūpa built by King Aśoka at the place where the Buddha formerly displayed his miraculous power to subdue heretics and preached the Dharma to awaken the celestial and human beings. To the west of the city was an ancient monastery, where Deva Bodhisattva once made a discussion with the

Arhat Uttara (meaning "upper") of this monastery. After the seventh round of the disputation, the Arhat could not answer the question set forth by Deva Bodhisattva, so by employing his miraculous displays secretly, he went to the Tuṣita Palace to consult Bodhisattva Maitreya. Bodhisattva Maitreya answered the question for him but said, "That Deva has been cultivating his merit for a long time and will attain Buddhahood of Proper and Equal Enlightenment in the Bhadrakalpa. You shouldn't belittle him." When Arhat Uttara returned, he answered the question previously asked by Deva Bodhisattva. Deva said, "The answer is obviously the view of Bodhisattva Maitreya, not one arises from your own wisdom." This was the place where after hearing those words the Arhat felt ashamed and rose from his seat to apologize to Deva Bodhisattva in sincerity.

From here going southward through a big forest for fifteen or sixteen hundred *li*, the Master reached the country of Draviḍa[29] (in the domain of South India). The capital of the country was called Kāñcīpura[30], the birthplace of Dharmapāla (meaning "dharma protector") Bodhisattva. As a son of a minister of this country, Dharmapāla was perspicacious when he was young. After he reached the age of twenty, the king appreciated his talents and wished to marry the princess to him. Having practiced long-term celibacy, Dharmapāla had already been relieved from attachment to desires. He felt greatly annoyed on the evening of his wedding, so he prayed before a Buddha image for protection, hoping to escape from such a trouble. Because of his utmost sincerity, a great deity appeared, carried him out of the city, and settled him into a buddha hall at a mountainous monastery about several hundred *li* away. He, however, was mistaken as a thief by the monks of the monastery. Then Dharmapāla explained to them. Upon hearing it, all hearers were amazed and could not help extolling his purity. Thus, he renounced his home and became a monk ever since. He was wholeheartedly devoted to the study of the Right Dharma, and consequently, he was able to master the convictions of various schools, especially good at writing treatises. He composed the *Śabdavidyāsaṃyukta Śāstra* in twenty-five thousand stanzas, and wrote several dozens of wide-circulation treatises to expound the *Śataśāstravaipuly*, the *Vijñaptimātratāsiddhi Śāstra,* and the *Hetuvidyā*. His noble virtues and great talents were related in a separate biography.

The city of Kāñcīpura was a seaport in South India, and from here, it took three days to travel to the country of Siṃhala along the sea route. Before the Master set out on his voyage, the king of Siṃhala had passed away, a famine broke out and thus social turmoil had arisen. At the time, the great virtuous monks of Siṃhala, including Bodhimegheśvara (meaning "residing in cloud of enlightenment"), Abhayadaṃṣṭra (meaning "fearless tooth"), together with more than three hundred others, arrived at the city of Kāñcīpura on their way to India. On meeting them, the Master asked, "I have heard that your country has great virtuous monks who have an intimate knowledge of the Tripiṭaka of the Sthavira school as well as the *Yogācārabhūmi Śāstra,* so I've planned to go to your country to further my study, but why have you teachers come here?" To reply, the monks said, "A famine eventuated with the demise of our king, and there is no one to rely on. We have come here because we have heard that Jambudvīpa continent is happy, peaceful, and abundant in food, and that as the birthplace of the Buddha, there are many holy traces of His presence. Regarding the knowledge of Dharma, we are unsurpassable in our country. If you entertain any doubts, you might ask us as you please." The Master cited some key passages of the *Yogācārabhūmi Śāstra* to inquire their explanation, but their explanations were no better than those by Ven. Śilabhadra.

It was said that there was a country called Malakūta[31](in the domain of North India) more than three thousand *li* away from the boundary of Draviḍa. And located by the seaside, it boasted of rare pearls and wondrous precious jewels. To the east of the capital city was a stūpa built by King Aśoka at the place where the Buddha once enlightened countless people by preaching the Dharma and displaying great supernatural powers. In the south of the country, there was the Mount Malaya by the sea, where there were deep ravines and high crags, with sandal trees and serpent sandal trees growing among them. A serpent sandal tree resembled a white sandal tree, but only because the wood nature of the former was cold, snakes usually coiled up in it before entering hibernation in winter, thus different from the latter. Also, there were fragrant Karpūra trees whose trunks looked like those of pine trees except that their leaves were different, so were flowers and fruits. When the wood was sappy, it didn't smell fragrant. However, after it was cut down and dried up, when broken, it would exude a scented white substance that looked like mica, which was what we called dragon-brain scent (camphor).

Also, the Master heard that in the northeast by the seaside there was a city, from which three thousand *li* in the southeast, there was the country of Siṃhala[32] (meaning "lion Catcher," not in the domain of India.), more than seven thousand *li* in perimeter. The perimeter of its capital city was more than forty *li.* The capital city was densely populated with cereals growing abundantly. The local people were stocky, swarthy, irascible, and impetuous. That was the general condition of this country. As an island of gems, the country produced a large amount of precious and rare things. Once upon a time there was a girl of North India who was sent to her marriage to a neighboring country, but on the road, she encountered a lion-king. In panic, the people who escorted her run away and left the girl alone in the carriage. The lion came over to see her, carried her on the back and went into the deep mountains. Afterwards, the lion hunted animals and gathered fruits to support her. As time passed by, she bore a son and a daughter, who looked like humans but had cruel and ferocious temperament. Gradually, the boy grew up.

Once he asked his mother, "What kind of creature am I, with an animal father and a human mother?"

Then the mother told him what had happened in the past. The son said, "Now that the human and the beast are of different creatures, why do not you leave the lion?"

The mother said, "It's not because I don't want to, but because I can't find a way to escape."

Thereafter, in order to make an investigation of the lion's route, the son often followed his father to climb the hill and cross the valley. One day, when he saw his father had gone far, he led his mother and younger sister down the hill to take a shelter in a village. Later, he, with his mother and sister, returned to his mother's homeland to look for the maternal uncle, but found there was none left in the blood lineage. They then settled down in the village. When the Lion-king returned and could not find its wife and children, it went out of the mountains in a fury, roared into villages and killed many passing-by men and women on the road. After the king of the country heard the report, he commanded his four armies[33] and many carefully-selected valiant men. One day they besieged the lion and attempted to shoot it with arrows; however, on seeing them, the lion bellowed even more furiously, paralyzing soldiers and horses to the ground, thus no one dared to draw near to it. Such situation had lasted for several days, and the king got nowhere with the lion. Then the king posted a public notice to the effect that anyone if he could slay the lion would be rewarded one billion gold coins.

The lion's son said to his mother, "It is hard for me to bear the coldness and hunger, so I want to answer the king's call. What's your opinion?"

The mother dissuaded him by saying,"You must not do so. Although it is an animal, it is still your father. If you kill it, how could you be called a human being?"

The son replied, "If I don't kill it, it will not leave, and maybe one day it will come to our village to look for us. Once the king knows the truth, he will have us executed, if that happened, the lion also would not be spared. Why so? Just because it is you and me who made the lion savage. How could we bring a great trouble to many people only to save one life? I have thought it over carefully, I might as well go to answer the call."

When the son went up to the lion, the lion became gentle. Upon seeing him, it bent over in gladness, bearing no mind of slight malice and harm. The son slit its throat and disemboweled it with a sharp knife. Although the son afflicted such a great pain on the lion, for bearing the deep affection and tender feelings, it showed the remarkable endurance without moving, and thus died. The king was delighted and amazed at the news, so he inquired of the son about the reason. At first, the son refused to tell the truth. After being interrogated insistently, he had to relate the story. The king exclaimed, "Alas! If not be an offspring of a beast, how could you have such a cold heart! As we have promised to give you a reward, we are not to break my words, but you killed your father, we can't permit you, such an unfilial and rebellious son, to live in our country." Therefore, he ordered the official in charge to give the family a large amount of gold and gems, and drive them to the wild. So, boarding two ships laden with gold and provisions, they were sent into the sea. From then on, they were drifting aimlessly. Later, the son's ship sailed to this Island of Gems, for seeing the island was full of precious and rare substances, he settled down here. Afterwards when some merchants with their families arrived at the island on the way to and back from seeking the valuables, the son killed the merchants but kept their women, left descendants for numerous generations. Since the population gradually multiplied, the monarchical state was established. Because the country's ancestor once caught and killed a lion, hence the name of the country—Lion Catcher. The daughter's ship floated to a place west to the country of Pārasī. The daughter was caught by a devil and hereafter gave birth to a large number of daughters, who later founded the West Great Women's Country. Indeed, another tradition goes that Siṃhala[34]was the name of a merchant's son. A man of quick wits, he escaped from the murder of Rākṣasis[35] and later became the king of a country. He came to this Island of Gems and killed all the Rākṣasis and established the capital here, hence the city was named after him. The narration of this story was in the *Record of the Western Regions*.

Originally the Buddha's teachings had not been available to this country. During the first one hundred years after the Nirvāṇa of the Tathāgata, Mahendra, the younger brother of King Aśoka, who abhorred and renounced the desires and affections, attained the four stages of sainthood of a *Śramaṇa*[36] successively. Then displaying various miraculous powers, he travelled to and fro this country in the air to reveal and advocate the Buddha's teachings, thus winning the people's veneration and faith. Consequently, monasteries had been constructed, and now there were more than one hundred monasteries, housing ten thousand monks following the teachings of both Mahāyāna and Sthavira schools. The monks at the monasteries were solemn, well-disciplined, and intelligent. They encouraged and admonished each other not to be sluggish. Next to the king's palace was a Buddha-tooth monastery several hundred *chi* high, which was adorned with variegated jewels, especially with a big Padmarāga ruby set on the spire of an ornamental post of the roof. At quite nights, when it was clear of cloud, the bright light of the ruby could be seen even ten thousand *li* away.

Nearby there was another monastery that was also adorned with an assortment of precious jewels. Within the monastery was a gold Buddha statue made by the former king of this country, and on the topknot of statue was a precious pearl that was priceless. Once upon a time, a thief wanted to steal the pearl but found the monastery was guarded so firmly that he could not enter it, so he dug a tunnel underground and went through it into the hall where the pearl was preserved. With every attempt of the thief to reach the pearl, the statue rose higher and higher on its own. Finally, he gave up his attempt and signed, saying, "Formerly when the Tathāgata was practicing the Bodhisattva Way for the sake of the sentient beings, he never begrudged his body and life, let alone his kingdom and property. Why does he become so stingy today? In view of this, I'm afraid what was said of him might not be true." Hearing those words, the statue stooped down to give him the pearl. Having got the pearl, the thief went out of the monastery to sell it. A man who recognized the pearl caught hold of the thief and sent him to the king. When interrogated about where he had got the pearl, the thief answered, "It is the Buddha who gave it to me," and then told the king the story. So, the king went to the monastery himself, and saw that the head of the statue was truly bending lower than before. On seeing this miraculous sign, the king developed a deep faith in the Buddha. He redeemed the pearl from the man with various precious jewels and set it back on the topknot of the statue, which was existing now.

In the southeast corner of the country, there was Mount Laṇkā that was inhabited by hosts of devils and deities. At a former time, the Tathāgata preached the *Laṇkāvatāra Sūtra* (in olden times known as Lengqie by mistake) in the mountains. Several thousand *li* over the sea to the south of this country was an island country called Nārikeladvīpa[37]. Its people were of short and small stature, more than three *chi* tall, having human bodies but bird beaks. They didn't till the fields, instead, lived on coconuts. For the country was separated by the rough sea, it was impossible for the Master to reach it; then, he inquired of other people about the country's situation and got the foregoing account.

From Draviḍa, the Master and more than seventy monks from the country of Siṃhala returned to the northwest to visit and worship other holy sites. Going for two thousand odd *li*, they reached the country of Koṅkaṇapura[38] (in the domain of South India). There were more than one hundred monasteries with over ten thousand monks, who studied both Mahāyāna and Hīnayāna teachings. Deva temples and heretics were also large in number. Beside the palace city was a great monastery holding more than three hundred monks of erudition and literacy. Within the monastery, a precious crown of Prince Sarvasiddhārtha (in olden times known as Prince Xida by mistake) was enshrined, which less than two *chi* high, was kept in a valuable casket. On festival days, it was exhibited on a high altar, and would send forth the miraculous light to those people who prayed with utmost sincerity. Beside the city was a monastery, at which there was a shrine hall preserving a statue of Bodhisattva Maitreya, which was carved from a piece of sandalwood, more than ten *chi* high. This was a statue made by Arhat Śrotakoṭīviṃśa, and it also frequently gave out auspicious light. To the south of the city were the woods of Tāla trees, more than thirty *li* in perimeter. The leaves of the trees were long and glossy, thus, traditionally used as a valuable material for people to write on in neighboring countries.

From here proceeding to the northwest through a large forest and across a wildness haunted by violent beasts, after about twenty-four or twenty-five hundred *li,* the Master came to the country of Mahārāṣṭra[39] (in the domain of South India). It was the ethos of this country that the life was undervalued but the moral integrity honored. The king was of the Kshatriya caste. He favored martial arts and was very belligerent. Therefore, military forces of his country were well-equipped and highly disciplined. If a general was defeated in a war, instead of being punished by military law, he would be humiliated by being given a suit of woman's costume to wear. Feeling ashamed, usually the defeated general would commit the suicide. The king himself commanded several thousand brave warriors as well as several hundred violent elephants. Every time on the battlefield, before the actual conflict, he would give the elephants alcohol to drink until they fell into the state of half-intoxication, then he would brandish the commanding flag to impel them to charge vigorously. Under such a brutal assault, undoubtedly, the enemy would be badly defeated. For this reason, the king was very haughty, holding the neighboring countries in contempt. Even King Śilāditya, a man who was confident in his own resourcefulness, farsighted wisdom and strong military forces, was unable to subjugate it when he went on punitive expeditions in person for several times. In Mahārāṣṭra, there were more than one hundred monasteries with over five thousand monks, who studied both Mahāyāna and Hīnayāna teachings. Besides, there were Deva temples as well as heretics who smeared ashes all over their bodies. Inside and outside the capital city were five stūpas in total, each about several hundred *chi* in height, and all built by King Aśoka on the traces left by the four Past Buddhas when they were travelling here.

From here going to the northwest for over one thousand *li,* after crossing the Narmadā River[40], the Master reached the country of Bharukacchapa[41] (in the domain of South India). Then moving on more than two thousand *li,* he came to Mālava[42] (the Southern Lāṭa country, in the domain of South India), a country of the genteel custom, and the people here had a preference for the arts. Among the five realms of India[43], only Mālava in the southwest and Magadha in the northeast could be said to have peoples who loved scholarships and venerated the worthy men, and who were eloquent and gracious. There were more than one hundred monasteries with over twenty thousand monks studying the Hīnayāna teachings of the Saṃmitīya School. Also, there were some heretics who smeared ashes all over bodies and some others who worshiped the Devás.

It was said that, sixty years ago, there was a king named Śilāditya, who was talented, erudite, benevolent, and benign. He not only loved and well-nurtured his people but also venerated the Triple Gem. From his enthronement to demise, he never spoke a harsh word nor put on an angry face; he never hurt the feelings of either his ministers or commoners, and never injured the bodies of mosquitoes or ants. In fear of harming the aquatic insects and microbes, he always had the water filtered before giving it to elephants and horses to drink. Because he prevented his people from killing, during his reign, beasts were friendly to people, even jackals and wolves quenched their venomous minds. Within his country, people enjoyed the peace and auspicious signs appeared frequently. He also had monasteries constructed, magnificently beyond imagination, where the statues of seven Buddhas[44] were enshrined and the great assemblies of charity regularly held. During his reign of more than fifty years, such meritorious undertakings had never been canceled even for a moment. Up to now, there was still a nostalgic memory among the people about his time. At a distance over twenty *li* away from the capital city, there was a pitfall beside a Brāhmaṇa village, where an overweening brāhmaṇa fell into the hell alive as the punishment for his slanders of Mahāyāna teachings. The narration of this story was in the *Record of the Western Regions*.

From here going to the northwest for twenty-four or twenty-five hundred *li,* the Master reached the country of Aṭali[45] (in the domain of South India), producing the pepper trees whose leaves were resembling those of the pepper trees grown in the region of Shu[46] in China, as well as the olibanum trees whose leaves resembling those of the birch-leaf pear trees in China.

From here going to the northwest for three days, he reached the country of Kheḍa[47] (in the domain of South India). From here going northward for more than one thousand *li*, he came to the country of Valabhi[48] (in the domain of South India), where there were more than one hundred monasteries with over six thousand monks who studied the Hīnayāna teachings of the Saṃmitīya School. When the Tathāgata was alive, he frequented this country. Memorials were established by King Aśoka at every place the Buddha visited. Now the king was of the Kṣatriya caste, named Dhruvabhaṭa (known as Dizhou, meaning "eternal lord"), who was the son-in-law of King Śilāditya of the country of Kanyākubja. The king was irascible, with a careless and impetuous disposition, but he recognized moral principles, valued scholarships, and believed in the Triple Gem. Every year, he convened a seven-day charity assembly to offer the monks of various countries with necessities, including the foods of high taste, precious objects, bedding, garments, even medicine and the sorts.

From here going to the northwest for more than seven hundred *li*, the Master reached the country of Ānandapura[49] (in the domain of West India); and farther going to the northwest for more than five hundred *li*, he came to the country of Suraṭha[50] (in the domain of West India) . From here proceeding to the northeast for eighteen hundred *li*, he reached the country of Gūrjara[51], and again going to the southeast for twenty-eight hundred *li*, he came to the country of Ujjayanī[52] (in the domain of South India). Not far from its capital city, there was a stūpa, built at the place where King Aśoka made a replica hell. From here going northeast for more than one thousand *li*, he reached the country of Jajhoti[53](in the domain of South India); and from here farther going to the northeast for more than nine hundred *li*, he came to the country of Maheśavarapura[54] (in the domain of Central India); then, going to the west from here, the Master returned to the country of Surāṣṭra. From this country travelling again to the west, he arrived in the country of Audumbatira[55] (in the domain of West India). At a former time, when the Tathāgata was living, he often visited this place. King Aśoka had stūpas constructed at all those holy sites, which were still in existence.

From here going westward for more than two thousand *li*, the Master reached the country of Laṅgala[56] (in the domain of West India) near the sea, which was the passage to the West Women's Country. From here to the southwest was the country of Pārsa[57], out of the domain of India. The Master heard that pearls, gems, brocade, fine linen, wheel horses and camels were abundantly produced in this country, and that there were two or three monasteries with several hundred monks following the Hīnayāna teachings of the Sarvāstivādah school. The alms bowl of Śākyamuni Buddha was enshrined in the royal palace. The city of Ormus[58] was located at the eastern frontier of the country which was bordered on the country of Hrom[59] in the northwest. An island to the southwest of it was West Women's Country, whose regular settlers there were exclusively all women. It produced rare and precious objects. Since it was affiliated to the country of Hrom, every year the king of the latter would dispatch some men to the island to mate with the women there. But it was a custom that if a boy was born, it would not be brought up.

From Laṅgala traveling to the northeast for more than seven hundred *li*, the Master reached the country of Pāṭāsila[60](in the domain of West India), where there was a stūpa built by King Aśoka, as high as several hundred *chi*. The relics enshrined in the stūpa often emitted the light. It was the very place where in former times, the Tathāgata, being a Ṛṣi (hermit), was killed by a king.

From here going to the northeast for more than three hundred *li,* the Master reached the country of Avaṇḍa[61](in the domain of West India). There was an old base of a monastery in the big woods to the northeast of the capital city, where in the past, the Buddha permitted Bhikṣus to wear *hanfuji* footgear (meaning "boots"). Also, there was a stūpa built by King Aśoka. Beside the stūpa, there was a Vihāra enshrining a standing Buddha statue made of blue stone, which frequently issued forth the bright light. Again, more than eight hundred paces southward from here in the big woods, there was another stūpa built by King Aśoka at the very place where in the past, when the Tathāgata stayed here for a cold night, he covered himself with three layers of clothes, and in the following morning he permitted his Bhikṣus to put on the double garments.

From here again going eastward for more than seven hundred *li*, he came to the country of Indus[62] (in the domain of West India), which abounded in silver, gold, brass, cows, sheep, camels, red salt, white salt, black salt, and so forth. The salt was often taken away as the medicine by humans from other places. When the Tathāgata was living, he traveled in this country for several times. At all those holy sites, King Aśoka had the stūpas constructed as commemoration. There were also the traces left by the great Arhat Upagupta when he was traveling around to edify the people.

From here proceeding eastward for over nine hundred *li*, the Master ferried over a river to its east bank and reached the country of Mūlasthānapura[63] (in the domain of West India). There was a tradition to worship Devás, so a Deva temple had been magnificently constructed, enshrining a statue of Sun God wrought in gold and adorned with a variety of jewelries. The peoples of neighboring countries often came here to pray for blessing. Within this temple, gardens, woods, springs, and ponds were linked by brick stairways. All visitors appreciated and praised the scenery.

From here proceeding northwest for more than seven hundred *li*, he reached the country of Parvata[64] (in the domain of North India). Beside the capital city was a great monastery with over one hundred monks, all of whom studied the Mahāyāna teachings. This was the place where Śāstrin Jinaputra (meaning "victorious son") composed the *Yogācārabhūmi Śāstra Kārikā,* and it was also the place where Śāstrin Bhadraruci and Guṇaprabha renounced home to become monks. There were two or three great virtuous teachers, under whom one could pursue abstruse knowledge, and so the Master had stayed with them for two years to study the *Mūlābhidharma Śāstra*, the *Saddharmasaṃparigraha Śāstra,* the *Satyaśāsana Śāstra* and others of the Saṃmitīya school.

From here going southeast again, the Master returned to Nālandā Mahāvihāra in Magadha. After he paid his visit to Right Dharma Store, he heard that there was a Tiladhāka Monastery in the west three *yojanas* away from Nālandā, where there was a virtuous monk named Prajñābhadra, a native of the country of Balapati, who, being a monk of the Sarvāstivāda school, was well-versed not only in the Tripiṭaka of his own school but also in Śabdavidyā and Hetuvidyā. Then the Master went to study with him for two months until all his doubts were eliminated.

Then the Master left for Zhanglin[65] Mountains where Śāstrin Jayasena, an upāsaka[66], lived. He was a native of Surāṣṭra, and was of the Kṣatriya caste. When he was a child, he loved learning, and he studied the Hetuvidyā first with the Śāstrin Bhadraruci, then he studied Śabdavidyā and the treatises of both Mahāyāna and Hīnayāna schools from Sthiramati Bodhisattva. What's more, he studied the *Yogācārabhūmi Śāstra* with the dharma teacher Śilabhadra. As regards the non-Buddhist books, such as the Four Vedas[67], astronomy, geography, medication, divination, he not only had a thorough knowledge of their fundamental convictions, but was acquainted with their branch subjects. Since the Śāstrin was conversant in both

Buddhist and non-Buddhist teachings, and was a man of high virtue, he was venerated by the people at the time. The king of Magadha was Pūrṇavarman, who esteemed saints and respected scholars. Having heard the prestige of Jayasena, he was quite delighted, and so he sent messengers to invite the Śāstrin to be his National Teacher, and promised to confer upon him twenty large villages as the fief. But the king's invitation was declined by him. After the demise of Pūrṇavarman, King Śilāditya also invited Śāstrin Jayasena to be the National Teacher, conferring eighty villages in the country of Uḍra as fief to him, which was again refused by the Śāstrin. King Śilāditya persistently offered his invitations, which the Śāstrin declined again and again. At last, the Śāstrin said to the king, "I, Jayasena, have heard that if a man receives the present from someone, he should bend to do anything as the repayment. Now it is urgent for me to solve the matter of birth and death, so how could I spare time to attend to your state affairs?" With those words, he bowed to the king and left. The king could not retain him. From then on, he taught the Buddhist scriptures to disciples in Zhanglin Mountains. Adherents of him, both monks and laity, often amounted to several hundred and even more. The Master stayed with the Śāstrin for two thorough years, learning the *Vijñānamātraparikalpana Śāstra*, the *Manasabhidheyatā Śāstra*, the *Abhayasiddhi Śāstra,* the *Asaṃgamanirvāṇa Śāstra*, the *Dvādaśāṅgapratītyasamutpāda Śāstra*, and the *Sūtrālaṃkāra Śāstra*. Besides, by consulting with him, the Master also resolved his doubts in the *Yogācārabhūmi Śāstra,* the *Hetuvidyā* and other texts.

One night the Master had a dream. In the dream, the houses and courtyards of Nālandā Mahāvihāra were desolate and declined, with no monks but buffaloes fastened in yards. He entered the monastery through the west door of King Bālāditya Court and saw a golden figure on the fourth ground of the mansion, with proper and solemn features, issuing a bright light illuminating the whole room. The Master could not suppress his great pleasure, and decided to ascend the building, but he could not find the way. So, he besought the golden figure to give him a hand. The figure said, "I'm Bodhisattva Mañjuśri. You could not come up to me for you have karmic hindrances." Pointing outside of the monastery, he said, "Look there!" The Master turned to the direction of the finger, and saw in astonishment that the villages and towns outside the monastery had already been burned to ashes. Then the golden figure continued, "You had better go back to your country as early as possible. After ten years, King Śilāditya will pass away. A great turmoil will occur in India, and the wicked humans will engage in plots to harm each other. That is what I want you to know." Finishing those words, the golden figure disappeared. The master woke up and was greatly astonished at the dream. He told this dream to Jayasena, and the latter responded, "The Three Realms[68] have never been in peace or security. Maybe it will happen in the future. Now that you have been informed of the danger, it is high time that you made you decision." From this we know that wherever a Mahāyāna practitioner goes and whatever he does, he must be protected by bodhisattvas. Formerly, when the Master was about to go to India, the venerable Śilabhadra was required (by bodhisattvas) in a dream to keep on living for his coming, and at present, when the Master detained in India, the Bodhisattva persuaded him to go back home soon by showing the impermanence of the world. If what the

Master had done didn't fit into the holy mind of bodhisattvas, how could they be so compassionate to show such omens? By the end of the Yonghui period (650–655) of the Tang Dynasty, when Wang Xuance[69], a national envoy, went to India, he witnessed that King Śilāditya had passed away and India was suffering from a serious famine, which was just in coincidence with what had been foretold in the dream of the Master.

According to the custom of the western countries, in the first month of the year, the relics of the Buddha at Bodhi Monastery should be exhibited. Both the laypersons and monks of various countries came to attend the opening ceremony, and so did the Master and Jayasena. They saw the relic bones were of different sizes, some as large as pearls giving out red or white light; and the relics of flesh, as small as peas, were ruby and glossy. Numerous people presented incenses and flowers as offerings, and after they eulogized and worshiped the relics, the relics were put back into the stūpa. At the first watch[70] or so in the night, Jayasena discussed with the Master about the different sizes of the relics. He said, "The relics I saw in other places are as small as rice grains; why the relics today we see here are so big? Are you curious about it?"

The Master replied, "Yes. I also wonder about it."

A moment later, the lamp in the chamber suddenly was dimmed out, but the room turned bright within and without. With a surprise, they came out of the room to have a look, and saw the stūpa where the relics were preserved was setting forth the light rays of five colors up into the sky. The light was illuminating the heavens and the earth so brightly that the stars and the moon were rendered invisible. At the same time, they smelt a kind of exotic fragrance permeating all over the yard. Subsequently, the news that the relics had shown the great miraculous manifestation was spread from one person to another, which made the multitude quickly assemble again to worship the relics and extol the rarity of the case. No longer than a single meal, the light gradually became dim; before it vanished, the last beam encircled the bowl that covered the relics for several times, and finally came into it. Then the vast circle became dark again, and the constellation reappeared. Seeing the sight, all the people were relieved of the entanglement of doubts. Having spent eight days paying homage to the Bodhi tree and holy sites, the Master returned Nālandā Mahāvihāra.

At the time, Śāstrin Śilabhadra asked the Master to deliver the lectures on the *Mahāyānasaṅgraha Śāstra* and the *Vijñānamātraparikalpana Śāstra* to other monks. Previously, the virtuous teacher Siṃharaśmi had already made a discourse on the *Mūlamadhyamakakārikā,* and the *Catuḥśataka*, expounding their essential points to break the doctrines of the *Yogācārabhūmi Śāstra*. The Master has not only been acquainted with the *Mūlamadhyamakakārikā* and the *Catuḥśataka*, but also been well-versed in the *Yogācārabhūmi Śāstra*; therefore, he didn't think there were contradictions or impediments between different theories, for the saints actually had established different doctrines for particular purposes. He also believed that it was just because of one's failure to have a thorough understanding of the Buddha's teachings that one felt confused and thus said the theories contradicted with each other. Therefore, the disagreements indeed were not caused by the Dharma itself, but the adherents of Buddhism were to blame. Having a pity on Siṃharaśmi's shallow knowledge, the Master visited him only for several times; however, Siṃharaśmi always failed to answer the questions and interrogations posed by the Master. Owing to this, the disciples of Siṃharaśmi gradually dispersed and followed the Master to study.

The Master also believed that the essential doctrines of the *Mūlamadhyamakakārikā* and *Catuḥśataka* were merely aimed to refute the delusion caused by the false conception that everything was what it appeared to be[71], and he didn't think that they were intended to rebut the other two characters of dharma: everything was depending on constructive elements[72] and everything had the all-round and perfect nature[73]. But Siṃharaśmi could not gain a proper comprehension, and when he read of "nothing to be attained" in two Śāstras, he falsely held that bhūtatathatā and other theories established by the *Yogācārabhūmi Śāstra* should be discarded. Siṃharaśmi often expressed his opinion as such. On this account, the Master decided to bring two teachings comprehensively together in a harmony in order to show they were not contradictory. Thus, he composed the *Nikāyasaṃgraha Śāstra* in three thousand stanzas. After he finished the *Śāstra*, he presented it to the Ven. Śilabhadra and the other monks to read, and won the praises from all of them; henceforth the *Śāstra* was circulated and studied all around. Siṃharaśmi felt ashamed, so he left for the Bodhi Monastery, where he asked one of his fellow schoolmates in the East India, named Candrasiṃha, to come and debate with the Master in order to avenge the previous humiliation. But, when that monk arrived at the monastery, in the presence of the Master, he was awed into silence and didn't venture to say a single word. Thereafter the reputation of the Master grew much more higher.

Before Siṃharaśmi went to the Bodhi Monastery, King Śilāditya had had a brass Vihāra, more than ten *zhang* tall, built beside the Nālandā Mahāvihāra, which was well known to various countries. Later, the king went on a military expedition to the country of Koṅgoda, and on his way, he arrived at the country of Uḍra. All the monks of this country were adherents of Hīnayāna school. Having no faith in Mahāyāna teachings, they even considered it as Śūnyapuṣpa[74] heretical teachings never preached by the Buddha.

On seeing the arrival of the king, they said ironically, "We have heard that Your Majesty had built a brass Vihāra beside the Nālandā Mahāvihāra. What a great accomplishment! Why didn't Your Majesty have a Vihāra constructed at the heretical temple of Kāpālikas[75]? If so, it seems to be much reputable."

The king demanded, "What are you getting at?"

They replied, "The teachings of Nālandā Mahāvihāra, as same as those of Śūnyapuṣpa, have no differences from Kāpālikas heretical teachings."

Formerly, an old brāhmaṇa named Prajñāgupta[76], Abhisheka[77] teacher of the king of South India, who was well acquainted with the teachings of the Saṃmitīya school, had composed the *Mahāyānabheda Śāstra* in seven hundred stanzas. The book won the esteem of all Hīnayāna teachers. And they proffered this book to the king.

"What our school preaches is shown in this book. Is there any follower of Mahāyāna school who could confute a single word of it?" they challenged.

The king answered, "We, your disciple, have heard that animals, such as foxes and small mice, often boast that they are stronger than a lion; however, they are frightened out of their wits when they actually see one. For you teachers haven't met the virtuous Mahāyāna teachers before, you are obstinate with your erroneous views. When you have a chance to meet the teachers of Mahāyāna school, I'm afraid you might submit yourselves as those animals in the presence of a lion."

They said, "If Your Majesty entertains any doubt about our confidence, why don't you assembly them to have a debate with us face to face?"

The king replied, "It is not a difficult thing to do."

Then on the same day, the king dispatched a messenger to deliver a letter written by himself to the venerable Śilabhadra, Right Dharma Store, at Nālandā Mahāvihāra. The letter read as follows:

"We, your disciple, arrived at the country of Uḍra on our expedition, and met the teachers of Hīnayāna school who, sticking to shallow doctrines, had composed a treatise to slander the Mahāyāna teachings. Besides their coarse diction, the justification for their convictions is also unreasonable and harmful, but they arrogantly ventured to expect a debate with you and the other teachers. We, your disciple, know that the virtuous teachers at the monastery are extraordinarily talented and wise. You have a good mastery of whatever you have learned. So, we presumptuously granted them the permission and enjoined our messenger to inform you about this issue, expecting you to dispatch four virtuous teachers to come to our temporary residence in Uḍra to have a debate with them as they required. The four teachers are supposed to be not only conversant with the convictions of both their own school and others, but also acquainted with the Buddhist and non-Buddhist knowledge as well."

Having received the letter, Right Dharma Store convened the monks to choose the proper ones from them, as a result, Sāgaramati, Jñānaprabha, Siṃharaśmi and the Master were selected to act on the order of the king.

Seeing Sāgaramati and others were worried, the Master consoled them by saying, " I have thoroughly studied the Tripiṭaka of various Hīnayāna schools in my country and in Kaśmīra, so I have a deep understanding of their basic teachings. Obviously, it is impossible to use those theories to refute the Mahāyāna teachings. Although I'm a person of paltry wisdom and shallow knowledge, I have the confidence to settle the debate. Wish you great teachers not to worry about it. Even if we could not win over them, I, a Chinese monk, am to blame. You won't be involved in." At his words, all the other three teachers breathed again and rejoiced. But later, King Śilāditya sent another letter, in which he said, "The great virtuous teachers who were formerly invited don't have to start right away. Please wait for a later notice."

At that time, there was a heretic of Lokāyata School coming to launch a debate. He listed forty points of his argumentation on a piece of paper and put it on the door to the monastery. Then he claimed, "If one of these points is to be refuted, I will have my head cut off as an apology." Several days passed, there had been no one to come to meet the challenge. The Master then asked his monastic servant to go out to peel the poster off, tear it to pieces, and trample on them. Irritated, the brāhmaṇa asked, "Who are you?" The man answered,

"I'm a servant of Mahāyānadeva." The answer made the brāhmaṇa feel very ashamed. He had already heard the name of the Master, and felt it beneath him to argue the matter out with a servant. At this time, the Master called the brāhmaṇa in. In the presence of the venerable Śilabhadra and other virtuous monks, the Master launched a debate with him about the basic principles of the brāhmaṇa's own school as well as the convictions of other various heretical schools.

The Master argued as follows:

"Some heretics, such as Pāśupatas (Bhūta)[78], Nirgranthas[79](the non-fastened), Kāpālikas (skull-chaplets wearers), and Jūṭakas[80], are different in their appearance and costume, while others, including Sāṃkhyas[81] (formerly known as Sengqu) and the Vaiśeṣikas[82] (formerly known as Weishishi), are different in their standpoints. Bhūtas practices the spiritual cultivation by smearing ashes all over the body, and so looks deathly pale just like a wild cat sleeping in the pit. Nirgranthas behaves eccentrically to keep naked or pluck the body's hairs, smugly taking those behaviors as virtuous deeds. With chapped skin and parched feet, he looked like pieces of touch wood lying by the river. Kāpālikas makes skull-chaplets and wears them on the head or around the neck. With sunken and dried-up sockets, in scrawny form, he looks like Yakṣas[83] at tomb. Jūṭakas filthily wears in rags, eats excrement, and drinks urine, which make them fishy, foul, and stinky, like a mad pig in the sty. Having mistaken what they have done for practicing the Way, those people are stupid, aren't they?

"According to the heretical theory of the Sāṃkhyas, twenty-five true principles (*tattvāni*) have been established in the following way: the primary matter (*prakṛti*) gives rise to the great principle (*mahat*) which in turn engenders the subjectifying sense (*ahaṃkāra*[84]); the Self-consciousness, on the one hand produces the Five Subtle Elements (*tanmātraṇi*)[85], which then cause the Five Gross Elements (*mahābhūta*)[86], on the other hand, begets the Eleven Organs *(indriyāṇi)*[87]. Totally, there are twenty-four entities provided for and enjoyed by *ātman* (*puruṣa*)[88]; so, when the spirit is released from them, it will attain purity. Meanwhile the Vaiśeṣika heretics hold the theory of the Six Categories of Cognition (*padārthas*), viz., substance (*dravya*), quality (*guṇa*), action (*karma*), universal genetic property (*sāmānya*), ultimate particularity *(viśeṣa*), and inherence (*sāmāvāya*), which are possessed by the *ātman*. When *ātman* is not emancipated, it is entangled in those six predicaments; whereas when it is disintegrated from them, it attains a state called *nirvāṇa*.

"Now let me refute the theory of Sāṃkhyas. Among the twenty-five principles, as you hold, the principle of the *ātman*, is of a particular nature, while the other twenty-four principles are interrelated into one substance—the entity of primary matter, which is of the three qualities(*guṇāni, dharmāḥ*), that is, *sattva* (goodness), *rajas* (passion), and *tamas* (ignorance), and by intermingling by those three, the *mahat* and other twenty-three principles came into being, also each of these twenty three principles having the three qualities as its substance. Now if *mahat* and the rest are all constituted by the three qualities, they should then be the same as an assembly or a forest, which are merely unsubstantial false conceptions. How can you say that they are true entities? Again, if *mahat* and the rest are all composed of the three qualities, then [any] one of them should be the same as [all] the others. And if one is the same as the others, then any one of them should have the same functions as all the others. But since this is not the case, why should you hold the view that the three qualities are the substantial nature of all the entities? Again, if one entity is just the same as the other entities, then the organs of mouth and eye, and so forth, should have the same function as the excretory organs. And if each organ has the functions of all the other organs, then the organ of the mouth ought to smell odors and the ear see colors. If it is not so, how can you hold the view that the three qualities are the substance of all things? How could a wise man have formulated such convictions? Moreover, if primary matter is unchangeable, it should be like the substance of *puruṣa*. How can it be transformed into *mahat* and the others? Again, if the *puruṣa* as you conceive it is unchangeable by nature, then it ought to be the same as primary matter and should not be the *puruṣa*. And if it is the same as primary matter, then its substance is not that of the *puruṣa* and ought not to enjoy the other twenty-four principles. In such a case, *puruṣa is* not the subject that is able to enjoy, nor are the twenty-four principles the objects to be enjoyed. Since there is neither subjectivity nor objectivity in the proposition, your principles can not be established."

Falling into silence, the brāhmaṇa could not produce a single word. He rose up and apologized to the Master by saying, "Today I'm defeated. To keep my previous promise, now I'm at your disposal." The Master said, "We are all the disciples of the Buddha Śākyamuni, and we never take anyone's life. Instead, I order you around as my slave." Filled with respect and pleasure, the brāhmaṇa was completely compliant. Then the Master led him back to his quarters. None of the people who heard it didn't sing praise with delight.

At the time the Master was about to go to Uḍra, before that, he sought and obtained the *Mahāyānabheda Śāstra* in seven hundred stanzas composed by the Hīnayāna teachers.

However, having read through it, he found several dubious points in it, then he consulted the brāhmaṇa previously defeated by him, and asked, "Have you ever attended lectures on this treatise?"

The brāhmaṇa answered, "I have attended lectures on this treatise for five times."

Then the Master asked him to explain the treatise for him, but the brāhmaṇa said, "Being your servant, how dare I lecture on it for Your Reverence?"

The Master encouraged him by saying, "It is the work of other school, and so I haven't read it before. Feel free to lecture on it for me."

The brāhmaṇa said, "If so, I'll explain it to you, but please wait until the midnight, in case your reputation should be hurt when people know you learn the Dharma from a servant."

Thus, when the night fell, keeping away from others, the Master invited the brāhmaṇa to make a discourse on the *Śāstra*; the Master only listened once and acquired all its doctrines. Then he sorted out some erroneous passages and employed the Mahāyāna doctrines to refute them. Consequently, he composed a treatise entitled the *Aghadarśanabheda Śāstra* in sixteen hundred stanzas, which he presented to the venerable Śilāditya and other fellow disciples. In admiration, all of them praised it by saying, "If we employ this comprehensive text to examine the views of the opponents, none can hold themselves." This treatise was experimental in conception, striking out a new path. Then the Master said to the brāhmaṇa, "You are a man of goodness, and for being defeated in the debate, you are condescended to be my servant. It is a shame enough for you to suffer. Now I set you free, and you can go anywhere as you like." Delightedly, the brāhmaṇa bade farewell to the Master and departed for the country of Kāmarūpa[89] in East India. There he told King Kumāra about the righteousness and virtue of the Master, which made the king very pleased. Then the king immediately dispatched an envoy to extend his appreciation as well as invitation.

ANNOTATION

1 It is identified with the modern Bhagalpur, on the southern banks of the river Ganges in the Indian state of Bihar.

2 The old site is supposed to be at the present Rājmahāl.

3 It is identified with the northern part of Bangladesh (Country of Bengal). The old site of the capital was present Mahāsthān about 12 kolometers north to Bogra.

4 It is supposed that this kingdom included the northern part of Burdwan, the whole of Birbhum, and the province of Murshidabad, including all those parts of the districts of Kishnaghur and Jessore.

5 Saṃmitīya (correct measures) school: one of the eighteen or twenty early Buddhist schools in India, and an offshoot of the Vātsīputrīya sect, which was formed approximately three hundred years after the passing of Śākyamuni. Like its predecessor, it claims the person as a carrier of skandhas endures, and as such was a representative (perhaps the most prominent one) of the

Pudgalavāda schools.

6 The heretic boasted that he possessed such an amount of knowledge that he had to wear a copper sheathing around his belly to prevent his knowledge bursting out.

7 The present Dacca district in East Pakistan.

8 The district of Prome in Burma.

9 This country is said to be Pegu and the Delta of the Irrawaddy in Myanmar.

10 Ancient capital of Thailand.

11 Modern Cambodia.

12 Modern Laos and part of Vietnam.

13 Probably in Java and Sumatra.

14 Modern Tamluk, the district headquarters of Purba Medinipur district of West Bengal, India. The present town is located on the banks of the Rupnarayan River close to the Bay of Bengal.

15 Modern Sri Lanka.

16 Modern Bhubaneswar, the capital of the Indian state of Odisha.

17 It is supposed to be present Puri, situated on the Bay of Bengal, a municipality in the state of Odisha in eastern India.

18 It is supposed to be present Ganjam, a town and a notified area council in Ganjam district in the state of Odisha, India.

19 It is supposed to be Rajamahendri at the lower reach of Godavari River which is India's second longest river.

20 One who by non-Buddhist methods has attained to the five super-natural powers, mainly "Higher powers" (iddhi-vidhā), such as walking on water and through walls; "Divine ear" or "Deva-ear" (dibba-sota), that is, clairaudience; "Mind-penetrating knowledge" (ceto-pariya-ñāṇa), that is, telepathy; "Remember one's former abodes" (pubbe-nivāsanussati), causal memory, that is, recalling one's own past lives; "Divine eye" or "Deva-eye" (dibba-cakkhu), that is, knowing others' karmic destinations.

21 It is supposed to be the ancient province of Vidarbha or Berar, with Nagpur as

the capital. It is distinguished from the Kosala in the north, of which Sravasti was the capital.

22 Logic, one of the Five Sciences (q.v). Take reference to the note 110 of Fascicle II.

23 Modern Telangana, India.

24 Dignāga 陈那 (a.k.a. Diṅnāga, c. 480–c. 540 CE) was an Indian Buddhist scholar and one of the Buddhist founders of Indian logic (hetu vidyā). Dignāga's work laid the groundwork for the development of deductive logic in India and created the first system of Buddhist logic and epistemology. Dignāga was born in Simhavakta near Kanchipuram and very little is known of his early years, except that he took as his spiritual preceptor Nagadatta of the Pudgalavada school before being expelled and becoming a student of Vasubandhu.

25 Modern Amāravatī at the lower reach of Krishna River.

26 Śāstrin: a teacher, a learned person.

27 Asura: a kind of demon, an evil spirit.

28 It is supposed to be Nellore in the Indian state of Andhra Pradesh. It is located on the banks of Penna River.

29 It is supposed to be an area between the south of Andhra Pradesh and the north of Tamil Nadu.

30 Modern Kānchipuram in the Indian state of Tamil Nadu, 72 km (45 *mi*) from Chennai – the capital of Tamil Nadu.

31 The country of Malakūta is supposed to include the modern districts of Tanjore and Madura on the east with Colmbatore, Cochin and Travancore on the west.

32 Sri Lanka.

33 Four armies: elephant force, horse cavalry, chariot force, armored infantry.

34 The detailed story could be found in fascial eleven of the *Great Tang Records on the Western Regionss* (*Datang Xiyu Ji*《大唐西域记》).

35 An ogress.

36 In Theravada Buddhism, they are the four progressive stages culminating in full enlightenment as an Arhat, so they are also called the four stages of enlightenment, including: srotāpanna (A Stream-enterer), sakṛdāgāmin (A Once-returner), anāgāmi (A Non-returner), arhat.

37 Nārikeladvīpa is described as an island several thousand *li* south of Ceylon.

38 It is supposed to be on the northern bank of the Tungabhadra River in India.

39 Its capital was supposed to be Nāsik to the northwest of Bombay, which lies on the western edge of the Deccan Plateau.

40 The Narmadā is a river in central India and the sixth longest river in the Indian subcontinent. It rises from Amarkantak Plateau near Anuppur district. It forms the traditional boundary between North India and South India and flows westwards over a length of 1,312 km (815.2 *mi*) before draining through the Gulf of Khambhat into the Arabian Sea, 30 km (18.6 *mi*) west of Bharuch city of Gujarat.

41 Mdern Broach at the mouth of the Narbada River.

42 Modern Malwa in west-central India occupying a plateau of volcanic origin.

43 See note 35 of Preface.

44 The seven ancient Buddhas, viz. Vipaśyin, Śikhin, Viśvabhū, Krakucchanda, Kanakamuni or, Kāśyapa, and Śākyamuni. The last four are said to be of the present kalpa.

45 This country is still unidentified.

46 Modern Sichuan 四川 Province, China.

47 Modern Cutch (also Kutch or Kachchh), the present day Kutch region of Gujarat north of the Gulf of Kutch.

48 It is supposed to be Kathiawar. The old site of its capital was present Wala to the northwest of Bhaonagar.

49 This country is identified with the triangular tract lying between the mouth of

the Banas River on the west and the Sabarmati River on the east.

50 Modern Kathiawar, a peninsula in Western India and part of the Saurashtra region.

51 It is supposed to be in Rājputāna in India. Rājputāna was a region that included mainly the present-day Indian state of Rajasthan along with parts of Madhya Pradesh, Gujarat and some adjoining areas of Sindh in modern-day southern Pakistan.

52 Present Ujjain, the largest city in Ujjain district of the Indian state of Madhya Pradesh.

53 The capital of this country is identified with the modern district of Bundelkhand.

54 It is supposed to be the old town of Mandala, the original capital of the country on the upper Narmada River.

55 It is supposed to be at India estuary in the south of Pakistan.

56 It is situated in the eastern part of Mekran. Mekran is a semi-desert coastal strip in Balochistan, in Pakistan and Iran, along the coast of the Persian Gulf and the Gulf of Oman.

57 Or Persia, present Iran.

58 Present Hormuz, Iran.

59 Refers to Eastern Roman Empire.

60 It is suggested that this country was in the Thar and Parker district of west India.

61 This country is regarded as corresponding to the region of Middle Sindh, and its capital as the old city Brahmanabad (Mansura).The city now lies 8 miles (13 km) south-east of Shahdadpur, Pakistan, and 43 miles (69 km) north-east of Hyderabad.

62 This country is regarded as corresponding to the region southwest to Punjab, Pakistan, at the confluence section of Sutlaj and Indus rivers.

63 Modern Multan, a Pakistani city and the headquarters of Multan District in

the province of Punjab, is Located on the banks of the Chenab River.

64 Present Halabba, Punjab, Pakistan.

65 The Staff Forest Mountain or Stickwood Hill.

66 Upāsaka: a Buddbist layman, or a lay practitioner.

67 There are four Vedas: the Rigveda, the Yajurveda, the Samaveda and the Atharvaveda.

68 The "three realms" is also called "three worlds," "three spheres," "three planes of existence," and "three regions." In Buddhism, the three worlds refer to the following destinations for karmic rebirth: (1)Kāmaloka is the world of desire, typified by base desires, populated by hell beings, preta, animals, ghosts, humans and lower demi-gods. (2) Rūpaloka is the world of form, predominately free of baser desires, populated by dhyāna-dwelling gods, possible rebirth destination for those well practiced in dhyāna. (3) Arūpaloka is the world of formlessness, a noncorporeal realm populated with four heavens, possible rebirth destination for practitioners of the four formlessness stages.

69 Wang Xuance王玄策 (fl. 7th century) was a Tang Dynasty guard officer and diplomat. In 648, Tang Taizong sent him to India in response to Harshavardhana's sending an ambassador to China. However once in India he discovered Harshavardhana had died and the new king attacked Wang and his 30 mounted subordinates. This led to Wang Xuance's escape to Tibet where he mounted a joint of over 7,000 Nepalese mounted infantry and 1,200 Tibetan infantry, then he attacked on the Indian state in June of 684. The success of this attack won Xuance the prestigious title of the "Grand Master for the Closing Court."

70 A period of time during seven to nine o'clock in the evening.

71 The nature that maintains the seeming to be real; nature of existence produced from attachment to all-pervasive discrimination.

72 Or the nature of dependent arising.

73 Or termed as bhūtatathatā in Sanskrit, also translated as the perfect true nature, absolute reality, perfectly accomplished nature of reality, etc.

74 Sky-flower heretics, or followers of illusion.

75 Kāpālikas, also interpreted variously as Digambara Jains, Pashupatas and Kapalikas. The word Kāpālikas is derived from kapāla meaning "skull", and Kāpālikas means the "skull-men." The Kāpālikas traditionally carried a skull-topped trident (khatvanga) and an empty skull as a begging bowl. Other attributes associated with Kāpālikas were that they smeared their body with ashes from the cremation ground, revered the fierce Bhairava form of Shiva, engaged in rituals with blood, meat, alcohol, and sexual fluids.

76 He is a follower of the Saṃmitīya sect who had composed a treatise in 700 verses which opposed the Mahāyāna teachings. In response, while living at Nālandā, Xuanzang wrote a Sanskrit work in 1600 verses to refute this text, called *The Destruction of Heresy*. In this context, the Saṃmitīya sect was regarded as heretical.

77 Consecrate someone by sprinkling water on his head.

78 Or Bhūtatīrthikas, a Shivaitic religious group, who are followers of Śiva, Śaiva or Shiva ascetics; a class of heretics who smeared themselves with ashes; ascetics who smeared their bodies with ashes.

79 Nirgranthas are Jain monks, who have no desire or defilements, also called Shramanas, which denotes they treat everything with equanimity.

80 Perhaps Śiva, Śaiva or Shiva ascetics, usually wearing the matted hair, or any knot or fillet of hair. *Jūṭa* means twisted hair.

81 Sāṃkhya school is one of the six āstika schools of Hindu philosophy, which is most related to the Yoga school of Hinduism. Sāmkhya is an enumerationist philosophy whose epistemology accepts three of six pramanas (proofs) as the only reliable means of gaining knowledge. These include pratyakṣa (perception), anumāṇa (inference) and śabda (āptavacana, word/testimony of reliable sources). Much of Samkhya literature appears to have been lost,

and there seems to be no continuity of tradition from ancient times to the age of the commentators. The earliest surviving authoritative text on classical Sāṃkhya philosophy is the *Sāṃkhya Karika* (c. 200 CE or 350–450 CE) of Īśvarakṛṣṇa. There were probably other texts in early centuries CE, however none of them are available today. Sāmkhya philosophy regards the universe as consisting of two realities, puruṣa (consciousness) and prakṛti (matter). Jiva (a living being) is that state in which puruṣa is bonded to prakṛti in some form. This fusion, state the Sāmkhya scholars, led to the emergence of buddhi (intellect) and ahaṅkāra (ego consciousness). The universe is described by this school as one created by purusa-prakṛti entities infused with various permutations and combinations of variously enumerated elements, senses, feelings, activity and mind. During the state of imbalance, one of more constituents overwhelm the others, creating a form of bondage, particularly of the mind. The end of this imbalance, bondage is called liberation, or kaivalya, by the Sāmkhya school. (Gerald James Larson 2011, *Classical Sāṃkhya: An Interpretation of Its History and Meaning*, Motilal Banarsidass, pages 36–47).

82 Vaisheshika School 胜论派 was founded by the Hindu sage Kaṇāda Kashyapa. *Vaiśeṣika Sūtra*, also called *Kaṇāda sutra*, is its fundamental sutra authored by Kaṇāda, likely compiled sometime between 6th and 2nd century BC and finalized in the currently existing version before the start of the Common Era. This philosophical school is known for its insights in naturalism, as a form of atomism in natural philosophy, which postulated that all objects in the physical universe are reducible to paramāṇu (atoms), and one's experiences are derived from the interplay of substance (a function of atoms, their number and their spatial arrangements), quality, activity, commonness, particularity and inherence. According to Vaiśeṣika school, knowledge and liberation were achievable by complete understanding of the world of experience. (Oliver Leaman, *Key Concepts in Eastern Philosophy.* Routledge, 1999, page 269.)

The *Vaiśeṣika Sūtra* is one of the earliest known systematic realist ontology in human history, presenting its theories on the creation and existence of the universe using naturalistic atomism, applying logic and realism.

83 A kind of spirit or demon.

84 Ahaṃkāra, literally "I-maker" or "the constructor of the 'I am'."

85 Or five rudimentary elements, including: hearing, touch, sight, taste and smell.

86 Refers to earth, water, fire, wind and space (or ether).

87 Or eleven "faculties", refers to eye, ear, nose, tongue, body, hand, foot, genitals, excretory organs, and mind.

88 Or ātman. The soul, the spiritual ego, or permanent person, which by non-Buddhists was said to migrate on the death of the body. Puruṣa is also the Supreme Soul, or Spirit, which produces all forms of existence.

89 Present Guwahati in Assam, India. It is situated on the south bank of the Brahmaputra River.

Fascicle V

Beginning with the Oracle Made by a *Nirgranṭha* about the Master's Return to China and Ending with His Arrival at the Western Canal of the Imperial Capital Chang'an

Before the arrival of the envoy sent by King Kumāra, a naked *nirgranṭha* named Vajra entered the chamber of the Master unexpectedly. Having long heard that the *nirgranṭha* was good at fortune-telling, the Master invited him to take a seat and inquired about his return to China, saying "I am a monk of China, and it has been quite a long time since I came here to pursue the Buddha Dharma . Now I intend to go back, I wonder whether I shall be able to reach my country or not. Remaining here or going back, what choice would be better? How long will I live? Please show me kindness to make a prediction for me."

To make the prediction, the *nirgranṭha* asked for a white stone to draw something on the ground. Then he told the Master, "You'd better stay in India, for both laity and monks in all Five Indias will show you respect; if you go back, you can reach China where you will also get respect, but not more than the respect you win here. As for your life span, you will live another ten years from today, but it is beyond my ability to know how your life would be prolonged by your merits and blessings."

Continuously, the Master asked, "If I am going to go back to China, how could I carry back such a large number of scriptures and images?"

The *nirgranṭha* answered, "Don't worry about it. King Śilāditya and King Kumāra will send someone to escort the Master on your journey back. Rest assured that you shall arrive in China without trouble."

"Those two kings I have never met before, how could they grant me such a favor?" said the Master doubtfully.

The *nirgranṭha* replied, "Now King Kumāra has already sent his envoy on the way to extend the invitation to you, and he will be here in two or three days. And if you meet King Kumāra, you will see King Śilāditya." After those words, the *nirgranṭha* left.

Then, the Master was determined to go back to China. He began to pack the scriptures and images after he worshiped them in solemnity. Having heard about the news, many virtuous monks came over to persuade him to stay by saying, "India is the very place where the Buddha was born. Although the greatest Holy One has attained nirvāṇa, his traces and tracks are still in existence here. It is sufficient for a person to spend his lifetime in pleasure by travelling around to worship and extol them. Now that you have already come here, why not do so? Moreover, China is a borderland. She sets at naught the talented people, and disparages the Dharma; thus buddhas have never been born there. It is also a place where the people are narrow-minded and defective with frailties, so sages and worthies don't want to go there. In addition, as a cold and rough land, it doesn't deserve your nostalgia."

The Master retorted, "First and foremost, the teachings preached by the Dharma Lord should be widely promulgated. How could we hold them privately to ourselves and leave the unenlightened people trapped in ignorance forever? What's more, in China, proprieties have been greatly appropriated and laws well constituted; the sovereign is sagacious and the subjects loyal; fathers are benign and sons filial; benevolence and righteousness are thought highly of; elders and saints are greatly respected. In addition, my fellow countrymen have gained an insightful perception of the profound and the subtle, and so their wisdom is in communion with deities; they have a thorough understanding of the laws of nature and know to take their actions accordingly, and so they have developed a culture whose brilliance could not be overshadowed even by Seven Luminaries[1]. They not only have invented the device for dividing time but also produced the twelve-pitch scale of music[2] through bamboo pitch pipes; they are capable of taming birds and beasts, also able to interact with the spirits and deities; having known how to adapt themselves to the alternation of Yin and Yang, they have benefited and pacified all living beings. Ever since the bequeathed Buddha dharma was spread into the East, the Mahāyāna teachings have been attached with the great importance, so that the crystal-water-like Samādhi is aspired by the people and the pure observance of Śilā by is widely performed. At present, my fellow countrymen tend to devote their minds to Bodhi.

They are eager to perform meritorious deeds and take the vows taken by bodhisattvas of the Ten Stages. Highly motivated by the goal of achieving the Three Bodies of a Buddha[3], and putting palms together to worship the Buddha, they have already been on the gradual path of learning and self-cultivation. A long time ago, they were greatly honored by hearing the name of the Holy One as well as His Dharma. As the news that the golden figure[4] appeared in the dream spread all over, the people have already begun to be acquainted with the wonderful teachings. Actually, no one dares to deny that two countries will make progress in seeking the truth neck and neck in the long run. How could you despise China and say that she has never been visited by buddhas?"

The monks replied, "According to scriptures, when various heavenly beings eat the same food, because of their different merits, they actually relish different taste. Both the Master and we are living in Jambudvīpa, but the Buddha was born here in India instead of in your country, thereby we know that your land is remote and uncivilized. As it's a land lack of blessings, we wish you not to go back to it."

The Master argued, "Once Vimalakīrti was asked why the sun appeared in Jambudvīpa, he answered that the sun was aimed to dispel darkness. Now my intention of returning home is of the same motive."

Seeing the Master didn't take their advice, those virtuous monks had to go with him to the venerable Śilabhadra to arbitrate.

The Ven. Śilabhadra asked the Master, "What's your decision?"

The Master replied, "As this country is the very place where the Buddha was born, certainly I don't dislike it, whereas my intention of coming here is nothing but to pursue the great Dharma for the sake of all living beings. Since I arrived here, it has been a great favor to me that you have delivered lectures on the *Yogācārabhūmi Śāstra*; after hearing it, all my doubts have been resolved. Besides, I have already visited and worshiped the holy sites and learned the profound teachings of various schools. Personally, I feel happy and satisfactory because my journey is truly worthwhile. But in order to make my fellow countrymen who have intimate affinity with Buddhism learn as much as I have learned here, I hope to bring back to China what I have learned here and to engage myself wholeheartedly in translation. In this way I could requite the kindness of teachers in India. Therefore, I could not linger here any longer."

Hearing those words, the Ven. Śilabhadra rejoiced and claimed, "What he said is the aspiration of the bodhisattva and is what I expect him to do. Please let him prepare for his return journey. You shouldn't detain him any longer." Finishing those words, the Ven. Śilabhadra came back to his chamber.

Two days later, King Kumāra of East India sent a messenger to deliver a letter to the Ven. Śilabhadra, which reads, "I, your disciple, wish to see the great virtuous monk from China. Please send him to me to gratify my longing." After receiving this letter, the Ven. Śilabhadra told other monks, "King Kumāra wants to invite Xuanzang to his country, but he has already been chosen by us to go to King Śilāditya to have a debate with the adherents of the Hīnayāna school. Now if Xuanzang goes to King Kumāra, how to satisfy King Śilāditya' s wish to see him? So, we shouldn't let him go." Then, the Ven. Śilabhadra told the messenger, "The Chinese monk intends to go back to China. I'm afraid that he has no time to go on the order of the king." The messenger returned but came back again with another invitation letter from King Kumāra, which reads, "Even if the Master wishes to go back to China, it's not troublesome for him to drop by my place. Please condescendingly give me a favor to come and don't decline my request once more."

But the Ven. Śilabhadra didn't send the Master, which put King Kumāra in such a rage that he dispatched another messenger to bring the third letter to the Ven. Śilabhadra, which reads, "We, your disciple, being an ordinary man, have been defiled by the pleasures of the mundane world, not knowing how to turn my mind to the Dharma. Now at hearing the name of that foreign monk, we felt delighted in both the mind and body, with a sprout of faith shooting forth. But time and again you didn't permit him to come to our country, and we think what you have done is nothing but to leave living beings in the endless darkness. Is it proper for a great virtuous monk to act in this way when he is expected to foster the bequeathed Dharma and to give guidance to human beings? With a strong admiration for the Master, we are sending this letter to you as a further request. If he still does not come to me, we will turn to be evil. Not long ago, even King Śaśāṇka was able to damage the Dharma and cut the Bodhi tree, why do you think we haven't got such a power? We shall summon my elephant army to attack your country and trample Nālandā Mahāvihāra into dust. The words we have uttered ring true as the dazzling sun. You teacher can wait and see."

Having received this letter, the Ven. Śilabhadra said to the Master, "For he is a king without a kind heart, the Buddha Dharma fails to prevail within his domain. Ever since your name came into his ears, it seems that he has developed a deep aspiration for buddha-truth. Maybe in one of the past existences, you could have been his beneficial friend. Please take the trouble to go there to meet him. Now it is a right time for a monk to fulfill his responsibility of benefiting living beings. As if to cut a tree, when the root is chopped off, the branches will wither by themselves; so, when you go to his country, please help the king generate a Bodhi mind. If so, his people would certainly follow suit. On the contrary, if we decline his invitation again, I'm afraid there will be a great trouble. Please don't hesitate to take this labor."

Then the Master bade farewell to the Ven. Śilabhadra and left with the messenger. Seeing his arrival, the king was very pleased. Leading his ministers, he saluted the Master by bowing before his feet and singing praises. Then he ushered the Master into the palace. Every day he arranged the music, foods, drinks, incenses, flowers, and other offerings to the Master in abundance. The king also volunteered to fast and observe the Precepts. The Master stayed for more than a month.

King Śilāditya returned from his military expedition in Konyodha. When he learned the Master was at the palace of King Kumāra, he was shocked and said, "We had invited him for many times, but he didn't come. Now for what reason is he there?" Then he dispatched an envoy to require King Kumāra to send the Chinese monk to him as soon as possible. But king Kumāra told the envoy, "My head might be available to you, but the Master cannot go right now." The envoy came back and made a report, which threw King Śilāditya into a fury.

He said to his attending ministers, "King Kumāra makes light of us. How dare he speak such harsh words to us because of a monk?"

He sent an envoy again to reproach King Kumāra with the words, "Now that you said your head might be available to us, you can give it to our envoy to take it back." Knowing he had made such an indiscreet remark, King Kumāra was full of fear. He had to set out immediately with the Master. Leading a well-disciplined troop of twenty thousand elephants boarding thirty thousand ships, against the currents they sailed along the Ganges to King Śilāditya. Finally, they reached the country of Kajuṅghira[5], where King Śilāditya and his forces had already stationed. Before King Kumāra had an audience with King Śilāditya, he first issued an order to have a temporary palace built on the northern bank of the Ganges, then crossed the river to settle the Master in the palace; then on the same day, King Kumāra led his ministers to pay a visit to King Śilāditya on the southern bank of the river. King Śilāditya was very pleased at seeing their arrival. After knowing that King Kumāra adored the Master, King Śilāditya didn't blame him for what he had said before, and instead, he only asked him where was the Chinese monk.

King Kumāra answered, "At my temporary palace."

King Śilāditya asked, "Why has he not come?"

King Kumāra answered, "As Your Majesty esteems the worthy and loves the truth, how could we send the teacher to meet Your Majesty in a careless manner?"

The king said, "You are right. You may go back to your place now. Tomorrow we shall come to invite him by ourselves."

King Kumāra returned and told the Master, "Although King

Śilāditya said he would come tomorrow, we are afraid he might come tonight. Let us wait for him. When he comes, the teacher needn't leave your chamber."

The Master said, "I will behave myself as the Buddhist teachings have taught me."

At about the first watch[6] of the night, the king did come. The report came too, "There are several thousand candles and torches in the river, along with the sounds of pacing drums."

King Kumāra said, "Here comes King Śilāditya."

Then ordering his men to lift candles, King Kumāra, together with his ministers, went out and walked for a long way to welcome King Śilāditya. When King Śilāditya was walking, several hundred golden drums were beaten rhythmically to accompany his every step; for this reason, these drums were named the rhythmic pacing drums. In India, only King Śilāditya enjoyed such a unique prerogative, and no other kings had the same honor.

When the Master arrived, King Śilāditya bowed with wholehearted reverence to the Master and pressed the head against his feet. After scattering flowers about and eulogizing the Master with poetic verses, he asked, "Why didn't the master come when we previously extended our invitation to you?"

The Master replied, "I have come from afar in order to seek the Dharma and to learn the *Yogācārabhūmi Śāstra*. I failed to come here to pay my respect to Your Majesty because when I received your order, I hadn't finished my study of the Śāstra."

Then the king continued to demand, "We know that the master has come from China. We have heard that in your country there is a piece of dancing melody called the *Prince of Qin*[7] *Who Broke the Formations*[8]. We don't know who the Prince of Qin is. For what meritorious accomplishments does he win such praises?"

The Master answered, "In my motherland, eulogistic songs are usually composed for a man who has virtues of a sage, or is capable of protecting and benefiting all living beings by eradicating the evil and the brutal. Such melodies are performed either in sacred ancestral temples or in humble villages as folk songs. The Prince of Qin is the Son of Heaven of China at present, and before his enthronement, he was bestowed with such a title by the former emperor. At the beginning when there was no lord to reign over, the country submerged in turmoil: corpses heaped up in fields and blood flowed in rivers and valleys; devil stars gathered at nights while the inauspicious and disastrous air congealed in mornings; the Three Regions of the Yellow River[9] were ravaged by corrupted officials as greedy as giant pigs, and the domain within the Four Seas[10] was scourged by people who were of no difference from brutal, evil and avaricious snakes. Being a son of the former emperor, to obey the mandate of heaven to be a great general[11], the Prince of Qin established his almighty authority and strengthened his army. Wielding battle-axes and brandishing spears, he eradicated those rebels who were as evil and brutal as whales, and liquidated the riots in sea and on land; henceforth, the country was pacified, with the Three Luminaries[12] shining high again. Therefore, the people enclosed in six quarters[13] expressed their gratitude by composing this song to eulogize him."

The king claimed, "It must be the heaven who appointed a man like him to be the lord of living creatures." Also, he said to the Master,

"We are to go back to our place first. We shall bid our welcome to you tomorrow. Hope you will condescend to go with us." Then he left.

In the next morning, a messenger arrived, who guided the Master and King Kumāra to a place next to the palace of King Śilāditya. King Śilāditya, in company with his more than twenty personal tutors went out to greet the Master and King Kumāra. Having taken their seats, variegated tasty foods were served. After the flowers were scattered about and the music performed, King Śilāditya asked, "I have heard that the teacher has composed the *Aghadarśanabheda Śāstra*. Where is it?" "Here it is." The Master passed him the *Śāstra*.

Then the king took it to read. After browsing it, the king was very glad and turned with a remark to his personal tutors, "We have heard that when the sun rises, the light of glowworms and candles would be dimmed, and when the thunder rumbles, the striking noises of hammer and chisel would be muted. It seems that all the doctrines held by you have been refuted in this book; would you like to make a response to it?" None of them dared to say anything. The king thus said, "Your teacher Devasena once flattered himself as the most distinguished in knowledge, claiming that he had surpassed all other philosophers. He is the very man who initiated the deviated views and always denigrated the Mahāyāna teachings; but on hearing this virtuous monk's coming, he has gone to Vaiśāli on the pretext of taking a pilgrimage to the holy sites. He absented himself from meeting the Master, from which we know the incompetence of your coterie." The king had a younger sister, a lady of wisdom and good disposition, who was well-versed in the Saṃmitīya teachings. At the time, she was sitting behind the king. When she heard the Master said that the Mahāyāna teachings were profound and comprehensive while the Hīnayāna teachings were shallow and limited, she was so satisfied and delighted that she could not refrain herself from lavishing praises.

King Śilāditya also said, "The treatise of the Master was great. We and the other teachers here are all convinced by it and developed a faith in the Mahāyāna teachings. However, we are afraid that the Hīnayāna adherents and heretics of other countries are still sticking to the stupid and delusive views; therefore we plan to hold an assembly on your behalf at the city of Kanyākubja. We will order all *Śramaṇas,* Brāhmaṇas and heretics of the Five Indias to attend it. Please elucidate the sublimely subtle teachings of the Mahāyāna school to defeat the evil intention of those slanders, and smash their arrogance by displaying your noble virtues." On the same day, the king issued an order to summon the scholars from various countries, inviting them to gather at the city of Kanyākubja to read the Chinese Master's treatise.

From the early winter to the twelfth month of the year, the Master and two kings sailed along the Ganges up to the site of the assembly. The people who came to take part in the gathering included eighteen kings of the Five Indias, more than three thousand monks conversant in both the Mahāyāna and Hīnayāna teachings, over two thousand brāhmaṇas, *nirgranṭhas*, other heretics, and more than one thousand monks from Nālandā Mahāvihāra. All of them had the profound literary capability as well as the excellent eloquence, aspiring to hear the true voice of the Buddha Dharma. They were escorted by entourage, and surrounded by elephants and carriages stretching broadly as permeating mist, with canopies and banners high rising like surging clouds. Such a dense mass crammed an area of several tens of square *li*. It was said that the population of Six Qi[14] was so large that when the people lifted their sleeves, a huge curtain was formed in the vast circle, and that Three Wu[15] were so overcrowded that when the people dashed their perspiration, a shower came down. But no matter how big those crowds were, they could not be compared with the bustling and spectacular scene at this moment.

In advance, the king ordered two thatched halls built at the gathering venue to lodge the Buddhist images as well as the congregation. When the Master arrived, the two thatched halls had already been constructed, so spacious that each of them could seat more than one thousand people. The king's temporary palace was built five *li* away from the west of the gathering venue. At the opening ceremony, walking at the front of the procession was the gold statue of Buddha cast in the royal palace. The statue was enclosed by a precious curtain and placed on the back of an elephant, with King Śilāditya dressing himself up to be Indra holding a white whisk as the right attendant while King Kumāra to be Brahmā holding a jeweled canopy as the left attendant, both of whom were adorned with celestial crowns, floral garlands, jeweled necklaces, and jade pendants. Behind the statue were two caparisoned elephants loaded with flowers to be scattered along the road. The Master and the king's personal tutors each rode an elephant, walking behind the king in the procession. In addition, three hundred elephants were distributed to other kings, ministers, and the great virtuous monks to ride, who lined the roadway on both sides, moving and lauding. Donning formally and brilliantly for the assembly in the early morning, the party started from the temporary palace and proceeded to the gathering venue. Upon arriving at the gate to the courtyard, they were asked to dismount from the elephants. The Buddha statue was held in both hands and carried into the hall. After the statue was placed on a jewel-encrusted pedestal, the two kings and the Master took turns to make their offerings. Then the eighteen kings were invited to come in to worship, and next came the most reputable monks from various countries who were truly learned, totally over one thousand, and next came brāhmaṇas, heretics, and well-known ascetics, totally more than five hundred; and last came more than two hundred ministers of various countries. Other clerics and laypeople lined up neatly outside the yard. King Śilāditya had the food served for the people both inside and outside the courtyard at the same time.

After the meal, one gold plate, seven gold bowls, one gold bathing jug, one gold monk's staff, three thousand gold coins, and three thousand cotton cambric robes of high quality were offered to the Buddha statue. The Master and other monks were also presented with offerings different from each other. After the almsgiving, the Master took his seat in a jewel-encrusted chair as the primary debater. He extolled the Mahāyāna teachings and introduced the tenet of the treatise. Then the *Śramaṇa* Vidyābhadra of Nālandā Mahāvihāra was asked to read the treatise aloud to the public. And the treatise was transcribed and then hung outside the gate to the meeting hall so that everyone could read it. If anyone could find in the treatise a single word illogical and refutable, the Master would be beheaded as an apology. But no one questioned a word of the treatise until the nightfall. Delightedly, King Śilāditya called it a day and returned to his palace. The other kings and monks also dispersed to their places. The Master and King Kumāra came back to their places too. In the next morning, the party congregated as they did on the previous day, receiving and worshiping the statue with the same ritual etiquette.

It was lasting for five days. When the Hīnayāna adherents and heretics saw their doctrines were to be smashed by the Master, they developed a malicious mind full of hatred and plotted to murder the Master. Knowing the conspiracy, the king issued an edict, saying, "It has been a long time since the heretical clique tried to corrupt the truth. They have misled and confused living beings by concealing the orthodox and correct teachings. If without those saints, how can we discern the false from the genuine? Today, here comes this Chinese teacher who has a lofty and broad mind. And because of his distinguished understanding of the profound doctrines as well as his rigid self-cultivation, he has already entered the truth. In order to guide the ignorant people who have gone astray to return to the Right Path, he has come to our country to promote the great Dharma and subjugate various heretic theories. Pitifully, there are still some arrogant and perverse persons, who, instead of confessing and repenting, have the audacity to develop malicious thoughts scheming to do some harm to the Master. If such behavior is tolerable, what else cannot be forgivable? Among you, anyone who dares to injure the Master in whatever way will be executed and anyone who dares to curse the Master will have the tongue cut off; however, one who intends to express his opinions in defense of his own theory is an exception."

Henceforward, devious and evil persons stopped their conspiracy.

When eighteen-day assembly concluded, there had been no one launching any debate with the Master. On the eve of the adjournment of the meeting, the Master again extolled the Mahāyāna teachings and lauded the meritorious deeds of the Buddha, which made countless people give up their false views and regain the right, and renounce the Hīnayāna school and turn to the Mahāyāna school.

Having more esteem for the Master, King Śilāditya offered him ten thousand gold coins, thirty thousand silver coins, and one hundred fine cotton cambric robes. Each king of eighteen kingdoms also offered the Master with rare and precious things. The Master, however, took none of them. Then King Śilāditya enjoined one of his attending ministers to adorn the Master's elephant with a canopy, and asked his high officials to accompany and safeguard him to cruise around the city, with the purpose of making the public know that the Master had established his unchallengeable theories. Although it was the tradition of the Western countries that the winner of a debate should enjoy an honor of sorts, the Master still declined it and didn't want to go. The king had to persuade him by saying "As this custom has been practiced from early times, it should not be violated." Eventually, as an alternative solution, a man held the cassock of the Master, cruising around the city while announcing loudly, "The Dharma Master of China has established the Mahāyāna teachings and refuted various heresies. In the past eighteen days, no one has launched a debate with him. Let the news be widely known." The revered congregation competed to confer various honorary titles on the Master. The Mahāyāna adherents lauded him as Mahā-deva, meaning "heavenly being of Mahāyāna"; the Hīnayāna adherents called him Mokṣa-deva, meaning "heavenly being of emancipation." After burning incenses, strawing flowers, and worshiping the Master, people made their departure. Henceforward, the Master's reputation of the high virtue began to spread far and wide.

There was a monastery sponsored by King Śilāditya, which was located to the west side of his temporary palace. At the monastery a Buddha's tooth relic was enshrined, about one inch and a half long, yellowish white in hue, often issuing a bright light. In the past, a king of Krīta caste[16] in the country of Kaśmīra eradicated the Buddha Dharma and dismissed the monks, which forced a bhikṣus into exile to India, where he told it to Tukhāra, a king of Himatala. The king fell into indignation after hearing of the destruction of Buddhism by such a lowly and degrading caste; so, dressing himself up as a merchant, he led three thousand warriors to go to Kaśmīra. They carried a large number of jewels and precious things and pretended to offer them to the king of Kaśmīra as gifts. Being avaricious, the king of Kaśmīra was very glad at hearing this news and dispatched his envoy to welcome them. Robust and valiant, the king of Himatala looked as awesome and dignified as a deity. When the two kings met, he came over to the throne of the Kaśmīra king, removed his hat and reprimanded him loudly, which shocked the Kaśmīra king to fall to the ground in horror; quickly, the Himatala king pressed him and had his head cut off. Then he turned to the surrounding ministers and said, "I am the king at the foot of the snow mountains. Knowing you had destroyed the Buddha Dharma, we have come here to punish you. But it is merely a fault of one person, you needn't bear the blame; so, you could set your mind at rest. Only those who used to incite the king to do the evil will be banished to other countries, and the rest will be spared from punishments." After the evildoers had been subdued, the monastery was rebuilt again and the monks were summoned to come back to receive the offerings. Then, the king returned to his country.

Having heard the country was pacified, holding his religious staff, the bhikṣu who formerly exiled to India set out on his homeward journey. On the way, he encountered a herd of elephants, coming up and roaring loudly. In panic, the bhikṣu had to climb up a tree to hide himself. But the elephants drained water by trunk to squirt him, and dug the tree with ivory. After a while, the tree fell. Then an elephant rolled the bhikṣu up on its back and carried him into a big forest, where the bhikṣu saw an elephant lying sick due to skin ulcer. One elephant led the hand of the bhikṣu to touch the sore skin of the sick elephant. Seeing a bamboo thorn there, the bhikṣu pulled it out, squeezed out the pus and blood, and tore off a piece of his robe to bandage the wound. After this treatment, the elephant soon recovered. The next day, elephants vied with one another to collect fruits and foods to entertain him. After the entertainment, one of the elephants handed a golden box to the sick elephant. The sick elephant took it and gave it to bhikṣu. After he received it, he was carried by an elephant out of the forest to the place where he was found. Then the elephants knelt at the feet of the bhikṣu to express their gratitude and left. The bhikṣu opened the box and found the Buddha's tooth relic, and so took it back to worship.

Recently, when King Śilāditya heard that there was a Buddha's tooth relic in the country of Kaśmīra, he came to the borderland to pay homage to it. However, the monks were too stingy to show it to others, so they ignored the king's request and hid it somewhere. Their king, on the contrary, was in fear of King Śilāditya, so he dug here and there until he found it, and presented it to King Śilāditya. Upon seeing it, King Śilāditya developed such a strong admiration that he appropriated it by force and took it back to his country to worship. Here was this very tooth relic. After the meeting, King Śilāditya offered the monastery with the golden statues, religious robes, and money. In addition, he ordered monks to guard the relic.

The Master had already taken leave of the virtuous monks in Nālandā Mahāvihāra and obtained images as well as scriptures. On the nineteenth day when the assembly was over, he intended to bide farewell to King Śilāditya and take on his return journey.

The king said, "We, your disciple, have mounted the throne for over thirty years. Because we often worried that our merits and virtues could not be increased and that the good causes made in our past lives could not be succeeded by new ones, we accumulated wealth as well as valuables, and paved a great assembly venue between the two rivers in the country of Prayāga. There we hold a seventy-five-day unlimited charity meeting every five years, inviting *Śramaṇas*, the brāhmaṇas, the poor, the lonely and the solitary within the five realms of India to attend. Up to now, five charity meetings have already been convened. Now we are going to hold the sixth one. Would you like to wait to see the sight and share this felicity with us?"

The Master replied, "In the process of practicing the Bodhisattva path, both the wisdom and virtue have to be cultivated; the intelligent men never forget to nourish the tree root when they harvest the fruits.

Now that Your Majesty was not miserly with your treasures or wealth, how could I refuse to stay a little longer? Please allow me to go with Your Majesty." The king was greatly delighted.

On the twenty-first day, they set out to the grand charity meeting venue situated in Prayāga. In the north side of venue was the Ganges and in the south the Jumna, two rivers flowing eastward from the northwest to converge here. At the confluence of the rivers, there was a big plain, fourteen or fifteen *li* in circumference, as flat as a mirror. From the ancient times, various kings came here to give alms, hence the name the Site of Almsgiving. It was said that at this very spot even a coin given in charity could accumulate much more merit than what was gained by giving a hundred or thousand coins in other places. For this reason, since olden times it had been held in high esteem. King Śilāditya had an almsgiving venue built in the plain. The venue was enclosed by a fence of reeds, with each side one thousand paces in length, and inside the fence there were dozens of thatched houses for storing the various valuables, such as gold, silver, pearls, red crystals, precious emeralds, sapphires, and others. Next to the thatched houses, several hundred long-houses were also constructed to store garments made of silk or spotted cotton cambric, gold and silver coins, and the like. Outside the fence, there was a separate place for food provision. In front of the treasury, more than one hundred rows of long rooms stood, like the lanes in the markets of the Tang's capital. Each long room could seat more than one thousand persons.

Previously, the king had already issued an imperial decree to summon the *Śramaṇas*, the heretics, the *nirgranṭhas*, the poor, the orphan and the childless to congregate at the almsgiving venue to receive alms. Besides them, those who hadn't returned home after attending the assembly at the city of Kanyākubja also came to the almsgiving venue, including King Śilāditya, in company with eighteen kings. When they arrived, monks and lay persons, more than half a million, had already congregated. Then King Śilāditya encamped on the north bank of the Ganges; King Dhruvabhaṭa of South India encamped west of the confluence of two rivers; King Kumāra encamped by the side of the floral woods on the south bank of the Jumna; the alms-receivers encamped west of King Dhruvabhaṭa's camp.

On the following morning, King Śilāditya and King Kumāra who embarked the warships, and King Dhruvabhaṭa who led an elephant army, all being followed by well-organized ceremonial guards, congregated at the venue where eighteen kings were lining up by rank. On the first day, a Buddha statue was placed in the thatched hall at the almsgiving venue, offered with the most valuable substances, the garments of high quality, and delicacies; simultaneously, the music was played and flowers were scattered. It was not until the nightfall that people dispersed. On the second day, a Sun God statue was placed there, which was offered with half the number of valuable substances and garments of the previous day. On the third day, a Īsvaradeva statue was placed, which was presented with the same number of offerings as those to Sun God. On the fourth day, more than ten thousand monks were offered with alms; seated in one hundred rows, each of them received one hundred gold coins, one pearl, one cotton cambric robe, food, flowers, and incenses. And after receiving the offerings, they left. The fifth group of alms-receivers were brāhmaṇas. It took more than twenty days to give alms to all of them. The sixth group to receive offering were heretics, and it took ten days to give alms to all of them. The seventh group were those coming from afar, and it took ten days. The eighth group were the poor, the orphan and the childless, and it took a whole month to give alms to them all. By this time, the five-year storage of national treasure had been exhausted, only leaving the elephants, horses, and weapons to suppress the riots and defend the country. What's more, all the valuable personal effects of King Śilāditya, as well as what he was wearing, including his attire, pendants, earrings, armlets, headdress, necklaces, and topknot pearls, were given out as alms, and none was left. As all possessions had been given away, the king had to ask his younger sister to give him rough and shabby clothes to put on. After that, he worshiped the Buddhas in ten directions in delight and put his palms together, saying, "We have accumulated a large amount of wealth and treasures in our life, but always had a fear that we could not deposit them in security. Today we have deposited them in the Field of Blessedness[17], truly being well-stored in safety. We hope that we could possess enormous wealth and acquire the supreme Dharma in our numerous future lives to offer to all sentient beings equally, and that we could achieve Ten Capabilities[18] as well as Two Adornments[19]."

After the conclusion of the charity meeting, the kings gave the people all kinds of precious substances, money, and goods to redeem the pendants, necklaces, topknot pearls, imperial garments and other things which had been given away by King Śilāditya as alms, and then returned those articles back to him. Only a few days later, his clothes and precious jewelry were the same as before.

With a strong desire to go back to motherland, the Master bid farewell to King Śilāditya. The king said, "We are just about to propagate the bequeathed Dharma together with Your Reverence; why are you going to leave so soon?"

The Master had to tarry for ten more days. King Kumāra also showed the same hospitality and tried to detain the Master by saying, "If the teacher could take up residence in our place to receive our offerings, we would have one hundred monasteries constructed for you."

Seeing the kings were so obstinate in their retention, the Master sincerely begged them to understand, and said, "As a country far away from here, China has heard the Buddha Dharma very late. The framework of Buddhism has been known there but the comprehensive and complete content is still unknown. For this reason, I have come here to seek the unknown. Owing to the earnest expectation of the saints in my homeland, my wish has now been gratified; thus, I dare not forget my commitment for a minute. In the scripture it is said that those who impede others from studying the Dharma will be born having no eyes in the future lives. If I am to be detained here, numerous practitioners in my homeland would lose the chance to benefit from the Dharma. How could we have no fear of the future retribution to be born without eyes?"

King Śilāditya replied, "We are impressed with your virtue, and so we hope we are able to worship and make constant offerings to you. But if our retention would make others to forfeit benefits, we feel restless and guilty. So, you are free to leave or remain as you please.

If you decide to leave, we wonder which route the teacher will take. If you are taking the way of the South Sea, we shall dispatch the envoy to escort you."

The Master answered, "Formerly I started from China and at her western border, passed by a country named Gaochang. The king of this country was wise and farsighted, who believed in the Buddha Dharma. Knowing I had been coming all the way for pursuing the Ultimate Truth, he rejoiced in my merit and showed admiration for me. He provided me with abundant traveling sustenance and expected me to stop over his country on my way back home. So, I could not let him down. I'd like to take the northern route back."

Again, the king asked, "How much provision and money does the teacher need?" The Master replied that he didn't need anything. "How could that be so?" said the king. And he issued an order to offer plenty of gold coins and other things to the Master. King Kumāra also gave the Master various precious substances. Actually, the Master refused to accept them save an aurṇika cape[20] given by King Kumāra, which was made of the finest wool (with the hairs thick at the top and thin at the bottom) and thus capable to protect him from the rain on the road. Then the Master bade farewell. The kings, together with others, saw him off for more than several ten *li* before turning back. At the departure, none of them could refrain from sobbing bitterly.

The Master loaded the war-horses of King Udita of North India with images, scriptures, and other articles, and proceeded slowly on the horseback, in company with King Udita. Later, King Śilāditya, in addition, gave an elephant to King Udita, and also gave him three thousand gold coins and ten thousand silver coins to cover the traveling expenses of the Master. Having been away for three days, King Śilāditya, King Kumāra, King Dhruvabhaṭa and others caught up with them again to see the Master off, each of them leading several hundred light cavalrymen. Their hospitality to the Master came to such an extent! What's more, four attendant officials, titled as Mahātāra (similar to officials without portfolio), were also dispatched to escort the Master on the journey. They were carrying a credential letter written on a piece of white cotton cambric cloth and sealed with the red ink paste, which was to be presented to the states along the route, requesting the local authorities to supply the Master with horses and escort him stage by stage until he reached the border of China.

From a big forest southwest to the country of Prayāga, proceeding for seven days, the Master reached the country of Kauśāmbi[21]. There he worshiped the holy site located in the south of the capital city where the Elder Ghoṣila gave a garden to the Buddha. After that, the Master, together with King Udita and his retinue, went northwest for one month or more while passed several states and paid homage to the Celestial Stairway again. Then proceeding northwest for three *yojanas*, the Master arrived at the capital city of the country of Vilaśāṇa, and stayed there for two months, where he met Siṃharaśmi and Siṃhacandra, two disciples of Right Dharma Store, who were giving lectures on the *Abhidharmakośa Śāstra*, the *Mahāyānasaṅgraha Śāstra,* the *Vijñaptimātratāsiddhi Śāstra,* and others. They received the Master in pleasure. The Master delivered the lectures on the *Yogaparikalpana Śāstra* and the *Abhidharmasamuccayavyākhyā Śāstra* too. After two months, he departed.

Again, going northwest for more than a month, passing by

several countries, the Master reached Jālandhara[22], the capital city of North India, and stayed there for another month. King Udita dispatched a guide for him. After going westward for more than twenty days, he arrived at the country of Siṃhapura. At the time there were more than one hundred monks, all northerners. Carrying the images and scriptures, they traveled together with the Master to go back to their homeland. They were walking along mountainous creeks for more than twenty days. Because bandits were rampant in the mountains, the Master always sent a monk to go first for fear of being robbed. When he encountered bandits, the monk would say as he was taught: "We have come all the way to seek Dharma. What we are carrying now are images, scriptures, relic bones, and nothing else. Please you, the almsgivers, give us protection rather than develop the malicious mind to do harm to us." The Master, leading other monks and travelers, proceeded behind. For several times they met the bandits who got away without harming them.

Advancing for twenty days, the Master came to the country of Takṣaśilā. Again, he worshiped the site where King Candraprabha gave away his head a thousand times in previous lives. Fifty *yojanas* to the northeast of this country was the country of Kaśmīra, whose king dispatched an envoy to invite the Master, but the Master refused because it was inconvenient to go there with elephants loaded with heavy cargoes. After staying for seven days, he resumed his journey, going northwest for three days until he reached the great Indus River, five to six *li* in breadth. The Master crossed the river on an elephant while other fellow travelers carrying scriptures and images sailed across the river in a boat. One of the travelers in the boat was appointed to take care of the scriptures as well as various seeds of rare flowers of India. When the boat was coming close to the midstream of the river, swift gales suddenly arose here and there, violently shaking the boat, nearly to overturn it for several times. In a great panic, the man who looked after scriptures fell into the water, yet was rescued by the concerted efforts of others. But unfortunately, fifty bundles of scriptures, various flower seeds and other things had been lost, with the rest property narrowly escaped damage.

At the time, King Kapiśā had already been in the city of Uḍakhāṇḍa[23]. Having heard the Master's coming, with veneration he went to the riverside to receive him.

He asked the Master, "I have heard that the teacher has lost the scriptures in the river. Haven't you taken the Indian flowers or fruits seeds, have you?"

In reply, the Master said, "Yes, I have taken them."

The king told him, "That is why your boat was turned over by the surging waves. From olden times, accidents of this sort have often happened to those who brought flower seeds and tried to cross the river."

Then the king and the Master entered the city. The Master was lodged in a monastery. For having lost the scriptures, he had to tarry there for more than fifty days, during which he sent some men to the country of Udyāna to copy the Tripiṭaka of the Kāśyapīya school. Having heard the Master was approaching, King Kaśmīra, despite the long distance, came over to pay homage to him in person. The king spent several days staying with the Master before going back to his palace.

In accompany with King Kapiśā, the Master proceeded northwest for more than a month and entered the domain of the country of Lampāka[24]. Some time ago, the king had already sent the prince back to the capital city to deliver the order that the people and monks there should get canopies and streamers prepared well awaiting outside the city to receive the Master. He and the Master, however, were advancing behind unhurriedly. When they arrived, they saw a spectacular view that thousands of monks and laity were waiting there, holding numerous canopies and streamers. In ecstasy, the people paid homage to the Master and sang eulogies to him. Swarming around, they followed the Master coming into the capital city, where he adjoined in a Mahāyāna monastery. Afterwards, the king held a seventy-five-day unlimited almsgiving meeting for the sake of the Master.

From here going due south for fifteen days, the Master reached the country of Varaṇa[25] and worshiped the holy sites there. Then going northwest, and then he came to the country of Avakan[26]and farther going northwest, he arrived at the country of Jāguḍa[27]. Then proceeding northward for more than five hundred *li,* he reached the country of Vṛjisthāna[28], and going eastward from it, the Master entered the country of Kapiśā. The king there held a seven-day almsgiving meeting for him. After the meeting, the Master departed. Then going northeast for one *yojana,* he arrived at the city of Grosapam[29], where he parted company with King Kapiśā and advanced to the north continuously.

The King of Kapiśā dispatched his minister who was leading more than one hundred people to escort the Master to cross the Snow

Mountains[30]. Carrying fodder, various foods, and other supplies, they had proceeded for seven days before reaching the summit of the mountains. The precipitous peaks of the rolling mountains were in different shapes, either lying flat or towering high. It was far beyond the words to delineate the hardships and dangers of the journey. For it was totally impossible to ride the horse, the Master had to go on foot with a cane. Trekking for seven days, he came to a high mountain, at the foot of which there was a village with more than one hundred households. The goats which the people kept were as large as donkeys. They lodged in this village on the day of their arrival and set out again at midnight, guided by the villagers riding mountain camels. It was a place replete with snow gullies and ice-covered creeks. If without the local guides, the travelers might easily slip down into them. The next day, they finally crossed the dangerous icy place. At that time there remained only seven monks and some twenty hired men, an elephant, ten mules, and four horses. On the following day, they arrived at the foot of another mountain. Following a winding trail, he climbed the ridge of the mountain which looked like being snow-capped from a distance but turned out to be white stones when coming close. The mountain was so high that even the gathering clouds and flying snowflakes failed to reach its summit. In the twilight they finally arrived at its top, where the bellowing wind was piercingly cold, and so strong that none of the travelers could stand straight. With neither grass nor trees, the huge rocky peaks rising high in a large number, looking like bamboo shoots in woods. Because of the great height of the peak and the strength of the winds, even birds were incapable to fly above, but merely fluttering their wings several hundred paces away on the northern or southern side of it. Reckoning in all the lofty mountains and peaks in Jambudvīpa, this mountain might be the highest of all.

The Master went down the northwestern side of the mountain range, and continuously walking for a few *li*, came to a small piece of flat ground. Putting up the camps, he spent the night there. In the following morning, he resumed his journey again. After five or six days, the Master went down the mountain and entered the country of Andarāb[31], in the old territory of Tukhāra. There were three monasteries with several tens of monks who were studying the teachings of the Mahāsāṃghika school. There was a stūpa built by King Aśoka. The Master had stayed there for five days. Then he went down the mountain by the northwestern side and proceeding for more than four hundred *li*, reached the country of Khost[32], also in the old territory of Tukhāra. From here again going northwest in mountains for more than three hundred *li*, he reached the country of Ghūr, bordering on the Oxus River, which was the eastern boundary of Tukhāra. The capital was located on the southern bank of the river. The Master had an audience with the king there, the grandson of Yehu Khan, who claimed himself to be a *yehu* for ruling over Tukhāra. After accommodating the Master in his official place for one month, Yehu ordered his court guards to escort the Master to continue the journey, with some more merchants.

He then went eastward for two days and arrived at the country of Munjān[33]. In its neighborhood were the countries of Arini[34], Rohu[35], Kṛṣma[36], and Pārghar[37], all of which were in the old territory of Tukhāra. From the country of Munjān, farther traveling westward, the Master entered a mountain and after going for more than three hundred *li,* reached the country of Himatala[38], also in the old territory of Tukhāra. Its customs were quite like those of Turks with the exception of the headdress of the married woman. The headdress was a wooden horn more than three *chi* high, with two prominent branches in front, symbolizing parents-in-law. The upper one represents the father-in-law, and the lower the mother-in-law. One of the branches would be removed accordingly with the death of one of the parents-in-law; if both parents died, the whole headdress would be discarded. From here going westward again for more than two hundred *li*, the Master reached the country of Badakshan[39], also in the old territory of Tukhāra. Detained by the cold weather and snow storm, he remained there for over one month.

From here traveling southeast in mountains for more than two hundred *li,* the Master reached the country of Yamgān[40]. And again going southeast on a dangerous trail for more than three hundred *li,* he came to the country of Kurān[41]. Then proceeding northeast for more than five hundred *li* he reached the country of Tamasthiti[42] (also known as Humi), which was situated between two mountains and by the Oxus River. This country produced good horses, small but strong. The local people had violent temper, lacking etiquette and culture. Moreover, they looked unsightly, particularly having eyes green in hue different from the people in other countries. There were about a dozen monasteries. The city of Khamdādh[43] was the capital, inside which there was a monastery built by the former king. At this monastery, hanging over a stone Buddha statue was a round canopy wrought in copper and gold, also adorned with variegated jewels.

Suspending in the air on its own, this canopy rotated along with the circumambulating of the devotees and stopped when the devotees stopped. No one could give the explanation for this miraculous phenomenon (A detailed account of the construction of this monastery was recorded in the other book[44]).

Proceeding from the great mountain of this country to the north, the Master came to the country of Śikni[45]. And traversing the country of Tamasthiti, he came to the country of Śāmbhi[46]. Then from here going eastward in mountains for more than seven hundred *li,* he reached the Pamir Valley, which was more than one thousand *li* long from east to west, and more than one hundred *li* broad from south to north. Since the valley was situated between two snow mountains amid Pamir range, all the year round the wind was blowing and snow falling without a moment's break even in springs and summers. Due to the severe cold, this land has little vegetation. So, it is not suitable for farming. The region was barren with no sign of habitation. In the valley was a large lake measuring three hundred *li* east-west and more than fifty *li* south-north, situated in the center of Jambudvīpa. Of the high altitudes, the lake extended out of the sight. Hundreds and thousands of different kinds of aquatic animals were making noises together, which sounded like the din produced by workshops in the market. Also, there were variegated huge birds, more than one *zhang* tall, whose eggs were as large as urns, might be so-called Tiaozhi[47] huge ova in olden times. A river branched out from the lake in the west, which reached the eastern border of the country of Tamasthiti where it joined with the Oxus and flowed westward into the sea. All the rivers on the right side converged in the same way. Another river branched out from the lake in the east, which reached the western border of the country of Kashgar where it joined with the Sītā River, and then flowed eastward into the sea. All the rivers on the left side converged in the same way. To the south of the valley, beyond the mountain there was the country of Balūra[48], rich in gold and silver minerals. The hue of gold looked like fiery. The breadth of this lake from south to north was the same as that of the Anavatapta Lake[49].

Proceeding eastward out of the valley, trekking up a dangerous mountain trail and wading across the thick snow for more than five hundred *li,* the Master reached the country of Kabandha[50]. Its capital was located beside a precipitous mountain range, with Sītā River at its back in the north. The Sītā River flew eastward into Salt Lake (Lop Nor)[51] . In the midst of flowing, it became a subterranean current and came out again at the Jishi Mountain (Mountain of Accumulated Stones). The river was the source of the rivers of the country. The king was wise and intelligent. He had ascended the throne for many years since the founding of this country, claiming himself to be a descendant of the *cina-deva-gotra* (meaning "offspring of the Han sun"). There was a monastery in his old palace built for the late Śāstrin Kumārajīva. The venerable Kumārajīva was a native of Takṣaśilā, who was perspicacious and brilliant. It was said that he was capable of reciting thirty-two thousand words and writing the same number of words every day. With great wisdom, he sported with various dharmas as a child playing with different toys; he was also fruitful in composing treatises. Totally, he had composed several tens of treatises, all of which were in wide circulation, thus he was regarded as the founder of the Sautrāntika School. At that time, there were four famous Śāstrins: Aśvaghoṣa[52] in the east, Deva in the south, Nāgārjuna in the west, and Kumārajīva in the north. They were honored as Four Suns, implying that they could dispel the delusions of living beings. Kumārajīva had enjoyed a high reputation, even the late king once launched a military expedition to attack his homeland in order to invite him back for worship.

More than three hundred *li* to the southeast of the city was a huge rocky bluff with two caves, in each of which there was an arhat entering the Samādhi of the Cessation of Mentality. Sitting straight and motionless, they looked bony but did not collapse and decay over past seven hundred odd years. The Master spent about twenty days in this country.

Then traveling northeast for five days, he was encountered by a gang of bandits. The merchants were so frightened that they climbed up the hill, and the elephants were chased so hard that some of them jumped into the river and drowned. After the bandits had gone away, the Master, again with the merchants, resumed their journey, gradually down to the east. Regardless of severe cold and hazards, proceeding for more than eight hundred *li* and getting out of the Pamir Ranges, the Master reached the country of Usar[53].

Two hundred *li* to the west of the city, there was a great mountain with lofty peaks and ridges, in which stood a stūpa. According to a story, several hundred years ago, the mountain was struck by a thunderbolt and split into halves. There appeared a bhikṣu, who was haggard but gigantic in stature, sitting in meditation with closed eyes, with hair all over his head hanging down to his shoulders. A woodcutter discovered him and made a report to the king. The king came to worship him in person. When the news spread, the gentry and common people far and near assembled to pay homage and make offerings, with flowers amassed like a mattress.

The king asked, "Who is this person?" and got the answer from a bhikṣu, "He is an arhat entering the Samādhi of the Cessation of Mentality. With the elapse of time, his hair has grown to such a length."

The king asked again, "In what way could we wake him up?"

The bhikṣu answered, "His corporeal body is sustained by material food, and it will be ruined once he is awaken from meditation. It is better to sprinkle his body with milk and ghee first to moisten his flesh and skin, and then strike a Ghaṇṭā[54] to wake him up. Perhaps by so doing, we would bring him out of his meditation."

The king said, "Good indeed."

Then following the advice of the monk, the king enjoined his man to sprinkle milk over the arhat and strike the Ghaṇṭā. Consequently, the arhat opened his eyes, looked around and asked, "Who are you in the robes of Dharma?"

"We are bhikṣus." was the answer.

He then asked, "Where is my teacher Tathāgata Kāśyapa now?" and got the reply, "He attained nirvāṇa a long time ago."

On hearing this, the arhat was depressed, yet he demanded again, "Has Śākyamuni Buddha attained the Supreme and Proper Enlightenment yet?"

The reply was, "Yes. He has already obtained the Enlightenment. After benefiting all living creatures, he has already attained nirvāṇa."

After hearing those words, the arhat lowered his eyes in

concentration for a long time. Then he lifted his hair with his own hands to rise up into the air, and caught a fire by performing the magic power. After his cremation, his remains dropped down on the ground, which the king and the people collected and built a stūpa for storage and commemoration. It was the very stūpa that the Master saw here.

From here going northward for more than five hundred *li*, the Master reached the country of Kashgar (formerly called Shule after the name of its capital city. The correct pronunciation was Śrīkrītāti. Shule was an erroneous name.) Then from here proceeding to the southeast for more than five hundred *li* and crossing the Sītā River and a lofty ridge, he came to the country of Chakuka[55] (formerly known as Juqu). To the south of the country was a great mountain, in which there were a lot of cavern chambers. In India, those who had attained some fruition in spiritual cultivation usually employed the supernatural power to come and live here; therefore, in this place the persons who entered nirvāṇa were large in number. Even at present, there were still three arhats abiding in chambers, who had entered the Samādhi of the Cessation of Mentality. Monks often came there to shave off their slow-growing beard and hair. In addition, the country has also preserved a large number of Mahāyāna scriptures, including dozens of copies, each with a hundred thousand stanzas.

From here again going eastward for more than eight hundred *li,* the Master came to the country of Kustana[56] (meaning "milk of earth," the interpretation of the local language; commonly known as the country of Hvamna. It was called as Odun by the Huns, as Hotan by the various *hu* tribes, as Kustana by the Indians; it was known as Yutian erroneously in olden times), more than half of which was covered by desert, and thus suitable to produce cereals and fruits. And it also produced carpets, fine felt and cotton cambric. Craftsmen here spun extremely fine silk and linen. This land abounded in the ores of white and black jade. The climate here was temperate. The local people knew etiquette and justice, also were fond of learning and music. Their refined and prudent proprieties made them distinguished from other *hu* tribes[57]. Its writing system was derived from that of India but with slight differences. Buddhism had been highly esteemed here. There were a hundred monasteries with more than five thousand monks, most of whom were studying the Mahāyāna teachings. The king was heroic, intelligent, valiant, dignified, benevolent and virtuous. He claimed himself to be a descendant of the God Vaiśravaṇa. The ancestor of the king was one of the princes of King Aśoka, who originally was in the country of Takṣaśilā, and later was driven to the north of the snow mountains. On account of rearing livestock, he migrated to wherever the water and grass was available; finally, he came here and founded the capital. Having married for a long time but without giving birth to a son, he had to pray at a temple to God Vaiśravaṇa for one, and thus got a son from the forehead of a god statue. At the same time, from the ground in the front yard of the temple miraculously surged out the fluid as sweet and tasty as milk, which was then taken to raise the kid. In this way the baby boy had been brought up. After the demise of the king, his son succeeded to the throne. The new king was well-known for being majestic and virtuous, annexing several countries by his military power. The present king was a descendant of him. Since the king's ancestor was nourished by milk from Earth, the country should be correctly called

Kustana, translated as Earth Milk country.

The Master entered its domain and arrived at the capital Bhāgya[57], in which a sitting statue of Buddha was enshrined, more than seven *chi* in height. Looking dignified with perfect features, the statue had a precious crown on the head. According to the old stories, this statue originally was seated in the country of Kaśmīra, and was later invited here. A long time ago, there was an arhat. Once he met a *Śramaṇa* who was afflicted with measles, about to pass away. Knowing this *Śramaṇa* wanted to eat vinegary rice cakes, the arhat employed his divine vision to find some in Kustana; then he went there on his deva-feet and begged some back for the *Śramaṇa.* After eating, the *Śramaṇa* was so satisfied that he vowed to be reborn in Kustana. Later on, his wish was realized and he was reborn into the royal family of Kustana. He succeeded to the throne and showed a distinguished talent, especially resourceful in military strategies. With an ambition to annex other countries, he climbed over the snow mountains to invade his homeland in the previous life. The king of Kaśmīra had to summon the generals and train his army to resist the incoming aggregation. The arhat said to the king of Kaśmīra, "It is no need to take military measures. I shall drive them away by myself." Then he went to the place where the Kustana king had stationed. He not only told the king the forehead-birth story, but also pointed out the king's faults. Directly, he told the king that those faults were caused by his greed and violence. And as a testimony, he showed the king the robe which he once wore as a *Śramaṇa* in the previous life. Seeing the robe, the king immediately regained a knowledge of previous lifetimes, so he felt ashamed of what he had done. Then he reestablished a friendship with the king of Kaśmīra and withdrew his troops. Carrying the statue he worshiped in his previous life, he planned to return to his country with the army; but when they arrived at this city, this statue refused to move, and even if the king and the soldiers bent all the maximum efforts, it still could not be moved a little. Thereafter, a monastery had to be built to enshrine the statue, and monks were invited to live in. The king offered his favorite precious crown to adorn the head top of the statue, which still could be seen at present. The crown was bedecked with many precious substances, winning a wide admiration.

The Master spent seven days in Kustana. Upon hearing the entrance of the Master into his country, the Kustana king came to the frontier to welcome him in person. Two days later, the Master resumed his journey. The king returned to his capital in advance, while leaving his son at the Master's service. After the Master had proceeded for two days, the king again dispatched his attendant officials to receive him. The Master stopped over to spend the night at a place forty *li* away from the capital. On the following day, the king, leading laity and monks, was already waiting for the Master on the left side of the road, with the music being performed and incenses burnt and various flowers offered. When the Master arrived, he was ushered into the city and lodged in a Hīnayāna Sarvāstivāda Vinaya.

More than ten *li* south of the capital was a great monastery built by the former king of this country for the arhart Vairocana (meaning "universal illumination"). In the past, this country had not been influenced by the Dharma teachings; later, an arhart came from Kaśmīra and sat in meditation in woods. When a man saw him, amazed at his build and garment, he made a report to the king. Upon hearing the report, curious about the arhat's appearance and behavior, the king came in person to see him.

He asked the arhat, "Who are you, alone in the woods?"

The arhat answered, "I'm a disciple of the Tathāgata. I'm residing here for the Dharma."

The king inquired again, "What does it mean by the title of the Tathāgata?"

The arhat replied, "The Tathāgata is one of the virtuous epithets of the Buddha. In former times, he was a prince named Sarvasiddhārtha[58], the son of King Śuddhodana. Because he felt sympathetic to the living beings who were painfully submerging in the sea of desires without the salvation and reliance, he renounced his enormous wealth, his large family, even his throne, and went alone to the desolate forest to practice the self-cultivation. After six years, he attained Buddhahood, thus obtaining a golden body of the buddha, and realizing the unsurpassed correct enlightenment[59]. Then he sprinkled the sweet dew of the Dharma at the Deer Park, and revealed his dazzling Maṇi[60] pearl on the Vulture Peak. In the course of his eighty-year lifetime, he had preached the Dharma to the sentient beings, granting them benefits and felicity. At last, conforming to the causality of transformation, he ceased his manifestations in the mortal world and attained nirvāṇa. Now, his bequeathed image and scriptures are still extant and in circulation. Owing to the past blessings, the king became the lord of the people. Please shoulder the responsibility to turn the Dharma-wheel continuously and become the reliance of all sentient beings. Is it reasonable for you to keep ignorant of Buddhism?"

The king answered, "Our past sins have been accumulated so enormously that we have been restrained from hearing of the name of the Buddha. Today, it's our fortune to have the saint coming here to show us the truth. Now that here remain image and scriptures, we'd like to uphold them in worship and become the practitioner of the Dharma."

The arhat replied, "If you are to convert to Buddhism sincerely, you should build a monastery first, and then, the divine image would come here of its own accord."

Then the king returned and meticulously selected a sacred site with his ministers. He issued an order to recruit the skillful craftsmen, consulted the arhat about the architectural style and started to build the monastery.

On the completion of construction work, he asked the arhat, "Here is the monastery, but where is the Buddha image?"

The arhat answered, "Only if you show your sincerity is the image coming soon."

Then the king led his ministers, gentry, and commoners, holding fire and flowers in their hands, waiting sincerely. In a moment, here came a Buddha statue in the air and descended on the lotus seat. Solemn and sublime, the statue was illumining all around with the dazzling light. On seeing this, the king expressed his adoration with joy. Then he invited the arhat to preach the Dharma to his people. Also, he and his countrymen gave offerings in abundance. This monastery was the first one constructed in this country.

Because the Master had lost some scriptures previously when he was crossing the river, no sooner had he arrived at the city than he sent someone to Kucha and Kashgar to seek the scriptures. Now he was detained by the king of Kustana and could not resume his homebound journey. Thus, he wrote a letter to report his experiences to the court of Tang with the effect that he had been to the Brahminic countries to seek the Dharma and now already arrived at Kustana on his return journey. He asked a young man from Gaochang to follow some merchants and take the letter to the capital Chang'an. The letter reads as follows:

I, *Śramaṇa* Xuangzang, beg to make the following statement:

I have heard that Ma Rong[61] was erudite, so Zheng Xuan[62] went to study with him in Fufeng; Fu Sheng[63] had the wisdom of discernment, so Chao Cuo[64] modestly acknowledged him as his tutor in Ji'nan. As we see, even a newly-established thought like Confucianism could make the ancient people take the trouble to cover a long distance to pursue, not to mention the divine traces left by various buddhas when they brought benefits to the world, and the wonderful teachings of the Tripiṭaka which is intended to resolve the entanglement of ignorance. How dare we fear the long-distance travel and not aspire to pursue them? Buddha was born in the West whereas his bequeathed teachings have come to the East. However, in my view, although the holy scriptures had been introduced into our land, the comprehensive and unified system had not been well established. For this reason, I often thought of furthering my study in India at any cost or consequences. Subsequently, in the fourth month of the third year of Zhenguan (629), I ventured to transgress the national regulations and set out privately for India. On my road I trod on the vast shifting desert, climbed over the high ranges of the snow mountains, passed through precipitous cliffs of the Iron Gate and witnessed rolling waves of the Hot Sea. Setting out from our capital Chang'an and terminating in the new city of Rājagṛha, my whole journey covers more than fifty thousand *li.* Customs I encountered were diverse in a thousand ways, and hardships and dangers set before me were myriad in number, but under the authoritative influence of Your Majesty, no hindrance could stop me from forging forward. Moreover, honorably treated with abundant etiquette and lavish offerings along the road, I even didn't feel any weariness or fatigue. At long last, I had my aspiration fulfilled. I visited Gṛdhrakūṭa Mountain and worshiped the Bodhi tree; I beheld the traces I had never seen and read the scriptures I had never heard of. I marveled at the unfathomable and miraculous wonders in this world; I witnessed numerous transformations from the power of *yin* and *yang*. As a messenger of your virtue and benevolence, I arose the adoration of those alien people for Your Majesty. Totally, I have spent seventeen years visiting and travelling. On my return journey, I started from the country of Prayāga, passed through the domain of Kapiśā, scaled the Pamir Range, crossed the Pamir Valley, and now I arrived at Kustana. Because my elephants were drowned in a river, there is no carriage available for transporting large amounts of scriptures and books, and I have to stop for a while. I am afraid

I could not meet Your Majesty at an earlier moment, no matter how strong my aspiration for seeing you soon. Thus, I send Ma Xuanzhi, a lay man from Gaochang, to follow some merchants to go to the capital to deliver my letter, so that Your Majesty would know of my intention beforehand.

Afterwards, the Master delivered lectures on the *Yogācārabhūmi Śāstra*, the *Abhidharmasamudāya Prakaraṇa Śāstra*, the *Abhidharmakośa Śāstra*, and the *Mahāyānasaṅgraha Śāstra*to the monks of Kustana. During the whole day and night he expounded these four treatises one after another. The king, laity, and monks, took refuge in the Master, listening to him and upholding the Dharma. Every day the listeners amounted to one thousand. Seven to eight months have passed, and the youth who had been dispatched to the capital returned, with an envoy sent by the Emperor to receive the Master, who brought an imperial letter of regards, running as follows:

Upon hearing the Master's coming back from the alien land after seeking the Way, we had boundless joy. You should come to us as quickly as possible. The monks in that kingdom who know Sanskrit language and understand scriptures should be brought to us too. We have already ordered Kustana and other kingdoms to dispatch guides to escort you back, thus, the manpower and carriages will not be in shortage. The governor of Dunhuang is commanded to receive you in the desert, and the governor of Shanshan[65] to receive you at Jumo[66].

After reading this letter, the Master resumed his journey all at once. The Kustana king presented the Master with abundant sustenance.

After leaving the capital city, forging eastward for more than three hundred *li*, the Master reached the city of Pima[67]. In the city, there was a sandalwood-carved statue, more than three *zhang* in height, very solemn and dignified. It frequently gave miraculous responses to prayers. It was said when a person suffered from a certain disease, if he pasted a piece of gold foil on the body of the statue corresponding to his painful part, he would recover soon; and when a person had a wish, if he prayed sincerely, his wish would come true. According to a legend, formerly when the Buddha was living in the world, King Udayana of the country of Kauśāmbi made this statue, and after the Nirvāṇa of the Buddha, it flew from that country to the city of Araurak north of this country, and later it came here of itself (the story was recorded in the other book[68]). It was also said there was a prophecy that after the extinction of the Dharma of Śākyamuni, the statue would enter the Dragon Palace[69].

Leaving the city of Pima, forging ahead to the east, the Master entered the desert. After more than two hundred *li,* he reached the city of Nina[70]. Continuously going eastward, he entered a great shifting desert where the sand drifted with the wind, without grass nor water. This place was often haunted by ghosts and evil spirits; and local people and animals easily succumbed to high temperature and fatal wind. There was no path. Wayfarers fro and back had to track the skeletons of humans or animals as road signs to find the way. What's worse, it was very difficult to advance on such a hard and barren land, which was already narrated in the proceeding text. Trekking for more than four hundred *li*, he reached the old territory of Tukhāra and again for more than six hundred *li*, he reached the old territory of Calmadana, the land of Jumo. Then he forged to the northeast for more than one thousand *li,* and arrived at the country of Navāpa, the land of Loulan. Having passed through all those places, at long last the Master came to the domain of his motherland. Having changed his horse for the one of the Tang, he dismissed the Kustana attendants, together with camels and horses. When the retinue were paid for their labor on official order, they declined and departed.

Upon arriving at Shazhou[71], once more the Master wrote a letter to the Emperor. At the time, the Emperor was at Luoyang Palace, when he received the letter, he knew the Master was approaching the capital. Then the Emperor ordered Fang Xuanling, Imperial Regent of the Western Capital, Left Puye[72] with the title of the Duke of Liangguo, to dispatch officials to wait and welcome the Master. Having heard that the Emperor was about to go on a punitive expedition to Liaodong[73], fearing that any possible delay on the road would spoil his chance to meet His Majesty, the Master doubled his speed and reached the Cao River[74] so quickly that the officials in charge of the reception were totally at a loss about how to welcome the Master in proper manners, for all the things involved in the reception ceremony had not been prepared yet. However, hearing the news, the local people, of their own accord, rushed out hurriedly and impulsively to greet the Master. They crammed the thoroughfares in such jostling closeness that the Master was unable to move forward. So, he had no choice but to stay over by the Cao River.

ANNOTATION

1 Traditional Chinese astronomy has a system of dividing the celestial sphere into asterisms or constellations.Seven Luminaries (*qiyao*七曜) consists of Sun, Moon and the five planets visible to the naked eye: Mars (*huo*火), Mercury (*shui*水), Jupiter (*mu*木), Venus (*jin*金), Saturn (*tu*土), corresponding to the five agents (*wuxing* 五行).

2 12 pitches of ancient Chinese music, which can be further classified into six *yanglü* 阳律 and six *yinlü* 阴律. The twelve-pitch scale is a standardized gamut of twelve notes. The series of twelve notes known as the twelve *lü* were simply a series of fundamental notes from which scales could be constructed. The gamut or its subsets were used for tuning and are preserved in bells and pipes. According to the chapter *Lüli Zhi*《律历志》in the *Hanshu*《汉书》, six lǜ pipes 六律 are: Huangzhong 黄钟, Taicu 太族, Guxian 姑洗, Ruibin 蕤宾, Yize 夷则, and Wuyi 亡射; six lǚ pipes 六吕: Linzhong 林钟, Nanlü 南吕, Yingzhong 应钟, Dalü 大吕, Jiazhong 夹钟, and Zhonglü 中吕.

3 According to Buddhism, we can understand Buddha through the threefold body or nature of a Buddha: Dharmakāya (Dharma-body): the body of Truth; Nirmāṇakāya (Transformation-body); Saṃbhogakāya (Enjoyment-body).

4 Refers to the Buddha. Emperor Ming (r. 58–75) of the Han Dynasty dreamed a golden deity flying in front of his palace, which foretold the introduction to Buddhism, so the golden figure is usually taken to refer to the Buddha.

5 Present Raj Mahal in south India.

6 Five watches of the night: (1) 7 to 9 pm; (2) 9 to 11 pm; (3) 11 to 1 am; (4) 1 to 3 am; (5) 3 to 5 am.

7 Emperor Taizong of Tang (r. 626–649), previous Prince of Qin, personal name Li Shimin 李世民, was the second emperor of the Tang Dynasty China, ruling from 626 to 649. He is traditionally regarded as a co-founder of the dynasty for his role in encouraging Li Yuan, his father, to rebel against the

Sui Dynasty at Jinyang in 617.Taizong is typically considered to be one of the greatest emperors in China's history and henceforth, his reign became regarded as the exemplary model against which all future emperors were measured. His era, the "Reign of Zhenguan"贞观之治 is considered a golden age in Chinese history.

8 This is a palace music and dance of the Tang Dynasty, also translated as the *Music of Prince of Qin Breaking up the Enemy's Front*. It was for banquets at first, but later was used to worship. According to the *Good Words of Sui and Tang* (*Suitang jiahua*《隋唐嘉话》), *Old Book of Tang-Treatise of Music* (*Jiutangshu yinyuezhi*《旧唐书・音乐志》) and *Extensive Records of the Taiping Era* (*Taiping Guangji,*《太平广记》), in 620, the Prince of Qin, Li Shimin defeated the army of the rebellion commander Liu Wuzhou刘武周 (?–620), the privates of Hedong 河东 danced and sang, the soldiers used the old melody which was popular among the Tang army to fill the new lyric, and that is the embryonic form of this Music. In early 627, Tang Taizong called Wei Zheng to write seven lyrics, Lü Cai to compose the music, formulated the music officially. Li Shimin made the *Picture of Dance of Breaking Up the Enemy's Front* himself, and improved the dance.

9 Three Regions of the Yellow River refers to the central China covering three commanderies: Henan 河南, Hedong 河东, Henei 河内.

10 The Four Seas were four bodies of water that metaphorically made up the boundaries of ancient China. There is a sea for each for the four cardinal directions. The West Sea is Qinghai Lake, the East Sea is the East China Sea, the North Sea is Lake Baikal, and the South Sea is the South China Sea. Two of the seas were symbolic until they were tied to genuine locations during the Han Dynasty's wars with the Xiongnu. The lands "within the Four Seas", a literary name for China, are alluded to in Chinese literature and poetry.

11 In 621, Li Shimin was made to be the great General Tiance 天策将军.

12 Sun, Moon, and the star.

13 Or the six directions: the four cardinal directions:south, north, east, west, and the up and down, generally denoting the universe. Here it refers to people within the territory of China.

14 After establishing the Han Dynasty, Emperor Gaozu 高祖, Liu Bang 刘邦 (r. 206–195 BC) appointed princes and vassal kings to help him govern the Han Empire and gave each of them a piece of land. His son Liu Fei 刘肥(died in 189 BC) was appointed as the Prince Daohui of Qi. During the reign of Emperor Hui, Liu Ying刘盈(r.194–188 BC), Qi was further divided into six parts, with each given to one of the six sons of Liu Fei.

15 Refers to a region including Wu Commandery吴郡, Wuxing Commandery 吴兴郡, and Kuaiji Commandery会稽郡 in ancient China, covering some places in modern Jiangsu 江苏 and Zhejiang 浙江 Provinces.

16 A sort of despised caste.

17 Field of Blessedness: a figurative term for those such as buddhas and monks who deserve offerings. Just as a field can yield crops, so donors can obtain good karmic results through their offerings to them.

18 Ten Capabilities: ten masteries possessed by a buddha or bodhisattva concerning: (1) lengthening or shortening life span; (2) samādhi; (3) material things; (4) actions; (5) births; (6) aspiration (or vow); (7) understanding; (8) supernatural abilities; (9) wisdom and (10) teachings.

19 Two Adornments: (1) adornment of wisdom and (2) adornment of good deeds such as alms-giving and keeping the precepts.

20 Woollen cape.

21 Modern Kosam, Uttar Pradesh, India.

22 Modern Jalandhar, a city in the Doaba region of the north Western Indian state of Punjab.

23 Modern Und to the north of Attock, in Punjab Province of Pakistan.

24 It is the modern Lamghan, near the source of the Kabul River. The Kabul

River emerges in the Sanglakh Range of the Hindu Kush Mountains in Afghanistan and empties into the Indus River near Attock, Pakistan.

25 Modern Bannu, the principal city of the Bannu District in southern Khyber Pakhtunkhwa, Pakistan.

26 Present the place southwest of Peshawar.

27 Modern Ghazni, the capital of Ghazni Province in Afghanistan. It is located in the central-east part of the country.

28 It is identified with Wardak about 40 miles north of Ghazni, in Afghanistan.

29 The capital of Kapiśā.

30 Refers to the eastern part of the Hindu Kush Mountains, Borossian Ridge, which is now the Kavak Pass in northeastern Afghanistan, about 3,500 meters above sea level.

31 Modern Inderab in the north of Kavak Pass in Afghanistan.

32 In the basin of the Khost River, the upper tributary of the Amu Darya in Afghanistan.

33 It is identified either with modern Talikhan east to Kondoz in Afghanistan, or with Munjan in Badakhshon.

34 Close to modern Hazrat-Imam, important ferry on the Amu Darya.

35 It is identified with Ragh, between the Kokcha River and the Amu Darya.

36 It is supposed to be modern Ishkashim in Afghanistan.

37 On the south bank of the Kokcha.The Kokcha River is in northeastern Afghanistan. A tributary of the Panj River, it flows through Badakhshan Province in the Hindu Kush.

38 It is supposed to be situated in the province of Badakshan or Daraim.

39 The capital of this country is supposed to be on or near the site of modern Fayzabad in Afghanistan. Feyzabad sits on the Kokcha River and serves as the provincial capital of Badakhshan Province.

40 Jerm of Badakhshan Province in the valley of Kokcha River.

41 It is in the upper part of the valley of the Kokcha River, with its capital

supposed to be modern Lajward.

42 Modern Wakhan, a very mountainous and rugged part of the Pamir, Hindu Kush and Karakoram regions of Afghanistan.

43 Located in the western part of Wakhan. Wakhan, on the left bank of the Ab-j Panja River.

44 Refers to the *Great Tang Records on the Western Regions* (*Datang Xiyu Ji*《大唐西域记》). Detailed record is in the fascial twelve of it.

45 It is identified with modern Shighnan, is an historic region whose name today may also refer to a town and a district in Badakhshan Province in the mountainous northeast of Afghanistan and also a district in Gorno-Badakhshan Autonomous Province in Tajikistan.

46 It is supposed to be the region around the modern Mastuj of Pakistan.

47 Tiaozhi is the name of an ancient country between the Tigris River and the Euphrates River in present-day Iraq.

48 Modern Baltistan, also known as Baltiyul or Little Tibet, is a mountainous region on the border of Pakistan and India in the Karakoram mountains just south of K2 (the world's second-highest mountain). Baltistan borders Gilgit to the west, Xinjiang Uygur Autonomous Region (China) in the north, Ladakh on the southeast and the Kashmir Valley on the southwest.

49 According to an ancient Buddhist cosmological view, the lake is lying at the center of the world. The name Anavatapta means "heat-free"; the waters of the lake were thought to be able to soothe the fires that torment beings. Anavatapta is also the name of the dragon that lives in the lake; having become a bodhisattva, it was free from the distresses that plague other dragons, which are tormented by fiery heat and preyed on by garudas. Lying south of Perfume Mountain, Lake Anavatapta is said to be 800 *li* in circumference and bordered by gold, silver, and precious stones. Four rivers issued from the lake. The earthly manifestation of the lake is often identified with Lake Manasarovar, which lies at the foot of Mount Kailash

(Gandhamadana or Perfume Mountain) in the Himālayas. The four mythical rivers are sometimes identified with the Ganges (east), the Indus (south), the Amu Darya (west), and the Tarim or the Yellow River (north).

50 Modern Taxkorgan Tajik Autonomous County (sometimes spelled Tashkurgan or Tashkorgan) , a county of Kashgar Prefecture in western Xinjiang, China.

51 Lop Nor is in southeastern Xinjiang Uygur Autonomous Region, east and lowest of Tarim Basin. It was a huge salty marshland covering 3000 square kilometers northeast of Xinjiang Uygur Autonomous Region. There were many names of Lop Nor, like salt marsh, dry sea by its character. Many rivers flew to Tarim Basin, such as Tarim River, Kongqi River, Qiemo River, Shule River and gathered as a huge lake, which was disappeared because of several rechanneled rivers. Lop Nor was ever a lively oasis with thousands of cows and horses, surrounding with green forests and clear rivers, but turned to an endless droughty Gobi Desert with no grass, river, bird. The land surface temperature is up to 70 degree centigrade (158 degree Fahrenheit). However, Lop Nor has Chinese richest sylvine mining resource with more than 2500 million tons of sylvine. After drought of Lop Nor, the ecological environment around it charged radically. Herbaceous plants died; euphratica forest was encroached by desert. The desert encroached to Lop Nor by three to five meters every year. Lop Nor was integrated with Taklimakan Desert soon, and this became a bare land. (https://www.discoverchinatours.com/travel-guide/korla/lop-nor/)

52 Aśvaghoṣa or Ashvaghosha 马鸣(c. 80 – c. 150) was a Buddhist philosopher, dramatist, poet and orator from India. He was the most famous in a group of Buddhist court writers, whose epics rivalled the contemporary Ramayana. Whereas much of Buddhist literature prior to the time of Aśvaghoṣa had been composed in Buddhist Hybrid Sanskrit, Aśvaghoṣa wrote in Classical Sanskrit.

53 Modern Shache (Yarkant) County or Yarkand County, a county in the

Xinjiang Uygur Autonomous Region, China, located on the southern rim of the Taklamakan desert in the Tarim Basin.

54 The bell.

55 Modern Yecheng County 叶城 in the Xinjiang Uygur Autonomous Region.

56 Modern Yutian County in the Xinjiang Uygur Autonomous Region.

57 Southeast of present Pishan 皮山 County, Xinjiang Uygur Autonomous Region.

58 Sarvārthasiddha, or Siddhārtha, meaning "all wishes realized", the name given to Śākyamuni at his birth.

59 Or anuttarā-samyak-saṃbodhi, the dharma realized by oneself, instead of being untaught by the teacher.

60 Maṇi: the best pearl.

61 Ma Rong 马融 (79–166), courtesy name Jichang 季长, was an Eastern Han dynasty government official and an influential Confucianist scholar. He was known for his commentaries on the books on the *Five Classics*, and the first scholar known to have done this. He also developed the double column commentary while doing it. His main students were Lu Zhi 卢植（139–192) and Zheng Xuan 郑玄(127–200). His biography appears in the *Book of Later Han*. He wrote the *Rhapsody on Long Flute* (*Changdi Fu*《长笛赋》); the *Classic of Loyalty* (*Zhong Jing*《忠经》), patterned after the *Classic of Filial Piety* (*Xiao Jing*《孝经》), bears attribution to his name.

62 Zheng Xuan, courtesy name Kangcheng (康成), was an influential Chinese commentator and Confucian scholar near the end of the Han Dynasty. He was born in modern Weifang, Shandong, and was a student of Ma Rong. Like his teacher, he was a member of the Old Text School that was challenging the state orthodox New Text School.

63 Fu Sheng 伏生(268–178 BC, or 260–161 BC), also known as Master Fu, was a Confucian scholar of the Qin and Western Han Dynasties. He was famous for saving the Confucian Classic *Shangshu*《尚书》(*Book of History*)

from the book burning of First Emperor of Qin. Fu Sheng was a native of Ji'nan prefecture 济南郡 (in present-day Zouping 邹平 or Zhangqiu 章丘, Shandong 山东 Province), and was said to be a descendant of the legendary ancient ruler Fuxi. He was a *boshi* 博士 ("erudite") of the Qin Dynasty. In 213 BC First Emperor of Qin ordered the Burning of Books and killed many Confucian scholars. Risking his life, Fu Sheng hid a copy of the books in the walls of his house. He later escaped his hometown in the warfare that soon broke out and eventually ended the Qin Dynasty. After the Han Dynasty was established in 206 BC, Fu Sheng returned home and retrieved the scrolls.

64 Chao Cuo 晁错(ca. 200–154 BC) was a Chinese political advisor and official of the Han Dynasty, renowned for his intellectual capabilities and foresight in martial and political matters. Chao took part in reviving from oblivion the *Book of History*. According to Sima Qian's *Records of the Grand Historian (Shiji)*, when Emperor Wen of Han (r. 180–157 BC) searched the country for copies of the *Shangshu*, Fu Sheng was the only person who could produce one. As Fu was already over 90 years old and unable to travel, Emperor Wen dispatched the official Chao Cuo to study the *Shangshu* from him.

65 In modern Ruoqiang 若羌 County in the Xinjiang Uygur Autonomous Region.

66 In the southwest of Qiemo 且末 Country in the Xinjiang Uygur Autonomous Region.

67 Located to the north of modern Cele 策勒 (Qira) County, in the Xinjiang Uygur Autonomous Region.

68 Refers to the *Great Tang Records on the Western Regions* (*Datang Xiyu Ji* 《大唐西域记》). Detailed record is in the fascial twelve of it.

69 According to tradition, *Prajñapāramita Sūtras* had been given by the Buddha to a great nāga who guarded them in the sea, and were conferred upon Nāgārjuna (c. 150–c. 250) later.

70 Located in the desert to the north of Minfeng 民丰 County in the Xinjiang Uygur Autonomous Region.

71 Present Dunhuang, a county-level city in northwestern Gansu Province, Western China. It has also been known at times as Shazhou and, in Uygur, Dukhan. Dunhuang is situated in an oasis containing Crescent Lake and Mingsha Shan (meaning "Singing-Sand Mountain"). Dunhuang commands a strategic position at the crossroads of the ancient Southern Silk Route and the main road leading from India via Lhasa to Mongolia and Southern Siberia, as well as controlling the entrance to the narrow Hexi Corridor, which led straight to the heart of the north Chinese plains and the ancient capitals of Chang'an (today known as Xi'an) and Luoyang.

72 Puye仆射, head of the important examination bureau of the government.

73 Emperor Taizong, Li Shimin sent punitive expeditions against Korea, which had once been part of the Han empire and was a tributary of the Tang at the time. The Koguryo throne was overthrown in 640, and the new ruler came to pose a threat to the kingdom of Silla in southern Korea, Tang's faithful tributary. The threat of a unified Korea encouraged Li to take action, and in 645 he invaded Koguryo. The expedition made slow progress and had to be withdrawn because of severe winter weather. A similar campaign failed in Korea in 646. Li planned to launch an even larger campaign in 649, but he died before it could be realized. Ultimately Li pushed Chinese power farther West than the Han Dynasty did and with Tang power expanded to the Pamirs Mountains (in present-day Tajikistan), trade flourished.

74 Today's Zao River皂河 , in the western suburb of Xi'an.

Fascicle VI

Beginning with His Arrival at the Western Capital in the First Month of the Spring of the Nineteenth Year of Zhenguan 645 and Ending with His Gratitude for the Preface Written by the Emperor to the Scriptures and the Emperor's Reply in the Sixth Month of the Summer of the Twenty-Second Year of Zhenguan (648)

On the day of Jingzi[1] of the first month in the spring of the nineteenth year of Zhenguan period (645), Fang Xuanling[2], Imperial Regent in the Capital and Left Puye with the title of the Duke of Liang, heard about the Master's safe return with Buddhist scriptures and images, and he dispatched Houmochen Shi, Great General of the Right Wuhou, Li Shushen, Prefect of Yongzhou[3], and Li Qianyou, Magistrate of Chang'an, to receive the Master. Then the Master entered the city along the canal, and was lodged in the capital posthouse (It's also said the Master was lodged in Vermilion Bird Street of the Capital). The spectators crowded around him like clouds.

On the same day, local authorities issued an order asking the monasteries to prepare canopies, carriages, flowers and banners for sending the scriptures and images to Hongfu Monastery, at which the people rejoiced, vying with one another to make lavish adornments. On the following day, the multitudes assembled at the southern end of the Vermilion Bird Street, where several hundred articles brought back by the Master from the Western Regions were exhibited in an orderly way, among which there were one hundred fifty grains of the flesh relics of the Tathāgata, also some Buddha images including a golden statue of Buddha's shadow image left in the Dragon Cave at Prāgbodhi Mountain in Magadha, three *chi* three *cun* in height[4] with the halo and pedestal; a sandalwood replica of Buddha's turning the Dharma Wheel for the first time at the Deer Park in Vārāṇasī, three *chi* five *cun* in height[5]; a sandalwood replica of the statue made by King Udayana of Kauśāmbi who desired to see the Tathāgata with his own eyes, two *chi* nine *cun* in height[6]; a silver replica of the Tathāgata's descending the treasure stairway from Heavenly Palace to Kapitha, four *chi* in height; a golden replica of Buddha's preaching the *Saddharmapuṇḍarīka Sūtra* and other scriptures at Vulture Peak in Magadha, three *chi* five *cun* in height; a sandalwood replica of the Buddha's shadow image left at the place where He subjugated the venomous dragon in Nagarahāra, one *chi* three *cun* in height[7]; a sandalwood statue of the Buddha's traveling in Vaiśāli for alms, and so forth. Besides there were also the Tripiṭaka works obtained by the Master from the Western Regions, including the Mahāyāna scriptures, two hundred and twenty-four works in total; the Mahāyāna treatises, totally one hundred and ninety-two works; fifteen works of Sūtra, Vinaya, and Śāstra of the Sthavira school; fifteen works of Sūtra, Vinaya, and Śāstra of the Mahāsāṃghika school; fifteen works of

Sūtra, Vinaya, and Śāstra of the Saṃmitīya school; twenty-two works of Sūtra, Vinaya, and Śāstra of the Mahīśāsaka school; seventeen works of Sūtra, Vinaya, and Śāstra of the Kāśyapīya school; forty-two works of Sūtra, Vinaya, and Śāstra of the Dharmagupta school; sixty-seven works of Sūtra, Vinaya, and Śāstra of the Sarvāstivāda school; thirty-six works on Hetuvidyā (logic); and thirteen works on Śabdavidyā (grammar). Totally there were amounted to six hundred and fifty-seven works bound in five hundred and twenty bundles and had been carried back by twenty horses.

On the same day, another order was issued asking monasteries to prepare the precious canopies and banners and other offering utensils, and gather at the Vermilion Bird Street on the early morning of the next day, the 28th of the month[8], in order to receive the scriptures and images as well as send them to Hongfu Monastery. Thereupon, mustering their enthusiasm, the multitudes competed with one another to prepare adornments as gorgeous as possible. Out of each monastery, banners, curtains, canopies, and precious altars as well as carriages were moving slowly, while the neatly-attired monks, nuns and others were following behind. Court and monastic musicians were performing in front and men carrying thuribles walking after, together they came to the Vermilion Bird Street where there were also some hundred other such worshiping utensils orderly arranged. The scriptures and images were carried through the streets amid the harmoniously tinkling sounds made by dangling jewelries, submerging in variegated flowers in profusion of colors. No one but might not sing panegyric and shed worries and concerns; and all gasped with amazement at the rarity of the occasion. Starting from the Vermilion Bird Street and terminating at the gate to Hongfu monastery, there were several ten *li* in between. On both sides of the road, capital citizens, scholars, court and local officials were reverentially lining up to witness the grand sight. The streets were crammed with the people and objects, and to prevent the trampling, the officials responsible for maintaining order had to require the people to stay where they were, prohibiting them from moving even when scattering flowers and burning incenses. Fumes were soaring up to the clouds and hymns winding around in the air. In the former time, when Tathāgata descended into Kapilavastu and when Maitreya ascended to the Tuṣita heaven, dragons and deities were making offerings and the celestial beings were flying about. Although the occasion at this moment was less spectacular, it indeed demonstrated the prosperity of the bequeathed Dharma in this era. On that day, every one saw five-colored auspicious clouds appearing in the sky north to the sun, stretching gorgeously for several *li* in perimeter and hovering above the scriptures and images as if they were welcoming and escorting them; actually, not until the scriptures and images arrived at the monastery did those clouds drift away.

Shi Yanzong's annotation: Having consulted the classics as well as historical literature, I have perceived that this auspicious phenomenon symbolizes the joy of Heaven and is usually complimented by the men of insight. In retrospect, dragons and deities made offerings and the celestial beings gave a cordial reception to the Tathāgata when he descended to Kapilavastu, also to Maitreya when he ascended to Tuṣita heaven. The occasion at this moment is less spectacular than the former ones, but the propagation of the bequeathed Dharma in the East has never been as thriving as it is at this point.

On the twenty-third day[9], His Majesty Emperor Wenwu[10] made an audience with the Master at Luoyang imperial palace. On the first day of the second month, they met again at Yiluan Hall. The Emperor received the Master with hospitality. After they took their seats, the Emperor asked, "Why didn't you inform us when you were to take your journey to the west?" The Master replied with apology, "When I was about to take my journey, I did submit petitions for several times, but my sincerity was so insignificant that I wasn't favored with official permission. Since my determination for pursuing the truth was very strong, I ventured to take my journey in secret. Actually, from then on I have always been preoccupied with the fear and guilty for taking action without authorization."

The Emperor said, "You are different from the lay people because you have renounced the household life to be a monk. We appreciate that you have risked your life to pursue the Dharma for the sake of sentient beings. So, it is no need for you to feel guilty. What we want to know is how you managed to reach that distant land separated apart from us by mountains and rivers, and how you traveled through places with peoples of different customs and mentalities."

The Master replied, "[Xuan]Zang has heard that it is not far for a man to visit Heavenly Lake if he can fly with a speedy wind, and nor is it difficult for him to ferry across the surging waves if he can sail in a dragon boat. Ever since Your Majesty was crowned, the turbulence inside Four Seas[11] has been wiped out so that Nine Regions[12] have swayed by your virtue and the space within Eight

Directions[13]enveloped by your benevolence. The breeze of your honesty cools the heat of warfare in the south China and your formidable force aroused awe in areas beyond Pamirs. The rulers of alien tribes, whenever saw a bird flying from the east, would bow in respect for it was supposed to be coming from the Superior Land (China), and how much more so when they met a human being like me who had ever received the edification from Your Majesty! Thus, solely relying on Your prestige, I could go and return without troubles."

The king said, "This is but the praises of the teacher. You flatter us."

Afterwards, the king inquired in detail about the situations of the lands stretching from the west of the Snowy Mountains to the territory of India, including climates, weather, seasons, products, customs, the traces of eight kings as well as sites of the Four Buddhas, also about the other pieces of information that hadn't been mentioned by the Marquis of Bowang[14] or recorded by the historians Ban Gu[15] and Sima Qian[16]. When traveled in cities and kingdoms, the Master kept his eyes and ears open *en route*; so, he was able to recollect what he had experienced with nothing left out. Thus, he could answer the questions set forth by the Emperor in a systematic and logical way. This made the Emperor glad, and he said to his attendant ministers, "In the past, Shi Dao'an was honored by Fu Jian[17] as a man of divine personality, and so revered by the whole court. Today the Master's remarks are elegant and refined, and his personality is pure and lofty. We think he is second to none but far more superior to those Buddhist forerunners."

At the time, Zhangsun Wuji[18], Duke of the Zhaoguo, responded,

"I agree with what Your Majesty has said. When I, your humble servant, was reading the *Spring and Autumn of the Thirty States and Dynasties*[19], from the biography of Dao'an I knew he truly was a lofty and erudite monk. But in his time, the Buddha Dharma just came to China, and there were not many translations of scriptures and treatises, so he merely acquainted himself with the branches and leaves rather than the root of the truth. Obviously, he could not have done better than the Master who embarked on a pilgrimage to the holy land to seek the sources of the subtle theories and follow the holy traces of nirvāṇa."

"Yes, indeed," confirmed the Emperor, then he turned to the Master and suggested, "Since the land of Buddha is far away from here, the divine traces and Dharma teachings haven't been fully recorded in the previous historical literature. Now that you have paid the visit to the land, why not compile a book to let the ill-informed people share your knowledge?"

What's more, after an observation, the Emperor perceived that the Master was competent for taking the position of premier, so he attempted to persuade the Master to give up practicing his Buddha Way and assist in secular affairs, which, however, the master declined by apologizing, "I, Xuanzang, was ordained as a monk at a young age and developed a firm faith in the Way of the Buddha. I have devoted myself to the profound teachings of Buddha so I learned very little about the Confucian theories. If Your Majesty compels me to abandon my monastic life, it could be likened to dragging a boat to land from the water. There is nothing good to the boat but makes it run aground and rot. I hope to practice the Way of Buddha all my life to requite the kindness of the country. If my wish could be fulfilled, it is but my greatest fortune." As the Master declined the offer insistently, he was spared.

At that time, the Emperor was preparing for a punitive expedition to Liaodong Peninsula[20], and his forces had already rounded up in Luoyang from every corner of the nation. Although very busy with military affairs, upon hearing the arrival of the Master, the Emperor immediately issued an order to send for the Master into court for an audience supposed to be short. They, however, had such a pleasant talk that they failed to realize the sun had already slipped to the west. Zhangsun Wuji (594–659), Duke of the Zhaoguo, had to remind the Emperor that it might be late for the Master to return to Honglu Monastery after the sunset. Then the Emperor said to the Master, "It is not to our heart's content to have a talk with you for such a short time, and we wish you could go with us to the east for inspection and sightseeing, so that in the spare time off commanding military actions, we could have a talk again. What do you think about it?"

The Master declined the invitation by saying, "I am afraid I am not able to accompany Your Majesty, because of coming back from such a long journey I have succumbed to some disease."

The Emperor asked, "As a man who is able to travel across the remote and perilous places alone, the journey I recommended to you makes no difference from moving a small step further. Why have you declined it?"

The Master replied, "With gallantry warriors at your command, Your Majesty is going to take on a punitive expedition to the east in order to fight back the invasion and wiping out the rebellious ministers. Rest assured you will achieve victories as glorious as the battles of Muye (1064)[21]and Kunyang[22]. Knowing my limitations, I do not think that I could give any assistance in the warfare; instead, what I will do is merely to consume expenses, which will make me feel abashed. In addition, the Buddhist precept prohibited me to witness warfare, so I dare not to break the rule set up by the Buddha. Humbly I wish you show me the divine mercy and spare me. If so, it would be the greatest prize to me." Hearing those words, the Emperor allowed his request and stopped persuasion.

Then, the Master entreated the Emperor by saying, "I have brought back more than six hundred Sanskrit works from the Western Regions, but I have not translated a word of them. I've known that there is a Shaolin Monastery[23] north to Shaoshi Peak in the south of Song Mountains. For being far away from the turmoil of markets and villages, it is lyrically serene with streams and rocks. Built by Emperor Xiaowen (467–499) of the Later Wei Dynasty, it was the very venue where Tripiṭaka-master Bodhiruci[24] did his translation. I wish to go there to translate the Buddhist scriptures I brought back for the sake of the country. Humbly I am waiting for the permission of Your Majesty." But the Emperor replied, "It is no need for the teacher to do the translation work in mountains. After the teacher went to the West, we had a Hongfu Monastery constructed at the Western Capital in honor of the late Empress Dowager Mu[25], in which there is a courtyard set apart for practicing meditation, quite reserved and tranquil. The teacher could go there to do your translation."

The Master accepted the favor and made another request by saying, "The ordinary people are so ill-informed that when seeing me coming from the West, they were deluded to watch the sight in swarms, thus much likely making my dwelling temple into a market-like place. It not only infringed the law but also disturbed dharma activities. For this reason, I beg to have some sentries in case any offenses might happen." Greatly pleased, the Emperor said, "Your request is truly wise to keep out of blame. We will take charge of it. The teacher could take a short stay here for three or five days before moving to Hongfu Monastery. Whatever you need, consult with Xuanling." Then the Master bade farewell and left.

On the first day of the third month, the Master returned to Chang'an from Luoyang, and dwelt in Hongfu Monastery. To make a preparation for his translation undertaking, he devised a roll of assistants he needed, including theory-consultants, literary composers, scribes, copyists, and so forth; then he presented it to Fang Xuanling, Duke of Liangguo, Sikong Minister, and Imperial Regent. Xuanling forthwith had a memorial written and sent a messenger to take it to the Emperor at Dingzhou[26]. Soon after, an imperial decree came, providing the Master with all he needed sufficiently.

On the second day of the sixth month, twelve venerable theory-consultants arrived, all of whom were well-versed in scriptures as well as treatises of both Mahāyāna and Hīnayāna schools. They were: *Śramaṇa* Lingrun and Wenbei of Hongfu Monastery, *Śramaṇa* Huigui of Luohan (Arhat) Monastery, *Śramaṇa* Mingyan of Shiji Monastery, *Śramaṇa* Faxiang of Baochang Monastery, *Śramaṇa* Puxian of Jingfa Monastery, and *Śramaṇa* Shengfang of Fahai Monastery, all aforementioned monks coming from the monasteries in capital; *Śramaṇa* Daochen of Fajiang Monastery in Guozhou[27];

Śramaṇa Xuanzhong of Yanjue Monastery in Bianzhou[28]; *Śramaṇa* Shentai of Pujiu Monastery in Puzhou[29]; *Śramaṇa* Jingming of Zhenyin Monastery in Jinzhou[30]; and *Śramaṇa* Daoyin of Duobao Monastery in Yizhou[31]. Also there arrived the nine literary composers: *Śramaṇa* Qixuan of Puguang Monastery, *Śramaṇa* Mingrui of Hongfu Monastery and *Śramaṇa* Bianji of Huichang Monastery in the capital city; *Śramaṇa* Daoxuan of Fengde Monastery in Zhongnan[32] Mountains; *Śramaṇa* Jingmai of Fuju Monastery in Jianzhou[33]; *Śramaṇa* Xingyou of Pujiu Monastery and *Śramaṇa* Daochuo of Xiyan Monastery in Puzhou[34]; *Śramaṇa* Huili of Zhaoren Monastery in Youzhou[35]; and *Śramaṇa* Xuanze of Tiangong Monastery in Luozhou[36]. There also arrived one philologist[37], *Śramaṇa* Xuanying of the Great Zongchi Monastery in the capital, and one Sanskrit-improver, *Śramaṇa* Xuanmo of the Great Xingshan Monastery. Besides, here came scribes and copyists, along with the materials provided by authorities.

Not until the first day of the seventh month did the Master begin to render the Sanskrit texts into Chinese. Firstly, he translated four works: the *Bodhisattvapiṭaka Sūtra*, the *Buddhabhūmi Sūtra,* the *Ṣaḍdvāradhāraṇī Sūtra* and the *Prakaraṇāryavācā Śāstra.* He finished the translation of the *Ṣaḍdvāradhāraṇī Sūtra* on the same day. The translation of the *Buddhabhūmi Sūtra* was completed on the fifteenth day of the seventh month. The translation of other two Sūtras were accomplished by the end of the year. On the first day of the first month in the spring of the twentieth year (of Zhenguan, 646), he started to translate the *Mahāyānābhidharmasaṃyukta-samudāya Śāstra* and completed it in the second month. He also translated the

Yogācārabhūmi Śāstra.

On the first day of the seventh month in the autumn, the Master presented the newly-translated works to the Emperor, with a letter attached as follows:

I, *Śramaṇa* Xuanzang beg to submit the following words:

The Eightfold Noble Path serves as the ferryboat or bridge by which a man could cross the sea of suffering, and the One Vehicle (Ekayāna) as the ladder or stairway by which one could ascend to nirvāṇa, but for the time was not ripe (for them to spread into China), they had been kept in storage within the regions west to Pamirs, not only unknown in the times of ancient sovereigns [He]xu and [Da] ting[38]but inaccessible to the people during the Zhou and Qin dynasties. Only when Kāśyapa-Mātṅga[39] arrived at Luoyang did those teachings enter the Central China and only when Senghui[40] travelled to Wu State[41] did the teachings infiltrate Jing and Chu[42] regions. Henceforward, ordinary people have laid causes for their final emancipation by practicing self-cultivation and common households have engaged themselves in setting up the Bodhi enterprises, by which the great and far-reaching benefits of disseminating the Dharma have been testified. Later, the venerable Zhiyan[43] and Faxian[44] sought scriptures from India, and Buddhasiṁha[45] and Kumārajīva[46] translated in succession, who promulgated the profound theories impressively. Unfortunately, however, all of them were living under the illegitimate governments; by contrast, I, Xuanzang, an insignificant man, am alone so fortunate to meet the sagacious monarch. To Your Majesty, I presented all the scriptures and treaties I had brought back, and because of your reverence for the holy words, I graciously have received your kind permission to translate them. Cooperating with theory-consultants and other monks, I have devoted wholeheartedly (to the translation) day and night without wasting even a single moment. A brush in hand all the time, I did my translation around the clock. Up to now, although I could not yet translate them all, there are still five works in fifty-eight fascicles have been finished, namely twenty fascicles of the *Mahābodhisattvapiṭaka Sūtra*, one fascicle of the *Buddhabhūmi Sūtra*, one fascicle of the *Ṣaḍdvāradhāraṇī Sūtra,* twenty fascicles of the *Prakaraṇāryavācā Śāstra* and sixteen fascicles of the *Mahāyānābhidharmasaṃyukta-samudāya Śāstra,* which have already been bound into eight bundles; besides, I have them copied separately and presented them to Your Majesty at the palace.

When the Buddha statue of Hongfu Monastery was molded, I saw Your Majesty coming to consecrate it by painting its pupils, and so I venture to implore Your Majesty to condescend again to pick up your divine brush to write an encomiastic preface to the newly-translated Buddhist scriptures and treatises because they are the texts translated for the first time in this gracious dynasty. May the enlightening and profound teachings shine as brightly as the sun and the moon! May the words written by Your Majesty exist as everlasting as Heaven and Earth! May the people one hundred generations later recite and chant your preface! And may the multitudes after one thousand years still behold it with reverence!

On the other day when they met in Luoyang, the Emperor required the Master to compose the *Record of the Western Regions*, and by now it had already been completed. On the fifth day (of the seventh month in the autumn), the Master presented another letter to the Emperor, which reads:

I, *Śramaṇa* Xuanzang, beg to submit the following statement:

According to the record of historians, the mountains of Panmu and Youling were the boundaries of the domain of the Yellow Emperor[47], and the whole territory of the Emperor Yao[48] from the west desert to the east sea was visited by Xia (Yu)[49] in his various vehicles. The white jade ring of Wangmu[50], Heavenly Queen of the West, was bestowed to the earthly lord who ruled the country with noninterference; and that the arrows made of red vitex twig growing in the eastern region of Yi tribe[51] were presented to the ruler who governed the country benevolently with no need for penal systems. All those glorious events, however, have gone with time, leaving nothing more but the records in ancient classics. In my humble view, since Your Majesty ascending to the Throne, you have seized the times to implement law and order and set up a good example to moralize the people. Your Majesty is not only mighty enough to hold the land in peace, but also able to confer benefits on the multitudes.

I think the pioneering exploits that you have done are no less than those achieved by the ancient emperors who made boats by excavating the tree trunks or invented bows by setting strings on a piece of wood. Your achievements are no less glorious than those made by Goddess Nüwa[52]in remote antiquity: she cut off the four legs of a turtle to make four pillars supporting the four corners of Earth; she heaped up reeds and cinders to stop the surging waters, and she reclaimed the square land and mended the dome of Heaven. You not only displayed the great seven military virtues[53] but also gave edification to people through expounding ten human ethics of Confucianism[54]. Your imperial grace could be likened to the headwaters of fountains and rivers, and your royal favors conferred on everything under heaven are like the rain in spring, never giving up moistening mugworts and reeds; thus in our nation, bushes of ganoderma in the recesses of forests are lavishly blooming and fountains are pleasantly gurgled with sprays of water. With a mighty force you have subdued barbarians, and rallying worthy ministers you have kept the whole empire in peaceful affluence; subsequently, orchestras are rehearsing at the Music Department and melodies are echoed in multi-layered pavilion, the purple air is enveloping the beautifully shell-inlaid royal palace and the white clouds are floating auspiciously over the jade casket holding the record of merits. You have pacified the tumultuous lands and extended your territory to distant places like Ruoshui[55] and Mengsi[56];

you have conferred your liberality upon remote places as Flaming Mountains[57] which is blistering all year around and Snow Mountains which is cold with the perennial ice; as a result, the envoys from foreign countries have come by sea and land to offer abundant tributes and pay allegiance to your authority. There are no such magnificent exploits and great sages recorded in historian books in national library. Formerly, the frontier of the Han (Dynasty) was expanded to Zhangye[58], however, not far from Jincheng[59], and Qin (Dynasty) barely reached Hepu[60] by stationing its troops in Guilin[61]. Alas, even the emperors of old times could not have done more!

Fortunately, I, Xuanzang, am living in the grand times of effectual governance and enjoying the peace at home and abroad. I developed a desire to travel to Brahminic domain to carry out meritorious deeds. My lifespan is as short as that of a morning dew and my vigor feeble as that of autumn katydid, but by relying solely on the divine influences of Your Majesty, I mustered my courage to take on a pilgrimage alone with my shadow in company. I have been to the holy places with a reverential heart and not caring about hardships, I took shelter in one caravanserai after another. I saw the huge ovum of Tiaozhi[62] with my own eyes to confirm what I had heard, also I had a glimpse of the solitary phoenix of Kaśmīra to prove the previous hearsay. Alas, as the time passed by, thanks to the blessing of Heaven, I have had all my wishes fulfilled. I scaled the snowy mountains, ferried across the Hiraṇyavati River[63], visited the Crane Grove and saw the Vulture Peak. I saw the road to Jatavana Garden still in existence and the city foundation of Rājagṛha standing quietly on the hill slopes. I visited all the holy sites to pursue the truth. Seventeen years slipped by before I returned to the imperial capital of my motherland. Totally, the countries I have traveled in and heard about are one hundred and twenty-eight[64].

In my personal view, what Dazhang and Shuhai[65] felt proud of was nothing but the extensiveness of the land they traversed; Kuafu[66], though ranged across the vast land at a wind speed, failed to inform us about the terrain conditions and customs of the people; Ban Chao[67] didn't reach very far, and Zhang Qian[68] travelled a lot but not broadly. In comparison, what I have written in this travelogue shows a different picture from the aforementioned. Although my record does not cover all the alien places, it does relate the various situations of the regions beyond Pamires. My narration tries to be accurate and true to fact, daring not to make any exaggeration by flowery language. After careful compilation and abridgment, the book was finally entitled the *Great Tang Dynasty Record of the Western Regions*, totally in twelve fascicles. Here what I present to you is a copy of this book, expecting under Your Majesty's honorable pen it would be modified and improved so that it would surpass the *Records of Diverse Matters (Bo-wu Zhi)* of Zhang Hua[69] in the Western Jin, and could also acquaint the people of present dynasty with rich knowledge just as what the *Geographical Record of Nine lands (Jiu Qiu)*[70] did in ancient times. But concerning my mediocre endowment, shallow knowledge, and my awkward writing style, I'm afraid my record should be full of omissions and defects. I'm worried that it is unworthy of Your Majesty's perusal.

On the sixth day, the Emperor answered the letter of the Master by saying:

We have read your letter and known your intention. As a man of noble disposition, you renounced secular affairs at a young age; by taking a precious ferryboat of Buddhist teachings, you have disembarked the yonder shore of the sea of suffering; searching for the wondrous Way, you have opened the door to the Dharma; expounding and propagating the grand doctrines, you have exterminated the sins of sentient beings. When the clouds of compassion are to roll up, you stretch them again to shelter all beneath the sky, and when the wisdom sun is to set down in the west, you make it rise to cast light in the world once more. Who else can do so if not you! With the shallow knowledge and clumsy endowment, we are always deluded by the material gains, therefore as to the abstruse teachings of the Buddha, how is it possible for us to speculate? The preface you required us to write for your Chinese versions of the Sanskrit scriptures is verily beyond our capacities. We shall read your new work the *Record of the Western Regions*. The above is written to Monk Xuanzang.

On the seventh day, the Master wrote another letter to the Emperor:

I, *Śramaṇa* Xuanzang, beg to submit the following statement:

With reverence and awe, I received Your Majesty's letter, by which I have been greatly flattered. I would like to follow Your Majesty's words to keep my integrity and strive to do better. Having little talent and less merit, I have been greatly honored to become a member of Sangha; very fortunately I've encountered a prosperous time of unification and peace. Also being blessed by Your Majesty, I developed the dauntless spirit to travel afar; and protected by the almighty power of the Tang Empire, finally I obtained the ultimate truth abroad. In remote regions, facing up to countless dangers, I resolutely held my sincerity; after I returned, in order to assist the propagation of the imperial edification, I decided to compile books brought back and recollected my memory about the alien states. It was of a great honor that I received the imperial decree ordering me to translate the scriptures and treatises, and now into fascicles and scrolls the Chinese versions have already been bound. All needed today is a preface to them.

Your Majesty possesses great wisdom, with your thoughts as vast as the widely stretching clouds and rich as lavishly blossoming heavenly flowers. You not only grasp the theories of *Xiang* (symbols) and *Xi* (their explanations) of the *Book of Changes*[71] but also surpass *Xian* and *Ying*[72] in elegant styles of arts. Your accomplishments overshadow other monarchs in the past, and your prestige is sure to pass down to the posterity in the far future. The divine power (of the Buddha) is so unfathomable that only your superb interpretation could expound, also the abstruse and time-honored teachings await nobody but Your Majesty to preface.

Therefore, I ventured to offend your authorities by entreating you to write a preface. However, your infinite graciousness is not yet granted a consent, because of which, I often make self-examinations and sign with pity, losing myself in disappointment. I have heard that the sun and the moon shine on high, but they never forget to shed their lights on doors and windows, that by their bypass flows, rivers and streams never forget to moisten cliffs and crags, and that the ethereal music played by the zither can never be muted just because a man is deaf, nor the glistening of the gold, jade and other rare treasures can be obscured because a man is blind. This is the way with things in the world. So, with a great respect, once more I venture to supplicate Your Majesty to write a preface to the Chinese versions of Buddhist scriptures and treatises. Just as a thunderstorm falls to the earth and the luminaries shed lights downwards, your generosity would be bestowed upon me. Your preface would be as immortal as Heaven and Earth, and as loftily superior as Sun and Moon. In addition, only by your divine pen would the wondrous words from the Vulture Peak spread far and wide, and merely by your splendid diction the abstruse scriptures of the Kukkuṭārāma[73] pass down forever. If Your Majesty consents to my request, not only the monks, insignificant in number, will be blessed with graciousness (of Buddhism), but all the deluded masses shall be extricated from worldly entanglements.

Thereupon the Emperor granted his request.

In the spring of the twenty-second year (648), the Emperor favored Yuhua Palace[74] with his presence. On the fourteenth day of the fifth month in the summer, the translation of the *Yogācārabhūmi Śāstra* was completed, totaling one hundred fascicles.

On the first day of the sixth month, an imperial decree was issued inviting the Master to the palace. On the way to the palace, messengers were sent in succession by the Emperor to ask the Master to proceed at leisure with fear that he might be tired. No sooner had the Master arrived than the Emperor granted him an audience at Yuhua Palace. In high good humor, the Emperor said, "We have come to this mountain palace to run away from the summer heat of the capital. The fountains and rocks here make us cool and help us regain our vitality to supervise and handle state affairs. But we missed you, and so we issued an order sending for you. The long walk must tire you out."

The Master extended his gratitude and said, "The multitudes are counting on Your Majesty for their livelihood, and so if you are not in good health, the people would be in apprehension. It is said that since Your Majesty came here, the food of imperial household has been fit for your health. Everyone rejoiced at this news. May the loftiness and health of Your Majesty be sustaining long as heaven! It is my great honor that you invite me here regardless of my mediocrity; as a matter of fact, filled with such a strong sense of gratitude, I am not tired at all."

Because the Emperor esteemed the Master as an erudite scholar with an elegant demeanor, he often pressed the Master to abandon the monastic life so as to assist him in state affairs. Formerly when they met at Luoyang Palace, the Emperor talked with the Master of such expectation. Now he repeated his request again by saying, "Such ancient emperors as Yao, Shun[75], Yu, and Tang[76], and even the sovereigns of prosperous Zhou and powerful Han dynasties, found it hard to take a complete view of a large amount of domestic and foreign affairs, let alone inspect them without assistance of others. For this reason, King Wu of Zhou[77], for example, had ten talented courtiers[78] and Emperor Shun had five ministers[79], to help them in governing the state and coordinate the relationship with neighboring countries; thus we know, without exception, almost to a lord, no matter how sagacious and wise they are, they must depend on their ministers. How could we, being unwise and ignorant, take action without relying on the assistance of the worthy and competent ones? We hope the Master will take off the dyed (religious) robe of Subhūti[80], put on the white (household) cloth of Vimalakīrti, and ascend to the post of minister; if so, you could present us with your counsels and sit at the government office to discuss the Way with us. What do you think of it?"

The Master replied, "Your Majesty just said that the state affairs were so abundant that even the Three Sovereigns and the Five Emperors[81] had to depend on the concerted efforts of sages and the worthy for it was hard for them to manage independently. Zhongni

(Confucius) once remarked: 'Where there were deficiencies of the monarchs, there what the ministers were adept in; so, the monarch could be likened to the head and his subordinates the limbs.' In my opinion, such saying is merely intended to admonish the mediocre people rather than those of superior intelligence, because if the ministers are so important, could it be said that King Jie of Xia[82] and King Zhou of Yin[83] hadn't got any ministers to assist them? Making an inference from this case, ministers are not so indispensable. Impressed with your superior wisdom, I respectfully believe that Your Majesty is governing the country on your own grand program, by which all affairs have come into their order accordingly. What's more, ever since Your Majesty followed the mandate of heaven to ascend to the throne, Heaven and Earth have been evolving harmoniously, and our country and neighboring nations have sustained well in peace, all of which are attributed to Your Majesty: you are neither slothful nor lascivious nor luxurious nor wasteful. On the contrary, you are working diligently and always take precautions in peace time against potential adversities, and you have achieved quite a compliment but you are not overbearing at all. What you have done is solely caused by your divine endowments bestowed on you from Heaven, and who else has done anything to your brilliance? Please allow me to cite several more evidences to clarify my point:

Your Majesty's resourcefulness of governance, your talent for leadership, your feats of resisting aggression and suppressing domestic rebellions, your grand enterprises of bringing prosperity and harmony to the masses, your intelligence and literary gift, and even your wholesome and upright physical features are all endowed by

Heaven, have nothing to do with others. This is my first point.

Having grasped essentials while deserted trifles, you highly valued the humanity and advocated the propriety. As a result, the frivolous custom has been removed from this degenerating age and the virtuous statecrafts of the past sage emperors have thus been restored; moreover, you have adopted a taxation system which levied a moderate amount and legal provisions meting out less severe punishment; thereby, the sentient beings within Nine Regions and Four Seas[84] are bathing in the waves of graciousness, living in peace and happiness. All the achievements mentioned above have been spontaneously produced from your holy mind, not arising from anyone else. This is my second point.

Your many gifts have branched out from your excellent understanding of the Way, and you have exercised your benevolence toward people in all quarters, from the sunrise east to the west beyond the Mount Kunlun[85], from the fiery southern land to the Great Wall in the north. Consequently, the aliens with various custom, some tattooing foot or drinking by nose, others donning *ko hemp* clothes with buttons on the left side, low their heads and go down on their knees to look forward to Your Majesty's graciousness as if they were waiting for the timely wind and rain. In the capital Chang' an, they usually make their guest houses replete with the rare and precious treasures that they are to present as tribute. All above are credited to Your Majesty's prestige alone, not to others. This is my third point.

Xianyun[86] is an old plague, which even the Five Sovereigns could not subdue, nor could the Three Emperors. Consequently, the region between the Yellow River and Luo River turned to be the wildness haunted by the uncivilized barbarians wearing disheveled hair, meanwhile the counties of Feng and Hao[87] were changed into the battlefields whistling with flying arrows; the Middle Kingdom[88] was on the decline whereas the Huns held sway. This had been the situation since the Yin[89] and Zhou Dynasties. In the Han Dynasty, Emperor Wu[90] deployed all military forces in his empire, and the great generals Wei Qing[91] and Huo Qubing[92] exerted all their energies, but what they did merely is the extermination of the branches and leaves with the root left intact. From then on, no other efficient military tactics had ever been heard of but the penalty expedition taken by Your Majesty that annihilated the plague by wiping out the lairs and nests of the Huns. Ever since, the Gobi Desert and regions beyond Mount Yanran[93] have been annexed to be fief lands where Chanyu[94], leading his anchormen and mounted masses, both men and women, came over to become your submissive subject. If such victory should be credited to ministers, then why before Your Majesty, although when there have been so many worthy ministers in the imperial courts since the times of Yu[95] and Xia, no victory as such has ever been achieved? Thus, I know where the Way prevails there is the victory. It is no need for Your Majesty to resort to others. This is my fourth point.

As Goguryeo[96], a tiny vassal state, didn't show courtesy to the suzerain country, the emperor of the Sui Dynasty[97] motivated all his military forces to take three punitive expeditions, but he could not capture even a single city, nor did he catch captives to a fair number; finally, he lost his six armies and returned in disgrace and embarrassment. By contrast, leading less than ten thousand cavalrymen, Your Majesty took only one expedition, first destroying the enemy's tactical formation at the temporary residence of the barbarian king, then breaking the fortified cities of Liao[dong] and Gai[mo][98]. Boosting the military morale, Your Majesty achieved the complete victory, with the foes slain and captured amounting to three hundred thousand. There seems no difference in the methods of deploying the soldiers and manipulating the generals, but the Sui House perished whereas the Tang House flourishes, from which I know the victory or defeat depends on the monarch rather than on others. This is my fifth point.

What's more, innumerable phenomena and myriads of lives must have come out under the influence of your virtues rather than under others, such as the perfect communion of Heaven and Earth, blazing brightness emitted from Sun and Moon, permeating harmonious atmosphere, rolling clouds, four divine beasts[99], unicorn, white wolves and foxes, red phoenix and magic grass, so conspicuously and multifariously muddled together that I could not mention them one by one. Your Majesty, however, always attempt to compare yourself with sage kings in ancient times, taking the king (King Wu of Zhou d.1043BC) as an example who made his achievements by relying on ten courtiers, frankly, to which I don't agree, for assuming you really need some assistants, you have already got many virtuous ministers as talented as Yi (Yin)[100] and Lü (Shang)[101]. In contrast to those ministers, I am mediocre and unintelligent, so what qualifications I have for participating in the management of state affairs? As a matter of fact, my ideal is to uphold precepts of a bhikshu and to elucidate as well as spread the bequeathed teachings of Buddha. For these reasons,

I plead Your Majesty not to press me to do what I am not qualified.

Hearing those words, the Emperor was greatly pleased. Then he said to the Master, "As to the matters you have mentioned above, how could we handle them alone without the blessing of Heaven and ancestors, and the assistance of ministers? If it is the wish of the teacher to propagate the profound truth, we shall not reverse your lofty ideal. Work hard! From now on we shall help you advocate the Way."

Comment by Shi Yancong: The Master has a thorough mastery of both the Buddhist and worldly knowledge, and with his glowing eloquence he was able to give expedient responses according to varying circumstances. How difficult it is! Formerly, Dao'an remonstrated with Fu Jian[102], but failed to stop the latter from his aggressive expedition; Daoheng and Daobiao[103] presented their views vehemently, but still could not change Yao Xing's[104] decisionor save him from the subsequent disgraceful defeat and grueling retreat. These great virtuous monks could by no means be compared with the Master in that the Emperor gave the immediate consent to the Master's requirements after hearing his refined argumentation. Thus, the noble character of the Master kept unsullied and his lofty ideal became even higher. On this account, it is no hard to conclude who is superior.

At the time, Chu Suiliang[105], Secretariat Director, also presented his view by saying, "The pacification of the country and happiness of the people have been realized under Your Majesty's holy virtues. We agree to the words of the Master that what we have done is nothing but merely the performance of our duties. Under the Sun and the

Moon, how dim is the light a glow-worm and a slow fire can give off!"

On hearing it, the Emperor smiled and responded, "It is not so. A precious fur coat could not be made from one fox. A great mansion must be constructed by bundles of timber and other materials. How is it possible for a monarch to make accomplishments all by himself? What the Master meant is to keep his moral integrity. He gave superfluous compliments on us."

Then the Emperor turned to the Master and asked, "What scriptures and treatises are you translating now?"

The Master answered, "Recently I have completed the translation of the *Yogācārabhūmi Śāstra* in one hundred fascicles."

The Emperor said, "This treatise is truly a voluminous work. Who composed it? What theory does it expound?"

The Master answered, "This treatise was composed by Bodhisattva Maitreya. The burden of it is to explain the Seventeen Stages of Bodhisattvahood."

The Emperor asked, "What does it mean by the Seventeen Stages?"

The Master replied, "They are: the stage of correlation of the five kinds of cognition, the stage of correlation of mental functions, the stage of having both deliberation and discrimination, the stage of having no deliberation but only discrimination, the stage of having neither deliberation nor discrimination, the stage of Samāhita[106], the stage of non-Samāhita, the stage of mental-activity, the stage of non-mental activity, the stage of achievement by hearing the Dharma, the stage of achievement by reflecting on the Dharma, the stage of achievement by practicing the Dharma, the stage of *Śrā*vaka[107], the stage of Pratyekabuddha[108], the stage of Bodhisattva, the stage of incomplete nirvāṇa, and the stage of complete nirvāṇa."

Then the Master made an outline and explained the general meaning of them one by one. Showing a great interest, the Emperor sent an envoy to the capital to fetch the *Yogācārabhūmi Śāstra.* After the treatise arrived, the Emperor read it intensively. Realizing that he had never known such grand and profound language and theories, amazingly, he turned to his attending ministers and said, "To us, reading Buddhist scriptures is quite like observing the sky and sea whose depths and heights are unfathomable. Here we have obtained such abstruse Dharma brought back by the Master from alien regions; however, we were too busy with state and military affairs to spare any time for learning the Buddha's teachings. Now when we come to study them, we have found their theoretical sources are sound and tenable, truly of no detectable boundaries. To put them in comparison with the worldly knowledge such as the nine schools of thoughts[109], typically Confucianism and Daoism, is like to juxtapose the vast sea with a small pool. We have discovered the fallacy that those three teachings[110] are of equal value. Obviously, this saying makes no sense."

Next an imperial decree was issued requiring the official in charge to select copyists from the Imperial Secretariat and asked them to transcribe the newly-translated scriptures and treatises, nine copies of each text. Then the copies were distributed to nine states—Yong, Luo, Bing, Yan, Xiang, Jing, Yang, Liang, and Yi—for circulation, for the purpose of acquainting the people all over the empire with the teachings they had never heard before.

At the time, Zhangsun Wuji, who was the Minister of Education and Duke of Zhaoguo, Chu Suiliang, who was the Secretariat Director[111], and others collectively presented a memorial to the Emperor, which reads:

> We have heard the Buddhist teachings are so abstruse that even heavenly beings find it difficult to comprehend them. Besides the profundity of theories, the language itself is often a hindrance to understanding. Your Majesty's governance is righteous and wise, being every bit in conformity with the Way, flying its brilliance up the bright sunshine; your beneficence is distributed universally, practicing edification to the Central Land[112]. What' s more, Your Majesty has protected and advocated the Five Vehicles[113], fostered the Triple Gem. For this reason, you are blessed to have the Master, a man of noble demeanor in this Age of Decline and a man met only once in a thousand years. Overcoming various obstacles to seek the scriptures and taking the perilous journey to pursue the Way, the Master has not only seen strange and peculiar custom with his own eyes, but also obtained the true teachings bequeathed by the Buddha; after he returned, he immediately devoted himself to the translation and propagation work, revealing the ultimate truth to people as if the Buddha preaching at this moment at the Āmravana Garden. When he opened his mouth to preach, the abstruse theories embodied in the refined words of those newly-translated scriptures

are of no difference from the sermons of the Buddha. As a matter of fact, all of these have been made possible by the influence of Your Majesty's high virtues. Stupid and ignorant as we are, we thus have gained the chance to read and hear (the truth), making us feel like riding a ferryboat to cross the raging sea of suffering. What's more, by propagating the translated works throughout the nation, your divine benevolence would benefit far and wide, nourishing multitudes of sluggish masses on the marvelous Dharma. How blessed your servants here are to have met with such an occasion which rarely occurs in a hundred million *kalpas*!

The Emperor replied, "It should be attributed to the great power of the compassionate aspiration of the Master as well as to your own merits accumulated in previous lives, not simply to me."

Previously the Emperor had already promised to write a preface to the newly-translated scriptures, but for state affairs were so heavy that he hadn't got the time to keep his words. Now that the Master put forward his request again, the Emperor began to moisten his brush with ink and set out to write. In a short time, he finished the composition of the preface, which was entitled the *Great Tang Preface to the Holy Teachings of the Tripiṭaka* in 781 characters, and placed it in the front pages of scriptures.

Then the Emperor, sitting at the Qingfu Palace, attended by officials and guards, and the Master taking the seat aside, ordered Shangguan Yi (608–665), a scholar of the Institute for the Expansion of Culture, to read the newly-indited preface to officials in presence.

The preface was written in the flowery style, and with brilliant and colorful wording, it sang compliments generously, which reads as follows:

> It is known that Heaven and Earth display visible demonstrations, sheltering and bearing all living things; whereas four seasons have no forms but brew cold and heat, transforming the whole world unwittingly. Therefore, by observing Heaven and Earth, even the mediocre and ignorant could have an inkling of the demonstrative phenomena; but to reflect on *yin* and *yang*, even the worthy and sagacious hardly make any thorough scrutiny of their numerous changes. In fact, Heaven and Earth, though embodying *yin* and *yang*, are easy to be recognized because they have visible forms; whereas *yin* and *yang,* though abiding in between Heaven and Earth, are difficult to fathom because they are of no visible entities. Thus, we know, for having visible demonstrations, Heaven and Earth can be examined without causing perplexity even to the ignorant; by contrast, for their forms being hidden, *yin* and *yang* throws the men, however wise they are, into befuddlement. Even more difficult it is to comprehend the Way to Buddhahood, because it values the emptiness, resorting to the supernatural powers to abide in nirvāṇa, and because it gives universal salvation to living beings of all sorts and reigns the worlds in ten quarters[114]. The supreme spirit soars up indefinitely whereas the divine power extends down ad infinitum. Inflating, the Buddha-way fills the universe, and

contracting, it can be embraced in a single thin hair. Neither arising nor perishing, going through a thousand Kalpas, it is by no means ancient but totally brand new; oblivious or visible now and then, it is bestowing a hundred blessings on the present age. The wondrous Buddha-way covers theories so abstruse that even the dedicated followers fail to perceive its boundaries; the dharma stream is lucid in quietude, from which one draws water but could not trace its source. Thence we know, how could an ordinary man who is ignorant and mediocre comprehend its essence and purport without being afflicted with doubts and bewilderment?

Having sprung up in the western land long before, the Great Teaching came to the Han Empire through the prophetic dream of the Emperor[115], and thus conferred the compassion onto the eastern land thereafter. In the immemorial time when the chaos was separated into Heaven and Earth, the material world began to evolve according to the Way even without the spread of Buddha's teachings, but it was not until an age when there arose the discussions on Buddha nature[116] that the people started to value the merits of Buddha and tried to follow suit in earnest. The historical Buddha returned to the ultimate truth by attaining His Nirvāṇa long ago and His golden body gradually faded out with the elapse of time, no longer mirroring the worlds of the trichiliocosm; at present, what has been left are only his graceful figure painted in pictures and his thirty-two auspicious physical marks resurfaced in people's imagination.

Thereafter, His abstruse words have been spread widely for the purpose of liberating the living creatures of the Three Realms, and His bequeathed admonitions propagated in order to guide sentient beings onto the ten stages of Bodhisattavahood. However, the true teachings are difficult to comprehend for they are hard to be generalized into one purport but the false doctrines are much easier for people to follow; therefore, a commotion of debates on what was the genuine and what was the erroneous has been going on continuously. Consequently, following the different intellectual traditions, the convictions concerning *being* and *non-being* (existence and non-existence) were regarded as either right or wrong, while the Great and the Small Vehicles took turns to prosper or decline with the changes of time.

Here is Master Xuanzang, acclaimed as a leading figure of the Buddhist community. Noble and perspicacious from a very young age, he has awakened to the Threefold Emptiness[117]; long in conformity with the divine spirit, he has accepted and practiced the Four Endurances[118]. Neither the breeze whistling in pine woods nor moonlight reflected in water could match his clearness and brilliance; neither the celestial dew nor bright pearls could measure up to his purity and grace. Wise enough, he was able to renounce all earthly attachments; and superbly divine, he could commune with the formless. Having transcended the Six defilements[119], he is not only remarkably outstanding among his contemporaries but also truly unsurpassable from the immemorial times to the far future. Contemplating in solitude, he was apprehensive of the decline of the true Dharma; indulging himself in the study of subtle theories, he was frustrated at mistakes and absurdness in the interpretations of the profound texts. So, he wished to systematically analyze and sort out the scriptures and treatises, with the purpose of improving what had been available, eliminating the false to preserve the true, and guiding the posterity. For this reason, he generated a strong aspiration for the land nourishing the pure Buddhism, and resolved to take on a journey to the Western Regions.

Holding a staff in hand, he advanced alone on his pilgrimage. By daylight, flying heavy snows blocked the road and blurred directions; at night, billowing sand storms blotted out the sky and obscured Moon. Trudging through mists and clouds, across mountains and rivers, he covered ten thousand *li*, in accompany with but his shadow; enduring severe cold and heat, neglecting frosts and snows, he followed the traces of ancients to move on. Thanks to his deep aspiration and heavy sincerity, the toil was greatly alleviated, and he finally achieved ideal. He has ranged across the Western Regions for seventeen years, and sought out the true teachings from the states along the route.

At the twin sala trees and by the eight rivers (of India)[120], he feasted himself on tasty flavor of the Way; at the Deer Park and on the vulture Peak, he paid homage to the miracles and unusual sights. Inheriting the supreme instructions of ancient sages, receiving the true teachings from the great worthy, he deplored the profound theories and thoroughly studied the marvelous truth. Thus, the Ekayāna and the Five Vinaya Sects of Hīnayāna[121] were speedily accumulated in his mind while the texts of the Eight Stores[122] and the Three Baskets[123] were flowing fluently from his mouth. From the places he visited, he brought back the Tripiṭaka[124] of great importance, totally amounting to the six hundred fifty-seven works, which he, thereafter, propagated in China by his translation. In so doing, he has introduced here the clouds of compassion from the western land to shower the dharma rain over the eastern land; thereby, the holy teachings once deficient in China are made complete, and the masses once sinful are blessed with happiness. The flames of burning houses have been extinguished by water and the misguided multitudes have come back from the road of delusion. After clearing the muddled waves of desire, living beings at long last reach the yonder shore of the suffering sea.

As we know, the evil-doer would fall into the three evil realms (animal, ghosts, hellish) because of the unwholesome karma; on the contrary, the good-doer would ascend to the good realms (heavenly, demi-god, human) because of the wholesome karma. So, to ascend or to descend depends on nothing but a man's own deeds. Only by growing on a high ridge could the flowers of an osmanthus tree be moistened by the celestial dew, and only by growing out of the turquoise water, the flying dust fails to defile the petals of a lotus. It is not because the osmanthus tree and the lotus are pure by nature, but because the ridge the former attaching to is so high that the ignoble can't ravish it, and the water the latter fostered by is so clean that the dirt can't taint it. Unconscious as the plants, they know to become perfect by relying on the advantageous conditions, so why could not a human being with consciousness and discernment resort to good circumstances to obtain felicity? May the circulation of these scriptures be as everlasting as the sun and the moon! May the blessings gained therefrom be as vast as Heaven and Earth!

Upon receiving the preface, the Master wrote a memorial to extend his gratitude:

I, *Śramaṇa* Xuanzang, beg to state:

I have heard that the six- *yao*[125] is able to make an exploration on the delicate situations, but is still confined to the phenomena of production and extinction, and that all things in the world are properly named, but the genuine suchness still could not be denoted. After examining the *Eight Trigrams* composed by Fuxi in remote times, we still find its subtlety unfathomable; although attributing all the prosperity of subsequent generations to the *Yellow River Chart* of Xuanyuan[126], we know little about it but gives free rein to our imagination. Humbly, I think that Your Majesty could be an incarnation of the Buddha, reigning the country as powerfully as a Gold Wheel King[127]. Having fought with distinction for the peace of the country passed down from the former emperors, you obscured the light of the sun and the moon by your brilliance. You not only enlarged the domain occupied by past sovereigns and dynasties, but also embraced the Dharma-dhātus[128] as numerous as the sands in the Ganges River. Monasteries are thriving as if the Jetavana Vihāra were removed to China, and the divine texts on palm leaves have been stored in the imperial library. Formerly, traveling ten thousand *li,* I went to Gṛdhrakūṭa Mountain with a religious staff in hand, and under Your Majesty's influential power, the long journey was just like a very short excursion, I felt I reached the twain Śāla trees as quickly as the lapse of a single meal without riding a thousand-petaled lotus flower to fly. I have exhausted all texts stored in the Nāga Palace[129] to collect the Tripiṭaka, and I have studied the Ekayāna to thoroughly master the bequeathed doctrines from the Vulture Peak. Thereafter, loaded on white horses, the Buddhist works have been brought back and, at the imperial court, I presented them to Your Majesty with sincerity. Then receiving a great favor, I was ordered to do the translation.

Although I am not as learned as Nāgārjuna[130], I have been given the privilege of transmitting the Lamp of Truth, at which I indeed felt so much embarrassed for my incompetence. Although I am not as literately talented as Aśvaghoṣa whose intelligence outflowed like water poured out from a bottle, I have gotten the chance to do translation, which I felt ashamed of. On the one hand, I'm afraid what

I have translated might be full of errors and absurdness, on the other hand, I feel very happy at this stroke of fortune of receiving the divine preface indited by Your Majesty. The words of the preface surpass those of the *Xiang* (symbols) and *Xi* (explanations) of the *Book of Changes*, and the reasoning of it opens the gate to all that is subtle and wonderful. Having received such holy response from Your Majesty, I am worried that I would not prove worthy of this high honor. I rejoiced over it as if I had obtained the prediction that I shall become the Buddha in the future. Not knowing how to express my great delight, I came to the palace to present this memorial to extend my gratitude.

After reading the memorial, the Emperor wrote a reply, in which he wrote:

We have not gotten the brilliant endowment, and we are ashamed that our words are not so rich or eloquent; besides, for we are not versed in the Buddhist teachings, we feel very embarrassed at the awkwardness of this preface we wrote yesterday. What we have done is just like contaminating the golden papers by dirty brush and ink, or throwing the bricks and pebbles into the piles of pearls. But unexpectedly we received your gratitude letter, which made us indebted to your compliments. After making a self-examination on ourselves, we felt all the more abashed. In fact, what we have done is neither worth your praises nor deserves your many thanks.

ANNOTATION

1 Jingzi refers to the seventh day, which may be wrong, because according to the tenth fascicle of this biography and Daoxuan's *Biographies of Tang Eminent Monks* (*Xugaoseng Zhuan*《续高僧传》), Xuanzang arrived in Chang'an on the twenty-fourth day of the first lunar month.

2 Fang Qiao 房乔(579–648), courtesy name Xuanling玄龄, posthumously known as Duke Wenzhao of Liang, was a statesman and writer who served as a chancellor under Emperor Taizong in the early Tang Dynasty. He was the lead editor of the historical record *Book of Jin* (《晋书》covering the history of the Jin Dynasty (265–420)) and one of the most celebrated Tang Dynasty chancellors. He and his colleague, Du Ruhui (585–630), were often described as role models for chancellors in imperial China.

3 Modern Guanzhong, a historical region corresponding to the lower valley of the Wei River.

4 Three *chi* three *cun* is about forty-three inches.

5 Three *chi* five *cun* is about fourty-seven inches. In other record, may be one *chi* five *cun*.

6 Two *chi* nine *cun* is about thirty-nine inches.

7 One *chi* three *cun* is about fifteen inches.

8 It should be the 25th of the month.

9 Here "the twenty-third day" should be wrong.

10 Emperor Taizong, Li Shimin (李世民598–649, r. 626–649). His full posthumous name is Wen Wu Dasheng Daguang Xiao Huangdi文武大圣大广孝皇帝.

11 See note 10 of Fascicle V.

12 Or Nine Provinces: is used in ancient Chinese histories to refer to territorial divisions or islands during the Xia and Shang Dynasties. The Nine Regions and Four seas have now come to symbolically represent the land under heaven, specifically China.

13 Eight Directions: east, south, west, north, southeast, northeast, southwest, northwest, symbolically representing China.

14 Zhang Qian张骞(?—114 BC)，born in Chenggu (present-day Chenggu County, Shaanxi Province)，was a famous explorer and imperial diplomat during the period referred to as the Western Han Dynasty. In 123 BC，Zhang Qian followed General Wei Qing in a major military raid against the Xiongnu. His guidance led to a number of victories, which succeeded in ending the harassment by the Xiongnu of the Han Dynasty. Zhang Qian was therefore conferred the title of Marquis of Bowang博望侯.

15 Ban Gu班固 (32–92) was a Chinese historian, politician, and poet best known for his part in compiling the *Book of Han*, the second of China's 24 dynastic histories. He also wrote a number of *fu* 赋, a major literary form, part prose and part poetry, which is particularly associated with the Han era.

16 Sima Qian 司马迁(206 BC–220 CE), was a Chinese historian of the early Han Dynasty. He is considered the father of Chinese historiography for his *Records of the Grand Historian*, a Jizhuanti-style (纪传体, history presented in a series of biographies) general history of China, covering more than two thousand years from the Yellow Emperor to his time, during the reign of Emperor Wu of Han.

17 Dao'an 道安(312–385) was a Buddhist monk of the Jin Dynasty (265–420), originating from what is now Hebei. Dao'an left home to join the monastic order at twelve. Ca. 335 CE he visited Linzhang and became a disciple of the famous Kuchean monk and missionary Fotucheng 佛图澄 (232–348). He was active in Xiangyang until the Former Qin ruler Fu Jian (337–385) captured the city in 379 and had Dao'an brought to live in Chang'an. He spent the last years of life translating and interpreting scripture as well as compiling a catalogue of scriptures.

18 Zhangsun Wuji 长孙无忌(died 659), courtesy name Fuji 辅机, formally the Duke of Zhao, was a Chinese official who served as a chancellor in the early

Tang Dynasty.

19 *Spring and Autumn of the Thirty States and Dynasties* (*Sanshiguo Chunqiu* 《三十国春秋》)was a history of the Eastern Jin period (317–420) compiled by Xiao Fangdeng萧方等 (528–549), courtesy name Shixiang实相, who was the oldest son of Emperor Yuan (梁元帝萧绎r. 552–554) of the Southern Liang Dynasty. The book was 31 *juan* "scrolls" long, collecting a large amount of historiographical sources and compiling a history of the Jin Dynasty and twenty-nine other polities existing during that time. The fragments of the book have been collected by the late Qing period (1644–1911) scholar Tang Qiu汤球 (1804–1881) in his *Collectaneum Shiliuguo Chunqiu Jiben* 《十六国春秋辑本》. It includes eighteen fragments of histories of the Sixteen States (300–430) that ruled over northern China during the Jin period, as well as some other texts about northern China during that period.

20 Emperor Taizong used Yeon Gaesomun's murder of the Goguryeo king as the pretext for his campaign and started preparations for an invasion force in 644.

21 The Battle of Muye牧野 (c. 1046BC) was a battle fought in ancient China between the Zhou and Shang. The victory of the Zhou led to the fall of the Shang. Muye is located in the north of today's Xinxiang City, Henan Province.

22 The Battle of Kunyang昆阳was fought between June-July in 23, between the Lǜlin绿林军 and Xin forces. The Lǜlin forces were led by Liu Xiu刘秀 (r.25–57), who later became Emperor Guangwu of Han汉光武帝, while the far more numerous Xin were led by Wang Yi王邑 and Wang Xun王寻. This was the decisive battle that led to the fall of the Xin Dynasty (9–23).

23 Also known as the Shaolin Temple, is a Chan (Zen) Buddhist temple in Dengfeng County, Henan Province.

24 Bodhiruci 菩提留支 (5th–6th centuries) was a Buddhist master from northern India. He was versed in mantra practices and the Tripiṭaka. Aspiring to propagate

the Dharma, in 502, the first year of the Yongping 永平 years of the Northern Wei Dynasty (386–534), he arrived in capital Luoyang. Emperor Xuanwu 魏宣武帝 (r. 499–515) valued him highly and commanded him to stay in the Yongning Temple 永宁寺 to translate Sanskrit texts into Chinese. His 39 translated works include the *Ten Stages Sūtra* and commentary, and the *Amitabha Sūtra* with commentary. Bodhiruci is regarded as the patriarch of the Dashabhumika School (地论宗Dilun zong), which used his *Ten Stages Sūtra* as its chief object of study.

25 Emperor Taizong's mother, Duchess Dou, the wife of Emperor Gaozu of Tang (566 – 635), Li Yuan 李渊.

26 Dingxian County 定线, Hebei Province.

27 Modern Hualong County化隆, Qinghai Province.

28 Modern Kaifeng开封, Henan Province.

29 Modern Puzhou蒲州, Shanxi Province.

30 The region east to Mianyang 绵阳, Sichuan Province.

31 Modern Chengdu 成都 and the surrounding area, Sichuan Province.

32 The Zhongnan 中南 Mountains, sometimes called the Taiyi 太乙 Mountains or Zhounan 周南 Mountains, are a branch of the Qin Mountains 秦岭 located in Shaanxi Province, south of Xi'an, China that extend from Wugong County in the west of the Province to Lantian County.

33 Modern Jianyang简阳, Sichuan Province.

34 Modern Yongji永济, Shanxi Province.

35 Modern Bingxian彬县, Shaanxi Province.

36 Modern Luoyang洛阳, Henan Province.

37 The monk scholar in Translation Bureau who took charge of using Chinese characters to record the pronunciation of Sanskrit language.

38 Hexu 赫胥 and Dating大庭 are two legendary Chinese sovereigns in remote antiquity.

39 See note 24 of Preface.

40 See note 103 of Fascicle I.

41 Wu (229–280), commonly known as Eastern Wu or Sun Wu, was one of the three major states that competed for supremacy over China in the Three Kingdoms period (220–280). It became an empire in 229 after its founding ruler, Sun Quan, declared himself "Emperor". Its name was derived from the place it was based in — the Jiangnan (Yangtze River Delta) region, which was also historically known as "Wu." Wu's capital was in Jianye, present-day Nanjing, Jiangsu Province.

42 Modern Hubei 湖北 and Hunan 湖南 Provinces.

43 See note 62 of Fascicle I.

44 See note 61 of Fascicle I.

45 See note 30 of Preface.

46 See note 106 of Fascicle I.

47 The Yellow Emperor, or Huangdi or Emperor Xuanyuan 轩辕 is one of the legendary Chinese sovereigns and culture heroes included among the Three Sovereigns and Five Emperors. Panmu and the Youling are two mythological mountains, the former is the eastern frontier, the latter the western one.

48 Emperor Yao (traditionally c. 2356–2255 BC) was a legendary Chinese ruler, with the family name of Yi, according to various sources, one of the Three Sovereigns and the Five Emperors. The clan name for Emperor Yao's tribe is Tang, so Yao is also known as Tang Yao 唐尧.

49 Yu the Great 大禹, born Si Wenming, was a legendary ruler in ancient China famed for his introduction of flood 女以文名 control, inaugurating dynastic rule in China by founding the Xia Dynasty.

50 In the *Classic of Mountains and Seas* or *Shan Hai Jing*《山海经》, Wangmu, also Queen Mother of the West 西王母(Xi Wangmu), the great goddess guardian of Mount Kunlun presented a white jade ring to the Yellow Emperor to show the friendship and veneration. Noninterference refers to a governing notion or method—taking no action that is contrary to Nature, which was

greatly advocated in ancient China.

51 The Dongyi or Eastern Yi was a collective term, referring to ancient peoples who lived in eastern China during the prehistory of ancient China and in lands located to the east of ancient China. The people referred to as Dongyi vary across the ages. They were one of the Four Barbarians in Chinese culture, along with the Northern Di, the Southern Man, and the Western Rong; as such, the name "Yi" was something of a catch-all and was applied to different groups over time.

52 Nüwa 女娲 is the mother goddess of Chinese mythology, the sister and wife of Fuxi, the emperor-god. She is credited with creating mankind and repairing the Pillar of Heaven. Her reverential name is Wahuang 娲皇(Empress Wa).

53 Refers to the seven military ethics mentioned in the *Twelfth Year of Duke Xuan of Lu* of *The Commentary of Zuo*《左传・宣公十二年》: the repression of cruelty 禁暴, the calling in of the weapons of war 戢兵, the preservation of the dominant position 保大, the firm establishment of one's merit 定功, the giving of repose to the people 安民, the harmonizing of all [the states] 和众, and the enlargement of general wealth 丰财.

54 Refers to the ten human ethics or duties mentioned in the *Conveyance of Rites* of the *Book of Rites*《礼记・礼运》: kindness in the father 父慈, filial piety in the son 子孝, gentility in the elder brother 兄良, humility and respect in the younger brother 弟弟, good behavior in the husband 夫义, docility in the wife 妇听, compassion in the elders 长惠, obedience in the juniors 幼顺, benevolence in the ruler 君仁 and loyalty in the subjects 臣忠.

55 Legendary river in Kunlun Mountains.

56 Legendary final setting place of the sun.

57 May refer to the Flaming Mountains, which are barren, eroded, red sandstone hills in the Tian Shan 天山 of Xinjiang Uygur Autonomous Region, and the soil surface temperature is very high, hence the name. They lie near the northern rim of the Taklamakan Desert and east of the city of Turpan. In

ancient times, the merchant traders traversing the Silk Route in Southeast Asia avoided the mountains by stopping at oasis towns, such as Gaochang高昌, built on the desert's rim at the foot of the Flaming Mountains and near an important mountain pass, Shengjinkou 胜金口.

58 Present Zhangye 张掖, Gansu Province, China. In 111BC, Emperor Wu (156–87BC) of the Han Dynasty set up Zhangye Prefecture.

59 The area northwest to present Lanzhou in Gansu Province and covering a part of Qinghai Province.

60 In today Guangxi Province, famous for the production of pearls, so also called Pearl Pu.

61 The prefecture of Guilin was set up by First Emperor of Qin in 214 BC, which was situated in Guangxi Province.

62 See note 47 of Fascicle II.

63 See note 22 of preface.

64 Here "one hundred and twenty-eight" should be one hundred and thirty-eight countries. The original text is wrong.

65 In legend, Dazhang 大章 and Shuhai 竖亥 are two persons who are good at walking in ancient times.

66 Kua Fu or Kuafu 夸父is a giant in Chinese mythology who wished to capture Sun.

67 Ban Chao 班超(32–102), courtesy name Zhongsheng 仲升, was a Chinese general, explorer and diplomat of the Eastern Han Dynasty. As a Han general and cavalry commander, Ban Chao was in charge of administrating the Western Regions while he was in service. He also led Han forces for over 30 years in the war against the Xiongnu and secured Han control over the Tarim Basin region. He was honored the Marquis of Dingyuan which means "pacifying the distant place."

68 Zhang Qian 张骞(d. 113BC), was a Chinese official and diplomat who served as an imperial envoy to the world outside of China in the 2nd century BC,

during the time of the Han Dynasty. He was the first official diplomat to bring back reliable information about Central Asia to the Chinese imperial court. He was honored the Marquis of Bowang which means "widly seeing." Zhang Qian's accounts of his explorations of Central Asia are detailed in the *Early Han historical chronicles*, *Records of the Grand Historian*, compiled by Sima Qian in the 1st century BC.

69 Zhang Hua张华 (232–300) was a Western Jin Dynasty (265–316) scholar, poet, and protoscientist. Zhang Hua's (c. 290 CE) "*Records of Diverse Matters*" (*Bowu Zhi*《博物志》) was a compendium of Chinese stories about natural wonders and marvelous phenomena. It quotes from many early Chinese classics, and diversely includes subject matter from Chinese mythology, history, geography, and folklore. The *Bowu zhi*, which is one of the first works in the literary genre of *zhiguai* 志怪"tales of anomalies; supernatural stories."

70 Or the *Record of Nine States* (*Jiuqiu*《九丘》), the earliest geography book of China.

71 Literally refers to *Xiang Zhuan* (or *Overall Image*, or the *Expressions of Symbolism*《象传》) and *Xici Zhuan* (*the Great Commentary*, or *the Appended Judgments*《系辞传》), generally representing the theories of *Yi Jing*.

72 *Xian* refers to *Xianchi* 咸池, the name of the ancient music piece legendary composed by Yellow Emperor and improved by Yao尧, and *Ying* to *Liuying* 六英, legendary composed by Diku 帝喾 or Zhuanxu 颛顼, generally used for Classical Chinese music.

73 See note 30 of Fascicle III.

74 Yuhua Palace玉华宫 was built in the earlier Tang Dynasty as an imperial palace and changed into a Buddhist monastery during the reign of Emperor Gaozong of Tang. It was located at Yijun County of Tongchuan铜川, Shaanxi.

75 Shun was a legendary leader of ancient China, regarded by some sources as

one of the Three Sovereigns and Five Emperors. Oral tradition holds that he lived sometime between 2294 and 2184 BC.

76 Tang 汤(c. 1675 – 1646 BC) or Cheng Tang, recorded on oracle bones as Da Yi, was the first king of the Shang Dynasty in Chinese history. He overthrew Jie, the last ruler of the Xia Dynasty.

77 King Wu of Zhou 周武王 was the first king of the Zhou Dynasty of ancient China. The chronology of his reign is disputed but is generally thought to have begun around 1046 BC and ended three years later in 1043 BC.

78 See *The Book of Documents-The Great Speech* (*Shangshu Taishi*《尚书・泰誓》), ten talented courtiers are: the Prince Regent Duke Dan of Zhou 周公旦, Duke Shi of Shao 召/邵公奭, Grand Duke Wang 太公望, is one of the names for a famous Chinese minister named Lü Shang吕尚, or Jiang Ziya姜子牙, who is also known by several other names), Duke Bi 毕公, Duke Rong 荣公, Taidian 太颠, Hongyao 闳夭, San Yisheng 散宜生, Nangong Shi 南宫适, Wenmu 文母 (refers to Taisi大姒, the wife of King Wen of Zhou, the mother of King Wu; or Yijiang邑姜, the wife of King Wu of Zhou, the daughter of Lü Shang).

79 According to *Lunyu-Taibo* (*Confucian Analects-TaiBo*《论语・泰伯》), Five ministers are said to be Yu 禹, Ji 稷, Xie 契, Gaoyao 皋陶, Boyi 伯益. "Shun had five ministers and the empire was well governed."

80 Subhūti 须菩提 was one of the Ten Great Śrāvakas of Gautama Buddha, and foremost in giving gifts. He is also sometimes referred to as "Elder Subhūti" (Subhūti Thera). He was a contemporary of such famous arahants as Śāriputra, Mahākāśyapa, Maudgalyayana, Mahākātyāyana and Ānanda.

81 The Three Sovereigns and Five Emperors were a group of mythological rulers or deities in ancient northern China who in later history have been assigned dates in a period from circa 2852 to 2070 BC.

82 King Jie 桀 (traditionally 1728–1675 BC) was the 17th and last ruler of the Xia Dynasty of China. He is traditionally regarded as a tyrant and oppressor

who brought about the collapse of a dynasty. Around 1600 BC, Jie was defeated by Tang of Shang, bringing an end to the Xia Dynasty that lasted about 500 years, and a rise to the new Shang Dynasty.

83 King Zhou 纣 was the pejorative posthumous name given to Di Xin 帝辛 the last king of the Shang Dynasty of ancient China. He was presented as the wicked ruler. When Zhou Dynasty's army defeated the Shang Dynasty at the Battle of Muye in 1046 BC, Di Xin gathered all his treasures around himself in the Palace, and then set fire to his palace and committed suicide.

84 The Nine Regions and Four Seas has now come to symbolically represent China.

85 The Kunlun Mountains 昆仑山 are one of the longest mountain chains in Asia, extending more than 3,000 kilometres (1,900 mi). In the broadest sense, it forms the northern edge of the Tibetan Plateau south of the Tarim Basin. The exact definition of this range varies. An old source uses Kunlun to mean the mountain belt that runs across the center of China, that is, Kunlun in the narrow sense: Altyn Tagh along with the Qilian and Qin Mountains. A recent source has the Kunlun range forming most of the south side of the Tarim Basin and then continuing east south of the Altyn Tagh. Sima Qian (*Shiji*, scroll 123) says that Emperor Wu of Han sent men to find the source of the Yellow River and gave the name Kunlun to the mountains at its source. The name seems to have originated as a semi-mythical location in the classical Chinese text *Shanhai Jing*《山海经》.

86 The Xianyun was an ancient nomadic tribe that invaded China during the Zhou Dynasty. Scholars identify the Xianyun with the Quanrong 犬戎 and Xiongnu.

87 Fenghao 丰镐 is the modern name of the twin city formed by the Western Zhou capitals of Feng and Hao on opposite banks of the Feng River near its confluence with the Wei River in Shaanxi, China. The ruins of Fenghao lie in present-day southwest Xi'an in Shaanxi Province.

88 It was a term developed under the Western Zhou Dynasty in reference to its royal demesne. It was then applied to the area around Luoyi (present-day Luoyang) during the Eastern Zhou and then to China's Central Plain before being used as an occasional synonym for the state under the Qing. It alludes to the "land of Chinese civilization" and was often used as a cultural concept to distinguish the Huaxia 华夏 people from perceived "barbarians."

89 Yin refers to the Shang Dynasty (1600–1046 BC); the Zhou Dynasty started in 1046BC and ended in 256 BC.

90 Emperor Wu of Han (141–87 BC), born Liu Che 刘彻, was the seventh emperor of the Han Dynasty of China, ruling from 141–87 BC. His reign resulted in vast territorial expansion, development of a strong and centralized state resulting from his governmental re-organization. As a military campaigner, Emperor Wu led Han China through its greatest expansion — at its height, the Empire's borders spanned from modern Kyrgyzstan in the west, to Korea in the east, and to northern Vietnam in the south. Emperor Wu successfully repelled the nomadic Xiongnu from systematically raiding northern China, and dispatched his envoy Zhang Qian in 139 BC to seek an alliance with the Yuezhi of Kangju (Sogdia, modern Uzbekistan). This resulted in further missions to Central Asia.

91 Wei Qing 卫青(died 106 BC), courtesy name Zhongqing 仲卿, born in present-day Linfen 临汾, Shanxi, was a military general of the Western Han Dynasty whose campaigns against the Xiongnu earned him great acclaim.

92 Huo Qubing霍去病 (140–117 BC) was a distinguished military general of the Western Han Dynasty during the reign of Emperor Wu of Han. He was the nephew of the general Wei Qing. Huo Qubing died in 117 BC at the early age of 24.

93 Or Khangai Mountains, a mountain range in central Mongolia, some 400 kilometers west of Ulaanbaatar. It's also known as Yanran Mountains in ancient China.

94 Chanyu was the title used by the nomadic supreme rulers of Inner Asia for

eight centuries and was superseded by the title "Khagan" in 402 CE. The title was used by the ruling Luandi clan of the Xiongnu during the Qin Dynasty (221–206 BC) and Han Dynasty (206 BC–220 CE).

95 Also Youyu有虞, is the clan name of Emperor Shun舜. According to traditional sources, Shun received the mantle of leadership from Emperor Yao 尧 at the age of 53, and then died at the age of 100 years. Before his death Shun is recorded as relinquishing his seat of power to Yu禹, the founder of the Xia Dynasty.

96 First campaign in the Goguryeo –Tang War. Goguryeo (高句丽37 BC–668 CE), also called Goryeo (高丽), was a Korean kingdom located in the northern and central parts of the Korean Peninsula and the southern and central parts of inner and outer Manchuria.

97 Refers to Emperor Yang of Sui (reign 581–618), personal name Yang Guang 杨广, was the second son of Emperor Wen of Sui, and the second emperor of China's Sui Dynasty. Emperor Yang was generally considered by traditional historians to be one of the worst tyrants in Chinese history and the reason for the Sui Dynasty's relatively short rule. His failed campaigns against Goguryeo, and the conscriptions levied to man them, coupled with increased taxation to finance these wars and civil unrest as a result of this taxation ultimately led to the downfall of the dynasty.

98 Gai refers to Gaimou盖牟 (Kaemo). In April 645, General Li Shiji's 李世勣 (594–669) army departed from Yincheng (present-day Chaoyang). On 1 May, they crossed the Liao River into Goguryeo territory. On 16 May, they laid siege to Gaimou (Kaemo), which fell after only 11 days, capturing 20,000 people and confiscating 100,000 *shi* (6 million liter) of grain. Afterwards, General Li Shiji's army advanced to Liaodong. On 7 June 645, they crushed a Goguryeo army of 40,000 troops strong, who were sent to the city to relieve the city from the Tang siege. A few days later, Emperor Taizong's cavalry arrived at Liaodong. On 16 June, the Tang army successfully set Liaodong

ablaze with incendiary projectiles and breached its defensive walls, resulting in the fall of Liaodong to the Tang forces.

99 Four divine beasts or mythological animals refer to Qinglong 青龙, Baihu 白虎, Zhuque朱雀 , Xuanwu 玄武 or kylin, phoenix, tortoise and dragon.

100 Yi Yin 伊尹 (?–1540 BC), was a minister of the early Shang Dynasty, and one of the honored officials. He helped Tang of Shang, the founder of the Shang Dynasty, to defeat King Jie of Xia. Oracle inscriptions of Yi have been found, evidence that his social status was high.

101 Jiang Ziya 姜子牙(fl. 11th century BC), also known by several other names, was a Chinese noble who helped kings Wen and Wu of Zhou overthrow the Shang in ancient China. Following their victory at Muye, he continued to serve as Zhou's prime minister. He remained loyal to the regent Duke of Zhou during the Rebellion of the Three Guards; following the Duke's punitive raids against the restive Eastern Barbarians or Dongyi, Jiang was enfeoffed with their territory as the marchland of Qi. He established his seat at Yingqiu (within modern Zibo淄博).

102 Fu Jian苻坚 (r. 357–385), courtesy name Yonggu 永固 or Wenyu 文玉, formally Emperor Xuanzhao of (Former) Qin (前)秦宣昭帝, was an emperor of Former Qin Dynasty, under whose rule (assisted by his able prime minister Wang Meng) the Former Qin state reached its greatest glory—destroying Former Yan, Former Liang, and Dai and seizing Jin's Yi Province (modern Sichuan and Chongqing), posturing to destroy Jin as well to unite China, until he was repelled at the Battle of Fei River in 383. For a variety of reasons, the Former Qin state soon collapsed after that defeat, and Fu Jian himself was killed by his former subordinate, Yao Chang 姚苌 the founding emperor of Later Qin, in 385.

103 Both Daoheng道恒 (346–417) and Daobiao 道标 were disciples of Kumārajīva. Yao Xing forced them to return to secular life, so they hid in Langya琅琊 Mountains.

104 Yao Xing 姚兴(366–416), was an emperor of the Later Qin 后秦. He was the son of the founding emperor Yao Chang (Emperor Wucheng).Yao Xing was an avid Buddhist, and it was during his reign that Buddhism first received official state support in China. The monk Kumarajiva also visited Chang'an at Yao Xing's request in 401.

105 Chu Suiliang褚遂良(596–658), courtesy name Dengshan登善, formally the Duke of Henan, was a Chinese official who served as a chancellor during the reigns of the emperors Taizong and Gaozong in the Tang Dynasty.

106 One's body and mind both fixed in meditation.

107 Śrāvaka means "hearer." The term is sometimes reserved for distinguished disciples of The Buddha, or, more generally, "Disciple."

108 Also self-enlightened buddhas.

109 The Nine Schools of Thought were the various Chinese intellectual currents of the pre-Qin period. They were: Confucianism (as interpreted by Mencius and others), Legalism, Taoism, Mohism, Agriculturalism, two strains of Diplomatists, the Logicians, Sunzi's Militarists, Naturalists. They were the primary schools during the Hundred Schools of Thought period of China during the Eastern Zhou Dynasty.

110 Confucianism. Daoism, and Buddhism.

111 Or the Chief Privy Councilor or the Chief /Head of the secretariat.

112 China.

113 Five Vehicles: the five degrees of religious advance among the Buddhists: (1) The vehicle of Buddha; (2) of the Bodhisattvas; (3) of the Pratyeka Buddha; (4) of the ordained disciple; (5) of the lay disciple.

114 Ten quarters refers to ten directions: north, northeast, east, southeast, south, southwest, west, northwest, up and down, denoting all directions; everywhere.

115 Emperor Ming (r. 57–75) dreamt of a golden deity interpreted as the Buddha and sent a delegation to India. They returned circa 67 CE with the monks

Kāśyapa-Mātaṇga and Dharmaratna (Zhu Falan), and white horses carrying Buddhist texts and images.

116 The discussion on Buddha nature, see note 144. During the Southern and Northern Dynasties and Sui and Tang Dynasties, there were two opinions existing in the Ground Treatise School (地论宗): the northern path viewed ālaya consciousness as an impure consciousness and upheld dependent arising of dharmas from ālaya consciousness, "当常(*dangchang*)" in Chinese , while the southern path viewed ālaya consciousness as one's inherent pure mind, one's Tathāgata store (Tathāgata-garbha), and upheld dependent arising of dharmas from dharma nature (dharmatā), which is true suchness, "现常(*xianchang*)" in Chinese.

117 Or Śūnyatā, translated into English as emptiness and emptiness, which has multiple meanings depending on its doctrinal context. It is either an ontological feature of reality, a meditation state, or a phenomenological analysis of experience. Here, the Threefold Emptiness refers to: Emptiness of the ego (or not-self: nature of the five aggregates of experience and the six sense spheres are empty), Emptiness of self-nature (all things are empty of intrinsic existence and nature), and Emptiness of both the ego and phenomena.

118 Four Endurances: the understanding of the following four: (1) all things do not arise; (2) all things do not perish; (3) all things do not have self-nature, for they exist because of causes and conditions; (4) all things are such that one should not let his mind dwell on them.

119 Six defilements: six qualities that are the cause of all impurity, i.e., sight, sound, smell, taste, touch, and idea.

120 According to the *Mahapari nirvāṇa Sutra*, eight rivers in India are Ganges River, Yamula River, Sarabhu River, Aciravati River, Mahi River, Hindu River, Oxus River, Sītā River.

121 After the demise of Buddha, there were five sects who had disagreement on

the vinaya.

122 The Mahayāna and Hīnayāna, each of them, contains the Sūtras, treatises, Vinaya and Mantras, altogether eight Stores.

123 The Tripiṭaka teachings for Śrāvaka, Pratyekabuddha and Bodhisattva.

124 The Tripiṭaka are the Sūtras (teachings of the Buddha), the treatises (discussions of the teachings and philosophical extrapolation), and the Vinaya (rules for the monastic life). Collectively, they are referred to as the Tripitaka; the "triple basket."

125 The basic unit of the *Zhou yi* or the *Changes* (a Western Zhou divination text) is the hexagram (卦 guà), a figure composed of six stacked horizontal lines (爻 yáo). Each line is either broken or unbroken.

126 Xuanyuan is the given name of the legendary Yellow Emperor, and literally, he once obtained The *Yellow River Chart* (*Hetu*《河图》), which, however, is to parallel to the *Eight Trigrams.* Actually, it implies the grand design and strategic plan of Xuanyuan, as what is recorded in the *Annals of the Five Emperors* (*Wu Di Benji*《五帝本纪》) of the *Records of the Grand Historian* (*Shiji*,《史记》):

"In the time of Xuanyuan, Shennong became enfeebled. The princes made raids on each other and harassed the people, but Shennong could not chastise them, so Xuanyuan exercised himself in the use of weapons of war, so as to be able to punish irregularities. The princes all came and did homage, but Chiyou, the fiercest of all, could not be subdued. Yandi (Flame emperor) wished to oppress the princes, so they turned to Xuanyuan, who practised virtue, marshalled his men, controlled the five elements, cultivated the five kinds of grain, pacified the nations, and went over all parts of his country. Training black bears, grizzly bears, foxes, panthers, lynxes, and tigers, he, with their aid, fought with 'Flame emperor' in the desert of Banquan, and, after three battles, realized his wishes. Chiyou was a rebel, who did not obey the Emperor's command, so Huangdi, levying an army of the princes, fought against Chiyou, captured, and slew him in the desert of Zhuolu. The princes all agreed that Xuanyuan should be the Emperor in place of Shennong, under the title Huangdi. Those in the empire who would not submit, Huangdi pursued and chastised, and when they were subdued he left them. He made cuttings in hills, opened roads, and was never at rest." https://ctext.org/shiji/wu-di-ben-ji

127 See note 56 of Fascicle II.

128 Dharma domains or realms.

129 The dragon palace, i.e. the Nāga Palace, which refers to the place where Nāgārjuna retrieved the Mahāyāna teachings. The term here is simply an allusion to Mahāyāna scriptures or teachings.

130 Nāgārjuna 龙树 (c. 150 – c. 250 CE) is widely considered one of the most important Mahāyāna philosophers. Along with his disciple Āryadeva 圣天, he is considered to be the founder of the Madhyamaka school of Mahāyāna Buddhism.

Fascicle VII

Beginning with the Composition of *A Statement on the Sacred Preface* by the Crown Prince in the Sixth Month in the Twenty-Second Year (648) and Ending with a Reply by the Master in the Second Month of the Spring in the Fifth Year of Yonghui (654)

In the sixth month of the summer in the twenty-second year of Zhenguan (648), Heavenly Lord and Great Emperor[1] lived at the Spring Palace[2], after reading the *Sacred Preface* respectfully, he indited *A Statement on the Sacred Preface*, which reads:

As to the propagation and promotion of the Buddhist teachings, a man of no wisdom is incapable of spreading its words far and wide; and as to the advocacy and elucidation of the profound doctrines, none but one with sagacious faculties could set their gist explicitly. The Holy Teaching of True Suchness (Tathatā) is the authentic source of all dharmas as well as the ultimatum of various scriptures, thus it is comprehensive in content and profound in theories. It reaches the innermost delicacies of *being* and *non-being* and embodies the quintessential nature of production and extinction. Because of being profuse in wording and inclusive in the Way, its source could not be easily traced by a man who explores it; because its language is explicit while the underlying meaning is implicit, its implications could not be readily speculated by a man who performs it. As we know, beneath the compassion of buddhas no wholesome deed has not been accomplished and under the edification of dharmas no unwholesome condition has not been eliminated. As we see, the dharma net of regulations and principles has already been cast, the right teaching of the Six Pāramitā[3] propagated, the afflictions of sentient beings relieved, and the very core of the Tripiṭaka revealed; therefore, the name (of Buddha) has flown to distant areas without being on wings, and the Buddha Way has stood firmly and shall do so forever without rooting in the soil. Both the Way and holy name have been passed on from remote ages to the present, bestowing prosperity to the world. Responding to the clamors of sentient beings by taking the manifestation-body, the Buddha shall be immortal throughout numerous kalpas. On the Vulture Peak, the morning bell and evening chanting are alternately ringing out, and at the Deer Park, the Sun of wisdom is shining when samādhi and prajñā are preached aloud; rising high into the sky, richly-ornamented canopies are flying together with auspicious clouds, while on the earth, farms, fields and forests are assuming colors gorgeous as heavenly flowers.

Blessed by Heaven with the felicity, His Majesty mounted the Throne. Henceforward, he has been ruling with noninterference the land within the eight quarters[4]. His virtue has not only influenced the people within the nation but also won the veneration of neighboring ethnicities and vassal countries. His beneficence is conferred even to the ancients and the palm-leaf texts are now stored in our national library; His kindness is extended even to insects and Sanskrit stanzas are preserved in golden caskets for the wide circulation. Waters of Anavatapta Lake has been drained into eight rivers[5] of the capital city of our grand nation and Mount Gṛdhrakūṭa has been linked to the green peaks of Hua[6] and Song[7] Mountains. Also I humbly believe: although the dharma nature is of great quietude, it could be attained by any devoted mind; although the true wisdom is mysterious and abstruse, it would clarify itself to the sincere and earnest. What His Majesty has achieved truly resembles a torch which illuminates the dark night or a rain which extinguishes the flaming house. Is it not a fact? Now as we see, just as a hundred rivers join together into the sea, myriads of the diverse doctrines are synthesized into one truth. How could King Tang of the Shang Dynasty (c.1600–1046 B.C.) and King Wu of the Western Zhou Dynasty (1045–256 B.C.)[8] be equaled to His Majesty?! Even the sagacious emperors Yao and Shun failed to compete with His Majesty in holiness and morality!

Intelligent and talented at a young age, Master Xuanzang

began to set his mind on Buddhism; in his childhood, he was already pure on the spiritual plane and when he grew up, he outgrew the world of vanity. Indulging himself in contemplation and hiding his traces in cloistered mountains, he resided in the Third Dhyāna[9] and cruised the Ten Stages of Bodhisattvahood. Having transcended the Six defilements[10], he became an outstanding scholar of Buddhism[11]; having mastered the gist of One Vehicle, he instructed and enlightened the people by skillful expedients. Because there were no solutions to his doubts in China, he resolved to seek the original texts in India. Finally, trudging across Ganges, he obtained the Mahāyāna texts and venturing beyond snowy mountains, he acquired the Hīnayāna texts. For pursuing the Way, he spent seventeen years abroad, and when he was proficient in all the Buddhist texts, he resolved to benefit the world. On the sixth day of the second month of the nineteenth year of Zhenguan (645), upon receiving the imperial order, the Master began to translate the important works of the Holy Teaching, totaling 657 works, at Hongfu Monastery. He hoped to drain the water from the dharma sea to cleanse the turbid world inexhaustibly, and he hoped to hand on the wisdom lamp to illumine the darkness perpetually. If it weren't for our wholesome karma accumulated from former existences, how could the Buddha's teachings have been so advocated and propagated?

May the dharma nature abide as eternally and brightly

as the three luminaries[12]! May His Majesty's felicity be as consolidated as Heaven and Earth! Reverentially I have read the preface composed by His Majesty to the newly-translated scriptures and commentaries. In my opinion, it is unprecedentedly prominent. Its arguments ring convincing to ear just like a piece of melodiously- performed music, and its words are overflowing smoothly and fluently just like a wind blowing or a cloud flying. I, Li Zhi, ventures to draft *A Statement on the Sacred Preface*, which resembles to add a grain of dust on a big mountain and throw a dewdrop into a river.

The Master submitted a letter to extend his gratitude, which reads:

I have heard that the Seven luminaries[13] shroud the whole world in their light because they are residing high in the sky, and the Nine Rivers[14] moisten all things because they are flowing on the earth. From it we can perceive the importance of the interdependent relationship as a law followed by the natural phenomena. Thus, I believe the propagation of the Dharma must depend on humans. Now Your Highness has given a full play to your literary gift by composing this essay to extol the Great Vehicle and glorify the True Reality[15]. In my opinion, its ideas are going on smoothly and fluently as a pearl is rolling or a windlass revolving; its language is beautiful, gleaming like the sun and the moon; and it rhythms properly, as melodious as the ancient music of *xian* and *shao*[16]. It is really a privilege bestowed by Your Holiness

> on me, humble as I am, but is fortunate enough. I submit this letter to extend my deep gratitude to your kindness.

Soon after, a reply by the Crown Prince was sent to the Master, which runs as follows:

> I, Li Zhi, am a man with meager talent and knowledge. As intelligence passes me by, I have not read much of the Buddhist works, so *A Statement on the Sacred Preface* written by me might be especially awkward and ill-informed. Unexpectedly I received your letter replete with compliments. In introspection, I felt ashamed and uneasy. I felt very guilty for having brought Your Reverence the trouble to give me so many thanks and compliments from afar.

Shi Yancong's annotation: On the publication of two holy prefaces, the people of all kinds, including the princes and dukes, ministers and officials, monks and laity, and masses, exulted with dances and songs, competing with one another to eulogize those meritorious writings. At the beginning, the two prefaces were merely circulated at the court, but less than twelve days, it was commended by the whole empire too. Once again, the shield of compassion clouds was strengthened and the light of wisdom sun intensified. People who wanted to convert to Buddhism surge in number, rushing to monasteries like billowing waves and rolling clouds. Confucius once said that superiors set the trend for inferiors in the way that wind is blowing over grass, in whatever direction the wind blows the grass always bends. Is it not an example to prove it? Also, that is why the Tathāgata always entrusted the dharma to the kings in former times.

At the time, Yuanding, Abbot of Hongfu Monastery, together

with other monks in the capital, wrote a petition to the Emperor for the permission to inscribe those two prefaces on metal vessels and stone slabs so as to preserve them well at temples, which was granted by the Emperor. Later, Huairen of Hongfu Monastery and other monks collected the individual characters from among the calligraphic works of Wang Xizhi (303–361)[17], General of the Right Army of the Jin Dynasty (265–420), and rearranged the order of those characters anew according to the two prefaces, and finally had them engraved on slabs.

On the first day of the seventh month, the Crown Prince planned to perform a posthumous religious ceremony for his mother Majestic Empress Wende[18] who relinquished the world early in her life, so as to requite her kindness and do a meritorious deed for her sake. He asked Gao Jifu (596–654), Great Officer of the Middle Class and Acting Director of the Crown Prince's Right Palace, to issue the following edict:

> I am a karmically imperfect person, so hapless to have caused misery to my beloved one. When I was very young, I lost my mother, since then a sharp sense of bereavement has been feeding on me all the time. Whenever I realized I was incapable of showing my filial piety to my mother any more, I was afflicted by a piecing pain deeply-rooted in bones. On various festival days and on every death anniversary of the late Empress, the grief arises from my heart. I missed my mother deeply but could do nothing at all. I often reproach myself for helplessness even to such an extent that all kinds of amusement, be music or songs, have totally lost interest

for me. I wish to requite her great maternal love but have not yet to do it. Alas! Even the grown-up crows know to nurture their parents, but I could not satisfy my desire to offer filial piety to my mother. I believe that the way to Enlightenment is extensive and beneficial, which must be able to grant blessings to the deceased. So, I wish to show my affection to my mother by taking the Three Refuges. I will order the official in charge to choose a suitable site among the deserted monasteries in capital for the construction of a new monastery to enshrine Majestic Empress Wende, and on the day of its completion, the ordination ritual of monks will be held. Moreover, the backdrop of fountains and woods should also be landscaped as perfect as the Trāyastriṃśa Heaven[19], and in this way I believe I would express my filial piety to my mother.

Thereafter, the official in charge carefully selected a site at the Jinchang residential quarter to the south of the palace city, facing the Qu Lake; formerly there used to be an ancient monastery named Jingjue, on the very site of which the new monastery was to be built. After having observed constellations and measured the land, the construction of the monastery was launched. The monastery followed the architectural style of the imperial palace and the Jatavana Park, and was constructed by the craftsmen with workmanship superb as that of ancient carpenters [Lu] Ban[20] and Chui[21], using high-quality timbers from Henghuo Mountains[22]. In the gardens, there were rocks of fine grain; in the woods were catalpa, cassia, camphor and palm trees. For decoration, pearls and jade, cinnabar and blue earth, ochre and chalk, and gold and jadeite were profusely employed. Multi-storeyed pavilions, complex halls, high-rising turrets and the spacious monks' chambers were distributed all over a dozen courtyards, totally 1,897 rooms, each being adequately furnished with beddings, daily utensils and other articles.

Later, His Majesty Emperor Wenwu[23] read the *Bodhisattvapiṭaka Sūtra* presented by the Master. Impressed with it, he ordered the Crown Prince to compose a postscript to the scripture. The postscript was written as follows:

> I have heard that Fuxi comprehended the extreme profundities, inspired by images on the tortoise shells[24], and that Emperor Xuanyuan understood the obscurity, conveying the refined and the abstruse by inventing characters with reference to birds' tracks[25]. However, examining the markings on the shell of tortoise from the Luo River[26] to open the secret gate seems to be far from getting the true source of reality; similarly, exploring the ancient divination books to probe all changes in the universe is not a way to gain permanent happiness. Still, their activities have been glorified in records of classics and historical literature, exerting influences on every corner of China; and their virtues have nourished sentient beings, conferring benefits on a myriad of generations all the same.
>
> Humbly, I believe that His Majesty, like a Wheel-turning King[27], governs the country with non-interference and extends his edification to the place as far afield as the Kukkuṭā garden. Although he resides in his magnificent

palace, his views are in conformity with the teachings preached on the Vulture Peak. Deserved the honorable title as the General Guide of Men, His Majesty shows the wisdom inconceivable to the reasoning mind; his words embody the Prajñā[28] that even the theories of *Xiang* (symbols) and their *Xi* (explanations) of the *Book of Changes* are no match for. Thus, by his writing, the profound teachings have been elucidated explicitly and the Eight Emancipations[29] spread far and wide; instructions of the Buddha have been introduced into China and the Four Dhyānas[30] practiced all around. Consequently, living beings in the three-thousandfold world are infused with hope, a hundred *Koṭis* Sumeru mountains annexed into the mundane world, the waters of Nairañjanā river drained into the pond of imperial palace and the garden of Anāthapiṇḍika enclosed into the Shanglin Palace[31]. The nature of Dharma is of emptiness and quietude, which could respond to various circumstance expediently; the True Teachings is profound and wonderful, which reveals the truth however enigmatic it is. All in all, under the guidance of authoritative power of the Throne, the dharma current flows inexhaustibly; for the Rock kalpa[32], the buddhas of various times could give edification to sentient beings ceaselessly. In addition, His Majesty has a well–proportioned build and wholesome faculties beyond description, so if a comparison is to be made between him and the other monarchs, the latter certainly cannot be mentioned in the same breath.

Since Heaven and Earth were created, the communication between Cīna[33] and India had long been hindered geographically by the drifting desert so that the divine texts remained in oblivion. Later, a golden deity was descending into the dream of the Emperor Ming (28–75 CE) of the Han Dynasty[34], marking the Buddhism came into China; and from the Jin Dynasty (265–420 CE), for the ever-growing eagerness and sincerity of the people, more and more Buddhist scriptures were brought into China on the backs of steeds. However, by using a gourd to ladle the water in Four Seas, one could not measure the amount of the water, nor could one know the location of seven luminaries only by peeping at them through a thin straw pipe. [In fact, what had been done in the past is just like this.] By the time His Majesty's influence spreads far and wide, his awesome power goes beyond the Iron Enclosing Mountains[35]; as the most sagacious emperor who propagates and advocates the dharma, his virtue reaches up to the Diamond Ranges[36]; thereafter, lands numerous as the sands in the Ganges are following the true teachings and the door of emancipation opens to the people who treading on the road to the Ultimate Truth. The Sanskrit stanzas preached at the Dragon Palace[37] echo in the astronomical observatory Qingtai of Chang'an while the Lion's Roar of the Buddha[38] inscribed on the palm-leaf is preserved in Imperial Library of the capital. Sprinkling the sweet dew to moisten sprouts as well as stalks, lowering clouds of wisdom to shelter all the birds and beasts, if without the influences of the sagacious emperor, how could the people have accomplished the grand deed of taking refuges in the Triple Gem?

The *Bodhisattvapiṭaka Sūtra* is a book that conveys the essential gist of the great enlightenment. Practicing by it, Gautama Buddha has realized the non-birth; accepting and holding onto it, Bodhisattvas have ascended the state of non-retrogression. Embodying the quintessence of the Six Pāramitā, disclosing the fundamentals of the Four Unlimited Mental States[39], this *Sūtra* serves as a ferry for a man to cross to the yonder shore or a ladder for him to attain to the perfect enlightenment.

Since the middle of the Zhenguan period (627–649) when Shendu[40] established friendly diplomatic relations with Tang, the edification of the Tang Empire has been exerted on the lands beyond the hot deserts while the precious treasures have been transported into China over the Hindu Kush Mountains. With the frequent cultural exchanges, the units of measurements were unified and so was the length of the axles of carts, ever since there has been no hindrance to the transportation. In order to seek the truth, Śramaṇa Xuanzang, holding a religious staff, went out of the Yumen Pass and proceeded straight to Vārāṇasī; after a long trek, he arrived in Tianzhu[41], birthplace of Almighty One (Buddha), where he obtained this scripture. As soon as he returned to Chang'an, he presented it to His Majesty and received the imperial order to translate it. Now the translation has been completed.

After paying my respects to His Majesty, I purified my mind and read this treasure of wonderful Dharma. Reverentially obeying the Emperor's order, I wrote this postscript, though insignificant it is, to sing praises for the *Sūtra*. I will ask the official in charge to append my article in the end of the scripture.

From then on, the Emperor showed more trust in and affection for the Master. He often consulted the Master on the doctrines of the Dharma, having talks with him on issues like how to do meritorious deeds, how to cultivate the field of blessedness, and so on. He kept company with the Master, unwilling to separate for a single moment. Also, the imperial orders were issued again and again to offer more items of sustenance to the Master, provide him with clothes of various seasons, and substitute utensils and articles of beddings for brand new ones from time to time. On the seventeenth day of the seventh month in the autumn, when the summer retreat was concluded, the Emperor presented a religious robe to the Master, worth a hundred gold coins, which was so dexterously made that even a careful observer could not tell the traces of stitches in and out. There had been a lot of previously-made religious robes in the palace storehouse, but none of them was thought to be good enough, so the Emperor asked the ladies in the harem to make a new one and its needlework cost several years, which at last turned to be his favorite. Every time the Emperor was on his inspection tour, he always brought the Master along with him. In the twenty-second year of Zhenguan period (648), the Emperor favored the Luoyang Palace with his presence. At the time there were two eminent monks, the Ven. Daogong from Suzhou and the Ven. Huixuan from Changzhou, both of whom were of noble character and well learned in Buddhist and non-Buddhist knowledge, so they were acclaimed by officials and commoners as well. The Emperor summoned them to the palace. After exchanged greetings, they took their seats. Those two monks were donning religious robes inherited from their late teachers whom the Emperor Wu of Liang (464–549) gave those robes to. As precious inheritance, the robes had been carefully preserved, and now for having an audience with the Emperor, they put them on. Scorning at the coarse craftsmanship of the robes, the Emperor had the newly-made religious robe fetched to show off to them, meanwhile asked them to write acclamatory verses.

The Ven. Daogong voiced his acclaim in the following poem:

The field of blessedness nourishes the virtue,
The holy teachings perfumed the seeds.
Although the threads are not gold,
Still well on patterns many a color goes.

Crimson and blue set each other beautifully off,
Into the silk threads emerald green intermingles.
There were stripes as well as pieces,
Dividing the field of Blessedness into separate patches.

The last two lines of the Ven. Huixuan's poem are:
If I may put it on for a moment, truly
My field of blessedness is to be cultivated.

In this verse the Ven. Huixuan indicated that they wished to put the robe on, but the Emperor refused, and gave each of them fifty rolls of silk instead. This robe was resplendent beyond all comparison. No one was qualified to don it save the Master, for he was a man of such high virtue. Together with the robe, a razor was also presented as a gift to the Master, and for these gifts, he wrote the following letter to express his gratitude, which runs as follows:

> I, *Śramaṇa* Xuanzang, bowed down with respect to receive a Kāṣāya and a razor granted by Your Majesty. Privileges have been bestowed on me so repeatedly and gracious favors accorded to me so impressively that I am full of awe and uneasiness, feeling like walking on the thin ice in early spring. Fortunately, I was educated to be respectful and peaceful, so at a very young age, I joined the monastic order to be a monk; however, I am yet to have my Three Karmas[42] well- modulated and amply repay the Four Graces[43]. For this reason, I don't deserve Your Majesty's consideration or beneficence. The robe of endurance[44] is shining brightly with well-merging colors of rainbow and the razor of wisdom has the sharp edge which can cut jade easily. I hope I can put on the former as the armor to subdue the devils of worries and take the latter to cut open the net of worldly defilements. I am worried that my honor would be defamed for its false name and that my inferiority and shallowness incur the criticism from others, at the thought of which I feel so ashamed and restless that I could do nothing but bend down in humility; meanwhile, despite my anxieties

and embarrassment, I have been greatly encouraged and put in a high-soaring spirit by your munificence. Again, I feel I am unworthy of Your Majesty's kindness, and uneasily I am writing this letter to extend my deep gratitude, which I'm afraid might disturb Your Majesty's serene mind. Trembling all over, I prostrate to express my gratitude for your grace.

When the Emperor was young, he toiled at the military affairs, after he assumed the reins of government, he had been preoccupied with the welfare of the people. During his military expedition to quell the riots in Liaodong, braving the wind and frost, he was weather-beaten. After he came back from the battlefield with his troops, his energy was flagging gradually, so he started to concern about the problem of the life and death. Since he made an acquaintance with the Master, he had followed the Eightfold Path and taken the Five Vehicles, thus was gradually restored in health.

Once he asked the Master, "If we intend to perform meritorious deeds, what should we do?"

The Master replied, "All living beings are submerged in delusion and ignorance, if without wisdom, they would never be awakened. It is the Dharma that nurtures the sprout of wisdom, and the propagation of the Dharma is verily held in mortal hands, so the ordination of monks is the most beneficial."

At hearing this, the Emperor was very delighted.On the first day of the ninth month in the autumn, an imperial decree was sent forth, which reads:

At the end of the Sui Dynasty, there was no correct governance, so the country split asunder. The domain within the Four Seas was falling into turmoil and disasters with riots erupting from eight quarters. We shouldered our responsibility to suppress the riots by taking the punitive expedition. Braving the wind and frost, sleeping on horseback, we experienced the innumerable hardships. After returning, although taking medicines, we haven't yet regained our health. Recently, we, however, have been gradually recovering. Is it not a good retribution for our meritorious deeds, is it? We order every monastery in the capital city and in other states of the empire to ordain five persons. Hongfu Monastery could enjoy the privilege to ordain fifty monks.

Within the domain of the empire, totally there were 3,716 monasteries, altogether 18,500 odd monks and nuns were ordained. Previously, in the last years of the Sui Dynasty, the monasteries were already in dilapidation, with monks and nuns nearly extinct, now because of this decree, the Buddhist followers were thus multiplied. The Emperor truly is a superior man! He followed the valuable words so wisely and timely!

The Emperor once said to the Master, "It is the *Vajracchedikāp rajñāpāramitā Sūtra* that gives birth to all buddhas, and if a man hears this Sūtra and doesn' t slander it, the merits he thus obtains are much more than he offers his body and life, or gives the precious jewels and pearls numerous as the sands in the Ganges River as alms. In addition, this Sūtra is profound in meaning and precise in diction, so it has always been preferred by the worthy and the true virtuous ones. We wonder whether the previously-translated version is faithful to the original text or not."

The Master replied, "The merits of upholding this scripture are every bit as what Your Majesty has believed. The people in the West also prefer and respect it. Recently I have read the old versions and found that there were a few omissions. The full title of the Sanskrit Sūtra is *Vajracchedikāprajñāpāramitā Sūtra,* but the old Chinese version simply rendered it into *Vajrapra*jñā *Sūtra.* Actually, the burdens of this Sūtra are that Bodhisattvas considered the discrimination as an affliction, and that the discrimination is a delusion of men which is as hard as *Vajra,* diamond, so can only be cut off by the wisdom of non-discrimination; hence the name *Vajracchedikāprajñāpāramitā Sūtra.* From it, we know the former version has lost two Chinese characters for *cchedikā (able to cut)* in the title. Besides, in the translation, one of the three inquiries, one of the two verses, three of the nine parables are missing. The terms *Sheweiguo* (for *Śrāvastī*) used in Kumārajīva's version and *Pojiapo* (for *bhagavat*) in Bodhiruci's are more or less acceptable."Then the Emperor suggested, "Since Your Reverence has already got the Sanskrit text, why not produce a new version to let the people know a full and complete one?"

Indeed, what makes scriptures valuable is the true teachings they convey, so it was no good to employ florid language at the cost of faithfulness. Therefore, the new Chinese version of the *Vajracchedikāprajñāpāramitā Sūtra* was produced faithfully to the Sanskrit text. When it was presented to the Emperor, it made him rejoiced.

In the tenth month in the winter, the Emperor, with the Master as his company, returned to the capital. Formerly, on the imperial order, the official in charge had already built a separate house west to Ziwei

Hall in the northern part of the imperial palace, naming Hongfa-yuan (House for the Propagation of the Dharma). Now the Master took up residence in it. During the daytime, the Emperor asked the Master to accompany him and talk with him whenever and wherever possible; at night the Master returned to his chamber to do translation, where he completed the translation of Asvabhāva Bodhisattva's *Exposition of the Mahāyānasaṅgraha Śāstra* in ten fascicles and Vasubandhu's *Exposition* of this work in ten fascicles, and the *Pratītyasamutpāda Sūtrain* in one fascicle, and the *Mahāyānaśatadharmaprakāśamukhaś āstra* in one fascicle.

On the fifth day [of the tenth month], the Crown Prince sent forth an order, saying:

> The construction of the Ci'en Monastery[45] is near completion. There will be lofty and grandiose mansions but a dearth of monks. I received a decree from the Emperor ordering three hundred monks to be ordained and fifty great virtuous monks to be invited in this sacred abode to practice the Way. This newly constructed preaching venue should be named as Great Ci'en Monastery. A Translation Studio should be built separately. Beams and ceilings should be painted in splendid colors and decorated with auspicious patterns. The plinths should be made of jade stones, the steps of bronze, the knockers of golden brass and the ground laid with beautiful tiles. All in all, everything should be exquisite and gorgeous. The Master is supposed to move into it to do his translation work and take charge of the monastic affairs at the same time.

Upon receiving this order in which the Master was required to be the abbot of the monastery, he presented a letter to the Emperor to decline the appointment:

I, *Śramaṇa* Xuanzang, beg to submit the following statement:

Bowing down respectfully to receive the imperial decree requiring me to be the abbot of Ci'en Monastery, and at this honorable appointment I feel quite uneasy. Very embarrassed and fearful, I am in the deep trepidation. My knowledge has never been systematic and my practices also empty and shallow, but I venture to take the vow to do my best endeavors to advocate and propagate the Buddha's teachings. Relying on Your Majesty's prestige, I traveled to the remote places for the pursuit of the Way. On the imperial order, I have been translating the scriptures and treaties brought back from India, hoping by doing so the dharma stream would moisten and nourish our country, and the holy teachings would spread around and pass on to the posterity. Indeed, I have been afflicted with a rash for a long time because of the arduous journey undertaken before. Although I kept striving on with my last strength, I, tired and incompetent, am still afraid that I will not be able to have my translation work completed. If so, I would be unworthy of the grace that the country bestowed on me. If so, I could not be absolved from punishment for my dereliction of duty. The decree that appoints me to take charge of the monastic affairs gives me another chance to be reprimanded. What if fish and birds exchange their nature? There must be no way for the former in sky and the latter in water. I think that Your Highness is a man with the heavenly-bestowed nature of benevolence and filial piety, from your innermost heart overflowing affection for and reverence to your mother. Haunted by the anguish of losing her, Your Highness has had this monastery constructed to augment the great blessings both in the nether and mundane worlds. To administer the monastic staff of it should be a responsibility to be shouldered by a man with managerial competence, for employing an incapable man is to make confusion and disorder. Thus, I sincerely hope you will exercise acute discernment again to choose favorable conditions for the propagation of the Dharma. Please condescend your compassion once more to examine my stubborn but loyal sincerity. If so, I, as a monk, shall never be guilty-stricken for doing something regretful. It is desirable if fish could enjoy the fun of swimming and birds the pleasure of flying. With utmost loyalty and sincerity, I submit this letter to have you know my desire. Fearful and shameful, I am filled with even more trepidation.

On the twenty-second day of the twelfth month, an imperial edit was issued to the effect that [Li] Daozong (600–653), Prince of Jiangxia and Director of Ceremonies, should command the nine courtly bands[46]; Song Xingzhi (?–651), Magistrate of Wannian, and Pei Fangyan, Magistrate of Chang'an, should lead the bands of their prefectures respectively; monasteries should get banners and canopies prepared, making them as solemnly splendid as possible; on the morning of the twenty-third day, all of them should assemble at the Anfu Gate Street to receive the Buddha images and escort the monks into the Great Ci'en Monastery. On that day people and objects were arrayed in thoroughfares. There were totally over fifteen hundred carriages adorned with over three hundred curtains as well as canopies, also with colorful silk banners and pendent streamers embroidered with patterns of dragons and fish. The day before some articles had already been removed from the palace and deposited in the Hongfu Monastery, including more than two hundred pieces of embroidery and paintings of Buddha, two Buddha statues, one gold and one silver, and five hundred satin and silk banners sewn with golden threads, etc. All of them, together with the scriptures, images, and relics of the Buddha that had been brought back from the western countries by the Master, were taken out from the Hongfu Monastery and placed in curtained seats of carriages. Now the procession was proceeding. The Buddha images were in the middle, with the large and luxurious carriages arranged on both sides on which the tall poles were erected with fluttering banners. Behind the banners, the images of Divine Lion King and other deities were set as vanguards. Besides, fifty big carriages were splendidly bedecked for those monks of great virtue to take, following behind which were monks of the capital chanting prayers and singing hymns, holding incenses and flowers in hands. Next came the civil and military officials leading their attendants and guards in ranks. On both sides of the procession, there were nine bands of the Board of Ceremonies in front with the musicians of two prefectures behind, with the harmonious tinkling of the drums and bells clamoring over the capital. People were made dizzy by the picturesque mixture of streamers and banners fluttering high, obscuring the sun. The procession extended as far as the eye could see, whose head and tail people could not tell. The Crown Prince dispatched his Chief Guard Yuchi Shaozong and Deputy Chief Guard Wang Wenxun to command more than one thousand palace guards to serve as carriers. The Emperor appointed Li Qianyou (593–668), Imperial Inspector, to be the Grand Chief, to assist Marquis of Wu in supervising the procession. The Emperor, together with the Crown Prince and the ladies of the harem, stood on the tower-arch of Anfu Gate, holding the incense burners in their hands and overlooking the procession with the delight. In the street, onlookers amounted to tens of thousands. When the images and scriptures arrived at the gate to the monastery, the Emperor ordered Duke of Zhao and Duke of Ying, together with Chief of Imperial Secretariat Chu Suiliang (596–658) to hold the incense burners to usher the images and scriptures into the hall for placement. Then, the Nine Bands of music, the Dance of Triumph and the other acrobatic feasts were performed in the courtyard of the monastery. After the performance, people dispersed.

The ordination of monks was scheduled to be held on the twenty-sixth day [of the twelfth month]. On the twenty-fifth day, the Crown Prince, escorted by his bodyguards, left the palace to spend the night at his old residence. On the morning of the following day, the Crown Prince came from the south of the monastery, followed by his honor guard holding flags decorated with feathers fluttering high, and reached the gate of the monastery. Alighted from his carriage, he walked into the monastery, after him the officials of all ranks. Having paid his homage to the Buddha images, he granted an interview with fifty monks of great virtue and told them why he had this monastery constructed. While he was speaking he was often choked by sobs, which made officials and monks present so touched that they shed tears with him. With regard to his deep filial piety, he could be commended as an Emperor Shun[47] of his time! After the talk, the Crown Prince ascended the eastern pavilion of the main hall and ordered Zhang Xingcheng (587–653), Deputy Manager of General Affairs to the Crown Prince, to claim an edict of amnesty to all prisoners in the capital and its neighborhood. Then he had the monks shaved and served with an alms meal. In addition, he presented the princes, dukes and their subjects with rolls of silk. After that, asking his men to clear the way, the Crown Prince descended from the pavilion to worship the Buddha images. Together with his concubines and others he visited all buildings in the monastery. When he stopped at the house of the Master, he indited a poem with five Chinese characters in each line and had it posted on the door, which reads:

Halting our royal carriage in front of the Hall of Bliss,
I gazed at the majestic capital from far off.
The Dharma Wheel is rotating under the sun,
While canopies are flying high into the clouds.

Decorated pavilions are perfumed by the incense puff,
And precious cassocks are gleaming in sunset glow.
Merging into the distant rainbow, streamers are
Sharing the brightness of the sun.

Attaining the Ten Stages[48] in tranquility,
Ekayāna supersedes the Three Vehicles[49] as a matter of course.

After visiting the monastery, the Crown Prince returned to his palace. At the time, both monks and laity were delighted, singing grandiose praises about the prosperity of the abstruse Way and the revival of bequeathed Dharma. They amazed at such an affair, for it had never happened in ancient or present times. On the same day, an imperial decree was issued asking the Master to return to the northern palace.

In the fourth month in the summer in the twenty-third year (649), the Emperor favored the Cuiwei Palace[50] with his presence, with the Crown Prince and the Master in his company. Besides handling the state affairs, the Emperor often talked with the Master about metaphysics and the Way even to the exclusion of any other things. In their talks, the Emperor inquired about the theories of the causation as well as the retribution, also about the holy relics left by the ancient sages in the Western Regions. In order to give those questions well-founded answers, the Master often quoted passages from the scriptures and treatises, which made the Emperor firm in his Buddhist faith, and for several times, the Emperor even pushed up his sleeves and signed with regret, saying, "We met the Master too late to carry out the Buddhist enterprises extensively!"

When the Emperor left the capital, he was slightly indisposed, but he looked no less majestic and wise than ever before. On the twenty-sixth day of the fifth month, he developed a slight headache, yet still put up the Master for the night in the palace. On the twenty-seventh day, the Emperor passed away at the Hanfeng Hall. This news had been withheld for some time; and not until the royal family returned to the capital was it announced to the public. The coffin was then placed at the Taiji Hall. On the same day, the inauguration ceremony for the Crown Prince to ascend the Throne was held, who in the following year, changed his reign title to Yonghui. At the demise of the Emperor, the people all over the empire wailed grievously as if they had lost their parents.

The Master returned to the Ci'en Monastery. From then on, he devoted himself to translating, without wasting a single minute. Every day, he made a timetable for himself, and if he failed to keep to it for being interrupted by whatever business during the daytime, he would complete his work at night. Every day, not until after the second watch[51] at night did he put down his pen and put away the scriptures; and before he went to sleep at the third watch[52] he worshiped the Buddha image and made self-cultivation; usually he got up at the fifth watch[53] in the morning to recite the Sanskrit texts and marked out the content with red ink for his translation that day. Every day, after the midday meal and at dusk he would spend some time in lecturing the newly translated scriptures and treatises, which attracted the monks and laity from all over the country to come to learn and to clear up their doubts and inquire about some theories. Besides, as the abbot of the monastery, monastic affairs of various kinds were also heaped upon him. In addition, there were messengers coming one after another from the imperial palace to consult the Master of such meritorious deeds as making ten complete sets of duplication of all scriptures and molding over two hundred gem-decorated *jiazhu*[54] clay statues of the Buddha. What's more, after sunset, usually there were over one hundred monks waiting in corridors and side chambers for the admonitions. The Master managed various affairs and answered all questions effectively with no defect and omission. Despite so many people and businesses he had to attend to, the Master always carried a refined bearing, never at a loss in management. When he talked with other virtuous monks, sometimes he told them the theories established by the worthy and the sagacious in the West, as well as the heterodoxy of varied schools, and sometimes he spoke of his study experiences of visiting different lecture centers in his youth. When he spoke, he was full of wisdom and passion, never showing a slight fatigue or stagnation. In such a manner he distinguished himself from others in astuteness, acuteness, and strength. What's more, there were some princes and ministers often calling upon him when they came to the monastery to pay homage to the Buddha or make repentance, and on those occasions, the Master expediently gave them flexible guidance to evoke their Bodhi mind, which made them, almost without exception, abandon their pride and extravagance; therefore, they thought highly of the Master and hold a reverential and solemn attitude toward him.

On the eighth day of the first month in the spring of the second year (651), Jia Dunyi, Governor of Yingzhou[55], and Li Daoyu, Governor of Puzhou[56], Du Zhenglun, Governor of Guzhou[57], and Xiao Rui, Governor of Hengzhou[58], assembled in the capital to discuss national affairs. In their spare time off duty, they went together to visit the Master, craving to receive the Bodhisattva Precepts, so the Master granted them with the precepts and extensively explained the practices of Bodhisattva. In addition, he exhorted them to be loyal to the Emperor and be benevolently kind to the subjects. Those gentlemen presented their well-earned wealth as offerings and left delightedly. Afterwards, they wrote a letter of thanks to the Master for his transmission of the Precepts and Dharma on them, which was later taken to the Master by a messenger. The letter reads:

We presume: not because of the desire of the physical body for food did Tathāgata accept the food offered by Cunda[59]; only because the Dharma is not something to be acquired did Vimalakīrti preach it at the request of Subhūti[60]. These stories are intended to show the facts that the ultimate truth is permanent and there is no duality between commoners and saints. Men are guided by using expedient methods and the Way is propagated through the phenomenal. The one who made offerings expressed their sincerity to the Dharma while the other who accepted them granted the bliss to the alms givers. How could we say when they did so, their mind was attached to discernment of self and others, or to the fame and the wealth?

Respectfully we believe that you have cultivated the root of virtue during numerous past existences rather than merely in the days when encountering a few buddhas. Therefore, you could penetrate all aspects of the Dharma, have a good command of twelve divisions of the Mahāyāna canon[61], acquaint yourself with the true teachings alone, and took a long trek to follow the holy traces of the Buddha.

Visiting the pure land of Gṛdhrakūṭa Mountain and bathing in the clear waters of Ganges, you entered the innermost dharma realm and studied under the well-learned teachers. A hundred generations have passed since the Buddha's Nirvāṇa, and notwithstanding, you finally collected His bequeathed texts on the ultimate truth and thoroughly explored the abstruseness preached by Him one thousand years ago. Serving as a boat to ferry a myriad of sentient beings across the sea of suffering, you never flaunt nor delude yourself; conferring benefits on all sentient beings, you hold the attitude of equality, never giving priority to anyone.

Ignoring the twofold emptiness[62], we have been forced by our karma to submerge in the Three Realms[63] incessantly. Like silkworms in cocoons, we are binding ourselves in reincarnation which goes on endlessly as a winch turns over the well. We developed a faith in Buddhist teachings, and with different capabilities we acquired the dharma at different levels. On the one hand, after taking the refuge in Triple Gem with homage, we adhered to the Four Propositions[64] and practiced meditation at secluded places; we abhorred mundane sufferings and desired for the permanent merriness. On the other hand, still having been trapped in Avidyā[65] from the time immemorial, we were unable to comprehend the ultimate truth, and failed to awaken to that the Buddha nature is abiding in each of us and that the phenomenal world is arising from our consciousness. As a result, our mind could not get rid of the desire for acquisition and we were sticking closely to the falsehood of finitude or infinitude. We were incapable of taking the Eightfold Nobel Path by removing the Eight Erroneous Practices[66] nor approaching the Way through practicing the None-way.

Alas! We could not find a boat to ferry across the sea [of suffering]! We could see nothing ahead but a black wall!

Yesterday when we were not occupied by mundane business, we paid a visit to you. In order to make us engender the mind for pursuing the unsurpassed Way, you conferred on us Bodhisattva Precepts and delivered us the Dharma talk we had never heard before. We are greatly indebted to what you have done to us. It's said that a single right idea could break through the limitless ignorance, and the Four Forms of the Unlimited Mind[67] would penetrate the practices in the infinite future. Bodhi seeds are sprouting from the worldly worries and the lotus flowers are growing out of fire, which are intended to illustrate that the nature of Tathāgata is none other than that of the mundane world and that there is no difference between the nirvāṇa and the birth-and-death. As the practicing Prajñā is meant the non-practicing of it, so attaining Bodhi is to acquire nothing at all. All at once, we people of meager intelligence had the opportunity to hear the Great Teachings. We accepted it with veneration, when we seriously pondered over it, we exulted beyond expression. Among the Six Pāramitas, the Dharma Dāna[68] is the supreme one; among the honorable Triple Gem, the Master is the best gem of monks. With disinterested motives, you are showing compassion to living beings just like the sun and the moon, which throwing their light down to the earth. We are looking up to you with gratitude just as sunflowers are turning with the sun. We dare not to hope we might follow the example of the Bodhisattva when he sacrificed his physical body for the pursuit of the Dharma, but perhaps we could learn from the little boy[69] who offered his only possession, a handful of earth, to the Buddha when he caught sight of Him. We are sending you some small gifts, enlisted separately, to express our gratitude and respect, with the hope that our sincerity would open up the field of merits. Please accept these insignificant gifts, dispose them at your will, and only by doing so would you render our offerings much more valuable, as if a dew is to be dropped into Bohai Sea[70] or a speck of dust thrown onto the Sumeru Mountain. That will be very, very fortunate indeed! Since it is still rather cold in spring, we hope you will take a proper care of yourself. This letter is presented for no other reasons but to express our emotions.

With homage from Jia Dunyi and others.

Such is the way the Master was adored by the worthy officials at the Imperial Court.

In the third month in the spring of the third year (652), the Master planned to build a stone pagoda south of the main gate of the monastery in order to preserve the scriptures and images he had brought back from the Western Regions. His intention was to insure them against loss and damage through vicissitudes or in the fire. The pagoda was designed to be as tall as thirty *zhang*[71], a landmark symbolizing the lofty foundation of the Tang Empire, and a replica of the memorial site of Śākyamuni Buddha. Then he presented to the Emperor a petition and a blueprint of construction. After reading it, the Emperor dispatched Li Yifu (614–666), imperial secretary, to inform the Master by saying: "The construction of the pagoda is of such a great undertaking that we are afraid the completion of it would not be in a short time, so it is best to build it out of bricks. Besides, we don't want to toil the teacher at it. Now, the garments and properties of the deceased in Eastern Palace and six imperial harems have already been collected to support your project, which will be sufficient to cover the whole construction expense."

Then bricks were used and the construction site was shifted to the west courtyard of the monastery. Each side of the pagoda base was one hundred and forty *chi*[72] in length. The pagoda was built after the architecture style of Western Regions rather than that of China. It had five storeys, plus a Wheel Sigh and a Dew Basin, totally one hundred eighty *chi*[73] in height. In the center of each storey, there were one or two thousand grains of Śarīras[74], totaling over ten thousand in the whole pagoda. The top storey was a stone chamber, with two steles (slabs) standing on the southern side, bearing the *Preface to the Holy Teachings of the Tripiṭaka* and *A Statement on the Sacred Preface*, indited respectively by two Emperors. The inscriptions were engraved in the calligraphy of Chu Suiliang (596–658), Premier, Right Puye and Duke of Henan.

On the day of laying the foundation stone, the Tripiṭaka Master stated his sincere wishes in a petition to the effect as follows:

> I, Xuanzang, mediocre and unlucky, was not born in the time the Buddha lived in the world; nevertheless, my insignificant goodness makes me get the chance to hear the teachings of the Buddha in the Image Period. How unfortunate it is if I had been born in the Dharma-ending age! If so, in whom should I take refuge? Fortunately, I

left the household life at a young age to be a monk in the monastery, thus I could look upon the divine Buddha images with my own eyes. Earlier in my childhood, I began to brew an aspiration for the Dharma. However, I tried to learn the bequeathed teachings but failed to get to the gist. When I heard about the self-cultivation of Bodhisattvas, despite my mediocrity I craved to be equal to them; when I was told about the Dharma preached by Tathāgata, wholeheartedly I showed my worship to Him. Thereafter I sought the instructions from various honorable teachers successively and extensively consulted the senior scholars.

It is the dream of Han Emperor that initiated the introduction of the Right Dharma into the East. But for a long time the detailed and complete elucidation on the truth hadn't been available because the route to the West was arduous and long, which made the scholars restrained by their biased views or/and limited to a particular aspect of theories; therefore, they often rivaled against each other, enmeshing themselves in disputes on whether or not sentient beings originally possessed, or were about to possess, the Buddha-nature; correspondingly, partisan groups cropped up with opposite opinions and often darted hatred at each other. This situation unavoidably brought distortion to the unique flavor of the Buddha's teachings. Consequently, learners fell into bewilderment, totally lost in the choice of the right way to follow. Often seeing into the direction of the Vulture Peak, I was feeling more and more melancholy, and just like

Bodhisattva Sadāpralāpa[75], I could not set my mind at rest, enduring many sleepless nights. Then, I prayed for blessings of the Buddha, and by relying on the power and influence of the country, I left my mother land where I was bound to live all my life, and threw my body into an alien place where a myriad of perils awaiting me. During my journey, reverentially I visited all the traces left by the former saints, and whenever I heard a scholar learned in Dharma, I made straight for his place to study from him. A feeling of self-pity welled up in my mind every time I reached a place where I saw what I had never seen before; and I was full of thanks and ecstasies when I heard what I had not heard before, might it be a word. I devoted all my resources to transcribing the scriptures and treaties needed in our country. Not until my vow had been fulfilled did I return to the imperial court. Very fortunately it was a prosperous time and the wise monarch ordered me to translate Buddhist texts into Chinese.

His Majesty, the late Emperor, was as supreme as Cakravartīrāja and his prestige resounded loudly like a roll of drums. Having shouldered the responsibility of inheriting and carrying forward the Buddhist teachings in the Image Period, he showed his holy sincerity by composing the preface to the Tripiṭaka canon. Afterwards, the Way was preached in the Spring Palace, so the reigning Emperor composed *A Statement on the Sacred Preface*. Both compositions have come to the scene just like the sun and the moon rising high simultaneously, giving out glazing brightness. Their melodious language resembles the music produced by drums and bells, and their inspiring thoughts, like the Seven Luminaries, would cast light on the world forever. Neither the White Horse Monastery[76] in the eastern capital nor the Caotang Monastery[77] in the western capital ever witnessed the great events of the translation of Buddhist scriptures of the same breath as the present occasion. To pity the living creatures for losing their reliance, the Buddha, and to prevent the Sanskrit Tripiṭaka from being mislaid or falling into oblivion, I have conceived of building a pagoda to store the Sanskrit texts. Also, two memorial steles are to be erected to bear the writings of sagely emperors, the *Preface* and the *Statement*, otherwise they would be forgotten forlornly for not being recorded. May they stand majestically forever! May a thousand buddhas behold them as we do! May the holy writings of Emperors endure as long as Heaven and Earth!

At the time, the Tripiṭaka Master carried baskets or crates with his own hands to transport the bricks and stones for construction. It took two weeks to build the pagoda.

On the twenty-third day of the fifth month in the summer, the great virtuous monks Jñānaprabha, Prajñādeva and others of the Mahābodhi Vihāra in Central India delivered a letter to the Master. Jñānaprabha had a good command of both the Mahāyāna and Hīnayāna texts, also the heretical works including the Four Vedas, the treatises of five branches of learning[78], and others. As a principal disciple of the venerable Śilabhadra, he was respected by all scholars in the five realms of India. It was true to Prajñādeva, who was conversant with the eighteen branches of the Hīnayāna School and able to give guidance to followers skillfully. They often exchanged ideas with the Master when he was travelling in the Western Regions. The two masters had gained much learning from the Hīnayāna teachings, but they didn't attach their interest to Vaipulya[79]. Seeing they stubbornly stuck to the biased views, the Master always criticized and retorted them. At the congregation in Kanyākubja City, when the Master fiercely denounced them, they felt ashamed and frustrated. After the Master left India, they had pined for him in respect, so they asked Dharmadīrgha, a *Śramaṇa* from their monastery to bring a letter full of eulogistic verses to the Master, together with two rolls of cotton cambric cloth as gifts. With deep sincerity, the letter complimented the Master as follows:

> The abbot Prajñādeva of Mahābodhi Vihāra at the Diamond Seat of the mysterious and auspicious World-Honored One, surrounded by a multitude of learned monks, begs to send this letter to the Mokṣācārya of the country of Māhacīna[80] who is most learned in the subtle teachings of scriptures, disciplinary texts and treatises, extending to him unlimited respect and hoping that he may live in good health with the least ailment and trouble. I, *bhikṣu* Prajñādeva, have indited the *Encomium Upon the Great Supernatural Transformation of Buddha* and other writings on the wisdom of inference[81] of scriptures and treatises, which I dispatched *Bhikṣu* Dharmadīrgha to present to you for your

perusal. *Upāsaka* Jñānaprabha, the unlimited-learned and senior scholar of this place, also sends his regards to you, and *upāsaka* Sūryalabdha bows himself to you in homage too. Together we are sending you two rolls of white cotton cambric cloth to represent our remembrance of you. Slight are the gifts but long is the route! If you don't mind, please accept them. Whatever scriptures and treatises you need, please give us a list, and we shall make copies and send them to you. May Mokṣācārya take a notice of the above.

To such a degree the Master was admired by the worthy of another land far off.

In the second month of the spring of the fifth year (654), Dharmadīrgha left for India and asked the Master for a reply. The Master then wrote a letter and packed some gifts too. Before handing the letter to the messenger, it was copied and sent to the Emperor for perusal. The letter reads:

I, *bhikṣu* Xuanzang of the Great Tang Empire, respectfully presented this letter to the reverend Tripiṭaka-master Jñānaprabha of the kingdom of Magadha in Central India. More than ten years have quickly passed since my departure. Being separated by distance, we have not heard of each other for a long time. Indeed, I am often preoccupied by the ever-increasing feelings of admiration and longing for you. You have sent *Bhikṣu* Dharmadīrgha to bring me your regards, telling me you are in good health, and on hearing it, all at once my mind was rendered brightly broad as if I looked upon your visage with my own eyes. My pleasure, however, is beyond my words. The weather is becoming warmer in this season. How are you getting on after the last letter? Some years ago, from a returned messenger I knew that Right Dharma Store, our great master, had died to verify his impermanence. I felt grief-stricken as if I had been cut by a knife, too strong an agony to endure. Alas! A lifeboat has sunk in the sea of suffering! Celestial and human beings lost their eyes! How could this heart-rending pain have gotten up so quickly? In my opinion, Right Dharma Store must have planted the meritorious seeds in past lives and accomplished great exploits immortal in history, so he was not only able to employ his superb natural endowment to perfect himself, but also to display his extraordinary talents to inherit the virtue of Āryadeva[82] and forward the glory of Nāgārjuna[83]. Having lighted the torch of wisdom again and erected the banner of the Right Dharma to guide masses once more, he extinguished the fiery flames on the mountain of heretical views, pacified the tidal waves of the overturned sea, led the tired into the places full of treasures and peace, and showed the right way to the people who went astray. How brilliant and magnanimous he was! He was truly the pillar of the Dharma Hall. He not only was well-saturated with the Three Vehicles and the Great and Lesser teachings[84], but acquainted himself thoroughly with heretical books either on annihilation or on permanence. He could clarify extremely complicated doctrines and explain the abstruse and hidden meanings of the theories, so both Buddhists and non-Buddhists were flocking to study under him, esteeming him as an eminent leader of Indian Buddhism. Moreover, as an untiring instructor, he gave his guidance day and night, and from his inexhaustible knowledge, the disciples gained what they wanted to their hearts' content. In order to consult him for the Way, I once attended to him as a learner, then I was fortunate enough to receive his instruction face to face. Under such a great learning environment, I, clumsy as I am, made a considerable progress, just like a vein, which naturally climbs up by twining round a tree. When I bid farewell to him, I received some pieces of advice from him that are still ringing in my ears today. I hoped he would be in good health and live a long life so that he could set an example to the posterity about how to glorify the Dharma. It never occurred to me that he could have returned to the eternity so soon. At present, no matter how nostalgically I pine for those days that I spent with him, the past is gone forever. Respectfully I assume that when you were young you began to receive his refined instructions, and as one of his favorite disciples for such a long time, you must think it very unbearable to part with him. What else we could do? Nothing at all! Alas! nothing we could do about it! This is a phenomenal world, what could we do to it?! So, I hope you will restrain your grief. In the past, after Great Enlightened One[85] hid His light off, Mahākāśyapa[86] inherited and carried out the great enterprise of Him; and after Sāṇakavāsa[87] passed away, Upagupta[88] continuously expounded his excellent convictions. Now that you have succeeded to his post after our dharma leader returned to his absolute reality, I expect you to employ your lucid and impassioned words to propagate the Dharma incessantly as the Four Seas[89] run permanently. May your wisdom and blessedness last long as the five great mountains[90].

Among the scriptures and treatises brought back by me, I have already translated the *Yogācārabhūmi Śāstra* and other texts, be long and short, totally about more than thirty works. As to the translation of the *Abhidharmakośa Śāstra* and the *Abhidharmanyāyānusāra Śāstra,* they are not yet completed, but will be finished this year. At present, the Great Tang Emperor on the throne has enjoyed all felicity and robust health. With the compassion of Cakravartīrāja king, His Majesty has been propagating the edification of the Dharmarāja (King of the Dharma). After having composed the preface to the newly-translated scriptures and treatises with his divine ink brush, he ordered the officials in charge to transcribe them for circulation within and without the empire, so neighboring countries also could uphold and study them. We are living at the end of Image Period of Buddhism, but the Buddha's teachings are still existing gloriously, harmoniously, and prosperously, same as those passed down from the Jetavana Garden in Śrāvastī.

Hope that you are informed of the above information. In addition, formerly when I was crossing the Indus River I lost a pack of scriptures, which are listed at the end of the letter. At your convenience, please send me new copies of them when a messenger is available. Also, there are some small gifts for you, wish you to kindly accept them. For such a great distance, pardon this meager offering.

With homage from Xuanzang.

Also he wrote a reply to the venerable Prajñādeva as follows:

I, *bhikṣu* Xuanzang of the Great Tang Empire, am respectfully writing this letter to the reverend Tripiṭaka-master Prajñādeva of Mahābodhi Monastery. As it has been a long time from our departure, my admiration for you has become much stronger; yet I could not find any solace because no tidings have been exchanged. Not until the *Bhikṣu* Dharmadīrgha arrived here with your letter that wishes me well in health and life did I feel delighted at hearing from you. Besides, I have received two rolls of cotton cambric cloth and one folder of eulogistic verses, a token of your deep friendship, which, as a person meager in virtue, I don't think I deserve, so I am verily feeling embarrassed and uneasy. The weather becomes ever warmer in this season. After writing me this letter, how is your health recently?

With an intimate knowledge of different schools and a careful study of the scriptures of the Nine Sections[91], you have erected the banner of the Right Dharma to direct Buddhist converts and stricken the drum of triumph to subdue those haughty heretics. You keep your noble obstinacy in front of the nobility and distinctively stand out among brilliant scholars; therefore, to my mind, you must live an easy and cozy life. I am humble and worthless, and in addition, I am suffering a decline in my vigor and strength nowadays. With my growing admiration, I miss you ever more.

Formerly when I visited your country, I was fortunate enough to behold your brilliance, later, at an assembly in Kanyākubja City, we became intimate after the debate. At the time, we were debating in front of many a king and thousands of disciples in order to judge the values of some theories, with one side upholding Mahāyāna doctrines while the other advocating the incomplete teachings of the Hīnayāna school. During our debates, the words and tones must have been high or low, but in order to defend the truth, we never took the personal feelings into account. Although the tart remarks made our relationship frozen hard, as soon as the assembly was over, our annoyance was released immediately. Now I have heard from your messenger that you are still feeling regretful and sorry for that event; please don't be so mindful of it. Your Reverence has a rich knowledge and a good eloquence; you are highly-motivated and lofty-minded; even the Anavatapta Lake is by no means equal to your learning in depth and width, and the flawless Maṇi pearl is no match for your pure and noble character. Being a role model for the following generations to learn from, you must belong to the superior. I hope you will go on to propagate the Right Dharma, striving for setting a good example for the people. As to the perfectness of the theories and the sophistication of the expressions, the Mahāyāna teachings are second to none, so it is verily pitiful that you have not developed a deep faith in it. You can be likened to a man who discards a cart drawn by a white bullock but takes pleasure in obtaining a deer cart or a goat cart. You are like a man who is fond of quartz instead of precious crystal. You are virtuous and perspicacious, so how could you be enmeshed in such a delusive view? What's more, it is impossible for the physical body, easily broken as an utensil, to be permanent, so it seems to be better for you to generate the bodhi mind as earlier as possible and adopt the right view solemnly, otherwise on the dying bed you would sigh with remorse. Now the messenger is returning home, and I asked him to hand you my letter, enclosed herewith some small gifts to express my deep gratitude for your kindness and wishes, which, however, is quite inadequate to show my admiration for you. This I want you to know. Formerly, on my journey back to my country, I lost a pack of scriptures when crossing the Indus River. Now attached is a list of them I particularly made. I shall very appreciate it if you will kindly send me new copies. I could hardly dwell upon other matters in this short letter.

Presented respectfully by *bhikṣu* Xuanzang.

ANNOTATION

1 Heavenly Lord and Great Emperor was the title conferred to Emperor Gaozong of Tang 唐高宗 (628–683) in 676, twenty-seven years after his ascension to the Throne. Emperor Gaozong (r.649–683), whose personal name was Li Zhi李治, was the third emperor of the Tang Dynasty. After the first month of the second year of Linde 麟德(665), much of the governance was in the hands of his second wife Empress Wu Zetian 武则天 (r.684–704) who ascended the throne and changed the name of the dynasty to Zhou in 690.

2 The East Palace was the residence of the Crown Prince, Li Zhi, who ascended the Throne in 649.

3 Six Pāramitā or Six spiritual perfections: giving, precept-keeping, patience, effort, meditation, and wisdom.

4 Used like ten quarters or directions, in old days meant in general the world, here typically referring to Tang Empire.

5 The ancient rivers of Chang'an were rivers of Wei 渭, Jing 泾, Feng 沣, Lao 涝, Yu 潏, Hao 滈, Chan 浐, Ba 灞.

6 Mount Hua 华山 is a mountain located near the city of Huayin in Shaanxi Province, about 120 kilometres east of Xi'an. It is the western mountain of the Five Great Mountains of China, and the highest is the South Peak at 2,154.9 metres (7,070 ft).

7 Mount Song 嵩山 is a mountain in central China's Henan Province, along the southern bank of the Yellow River. It is known as the central mountain of known as the central mountain of the Five Great Mountains of China. Its summit is 1,500 meters (4,900 ft) above sea level.

8 Tang 汤 is the first king of the Shang Dynasty who overthrew (c. 1600 BC) the Xia Dynasty; and King Wu 武王 was the first king of the Zhou Dynasty who overthrew (c. 1046 BC) the Shang Dynasty.

9 The Pāli canon describes eight progressive states of Dhyāna. Four are called

meditations of form, and four are formless meditations. There are four stages of deep meditations of form: (1) First Dhyāna — the five hindrances have completely disappeared and intense unified bliss remains. Only the subtlest of mental movement remains, perceivable in its absence by those who have entered the second Dhyāna. The ability to form unwholesome intentions ceases. The remaining qualities are: directed thought, evaluation, rapture, pleasure, unification of mind, contact, feeling, perception, intention, consciousness, desire, decision, persistence, mindfulness, equanimity and attention. (2) Second Dhyāna — all mental movement utterly ceases. There is only bliss. The ability to form wholesome intentions ceases as well. The remaining qualities are: internal assurance, rapture, pleasure, unification of mind, contact, feeling, perception, intention, consciousness, desire, decision, persistence, mindfulness, equanimity, and attention. (3) Third Dhyāna — one-half of bliss (joy) disappears. The remaining qualities are: equanimity-pleasure, unification of mind, contact, feeling, perception, intention, consciousness, desire, decision, persistence, mindfulness, equanimity and attention. (4) Fourth Dhyāna — The other half of bliss (happiness) disappears, leading to a state with neither pleasure nor pain, which the Buddha said is actually a subtle form of happiness. The breath is said to cease temporarily in this state. The remaining qualities are: a feeling of equanimity, neither pleasure nor pain; an unconcern due to serenity of awareness; unification of mind, contact, feeling, perception, intention, consciousness, desire, decision, persistence, mindfulness, equanimity and attention.

10 Six defilements: six qualities that are the cause of all impurity, i.e., sight, sound, smell, taste, touch, and idea.

11 In original Chinese text, Kapilavastu 迦维 is used to symbolize Buddhism.

12 Sun, Moon and stars.

13 See note 1 of Fascicle II.

14 Nine branches of the Yellow River, generally refers to the rivers and streams.

15 Refers to tathatā, the ultimate nature of all things, also the samādhi of reality, in which the unreality of the phenomenal is realized.

16 Refers to the music *Daxian*大咸 in the times of Emperor Yao and *Dashao* 大韶in the times of Emperor Shun, later generally representing the ancient music of China.

17 Wang Xizhi 王羲之 (303–361) was a famous Chinese calligrapher. One of the most celebrated calligraphers in Chinese history. He is said be the exemplar of the high art of calligraphy, a master of every form but particularly of the running script (xingshu Chinese 行书). Born in Linqin County in Shandong Province, he lived in present-day Shaoxing, Zhejiang, most of his life. None of his original works remain today. His most famous work is the "*Preface to the Poems Composed at the Orchid Pavilion* (*Lanting Xu*《兰亭序》).

18 Empress Zhangsun 长孙皇后 (601–636), formally Empress Wendeshunsheng 文德顺圣皇后（literally "the civil, virtuous, serene, and holy empress") or, in short, Empress Wende 文德皇后, was the wife of Emperor Taizong and the mother of Emperor Gaozong. She was of Xianbei origin and well educated.

19 Formerly, the Buddha went up to Trāyastriṃśa Heaven to preach the Dharma for his mother.

20 Lu Ban (c. 507–444 BC) was a carpenter, engineer, and inventor in the Zhou Dynasty. He is revered as the Chinese god of builders and contractors.

21 A legendary figure in remote ages of Yao and Shun, who was an inventor of some agricultural tools, such as bow, plough, spade, and so forth.

22 Also called Mount Heng 衡山 or Mount Huo 霍山. It is a mountain in south-central China's Hunan Province known as the Southern Mountain 南岳 of the Five Great Mountains of China.

23 See note 10 of Fascicle II.

24 Refers to the *Hetu* "河图" "Yellow River Chart" and the *Luoshu* "洛书" "Inscription of the River Luo", two cosmological diagrams used in ancient China. The "Inscription of the River Luo" is first mentioned in the book

Guanzi《管子》, where it is said that a dragon turtle (longgui 龙龟) left the waters of the River Luo, so that an inscription was seen on its back, actually also a pattern of the shell that could be interpreted as the eight trigrams in a constellation different from that on the *Hetu*. The turtle appeared during lucky times when virtuous rulers reigned the empire and ceased to be seen when bad and selfish men governed the world.

25 According to the legend, the Emperor Xuanyuan (Yellow Emperor) asked his official historian Cangjie 仓颉 to invent Chinese characters with reference of birds' tracks.

26 Traditionally, Fuxi is regarded as the originator of the *I Ching*(also known as the *Yi Jing* or *Zhou Yi*), which is attributed to his reading of the *Hetu* and the *Luoshu*. According to this tradition, Fuxi had the arrangement of the trigrams of the *I Ching* revealed to him in the markings on the back of a mythical dragon horse (sometimes said to be a tortoise) that emerged from the Luo River. This arrangement precedes the compilation of the *I Ching* during the Zhou Dynasty. This discovery is said to have been the origin of calligraphy. Fuxi is also credited with the invention of the *Guqin* musical instrument, though credit for this is also given to Shennong神农 and Yellow Emperor.

27 Or Chakravartin (Wheel-turning King): a universal monarch, is an ancient Indian term used to refer to an ideal universal ruler who rules ethically and benevolently over the entire world.

28 Prajñā or wisdom is insight in the true nature of reality, namely impermanence, dissatisfaction or suffering, non-self and emptiness.

29 Also, eight kinds of liberation. Eight forms of emancipation obtained through the eight kinds of meditation. The ultimate aim is freedom from Earthly desires of the threefold world. They are:

(1) emancipation from thoughts of external things by meditating on their impurity;

(2) further advancement of the first emancipation by continuing meditation on impurity;

(3) emancipation obtained by meditating on the pure aspect of things in the outside world;

(4) emancipation from thoughts and bonds of material objects and entering meditation on the Realm of Boundless Empty Space;

(5) emancipation from thoughts of boundless empty space and entering meditation on the Realm of Boundless Consciousness;

(6) emancipation from thoughts of boundless consciousness and entering meditation on the Realm of Nothingness;

(7) emancipation from thoughts of nothingness and entering meditation on the Realm of Neither Thought Nor No Thought;

(8) emancipation from, or extinction of, all workings of the mind, which is the source of earthly desires.

30 Four Dhyānas: the four stages of meditation that correspond with the four dhyāna heavens, which are still in the realms of samsara.

31 Shanglin Palace was an imperial palace, built by Liu Che刘彻, Emperor Wu of Han (156–87BC), in 138 BC, on an old site of the Qin Dynasty. It is famous for its a large scale and grandiose landscape, being a typical example of the architectural palace during the Qin and Han dynasties. It was constructed as a pleasure park with artificial water features, with the Jianzhang Palace as the royal residence and many subsidiary structures. The park contained all manner of exotic flowers, tropical plants and trees and was given several statues including a whale and replica of the Milky Way. There was even a menagerie which included exotic birds, a rhinoceros, and an elephant.

32 Rock kalpa 盘石劫or拂石劫, also, rock-rubbing kalpa. One of several definitions of a kalpa used to illustrate its measureless length of time. According to *The Treatise on the Great Perfection of Wisdom*, a kalpa is

longer than the time required to wear away an immense cube of rock forty li (one li is about 540 meters) on each side if one were to brush it with a piece of cloth once every hundred years. In the *Miscellaneous Agama Sūtra*, the length of each side of the rock is given as one *yojana* (about 7 kilometers).

33 Ancient Indian name for China.

34 It is said that the Emperor Ming had a dream in which a golden image appeared in the west. So moved was he by this strange dream that he sent a group of envoys beyond the western borders of China to find out what they could about this image. This was in about 64 CE. the envoys returned three years later accompanied by two monks, Kāśyapa Mātaṅga and Dharmaratna. The monks brought with them a text called *The Sūtra of the Forty-Two Sections* and the emperor built them a monastery called the White Horse Monastery, after the horse that had carried the text and the monks' supplies.

35 Or Chakravada. The Iron Enclosing Mountains supposed to encircle Earth, forming the periphery of a world. Located at the center of the world, Mount Sumeru is surrounded by eight concentric mountain ranges, which are separated by eight concentric seas. The Chakravada are the eighth and outermost of these mountain ranges and are made of iron, while the other seven are made of gold.

36 Mount Sumeru.

37 See note 69 of Fascicle V.

38 The lion's roar is a metaphor for Buddha's authoritative preaching. Buddhist preaching is equal (in power over demons, heretics and misery) to the power of a lion's voice over animals.

39 Four Unlimited Mental States(Caturapramāṇāḥ): (1) boundless kindness (Maitrī); (2) boundless pity(Karuṇā); (3) boundless joy(Muditā); (4) limitless indifference to distinctions of friend and enemy, love and hate, and so forth (Upekṣā).

40 Shendu身毒, the Chinese name for ancient India subcontinent.

41 Tianzhu天竺, the Chinese name for ancient India subcontinent.

42 Refers to physical, verbal, and mental functions, i.e. thought, word, and deed.

43 Four kinds of grace: parents' grace, all living being's grace, king's or teacher's grace, and Triratna's grace or patron's grace.

44 One of the other names of cassock or Kāṣāya (jiasha袈裟) , the robes of fully ordained Buddhist monks and nuns.

45 Or the Great Compassion Temple.

46 The nine courtly music bands were popular during both the Tang and preceding Sui dynasties, performing the traditional Chinese music and the music of neighboring countries as well. In general, nine bands included: traditional Han music (qingyue清乐or hanyue汉乐); Libi music礼毕曲 (the ceremonial finale) which followed the folk lyrics of the Sourthern dynasty(420–589); Uzbekistan music such as Kangguo music康国乐 and Anguo music安国乐; Xinjiang music, such as Shule music疏勒乐, Kucha music(or Qiuci龟兹乐), and Xiliang music(or Wesrern Ling西凉乐) that was derived from Qiuci music; Indian music; Korean music.

47 Shun was renowned for his modesty and filial piety. Legend has it that Shun's birth mother died when Shun was very young. His father was blind and remarried soon after Shun's mother's death. Shun's stepmother then gave birth to Shun's half-brother Xiang象 and a half-sister. Shun's stepmother and half-brother treated Shun terribly, often forcing Shun to do all the hard work in the family and only gave him the worst food and clothing. Shun's father, being blind and elderly, was often ignorant of Shun's good deeds and always blamed Shun for everything. Yet, despite these conditions, Shun never complained and always treated his father, his stepmother, and his half-brother with kindness and respect. When he was barely an adult, his stepmother threw him out of the house. Shun was forced to live on his own. Later, Shun's stepmother and half-brother always conspired to kill Shun. Once, Xiang lit a barn on fire, and convinced Shun to climb onto the roof to put the fire out, but

Xiang took away the ladder, trapping Shun on the burning roof. Another time, Xiang and his mother conspired to get Shun drunk and then throw him into a dried-up well and then buried him with rocks and dirt. But fortunately, Shun survived many such attempts on his life. Yet, he never blamed his stepmother or his half-brother, and forgave them every time. Eventually, Shun's stepmother and half-brother repented their past wrongs. Shun wholeheartedly forgave them both, and even helped Xiang get an office.

48 The Ten Stages of the Perfect Truth. See note 6 of Preface.

49 Three Vehicles: the three paths to enlightenment: (1) the Śrāvaka-vehicle; (2) the Pratyekabuddha-vehicle; (3) the Bodhisattva-vehicle.

50 Located in Mount Qinghua south of Chang'an.

51 The second watch is about from 21:00 to 23:00. In ancient China, *xu*戌 was referred to as the first watch, *hai*亥 the second watch, *zi*子 the third and *chou* 丑 the fourth, and so forth.

In ancient China, there were 12 shi时 in a day, which were used to stamp the time. The 12 *shi* are: midnight, crowing, dawn, sunrise, breakfast, ante, noon, post, dinner, sunset, dusk, and quieting. Earthly branches are used to name the 12 *shi*: *zi*子 (23:00 to 01:00), *chou*丑 (01:00 to 03:00), *yin*寅(03:00 to 05:00), *mao*卯(05:00 to 07:00), *chen*辰(07:00 to 9:00), *si*巳(9:00 to 11:00), *wu*午(11:00 to 13:00), *wei*未(13:00 to 15:00), *shen*申(15:00 to 17:00), *you* 酉(17:00 to 19:00), *xu*戌(19:00 to 21:00), *hai*亥(21:00 to 23:00). The time length of a *shi* is two hours. The first *shi* covered the time around midnight from 00:00 to 02:00 until the Tang Dynasty and from 23:00 to 01:00 during the Song Dynasty.

52 The third watch is about 23:00 to 01:00.

53 The fifth watch is about 03:00 to 05:00.

54 *Jiazhu* technique is a popular art craft of making clay statues in the Tang Dynasty, and the procedure is as follows: make an unpainted clay idol; cover it with a piece of ramie cloth, which then is painted with lacquer; finally put

out the clay idol, thus the hollow image is made.

55 Present Hejian 河间and its neighborhood, in Hebei Province.

56 Present Puzhou蒲州and its neighborhood, in Shanxi Province.

57 Present Mianchi渑池and its neighborhood, in Henan Province.

58 Present Zhengding正定 and its neighborhood, in Hebei Province.

59 In the *mahā parinirvāa sūtra*, Cunda was a blacksmith who gave the last meal as an offering to Buddha. Falling violently ill, The Buddha instructed his attendant Ānanda to convince Cunda that the meal eaten at his place had nothing to do with his passing and that his meal would be a source of the greatest merit as it provided the last meal for a Buddha.

60 Shande 善德 refers to Subhūti. In Chapter "*The Reluctance of the Bodhisattvas*" of *The Holy Teaching of Vimalakīrti*, the Buddha asked the merchant's son, Subhūti, to go to Vimalakīrti to inquire about his illness. Subhūti replied, "Lord, I am indeed reluctant to go to that good man to inquire about his illness. Why? Lord, I remember one day in my father's house when, in order to celebrate a great sacrifice, I was bestowing gifts upon religious devotees, brahmins the poor, the wretched, the unfortunate, beggars, and all the needy. On the seventh and final day of this great sacrifice, the Vimalakīrti came there and said, 'Merchant's son, you should not celebrate a sacrifice in this way. You should celebrate a Dharma-sacrifice. What is the use of the sacrifice of material things?' Subhūti asked him, 'How does one give a Dharma-sacrifice?' Then Vimalakīrti answered this question in details.

61 Twelve divisions of the Mahāyāna canon: (1) sūtra; (2) geya; (3) gāthā; (4) nidāna; (5) itivṛttaka; (6) jātaka; (7) adbhuta-dharma, i.e. the abhidhama; (8) avadāna; (9) upadeśa; (10) udāna; (11) vaipulya; (12) vyākaraṇa.

62 See note 34 of Preface.

63 See note 68 of Fascicle IV.

64 The Four Propositions may refer to: the four terms of differentiation of all things into the existing (phenomenal), non-existing (noumenal), both, and

neither.

Or four sayings after the attainments of arhats: All rebirths are ended, the noble life established, my work accomplished and no further existence is mine.

Or the Four Dharma Seals, as follows: (1) processes are impermanent; (2) experiences boil down to suffering; (3) Dharmas have no selves; (4) Nirvāṇa is silence and stillness. Because suffering is the consequence of the impermanence of everything in the life of a sentient being, including itself, the second Dharma Seal can be omitted from the list to make the Three Dharma Seals.

Or The Four Bodhisattva Vows, or The Four Vast/Great Vows：

Sentient beings are countless; I vow to deliver them all.

Afflictions are endless; I vow to eradicate them all.

Dharma Doors are measureless; I vow to learn them all.

Buddha bodhi is unsurpassed; I vow to attain it.

65 Avidyā is commonly translated as "ignorance" or "delusion." Avidyā is held to be the root cause of one's coming to exist in this plane of affliction, continuing to crave and cling to it, and repeatedly returning without understanding. Avidyā is explained in different ways or on different levels within different Buddhist teachings or traditions. On the most fundamental level, it is a misunderstanding of the nature of reality; more specifically–a misunderstanding or mis-perception of the nature of self and of phenomena. On a more general level, Avidyā can be defined as not understanding the full meaning and implication of the Four Noble Truths.

66 Eight Erroneous Practices: the practices that are against the Eightfold Noble Path.

67 Kindness, pity, joy and self-sacrifice.

68 Dāna is generosity or giving, a form of alms. In Buddhist thought, it has the effect of purifying and transforming the mind of the giver.

69 The King Aśoka was this little boy in one of his previous lives.

70 The Bohai Sea or Bo Sea 渤海, is the innermost gulf of the Yellow Sea and Korea Bay on the coast of Northeastern and North China. It is used to represent the great sea in ancient China.

71 About 90 meters.

72 About 46.67 meters.

73 About 60 meters.

74 Śarīra is a generic term referring to "Buddhist relics", although in common usage it usually refers to pearl or crystal-like bead-shaped objects that are purportedly found among the cremated ashes of Buddhist spiritual masters.

75 Sadāpralāpa: Sadāprarudita, a Bodhisattva mentioned in the *Prajñā-Pāramitā Sūtras*.

76 Or the White Horse Temple, is located about seven miles away from Luoyang City. It is the first Buddhist temple in Chinese history ever since Buddhism came to China.

77 The Caotang Temple is located at the northern foot of the Guifeng Peak in the Caotangying Village of Huyi District, 50 kilometers southwest of the city of Xi'an. It is the ancestral temple of the Three-Treatise or the Middle Doctrine School, where Kumarajiva once translated Buddhist scriptures.

78 Or five studies (panca-vidyā,五明). These are: (1) language and composition; (2)science and technology; (3)medical arts; (4) logic, and (5) inner knowledge in a certain discipline .See note 110 of Fassicle II.

79 Extensive Mahāyāna.

80 China.

81 Anumanapramana in Sanskrit. Comparative or logical inferences, e.g. fire from smoke.

82 See note 134 of Fascicle II.

83 See note 120 of Fascicle II.

84 Mahāyāna and Hīnayāna.

85 One of the titles of the Buddha.

86 See note 24 of Preface.

87 Sāṇakavāsa was a disciple of Ānanda, and is considered the third Indian Patriarch in Zen Buddhism.

88 Upagupta (c. 3rd century BC) was a Buddhist monk. Upagupta's teacher was Sāṇakavāsa.

89 See note 10 of Fascicle V.

90 The Five Great Mountains or Wu Yue 五岳 are arranged according to the five cardinal directions of Chinese geomancy, which includes the center as a direction. The five mountains are among the best-known natural landmarks in Chinese history, and since the early periods in Chinese history, they have been the ritual sites of imperial worship and sacrifice by various emperors. They are: East Great Mountain (Dongyue 东岳)—Tai Shan泰山; West Great Mountain (Xiyue西岳)—Hua Shan华山; South Great Mountain (Nanyue南岳)—Heng Shan衡山; North Great Mountain (Beiyue 北岳)—Heng Shan恒山; Center Great Mountain (Zhongyue中岳)—Song Shan.

91 See note 45 of Fascicle II.

Fascicle VIII

Beginning with the Translation of the *Nyāyamukha Śāstra* in the Fifth Month of the Summer in the Sixth Year of Yonghui and Ending with the Memorial of Thanks Presented by Officials for the Stele Inscription Indited by the Emperor [Gaozong] for the Monastery in the Third Month of the Spring in the First Year of Xianqing[1]

On the fifth day of the fifth month of the summer in the sixth year (of Yonghui, 655), besides his regular translation work, the Master also tried to render the *Nyāyamukha Śāstra* into Chinese. Formerly he had already translated the *Hetuvidyā* at the Hongfu Monastery. Each of the two treatises consisted of one fascicle, explaining the logic procedures of argumentation and refutation, also showing the methods of inference and direct perception[2]. The monk translators at the monastic translation center vied with one another to compose commentaries on these theories. At the time, a monk translator named Qixuan showed these two translated treatises to Lü Cai (606–665)[3], Chief of the Palace Medical Service. After Lü read them, he arbitrarily made some alterations on the reasoning methods of the treatises and pointed out the strong and weak points of them by composing *A Diagrammatic Exposition and Refutation of the Annotations of Hetuvidyā*, to which the preface runs as follows:

It has been well known that the growing and declining follows the law of Heaven and Earth. How vast *Qian*[4](Heaven) is! How complete *Kun*[5] (Earth) is! Hexagrams demonstrate the principles of changeability and transformability; nevertheless, such theories still do not transcend the mundane world and their corresponding practices are still confined to the phenomenal under heaven. As a result, we could not make any deduction beyond the universe by simply observing the vital energy of the heavens and the earth, nor could we venture any further prediction about anything transcendental even if we comprehensively know *yin* and *yang*. I have never heard that *xiang*[6] (symbols) and *xi*[7] (explanations) in the *Book of Changes* opens the gate to the Eightfold Noble Path nor that before the formation of the material world, the teachings of two categories of wisdom[8] had already been propagated. That is why both the convictions of voidness and reality must of necessity be applied to achieve twofold insight, and only by wholeheartedly contemplating on both the ultimate truth and conventional truth could the non-dualism be obtained. The river of desires would be ferried across by taking the boat of Six Pāramitā and the mansion on fire be evaded by driving the three kinds of carts. From the above, we know how the almighty power of the Dharma Lord has been displayed. Surpassing all living beings, the Buddha is completely free from all delusions on His own; awakening to the truth alone by subjugating various devils, He has enlightened both Himself and others. When His karmic action began to operate, His power was as strong as that of rumbling thunder and flashing lightning. However, just as the fire dies out when the firewood is consumed, His life came to an end when the conditions for His worldly manifestation were exhausted. Although His incarnations show us His comings and goings, He indeed has no birth or living from perspective of the eternal reality; with the purpose of preaching the truth to save the sentient beings, He made transformations responsively to different requests. His blessings and illustrious virtues reach as far as the imagination can go! When a bud burgeons forth in its initial stage of growth, the vigor of its life could be seen, so we would be born in the pure land because of the auspiciousness and blessings we enjoy at this time and place.

In my humble opinion, since the Tang Imperial House held sway over the empire, the successive emperors, [like Cakravartin] brandishing Gold Wheels[9], have reigned over the four quarters. Taking supreme position, they pacified a myriad of places. Like Sunshine, their wisdom is shining high up to Six Desire Heavens[10], while their edification is casting down like the dharma clouds over Ten Stages of Bodhisattvahood. Their influences have been expanded far beyond the desert in the west, touching the Land of Happiness[11], and to the sea in the east, even cloaking the

Land of Joy[12]. Their prestigious edification has covered the boundless land, having the transportation and language normalized under the highest heaven of the form-realm[13]. Thereby, a hundred Koṭis of Sumeru Mountains are enshrined to receive sacrifices in turns, and three thousand Dharma Realms are bathed in the imperial prestige. Consequently, five parts of India are rendered into an ethnic turf of our capital's Gao Street[14] and eminent promotors of Buddhism[15] are invited to translate Sanskrit texts into Chinese at the Imperial Library.

Now here is a Tripiṭaka master, Reverend Xuanzang, who might be likened to Śākyamuni of our present time. He was perspicacious at a young age and when he grew up, he became a learned and versatile scholar. Pure in morals and conducts, he is an industrious practitioner of monastic commandments and precepts. A true pillar of the Triple Gem, he is a role model for the fourfold community[16]. For it has been too long a time since the teachings of Śākyamuni spread eastward into China, the Master was worried that the right and the wrong convictions could have been inseparably mixed like milk in water. He thought that if not to verify the True Reality at Kapilavastu or not to check the original scriptures at Magadha, the Buddhist canon would not be ensured in authenticity and the ultimate truth be established soundly. Fortunately, he came at a harmonious and peaceful time when there were no disturbances or clashes, which made it possible for him to cross the Great Desert and scale the Pamir Range. During his journey, neither taking the easier route where he could taste the betel leaf nor carrying with him any asarum grass[17] to speed the horse to render the long journey short, he went straight to his destination. At last, he not only arrived at the source of the Yellow River but ferried across the Ganges east of Kapilavastu; he not only collected palm leaf scriptures at Gṛdhrakūṭa Mountain but also perused the valuable words at various monasteries. Having visited more than one hundred countries, he has obtained over seven hundred scriptures and treatises that were transported by carriages and post-horses of garrison stations. Finally, he brought back these texts to the imperial capital, presented them to His Presence and explained the theories to His Majesty face to face.

This *Hetuvidyā* is one of the Sanskrit texts obtained by the Tripitaka Master. As for theories, it covers the Three Vehicles, and for practices, it embraces a hundred dharmas[18]. It studies the doctrines of both voidness and reality, and elaborates the theories of both Buddhist and non-Buddhist schools. Its wording is concise and precise; its theories are well-knit and comprehensive; its expressions are elaborate, and its meanings are magnificent. Some learners had studied it throughout their lives but still could not make out its profound meanings; others even failed to find out its origin after exploring it for many years. Since the book was regarded as a gate to various subtleties, it was the first to be translated into Chinese. There were several teachers, namely the venerable Shentai, the venerable Jingmai, and the venerable Mingjue, endowed with divine intelligence, who were ambitious and enterprising. They were well-versed in various scriptures, gaining a thorough comprehension of whatever they learned. Under the imperial decree, they were invited, later than others, to participate in the translation congregation, where they gained the opportunity to consult the Tripiṭaka Master face to face. Holding the scriptures in hand, they were instructed directly by the Master who, being proficient in preaching the Dharma, elucidated the abstruse and profound texts wonderfully. The venerable Tai and others made their notes, each in his own way, of what they had heard from the Master; and afterwards, they composed treaties on this scripture. On the completion of these expository writings, they planned to publicize them. Thus, before their circulation, few had a chance to read them.

The venerable Qixuan was an old friend of mine when I was young. In the past when I lived in seclusion in Mount Song, he often dropped in on me in his spare time. Later when I served as an official in the imperial capital, he came to visit me in a shabby alley. Since the first time I received instructions from him, more than thirty years have passed. It is beyond my words to describe how earnest and sincere is the friendship between us. Indeed, he is a man of pure and high moral integrity, rigorously observing the Buddhist disciplines. He had an intimate knowledge of One Vehicle and confined his actions to what is stipulated in the *Sarvāstivādavinaya.* Seeing that he was living a simple and austere life, I often tried to persuade him to live a life subject to the mundane conventions. However, monks and laity are following different codes in behaviors, so a host of the arguments always arose in our jests. Once he said to me composedly, "Dānapati, you have made a thorough research into the *Six Classics*[19], and was saturated with the various ideologies of the Hundred Schools[20]. You could deduce the interactive movements of *yin* and *yang,* also detect the slightest variations of musical tones made by pitchpipes[21]. Moreover, I have heard that you had never read the *Taixuan jing (Great Mystery Classic)*[22], but you were able to explain it to the Emperor the moment you were inquired, and that you had never played the lost chess game Xiang Xi[23], but after exploring the literature for ten days, you recreated it on your own. Thus we can see that even with limited mortal faculties, you try your utmost to do a thorough research on any knowledge you encountered. The teachings of the Buddha are so subtle, grand and unfathomable that they are totally different from any other knowledge, so even if you exert yourself to learn and study, I don't think you even know where you could properly put your mind. Why should you always interpret the Buddhist theories on your own to incur the jeers?" Later, when the translation of *Hetuvidyā* was firstly published, the venerable Qixuan thought its meaning was profound and abstruse, so he made a copy of it before others did so, and gave it to me, also with a letter attached, saying, "It is very difficult to make a comprehensive study on the wondrous profundity of this scripture. When scholars, even of high intelligence and broad knowledge, heard it, most of them would still fail to understand it. Now, if you could acquire a good understanding of it, you will be esteemed as a master of both Buddhist and non-Buddhist learning."

It is true that I had not heard of this scripture before, for it was introduced into China not a long time ago, so at the thought of it, I felt ashamed and was afraid that I would fail in this challenge. But in order to answer the letter, I had no way but tried my best to read the treatise under the pressure. Resorting to its uncontroversial and accurate expressions (mutually accepted by proponent and opponent), I tried to probe into its profound meanings, and employing the methods of comparison and inference, I worked hard to seek its subtle gist. By doing so persistently, I had myself more or less acquainted with the theories of this school. Later, I borrowed three commentaries composed by different dharma teachers, and made a further study on all of them. Eventually, I find that the literary styles of those dharma teachers are flowing coherently and that their explanations are forcefully convincing, but since the views they adhere to are diverse, so what they have concluded seems to be contradictory to each other. I wonder why their thoughts are veering into opposite directions if they have obtained the same theories from the Tripitaka Master. If the disputes arise from inside the Buddhism, it seems to be unavoidable that the insolence of offensive remark from the outside would obtain a chance to seep into. Although the Buddha preached the Dharma with but one voice, He actually granted the permission to different living beings to perceive it in his own language according to his own needs. Then why should a layman, clad in white, be eliminated from the rank of living beings?

Thus, off my official duty, I ventured to make this commentary in my spare time. In my commentary, taking reference to the opinions of the aforementioned three Dharma teachers, I have done much to advance their correct ideas to be more perfect, but refute and discard their dubious points. Divided into three fascicles, my treatise is thus called *Annotated Commentary on Theoretical Propositions and Refutation,* in which the black words are the original text of the scripture, and the red words preserve the old views of three Dharma teachers and below them, there are black words again that are my newly written commentaries with the aim to clear up those teachers' dubious points, totally more than forty items. I did not make notes on insignificant issues. Moreover, since some expositions are too obscure to be understood by readers, I drew a few theoretical diagrams to take as references. In addition, I drew a separate diagram as large as one square *zhang* to illustrate my recent annotations. Since nobody outside the Buddhist circle has a thorough comprehension of the *Hetuvidyā* , I have no one to consult; so if someone says that I was born with the knowledge, though I am not flattered at all, I know only when a man becomes so well-learned that he finds no need to set forth further inquiry could he be called a "Transmitter of the Lamp", and only when a man could infer other subjects from one subject could he then be honored as a virtuous and worthy man. I have never learned the *Śāstra* in life, it is really imprudent to pick up the writing brush to indite this commentary. Without the guidance of other teachers, is it possible to avoid illogical and unsystematic views in my comments and explanations?

I have heard that once when a Yakṣa on the Snow Mountain was preaching the Dharma on the life and death, the beasts exclaimed in joy for they heard the truth never known before. When the Yakṣa's words were plausible and convincing, even the heavenly beings showed great veneration to him. Probably my comments and explanations are of the similar case. If you Dharma teachers could put my low and mean status aside for a minute, give due consideration to my composition here, and if you could respect its value and absorb its correct ideas, rather than belabor whether those ideas are coming from a lay person or a monk, then the true Way of the Buddha would never drop into the dust. The propagation of Buddhism needs to be undertaken by numerous people, so could there be any dogmatism on it? However, just because of bearing the preconceived notion of the self and others, it is hard for people to tell right from wrong. Now although I am able to comprehend the theories at hand completely and correctly, it is still a need for me to consult the Tripitaka Master.

On the first day of the seventh month in the autumn, the monk translator Huili heard about this matter and showed his great concerns and wrote a letter to Left Premier Yu (Zhining), Duke of the State of Yan, pointing out the harm supposed to be done by Lü's *A Diagrammatic Exposition and Refutation of the Annotations of Hetuvidyā* :

I, Huili, have heard that the teachings established by various buddhas are recondite in language and profound in theories, lofty and broad as vault of heaven and expansive as the vast sea. When discussing the problems such as the inherent nature or the demonstrations of tathatā (the true reality), even those at the tenth stage of Bodhisattvahood could not but lose in bewilderment; when talking about causation of a tiny grass, even those who are free from reincarnation fail to figure out. So, what an ignorantly vain hope it is if a man, being entangled by the Eight Erroneous Practices[24] and submerged in the Four Inverted Views[25], should wish to make out syllogisms of Buddhism[26] by distinguishing and manifesting similarities and discrepancies between it and other theories!

As far as I know, the translation master of the Great Ci'en Monastery possesses the wisdom and aptitude accrued from his precepts and meditation in numerous previous lives, and with lofty moral sentiments, he is unrighteous and pure in deeds, which make it possible for him to visit the holy land alone in search for the subtle teachings of the Buddha. Synthesizing the Tripiṭaka canon in his bosom and grasping the Four Āgama in his palms, he not only inherited the sublime personality of the virtuous forebears, but also carried their bequeathed demeanor forward in his time. He serves as a boat in today's decadent world to ferry people across the sea of sufferings, and functions as a model for the monastic community to follow. The texts he has already translated are more than three hundred scrolls, among which there is a short treatise entitled *Hetuvidyā,* with the purport of how to make argumentation and refutation and of what procedure to follow to confute the erroneous views. Although it is not an essential doctrine of unfathomable Buddhist teachings, it is still beyond the knowledge of those impertinent people.

Recently I have heard that Lü Cai, Chief of the Palace Medical Service, a man with ordinary faculties, plagiarized the views of various teachers and composed a diagrammatic explanation on the meaning of hetuvidyā. In my opinion, just because he fails to gain an insight into it, inevitably he has developed some heretical views. In order to pursue the fame and praises, he has recklessly made far-fetched interpretations. What he has done not only libels the correct views of virtuous scholars but indulges himself into the self-conceit that makes his false ideas go unchecked. In front of nobles and influential officials he boasted himself, and amid the ordinary people he made a clamorous display of himself. He didn't save energy or mentality in doing so, even without a slight shame at this effrontery. It is verily inconceivable that a man like him with rich experiences of the fickleness of the world could constantly keep such a secular passion and never be bored with it. Taking the position of the Chief of the Imperial Medical Bureau, he developed confidence that he was adept in mundane affairs, which indeed further grew into a false belief that he could fully understand the ultimate truth. Is there any difference between him and a house mouse when the mouse deems it simple to reach the Langfeng Peak[27] of the Mount Kunlun just because it once strode over a caldron? Or is he different from a spider who sees it easy to weave a web over thorns, so erroneously believes that it can do the same on a large mulberry? Knowing nothing about his limits, he is of no difference from them at all! It is said that the loudest sound is the silence and the greatest eloquence sounds like stuttering. Vimalakīrti, though well-versed in reasoning, kept silent in the city of Vaiśāli; and Confucius, a man of high virtue, was prudent and modest in front of his fellow countrymen. [Huang] Shudu (75–122)[28] won the fame for being as generous as an ocean, and [Li] Yuanli (110–169)[29] was esteemed as a moral model of his time, but I have never heard that they sang praise for themselves and clamored for the commendation from government officials.

With this letter from Huili, the matter was settled.

On the first day of the tenth month in the winter, on hearing the settlement of this matter, Liu Xuan, an official scholar of Board of Rites, wrote *A letter of Homage in Verse* to pose a challenge again to the monks who were in the translation work, saying:

Homage to all buddhas,
Praying for the protection by Thy divine powers;
Sincerely I present this statement,
Not to disparage or blasphemy anyone.

Submerged in the deep darkness,
The ignorant longs for enlightenment;
Floating on the vast sea of desire endlessly,
Seldom we espy so much as a ferry boat.

Variant views vie with one another,
And we desire in earnest a unified one;
Free from attachment as well as existence,
Our argument walls against mistakes and distortion.

Arrogance arises in the discussion of the Eightfold Noble Truth,
And sophism plays itself in one hundred ways of negation;
Attachment and non-attachment are both on the same forum,
And defilement and purity are usually mingled inconspicuously.

Choose the gold while abandon the debris,
And polish the jade to add its light;
The Buddha shines wisdom light all over the world,

And on the exploration of the subtle truth we concentrate.

For the genuine heart opens the great Way,
In debate, no one dares to slander nor defame;
Straightforwardness in debates proves the lofty virtue,
While obsequiousness is deemed as the degeneration.

Wish Thee to be patient with my words,
For the improvement is supposed to be made;
Wish Thee to show a pity on my sincerity,
And grant me Thine admonitions in return.

The *Homage* reads:

In the past, Śākyamuni Buddha was born in the imperial palace, and later showed his demise between the twin Śāla trees. Henceforward, his subtle words have been propagated far and wide, revealing the ultimate truth to all beings; thereby the land has been protected by his compassion and living beings enlightened beneficially. Like a tree casting its shade, the teachings of the Buddha were widely circulated in the west; and as stūpas were set up all over the land, the bequeathed Dharma thus came over to the east. The introduction of Buddhism into China was inaugurated during the last years of the Han and Wei dynasties, and under the reign of Fu [Jian] (337–385) and Yao [Xing](366–416), the transmission of Buddhism came up to its brilliance. Afterwards, the eminent monks appeared every once in a while, the learned and virtuous scholars also emerged one after another. Since then, the sun of wisdom has been hanging high and the Dharma wheel rotating incessantly. The merits of the introduction of the Buddhism into China have been attributed to Kāśyapa-Mātṇga and Faxian, while the explanation and propagation of Buddhist teachings credited to Kumārajīva and Dao'an; besides, Shankai[30] travelled to Luofu, and not long time ago, during the Jin Dynasty (265–420), [Fo]tucheng cropped up in the states of Zhao and Wei. In fact, it is hard for me to give a detailed description of their blunt words and uncompromising staunch attitude in discussions, but in brief, but in brief, none of them failed to discuss the theories of voidness and existence as taught by Ekayāna, or the doctrine of the suffering and the cause of suffering [as explained by] the Four Nobel Truths[31]. However, when they illustrated the concept of existence by employing the linguistic exposition, they still could not break away from *you-wei*[32]. As we know, only by restraining from words could the Way be made manifest, according to the absolute quietude. It resembles a man who is holding to a theory of abstruseness to seek for the abstruseness; the latter cannot be revealed by the former, because only by resorting to something abstruse but meanwhile forgetting it might the abstruse be the abstruseness.

Although the meanings are usually implied by the varied expositions, the noumenon is truly something beyond language; after all, to direct living beings to nirvāṇa needs to resort to verbal explanations, just as to catch fish needs a net and rabbits a snare[33]. Therefore, controversies arouse one after another once the language is employed, just as in a war both sides brandish weapons at each other. The loser holds his breath in cautiousness and fears whereas the victor claims his triumph loudly. If we are to subjugate devils and conquer the heretical views, we should be dauntless and well-eloquent with the power of refutation, otherwise the heretical would display themselves conspicuously and offensively, darting unbridled insolence at us. We should devote ourselves to the Way and practice it wholeheartedly. Only by setting up a dharma banner and striking a dharma drum would the tough foes be defeated, and only by turning a dharma wheel would evil powers be subdued. On the contrary, if we lack the fighting-will in front of the challenge, or employ dodgy arguments in discussion, we will have no way to promote the Triple Gem.

Lü Cai, Chief of the Palace Medical Service, has already entered the dharma gate of emptiness and existence, also stridden on the path of right view. In theory and practice, he matches for the virtuous forerunners. His insight is no less penetrating than that of the former sages, his diction is convincing, his theory is distinctly clear, he undertakes noble deeds, and he is a man of high virtue. He has already bathed in the current of Eight Kinds of Emancipation[34] and awaken to the Seven Links of Enlightenment[35]. Just as Vimalakīrti visited the Āmravana Garden, what Mr. Lü does is also to promote the perfect teachings; like Sadāpralāpa, who left home to pursue the truth after Dharmodgata[36], Mr. Lü is bound to seek the Way when he heard of it. With the purpose of spreading the teachings of Buddha, Mr. Lü composed this commentary to propose and refute the *Hetuvidyā*. If what he has discussed in the treatise is right, surely his correct views should be recognized; if there is something wrong in his exposition, certainly his flaws should be pointed out. Now I see monk scholars are gathering in the capital, all of whom are well-versed in Buddhist scriptures and treatises. Having heard that Mr. Lü was to seek the advice from the monks, both the court and the commonalty waited earnestly for their response. We are expecting that an inexhaustible transmission of the Dharma would clear away the sources of restlessness and worries, dissolve the accumulation of doubts and anger, ideally obliterating them once and for all.

Li Chunfeng (602–670)[37], Court Astronomer, upon hearing about this matter, wrote me the following words:

"I, bearing the Right Path in heart, have practiced the self-cultivation. I believe that the phenomenal entity is the mysterious embodiment of the Great Enlightened One and *wuwei* is the dharma-body of the Cultivator of Men[38]. Also, I believe that as the sun is dazzling high to aid the operation of the supreme Mystery, so the worthy monks elucidate the dharma to promote the subtle doctrines of the Dao of the Heavenly Master[39]. This is what I believe in and where I set my mind on. I am, however, very cautious not to pass off a yellow leaf as a piece of gold nor a pheasanta as a phoenix; I dare not to act as Nanguo[40] to pretend to know what I don't know, nor to confuse the right and the wrong, otherwise it is like to mix the waters of Zi and Mian Rivers together, regardless of their different tastes. So, if anything controversial arises, is it what I want to see? Is it what I want to see?"

Barely two thousand years have passed since the Buddha passed away at the Cane Grove. Actually, the Right Dharma has been obsolescent and the Dharma degeneration age set on foot; as a result, the unfathomable truth has been hidden rather than manifested, and the Way of Awakening is going to sink into oblivion. Master Xuanzang practiced dhūtanga[41] and traveled over a long distance to visit Kapilavastu. With his own eyes he beheld the Bodhi tree and the Hiraṇyavati River[42], he stepped on the soil of the seven spots where the *Avataṃsaka Sūtra* was preached in eight assemblies, he entered the city of Vaiśāli and climbed Vulture Peak, and he verified the legends of the Śāla Grove as well as of the precious stairway. As for other places he visited, such as Rājagṛha, Dantaloka Mountain, Ganges, there is no need for me to go into details here. Along the route, eminent monks in the Western Regions jumped at the chance to make discussions on the Prajñā with him, meanwhile he consulted the learned Indian teachers to settle questions of the Eastern land. Consequently, he not only held to the Vinaya Piṭaka firmly and persistently, but also grasped the gist of the

Abhidharma; he had the full comprehension of Sūtras through śabda-vidyā[43] and obtained the supreme wisdom by tackling the knotty questions. He cherished in his bosom all dharmas, be they small or great, and understood through his perspicacity all theories, be they deep or shallow. Thus, Tripiṭaka was an honorable name denominated in Cīna, and the title Maha was universally addressed in Kapilavastu. His deeds deserved those titles, except which nothing might be sufficient to give him praises!

Mr. Lü is an erudite scholar, conversant in various convictions, and clear about the importance of words and deeds. As to the Buddhist teachings, he is endowed with an inborn knowledge; and no need for learning and practice, he has congenitally acquired incomparable eloquence. Because Buddhism logic is abstruse and hidden, various interpretations of it have arisen one after another but none has reached a complete picture, which is like that the blind men conceive different images of an elephant for touching it at different parts, or that the empty bowls hold various food with variegated tastes. Now that Mr. Lü has already showed a strong attachment to his curiosities, the Master is supposed to give him instructions, which would also fulfill the expectation of both laypeople and clerics. The autumn mist has fallen while the people are heeding to the bell's ringing; when clouds are spreading all over the sky, thunders are expected to roar around. Just as a donkey is unable to bear the trample of a dragon nor an elephant, so the abstruse and subtle teachings of monks are expected to be beyond the understanding of the laypeople. But in the far distant past, when Mañjuśri, Buddha of the Superior Dragon Race, argued with Vimalakīrti, the latter, indeed, resolved the doubts of the former, from which we know that the theoretical accomplishments achieved by a Bhikṣus could possibly be acquired by an Upāsaka. Here I have ventured to express my aspiration, expecting it not to give you any trouble, that the Tripiṭaka Master would give us instructions if there be any doubts and ambiguities, so that we could share the guidance received from you with the fourfold community. Only when hindrances are eliminated forever will the Right Path be paved for living beings. It is the right way to make the Triple Gem prosper, is not it? Apart from what I have mentioned above, I am ill-informed of other issues.

Stated with respect from your disciple Liu Xuan.

On the fourth day of the tenth month, the monk translator Mingjun wrote a verse in response to the letter of the official scholar Liu Xuan, pointing out the merits as well as demerits of his letter:

Hurray for the Great Sage,
His perfect enlightenment is fully illustrious;
Like echoes always following sounds,
None of the slightest could escape the perception of Him.

If it were not for the permanent happiness,
Who would like to take refuge in Him?

A worthy teacher deserves the worship,
For he gives guidance to us ignorant beings.

Like numerous rivers billowing into the sea,
Heretical views are to be swallowed by the one-truth in the end;
With some convictions being accepted while others rejected,
The right truth neither increases nor decreases.

Heretics are galloping on the Eight Evil Ways[44],
Vying for vain name by conjuring the verse of four lines;
By covering up the mistakes, confusing the right with the wrong,
They ignore quintessence but dwell on triviality.

Ice melts under the warmth of sunshine,
Lustrous pearls are spotted in the clean water;
The supreme virtue is to be manifested,
And the great Way will advance with no hindrance.

Although praises and disparagement have been hurled alternatively,
No harm nor good could be done to the bequeathed glory;
Lofty is the venerable sage who is,
Compassionate toward all living beings.

We are expecting the judgment from the worthy,
So as to discern the right and the wrong;

In order to release my restraint feelings,

I am writing this letter to express my blunt views.

The responsive letter says:

A moment ago, on the Sacrificial Marking Post I read the *Message of Homage.* Having read it, I was dazzled by its high-sounding words! Scanning it thoroughly, I also sighed at its elegance. Truly it is beautiful, isn't? But, alas, I feel sorry for it! The rolling waves at the sea of desires surge high in sky and the mountain of heterodox views obscures the sun. Attaching to an inherently-existent self, how could people incessantly fall into heterodox views? For haughtiness invites obstinacy, which makes them sink into the sea of desires endlessly.

Some holding sixty-two views[45] run riot to lodge themselves in the erroneous ideas, and other heretics of ninety-five types worship their gods on all fours, not knowing how to come back to the truth. Because Tathāgata took the great compassion as his original vow, even without the formerly-established causal conditions, He still responds to various calls of the sentient beings. Inwardly, He possesses the Four Kinds of Wisdom[46]; outwardly, He displays the Six Supernatural Powers[47]. By employing the Ten Powers[48] to subdue devils and by manipulating the Seven Rhetorical Powers[49] to put down heresies, He dries up the Sea of Desires to bring all the sentient beings to the bank of the Threefold emptiness[50] and topples down the mountain of heterodox views to lead the people to walk on the Eightfold Right Path. In order to reveal the causes and show the effects, to return to the beginning and find the root, He has employed both the wisdom and compassion adroitly and wonderfully. How great He is! His exploits are truly beyond expressions! In the past, when the Buddha achieved the enlightenment under the Bodhi tree, a hundred Koṭis of sentient beings were influenced beneficially, bathing themselves in His edification; after He attained His Nirvāṇa in the grove of Śāla trees, His bequeathed teachings have been promoted all over the Three Thousand Worlds. The Sun of Buddha inclined to the West while the light from it was shining over the East, which was shown in a night when the Duke Zhuang of Lu (died in 682 BC) witnessed a gleam of auspicious light[51], and also in a dream where the Han emperor was informed of the coming of the Buddha's teachings. Then, Kāśyapa-Mātṅga and Dharmāraṇya held up the torch of wisdom to light the road ahead, on whose heels Buddhasiṃha and Kumārajīva transmitted the Dharma lamp. They translated scriptures, preached the Dharma, revitalized the degenerate era by performing supernatural powers, put down the heresy with brilliant theories, and resided in Dhyāna while solemnly practiced wholesome deeds in the mundane world. In succession, they combed out the messy web of convictions and retied the broken knot of inheritance. They were highly esteemed by the Han Chinese and various ethnicities for their noble character and integrity; in their undertakings of edification, even deities and spirits spared no effort to assist them. In this way, as the generations passed, the enterprises of the Buddha have been carried on in prosperity. However, what I could mention here is only a brief account of their merits and virtues, which indeed should be related in much more details.

The Tripitaka Master is extraordinarily excellent for his intellectual endowments and elegant demeanor. With a rich knowledge in scriptures and treatises, he is submerged in the one flavor of the Buddha's teachings while receiving the Five Vehicles[52] without omission. He was depressed that the former sages had departed from us ever farther and worried about that the teachings available in China are incomplete; therefore, he bore an aspiration to retrieve the supreme and entire teachings of the Buddha, thus devoted himself single-mindedly to perusing the Way. Once he decided to trace the genuine teachings in India, he planned his journey independently, disregarding that he would set off with the sole company of his own shadow. Adjusting his clothes, taking his religious staff, going out of the Yumen Pass, he took on the long journey straight to the Hiraṇyavati River[53]. In the monasteries of India, he not only cleared up his doubts, but deplored the abstruseness and gained an insight into the subtleness. Later, bringing the truth back to his holy motherland, he demolished absurd convictions and promoted the Buddha's edification. He completed the incomplete texts of his time, spreading the perfect Vaipulya theories of Mahāyāna much wider than his forebears had done. The supreme theories he has elucidated wonderfully get to the innermost arcane of no-discriminatory notions; the genuine nature [of mind and all things] is the true emptiness, overstepping the boundary of the mundane world. If one has a desire for obtaining something, he would miss the genuineness; if one adheres to emptiness, he would also spoil the reality. The depth of truth could only be achieved by extricating the two extremes[54] and forgetting the Middle Way[55], so even if one expels desire repeatedly, it is still hard for him to reach its profundity, also how could one reach the ultimate truth even if he empties the emptiness? How important it is! How wonderful! What an ultimate truth! How inclusive! So, let us engrave it in the heart and abide by it as the Dharma. In mind, it is the Dharma; in words, it is the teachings. In terms of the Dharma, it is divided into the individuality and generality; in terms of the teachings, there are negative or hidden expositions as well as positive or open ones. How can an imprudent person with superficial knowledge fancy to have a thorough knowledge of these essential doctrines and superior theories only after having had a glimpse of them? Wholeheartedly, the Master has given a full play to his intelligence, thoroughly expounding the root theories and rectifying the branches. Having clarified the doctrines of mysterious texts, he has triggered off the understanding of the abstruse theories. The sound of a drum is concealed, but gives forth loudly or faintly according to the force of striking; the sea drains water from everywhere, be from a thin stream or a broad river. There have come many great virtuous scholars and eminent monks from the foreign lands, who intended to inquire about the Way from the Master. In order to solve doubts and questions accumulated through a long time, every one of them was eager to be instructed by him face to face. Although they finally drank to their fill from the river of knowledge, it was still hard for them to measure the depth of the learning of the Master, which could be likened to a man who is alarmed by a very loud sound, but fails to know how far the distance the sound comes over. As regards to Hetuvidyā, it is only an insignificant doctrine of logic, because the direct perception and inference is simple and shallow, merely teaching the beginners the methods and rules of making argumentations. In fact, other theories including the crucial and pivotal doctrines of the Buddha's teachings, the various functions and accomplishments of subtle noumenon, etc., are all related in other unfathomable texts rather than here in *Hetuvidyā*.

Lü Cai, Chief of the Palace Medical Service, is truly bold and forthright. Being versatile since his early days, he has been magnanimous and erudite. He is said to be conspicuously knowledgeable because he has studied the ancient classics and perused the books on unusual teachings. Able to infer others from one fact, he is conversant with various occult arts; he is well-known for his convincing eloquence in debates, so being illustrious among the literati of Hanlin Academy[56]. Exuding a pride, he is always taking the lead to articulate. Based on the five processes[57] and six *yaos*[58], he often ventured to compose his writings and display his clever talks. Once, merely by giving a glimpse of the *Taixuan jing* (*Great Mystery Classic*), he gave a prompt answer to the inquiries raised to him (by the Emperor) about the book, and another time, he revived the lost game of chess at his first attempt. It seems that Maoxian[59] of the Jin Dynasty and Manqian[60] of the Han Dynasty are far from being equal with him. Curiously, after he has extensively acquainted himself with knowledge of various fields, he still has got ample time to show his admiration to the Mahāyāna Buddhism, bearing a constant sincerity. One day, just because of a frivolous debate with his friend, he suddenly developed an aspiration for Hetuvidyā. With no instructions of other teachers, only by making a comparison of various commentaries, he has found so-called faults and flaws to denounce the Hetuvidyā, showing his wanton interpretation recklessly. He invoked clamorous discussions at the imperial court and was impertinently opinionated in his writing. When we examine his will, there is nothing to blame; but when we assess his knowledge, he is not supposed to know well enough.

His treatise was written in one fascicle of five pieces of paper, in which he makes an analysis of the three commentaries [of monks] after having read them through. He points out forty errors from those commentaries but does not raise a single right point of his own. He raises no single right point of his own but he says he is right, while there are no flaws in the commentaries but he says there are. What he claims to be wrong is in fact not wrong and what he states to be right is not right at all. What he states to be right is indeed not right so all he considers to be right is something wrong; and what he claims to be wrong is in fact not wrong, so all he believes to be wrong are always right. Since what he condemns to be wrong is always right, so when it is right, not because he says it is right. Since what he approves to be right is always wrong, so it is wrong not because he says it is wrong. Because of such erroneous views, he incurs censure upon himself. In addition, cause (hetu)[61] has two aspects: one is to produce, the other is to illuminate. He confuses them as the same which indeed are different. Both the illuminator and the illuminated are given with one name, so he fails to know that they are different from each other. Again, of the two component parts (the subject and the predicate) of a proposition (pakṣa), he retains the subject while giving up the predicate as the proposition. As for the substantial meaning of an example (dṛṣṭānta) and the object on which the example depends, he rejects the substantial meaning, while keeping the object on which the example depends as the example. Because of the misconceptions described above, there arise many other groundless views. And for being confused by "*jicheng*"[62] of the proposition, he provokes seven confutations. Merely by a diligent self-study on the *Nyāyamukha Śāstra* and the *Hetuvidyā* without consulting other teachers, he interprets the text literally and misreads some words. Besides, he mistakes the *Sāṃkhya Śāstra* for the *Śabda Śāstra* and the *City of Birth* for the *City of Death*. He makes errors not only in the formula of separation and combination of the proposition, but also in the sequence of the antecedent and the consequent in a syllogism. What's more, he uses the vulgar colloquial slang or erroneous rhymes to transliterate the Sanskrit terms. He cites seven noun cases which simply resemble one case in Sanskrit language—the vocative, the eighth case—while he disregards the other seven different cases of the Sanskrit language. No one knows whence these miscellaneous errors and ridiculous mistakes do come from.

In addition, the Vaiśeṣika School holds that atoms are permanent and infinite in number but infinitesimal in body. When they amalgamate, offspring atoms are produced, which are reduced to half of the number of permanent infinitesimal atoms but twice as large as them. In the end, only one atom remains, whose body crams the whole universe. Mr. Lü quotes the lines from the *Appended Judgments of the Book of Changes*: 'In the beginning there is the Great Ultimate (*taiji*). It engenders two Primal Forces, *yin* and *yang*, which in their turn give rise to the Four Forms. The Four Forms give rise to the Eight Trigrams from which all things are created.' And then he states that the latter, the Great Ultimate, is the same as the former, the permanent infinitesimal atom in sense, although they are different in expression. As we know, however, the Great Ultimate is formless, but engenders things in various forms, and the origin of all things is one vital force which turns into myriad things. How could he make an analogy between the production of one from many with the production of many from one? By making such an analogy, he might want to show that he has got an extensive knowledge, but I wonder what is the theoretical base for his absurd understanding. Suppose it is a good example cited to exemplify the conception of production in Buddhism, but it cannot be avoided that such an analogy would degrade the Buddhist teachings into a heterodox view. How should a person mix the right with the wrong for seeking the compliments from his contemporaries? Unless he bears a personal grudge against others. Why should one go so far like this? Errors, flaws, and chaos are scattered all over his treatise, which I don't mean to dwell excessively upon. He impertinently indulges himself so much that he has fallen into such an awkwardness. If the root of a tree is not put straight, naturally, its branches and leaves are inclined to one side. Adhering to something erroneous in order to invent doubts, and thereby bringing forth arguments based on those doubts, is it not a vain attempt to seek a straight shadow from something crooked? What I have cited above are only a few examples to make readers have a general idea, if one expects to know more about his serious errors and other blunders, rejoinders would be given separately. As a man of intelligence and sensibility, how should Mr. Lü have behaved so imprudently? In the explanations of the ultimate truth and of the conventional knowledge, the difference between difficulty and ease is as striking as that between clouds in the sky and mud on the earth. The disparity between these notions is as large as the space separating the state of Chu and State of Yue apart. Buddhist teachings are grandly expansive and the Right Dharma is esoterically profound, so a superficial understanding and elucidation of them falls totally in vain. It is no use for a man throwing a handful snow into the flames of a great furnace. It is also impossible for a small boat made of lumbers glued together to ferry across the vast sea.

Mr. Li, Court Astronomer, has a meticulous mind and cherishes high aspirations. As an expert in Nine Principles of Mathematics[63], he has comprehensively grasped the divination method by using six lines of a hexagram; having made an extensive research on ancient texts, he could make prophecies by observing the colors of clouds; so he is contemptuous of Wei Hong[64]' s lack of generosity and disdainful towards Bi Zao[65]'s unskillfulness in prophecy. His spirit is unobstructed, where his reputation does lie. Now that you cite his view in your letter, I make a response to it here. He viewed the phenomenal entity is the mysterious embodiment of the Great Enlightened One and *wuwei* is the dharma-body of the Cultivator of Men. Only through infusion (paribhā-vanā) can one achieve the awakening at different levels but on spontaneity would one never attain Buddhahood. Similar words might bear the clashing connotations and synonymous expressions might depart from one another due to different imports. I hope he could take reconsideration of the wondrous Dao of Heavenly Masters School of Daoism. Formerly, Heavenly Master Kou [Qianzhi][66] was highly recommended to the imperial court by Mr. Cui [Hao][67], and together they caused the disaster to Buddhism, so what else new can we say now? Buddhism and Daoism are not so clearly separated as the waters of Zi and Mian rivers, but to confuse them is truly to mistake the brass for the gold.

I think you (the official scholar Liu Xuan) are a man of profound and extensive thoughts, getting a thorough knowledge of ancient classics. Preserving the propriety and righteousness in mind, you handle the worldly affairs expediently. Solemnly and magnanimously, your immaculate integrity soars high up to the clouds, and your gentility pacifies the tumultuous world. As a man of letter, you have won your reputation in the literary field; and as a scholar, you have held the important official position among Confucian literati. You have collected the nine categories of the Great Law of Governance[68] and conducted careful research on the convictions of the two Dai's[69]. As to three hundred regular rules mentioned in the *Rites of the Zhou* and three thousand minor codes of conduct in the *Etiquette and Rites*[70], there is nothing you haven't been familiar with; therefore, the theoretical principles are always at your fingertips and the practical matters are held in your palm of one hand. The way by which you arrange and display the sacrificial vessels and dais has been regarded as a standard to follow by the people, and you are always consulted with the amendments and ratification of public measures when necessary. Therefore, satirical poems like "Xiangshu"[71] have never been heard again whereas the eulogistic poems like "Yuli"[72] are now prevailing everywhere at the court. Your name and your actuality are perfect in agreement. Sincerity and respectfulness are your inborn endowments. You have a long-cherished aspiration to propagate and protect the Buddhism, so when witnessing this clamorous debate, you partook the shame and compunction by expressing your opinions in the letter in order to clear up the vague views. If you were not well-versed in the knowledge of Buddhism and non-Buddhism, nor familiar with the neighboring schools of ideologies, how could you eliminate the evil, exalt the virtuous, benefit the mundane world and preserve the truth? In the past, there were three thousand disciples of the venerable Kumārajīva, all submitting themselves to the Way; in the present congregation, the monks of the same high virtues are as many as the throng on the market. I, a humble monk, with the mediocre disposition, am taking the back seat in the translation congregation. I am lucky to hear the truth in the morning, but when I reflect upon myself in the evening, I often feel very ashamed for not being diligent enough. In my opinion, all the three virtuous monks who wrote commentaries have a thorough knowledge of Five Vehicles, whose high virtues are difficult for others to speculate on and whose remarkable literary attainment is also hard to reach. When the divine bird Shangyang[73] is dancing on one foot, the rain must fall; when a quick thunder is to rumble, there must be no time to cover the ears. There is a consensus, as an ancient saying goes 'If there is a tree branch for a bird to alight on, why the bird should take the trouble to look for Denglin forest[74]? When a pool is deep enough for a fish, there is no need for the fish to resort to a vast sea.' So, despite my stupidity and insignificance, I was expected to make the reply. I refused, but didn't get permission. Then I wrote this letter to roughly present my ideas. Although my words are not worth serious consideration, my views might be adoptable. Reflecting on my mediocrity and imprudence, I felt more and more ashamed and fearful. This writing is a response to the article mentioned above, beside which, nothing more I want to say.

Stated by Shi Mingjun.

On the seventh day of the tenth month, Liu Xuan received the letter and incited Lü Cai, Chief of the Palace Medical Service, to report the matter to the Emperor. Then an imperial edict was issued sending a group of officials and scholars to the Ci'en Monastery to invite the Tripitaka Master to hold a decisive debate with Mr. Lü. During the debate, Lü was unable to advance any further convincing arguments to justify himself, so he apologized and withdrew.

On the first day of the first month in the spring of the first year of Xianqing (656), Crown Prince [Li] Zhong (643–664)[75] dared not to hold his position much longer for he was not a son of the Empress, so following the example of Taibo[76], he presented petitions once and again to the Emperor asking for the permission to his withdrawal. The Great Emperor at last consented and appointed him the Prince of Liang, granting him ten thousand rolls of silk fabrics and an imposing mansion of the first grade. In the same month, [Li] Hong (562–675)[77], Prince of Dai, was conferred as Heir Apparent.

On the twenty-third day, a monastic feast for five thousand monks was set up at the Great Ci'en Monastery for the sake of the new Crown Prince. Each monk was offered three pieces of silk fabrics as a gift. Besides, the Emperor dispatched some courtiers to offer incenses at the monastery. At the time, Xue Yuanchao (622/624–685), Vice-Director of the Chancellery, and Li Yifu (614–666), Vice-Director of Secretariat, paid a visit to the Master. They asked the Master, "The translation of Sūtras has always been a magnificent enterprise to Buddhism. We wonder what else we could do to carry it out more effectively. Also, we don't know what the translation procedure was in ancient times."

The Master replied, "Since the Dharma Piṭaka is extremely recondite, it is quite difficult to circulate and elucidate it. On the one hand, it is the responsibility of Śākya monks to uphold and expound it; on the other hand, its protection and establishment relies on the efforts of kings and emperors. Only on a sea could a ship travel a thousand *li*, and by winding up a pine tree, vines could soar a ten thousand inches high, from which we can see if the Dharma

Piṭaka will confer its benefits far and wide, favorable conditions are indispensable. It is unnecessary for us to trace far back to the Han and Wei dynasties to dwell upon the ancient situations. Let me now give you an introduction to the work done by those emperors and ministers, except monks, during the reigning periods of the Court of Fu (351–394) and Court of Yao (384–417), and examine how they assisted in translation and propagation of scriptures and treatises. At the time of Fu Jian (r.357–384), when Dharmanandi (dates unknown) translated, Vice-Director of Chancellery Zhao Zheng (fl.375–384) worked as his amanuensis. At the time of Yao Xing (r. 394–416), the king himself and Marquis of Ancheng Yao Song (fl.394–416) served as amanuenses of Kumārajīva. During the Later Wei Dynasty (386–534), when Bodhiruci translated, Premier Cui Guang (450–523) not only assisted as his amanuensis but also wrote a preface to the translated texts. The same was true of other dynasties, such as the Qi (497–502), Liang (502–557), Zhou (557–581), and Sui (581–618). At the beginning of the Zhenguan period (627–649), when Prabhākaramitra (564–633) was translating, some lords were ordered to supervise and scrutinize the translation work, including left Premier Fang Xuanling; Li Xiaogong (591–640), Prince of the Prefecture of Zhao; Du Zhenglun (?–658), Chief Chamberlain to the Crown Prince; Xiao Jing (dates unknown), Chamberlain for Palace Revenue, and others. At present, however, we haven't been privileged with such arrangements. By the way, His Majesty has had the Ci'en Monastery constructed for the commemoration of Holy Empress of Cultural Virtue[78]. It is so spectacularly imposing and beautiful that no parallel could be found in ancient and modern times. I think it should be the most effective way to glorify Holy Empress of Cultural Virtue by setting up a memorial stele to spread her virtuous name to the subsequent generations, but there has not been one, so if you gentlemen could send my words to the Emperor, this idea would be realized."

The two officials promised to do so and then left. In the following morning, when they went to the court, they reported to the Heavenly Emperor the Master's wishes, which were all granted.

On the twenty-seventh day, Cui Dunli (dates unknown), a minister without portfolio, Secretariat Director and concurrently Chief Chamberlain to the Crown Prince with the rank of Imperial Inspector and Supervisor of the Compilation of National History with the honorary titles of Pillar of the Nation and State-founding Duke of Gu'an County, announced an imperial decree which runs as follows:

> Since the scriptures and treatises translated by the monk Xuanzang of the Great Ci'en Monastery are the latest versions, whose language and meaning need to be assured of consummation and accuracy. It is befitting to appoint Yu Zhining (589–665), Grand Tutor to the Crown Prince, Cabinet Minister, Left Puye[79], Duke of the State of Yan; Lai Ji (610–662), Secretariat Director, concurrently Minister of the Board of Official Personnel Affairs with the rank of Imperial Inspector and State-founding Baron of Nanyang County; Xu Jingzong (592–672), Minister of the Board of Rites and State-founding Baron of Gaoyang County; Xue Yuanchao (623–685), Acting Palace Attendant, concurrently Left Attendant to the Crown Prince with the

rank of Imperial Inspector and State-founding Baron of Fenyang County; Li Yifu (614–666), Acting Deputy Chief of the Imperial Secretariat, concurrently Right Attendant [to the Crown Prince] with the rank of Imperial Inspector and State-founding Baron of Guangping County; Du Zhenglun (?–658), Deputy Chief of the Imperial Secretariat, and some others to peruse the translations from time to time. Provided there might be something improper and unfitting, they are supposed to give the necessary polish or improvement correspondingly. Should more scholars be needed, two or three persons could be recruited as required.

After the court interview, Palace Attendant Wang Junde (?–670) was dispatched to pass on the words of the Emperor to the Master: "The officials including Yu Zhining and others you need as translation assistants have already been assigned to you. We wish to indite the inscription of the stele with Our own hands. We don't know whether these arrangements suit your mind or not. We are sending this message to inform you."

Upon receiving this message from the Emperor, the Master's long-cherished aspirations were quite satisfied. In front of the messenger, the Master had a mixed feeling of happiness and sadness, shedding tears on his robe and sleeves. On the following day, leading his disciples, the Master went to the imperial palace to submit a gratitude letter to the Emperor. (Original note: The letter has been lost)

It was in the second month of the year. There was a Bhikṣuṇī named Baocheng, a daughter of Xue Daoheng (540–609), Governor of Xiangzhou and Duke of Linghe of the Sui Dynasty. She used to be a consort *jieyu*[80] under Emperor Shenyao (the posthumous title of Emperor Gaozu[81]). Besides being an outstanding beauty within the imperial harem, she proved herself to be a woman of great virtue, and a worthy candidate to be recorded in historian books on eminent women. Her father was famous for erudition and so was she. Having inherited the cultural tradition of her family, she was well-versed in Confucian classics and historian books as well, particularly adept at writing. When the Emperor Gaozong was young, he studied under her; so, after succeeding to the throne, he treated her with great respect and courtesy, and by appointing her to be Lady of Hedong Prefecture, he extended his gratitude for her kindness of teaching him. As knowing the lady desired to be a nun, the Emperor gratified her by having a nunnery called Helin constructed separately inside the Forbidden Palace for her lodging, also with a stele erected to bear the words eulogizing her virtue. Several tens of her attendants were also ordained as nuns. Four kinds of requisites[82] [of a monastic priest] were provided at public expense. When the time for her to be fully ordained is approaching, an imperial decree was issued on the tenth day of the second month, inviting the Master and other nine great virtuous monks, together with an attendant for each of them, to come to Helin Nunnery to grant the full ordination to Bhikṣuṇī Baocheng, the Lady of Hedong Prefecture. Ten carriages decorated with precious treasures, together with ten others carrying musicians and their instruments, had already been ordered to wait inside the Jingyao Gate in advance. After that, horses were sent to the monastery to receive virtuous monks into the city gate where they boarded the carriages to proceed to the nunnery, with great virtuous monks advancing in front, and a consort of musicians performing behind. It was the second month in the spring, so the natural beauty was impressively spectacular. Along the roads lined with the freshly green willow trees and pinkish red peach blossoms, under the jasper pine trees enveloped in the transparently blue thin mist, carriages adorned with brocade curtains and purple canopies were moving on in a gracefully gliding manner, making the whole procession look like the scene when the Buddha and His monks were repairing from the Jetavana Garden to the city of Rājagṛha. Upon their arrival, they were lodged in a separate chamber, and an altar was then erected for the ordination rite for Baocheng and more than fifty other ladies. Among those virtuous monks, the Master alone was the Ācārya (preceptor), and the rest were present as witnesses. The ordination rite had lasted for three days. After it, the skillful artisan named Wu Zhimin was ordered to draw the portraits of ten guest masters for enshrinement. Next to Helin Nunnery, another nunnery had been built some time before, named Deye, accommodating several hundred nuns. At this occasion, Bhikṣuṇīs at Deye nunnery also invited the Master to confer the Bodhisattva Precepts on them, so the Master went there too. Not until he finished the ceremony did he depart and return. A large number of donations and offerings heaped up in front of the Master. Then eunuch Wang Junde leading some servants with flowery canopies escorted the Master back to the Ci'en Monastery; at the sight, the onlookers on both sides of the streets spontaneously developed the mind of kindness. Later, the name of Helin Nunnery was changed to Longguo.

Shortly afterwards, the Emperor completed the inscription of the stele, and ordered Zhangsun Wuji (594–659), Lord of Military Affairs, to show it to all the noblemen. It reads:

We have heard that in the very beginning of Creation when all things started to come into being, the tangible was supported by the earth and sheltered by the firmament. Although the two luminaries, Sun and Moon, are shining visibly in the sky, we could not conjecture their waxes or wanes; the Four Seas demarcate the land; nevertheless, we fail to know their vastness. What's more, the dharma gate[83] is non-active and transcendentally tranquil, though displaying the existence before the extinction; the holy teachings are comprehensively inclusive, demonstrating themselves in forms but indicating the formless; thereby, the Way has issued its light for boundless Kalpas, generously giving edification to all sentient beings. Vivid in our memory, when the Buddha was born into the imperial family, lotuses put forth their blossoms to support His first steps, the divine pond emitted the light and trees bent their branches down. At Deer Park, He preached His first sermon in the virtuous voice, and in Dragon Palace[84], He convened with numerous Bodhisattvas. He gave blessings to sinful sentient beings and invigorated the degenerated mortal world. In His former existences, He kept self-cultivating diligently and dauntlessly, regardless of remaining his bones in the gruesome graveyard, which inspired even the most stupid to imbibe the Way; He indulged himself in pursuing the truth recklessly, even sacrificing himself for the half-verse preached in the Snow Mountains[85], which made the most intelligent show their heartfelt admiration. The dharma rain is trickling down to extinguish the flames of the burning house; the sun of wisdom is shining high to bring light to the world after driving the darkness away. Having perused the history books bound with light yellow silk covers and acquainted ourselves with all schools of knowledge and occult arts, we think it is the teachings of Śākyamuni that is the loftiest and surely will exist forever.

Our mother, the late Empress Wende, resembling a jade tree with luxuriant foliage, had thrived the royal family as those worthy Empresses of sage emperors did in ancient times. She is worthy of being recorded in history books for her unparalleled and widely-known feminine virtues. She has exemplified for the ladies at the inner palace, and her noble kindnesses will exert influences in the future perpetually. However, we are alarmed that, like the moon wanes, her chaste light was obscured forever and her feminine virtue submerged together with her life, invisible to us any longer. Stroking her dressing mirror, we became ever more sentimental day after day, missing our mother deeply but didn't know where to find her. In the past, Zhong You heaved a sigh of sadness at the sight of his emolument of one thousand *zhong*[86] of millet[87], and Yuqiu felt sorrowful at his three losses[88]. The agony from the demise of our beloved mother was so acute that we had been preoccupied all the time by a plan to build a memorial monastery for her. Later, a premium site was chosen, which not only backs on to the suburb Bin district[89], adorned by beautifully luxuriant trees and thriving farmhouses, but faces the Zhongnan Mountains, encircled by high peaks resembling the petals of lotus flowers. To its left, eight rivers are flowing by, forming ponds with lucid waters, like mirrors scattering all over the fields, and to its right, the roads are leading to various directions, on which carriages are moving with canopies fluttering into clouds. It is verily an impregnable and secure terrace under the sky! Also, a supreme land in the capital! Now on the very land stood the monastery that is beautifully enclosed with engraved rails and winding corridors, and decorated pavilions towering high. When the three-legged crow[90](sun) soars in the pink clouds of the early morning, the palatial halls are tinted brightly in various hues; when the Jade rabbit[91](moon) appears in the night sky, the buildings are glowing brilliantly in the moonlight. The fine paths of gardens are permeated with fragrance of autumn orchids and the orderly-distributed courtyards are dyed in purple mist; the rocks are perfumed by the winter osmanthus and inside the closed doors are clumps of flowers blooming red. Looking ahead, lamps are shinning like flowers in full bloom, with flames jumping out of the wicks, swirling high up like cranes; the flapping banners are overflowing the colors of the rainbow, marking the imposing buildings of monastery from afar. Stairways are of various heights, with their jade-laid steps being moistened by dew; the refined curtains knitted by strings of pearls could be rolled either up or down, emitting the light obscuring the starry night. The low hills are flushed by the rosy dawn and the quiet ponds enveloped by bluish green mist. Ornamental pendants worn at waists are harmoniously tinkling with the evening bells; and in the morning twilight, drizzling winds are shimmering the tunes of Buddhist hymns. We think that even the Heavenly palace of Incense Buddha is no more beautiful than this monastery, not to mention the immortals' mansions Langfeng remotely on top of Kunlun Mountains, which also could not be as such exquisitely decorated.

Master Xuanzang is second to none in the Buddhist community. He is a man of lofty quality and solemn demeanor, pure and bright like a cool breeze rustling through pine trees. His thoughts are extraordinarily distinctive and deep, resembling the colorful clouds glorifying the sky. He was born with unprecedented wisdom, and from a very young age, he began to culture tranquility and genuineness in his mind. Being prominent among his contemporaries, his accomplishments have outshone Zhu Daosheng (355–434)[92] and Huiyuan (334–416)[93], and he sets up an example for the following generations, even Buddhasiṃha[94] and Kumārajīva (344–413)[95] could not be equal to him in this respect. Worrying about the obsolescence of the honest and simple customs of the olden times, apprehensive about the prevalence of vulgar conventions in our age, saddened by the endless darkness of the night and grieved at the permanent loss of the truth, he ventured dauntlessly into the alien lands to feed on the teachings he had never comprehensively heard of. Sailing beyond the Milky Way[96], he shook the tin rings of his mendicant staff above clouds. On the expansive sea of billowing waves, he voyaged across the terrifying tides rolling high; on the broadly stretching land covered by heavy frost, he forged ahead in the coldness, losing his figure in the shadowy distance. Trudging on the plain, winds from all directions blew open his robe; trekking in the snow mountains, biting gales rendered his clothes thin and light. In broad daylight, his skin was burnt by the scorching sun hanging low over the shifting desert; at nights in the moonlight, he kept his shadow as his sole companion; at the early twilight, often after scaling dangerous peaks was there nothing left but his solitary body moving on.

The Master exerted efforts to acquire wisdom, and did his utmost to explore the ultimate truth; he learned the Buddhist teachings wholeheartedly, and made a thorough study on the most in-depth of the doctrines; at last, he has obtained more knowledge than that of former saints and gained insight into what had not been mentioned in the available texts. Consequently, the golden Buddhist scriptures were thus introduced into the East, continuing the teachings that were about to vanish; the valuable verses were brought into China from the West, supplementing the incomplete texts here in the East. Later, for undertaking the enterprise of translation, he lodged here in the Great Ci'en Monastery. By expounding the abstruse teachings, he has greened the trees of the Jetavana Garden once again; by opening the secret door to dharma, he has pacified disturbing waves of thoughts in meditation.

We indulged ourselves in the Eightfold Path and cherished an aspiration for nirvāṇa (Śāla trees) for we wish to share with the deceased the immense bliss we have gained from doing so. Let us pray that our mother will gain a liberation by practicing the Six Pāramitās and her spirit will visit the imperial palace. Let us pray that our mother will enter Four Dhyānas[97], and her spirit will dwell in Heavenly residence of immortals. Alas! The harmonious condition of the universe is easily gone, resulting in the ebb and flow of the seasons with weather changing from cold to hot; Sun Goddess pilots her six-dragon chariot across the sky, driving the time to pass by, never ceasing day and night. Some dramatic changes would happen to the world some future day when the expansive ocean gives place to the farming lands or high peaks are lowered to ravines, against which, we respectfully have these words inscribed on the solid slab, intending to keep the facts and invoke compliments from posterity.

The inscription reads:

The three luminaries[98] are shining over the phenomenal world,
And myriad things undergo constant changes;
Human life is short and transient,
And the vicissitudes of time are ruling all.

Moral codes have long been obsolescent,
While decadent customs have been gradually sprouting out;
Waves of desires roll up with the flood of consciousness,
While the mists of karma surge the chaotic passions up.

Singing praises to the great Cultivator of Men,
Who was born in Kapilavastu;
With his subtle Way embodied by profundities,
He has revealed the unfathomable truth residing in quietude.

Vulture Peak stands not far from here,
And Dragon Palace opens its door to all;
The Sun of wisdom is shining high above,
While the clouds of compassion are spitting rains down.

Review holy teachings in my memory,
Heed the virtuous voices in my mind's ear;
The sublime truth has been valued throughout the past eons,
And the Way of Buddha will be second to none from now on.

Beneficently the Buddha appeared in the world,
Later his traces vanished between the Śāla trees;
The dream of Han Emperor Ming is still being talked about,
Whereas suddenly down the bright star[99].

Sad to see the dressing mirror of Our mother,
Alone in the grand mansion, bitterness feeds on me;

Royal garden Zhuolong becomes bleak and barren,
And imperial harem Jiaofeng[100] is haunted by depression too.

Stealthily, the coldness of frost and dew is permeating mornings,
Secretly, the sorrow for losing Our beloved mother surging up in evenings;
Ascending to Heaven in a cloud carriage,
Permanently, she is enjoying herself in the grand bliss.

Buildings have been constructed in a grandiose style,
Engraved with flowery patterns pleasing to eye;
Purple pillars are supporting the moon,
Crimson beams merging into the rosy dawn.

Through windows in breaks the foliage of trees,
While across the pond does the cozy breeze blow the flowers up and down;
Canopies are bending down where phoenixes alight,
And beside the bridge is a rainbow slanting above.

Though being endowed with wisdom and extraordinary gift,
The Master pursues tranquility, aspiring for a simple life;
A great personage appears once in a thousand years,
He strolls alone in the Threefold Emptiness.

At the Jetavana Garden he tasted the flavor of Way,
And in the snow mountains he braved the wind and gales;

The lamp of wisdom was lighted once more,
And again, the right truth was held in esteem.

Four seasons are taking turns to come and go,
While Sun deity in six-dragon chariot is galloping around;
Long night was dawned after the sepulchral darkness vanishes off,
And the dharma door opens in the morning sunrise of the eastern sky.

His lofty virtues exemplify for the following generations,
And his glorious deeds will receive compliments from all;
Beautifully the refined writing would be engraved,
As we hope the merits shall be carried forever on.

On the sixth day of the third month, the honorable gentlemen received the Emperor's composition, and they went to the court to express their gratitude by submitting a memorial, saying:

Kneeling to appreciate your handwriting beautiful as the blooming heavenly flowers, we feel like beholding the rare treasures of the Yellow River; respectfully pronouncing your superb words, we get into its rhythm sweet as the melodies of Yun and Ying[101]. The content of your writing, not only embraces the moral codes acceptable to the myriad generations, but also covers grand programs suitable for creating flourishing age for one thousand years. Utterly delighted to read it, and gasped with admiration, we find no bounds to our pleasure.

Humbly we believe that the sun of wisdom from the West is illumining brightly, driving away the vast darkness of the ignorance, and that the dharma current is flowing into the East, revitalizing the plants by moistening their aged roots. Edification shows no differences in different places and the principles of material world are very much the same everywhere, so the Buddhist texts have been valued by the peoples all the way since ancient times. With veneration we think that Your Majesty has been reigning over the country with regal gumption and has handled the worldly affairs well with acute discernment. On the one hand, Your Majesty has carried the moral principles of filial piety forward; on the other hand, you attached particular importance on the Way of emancipation from life and death. You have relocated the Jetavana Garden in this supreme land, beckoning the prominent to come and live with pleasure. Now the picturesque landscape is nurturing the eminent practitioners. Again, without hesitation, Your Majesty has issued the imperial edict to erect the lofty stele inscribed with your superb writing that contains your boundless splendiferous ideas and shows your cross-broad vision as well. Your ideas reach beyond the frontier of the *Xiang[zhuang]* and *Xi[zhuang]*[102], even penetrating the very arcane of the universe. Although we, your subjects, know little about the true teachings, we are fortunate enough to be granted with a chance to read your divine composition. Despite our poor understanding, we attempt to appreciate it but fail to be at its level, just as a small pit could not be compared with the huge pond where the divine turtle lives, or as the ephemeral mayflies fail to imagine the longevity of a divine cane. In pleasure, we cannot help singing and dancing with joy, bearing your composition forever in our minds. With incommunicable excitement welling up in heart, we read it throughout again and again. Alas, our pleasure verily goes beyond expression.

ANNOTATION

1 From June 655 to March 656.

2 Buddhism accepts two pramāṇa 量 as valid means to knowledge: pratyakṣa (现perception) and Anumāṇa (比inference).

pratyakṣa-pramāṇa 现量：Reasoning, from the manifest, pratyakṣa. (1) Immediate, or direct reasoning, whereby the eye apprehends and distinguishes colour and form, the ear sound, etc. (2) Immediate insight into, or direct inference in a trance 定 of all the conditions of the ālayavijñāna; to be seen clearly.

Anumāṇa-pramāṇa 比量: Comparison and inference; it is defined as 比 comparison of the known, and 量 inference of the unknown., e. g. the inference of fire from smoke.

Buddhism also considers scriptures as third valid pramāṇa, such as from Buddha and other "valid minds" and "valid persons." This third source of valid knowledge is a form of perception and inference in Buddhist thought. Valid scriptures, valid minds and valid persons are considered in Buddhism as Avisaṃvādin (圣教/圣言量, incontrovertible, indisputable).

3 Lü Cai吕才 (606–665), a philosopher in the early Tang Dynasty.

4 Refers to the first hexagram: Qian 乾(Heaven), originator or the creative. In the *Commentaries on the Book of Changes*《易经・彖传》, Hexagram No. 1, Qian: "Vast is the 'great and originating (power)' indicated by Qian! All

things owe to it their beginning: it contains all the meaning belonging to (the name) heaven." (大哉乾元，万物资始，乃统天). For English translations: https://ctext.org/book-of-changes/qian/ens

5 Refers to the second hexagram: Kun坤 (Earth), the receptive. In the *Commentaries on the Book of Changes*, Hexagram No. 2, Kun: "Complete is the 'great and originating (capacity)' indicated by Kun! All things owe to it their birth; it receives obediently the influences of Heaven." (至哉坤元，万物资生，乃顺承天). For English translations: https://ctext.org/book-of-changes/qian/ens.

6 Refers to the *Treatise on the Symbolism of the Hexagrams* (*Xiang Zhuan*《象传》).

7 Refers to *The Great Treatise* (*Xi Ci*《系辞》).

8 Buddha-wisdom of the phenomenal (权智) and Buddha-wisdom of the absolute reality (实智).

9 Chakravartin, a king who rules over all four of the continents posited by ancient Indian cosmography (i.e., a universal monarch). In Buddhism, the chakravartin was considered to be the secular counterpart of a buddha (enlightened one), with whom he shared many attributes. Gold Wheel (Cakra): a powerful weapon of Chakravartin.

10 In ancient Indian cosmology as adopted by Buddhism, the six heavens located in the world of desire and situated between Earth and the Brahma Heaven. Beings in the six heavens are dominated by desire. The six heavens, or Six heavens of the world of desire are, in ascending order, Heaven of the Four Heavenly Kings 四天王天, Heaven of the Thirty-three Gods 忉利天, the Yama Heaven 须焰摩天或夜摩天, the Tushita Heaven 兜率陀天, Heaven of Enjoying the Conjured 乐变化天, and Heaven of Freely Enjoying Things Conjured by Others 他化自在天. Heaven of the Four Heavenly Kings is located halfway up Mount Sumeru, and Heaven of the Thirty-three Gods, at its summit. The other four heavens are in the air, that is, between the summit of Mount Sumeru and the Brahma Heaven. among them, Heaven of Freely

Enjoying Things Conjured by Others, often called the sixth heaven, is known as the abode of the devil king.

11 Amitabha's Pure Land of the West.

12 Also, The Land of Exceeding Great Delight 妙喜世界, is the eastern paradise reigned over by the Buddha Akshobhya. It is believed that whoever is reborn there can never fall back to a lower level of Consciousness. The name Akshobhya (Aksobhya) means " Immovable" or " Unshakable." In Chinese he is called A-Chu-Fo 阿閦佛.

13 Here the Chinese 有顶, also called色究竟天(Akaniṣṭha heaven), literally refers to the final limits of the material world, which means the pure abodes whose characteristic is that there is nothing above them, and there are no features from elsewhere that surpass them. Akaniṣṭha means "not below" or "above all." So, the name "Akaniṣṭha" is used throughout the Buddhist teachings to refer to different abodes, which all share the common characteristic of being the highest, in relation to specific criteria. According to Mahāyāna, it is the highest heaven of the form realm.

14 An ancient street in Chang'an, used to be the center for the merchants from the Western Regions.

15 The original text in Chinese is translated literally as eighteen Wei Tuo 韦驮, a metonymy for Buddhism translators. Wei Tuo, also known as Skanda, was said to be the general in his eighteen previous lives. He is a Mahāyāna bodhisattva regarded as a devoted guardian of Buddhist monasteries who guards the teachings of Buddhism. In Chinese temples, Skanda faces the statue of the Buddha in the main shrine. In others, he is on the far right of the main shrine, whereas on the left is his counterpart, Sangharama (personified as the historical general Guan Yu). In Chinese Sūtras, his image is found at the end of the Sūtra, a reminder of his vow to protect and preserve the teachings. Here Skanda is the metonymy of eminent monk translators, who serve as protectors of Buddhist bequeathed teachings.

16 The fourfold community or the four members of the Buddhist community (parisā), consisting of Bhikṣu(s) Bhikṣuṇī(s), laymen and laywomen.

17 It is said in *The Classic of Mountains and Seas* (*Shanghai Jing*《山海经》), the aroma of asarum grass(杜衡) could speed the horse.

18 There are six categories of mental qualities, which have fifty-one dharmas, besides there are eight dharmas of mind, eleven dharmas of matter, twenty-four dharmas not associated with mind, and six dharmas not produced by cause, making a total of one hundred dharmas in five divisions, which make up all the elements of existence.

19 The Six Classics are:(1) *Classic of Poetry*: A collection of 305 poems divided into 160 folk songs, 105 festal songs sung at court ceremonies, and 40 hymns and eulogies sung at sacrifices to heroes and ancestral spirits of the royal house. (2) *Book of Documents*: A collection of documents and speeches alleged to have been written by rulers and officials of the early Zhou period and before. (3) *Book of Rites*: Describes ancient rites, social forms and court ceremonies. The version studied today is a re-worked version compiled by scholars in the third century BC rather than the original text, which is said to have been edited by Confucius himself. (4) *Book of Changes*. (5) *Spring and Autumn Annals*: A historical record of the State of Lu, Confucius's native state, 722–481 BC. (6)*The Classic of Music* is sometimes considered as the sixth classic but was lost in the Burning of the Books.

20 Hundred Schools of Thought were philosophies and schools that flourished from the 6th century to 221 BC, during the Spring and Autumn period and the Warring States period of ancient China.

21 The pitchpipes , in Chinese 律吕, are the most fundamental for Chinese music theory as a system of the twelve pitchpipes (shi'er lü 十二律) that is composed of a scale of twelve pipes. Six of the pipes were called lǜ (liülǜ 六律), the others lǚ (liülǚ 六吕). These were later called the six yang pipes (liü yanglü 六阳律) and the six yin pipes (liü yinlǚ六阴吕).

22 The *Taixuan Jing*《太玄经》is one of Yang Xiong's most important philosophical books. Yang Xiong (扬雄53 BC–18 CE), courtesy name Ziyun子云, was a philosopher and writer of the late Former Han period (206 BC–8 CE). Yang Xiong also wrote the gloss books *Fayan*《法言》, *Xunzuan*《训纂》, *Fangyan*《方言》and Cangjie Xunzuan《仓颉训纂》. The *Taixuan jing* is a theory of worldview that is partially philosophical and partially mantic. The origin of the universe is the great mystery (*taixuan*太玄).

23 *Xiangxi* 象戏 was an ancient chess game popular in the period of the Wei, Jin and Northern and Southern dynasties. It is said to be created by Yuwen Yong 宇文邕(r. 560–578), the Emperor Wu of the Northern Zhou. Yuwen Yong was a great fan of xiangqi (象棋chess), and wrote a book about it, *Xiang jing*《象经》, in 569 AD.

24 The eight heterodox practices, also Eight Erroneous Practices: the practices that are against the Eightfold Noble Path.

25 The four false beliefs; the four wrong views; the four inverted beliefs in regard to the doctrine of permanence, pleasure, personality, and purity.

26 The syllogisms of Buddhism mainly refer to the Trairūpya (triple inferential sign) introduced by Vasubandhu.

The Trairūpya is a logical argument that contains three constituents which a logical "sign" or "mark" (linga) must fulfill to be "valid source of knowledge" (pramana):

It should be present in the case or object under consideration, the "subject-locus" (pakṣa).

It should be present in a "similar case" or a homologue (sapakṣa).

It should not be present in any "dissimilar case" or heterologue (vipakṣa).

27 The Kunlun 昆仑 or Kunlun Shan is a mountain or mountain range in Chinese mythology, an important symbol representing the axis mundi and divinity. The mythological Kunlun is not confused with the real Kunlun Mountains of the Tibetan Plateau. Different locations of the Kunlun have been given in

the various legends, myths, and semi-historical accounts in which it appears. These accounts typically describe Kunlun as the dwelling place of various gods and goddesses, where fabled plants and mythical creatures may also be found. Langfeng peak is said to be the summit of it.

28 Huang Xian 黄宪(75–122), courtesy name Shudu 叔度, was an eminent worthy man in the Eastern Han Dynasty. For more information, refer to the *Book of the Later Han: Biographies of Huang Xian*《后汉书·黄宪传》.

29 Li Ying李膺(110–169), courtesy name Yuanli 元礼, was an eminent worthy man in the Eastern Han Dynasty. For more information, refer to the *Book of the Later Han-Biographies of Partisan Prohibitions* (后汉书·党锢列传). Or Wang Jun王筠(482–550). His courtesy name also is Yuanli 元礼, who was a famous man of letter of Liang Dynasty (502–557) of Southern Dynasties. For more information, refer to *The Book of Liang:Biographies of Wang Jun* (*Liangshu-WangjunZhuan*《梁书·王筠传》), which was compiled under Yao Silian 姚思廉(died 637), completed in 635.*The Book of Liang* is part of the *Twenty-Four Histories* (*Ershisi Shi*《二十四史》) canon of Chinese history.

30 According to the *Biographies of Eminent Monks*(*Gaoseng Zhuan*《高僧传》), Shan Kai 单开, or Shan Daokai 单道开 was a Dunhuang敦煌 monk. During the Eastern Jin Dynasty (317–420) he went to Mount Luofu 罗浮山, a sacred mountain situated on the north bank of the Dongjiang in the northwest of Boluo County, Huizhou in Guangdong Province. Later on, many other monks followed suit and established Buddhist monasteries on this mountain.

31 Four Noble Truths: (1) life is suffering; (2) defilements are the cause of suffering; (3) all suffering can be ended; and (4) the way to end suffering is the Eightfold Noble Path (q.v).

32 Literally means "taking actions", a term opposite to *wuwei*, a very crucial term often in Daoist philosophy. *wuwei* literally expresses the idea of "not to

act", but it doesn't mean to do nothing at all, and it emphasizes restraint from certain actions, which are seen as conflicting with the Dao.

33 Take reference to the *Chapter External Things* of the *Zhuangzi*: "A fish trap is there for the fish. When you have got hold of the fish, you forget the trap. A snare is there for the rabbits. When you have got hold of the rabbit, you forget the snare. Words are there for the intent. When you have got hold of the intent, you forget the words. Where can I find a man who has forgotten words, so I can have a few words with him?" (《庄子・外物》："荃者所以在鱼，得鱼而忘荃；蹄者所以在兔，得兔而忘蹄；言者所以在意，得意而忘言。")

34 Eight Emancipations: emancipation from attachment to forms and desires through eight types of meditation. Also, eight kinds of liberation. The ultimate aim is freedom from Earthly desires of the threefold world. They are:

(1) emancipation from thoughts of external things by meditating on their impurity.

(2) further advancement of the first emancipation by continuing meditation on impurity.

(3) emancipation obtained by meditating on the pure aspect of things in the outside world.

(4) emancipation from thoughts and bonds of material objects and entering meditation on the Realm of Boundless Empty Space.

(5) emancipation from thoughts of boundless empty space and entering meditation on the Realm of Boundless Consciousness.

(6)emancipation from thoughts of boundless consciousness and entering meditation on the Realm of Nothingness.

(7) emancipation from thoughts of nothingness and entering meditation on the Realm of Neither Thought Nor No Thought.

(8) emancipation from, or extinction of, all workings of the mind, which is

the source of earthly desires.

35 Seven Links of Enlightenment: (1) mindfulness, (2) discrimination between the true and the false, (3) vigor, (4) joy (5) ease of body and mind, (6) concentration, and (7) equanimity.

36 Dharmodgata (昙无竭菩萨Dommukatsu-bosatsu) is a bodhisattva described in the *Wisdom Sutras* (*Aṣṭasāhasrikā Prajñāpāramitā* and *Pañcaviṃśatisāhasrikā Prajñāpāramitā*). Bodhisattva Dharmodgata lived in his palace in the City of Fragrances (Gandhavatī). While satisfying the five desires and being accompanied by sixty-eight thousand women, he preached the doctrine of the perfection of wisdom three times a day. The people in the city held him in high esteem and presented him with offerings. Those who listened to his sermon and embraced it were saved from falling into the evil paths of existence. From Dharmodgata, Bodhisattva Ever Wailing (Sadāpralāpa) learned the teaching of the perfection of wisdom, mastered six million types of meditation, and finally attained supreme wisdom. In the *Wisdom Sutras*, Bodhisattva Dharmodgata is described as a "good friend" who leads Bodhisattva Ever Wailing to enlightenment in lifetime after lifetime.

37 Li Chunfeng李淳风 (602–670) was a Taoist, mathematician, astronomer, and historian who was born in today's Baoji, Shaanxi during the Sui and Tang dynasties. He was first appointed to the Imperial Astronomy Bureau to help institute a calendar reform. He eventually ascended to deputy of the Imperial Astronomy Bureau and designed the Linde calendar 麟德历. Li died in Chang'an in 670. The book *Massage-Chart Prophecies* (Tuibeitu,《推背图》) is generally credited to Li. The book is a collaboration of attempts to predict the future using numerology.

38 Generally, there are ten honorific titles of all Buddhas: The One That Has Come (Tathagata, 如来)，Worthy of Offerings or Worthy of Worship 应供，Truly Omniscient正遍知，Perfect in Illumination and Conduct(or Perfect in

understanding and practice明行足)，Well Departed善逝，Supreme Lord (or Unsurpassed One无上士)，Cultivator of Men(or Tamer of Men, or Passions Controller调御丈夫)，Teacher of Gods and Men(or Teacher of heavenly and human beings天人师), The World Honored Enlightened One世尊.

39 Refers to Daoism, for one of the most important schools of Daoism is the Heavenly Masters School (Tianshi Dao) with Zhang Daoling (张道陵 ?–156) as founder.

40 A story in *Hanfeizi*《韩非子》, fugitively refers to someone who masquerades as having an ability: Whenever King Xuan of Qi had men play the *yu* (a musical instrument), there had to be 300 men playing simultaneously. A reclusive scholar, by the name of Nanguo (lit. southern wall of a city), who was unable to play the instrument, asked if he could join the ensemble and play the *yu* for the king. King Xuan was delighted by this, and dispensed enough food rations for several hundred musicians. Then, King Xuan died, and King Min took the throne. He preferred to listen to the *yu* players play one by one, so the reclusive scholar fled.

41 Dhūtanga means a set of practices leading to the state of or appropriate to a dhūta (pp. of dhunāti), that is to a scrupulous person who shakes off one's desire for creature comfort in food, clothing, and shelter, living a scrupulous way of life.

42 Or the Lilajan River (also known by its older name: Niranjan River and also mentioned as Nilanjan River) flows through the Chatra and Gaya districts in the Indian states of Jharkhand and Bihar. Some people refer to this river as the Falgu River. As Bodh Gaya is on the shores of Lilajan (Niranjan) many legends are associated with this river concerning Buddha. It is said that Buddha bathed in the nearby Niranjan (now called Lilajan) River after attaining enlightenment.

43 The science of language: science of sounds or words, grammar, philology, etc.

44 Or Eight Evil Ways (八邪行). The opposite of the Eightfold Right Path. They

are: (1) evil views; (2) evil thinking; (3) evil speech; (4) evil actions; (5) evil livelihood; (6) evil endeavor; (7) evil mindfulness; (8) evil samādhi.

45 Sixty-two views refer to the wrong views held by ancient Indian philosophers. One set of 62 views argues about each of the five aggregates of a sentient being: in the past it is permanent, impermanent, both, or neither; in the present it is with boundary, without boundary, both, or neither; in the future it is going, not going, both, or neither. To these 60 views, two polar opposites, perpetuity and cessation of existence, are added to make a total of 62. Another set of 62 views includes 56 views of self and 6 views of existence. They hold that each of the five aggregates of a sentient being in the desire realm and the form realm, and each of the four aggregates of a god in the formless realm is a self, not a self, both, or neither, totaling 56 views. In addition, one's perpetuity and cessation of existence in the Three Realms come to 6 views.

46 Four kinds of wisdom-knowledge 四智, or Four Wisdoms. A Buddha has the virtue of complete wisdom-knowledge, which includes: (1) Ādarśa-jñāna 大圆镜智, the wisdom of "Mirror-like Awareness", "devoid of all dualistic thought and ever united with its 'content' as a mirror is with its reflections"; (2) Samatā-jñāna (平等性智), the wisdom of the "Awareness of Sameness", which perceives the sameness, the commonality of dharmas or phenomena; (3) Pratyavekṣaṇa-jñāna (妙观察智), the wisdom of "Investigative Awareness", that perceives the specificity, the uniqueness of dharmas; (4) Kṛty-anuṣṭhāna-jñāna (成所作智), the wisdom of "Accomplishing Activities", the awareness that "spontaneously carries out all that has to be done for the welfare of beings, manifesting itself in all directions."

47 See note 49 of Fascile III.

48 Ten Powers (daśa-bala, 十力). Because a Buddha's wisdom-knowledge is indestructible and unsurpassed, it is called powers. He has perfect wisdom-knowledge of: (1) everyone's right or wrong action in every situation, and

its corresponding karmic consequences; (2) the karmic requitals of every sentient being in the past, present, and future; (3) all stages of dhyāna, liberation, and samādhi; (4) the capacity of every sentient being; (5) the desires and or moral direction of every sentient being; (6) the different levels of existence; (7) the consequences of all actions, with or without afflictions; (8) the transmigratory states of all sentient beings and the courses of karma they follow; (9) all future rebirths of every sentient being and their karmic reasons; (10) the permanent ending of all His afflictions and habits upon attainment of Buddhahood.

49 The seven rhetorical powers or methods of bodhisattvas — direct and unimpeded; acute and deep; unlimited in scope; irrefutable; appropriate, according to receptivity; purposive or objective (i.e. nirvāṇa); proving the universal supreme method of attainment, i.e. Mahāyāna; seven rhetorical powers.

50 Śūnyatā, translated into English most often as emptiness and sometimes void, is a Buddhist concept which has multiple meanings depending on its doctrinal context. It is either an ontological feature of reality, a meditation state, or a phenomenological analysis of experience. Three Emptiness refers to: (1) The emptiness of a sentient being 人空 composed of Dharmas, such as the five aggregates, and dependent on causes and conditions; (2) the emptiness of a dharma 法空, such as any of the five aggregates, dependent on causes and conditions (see eighteen emptinesses); (3) the emptiness of both 俱空.

51 Recorded in the *Master Lü's Spring and Autumn Annals*《吕氏春秋》and *Wei Shu*《魏书》that when Sakya was born, it was on the night of fifth day of the fourth month in the summer of the seventh year of the reign of the Duke Zhuang of Lu (687 BC) that there were no stars but shooting meteors lighting up the night.

52 Yāna in Sanskrit, refers to a mode or method of spiritual practice in Buddhism,

and in particular to divisions of various schools of Buddhism according to their type of practice. In Mahāyāna Buddhism, the Five Yānas are five paths to liberation: (1) Puruṣayāna-the human vehicle. This is the very beginning of the spiritual path; (2) Deváyāna-the practice of ethics and meditation; (3) Śrāvakayāna-the practice of renunciation and the Four Noble Truths; (4) Pratyekabuddhayāna-practice concerned with dependent arising; (5) Bodhisattvayāna-practice of the Six Perfections.

53 See to note 22 of Preface.

54 Refers to two extreme views/beliefs, such as annihilation and immortality, being or non-being, or existence and non-existence.

55 The truth of non-duality; the truth of neither existence nor non- existence, etc.

56 Hanlin Academy (Hanlin yuan翰林院) was founded in 725 CE by Emperor Xuanzong 唐玄宗 as a place of study for scholars, artists, writers, and astrologers in Chang'an. Membership in the academy was confined to an elite group of scholars, who performed secretarial and literary tasks for the court. One of its main duties was to decide on an interpretation of the Chinese classics. This formed the basis of the Imperial examinations, which aspiring bureaucrats had to pass to attain higher level posts. Painters working for the court were also attached to the academy.

57 The theory of the Five Processes 五行 as expressed in *the Grand Norm/Plan* 洪范, a chapter of the Confucian Classic *Shangshu*《尚书》in the Western Zhou (1030–722 BC). They are: metal, wood, water, fire and earth.

58 Six *yaos* (lines, either broken or unbroken) formed a hexagram (combined by two trigrams) and their interpretations. The basic symbols in them were "—" and "– –", called respectively the *yangyao* (the positive line) and the *yinyao* (the negative line).

59 Zhang Hua张华 (231–300), courtesy name Maoxian 茂先, was a famous man of letters and statesman of the Western Jin dynasty (266–316).

60 Dongfang Shuo 东方朔(154–c. 93 BC) , courtesy name Manqian 曼倩, was a

Han Dynasty scholar-official, *fangshi* 方士(master of esoterica), author, and court jester to Emperor Wu (r. 141–87 BC). In Chinese mythology, Dongfang is considered a Daoist immortal.

61 Hetu: cause, condition, reason.

62 *Jicheng* 极成, a terminology in Hetuvidyā, means a proposition which both sides are already in full agreement on.

63 Nine Principles of Mathematics 九数 firstly appeared in the *Rites of Zhou*, a work on bureaucracy and organizational theory. The book appeared in the middle of the 2nd century BC and edited by Liu Xin 刘歆 (c. 50 BC–23CE). Nine Principles of Mathematics was mentioned in the book but without further detailed explanation.

64 Wei Hong卫宏，courtesy name Jingzhong敬仲，was a scholar during the reign of Guangwu Emperor (6B.C–57 AD) of the Eastern Han Dynasty.

65 Bi Zao 裨灶 was a famous prophet in Zheng state during the Spring and Autumn Period and Warring States Period (770–221 BC).

66 Kou Qianzhi寇谦之(365–448) was a Daoist reformer who re-envisioned many of the ceremonies and rites of the Way of Heavenly Master form of Daoism and reformulated its theology into a new movement known as The Northern Heavenly Masters. His influence was such that he had Daoism established as the official state religion of the Northern Wei Dynasty (386–534); this act, however, embroiled Daoism in long and often bloody factional political struggles.

67 Cui Hao 崔浩 (died 450 CE), courtesy name Boyuan 伯渊, was a prime minister of the Xianbei Dynasty Northern Wei. Largely because of Cui's counsel, Emperor Taiwu of Northern Wei was able to unify northern China, ending the Sixteen Kingdoms era and, along with the southern Liu Song, entering the Southern and Northern Dynasties era. Also because of the influence of Cui, who was a devout Daoist, Emperor Taiwu became a devout Daoist as well.

68 Refers to the Nine Divisions (Jiuchou九畴) mentioned in the *Hongfan* (《洪范》The Great Norm/Plan), a chapter of the Confucian Classic *Shangshu* (《尚书》), which assumes control over Earth consisted of "nine divisions" (Jiuchou 九畴): （1）Knowledge of the Nature of the Five Processes (the Five Elements五行); (2) The Five Personal Matters 五事; (3) The Eight Objects / considerations of Government 八政; (4) The Five Dividers of Time 五纪; (5)Royal Perfection 皇极; (6)The Three Virtues 三德; (7) The Examination of Doubts by Prognostication 稽疑; (8)The Various Verifications in Divination 庶征; (9) The Five Sources of Happiness (wufu 五福) and the Awing Use of the Six Occasions of Suffering 六极. The correct observation of these nine divisions would result in excellent rule ("royal perfection") and a prospering empire. It describes the world view of the period of Zhou (11th cent.–221 BC) in metaphysical terms. Sima Qian 司马迁(145 or 135 – 86 BC) purports (ch. 4 Zhou Benji《周本纪》) that once King Wu 周武王 of the Zhou Dynasty interviewed Prince Jizi 箕子, the last surviving noble of the Shang Dynasty (17th–11th cent. BC), about the "Way of Heaven" 天道. The answers of the Prince are to be found in the Hongfan. Kong Anguo (孔安国 late 2nd cent. BC) was of the opinion that the set of nine rules was designated according to the so-called *Luoshu* "洛书" diagram to be seen on the back of a turtle emerging from the River Luo.

69 Dai De 戴德 and his nephew Dai Sheng戴圣, birth and death of them unknown, Confucian scholars of the Former Han Dynasty. Both of them helped compile the *Record of Rites* (*Liji*《礼记》).

70 *Jingli*《经礼》refers to the *Rites of the Zhou* (*Zhouli*《周礼》), which is a description of the putative organization of the government during the Western Zhou period (11th cent.–770 BC). *Quli*《曲礼》refers to the *Etiquette and Rites* (*Yili*《仪礼》). With the *Record of Rites* (*Liji*《礼记》), there are the *Three Classics on Rites* (*Sanli*《三礼》), one of the Thirteen Confucian Classics.

71 Refers to the *Rat*《相鼠》, a poem in the *Odes of Yong Airs of the States of the Classic of Poetry*《诗经·鄘风》, criticizing the improper manners.

72 Refers to the *Yuli*《鱼丽》, a poem in the *Lesser Court Hymns of the Classic of Poetry*《诗经·小雅》, praising propriety.

73 The Shangyang 商羊, in Chinese mythology was a rainbird. It was one of several important mythical birds in Chinese tradition. The Shangyang was particularly associated with the Lord of Rain. According to the *School Sayings of Confucius* or *Family Sayings of Confucius* (*Kongzi Jiayu*《孔子家语》), once the Shangyang was supposed to have visited the royal court at Qi, where it performed a dance upon its one leg, whereupon an embassy was sent inquire of the meaning of this event to Confucius in the neighboring state of Lu: the Shangyang was known to Confucius, who predicted imminent heavy rain and advised the digging of drainage and the raising of dikes. As a result of following the sage's advice, Qi was spared calamity due to the ensuing inundation, whereas the other states who did not heed the advice were heavily damaged.

74 Denglin Forest邓林 refers to the peach forest left by Kua Fu when he died. In *Kuafu Chasing Sun* (*Kufu Zhuiri*《夸父追日》), a story in the *Classic of Mountains and Seas* (*Shanhai Jing*《山海经》), Kuafu, leader of a group of mighty giants, aspired to catch up with Sun. At that time, the world was desolate and uncultured, infested with vipers and beasts. Kuafu kept hanging the ferocious snakes he caught on ears for decoration, or grabbed them in hands waving proudly. In a year when the weather was extraordinarily hot, the plants were scorched, the rivers were dried and people were suffering from the intense heat of Sun. Kuafu swore to catch Sun and tame it to serve for all. Sun moved fleetingly in the sky, while Kuafu chased it like wind on the ground. When he shook off the dusts in his shoes, the dusts became a hill; he used three stones to support his boiler when he was cooking, and the stones later became three mountains. He caught up with Sun finally after nine

days and nights. However, Sun was so scorching that he felt thirsty and tired and went to the Yellow River and the Wei River to quench his thirst. But the water from these two rivers was not sufficient to satisfy him and he decided to go to the Great Lake to drink its water. Before he got there he died of thirst on the way. Before his death, Kuafu cast his walking stick away, and the place it fell off immediately grew a huge lush peach forest, which was called Denglin. The forest was flourishing all year round, which provided shades and peaches for the passersby and hard-working people to quench thirst.

75 Li Zhong 李忠 (643–665), courtesy name Zhengben 正本, was the oldest son of Emperor Gaozong and was created crown prince in 652. He was forced to yield the crown prince position to his younger brother Li Hong 李弘 (652–675), born of Empress Wu, in 656. He was later further reduced to commoner rank and put under house arrest, and when the chancellor Shangguan Yi 上官仪 (608–665) failed in his attempt to persuade Emperor Gaozong to depose Empress Wu in 664 and was executed, Empress Wu took the opportunity to accuse Li Zhong of being complicit in Shangguan's plans. Around the new year 665, Emperor Gaozong ordered Li Zhong to commit suicide. He was posthumously honored an imperial prince, but not a crown prince, during the second reign of his brother Emperor Zhongzong 唐中宗 (李显 Li Xian 656–710).

76 According to Sima Qian (145–90 BC), Taibo was the founder of the State of Wu. Taibo 太伯or 泰伯 was the eldest son of King Tai of Zhou周太王, his birth and death dates are unknown. Taibo had two younger brothers, Zhongyong and Jili. King of Zhou wished to make his youngest son Jili to inherit the reins of power, so Taibo and Zhongyong traveled southeast and settled in Meili in present-day Jiangsu province. There, Taibo and his followers set up the State of Wu, and made Meili its capital. Taibo's grand nephew, King Wu of Zhou overthrew the Shang Dynasty and started the Zhou Dynasty.

77 Li Hong 李弘 (652–675), formally Emperor Xiaojing孝敬帝 (literally, "the filial and respectful emperor") with the temple name of Yizong 义宗, was a crown prince (not emperor, despite his formal title) of the Tang Dynasty. He was the fifth son of Emperor Gaozong and the oldest son of his second wife Empress Wu (later known as Wu Zetian), and he was made the crown prince in 656. As he grew older, he often came in conflict with his ambitious mother Empress Wu, and it is commonly believed by traditional historians that she poisoned him to death in 675. His father Emperor Gaozong, then still reigning, posthumously honored him with an imperial title.

78 Empress Zhangsun长孙皇后 (personal name unknown, 601–636), formally Empress Wendeshunsheng 文德顺圣皇后 (literally "the cultural, virtuous, serene, and holy empress") or, in short, Empress Wende 文德皇后, was the wife of Emperor Taizong and the mother of Emperor Gaozong. She was of Xianbei origin and well educated.

79 Or the Left Vice-Director of the Department of State Affairs.

80 Or Lady of Handsome Fairness (*jieyu*婕妤), created by Emperor Wu of the Han Dynasty, is one of the ranks of imperial consorts. The ranks indeed have varied over the course of Chinese history but remained important throughout owing to its importance in management of the inner court and in imperial succession, which ranked heirs according to the prominence of their mothers in addition to their strict birth order.

81 Emperor Gaozu of Tang (566–635), born Li Yuan, courtesy name Shude叔德, was the founder of the Tang Dynasty, and the first emperor of this dynasty from 618 to 626. His posthumous title was Emperor Shenyao 神尧.

82 See note 31 of Fascicle III.

83 Or gate/door to enlightenment. In Buddhism, as the living beings are thought to have 84,000 delusions, so the Buddha provides 84,000 methods of dealing with them. Also refers to the doctrines, or wisdom of Buddha.

84 See note 129 of Fascicle VI.

85 This allusion comes from the *Mahāyāna Mahāparinirvāṇa Sūtra* (《大般涅槃经》) *or Nirvāṇa Sūtra*: the Buddha in a former incarnation was a great man of the Himālayas, he had already heard the former two verses–Whatever is phenomenal is impermanent, the law of creation and destruction (诸行无常，是生灭法), and in order to obtain the following two verses from a rākṣasa–Arising and ceasing are extinguished, Entry into nirvāṇa is true bliss(生灭灭已，寂灭为乐), he sacrificed his life.

86 Chinese ancient unit of measurement.

87 Zhong You 仲由(542–480 BC), commonly known by his courtesy names Zilu 子路 and Jilu 季路, was one of the best known and most faithful disciples of Confucius. Among Confucius's disciples, he was the second in terms of ability and accomplishment in statesmanship, after Ran Qiu. Zhong You is one of the Twenty-four Confucian paragons of filial piety. According to legend, he was from a poor family and often foraged wild greens to feed himself, but he would carry rice from more than 100 *li* away for his parents. When he grew up and became an important official, his parents had already died. He lived a life of luxury, but pined for the days of his youth. He often sighed: "How I wish I could return to the old days, when I ate wild greens and carried rice for my parents!" It is said that he heaved a sigh of sadness at the sight of his emolument of one thousand *zhong* of millet because it reminded him of his mother who died poor.

88 Master Yuqiu 虞丘子 was a prime minister serving the administration of King Zhuang of Chu (?–591 BC) during the Eastern Zhou Dynasty (770–256 BC). Once Confucius saw him weeping beside the road and asked for the reason. Yuqiu replied that there were three losses made him cry: first, when he was young he travelled off to study, but when he returned home his parents had already died, so he lost the chance to serve them with filial piety; second, although he had cherished a lofty ideal of serving a sagacious lord but it seemed that he would have no chance to realize his ideal; thirdly, he had

spent most of his life ranging around, so he was estranged from his family and country fellowmen, thus when growing old, he would not be properly provided for.

89 Present Binxian County 彬县 in Shaanxi Province.

90 The three-legged (or tripedal) crow 三足乌 is a creature found in various mythologies and arts of China. It is believed to inhabit and represent Sun.

91 According to the folklore in China, Moon rabbit or Jade rabbit 玉兔 is a rabbit that lives on Moon as a companion of Moon goddess Chang'e, constantly pounding the elixir of life for her. It represents Moon.

92 Zhu Daosheng 竺道生(355–434), was an eminent Chinese Buddhist scholar during Six Dynasties era. He is known for advocating the concepts of sudden enlightenment and the universality of the Buddha nature. Born in Pengcheng, Daosheng left home to become a monk at eleven. He studied in Jiankang under Zhu Fatai, and later at Lushan (Mount Lu) monastery with Huiyuan, and from 405 or 406 under Kumarajiva in Chang'an, where he stayed for some two years perfecting his education and also assisted Kumarajiva in his translation work.

93 Huiyuan 慧远 (334–416) was a Chinese Buddhist teacher who founded Donglin Temple on Mount Lushan in Jiangxi province and wrote the text On Why Monks Do Not Bow Down Before Kings in 404 AD. He was born in Shanxi province but after a long life of Buddhist teaching he wound up in Jiangxi province, where he died in 416. Huiyuan was posthumously named First Patriarch of the Pure Land School of Buddhism.

94 See note 30 of Preface.

95 See note 106 of Fascicle I.

96 In ancient Chinese mythology, the Milky Way was regarded as a river of stars in sky; here it implies rivers over land as numerous as the stars in the Milky Way.

97 See note 30 of Fascicle VII.

98 Sun, Moon and stars.

99 In the original Chinese text, *zhouxing* 周星 is used. In Chinese classics, it usually refers to Jupiter, the largest planet of the solar system. Jupiter passes through the Zodiac (ie, twelve times) every year. It circles the heavens in about twelve years, so it is called *zhouxing* or Zhou Star. 周*zhou* means a full circle. Here it is a metonymy for the mother of the Emperor.

100 Zhuolong 濯龙 is the name of the royal garden in the Han Dynasty(202–220 AD) and Jiaofeng 椒风, the name of imperial harem, both of which here represent the kind.

101 Yun refers to *Yunmen* 云门, the name of the ancient music piece legendarily composed by Yellow Emperor, and *Ying* to *Liuying* 六英, legendarily composed by Diku 帝喾 or Zhuanxu 颛顼.

102 Refers to the *Treatise on the Symbolism of the Hexagrams* (*Xiang Zhuan* 《象传》) and the *Great Treatise* (*Xici*《系辞》) of the *Book of Changes.*

Fascicle IX

Beginning with a Letter of Gratitude for the Completion of the Stele Inscription of the Ci'en Monastery in the Third Month of the First Year of Xianqing and Ending with a Letter of Gratitude for Emperor's Solicitude Letter for His Illness in the Eleventh Month of the Second Year

On the ninth day of the third month in the spring of the first year of Xianqing (656), the composition of the stele inscription for the Ci'en Monastery was completed by the Emperor with his own hand. Then Xu Jingzong, Minister of the Board of Ceremonies, dispatched a messenger to deliver the composition to the Master; meanwhile, the Court of State Ceremonials sent an official document to the monastery. On the tenth day, the Master led the monks of the monastery coming to the royal palace to express their gratitude by submitting a letter that reads:

I, *Śramaṇa* Xuanzang, beg to state:

I have received the document from the Court of State Ceremonials. I bow to accept your imperial notice to the effect that Your Majesty condescendingly took up your sacred ink brush to write the inscription for the Ci'en Monastery and have completed it now. With the advent of monarchical grace and under the inspiration of the imperial words, the door to the mystical Way becomes much loftier and the Buddhist monks are thus greatly glorified. Looking down on the fertile soil, we are ashamed of our mediocrity, and looking up to the firmament, we feel abashed at our incompetence. I have heard that the merit of Creator is to multiply the creatures and have them educated, and that the Way of saints is to demonstrate the sentiments by employing the language. Yet to draw the sixty-four hexagrams or coin the words is nothing but the vain talk about materialistic world; to set each component *yao* to symbolize different situation also could go nowhere beyond the phenomenal world. The virtues of Fuxi[1] were extolled in former times and the noble integrity of Ji[2] stood above the later generations, which, however, are of trifling importance in comparison with the following deeds: carrying out various enterprises by following the inmost doctrines of things, elucidating the Eight Considerations of the Governance[3] by refined words, expounding the Way by composing treatises, and leading the mortals to attain the Three Insights[4], etc. Actually, the doctrines embodied in thy writing proclaim everything under Heaven; the sentiments expressed by it are more brilliant than the sun and the moon. Ranking the superiority, this composition is the best of all.

Humbly I believe that Your Majesty, as powerful as Cakravartīrāja, is swaying over the empire and bringing the nation into its prosperous fortune. You are perfected in virtue as a sage and great in achievements as a deity, overflowing your edification to the four continents[5] and extending benevolence to the Nine Realms[6]. Your many aptitudes were evinced at birth and your great intelligence was bestowed by Heaven. Grieving at the sight of the dressing mirror of your deceased mother, you have had a monastery constructed to commemorate her. As soon as the lofty banners were erected, a stele inscription of beautiful rhythm was completed, whose gentler diction is resembling the blossoming heavenly flowers, and whose witty words are surging like waves on sea. Swallowing up a sea of ink, your writing brush expresses ideas brewed in the Dragon Palace[7]; and pouring out a river of characters, your writing washes sentient beings in the bequeathed teachings from the Crane Grove[8]. Abstruse and canonical, comprehensive and compact, your composition covers eight Buddhist Piṭakas[9] as well as six Chinese Classics[10]. The relics of the Jetavana Garden are thus elevated higher in importance due to your valuable thoughts and the remnant fragrance of Vārāṇasī Park keeps lingering because of the circulation of your refined writing. Far from being merely showing the way to those who go astray by exposing at length the rises and falls of the dreamlike life, this composition disciplines all beings in the four quarters under Heaven and gives guidance to all within the Three Realms[11].

Despite that my words and deeds are of little significance, I have still been honored as a member of monastic community; notwithstanding my humble position, I have been granted by Your Majesty with gracious regards time and again, which makes me lost in exclaiming over my good fortune. I, on the one hand, feel uneasy for not being qualified to have I received the teachings from Kanyākubja (city), yet on the other hand, I rejoice in having been born in this prosperous time of the Image Period of Buddhism[12]. I am ashamed and delighted at the same time. In my heart the two feelings are intermixed. With the sincerity and deep gratitude, I have come to the Imperial Court to present this letter of thanks.

On the eleventh day, again the Master thought to himself: bestowed by Heaven with intelligence and literary talent, the Sovereign was sagacious and versatile; his literary works were no less elegant than those of the rulers of Wei[13], and his calligraphic art exceeded that of the lord of Han[14]; now that his essay would be graved on the stele, why not ask him to take up his divine brush to write the characters for the stele inscription? With this idea, the Master went to the palace to present a letter to the Emperor, entreating him to write the inscription with his own hand, which runs as follows:

I, *Śramaṇa* Xuanzang and others beg to state:

Respectfully we think that the unfathomable force demonstrates itself by taking transformations to correspond to different circumstances. How tremendous! How comprehensive! Being substantial and all-embracing, the most meritorious deed of an emperor is to give edification to the masses whenever they are in need. As we know, only when the sun and the moon are both clear and bright can the course of universe be wholly set in motion; and not until grass and trees are growing exuberantly is their virtuous duty of decorating the earth utterly fulfilled. So, we humbly believe that because of your intelligence that has been applied to a myriad of things and of your benevolence that has been displayed throughout the Three Realm, the great teachings of Buddhism thus have been respected widely and its abstruse doctrines elucidated extensively. It seems contemptible that the King Mu of the Zhou[15], though was fond of the Way, still failed to keep the appointment made in the decorous exchange of poems with Queen Mother of the West when he was appreciating the lyric at the Lake Yao, and that the Emperor Ming of the Han Dynasty, though showed veneration to the Dharma, did nothing else but constructed the White Horse Temple[16]; on the contrary, Your Majesty not only condescended to compose this holy essay but also permitted it to be engraved on the fine jade (stele) to spread the abstruse doctrines widely and to moralize the posterity. The essay reads as melodiously rhythmical as the antique music Liuying[17], and it also bears profound thoughts as brilliant as the glaring light emitted from the five constellations. Having changed secular conventions through the utmost sincerity, and fulfilled the Buddha's great oath by rectifying the decadent age, what you have done even surpassed the disclosure of the true Suchness or revelation of the abstruse profundity! Now the essay has already been completed and is yet to be inscribed on a refined slab, why not pick up your divine writing-brush again to leave your holy calligraphic art forever?

When the elegant music in ancestral shrine is performed by the ensemble beating of drums, chimes, and bells mounting on rack *sun*, vulgar songs are disqualified to be sung in chorus; once the dawn falls on the dragon land[18], what torch could give more light? If a man lacks a personality as accomplished as two superb musician (Bo) Ya[19] and (Shi) Kuang[20], or if he is not as powerful as Deity of Sun Xi He , who is controlling Sun chariot masterly, how is he able to beat the drum of Dharma resonantly and to add the resplendent hues to the Sun of wisdom? We call up our courage to supplicate Your Majesty to grant us a great favor by taking up your divine ink brush to make your fine work of calligraphy for the stele inscription; thereby, you will not only get the upper hand over the ancestral emperors for your turns of the brush, but also distinguish yourself from the sagacious monarchs of the following generations for your reputable styles and techniques. Your jade-precious writing-brush will utter resounding voices, by which the ignorant masses would be enlightened; and your marvelous strokes, like a phoenix flying and a dragon coiling, will blaze open the eyes of the blind. Consequently, the teachings of Buddha could be brought into such a prosperity in this Image Period that sentient beings would be made to submerge in the loving-kindness; what's more, the compliments on the peace and prosperity of the present age expressed by your writing would also maintain the imperial lineage in bliss forever.

Without measurable talent, I am short in vision, but fortunate enough to become a member of the monastic order, which makes me feel very grateful. Feeling embarrassed that I have had a shallow knowledge of Buddhism and not been so well-disciplined in vinaya, I do not think I deserve your praises and encouragements. Scrupulous and awesome at the favors you have granted to me so often, nowhere could I find to conceal my shame. Having brewed my sincerity and eagerness for a long time, I call up my courage in earnest and expect you to grant my request once more.

Now I venture to give you disturbance again, which indeed makes me tremble with fear, feeling like walking on the thin ice or the burning charcoal.

The entreaty was declined. On the twelfth day, the Master submitted a petition again, which reads:

Yesterday with a great pleasure I received the reply from Your Majesty, not giving consent to my request. Nevertheless, I still bear the extravagant hope of being favored by the imperial handwriting. I presume that a tree could be perfumed when the magnolia climbing on it is in full blossom, and that when kneeling at the precious jade stairway of the royal palace, one should have a chance to be honored with a favor endowed from the lord. I humbly consider that Your Majesty is ruling with impartiality and clean politics, governing the state with noninterference, and bringing the peace to the land. In addition, endowed with perspicacity and literary capacity, Your Majesty demonstrates your versatility whenever concentrating your mind. The grand program of administration[21] was conspicuously promoted on the riverside of Luo, and the excellent calligrapher of cursive style[22] attained excellence because of the diligent practices at inkstand. On the one hand, I received the previous favor bestowed by Your Majesty with great care as if I were holding the image of the of Ruomu[23] flower reflected in a gold mirror; on the other hand, I venture to look forward to your further kindness earnestly like watching for the shadow of osmanthus tree[24] on the silver moon. Just as two pieces of split jade await to be joined together, and as the light we admire should be issued from both the sun and the moon, so your brilliant composition would be promulgated with the assistance of your divine handwriting. Only by a combination could its indescribable subtlety be finally revealed. I touch the ground with my forehead, although bearing an aspiration, I still dare not to entertain high hopes in this regard. Regardless of being offensive, I submit this request at the risk of my humble life.

At the request of this petition did the Emperor begin to write with his holy ink brush, at which the Master's pleasure was beyond expression, so he wrote another letter to extend his gratitude, saying:

I, *Śramaṇa* Xuanzang, with due respect to Your Majesty, beg to state:

I have received your edict granting the honor to me by promising to scribe the composition for the stele of the Great Ci'en Monastery with your own hands. Hardly had the edict which is stamped with the Imperial Seal arrived when Your Majesty's profuse benevolence began to heap up on me; feeling so ashamed of my unworthiness that I fell into a complete loss. I have heard that when a strong crossbow is drawn full, a flying squirrel is unable to pull its trigger; when a resounding bell is in silence, a slender stem of herb cannot ring it again. I had never thought that your kindness, like the aureole of the sun and the moon, would come down to the Gate of Emptiness, and that your favor would fall on the monastery like the rain moistening the earth. For all those I wished, yet I dare not to seek after.

I humbly believe that, born with auspicious omens, grasping the credential of Heavenly Command, Your Majesty succeeded to the Throne. In meritorious achievements you equal Emperor Xuanyuan[25] and exceed Emperor Zhuanxu[26], and with greater momentum, your governance overwhelms the Xia and Yin dynasties. Your Majesty has elucidated various wonderful teachings to educate the people in this age, and you are versatile and talented enough to bring prosperity to the mundane world, so that the populace within the country are bathing in your benevolence, and the peoples outside obtain benefits from your wonderful edification.

The Dharma, however, a bridge as well as a ferry to cross the sea of suffering, could not be traced back to its source if not being elucidated by supreme saints; the hidden assistance of divinities could only be manifested by a man who is but a perfect sage. Only when an aspiration reaches to its earnest could Heaven be touched, correspondingly, the divine blessing could be prayed for, and that is why the grace of Your Majesty descends on me. The splendid composition that Your Majesty has deigned to write is much more precious than the rare treasures, and your exceptional calligraphy, after being circulated around, is sure to outshine the priceless valuables. All living beings will be grateful and joyous, particularly in double will be the exultation of the Buddhist monks. Even the beautiful music performed in the celestial palace is not supposed to be as rhythmical as your composition. Compared with your writing, the topknot pearl of the Wheel-turning King could not be more valuable, could it? It would be engraved on a durable slab which is to be planted in the temple's blissful courtyard. At the very sight of it, the ignorant and the deluded will open their eyes and their ears; by it, the brilliant torch of Dharma will be relayed down to the future generations. If the people could read the precious composition with reverence and truly appreciate your refined calligraphy, they would surely develop the Bodhi mind; if they recite the powerful words to explore the abstruse, they would thus obtain the Prajñā. After many kalpas innumerable as mustard seeds, the brilliant beauty of this composition will still be visible; even after oceans are transformed into fields, your graceful style will not perish at all.

I am mediocre, and always feel uneasy about what I have practiced. When I was greatly honored to be ordained as a monk, I was determined to expound the abstruse doctrines of Buddhism; later, by relying on the imperial prestige I was able to visit Kapilavastu[27]and other places; as soon as I returned, I set out to do translation; thereafter, undeservedly I received the imperial encouragements persistently. I was bathing in the generous kindness during the Zhenguan period (627–649), and since the Younghui period (650–655), I have been privileged even more immensely. I have received praises poured from the divine brushes of the late emperor and Your Majesty; what's more, I have even gotten the customized writings from you, two generous sovereigns. In view of my stupidity and inferiority, I am full of embarrassment and uneasiness. From daybreak to nightfall, I am totally preoccupied by a sincere eagerness to requite the kindness of you two monarchs. However, your kindness is as deep as the huge pool while my repayment whatsoever is just like a drop of water, so what difference can a drop make in the pool? The favors heaped up to me are as high as the majestic mountain, so it is impossible for my gratitude, small as a grain of dust, to repay the debt of kindness that I owe you. Therefore, all I should do is to resort to prajna and employ it indefinitely and expediently in order to augment the blessedness and protection bestowed on the empire by the Imperial Ancestral Temple, making the Tang as long as the Zhou Ddynasty[28], and even much longer. With extreme fear and respect, I wrote this gratitude letter and asked Palace Attendant Wang Junde to submit it to Your Majesty. Offending your august prestige unscrupulously, I am crouching with trembling and trepidation.

On the eighth day of the fourth month in the summer, the inscription written by the Emperor himself was engraved on the slab by craftsmen, which was about to be sent to the monastery. With gratitude for the Emperor's generosity, the Master made a good preparation for the reception. Having richly-ornamented pennants, canopies, curtains and streamers well arranged on the roadsides and flowers strewn, he led his monk disciples of the Ci'en Monastery as well as other monks and nuns in the capital to come to Fanglin Gate to receive the stele which bore the inscription. Also here came an imperial decree ordering the musicians of the nine bands of the Board of Rites and orchestras of Chang'an and Wannian counties to perform music in the delivery procession. Among more than three hundred pieces of ceremonial articles, even the lowest canopy seemed high above the clouds and the shortest pennant fluttered as if into the sky. The very carriages for musicians were over one hundred in total. Proceeding seven days, they all assembled at the Anfu Gate Street in the western corner of Chang'an City. At the night, it rained, which made the following day inconvenienced; then another imperial decree came, ordering the processions to stay where they were and wait for the further instruction; meanwhile the Master had to come back to the monastery. Then two days later, it turned fine and clear. A new imperial decree came requiring the arrangements to be laid out as before. On the morning of the fourteenth day, canopies, streamers and other things were again lined up, extending for thirty *li*, picturesquely replenishing the road from Fanglin Gate to the Ci'en Monastery. Ascending the tower-arch of Anfu Gate, the Emperor was pleased with the sight below. There were over one million men and women in the capital witnessing the scene. On the fifteenth day, seven men were ordained to be monks and an alms feat for two thousand monks was set out, with the nine bands of the Board of Rites and other orchestras together performing music in front of the Buddha Hall. Not until the night fell did the people disperse. On the sixteenth day, the Master, leading his disciples, came to the imperial court to extend his gratitude for sending the stele to the monastery. The letter of thanks was presented to the Emperor, which reads as follows:

> I, *Śramaṇa* Xuanzang and others beg to state:
>
> On the fourteenth day of this month, we deferentially received Your Majesty's decree sending the stele bearing the imperial inscription to the Great Ci'en Monastery, accompanied by the music performed by the nine bands. At this time as peaceful and prosperous as that of Yao and Shun, the sun and the moon throw their light, intensifying the brightness of the torch of wisdom, and the vast sea surges waves, replenishing the broad river of Dharma. Standing as an immortal monument, the high-rising stele is bearing the divine writing that is splendid as the glaring candlelight. Its rich thoughts resemble the colorful clouds shining in the morning upon Gṛdhrakūṭa Mountain and

its words the numerous stars shining above the celestial peaks. Both laypeople and clerics, like rolling-forward clouds impelled by lightning, are rushing to appreciate it, all gasping in admiration at its rarity. Looking back at the history, the Eight Trigrams[29] bequeathed the written teachings to the subsequent generations, and the elucidations of six *yaos* made up the appended texts of the *Book of Changes*; the movements of birds inspired the invention of Chinese characters and weeping over a Kylin caught, Confucius stopped writing the *Spring and Autumn Annals*[30], Nevertheless, he left his masterpieces to us. In my opinion, all of them remind the world of the accomplishments made by the ancient saints who, besides, instructed the contemporaries expediently and exemplified the posterity, moralized the living beings and encouraged their virtuous demeanor. The sacrificial ritual to Heaven[31] held by the First Emperor of Qin (259–210 B.C.) is commemorated in stone carvings, and the exploits of the emperor of Wei[32]are documented on the stele Daxiang, which made them esteemed and praised, preeminent above other rulers. Nevertheless, they still could not be compared with Your Majesty because you yourself composed this divine essay, and displayed your artistic brushwork as well. Your masterpiece reads as rhythmical as the refined tune played at the ancestral temple and your powerful strokes leaves gorgeous traces in the calligraphy history. Pursuing the truth obtained from the Dragon Palace, your composition surpasses the teachings embodied in the *Zhuangzi*, the *Laozi* and the *Changes*; exceeding the calligraphic art of ancient times, your brushwork shows its excellence in the eight styles of characters[33]. Riding on the surging waves of spring water, your thoughts are on wings; like the autumn dew dripping in good time, the profound theory thus is transmitted far and wide. By propagating the subtle theory of the One Vehicle (Ekayāna) and by praising the abstruseness of Six Pāramitā, your edification has spread all over the Three Thousand Worlds and your prestige has reached the other side of a hundred *Koṭis* Sumeru mountains. The subtle teachings bequeathed from Vārāṇasī have been manifested ever more clearly by the divine words of Your Majesty; and the bodhisattvas in the bamboo grove have also become more distinguished under your divine brush. Consequently, having broken their nets of doubt, the heretical and heterodox retracted from the wrong path and resumed the Buddha's instruction; having his worries eliminated, even the demon god Papiyas demolished the mountain of deviant knowledge and took the Buddhist truth. People in the mundane world are awaken too, staying out of the erroneous way and escaping delusive dreams; they began to liberate themselves from sufferings by practicing self-cultivation. Since the teachings of Image Period arrived in the Eastern land, six hundred years have already passed, and the propagation of Buddhism has never been so prosperous as it is at present. In the past, when the Emperor Ming of the Han Dynasty got a dream, he felt it necessary to consult Fuyi

(?–about 90)[34] about the omen in it; when King of Wu State (182–252) was about to covert to Buddhism, he had to settle his doubts by conferring with Kan Ze (about 170–243)[35]. However, from that time on, nothing else of the kind has been worthy to be mentioned. Better than those rulers, Your Majesty has given edification skillfully according to various circumstances and thus the fortune of the country is sure to be greatly promoted. As the wholesome deeds must be rewarded with good retribution, so the consolidation of the empire foundation is sure to be attributed to Your Majesty. Resembling the King of the Golden Wheel, you have governed the country with distinction, making achievements which are beyond measurement; the same as the celestial Emperor of the Precious Crown, you will preserve your throne forever.

Xuanzang and other monks don't deserve the imperial graciousness. With a great fortune, we have staged on the Bodhi platform, so we hope to spread the clouds of compassion and strike the dharma drum once more, to revitalize the teachings of Triratna[36] and pave the Eightfold Noble Path permanently; however, when looking back to the past, our devotion and endeavor seemed to be very insufficient. So facing your instructions and praises, we felt verily embarrassed and abashed. Looking up to the firmament, we contemplate on the grace conferred from Your Majesty, and staring down into the deep ravine, we feel ashamed of what we have done. With the great sincerity to extend our deep gratitude, we come to the Imperial Court to express our thanks by presenting this letter.

On the arrival of the stele, the official in charge ordered a separate chamber to be built for its placement at the northeast corner in front of the Buddha Hall. The chamber was constructed and furnished as the pagoda for Buddha's relics. It had double-arched roofs supported by overlapping beams, clouds-patterned lintels, and colorfully decorated ridgepoles, with golden flowers shining upwards and high-hanging bells issuing light downwards, with a relief sculpture of immortals holding plates for the celestial dew.

What calligraphy the Emperor was adept at were Regular Script, Official Script, Cursive Writing and Freehand Cursive, especially the style of "flying white." The characters of the composition inscribed on the slab were of Freehand Cursive style whereas the four characters indicating the reign title "Xian Qing Yuan Nian" were of "flying white" style, which indeed exhausted the wondrous exquisiteness of handwriting art. The people rushing to appreciate it amounted to several thousand every day. Only those civil and military officials above the third rank were permitted to make rubbings. In the far distant past, after abandoning the old method of recording affairs by knotting the rope, ancients used the written characters as a substitute. Seal Script has been classified into the Small Seal and the Large Seal, while the Regular Script and Cursive Style could be distinguished by their running tendencies of strokes. The writing brush is dexterously controlled to produce the various styles, such as "hanging needle," "dropping dew" "cloudy vapor" "tinny ripples" "style of inscription on metal vessels" and the "service style", which is also known as the "running clerical style," with characters eight *fen* square, for writing official documents. The forerunners, each of them, though grasping a particular skill, still being incapable of mastering all styles. For instance, Emperor Yuan (74–33B.C.)[37] of the Han was good at writing the Clerical style for recording history; Emperor Wu of Wei (155–220)[38] was expert at the Cursive and Running (Freehand Cursive) styles; Zhong You (151–230) was skilled in three styles[39]; Wang Zhong[40] was at home in writing eight-fen-square characters; Liu Shao (Born between168–172 and died between 240–249) and Zhang Hong of the Wei Jin dynasties (220–420) were famous for "flying white " style; and Boying (?–about 192) and Ziyu (77–142)[41] won their names as "sages of Cursive Writing." Although Wang Xianzhi (303–361 or 321–379), Chief of the Imperial Secretariat, and Wang Xizhi (344–386), Right Army Commander, made themselves masters of more than one beautiful style, they still failed to be adept at the rest styles. That is why when Wei Wenxiu (of the Jin Dynasty) saw two Wangs' handwriting, he commented, "Although two Wangs are commonly regarded as experts of calligraphy, they are still far from knowing calligraphic art." In terms of the elegance and sharpness of strokes as well as the vigor revealed by the structures of characters, the Emperor was indeed matchless, for he was acquainted with various styles of the ancient calligraphists, even more versatile than the precedent saints. Since His Majesty's handwriting was exceptionally brilliant and his literary ability was extraordinary outstanding, he is truly worthy of his name.

Because the Master studied too hard in his youth and because he trudged up the icy and snowy mountains on his westbound journey, he developed a sort of cold illness. Every time he was attacked by it, he felt clogged in chest, which made him suffer. Over the past few years, solely by relying on the medicines was his life spared from the danger. In the fifth month of this summer, for incautiously seeking coolness in the hot weather, he succumbed again to the old disease and was approaching to the last moment of his life, at which both the laypersons and monks were greatly worried. Having heard about it, the Imperial Secretary made a report to the Emperor. Then the Emperor issued an order assigning an experienced imperial physician, Jiang Xiaozhang, and an acupuncturist, Shangguan Cong, to attend upon the Master. All the required medicines were supplied from the palace. Several Imperial Guards were sent as correspondents who were supposed to take shifts several times each day to make inquires of the physical condition of the Master and then report to the Emperor. Even the sleeping quarters of the Master were arranged by adroit attendants dispatched from the inner court. The Master was so highly cherished by the Emperor that even the affection of a loving father toward his single son was no stronger than it. Xiaozhang and others kept attending to the Master and treating him with effective medicines day and night; consequently, after five days, he recovered, which made people both inside and outside the palace finally breathed again. For having received the gracious kindness from the Emperor like this, the Master presented a letter on the following day to express his gratitude, which reads:

I, *Śramaṇa* Xuanzang, beg to state:

I was so inept to take care of my physical body that my cold disease was aggravated, which even made me rest near death, almost depart this age of prosperity. Fortunately, Your Majesty bestowed mercy on me, and compassionately sent experienced physicians to treat me. As soon as the acupuncture needle and medicine were applied, I began to drag out my feeble existence and restore vigor from my worsening condition. I recovered so well that now I count myself fortunate to see this thriving age again and follow your wise instruction once more, which to me, is far more significant than the permanent elimination of my disease. Examining myself, I am mediocre and humble, but I have been granted with such special favors from Your Majesty for so many times. Despite my insignificance, I have received generous kindness from you, which I don't know how to requite, so I think what I shall do is to rely on the Power of Wisdom to requite your deep benefaction extensively. I am still weak and weary, and not able to come to the palace to extend my gratitude to you face to face. With much fear and respect, I am sending my disciple Mahāyānaprabha[42] to present this letter to your Presence.

After reading the letter, the Emperor dispatched the palace attendant Wang Junde to console the Master by saying, "It is quite natural that you still feel feeble after taking medicines. May Your Reverence take good care of yourself. You should know better not to exert yourself [to the translation] too soon." Receiving this consolation from the Emperor, the Master was full of delight and awe. Then he presented another letter of gratitude to the Emperor, which reads:

I, *Śramaṇa* Xuanzang, beg to state:

I was afflicted by the disease brought about by my karma accumulated in the past existences. In an instant of breath, I nearly departed the age of prosperity. Beyond my expectation, the Emperor and the Empress condescendingly showed a lot of compassionate concern on me by sending imperial messengers to console me even more than ten times. My life was finally saved by your divine medicines, of which even by taking one pill I was effectively treated. Bathing in your holy benevolence, I have been truly relieved from bitterness and suffering; after medical treatment, I regain my health at present. I had never anticipated that my dispersing spirit would be called back by Your Supreme Emperor, and that my living-out lifespan could be prolonged in this mortal world. When looking at myself, I often wonder, mediocre and humble as I am, how could I deserve so many privileges? Thumping my chest in deep abashment, I am totally lost in finding words to express my feeling. The extraordinary grace I have received from you is so inexhaustible that it seems insufficient for me to requite your kindness even by smashing my insignificant body into pieces. So, all I could do is to do my utmost to worship the Buddha and recite the scriptures, because only by doing so with the exertion of all my mind and strength am I surely able to requite your exceptional kindness, and only by doing so could I breathe again, relieving my endless self-accusation. Respectfully, I am submitting this letter to extend my gratitude to Your Majesty. Full of joy and awe, I am indeed lost in what to do. I'm afraid my letter presented here is like a defilement to your eyes, and at the thought of this, I developed much more trepidation and shudder.

In the eleventh year of Zhenguan (637), an imperial edict was issued, saying, "Laozi is our forefather, so his name and titles should be placed before those of the Buddha." Then, Fachang, a monk of Puguang Monastery, and Puying, a monk of Zongchi Monastery, and several hundred others gathered at the court to express a protest, but in vain. In fact, after the Master came back from India, he repetitively presented petitions on this issue. The Emperor Wen[43] promised to have a debate held on it but he passed away before the debate. In the sixth year of Yonghui (655), another imperial edict was issued to the effect that if a Buddhist monk or a Daoist priest who was suspected to have committed crimes, he could be interrogated under the secular judicial procedure. Actually, the officials in remote regions misread the intent of the edict whatsoever, so the suspect priests were afflicted and mortified with unscrupulous application of cangue and cudgel, for the law case, be it grave or minor. This made the Master worried very much. The Master feared that he might not be able to serve the incumbent Emperor long because of his illness, so he asked someone to bring a petition to the Emperor on the two issues mentioned above, pointing out detrimental results which might be brought out, and intentionally wound up the petition by saying, "I might die at any moment, so I'm afraid that I would not have a later chance to meet Your Majesty, so I give you this advice sincerely. Now leaning upon my pillow, I am full of fear and trepidation."

Then a messenger came back with a reply from the Emperor, saying, "We have already known what you stated in the petition. The position of Buddhism and Daoism were designated by the preceding emperors, it is hard to change; however, we might as well deliberate over this matter later. As to the edict about the application of the secular judicial procedure to monastic priests, it will be abolished. The Master should be rest assured. Please take some medicine for your own good."

On the twenty-third day, an edict was issued, saying: "Daoist teachings are characterized by serenity and nonactivity while the Buddhist scriptures by abstruseness and subtlety. Both serve as bridges and ferries for living beings to cross the sea of suffering, so win the admiration from the Three Realms. However, nowadays the Dharma begins to fall into decay and human beings thus become degenerated, as a result, the stipulations and laws are too often violated, which make it necessary to employ the jurisdiction expediently to mete out punishment as admonition. It is not intended to disparage the Dharma by placing the secular jurisdiction above it, but to prevent people from doing evil and encourage them to be good. Now that the ordained have their own disciplinary rules, they should know how to regulate their behaviors, and if again they are subjected to another additional legal system, we are truly afraid that would cause a lot of troubles and anguish, so the former edict that puts Daoist priests and priestesses as well as Buddhist monks and nuns under the secular jurisdiction will be abolished. Henceforth if they commit any offense, they should be dealt with by their monastic rules and regulations."

Receiving this great grace from the Emperor, the Master

submitted a letter to extend his gratitude, which reads:

I, *Śramaṇa* Xuanzang, beg to state:

With great veneration I have received the imperial decree to the effect that the traditional monastic stipulations, rather than the secular penal code, would be applied to monks and nuns who might commit offense. Suddenly, the unexpected privilege fell on Buddhists and the enormous grace descended on the religious establishment again. How wonderful it is that we are bathing not only in the imperial grace but also the effulgent light of the Way! I bent my back to kowtow, in reverence and awe, feeling excited. I humbly believe that after the Dharma Lord attained nirvāṇa, His edification has been transmitted down into this Dharma-image age, in which the wise rulers of successive generations are those whom we should rely on to preserve monastic regulations. Your Majesty ascended the throne with the Imperial Seal representing the mandate of Heaven, and a King of the Golden Wheel, you are practicing the right way of governing. Showing a preference for the teachings of Śākyamuni Buddha, you have always been preoccupied with how to make them publicized and elucidated well, and for this reason, you have highly valued those who took off the ornaments to enter the Door to Abstruse Dharma, and treated monks differently from the mundane persons. Even when a monastic priest submerges in the Five Turbidities[44] or infringes disciplines, Your Majesty makes allowance for him just because he is donning the three garments[45] therein lies the field of blessedness. By doing so, you have cut open the dense net of the law to bestow much leniency and benevolence on Buddhist monks and nuns; articulating the fair words from your golden mouth, you have transferred your merits thus obtained to all sentient beings. Deities are so delighted that they respond by showing auspicious omens; the monastic orders, cherishing the grace, strengthen their resolve to follow the Way much more firmly and constantly. If there is a monk who ignores this absolution, he is to incur calamity upon himself, because he not only violates monastic disciplines established by the Buddha, our great teacher, but also defiles the profound kindness of Your Majesty, our saintly monarch. And when the wise deities are justified to reprimand and punish him, there seems to be no need to wait for the punishment to be meted out by the impartial national laws. Mediocre and stupid as I am, it is very fortunate for me to be on the path of Dharma. Every time the generous grace was granted to me, I was feeling embarrassed and fearful. This time Your Majesty bestowed benevolence upon me again, which made me fall in more awe and uneasiness. But as I have been ill lately, I could not pay you a visit at the palace by convention, so with much fear and respect, I am sending my disciple Mahāyānaprabha to present this letter to your Presence.

Thereafter, monks and nuns began to set their mind at practicing meditation and reciting scriptures. Seeing this, the Master was overwhelmed by a mixed feeling of grief and joy, unable to restrain himself from shedding tears, even wetting his sleeves and the front of his garment, yet at the same time being uplifted by the great joy and encouragement. Then he presented another letter to the Emperor, saying:

I, *Śramaṇa* Xuanzang, beg to state:

I, with veneration, have received Your Majesty's edict canceling the law article which was to apply the secular legal procedure to monk suspects, which fills my heart with so much gratitude and joy that I don't know how to express. Humbly I believe, it is the monarch who determines the prosperity or decline of the right Dharma by promoting or suppressing it, and the ruler who manipulates the adequacy or deficiency of ethical codes by performing the nonactivity at different extents. Since Your Majesty followed your heaven-bestowed fortune to be an emperor, you have employed your pure and bright wisdom to discern the Way from Six Arts[46], and distinguish Buddhism from Confucianism; thereby the bolt of the door of non-dualism was opened and the path for one vehicle was widely paved. In the Secretary Department of the capital, you are propagating the teachings preached at the Dragon Palace[47] and the Vulture Peak, and throughout the land of our country you are transmitting the sounds of bells and the chanting from the temples. What you have done is intended to bring happiness and goodness to the masses so to cleanse their karma. It is an auspicious time for the dharma door and it is a good fortune for the whole empire! Not long ago, the monastic community deserved the blame for its managerial incompetence and inappropriate instruction. Some undisciplined monks not only deteriorated the Buddha's teachings but also violated the national legislation, so much so that an individual committed an offense, all the rest suffered shame. The majestic authority of the Emperor was so offended that the secular penal code was thus ordered to be applied to the monks, intending to eliminate the illegal by punishment and admonition. All the monks were shocked and horrified, entangled in shame and fear day and night. You, however, with the discernment superb as a heavenly being, were inclined to display your benevolence all around; and in addition, since you are holding a firm belief and confidence in the abstruse teachings of Buddha, you decided to conceal the filth by your generous forbearance; finally, you have bestowed the special grace to attenuate the severe punishment, not because the offender deserves the mercy but because the dignity of the Dharma should be taken into account with reverence. Thereby, the fish in the net are set free to swim again in the Chang and Han rivers and the birds in the cage are released to soar up once more in the vast sky; the turbidity of dharma water is cleansed and the barren blessedness field is turned to be fertile. Monks are feeling deeply grateful for your kindness. Encouraged, they resolved in earnest to remove the unwholesome so as to live up to your expectations on them. Wholeheartedly worshiping the Buddha and single-mindedly reciting scriptures, they will surely requite the utmost kindness of Your Majesty. Respectfully I think that the Emperor and the Empress will enjoy abundance of happiness forever for you have achieved great exploits by ensuring the uninterrupted continuity of the heritage of the Three Jewels, and that, by displaying infinite compassion, you also will bestow peace and welfare on the numerous generations in the future. An empire of prosperity and auspiciousness, China now is as beautiful as Kapilavastu[48]. Jumping and dancing with great joy, I am feeling extremely grateful. So, I am writting this letter to extend my gratitude. If there is, any offence to Your Majesty, I would feel more fearful and uneasy.

The Emperor read the letter and knew that the Master had been recovered. Then he dispatched messengers to welcome the Master into the palace, settling him in the western pavilion in the court of the Ningyin Palace to receive offerings. There the Master was devoted to his translation and went out once after every twenty or thirty days.

In the tenth month of this winter, the confinement of the Empress was approaching, thus she took refuge in the Triple Gem and prayed for the blessing from divine power. The Master told the Emperor, "The holy body of Her Majesty will be in good condition, suffering no pain at child-birth. The infant shall be a boy. After it is born safely, please let it be ordained at the monastery. Please grant me the permission." On the fifth day of the eleventh month[49], the Empress offered the Master with a Kāṣāya and many other articles, totally several tens of them in number, for which the Master wrote a letter to express his thanks, which runs as follows:

I, *Śramaṇa* Xuanzang, beg to state:

With great excitement and uneasiness I have received the Kāṣāya and other articles bestowed upon me, which made me totally lost in words. Neither the superior garments sewn by golden threads that have been passed down from preceding worthy gentlemen nor the priceless robes that were mentioned legendarily in sacred texts could be as refined and exquisite in craftsmanship as this one right in front of me. As to the evenly spreading of rich and light shades of color on the silk, the famous painter Jing Jun[50], cannot surpass in the elaboration; as to the delicate needlework of dense sewing, Li Lou[51], the person with an extraordinarily sharp vision, fails to discern the stitches. When I put it on, I felt that the I was captured by the hues of twilight mists in the chamber and that my whole body was perfumed by the fragrance of orchids; turning around and looking at myself, I felt my personal value and dignity were augmented at once. In olden times, Dao'an[52], whose words were greatly valued in the Later Qin Period, was never granted with such a favor, nor was Zhidun (314–366)[53] ever endowed with such a grace, even though he was venerated and complimented by the people in the Jin Dynasty. Only I, Xuanzang, mediocre and shallow-minded, have received such a generous preference from the Emperor and the Empress. Considering the favor bestowed on me meanwhile making a self-examination, I have felt more perspiration and trepidation. With great sincerity, may the

Emperor and the Empress have numerous descendants and enjoy the unlimited happiness forever. May the Emperor and the Empress reign the world with correct and bright administration and preserve the throne perpetually. May you shelter and nurture living beings as permanently as heaven does. With extreme shame and reverence, I am writing this letter to extend my gratitude to your Presence. Your gifts are generous whereas my words are slight, so it's such a pity that my thanks cannot be suffice to express to the Emperor and the Empress.

After the time of *shen* (3–5 P.M.) on the fifth day, a red bird came suddenly and alighted on the imperial tent, at which Xuanzang was greatly delighted, so he wrote a letter of congratulations, saying:

I, *Śramaṇa* Xuanzang, beg to state:

I have heard that a white turtledove cropped up to augur the enthronement of the Yin Emperor (1670–1587 B.C.)[54], and a red bird appeared as a good omen for prosperity of the Zhou Dynasty under the reign of King Wen (1152–1056 B.C.)[55]. From them, we know that it has been a commonplace phenomenon that the Great Heaven descends auspicious signs to denote human accomplishments. After the time of *shen* and before the time of *you* (5–7P.M.), I saw a bird alighting inside the curtain of the courtyard of Xianqing Hall, whose back, abdomen, and feet were covered with red feathers. It came from the south, and after entering the tent, it hopped back and forth in front of the throne of the Emperor in an easy manner. Realizing the bird was extraordinary, I said to it, 'The Empress is in her pregnancy, and yet to deliver, about which I am full of worries and concerns. May you bless the safety of her delivery. If my prayer would be answered, please show me some propitious sign.' Then, obviously knowing my intention, the bird indicated a sign of safety by whirling around and stamping its feet repeatedly. To my heart's full content, I was delighted. Then, I raised my hand to beckon it while walking forward slowly. When I was close to it, it wasn't frightened, and when I stroked it, it wasn't startled. This event was witnessed by men around me. Then, in order to requite its goodwill, I intended to instruct it to take refuge in the Triple Gems. I followed it up and down, but before I could catch it, it flew away.

In my humble opinion, such a rare case happened because the high virtues of the Emperor and the Empress are in communion with deities and spirits. You have bestowed your gracious kindness on the myriads of people, and you have had the propriety perfectly observed and the music melodiously performed within the domain of the empire, and your benevolence is generous and your righteousness influential, all of which thus summoned the tribe of feather to present the auspicious omen and the divine bird to afford service, prophesying that your descendants would be flourishing and your nation enjoy a continuing prosperity for eight hundred years as long as the Zhou Dynasty (c. 1046 BC–256 BC). Obviously, it is a fortunate omen, the divine award bestowed by Heaven, and as in olden times so it could also be witnessed in the contemporary era. I am humble but fortunate enough to have seen such a propitious omen, at which I feel so delighted that I dare not keep silent about it, so I wrote this letter to give a brief report to your Presence. As regards to other pieces of information about its imposing-looking feathers and wings, its masculine dignity, its historical record, and its remote habitat, they are beyond what I know. Stated the above with reverence.

No sooner the letter had been presented to the Emperor than a messenger came to the Master with an imperial edict, saying:

The Empress has finished her parturition and given birth to a boy as you predicated. The baby is endowed with pleasant and handsome features, and when it was born, the courtyard was illuminated by the divine light rising high up into the sky. With boundless delight, the people were dancing with joy within and outside the palace. We will certainly keep our promise. May the Master protect and care for the baby, and name it Buddha Light Lord[56].

Then the Master presented a congratulatory letter, which runs as follows:

I, *Śramaṇa* Xuanzang, beg to state:

I have heard that the ultimate Way displays itself and enlightens human and heavenly beings by divination, and your utmost expectation was finally answered by the delivery of a sagely child, so brilliant and holy. I humbly believe that the Emperor and the Empress possess the wisdom of the Threefold emptiness[57], thus giving instructions to the living beings dwelling in this land, and that being high in the supreme position, you have devoted to the Double Truth[58] and taken the One Vehicle. At the Empress' palace, the moment the good news of giving birth to the prince came, the great vow to attain Bodhi was made; when the sagely boy was still in the womb, the omen of its attainment of the Buddhahood was shown. The Buddha with ten honorable titles bestowed blessings upon the baby out of the great compassion, while numerous deities protected the inner chamber with deep reverence; when sufferings and calamities were cleared away, the boy was born in safety and peace. In the past when the Buddha was born, seven lotus flowers solemnly supported His first steps while nine dragons sprouted down water to bathe His body. At present, the baby is determined to step inside the gate of the Abstruse and it would be sheltered forever under the shade thrown by the Bodhi tree. When [Jiang Yuan[59]] stepped into a footprint left by the supreme deity Shangdi, an auspicious sign was shown for the birth of Hou Ji, which was regarded as an extraordinary response from Heaven, but however spectacular that case is, it is not sufficient to be compared with the present blessing of the Buddha who bestows us a boy of resourcefulness. For the blessings the Emperor and the Empress have gotten from Heaven, the whole empire is resounding with the songs of delight; having known a pony in the dark purple[60] cropped up in the royal family, the monastic community obtained a dauntless courage to peruse the Way. Humbly I wish you will not change your mind and let the boy put on the Dharma robe so that it will get free from the mundane attachments and accumulate wholesome karma for its future lives. Moreover, as a son of the Emperor, his status is majestically high, at the same time, as the lord of Dharma, his position is also dignified and distinguished. He is supposed to achieve boundless merits and serve as the bridge and ferry for the posterity, as long as the Emperor and the Empress' gracious words would be kept unblemished and your great vow could remain unchanged. I believe that even if a man practices Dana by giving away his properties that amount to all treasures in the world, it still could not match the merit you would obtain by offering your Prince to the Sangha. I believe that the wholesome karma accumulated in the Ten Stages of Bodhisattvahood is still not sufficient to cultivate the field of blessedness like this one you would cultivate by offering your Prince to the Sangha. All in all, may the Emperor and the Empress coagulate your hundred blessings into a golden flower illuminating as the North Star! May you enjoy a long life covering a myriad of springs! May your physical bodies be strong as the South Mountain! May you cram your long lives with all entertainments to your hearts' content! May you practice the compassionate actions in the endless *kalpas* to come! May the honest and brilliant Crown Prince inherit and carry forward the enterprises of the Emperor and the Empress! May your favorite subordinates be beneficial in their assistance of governing! Your son in swaddling cloth is sure to be blessed with more fortune day after day! Your son is sure to exemplify royal integrity for the posterity! Your son is sure to leave imprint on the grass seat of monk as a celebrated practitioner! Unexpectedly, I was favored by a good fortune to take shelter in the forbidden palace. Such distinguished status is not due to the exaltation of my virtue, but to the kindness conferred on me by the Emperor and the Empress. I count myself fortunate to witness the inauguration of the nation's heyday as well as the firm foundation newly-laid for the Buddhist undertakings. I felt a tremendous sense of exultation which would not be eliminated even if I should be ground to dust. With extreme jubilation, I present this letter to your Presence in congratulations. Imprudently being offensive to your majestic stateliness, I am trembling with more anxieties.

On the third day after Buddha Light Lord was born, the Master presented another petition, which reads:

I, *Śramaṇa* Xuanzang, beg to state:

To daily improve of one's character is greatly advocated by the *Book of Changes*, and to have numerous offspring is eulogized in the *Book of Songs*; by following those doctrines, the throne of the Zhou Dynasty could be handed down for a long time and prosperity of the Han Dynasty could sustain for centuries. The Yellow River's source is remote and its course long, so at a section named Dragon Gate, the water there whirled and surged turbulently; osmanthus trees take their root deeply into the soil, so they thrive exuberantly with fragrant clouds of flowers. Hence in my humble opinion, thanks to the successive sagely emperors before you, Your Majesty can fulfill your monarchy destiny. Those sagely emperors devised effective methods and convictions for governing the country, displayed benevolence toward the people and well-regulated the nation with righteousness, thus forming an unbroken tradition prevailing over a long time. Emperor Gaozu and Emperor Taizong ascended the throne and laid a sound foundation for descendants; since then, the Tang Dynasty has flourished and surely will keep prosperous forever. It is just like a tree with a deep root, which is able to thrive and like a stream with a remote source, which is able to run a long course. After Your Majesty followed the mandate of Heaven to ascend the throne, meritorious undertakings have been carried out even more magnificently. In terms of the recovery of original-purity and simplicity, you have done better than Three Emperors and Five Monarchs; and in terms of the establishment of proprieties and the promotion of the refined music, you have advanced even further than the emperors of Shang and Zhou Dynasties. Instead of sitting back complacently in the imperial power and paramount authority, you are constantly fretting about the welfare of multitude, working all hours, getting out of your bed before daybreak and usually having your dinner after sunset; consequently, our country with a vast territory is in peace and clearance. Even the prosperity built up by King Cheng and King Kang of the Zhou Dynasty[61] can't match what you have done. Thus, the auspicious clouds of various colors are spreading above, and rivers and seas below serene with no surging waves. The land under the sun is fashioned with Chinese culture, and the hometown of dragon[62] is bathing in your edification. How grandiose and majestic it is! It is difficult to relate by words. How hard it is for a man to come by such a flourishing age! By practicing the Way, you had won the response from Heaven so the deity blessed you with a son delivered on such a propitious day of this propitious month. Celestial tree spreads its branches abundantly, and the imperial family surely is expanding luxuriantly. All living beings within the empire rejoiced at the news, bearing high expectations on the boy. As for me, I am a hundred times happier than others, for what makes me feel delighted is not merely the safety of Her Majesty's delivery, but the Tathāgata has gotten one more successor. Earnestly, I hope the Emperor and the Empress will not withdraw the decree that permits the prince to enter the monastic community, because only by putting on the religious robe, taking a Buddhist name, accepting the Three Refugees and joining the rank of Sangha, will the prince be turned from a descendant of the human king into a successor of the Dharma Lord. The prince surely will renew and promote the Buddhist edification in this Image Period by elucidating and propagating the abstruse teachings. Also, he will revitalize the Buddhist order and encourage it to pursue enlightenment. Following the example of Arhat Pure-Eye (Vimalanetra)[63] and tramping the track of Arhat Moon-Shelter (Candrachattra)[64], he will sever two entanglements[65] and attain Samyak-sambodhi[66]. His physical body will be as sublime as Sumeru and be adorned by aureole brighter than the sun and the moon. In the future, he will shade the great chiliocosm by the clouds of compassion and hold the torch of wisdom to illumine a hundred Koṭis of continents. By striking the Dharma drum to defeat the devils, by brandishing the flag of victory to subdue the heretics, by saving the sinking ship from the turbulent sea, by extinguishing the spreading fire on the evil mountain, by drying up the river of vexations, and by breaking the massive egg brewing ignorance, he, a true regulating hero, will surely become a teacher for beings in both celestial and earthly realms. Sincerely I wish that under the blessings of their grandson, the spirits in the ancestral shrine would ascend the yonder shore (crossing the sea of suffering to achieve nirvāṇa), and that, sharing the glorious fortune of your son, the Emperor and the Empress would live in prosperity and govern the empire long. Only a son like the prince who brings honor to his parents could be said to be filial, which is also the reason why Śākyamuni Buddha renounced his kingdom and took the Bodhi Path. How could the trivial kindness of the Prince of Dongping[67] and the mediocre ability of Chen Si[68] be compared with the boy in the superiority and profundity? Solemnly donning the religious robe and carrying an alms bowl, I am waiting for a Well Come guest[69]; brushing the seat to scrape away the dirt, I have it ready for him taking a carriage coming from the imperial city[70].With extreme veneration and joy, I am looking forward eagerly. I present this letter to your Presence. Being offensive to your majestic authority, I am feeling regretful, trembling more violently with fear.

Without hesitation, the prince was helped to take the Three Refugees and put the Kāṣāya on. He was then protected and cultivated by the Grand Tutor in the palace, yet his dwelling chamber was arranged near to that of the Master. On the fifth day of the twelfth month, when Buddha Light Lord was one month old, an imperial edict was issued ordering seven persons to be ordained for the prince's sake and inviting the Master to shave the head of Buddha Light Lord.

The Master presented a letter of thanks as follows:

I, *Śramaṇa* Xuanzang, beg to state:

Following your gracious edict, yesterday I tonsured the head of Buddha Light Lord and had seven other men ordained as monks. The hair sheaved off from the prince indicates the extinction of his vexations. The seven ordained monks are attendants to serve him. Consequently, the palace of Pāpīyān[71] is shaken, and celestial beings in the pure-dwelling palaces of the fourth Dhyāna Heaven are greatly encouraged. Now that the great vow has been kept so well, the incoming blessings would be much greater. How should my humble mortal hands have had such an opportunity to serve the holy skin? And how lucky those mediocre persons are, who have been honored to enter the Way on such a grand occasion! Both the superiors and inferiors are thus greatly inspired, lost in a mixture of excitement and pleasure. Personally, I believe that the first care should be given to a newborn baby, and the final emancipation begins with the taking off ornaments [to be a monk]. I also think that the spiritual plane of the Emperor and the Empress transcends higher above the mortal world, while the happiness that you bring descends to the mundane world; thus, you are qualified to practice the virtue-cultivation and to open the gate to Abstruse Teachings. May the Throne be blessed with prosperity and the court be held in harmony! May Your Majesty reign over ten billion worlds and your dynasty last for thousands of years!

Apart from being safely guarded by good deities and well breast-fed, Buddha Light Lord, your extraordinary son, is also blessed by buddhas who compassionately putting their hands on his head[72], so his gracious demeanor would be improved and he would be made of a man with perspicacity and profundity to inherit and carry forward the undertakings of Buddha. Those newly-ordained monks, having already been granted with the deep grace from the Emperor, should resume the path of Way earnestly and devote themselves wholeheartedly to observing precepts and cultivat themselves, only by doing so could they requite your goodness. Full of gratitude and respect, I am submitting this letter to your Presence.

On that day the Master congratulated again on the full-month of Buddha Light Lord. Together with a religious robe and other items as gifts, he submitted a letter again, which reads:

I, *Śramaṇa* Xuanzang, beg to state:

An eagle needs time to practice how to soar up high against winds; the waning moon becomes bright full again after over ten days, from which we know even those endowed with unusual aptitude or shining in the high sky should renew themselves to display their excellence later. I believe that Buddha Light Lord, with an innate quality of supreme goodness, will generate auspiciousness; manifesting equilibrium and harmony, he will cultivate high virtues. Since the Prince was born of perspicacity and dignity, the spirits in the ancestral shrine have had expectations on him. Both in his sleeping and waking hours he is blessed by Heaven. He is jade-like handsome and graceful in manner, and apparently becomes more charismatic day by day. If it were not for your wisdom brilliant as the sun, for your thoughts cleansed by the dharma stream, for your resolute promotion of the Buddhist teachings, and your generosity to the Buddhist practitioners, how could the Emperor and the Empress have been blessed with the birth of a baby prince who is sucking the milk at ease in swaddling clothes, free from the injury and disaster, and perspicacious at such a young age? Now, as the crescent moon shining before our eyes is bound to be full in the near future, so the prince already having the makings is to be a sage; as the lucky grass *mingjia*[73] sprouts its new stalks during its monthly period of growth, so the prince's eyes pure like lotus flower would become ever brighter. Therefore, the Emperor and the Empress inside the imperial palace are gratified and the masses outside exhilarated. Seven groups of Buddhist believers[74] entrust themselves to the prince and the ministers and ordinary people[75] are waiting for his future instruction. How would he merely become a man who will leave his traces in the historian's book or a prince who is compatible with his distinguished position? It is a great honor to me that I have been generously preferred and protected by the Emperor and the Empress. I dare not to expect to establish a relationship with the prince as one between a teacher and a student, instead, together with him, I desire earnestly to seek Buddhahood. Thus, I venture to present this casket in which there is a one-fascicle copy of the *Prajñāpāramitāhṛdaya Sūtra* inked in gold letters. Besides, there is one copy of the *Story of the Scripture of Requiting Favors,* a Kāṣāya, an incense burner, an incense table, a bathing jug, a reading shelf, a rosary, a monk's staff (Khakkara), and a vessel containing bathing powder, all of which are indispensable religious utensils, being presented to express my pleasure and wishes. I expect those items would be the additional toys for the newly-born boy, to bring blessings to him, to assist him to clear obstacles on his future road and eradicate the evil for his bright prospect. I hope when the good deities see the prince, they will be greatly pleased, hence to strengthen his great vow. What I have offered indiscreetly are just of ordinary use, which makes me indeed apprehensive. May the Emperor and the Empress gain the supreme dignity, and like the North Star surrounded by numerous stars, be helped by wise and competent subordinates! May the Emperor and the Empress' prestige, just like the sun and the moon throwing their light throughout the world, spread far and wide! May the Emperor and the Empress bring the happiness to myriads of people and enjoy a life of ten thousand springs! May the prince, like Bohai sea getting water from all rivers, drain the talented people all around, from whom the best ones could be selected for use! May the royal son be imposing and forceful, driving his chariot galloping around the expansive frontiers! May a thousand buddhas give a benediction to Buddha Light Lord by touching his head so that his physical body would be adorned with the marks of a hundred kinds of good fortune! May his moralization become more articulate day by day, by which he would set up moral standards to rectify the world! With extreme gratitude, I am submitting this letter to your Presence.

In the second month in the spring of the second year (of Xianqing, 657), the Emperor favored the Luoyang Palace with his presence, being accompanied by the Master, together with five monk translators, each of whom was attended by one disciple. All their daily requisites were provided at public expenses. Buddha Light Lord set out before the Emperor, and the Master went together with the prince, while the other monks followed behind. Upon their arrival, they were lodged at the Jicui Palace.

In the fourth month in the summer, the Emperor and his party went to summer resort at the Mingde Palace[76], again with the Master as his companion. The Master was accommodated at Feihua Hall which was bordered by Zao Stream in the south and Luo River in the north. It was once named as Xianren Hall in the Sui Dynasty.

In the fifth month, an imperial edict was issued inviting the Master to return to the Jicui Palace to resume his translation work. Receiving the edict, the Master wrote an application letter for leave, saying:

> I, *Śramaṇa* Xuanzang, beg to state:
>
> It is a great honor for me to have received the imperial edict permitting me to resume my translation work at the Jicui Palace. Looking up to such generous treatment, I greatly appreciate your deep affection for me, but at the thought of being separated from you, I feel extremely depressed and sorrowful. Over a long time, I have been awarded with honor and acclaim from Your Majesty, despite the fact that I had neither achieved great accomplishments nor performed any extraordinarily meritorious deed. In virtues I am inferior to the scholar-officials, but you have granted me with heavy favors over and over again even disregarding the rules of rewarding. When I measure my ability, I feel fearful for my little talent and less learning; nevertheless, I have been safe and sound under your absolution.

Humbly I believe that the Emperor and the Empress are sagely wise, magnanimous and compassionate enough to nourish multitudes, not only meeting their diverse needs but resting every individual in security and serenity. Now separated by the stairway of the palace hall, listening to the tinkling bells of your carriage, I am sentimentally melancholy at the thought of leaving you; however, catching a mere sight of the mountain ridge covered with cogon grass afar where I am going to do my translation, my conviction is suddenly bolstered in my heart that you will live cozily and healthily, so I feel joyfully relaxed again. May the royal family have a long life as if you were taking the Peaches of Immortality[77] ! May the imperial residence be in an everlasting peace! May the sweet fountain at the palace be heat-relieving which gives you a lot of pleasure as if you were cruising in the mythical Jade Pool[78]! May the capital trees in this hot season be cooled by the coming autumn! May the cool wind visit this burning summer soon! When the capital is awaiting your carriage to return on the slab-paved path in fields, I will hold my religious staff standing reverentially in the high forest. Hail long life to you, and willingly I shall attend on you in my numerous lives. With utmost gratitude and affection to you, I am submitting this letter to bide farewell to Your Majesty. For my indiscretion, I am haunted by the alternating feelings frosty as ice and torrid as fire.

When the Master was in the capital, he had already translated the

Abhidharmajñānaprasthāna Śāstra in thirty fascicles but had not yet completed the translation of the *Mahāvibhāṣā Śāstra*. Then an edict came to the Master ordering, "Among the scriptures and treatises which are to be translated, those which haven't had Chinese versions should be translated first, and others already in Chinese should be translated later."

Then the Master submitted a memorial, saying:

> I have heard that even mediocre emperors tried to be the equals of previous sages, and that sacredness of masterpieces must be ascribed to the divine brush of the sagacious monarch. The late Emperor has governed the country by working out the grand programs which will exert seminal influences on the future generations. Enclosing the extensive land as the imperial city, depositing the palm-leaf scriptures in the archives of ancient classics, he has not only specially allotted the places for translation but also condescendingly wrote the preface to the Chinese versions of Buddhist scriptures. Surely what he has done will light the future generations forever and pass his high prestige down for thousands of years! Your Majesty renews the grand mission of forebears and throws your own brilliance even farther and wider; your superb administrative skills are daily improved while you spare no effort to give appreciation and support to those distinguished men. I enjoyed the undeserved favor from Your Majesty, and with great reverence, I often received your wise edicts, to these favors, however, every time stroking my insignificant body in introspection, I could

not help holding my breath with the deep abashment.

The other day in the last month, I received a letter from you to the effect that among the scriptures and treaties to be translated, those without Chinese versions should be translated first whereas others with Chinese versions should be translated later. The *Mahāvibhāṣā Śāstra,* a work in two hundred fascicles, is the exposition of the *Abhidharmajñānaprasthāna Śāstra.* Only a half of it has been previously rendered into Chinese about over one hundred fascicles, in which there are a lot of errors and mistakes, so I have to correct them, even translate it again. Since last autumn, I have already translated more than seventy fascicles, and there are still more than one hundred thirty fascicles yet to be translated. For this treatise is very important, I hope you will permit me to continue to translate it. Among the rest scriptures and treaties, if there are some in abridgment, or have errors and mistakes, I hope you will permit me to translate them too, making them faithful to the holy teachings.

The Emperor granted the Master's request.

At a young age, the Master left Luoyang, which used to be the capital of the Sui Dynasty. Now in the retinue of the Emperor, he got a chance to go back to his hometown to pay a short visit. He went to the old house of his family and inquired about his relatives and old acquaintances, but he found all of them had already died except his elder sister who married into a Zhang family at Yingzhou, and then he sent for her. When they met, they were overwhelmed by both grief and joy. From his sister he knew of the location of his parents' tombs, so he went there in person to hold a memorial ceremony for his departed parents. As a long time slipped away, the tombs were in a state of disrepair. The Master then planned to select another suitable place as the reburial site. Although having this plan on his mind, he dared not to make any arbitrary action. Instead, he submitted a request letter to the Emperor, which runs as follows:

I, *Śramaṇa* Xuanzang, beg to state:

Without Heaven's blessing, I lost my parents at a very young age; what's worse, because of the chaos of the Sui Dynasty, the burial ritual was carelessly carried out in a hurry. Time flies, and more than forty years have passed. Now the tombs have fallen into dilapidation, nearly vanishing from the view. Reminiscing about my deceased parents, I could not check the upsurge of my emotion. Together with my only elder sister, I intended to gather my parents' remains and carry them away from the original shabby place and rebury them on the western plain. By doing so, I hope I could requite my parents' immense love and their care on me and express my unlimited gratitude to them. Yesterday, I was favored with an imperial edict allowing me to go out on an inspection tour for two or three days. Without any brothers I have only one elder sister. I made a divination for the propitious date for the reburial of my parents' coffins, and was indicated that the twenty-first of this month was suitable.

At present, even some necessary funeral articles have not been prepared, not to mention other related things;

so, I am afraid that I could not deal with the whole matter appropriately during a two-or-three-day leave. I implore Your Majesty to grant a heavenly grace on me again and permit me to return after I finish the reburial ritual. What's more, a dignitary Brāhmaṇa guest has come here to stay with me, if the funeral is to be handled too hastily and simply, I am afraid he might sneer at it. I have been haunted by extreme anxieties, which I really find unbearable, so reverentially, I present this letter to your Presence. Prostrating myself before you, I supplicate you to show the mercy on me and comply with the request of the orphan.

After reading the letter, the Emperor granted the request made by the Master. Then an imperial edict was issued ordering the official concerned to assist the Master in handing the reburial ceremony, with the necessities provided at national expenses. Receiving this privilege granted by the Emperor, the Master wrote a letter again to extend his gratitude, saying:

I, *Śramaṇa* Xuanzang, beg to state:

Although my sins are serious, the deities in charge of punishment didn't mete out the death penalty on me, and thus I have dragged out my life to this day. The solar terms take turns to incur the seasonal changes of climate; the moon waxes and wanes incessantly. The graves of my parents are in a state of dilapidation now, overgrown with weeds, thistles and thorns. I have been considering to relocate the graveyard for many years, but because of being far away from my hometown, I could not have my wish fulfilled.

Fortunately, as a retinue member of your Imperial Carriage, I finally had a chance to go back to my hometown. Showing understanding and sympathy for my long-cherished wish, you permitted me to rebury my parents' coffins. As to all the necessities for the burial, the Emperor and the Empress kindly granted me the beneficence again by providing various assistances. What you have done to me is just like the light of the sun and the moon that shines even on debris, or the drops of rain that moisten everything with no exception of the wild weeds. I feel extremely grateful, filled with mixed emotions of fear and joy. You display your benevolence towards the living and the deceased as well, which will be engraved in my mind forever. I present this gratitude letter to your Presence. Considering the importance of this affair, a person as humble as me could never express thanks to the full.

With the Emperor's permission, the Master removed the tombs of his parents. All expenses of the funeral were covered by the national treasury. At the time, over ten thousand monks and laity from Luoyang and suburbs attended the ceremony.

After the Emperor Xiaowen (r. 471–499) of the Later Wei Dynasty removed his capital from Dai[79] to Luoyang, he had Shaoling Monastery[80] built on the north side of Mountain Shaoshi. The monastery was divided into the upper and lower sections on a hill slope, having twelve courtyards distributing over the high to the low altitudes. Situated on the east side of the Song Mountain, the monastery faced the Shaoshi Peak in the south and backed on a high ridge in the north, with three streams gliding around. In the mountain, rocks and precipices were towering high, fountains sparkling and gurgling, pine lichens (usnea) twinning around giant bamboos, and cassia, cypress, lycium and catalpa trees lushly growing. Showing a spectacular natural scenery, the mountain was fresh and serene, which was truly a good spot on the domain of the nation. Its western terrace was the most beautiful, where Bodhiruci once translated the Buddhist scriptures and where Dhyāna Master Buddhabhadra sat in meditation whose body was still preserved in a stūpa there. At the end of Daye period (605–616), once a gang of insurgents attempted to burn the stupa but they found it incombustible, which made the people near and far quite amazed. At the foot of the mountain range where the monastery was situated was Goushi County, to the southeast of which was Chen Village located in Phoenix Valley, also known as Chenpu Valley, which was the very place where the Master was born.

On the twentieth day in the ninth month of the autumn, the Master wrote a petition to entreat the Emperor to permit him to translate scriptures in the Shaolin Monastery. The petition reads:

I, *Śramaṇa* Xuanzang, beg to state:

I have heard that the road leading to enlightenment is long and far, so a man who is eager to step on it must first have supplies and provisions well prepared. I also have heard that the river of the life and death is deep and broad, so when a man wants to cross it, he needs to take a boat or a raft. Here, the "supplies and provisions" don't refer to the rice or the like that are to be prepared in the night before a man sets off for a journey, but refers to the supreme deeds guided by the Three Studies[81] and the Three Kinds of Wisdom[82]; again, the "boat or raft" has nothing to do with an actual boat, a raft or the like, but implies the pure Karma that a man obtains by performing the Eight kinds of Endurance[83] and of Prajñā[84]; therefore, numerous buddhas have come to the yonder shore just because they have possessed all of them. By contrast, the mortal people have been trapped in the life-and-death reincarnation merely for the lack of them. For this reason, all the vast Three Realms are floating on the river of Seven Outflows of afflictions[85] and the huge populations of Four Modes of Birth[86] are submerged in the waves of Ten Fetters[87]; as a result, everyone is rolled about by the circling waves, bound to the illusory worlds deliriously, and infatuated so much that he fails to shake free even after a Rock kalpa; what's worse, he even becomes more obstinate after a Mustard kalpa[88]. Sentient beings don't know to get out of the burning house by riding on the three kinds of carts, or to reach the mansion full of treasure by walking along the Eightfold Noble Path; what a pity it is! Now it is not because of the late autumn climate that makes me sigh but because I express the same sentiments as those of Confucius when he once sighed at the gains and losses of the people. I am so sentimental that I could not take in food at meals and I always sit up easily from my sleep. I perceive that my physical body has been formed by various conditions which temporarily congregate and that my thoughts have never rested for a single moment.

My thoughts are more precarious and fragile than the trees on the riverbank or the liana on the well wall, and they are more unstable and ramshackle than the city constructed in the air or foams arising from the water. Therefore, I have never expected my life to sustain long, knowing it might come to its end at any moment in some morning or evening. Time flies, like incessantly flowing water, and suddenly I realized I was sixty years old. As years elapse, I know my lifespan. When I was young, highly motivated by the desire for Buddhist Dharma, single-mindedly looking for good teachers and worthy friends, I spent many years ranging across various countries and states; as a result, I was greatly exhausted by the long journey, and in recent years, I even felt all the more decrepit. Considering the elapsing time and my present physical condition, how long shall I live? Now the prerequisites for the final emancipation have not been adequately prepared while the future days are left no more, at which I heave sighs every day in sadness. Such feelings could not find full expression in my writing.

Humble as I am, I count myself fortunate to meet with sagacious sovereigns, so that I have received benevolence from the late emperor and taken the enormous favor from Your Majesty, which make me bathe in the grand kindness for a long time. I have been highly esteemed, enjoying a plenty of compliments, and my prestige has been boosted locally and farther afield; I am a man, without wings, flying to the clouds and Galaxy. Having been offered with the Four Requisites[89] so abundantly, I have surpassed my contemporaries in resplendence of privilege bestowed by the Emperor and the Empress; looking back into the history, I could not find any ancient so favorably treated as me. What virtues and merits do I possess that could earn me so many favors? It is just because of the extensive beneficence and magnanimity of the Emperor and the Empress that I have been cared about so much; in fact, I am quite like a stone produced in Mount Yan[90] which is mistakenly cherished as a jade, or an inferior horse highly valued as a superb steed. When I make a self-examination, I solely feel ashamed and embarrassed. Ancient thinkers advocated the refined doctrine that the completeness should be avoided and the fullness be detested; also, one of the maxims shared by all buddhas is that a man should be content with reduction in desires. I must admit my lack of learning and talent. I realize that my fame and deeds do not match. It is unfitting for me to be so bold as to over-enjoy the kindness and compassion of the Emperor for too long. I entreat you to allow my humble bulk to end its span in forests of a mountain, where I will pay homage to Buddhas, recite scriptures, and do meditation, with the purpose to repay the rewards and preferment granted to me by the Emperor and the Empress. Dignified as a Cakravartin King, Your Majesty is giving edification as a Dharma Lord, thus I am indebted to you for your kindness of requiring me to translate the scriptures I brought back from the Western Regions. But because of my incompetence, I am afraid I am barely capable of executing such a difficult task; since I received your imperial order, I have felt uneasy from morning to night every day. Up to now I have translated more than six hundred fascicles of texts that reveal principal gist of Tripiṭaka and Four Āgamas, cover pivotal works of the Great and Lesser vehicles, illustrate a comprehensive collection of the practices and stages of saints, and display the eighty-four thousand dharma gates. These works have been eulogized by the peoples in the Western Regions and regarded as mighty canons functioning to defend and pacify a nation or region. In fact, every conceivable doctrine and theory could be found in the newly-translated texts, just like a man looking for a lumber in the Magic Denglin Forest[91], he could get whatever size he wants, or like a man collecting pearls at the seaside, he could obtain pearls of any shape, be square or round, at his will. The same is true to the learners with various purposes. I intend to requite the kindness of the country by doing the translation work, which, although insignificant, is supposed to compensate one ten-thousandth of your kindness.

A two-wheel cart cannot run with a single wheel; in order to eliminate afflictions, meditation (Dhyāna) and wisdom (Prajñā) should be applied simultaneously. To obtain wisdom needs to do research on scriptures and treatises while to enter Dhyāna needs to do meditation in woods. Although I had intimate knowledge of both when I was young, I scarcely have had any time to practice the Four Dhyānas[92] and Eight Degrees of Mental Concentration[93]; therefore, now I desire to indulge myself in the practice of meditation to tranquilize my mind, as if to make the muddy water clear. By doing so I will subdue my ape-like mind which is always impressionable and restless, and will harness my elephant-like thoughts which are running around randomly. But If I could not reside in a mountain to shut the world out, I shall not succeed in achieving my goals.

I have heard that the Shaoshi Peak of Mount Song truly is eminent and holy within territory. There are high-rising ridges and cliffs overlapping upon one another, and there are peaks and ravines of exceptional shapes, whence wind and clouds are generated while wisdom and benevolence are brewed, and there fruits and medicinal herbs are growing lushly and abundantly, with dodders and ficus pumila fresh and pure. There are Shaolin Saṃghārāma[94], the Xianju Monastery and other temples scattering around, some being built on rocks while others situated in valleys, all of which are circled by streaks of woods and winding creeks, and there Buddhist rituals are often held in solemnity in spacious halls and chambers. Concerning it is the very place where Tripiṭaka-master Bodhiruci was doing his translation work during the Later Wei Dynasty(386–535), it might be a suitable place for me to reside in, to practice meditation and do contemplation. In the past, the two Shus[95], courtiers of the Han Dynasty (202 BC–220 CE), knew to resign their high positions and abandon their enormous wealth to retire to seclusion; Chao Fu and Xu You[96], two ordinary men, knew to abide in trueness to maintain their personal purity. Now see how I stand. A long time ago I renounced my household life to pursue the Dharma but up to now I have still been confined to metropolis. Whenever the fresh breeze blows, it stirs my shamefulness and makes me feel uneasy.

Respectfully I believe that Your Majesty is much more brilliant than seven luminaries[97] and the light from your wisdom could penetrate the deepest nether world[98]. Again, I venture to supplicate Your Majesty to take my stubborn sincerity into consideration and grant me a special permission, so that I could turn away from the turmoil and mundane world to hide my traces from the mortals. I'd like to keep company with herds of elk and deer, live with wild ducks and cranes. By taking up residence on a piece of rock or seeking shelter in the shade of a tree, I shall guard and check my ape-like mind, and contemplate the reality of all things. I shall prevent the Four Māras[99] and Nine Bonds[100] from creeping up stealthily in my mind, and ensure the Five Endurances[101] and Ten Activities[102] to be generated successively. Only by doing so could I build a stairway up to the final enlightenment and make a ferry to reach the yonder shore. I ensure that outwardly, the edification of Your Majesty is not to be blemished by my deeds, and inwardly, my self-cultivation will be rectified and improved. If I might do so to the end of my life, it would be a great favor bestowed on me! If you grant me your permission, the refined bearing of Huiyuan (334–416) of Mount Lu would reappear and the pure moral integrity of Daolin (314–366) of Shan Hill[103] would be inherited. Besides practicing meditation. I also hope to spare time to resume my translation work, which is of a great pleasure to me. Now I am coming to the palace to present my petition to your Presence. Unwittingly offending Your Majesty's authority, I am trembling all over even more.

The Emperor perused the letter but declined the request of the Master.

On the twenty-first day of the same month, the Emperor wrote a reply letter to the Master, saying:

> Having read your letter, we have come to know that you would like to set up a model for the contemporary people by concealing your traces in mountains as Daolin and Huiyuan, and to contemplate in meditation tranquilly as Buddhasiṁha[104] and Kumārajīva[105]. Your modestly restrained manner, your virtue and integrity are greatly appreciated by us. We, scarcely having made any achievements and attained adequate knowledge, are not qualified to devote to what is the lofty and abstruse; however, despite we are superficial and ill-informed, we should know better than to approve your proposal. Serving as a bridge and a ferry in the Three Realms, the Master gives guidance to the Beings of Four Modes of Birth. Wisdom makes your mind lamp much brighter, never being obscured by the dusts of passions and desires, while meditative concentration stops your flowing

ideas, never being disturbed by waves of perception and discernment. You have already been dwelling in virtue and its power, is there any need for you to retire in the ridges of Taihua Mountain[106]? Residing in serenity and emptiness, is it necessary for you to regard the Mount Shaoshi so indispensable for self-cultivation? Wish you to take back your words and stop making further request. In ancient times people praised those real recluses who were living in noisy markets or vain courts, while in the present age it seems to be more commendable if a man could propagate what he has seen and heard (about the bequeathed teachings) in the world of mortals.

Since the imperial decree ordered the Master to stop the further request, the Master didn't dare to say anything more. Hardly had he received the imperial decree when he wrote a letter to extend his gratitude, saying:

I, *Śramaṇa* Xuanzang, beg to state:

The reply written by Your Majesty has already been brought to me by messenger Li Junxin. Written in vermilion, strokes of your handwriting are beautifully vigorous, and wise as the mystic diagram that emerged from the Yellow River[107]; your phrases are also very resplendent. Moreover, the energetic movement of your calligraphy pulsates like the rising peaks of high mountains and your emotional appeal demonstrates the heroic spirit. I haven't expected that in the late autumn I could have the chance to read such a piece of writing as beautiful as spring, and that suddenly, I, though living in the plain between Yi and Luo rivers[108], could be fortunate enough to behold precious jade from the Kunlun[109] and Jin mountains[110]. Holding the letter in hands, I leaped with joy. In ancient times, the epistle[111] written by King of Wei State[112] on wooden strips to Jizhong (177–230)[113] was merely intended to express the sad feelings of departure, while the letter of protest written by Huiyuan[114] to Emperor Jin[115] merely proclaimed the right that the monks should enjoy the public-provision of rice, but neither suggested how to take lodge in serenity and emptiness nor indicated how to set up the hermitage in marketplace or at court. Thus, we know that the sagacious mind of Your Majesty does contain both the Way and secular affairs, bearing the knowledge of both voidness and reality (existence and non-existence); thereby Your Majesty has exceeded Fuxi and Xuanyuan to reach a higher spiritual plane, and has won the hearts of all, leaving Cao of Wei[116] and Sima of Jin[117] far behind. I am a man with the disposition as plain as white silk, not being accustomed to the luxuriously flashy colors like red and blue. In addition, my body is as fragile as wild grapes, always expecting to wind up the strong trees like a pine. Therefore, I wished to live in misty twilight at Mount Shaoshi and keep company with springs and rocks of Mount Song. I hope, by doing so, I would escape the endless submergence in the river of death and birth, and extinguish the fire of desires. That is why I ventured with utmost ignorance to submit the letter to your Presence at risk of my life. Heaven bestows its compassion even on a wild duck or a quail; the fine drops coming from the clouds moisten everything on earth, never forsaking a small spider. The imperial edict, not granting my request but still favoring me with praises, was well-intended to maintain my dignity properly. As my five sentiments[118] are all trembling in awe, I even don't know which one to abide by at that moment. Now I withdraw my request and dare not to make it again. Respectfully I am writing this letter to extend my gratitude, shuddering even more in awe.

The fifth day of the eleventh month in the winter was the first birthday of Buddha Light Lord. Again, the Master presented a religious robe as a gift, attached herewith a letter as follows:

I, *Śramaṇa* Xuanzang, beg to state:

When orchids are blooming in flower nursery, passers-by would stop to admire, and when cassia trees grow prosperously along the banks of a lucid creek, pedestrians would be intoxicated with the fragrance. Even flowers and trees can bring us pleasures, not to speak of a newly-born baby in a royal family. Humbly I believe that with divine wisdom, bearing a graceful demeanor, possessing heaven-and-earth-like virtues, the Emperor and the Empress have placated and pacified various regions of the country, nurtured and raised the people as your own children. Having had a lot of monasteries constructed, you have accumulated many meritorious fortunes, which could not only ensure your Throne to be held forever, but consolidate your empire as firm as diamond. Attributed to your wonderful cultivation and edification, Crown Prince[119] has grown ever more intelligent and vigorous as time goes by; Prince of Lu[120] also has become ever more extraordinarily talented. Buddha Light Lord, he is particularly perspicacious at such a young age. One may well say that they will surpass the emperors of the Zhou and Shang dynasties, and match Yellow Emperor in sublimity. Generation after generation, the royal family is sure to multiply prosperously for ten thousand years. As a mediocre and insignificant person, I have been privileged to have audiences with the princes frequently. In my inner heart I am ecstatic about it. Today is the first birthday of Buddha Light Lord, so I present the gift as congratulations. Baring my humble heart, sincerely I offer a religious robe to him, in the hope that the prince shall be safeguarded by thousands of deities and enjoyed hundreds of fortunes. May he be sound in his sleeping and be composed when he is awake! May he be well-fed with milk and a balanced diet! May he perpetuate the prosperity of the Triple Gem, subjugate the four Māras, practice the Bodhisattva deeds and succeed in carrying out undertakings of Tathāgata! I am extremely delighted to behold him handsome, healthy and perspicacious, who is like a jade flower growing splendidly and vigorously on a divine branch of a celestial tree. Respectfully I submit this letter and the robe to your Presence. Unwittingly offending Your Majesty's solemnity, I am trembling all over even more.

At the time, the Master was doing his translation at the Jicui

Palace. He was totally engaged in it, without any momentary lapses, and eventually, he fell sick from constant overwork. When the Emperor knew it, he felt quite worried. Before long, Lü Hongzhe, palace physician, was dispatched to treat the Master. He went to see the Master with an imperial letter. The Master received it with a mixture of sadness and joy. He then wrote a letter to extend his gratitude as follows:

I, *Śramaṇa* Xuanzang, beg to state:

Messenger Lü Hongzhe has arrived with the imperial edict which not only expresses sympathy and solicitude to my illness, but also grants me permission to go out of the palace to recompose myself. At this unexpected arrival of your compassion, my huddled body carries itself straight up as if I were in the presence of the Crown, and I becomes refreshed all at once as if I were plunged into a cool spring. As I have not preserved my health in the right way, I have fallen ill, suffering from various diseases. Since I left you, I have been troubled by diseases doubly. I have been afflicted by continuing pain in heart, stuffiness in back, soreness in bones, and ache in muscles, so I often lose my appetite and suffer from insomnia. Aware that my strength was declining, I was afraid that if the unthought-of might happen, the palace would be contaminated (by my dead body), so I decided to go out of the palace to discard my humble body in gullies. Fearing my plan would disturb Your Majesty, I dared not to report it to your Presence, so with my Gate Pass, I left the palace for the monastery without authorization. In the monastery, however, due to exhaustion and fatigue, my diseases become more serious, so much so that I often thought that I would depart this age of peace and prosperity. Afterwards, thanks to Zhang Dezhi, the court physician of the Palace Medical Department, who treated me with acupuncture, my health was gradually recovered and I barely survived. Considering my crime of taking arbitrary actions, I am waiting for Your Majesty's condemnation and punishment. Respectfully I believe that the sun and the moon issue their light forever upon the stupid and the clumsy, and that rivers and seas are always inclusive and lenient. Nevertheless, the benevolence could not be bestowed on the extremely humble man whatsoever again to make the regular civil and penal code violated, could it? I hope that the justice will be upheld by sending me to the Imperial censor[121]. In this way, the solemnity of jurisdiction would be maintained. If imprisonment is too slight to mete out the punishment on me, I don't mind waiting for a more severe one, even the death penalty. At this moment my residual soul and feeble body are lingering on, Your Majesty confers gracious favors on me once again; I could requite you with nothing but take your words to heart and engrave them in my flesh and bones. At present I am in an extraordinary miserable condition, and I don't think I could live for long. I am not afraid of death but what I feel sorry is that before I could requite your kindness, my life might be exhausted to its end.

I am greatly impressed with Your Majesty's industriousness

that in order to train the troops, you not only spare no pains to take hunting expeditions in person, but also study the martial and military arts and give lectures on them. You have shown your kindness by releasing the captivated Kylin[122] and recorded the loyalty of a man who offered the phoenix[123], so you have gathered the people from far and near around you, with status high and low, be talented or mediocre, all of whom are elated and happy. Following suit, the God of the wind[124] sweeps away dust, and mountain deities protect the wild animals and plants as well. Respectfully I think that whether you act or not, you are always in the utmost happiness and fortune. Having explicitly promulgated legal code for a hundred days (before taking the expedition), you returned after twelve days; belittling taking distant expeditions around, like what King Mu of Zhou[125] did on his eight steeds, you turned back in victory, no need to embark on a long journey. The imperial carriage could stop but the solicitude you gave me will never cease to warm me. In coping with matters in hand, I am on tenterhooks for I fear to commit dereliction of duty at the end of my life. With extreme uneasiness, I present this letter to your Presence, waiting for punishment at any moment. Being confounded and at a loss, I am crouching to hear from you.

After perusing the letter, the Emperor was very delighted. Three days later, he dispatched an envoy to invite the Master to the Palace to receive the offerings of the Four Requisites for some following days. After that, another imperial edict was issued sending the Master back to the Jicui Palace to resume his translation work.

During the twelfth month in the winter, Luoyang where the Luoyang Palace was situated was made to be the Eastern Capital[126]. As the precincts of the new capital were narrow and cramped, so Sishui county of Zhengzhou[127] and Heyang County of Huaizhou[128] were then delimited into the eastern portion of the new capital. In the west, Guzhou, as an administrative area, was abrogated, and Yiyang[129], Yongning[130], Xin'an[131], Yingchi[132] and other counties were incorporated into the capital instead. Considering his hometown having been honored as a part of the capital, the Master wrote a letter of congratulations, saying:

> I, *Śramaṇa* Xuanzang, beg to state:
>
> I have heard that the star *chunshou*[133] bestowed the Qin region to the Qin Dynasty, thus Chang'an was constructed as impregnable as an iron city, which shows that the enthronement must be destined by Heaven. Also, I heard that in the Xia Dynasty when the divine chart was presented by tortoise[134] from Luo River, Jade Spring (Luoyang) soon began to be built as the political seat in the Central Plain[135]. From this we know that the capital and its environs seem to be important, where the heavenly omens are descended, and the great programs of the monarch are implemented. Ever after, eulogies spread afield and the prosperity is expected. Now, the very law is continuously operating and actions have been taken accordingly.
>
> Humbly I believe that the Emperor and the Empress have administrated the nation with the complete judicial system,

enforced the law impartially and fulfilled the requests of the people actively. You imitated Yu[136] to take the inspection tour around, and then resided in Luoyang, an important area of the Central Plain. On the one hand, following the traditional custom of constructing a magnificent capital city, you have had the inner and outer capital cities built in the same architecture style of Haojing[137]; on the other hand, to avoid building the residence too luxuriously, you didn't drive laborers to do the heavy manual work as they used to do in the old days. In this new capital, in order to conduct state affairs well at hand, the Emperor and the Empress detested living in comfort, and always rose early in the morning. If it were not for a compromise between Hua (Chinese) and Yi (the foreign tribes) and a unification of the different systems of taxes and corvee, how could your compassion be constantly bestowed (on Luoyang) and your decree (of making Luoyang as the eastern capital) be proclaimed irrevocably? The moment your decree was issued, the mountains and rivers took on a flourishing look; when it was carried out, mist and clouds of various colors began to fly amazingly. The flying ridges of houses are brilliant in the sunshine; the air on roads is vibrated with fresh breezes. The blessings of the deities are spreading far and wide while human relations are preserved in virtue and harmony. Even the bream of Wuchang[138] would take pleasure in removing from their habitat to the new capital city; cranes in Yun and Ting mountains[139] contend to attend on carriages of the Emperor and the Empress escorted by their entourage in front and behind. The geographical dependence of the State of Zheng[140] and the Western Jin[141] was scorned for being narrow; the tactic put forward by Liu (Jing) and Zhang (Liang)[142] was depreciated as being lopsided; even kings of the Zhou Dynasty did not take a broad and long-term view as this one, so they invited trouble to establish Feng (hao) and Luo(yang)[143] as their capitals at different times. By contrast, holding the nation in control, the Emperor and the Empress constructed Yi (River) and Xian(yang)[144] simultaneously, so that the royal family will be in prosperity forever and the nation's high destiny will last long. Currently, the Emperor and the Empress are able to either feast foreign guests at the Pingle Palace[145] at Luoyang in the east, or entertain them at the Jianzhang Palace[146] at Chang'an in the west. Musicians are playing the s*heng*[147] to prolong the bliss for eternity, and men of letters, with their extraordinary literary talent, are chanting the eulogies to the Emperor and the Empress. How altruistic and just the Emperor and the Empress are! How difficult to describe your loftiness! Being a man of no use, I have hardly rendered any service, which makes me feel ever more scared. But now my birthplace has been honorably incorporated into the environs of the capital where three rivers[148] are flowing across. It is a true fortune only once in a thousand years that my hometown develops into the brand new. The old cottage of my family was ruined, but my humble life is still here in existence as a blade of grass. I am delighted to see that my native place is under the administration of the capital area. Thus, I do not feel embarrassed as previously it was shut outside the pass. Jubilation of building a capital is well worth a celebration by the people near and far; all the more so, the people particularly wish you the best of health. Overwhelmed by extreme happiness, I cannot help clapping my hands. At present, I am submitting this letter to extend my gratitude.

In the first month in the spring of the third year (658), the Emperor returned to the Western Capital. The Master accompanied him.

ANNOTATION

1 Fuxi 伏羲 is a culture hero in Chinese legend and mythology, credited (along with his sister Nüwa 女娲) with creating humanity and the invention of hunting, fishing and cooking as well as the Cangjie 仓颉 system of writing Chinese characters c. 2,000 BC. Fuxi was counted as the first of the Three Sovereigns at the beginning of the Chinese dynastic period.

2 Refers to King Wen of Zhou 周文王(1152–1056 BC), born Ji Chang姬昌, who was posthumously honored as the founder of the Zhou Dynasty and titled King. It was his son Wu who conquered the Shang following the Battle of Muye.

3 Refers to the eight objects of government (*bazheng*八政) mentioned in the *Shang Shu-Grand Norm*《尚书・洪范》: food; wealth and articles of convenience; sacrifices; (the business of) the Minister of Works; (that of) the Minister of Instruction; (that of) the Minister of Crime; the observances to be paid to

guests; the army.

4 Or Trividyā. See note 101 of Fascicle I.

5 Four continents — the four island-continent which surround Mount Meru according to the Buddhist cosmology. They are: Pūrvavideha in the East, which is semi-circular and white in colour; Jambudvīpa in the South, which is trapezoidal and blue (this is the continent we human beings live in); Aparagodaniya in the West, which is circular and ruby red; Uttarakuru in the North, which is square and green.

6 Refers to the nine realms of subjection to the passion, i.e. all the realms of the living except the tenth and the highest—the Buddha Realm. The ten realms, sometimes referred to as the ten worlds, are part of the belief of some forms of Buddhism that there are ten conditions of life which sentient beings are subject to, and which they experience from moment to moment. These realms can also be described through the degrees of enlightenment that course through them. They have been translated in various ways. They are divided into the Six Realms, followed by higher states of enlightened consciousness that lead to final Buddhahood. The Six Realms are: Hell, the Hungry Ghosts, the Beasts, the Asuras, Humans and lastly Heaven, or the realm of the gods. Above these lie the four holy states: the Śrāvaka, the Pratyekabuddha, the Bodhisattva and finally completely enlightened Buddhahood.

7 See note 129 of Fascicle VI.

8 The Buddha made his journey to Kushinagar, at the age of 80, entered nirvāṇa in a grove, lying down on his right side in the auspicious position on a couch between twin Śāla trees. After the nirvāṇa of Buddha, trees there were turned to be white mournfully, thus like a flock of cranes alighting on the branches. Later on, the term also generally refers to the grove outside/inside a monastery, more often to the monastery.

9 Theravada Buddhism and Mahāyāna Buddhism respectively has four canons (Piṭakas), including discipline (Vinaya Piṭaka), scriptures (Sūtra Piṭaka),

commentaries (Abhidharma Piṭaka) and mantra (dhāraṇī). Totally they have eight Piṭakas.

10 See note 19 of Fascicle VIII.

11 See note 68 of Fascicle IV.

12 See note 120 of Fascicle I.

13 Refers to Emperor Wu of Liang梁武帝 (r. 502–549), personal name Xiao Yan 萧衍, courtesy name Shuda 叔达, nickname Lian'er 练儿, was the founding emperor of the Liang Dynasty. His reign, until the end, was one of the most stable and prosperous during the Southern Dynasties. Emperor Wu created universities and extending the Confucian civil service exams, demanding that sons of nobles study. He was well read himself and wrote poetry and patronized the arts. Although for governmental affairs he was Confucian in values, he embraced Buddhism as well. He himself was attracted to many Indian traditions. He banned the sacrifice of animals and was against execution. It was said that he received the Buddhist precepts during his reign, earning him the nickname Bodhisattva Emperor. The Emperor is the namesake of the *Emperor Liang Jeweled Repentance* (*Lianghuang Baochan* 《梁皇宝忏》), a widely read and major Buddhist text in China. Emperor Wu is remembered by many Buddhists today for the many contributions he gave to the faith.

Or refers to Cao Cao曹操 (155–220), courtesy name Mengde孟德, was a Chinese warlord and the penultimate Chancellor of the Eastern Han Dynasty who rose to great power in the final years of the dynasty. As one of the central figures of the Three Kingdoms period, he laid the foundations for what was to become the state of Cao Wei and was posthumously honoured as "Emperor Wu of Wei." 魏武帝.

14 Refers to Emperor Zhang of Han汉章帝 (56–88), personal name Liu Dan 刘炟, was an emperor of the Han Ddynasty from 75 to 88. He was the third emperor of the Eastern Han. Emperor Zhang was a famous calligrapher in

Ancient China and especially skilled in cursive script, now called *zhangcao* 章草. Han society prospered and its culture flourished during this period.

15 King Mu of Zhou 周穆王, full name Ji Man姬满, was the fifth king of the Zhou Dynasty. The dates of his reign were 976–922 BC or 956–918 BC. Mu was reputed in narratives to have lived until the age of 105 and to have traveled to the mythical mountain known as Kunlun to taste the Peaches of Immortality. A popular later work is the *Tale of King Mu, Son of Heaven* (*Mutianzi Zhuan* 《穆天子传》), a fourth-century BC romance, describes Mu's visit to the Queen Mother of the West, the ancient mother goddess of China associated to the mythical Kunlun, the axis mundi. In Chinese mythology, Peaches of Immortality are consumed by the immortals due to their mystic virtue of conferring longevity on all who eat them, and Lake Yao (*yaochi* 瑶池) is a mythological lake in the divine paradise of Kunlun. King Mu of Zhou feasts at Lake Yao in Chapter 3 of the *Tale of King Mu, Son of Heaven* with a banquet, wine, gifts, and decorous exchange of poems with some sense of his being subsequently rejuvenated or at least blessed with posterity. The implications of the poems seem to cast the Queen Mother of the West as a vassal whom King Mu confirms in ruling her own land.

16 The White Horse Temple 白马寺 is, according to tradition, the first Buddhist temple in China, established in 68 AD under the patronage of Emperor Ming in the Eastern Han Dynasty capital Luoyang.

17 The name of a piece of Chinese ancient music, legendarily composed by Di Ku 帝喾 or Zhuanxu 颛顼, who are mythological emperors of ancient China, two of the Five Emperors of the Three Sovereigns.

18 Dragon Land 龙乡 is modern Kaifeng City in Henan Province, which was said to be famous for raising best roosters; the rooster crowing in Dragon Land implies the coming of the daybreak.

19 Boya 伯牙 was a *qin* (a music instrument in ancient China) player from the Spring and Autumn Period or the Warring States Period. He was known by

his first name of "Boya," although his surname may have been Yu 俞, thus his complete name is sometimes given as Yu Boya 俞伯牙. He is associated with the *guqin* 古琴 pieces *Gao Shan* 高山（High Mountains) and *Liu Shui* 流水(Flowing Water). The story of Boya and Zhong Ziqi 钟子期, his close and sympathetic friend, exemplifies the Chinese ideal of friendship. *qin*, a musical stringed instrument with strings stretching over a flat sounding box in ancient China, similar to zither; it is laid flat and played with fingers.

20 Shikuang 师旷(Master Kuang), style name Ziye子野, was a famous music master in Jin (southern Shanxi Province) during the reign of Duke Ping (r. 557–532), who was born blind but had a good taste in music. There are numerous stories about him, many concerning the *qin*.

21 The grand program of administration refers to the *Great Norm/Plan* (*Hongfan* 《洪范》).

22 The calligrapher of cursive style may refer to Zhang Zhi (张芝?–a. 192), courtesy name Boying 伯英, a famous calligrapher in the Eastern Han Dynasty. He was diligent by exercising his calligraphy near to a pool, eventually blackening the pool water, and even practicing calligraphy on his clothes. The later generations appraised him as the greatest master of cursive hand for his uniqueness and perfection. So he was famous for his typical cursive style called *zhangcao* 章草.

23 In ancient Chinese mythology, Ruomu 若木 is a divine tree for Sun to alight on. A similar tree, known as Fusang 扶桑, which refers to several different entities in ancient Chinese literature, often either a mythological tree or a mysterious land to the East. Ruomu exists in the west, and each morning Sun was said to rise from Fusang and fall on Ruomu. Chinese legend has ten birds (typically ravens) living in the tree, and as nine rested, the tenth would carry Sun on its journey.

24 Chinese mythology held that a self-healing osmanthus tree grows on Moon and was endlessly cut by Wu Gang, a figure in traditional Chinese folklore

and religion who is known for endlessly cutting it on Moon.

25 See note 47 of Fascicle VI.

26 Zhuanxu 颛顼, also known as Gao Yang 高阳, was a mythological emperor of ancient China. In the traditional account recorded by Sima Qian, Zhuanxu was a grandson of the Yellow Emperor who led the Shi clan in an eastward migration to present-day Shandong, where intermarriages with the Dongyi clan enlarged and augmented their tribal influences. At age twenty, he became their sovereign, going on to rule for seventy-eight years until his death.

27 The birth place of Buddha.

28 The Zhou Dynasty is notable for lasting for a long time, from 1046 to 256 BC, about 791 years.

29 A trigram is a combination of three unbroken (positive or *yang*) or broken lines (negative or *yin*) originally used in divination, in the *Book of Changes*.

30 As the Kylin 麒麟 is believed to be a benevolent creature, its appearance is regarded as an auspicious sign. It is also believed that the Kylin would only appear during the reign of a good ruler, or shortly before the birth or death of a sage. According to popular belief, the birth of one of China's greatest sages, Confucius, was made known when a Kylin appeared to his pregnant mother. This Kylin coughed up an inscribed jade tablet that foretold the future greatness of the child in the womb. Furthermore, when a Kylin was caught and injured by a charioteer, Confucius regarded it as a foreshadowing of his death, so he stopped writing *The Spring and Autumn Annals* or *Chunqiu*《春秋》. Thereafter, *Chunqiu* is also called *Lin Jing*《麟经》.

31 Traditionally, Chinese emperors held sacrificial ceremony to pay homage to Heaven at Mount Tai泰山 as an announcement of their imperial inauguration. They pay homage to Earth at Mount Liangfu梁父山.

32 Cao Cao (155–220), Emperor Wu of Wei, died in March of the 25th year of Jian'an period (220), and one of his sons, Cao Zhi 曹植 (192–232) composed the inscription for stele named *Daxiang* 大飨 to eulogize the virtues and

achievements of Cao Cao. Another son, Cao Pi 曹丕 (r.220–226), Emperor Wen of Wei, rewarded the army with a great feast in 222, which is recorded in an inscription on a tablet, also named *Daxiang*.

33 The *zhuan* script (seal character) was the earliest form of writing after the oracle inscriptions, which features in cursive lines and various writing forms, resembling the tracks of birds. However, this caused the problem of non-simplicity. It's said that the first effort for the unification of writing took place during the reign of King Xuan (r. 827–782 BC) of the Western Zhou Dynasty, when his grand historian (*taishi* 太史) Shi Zhou 史籀 compiled a lexicon of 15 chapters, standardizing Chinese writing under script called *zhuan*. According to the *Explaining Graphs and Analyzing Characters* (*Shuowen Jiezi*《说文解字》) by Xu Shen 许慎 (c. 58–c. 148), there were the eight writing scripts in Qin Dynasty 秦书八体：large seal script 大篆, small seal script 小篆，*kefu* (刻符as credential symbols)，worm script (*chongshu* 虫书)，*moyin* (摹印, a kind of script on the signet), *shushu* (署书a kind of script on the seals), *shushu* (殳书, a kind of script on the weapons), and official script (*lishu*隶书).

34 Fu Yi 傅毅(?–a.90), courtesy name Wuzhong 武仲, was a famous writer of the Eastern Han Dynasty. According to the *Master Mou's Treatise Settling Doubts* (*Mouzi Lihoulun*《牟子理惑论》), a classic Chinese Buddhist text, Fu Yi told Emperor Ming that the golden man in his dream was Buddha.

The Mouzi Lihoulun comprises a purportedly autobiographical preface by Master Mou, a late 2nd-century Confucian scholar-official who converted to Buddhism, and an imaginary dialogue of questions and answers about Buddhist practices.

35 Kan Ze阚泽(a. 170–243), courtesy name Derun 德润, was a famous scholar, politician during the Three Kingdoms Period. When Kang Senghui 康僧会 (Vietnamese: Khương Tăng Hội; died 280), a Buddhist monk and translator, came to the State of Wu, the king of Wu, Sun Quan孙权(r. 229–252)

consulted Kan Ze about it.

36 Triratna: The Three Jewels; The Triple Gem; The Three Treasures: Buddha, Dharma, Sangha.

37 Emperor Yuan of Han 汉元帝 (75–33 BC) was born as Liu Shi 刘奭. He reigned from 48 to 33 BC.

38 Refers to Cao Cao.

39 Ancient script, the Seal Style and the Clerical Style.

40 Wang Zhong王仲, style name Cizhong次仲, a calligrapher of the Eastern Han Dynasty (25–220), also said to be of the Qin Dynasty (221–207 BC) , is regarded as a founder of the Official Script.

41 Zhang Zhi 张芝, style name Boying 伯英, whose birth date is unknown, died in about 192 AD. Cui Yuan崔瑗, style name子玉， a calligrapher of the Eastern Han Dynasty (25–220). Both of them are said to be expertise in the Cursive Style.

42 Or Puguang普光, a disciple of Xuanzang.

43 Refers to Emperor Taizong of Tang.

44 Refers to Emperor Taizong of Tang.

45 Refers to the three regulation garments of a monk, kaāṣāya 袈裟, i.e. saṅghāṭī 僧伽梨, assembly robe; uttarāsaṅga 郁多罗僧, upper garment worn over the antarvāsaka 安陀会, vest or shirt.

46 During the Zhou Dynasty (1122–256 BC), students were required to master the Six Arts 六艺: Rites, Music, Archery, Charioteering, Calligraphy, Mathematics. The Six Arts were practiced by scholars and they already existed before Confucius, but became a part of Confucian philosophy.

47 See note 129 of Fascicle VI.

48 According to Buddhist tradition, Kapilavastu is the name of the ancient city where Siddhartha Gautama was raised and lived until the age of 29, when he renounced worldly life. There is some controversy about the exact location of Kapilavastu. Some versions say that it is located in present-day Rummindei,

in the Terai region of Southern Nepal, about 10 kilometres west of Lumbini (the birthplace of the Siddhartha Gautama) not far from the Indian-Nepalese border. Other versions hold that Kapilavastu is located in Northern India, and that the Piprahwa village used to be within Kapilavastu.

49 Here the date could be wrong because the fifth day of the eleventh month was the birth day of Li Xian 李显(r. 683–684 and 705–710), the third son of Wu Zetian. According to other script, it might be the first day of the eleventh month.

50 According to the *Shuo Yuan* 《说苑》, variously translated as *Garden of Stories*, *Garden of Persuasions*, *Garden of Talks*, etc., a collection of stories and anecdotes from the pre-Qin period to the Western Han Dynasty, Jing Jun was a native of Qi State in the Warring States Period, who was good at painting.

51 Li Lou 离娄 is a legendary figure mentioned in the *Mencius,* who had an extraordinarily sharp vision.

52 See note 17 of Fascicle VII.

53 Zhi Dun支遁 (314–366) was a Chinese Buddhist monk and philosopher.

54 The Yin Emperor refers to the founder of the Shang Dynasty or Yin Dynasty, Shang Tang商汤, also called Cheng Tang 成汤 (1670–1587 BC) . According to traditional historiography, Shang Dynasty ruled in the Yellow River valley in the second millennium BC.

55 King Wen of Zhou 周文王 (1152–1056 BC) was king of Zhou during the late Shang Dynasty.

56 Li Xian 李显, and at other times Li Zhe 李哲, was Emperor Zhongzong of Tang, the fourth emperor of the Tang Dynasty, ruling briefly in 684 and again from 705 to 710. Emperor Zhongzong was the third son of Emperor Gaozong of Tang and Empress Wu (later known as Wu Zetian). He succeeded his father in 684. His mother, however, deposed him less than two months later in favor of his younger brother Emperor Ruizong. The former emperor,

demoted to a princely rank, was sent in exile in the provinces and placed under house arrest. Six years later, Emperor Ruizong in turn relinquished the throne to his mother and Empress Dowager Wu officially proclaimed herself empress regnant, while Emperor Ruizong was made crown prince. By 698 the court was caught in the middle of a bitter power struggle. In an attempt to decrease the power struggle, Empress Wu liberated the former emperor from his 14 years of seclusion and recalled him to the capital in April 698. He was reinstated as crown prince in October 698, taking the place of his brother. On 20 February 705, a palace coup deposed Wu Zetian and Emperor Zhongzong was restored as emperor three days later. Emperor Zhongzong reigned for five years but was a rather weak and easily influenced ruler. Real power was in the hands of his empress consort, Empress Wei and her lover Wu Sansi (Wu Zetian's nephew). In 710, Emperor Zhongzong died, allegedly poisoned by Empress Wei, who then installed his son, Li Chongmao, as Emperor Shang. Empress Wei, who had failed to install her daughter Li Guo'er, the Princess Anle, as heir to Emperor Zhongzong, thought that Li Chongmao, born of Zhongzong and a concubine and who was only 16 years old, would be easy to control and allow her to preserve her power. The scheme failed, however, when Princess Taiping, the sister of Emperor Zhongzong, launched a coup two weeks later with her nephew Li Longji (later Emperor Xuanzong), son of the abdicated Emperor Ruizong, and overthrew Empress Wei and the young emperor. Emperor Ruizong, the father of Li Longji and the older brother of Princess Taiping, was restored as emperor.

57 See note 117 of Fascicle VI.

58 Dvi-satya: Saṃvṛti-satya (common/conventional truth) and Paramārthasatya (absolute/ultimate truth).

59 Jiang Yuan 姜嫄 is an important figure in Chinese mythology and history, who was the mother of Qi (also known as Houji后稷), credited in Chinese mythology with founding the Ji clan who went on to establish the Zhou Dynasty. In the

Zhou hymn "*Birth of Our People*" – credit Qi with a miraculous birth after Jiang Yuan stepped into a footprint or toeprint left by the supreme deity Shangdi上帝. The hymn records her as attempting to abandon him three times (his name Qi means "the Abandoned One").

60 The divine horse of the Wheel King.

61 King Cheng of Zhou was the second king of the Zhou Dynasty. The dates of his reign were 1042–1021 BC or 1042/35–1006 BC. King Kang of Zhou was the third sovereign of the Chinese Zhou Dynasty and son of the King Cheng of Zhou. The dates of his reign were 1020–996 BC or 1005–978 BC. King Kang followed his father King Cheng's policy and expanded the Zhou territory in the North and in the West.

62 China.

63 Arhat Pure-Eye (Vimalanetra) is the two-hundredth Arhat of five hundred Arhats. In the chapter XXV. Ancient Devotion of *The Lotus Sutra*, The young princes Vimalagarbha and Vimalanetra were two sons of the king Subhavyûha, out of compassion for their father who didn't believe in Buddhism andheld the wrong views, displayed some miracle, " Immediately the young princes Vimalagarbha and Vimalanetra rose into the atmosphere to a height of seven Tâl trees and performed miracles such as are allowed by the Buddha, out of compassion for their father, the king, Subhavyûha. They prepared in the sky a couch and raised dust; there they also emitted from the lower part of their body a shower of rain, and from the upper part a mass of fire; then again they emitted from the upper part of their body a shower of rain, and from the lower part a mass of fire. While in the firmament they became now big, then small; and now small, then big. Then they vanished from the sky to come up again from the earth and reappear in the air." At the sight of the miracle produced by the magical power of the two young princes, their father, the king Subhavyûha, was converted.

64 An elder of Vaiśālī, who at the Buddha's bidding sought the aid of Amitābha,

Mahāsthamaprāpta and Guanyin, especially the last, to rid his people of a pestilence. Also in the ChapterXIII *Dharmapūjā* or *Serving the Dharma* of the *Vimalakīrti Sutra*, the Buddha was the prince Moon-Shelter (Candrachattra) in one of his previous lives.

65 It might be two kinds of Bondages of monks: one is the avarice for nourishing oneself by gain; the other is the avarice for reputation.

Or two kinds of hinderances 二障：

A. (1) Affliction hindrances 烦恼障, which lead to another two kinds of hindrances: evil karmas and corresponding requitals (see three kinds of hindrances); (2) hindrances to wisdom-knowledge (jñeyāvaraṇa, 智障), which are one's ground-abiding ignorance 住地无明, the root ignorance 根本无明.

B. (1) Affliction hindrances as in A (1); (2) hindrances to liberation, which prevent one from attaining the Samādhi of Total Suspension of Sensory Reception and Perception.

66 The perfect universal wisdom of a Buddha; correct equal or universal enlightenment; fully Enlightened one.

67 Liu Yun刘云 (?–4 BC), grandson of the Emperor Xuan of the Han Dynasty.

68 Cao Zhi曹植(192–232), courtesy name Zijian子健, was a prince of the state of Cao Wei in the Three Kingdoms period, and an accomplished poet in his times. His style of poetry, greatly revered during the Jin Dynasty and Southern and Northern Dynasties, came to be known as the Jian'an style. Cao Zhi was a son of Cao Cao, a warlord who rose to power towards the end of the Eastern Han Dynasty and laid the foundation for the state of Cao Wei.

69 According to the *Ekottarāgama*, Buddha addressed those who are willing to come up to be a disciple of the Buddha as Bhikṣu "Well Come"; here it is alluded to the prince.

70 Alluded to the story: When Sakyamuni Buddha was a prince, having seen the absurdity of mundane life, he decided to renounce the home. At midnight he saddled his favorite horse, and with a charioteer, they went out of the capital

city to reach the border of the kingdom of Magadha. There, Siddartha cut off his beard and his hair, and said farewell to his charioteer and his horse. Then he exchanged his jeweled clothes for the rags of a beggar, and had gone his way of self-cultivation.

71 Also Māra.

72 To lay the hand on the top of the head, a custom of Buddha in teaching his disciples, especially granting the assurance of future enlightenment.

73 *Mingjia* 蓂荚, also *lijia* 历荚, in Chinese myth, is a kind of lucky grass.

74 Refers to seven groups of disciples, including the five monastic groups: bhikṣus (monks), bhikṣuṇīs (nuns), śrāmaṇeras (novice monks), śrāmaṇerikās (novice nuns), śikṣamāṇās (novice nuns in their last two years before ordination) and the two lay groups: upāsakas (laymen) and upāsikās (laywomen).

75 In the original Chinese text, "Four gates 四门" is used, which refers to the entrances in different directions of Mingtang 明堂 which in ancient China, was the palace for an emperor to declare punishment and prize or instructions, so "Four gates" is used to mean the guests or the ministers and ordinary people.

76 In the Sui Dynasty, it was called the Xianren Palace 显仁宫, build by Yuwen kai 宇文恺(555–612) under the order of Emperor Yang of Sui 隋炀帝(r.604–618) in about 605AD, situated in today Yiyang 宜阳, Henan Province.

77 In Chinese mythology, Peaches of Immortality are consumed by the immortals due to their mystic virtue of conferring longevity on all who eat them.

78 The dwelling place of immortals.

79 Modern Datong 大同, Shanxi Province.

80 The Shaolin Monastery is located in Dengfeng County, Henan Province. The Shaolin Monastery was built on the north side of Shaoshi, the central peak of Mount Song, one of the Sacred Mountains of China, by Emperor Xiaowen of the Northern Wei Dynasty in 495 AD.

81 The Three Studies: discipline(Vinaya), meditation (Dhyāna) and wisdom (Prajñā).

82 Generally there are three kinds of saying:

A. also called the Three Modes of Attaining Wisdom三慧: Wisdom from reading, hearing, instruction闻慧; Wisdom from reflection,and so forth思慧; Wisdom from practice (of abstract meditation) 修慧.

B. The Three Kinds of Wisdom-knowledge 三智: (1) overall wisdom-knowledge (sarvajña,一切智), which is the emptiness of everything, acquired by an Arhat, a Pratyekabuddha, and a holy Bodhisattva; (2) discriminative wisdom-knowledge 道种智, which is a holy Bodhisattva's growing wisdom-knowledge of the differences of all things; (3) knowledge of all wisdom-knowledge (sarvajña-jñāna, 一切种智), or omniscience, which is a Buddha's perfect wisdom-knowledge of all beings and all things in their general and particular aspects, and of the non-duality of emptiness and myriad displays of illusory existence.

C. (1) earthly or ordinary wisdom世间智; (2) supra-mundane, or spiritual (śrāvaka and pratyeka-buddha出世间智) wisdom; (3) supreme wisdom of bodhisattvas and Buddhas出世间上上智.

The Three Kinds of Wisdom here in the text may refer to the first saying A.

83 The eight kṣānti, or powers of patient endurance, in the desire-realm and the two realms above it, necessary to acquire the full realization of the Four Noble Truths 四谛; these four give rise to the endurance or patient pursuit that results in their realization四法忍. In the realm of form and the formless, they are called the 四类忍.

84 By patient meditation the false or perplexed views见惑 will cease, and the eight kinds of Prajñā or gnosis八智 be acquired; therefore Prajñā results from endurance and the sixteen, eight endurance and eight Prajñā 八忍八智or 观, are called the sixteen mental conditions十六心 during the stage of enlightenment, when illusions or perplexities of view are destroyed. Such is

the teaching of the Wei-shi School唯识宗, or the Consciousness-only School.

85 āsrava 漏, or discharge, or leakage, or outflow of afflictions, is characteristic of sentient beings in their cycles of birth and death. It is also defined as another term 烦恼, i.e. flowing, running, discharge; distress, pain, affliction. For example, anger is an affliction in one's mind, which is discharged through one's body and voice. Any discharge is a display of one's affliction and does not decrease it. The Seven Discharges are respectively caused by: (1) contamination of views, or the illusion of viewing the seeming as real. (2) The three root afflictions, coming from the three poisons: greed, anger, and delusion. (3) six faculties: eye, ear, nose, tongue, body, and mental faculty. The first five are physical, and the last one is mental. (4) various evil deeds and evil persons. (5) four necessities, usually including food and drink, clothing, bedding, and medicine. (6) three states of Vedanā, i. e. sensation, are divided into painful, pleasurable, and freedom. When things are opposed to desire, pain arises; when accordant, there is pleasure and a desire for their continuance; when neither, one is detached or free. (7) leakage of mindfulness, or stream of delusive memory.

86 Or the four forms of birth or four kinds of birth: (1) 胎生 jarāyuja, viviparous, as with mammalia; (2) 卵生 aṇḍaja, oviparous, as with birds; (3) 湿生 or 寒热和合生 saṃsvedaja, moisture, or water-born, as with worms and fishes; (4) 化生 aupapāduka, metamorphic, as with moths from the chrysalis, or with Devás, or in the hells, or the first beings in a newly evolved world.

87 Ten Fetters 十缠 are: (1) no sense of shame; (2) no sense of dishonor; (3) jealousy; (4) stinginess; (5) remorse; (6) torpor; (7) restlessness; (8) stupor; (9) rage; (10) concealing one's wrongdoings.

88 Both Rock or Mustard kalpas refer to infinite amount of time. Buddha had not spoken about the exact length of the maha-kalpa in number of years. However, he had given several astounding analogies to understand it. Imagine a huge empty cube at the beginning of a kalpa, approximately 16

miles in each side. Once every 100 years, you insert a tiny mustard seed into the cube. According to the Buddha, the huge cube will be filled even before the kalpa ends. Imagine a gigantic rocky mountain at the beginning of kalpa, approximately 16 x 16 x 16 miles (dwarfing Mount Everest). You take a small piece of silk and wipe the mountain once every 100 years. According to the Buddha, the mountain will be completely depleted even before the kalpa ends.

89 See note 31 of Fascicle III.

90 According to the *Classic of Mountains and Seas* or *Shanhai Jing*《山海经》, a Chinese classic text and a compilation of mythic geography and myth, Mount Yan produces stones look like jade.

91 Kuafu 夸父 is a giant in Chinese mythology who wished to capture Sun. He followed Sun from the East to the West, draining the Yellow River and the Wei River (all rivers and lakes crossing his path) to quench his burning thirst. As he searched for more water, he died of dehydration. The wooden club he was carrying grew into a vast forest of peach trees called Denglin Forest 邓林 with magic power.

92 See note 30 of Fascicle VII.

93 The concentration of cessation灭尽定, entering into the concentration of total extinction of mental activity and other eight degrees of mental concentration, i.e. the four Dhyānas corresponding to the four divisions in Heavens of form, and the four degrees of mental concentration on the emptiness, corresponding to Heavens of formlessness.

94 Or saṅghāgāra, 伽蓝in Chinese, means monks' dwelling.

95 Shu Guang疏广(?–45 BC) and his nephew Shu Shou 疏受 of the Han Dynasty.

96 Both Chao Fu 巢父 and Xu You 许由 were legendary hermits in Chinese ancient times. Emperor Yao (traditionally c. 2356–2255 BC) wanted to give them the royal throne but was refused. Instead, they became recluses so as to

maintain their personal purity.

97 See note 1 of Fascicle II.

98 In the Chinese concept of cosmology, the sky is divided into nine divisions 九重天 and Earth is also in nine layers correspondingly. The deepest part in the nether earth is called *jiuyou* 九幽.

99 The Four Māras or Destroyers: the māras of the passions 烦恼魔, the skandha-māras 蕴魔, death-māra 死魔 and the māra-king 他化自在天子魔.

100 The Nine Bonds bind men to mortality: love, hate, pride, ignorance, (wrong) views, possessions (or grasping), doubt, envy, meanness (or selfishness).

101 The Five Endurances, refers to the five stages through which a Bodhisattva deepens his insight into the Dharma: (1) before the Ten Stages of Bodhisattvahood (q.v); (2) the first, second, and third stages of the Ten Stages; (3) the fourth, fifth, and sixth stages of the Ten Stages; (4) the seventh, eighth, and ninth stages of the Ten Stages; (5) the tenth stage and the stage of Buddhahood. About the Ten Stages of Bodhisattvahood, see note 6 of the preface.

102 The ten necessary activities in the fifty-two stages of a bodhisattva, following on the ten grades of bodhisattva faith 十信 and The ten stages, or periods, in bodhisattva-wisdom, prajñā 十住; the two latter indicate personal development. These ten lines of action are for the universal welfare of others. They are: (1)joyful service; (2)beneficial service; never resenting; (3)without limit; (4)never out of order; (5)appearing in any form at will; (6) unimpeded; (7)exalting the pāramitās amongst all beings; (8)perfecting the Buddha-law by complete virtue; (9)manifesting in all things the pure, final, true reality; (10)ten practices.

103 Zhidun支遁 (314–366), courtesy name Daolin道林, was a Buddhist monk and philosopher, who spent many years in a temple in Shan County 剡县, in today Shengzhou city 嵊州市, Zhejiang Province.

104 See note 30 of Preface.

105 See note 106 of Fascicle I.

106 Might refer to Mount Hua 华山, also called Taihua Shan 太华山. See note 6 of Fascicle VII.

107 Refers to *Hetu* "河图".

108 The Luo River 洛河 is a tributary of the Yellow River in China. It rises in the southeast flank of Mount Hua in Shaanxi Province and flows east into Henan Province, where it eventually joins the Yellow River at the city of Gongyi. Although not a major river by most standards, it flows through an area of great archaeological significance in the early history of China. The Luo's main tributary is the Yi River伊河, which joins it at Yanshi, after which the river is called the Yiluo River伊洛河, nurturing the so-called the culture of He-Luo 河洛文化 of China.

109 The Kunlun Mountains are one of the longest mountain chains in Asia, extending more than 3,000 kilometres (1,900 *mi*). In the broadest sense, it forms the northern edge of the Tibetan Plateau south of the Tarim Basin. The exact definition of this range, however, varies. Kunlun is also the name of a mythical mountain believed to be a Taoist paradise in China. Kunlun is known to be rich in fine nephrite jade.

110 Bian He 卞和 found a piece of jade stone, Heshibi 和氏璧, on Mount Chu, also called Mount Jin, in the State of Chu during the Spring and Autumn and Warring States Periods (722–222 BC). It was first made into a jade disc, then into the Imperial Seal of China by Qin Shi Huang (259–210 BC).The story of how this precious jade was discovered has come from Han Fei韩非 (280–233 BC) in his book of the same name, in the beginning of Chapter 13: *He Shi*. As "Shi" in the title means "surname," the title is referring to Bian He卞和. The Heshibi or He's Jade Disc, played an important part in many historical stories in Ancient China. The most famous one is "*Returning the Jade Intact to Zhao* 完璧归赵".

111 Refers to the *Letter to Wu Zhi* (*Yu Wuzhi Shu*《与吴质书》), was written in

219 by Cao Pi曹丕.

112 Cao Pi 曹丕(r.220–226), courtesy name Zihuan子桓, was the first emperor of the state of Cao Wei in the Three Kingdoms Period. Cao Pi was also an accomplished poet and scholar, just like his father Cao Cao and his younger brother Cao Zhi. He wrote *Yange Xing*《燕歌行》, the first Chinese poem in the style of seven syllables per line 七言诗. He also wrote over a hundred articles on various subjects.

113 Wu Zhi吴质 (177–230), courtesy name Jizhong 季重, was a famous litterateur during the Three Kingdoms Period (184/220–280).

114 Refers to the text *On Why Monks Do Not Bow Down Before Kings* (*Shamen Bujingwangzhe Lun*《沙门不敬王者论》) written by Huiyuan慧远 (334–416) in 404 AD. Huiyuan was born in Shanxi province, and later founded the Donglin Temple on Mount Lushan in Jiangxi province where he died in 416. Although he was born in the north, he moved south to live within the bounds of the Eastern Jin Dynasty.

115 Emperor Xiaowu of Jin 晋孝武帝(r.372–396), personal name Sima Yao 司马曜, courtesy name Changming 昌明, was an emperor of the Eastern Jin Dynasty (265–420).

116 Refers to Cao Cao. He was also skilled in poetry, calligraphy and martial arts and wrote many war journals. He has also been praised as a brilliant ruler and military genius who was quite skilled in statecraft.

117 Refers to Sima Shi司马师 (208–255) and Sima Zhao司马昭 (211–265). Sima Shi, courtesy name Ziyuan子元, was a military general and regent of Cao Wei during the Three Kingdoms period of China. After Sima Yan (the son of Sima Zhao) became emperor, he, recognizing Sima Shi's role in his own imperial status, posthumously honored his uncle as Emperor Jing of Jin 晋景帝, with the temple name Shizong 世宗and his father Sima Zhao as Emperor Wen of Jin 晋文帝, with the temple name of Taizu 太祖.

118 Five sentiments may refer to merriness, angry, worry, sadness, and fear.

119 Reforsto Li Hong 李弘 (652–675). see note 77 of Fascicle VIII.

120 Li Xian李贤 (653–684), courtesy name Mingyun 明允, formally Crown Prince Zhanghuai 章怀太子, named Li De 李德, from 672 to 674, was a crown prince of the Tang Dynasty. He was the sixth son of Emperor Gaozong, and the second son of his second wife Empress Wu (later known as Wu Zetian). He was known for writing commentaries for the *Book of Later Han*, the official history of the Eastern Han Dynasty. He became crown prince in 675 after his older brother Li Hong's death, but soon fell out of favor with Empress Wu herself. In 680, Empress Wu had her associates accuse Li Xian of treason, and he was demoted to commoner rank and exiled. In 684, after Emperor Gaozong's death, Empress Wu, then empress dowager, had her associate Qiu Shenji 丘神绩 visit Li Xian to force him to commit suicide. In 655, he was granted to be Prince of Lu.

121 Imperial censor(宪司 or 御史): ancient Chinese official in charge of inspecting other officials. Censorate, the surveillance agency.

122 Implying that the Emperor is benevolent and merciful. See note 30 of this fascicle.

123 Implying that the Emperor could award people according to their contributions. It may allude to a Chinese idiom—presenting the pheasant to the king of Chu State 山鸡献楚, which comes from *the Master Yinwen-the Great Dao* (Yinwen Zi Dadao Shang《尹文子・大道上》)：

A man walked, shouldering a load with a pheasant, and a passer-by asked him, "what is it?"

He lied to him and said, " It is the Phoenix. "

"I only heard that there was a Phoenix. Today I really saw it. Do you sell it or not? " asked the man.

The man with the pheasant answered," It's for sale. "

The passer-by gave him ten ingots of gold, but the man did not sell it. So the passer-by doubled it and bought the pheasant. The passer-by prepared to dedicate it to the king of Chu, but after a night the bird died. The passer-by did not cherish money, but only kicked himself for not presenting a phoenix to the king of Chu. The people in the country heard it and reported the matter to the king of Chu. The king of Chu appreciated his loyalty very much and gave him a great reward, ten times more than the money he bought the bird.

124 Refers to the Chinese god of the wind named Feilian 飞廉, also known as Fengbo 风伯, a mythological figure with the head of a deer and the tail of a snake and is one of assistants of Chiyou 蚩尤.

125 Refers to King Mu of Zhou周穆王 (c. 1054–949 BC). He was the fifth king of the Zhou Dynasty. The dates of his reign were 976–922 BC or 956–918 BC. Mu was more ambitious than wise. During Mu's reign, the Zhou Dynasty was at its peak, and Mu tried to stamp out invaders in the western part of China and ultimately expand Zhou's influence to the east. In the height of his passion for conquests, he led an immense army against the Quanrong, who inhabited the western part of China. His travels allowed him to contact many tribes and swayed them to either join under the Zhou banner or be conquered in war with his army. This expedition may have been more of a failure than a success, judging by the fact that he brought back only four white wolves and four white deer. Unintentionally and inadvertently, he thus sowed the seeds of hatred which culminated in an invasion of China by the same tribes in 771 BC. In his thirteenth year the Xu Rong, probably the state of Xu in the southeast, raided near the eastern capital of Fenghao. The war seems to have ended in a truce in which the state of Xu gained land and power in return for nominal submission.

126 Chang'an was also known as Xijing 西京 or the "Western Capital," relative to its position to the capital at Luoyang as the "Eastern Capital."

127 Present Sishui and its surrounding areas west of Xingyang City, Henan Province.

128 Present Qinyang City and its surrounding areas, Henan Province.

129 Present Fuchang County, west of Yiyang city, Henan Province.

130 Present the area northeast of Luoning, Henan Province.

131 Present Xin'an City and its surrounding areas, Henan Province.

132 Present the area west of Mianchi, Henan Province.

133 The star *chunshou* 鹑首, according to Chinese Astrology in ancient times, was usually associated with the Qin (today Shannxi Province) region, with Chang'an as the capital of the Qin Dynasty, called the western capital.

134 Refers to *Luoshu* diagram to be seen on the back of a turtle emerging from the River Luo.

135 The Central Plain (Zhonji中畿or Zhongyuan中原), also known as Zhongtu 中土, or Zhongzhou 中州, is the area on the lower reaches of the Yellow River which formed the cradle of Chinese civilization. It forms part of the North China Plain. In its narrowest sense, the Central Plain covers modern-day Henan, the southern part of Hebei, the southern part of Shanxi, and the western part of Shandong Province. A broader interpretation of the Central Plain's extent would add the Guanzhong plain of Shaanxi, the northwestern part of Jiangsu, and parts of Anhui and northern Hubei. Since the beginning of recorded history, the Central Plain has been an important site for Chinese civilization. In the pre-Qin era, present-day Luoyang and its nearby areas were considered the "Center of the World," as the political seat of the Xia Dynasty was located around Songshan and the Yi-Luo river basin.

136 Yu禹or Yu Shun禹舜, or Shun 舜, also known as Emperor Shun 帝舜 and Chonghua 重华, was a legendary leader of ancient China, regarded by some sources as one of the Three Sovereigns and Five Emperors being the last of the Five Emperors. Oral tradition holds that he lived sometime between 2294 and 2184 BC.

137 Hao or Haojing 镐京, also called Zongzhou 宗周, was one of the two settlements comprising the capital of the Western Zhou Dynasty (1066–770

BC), the other being Feng or Fengjing 沣京. Together they were known as Fenghao and stood on opposite banks of the Feng River 沣河 with Haojing on the east bank. Archaeological discoveries indicate that the ruins of Haojing lie next to the Feng River around the north end of Doumen Subdistrict 斗门街道 in present-day Xi'an, Shaanxi Province. It was the center of government for King Wu of Zhou (r. 1046–1043 BC).

138 Sun Hao 孙皓 (243–284), the fourth and last emperor of the state of Eastern Wu during the Three Kingdoms period, turned out to be a cruel, extravagant and incompetent monarch. The state of Eastern Wu was eventually conquered by the Jin Dynasty in 280, ending the Three Kingdoms Period. He undertook a costly move of the capital from Jianye to Wuchang, which was regarded by people as the most unfortunate and stupid choice. So it is said that people at that time hated such a choice and refused to eat the Wuchang bream 武昌鱼, a species of cyprinid fish native to the Yangtze basin, even if it was tasteful.

139 Yun and Ting are two mountains where ancient Chinese offered sacrifices to Heaven and Earth known as Fengshan 封禅.

140 The State of Zheng郑国 was established by Wang Shichong 王世充 (567–621), whose courtesy name was Xingman 行满, a general of the Chinese Sui Dynasty. He deposed Sui's last emperor Yang Tong杨侗 (604–619) and briefly ruled as the emperor of a succeeding state of Zheng. In 619, he took Luoyang as the capital. After becoming emperor, however, he was unable to withstand military pressure from Tang Dynasty forces, forcing him to seek aid from Dou Jiande 窦建德 the Prince of Xia. After Dou was defeated and captured by the Tang general Li Shimin (the later Emperor Taizong), Wang surrendered. Emperor Gaozu of Tang spared him, but the Tang official Dugu Xiude 独孤修德, whose father Dugu Ji 独孤机 had been executed by Wang, assassinated him.

141 The Jin Dynasty is usually divided into Western and Eastern Jin eras. The

Western Jin (266–316) was established as a successor state to Cao Wei after Sima Yan司马炎(r. 266–296)usurped the throne, and had its capital in Luoyang, later in Chang'an (modern Xi'an); Western Jin reunited China in 280, but fairly shortly thereafter fell into a succession crisis, civil war, and invasion by the "Five Barbarians (Wu Hu)." The rebels and invaders began to establish new self-proclaimed states in the Yellow River valley in 304, inaugurating the "Sixteen Kingdoms" era. These states immediately began fighting each other and the Jin Empire, leading to the second division of the dynasty, the Eastern Jin (317–420) when Sima Rui司马睿(r.317–323) moved the capital to Jiankang (modern Nanjing). The Eastern Jin Dynasty was eventually overthrown by the Liu Song.

142 Liu Jing刘敬 (year of birth and death unknown), with original name Lou Jing娄敬, was a general of the Western Han. In 202 AD, he passed Luoyang on the way to Longxi陇西 to defend the frontier and suggested to Liu Bang 刘邦(256–195), the Emperor Gaozu of Han, that the capital of Han should be moved from Luoyang to Guanzhong plain of Shaanxi, with which Zhang Liang 张良(c. 3rd century BC–186 BC) showed his agreement. Following their advice, afterwards, liu Bang chose Chang'an as the capital of Han. Zhang Liang, courtesy name Zifang子房, was a strategist and statesman who lived in the early Western Han Dynasty. He is also known as one of the "Three Heroes of the early Han Dynasty" 汉初三杰, along with Han Xin 韩信 and Xiao He 萧何.

143 Refer to Fenghao 丰镐 (present-day xi'an) capital of the western zhou and cheng zhou 成周 (present-day Luoyang), capital of the Eastern zhou.

144 Yi River伊水 runs in the west of Henan Province and flowed into the Luo River in Luoyang, so here it refers to Luoyang. Xianyang咸阳 was the capital of the Qin Dynasty, which was in the same administrative area with Chang'an; thus, here it refers to Chang'an.

145 The Pingle Palace was an amusement palace, firstly built during the reign of

Emperor Ming (r.57–75) of the Han Dynasty, located outside the west gate to Luoyang city.

146 Jianzhang Palace was constructed magnificently and spectacularly in Chang'an in 104 BC, the first year of the reign of emperor Wu (r.141–87 BC) of the Han Dynasty.

147 Sheng 笙 is a Chinese mouth-blown free reed musical instrument consisting of vertical pipes. It is a polyphonic instrument and enjoys an increasing popularity as a solo instrument. In the *Deer Bleat*《鹿鸣》of the *Book of Odes*《诗经》, the "playing Sheng" is regarded as the imperial music to entertain the distinguished guests. Later, it also implied the eagerness of seeking after the men of worth and ability.

148 Refers to Luoyang, where are three rivers: the Yellow River, the Luo River and Yi River.

Fascicle X

Beginning with the Master's Return to the Western Capital Chang'an Accompanying the Emperor from Luoyang in the First Month of the Third Year of Xianqing Period (658) and Ending with His Demise at the Yuhua Palace in the Second Month of the First Year of Linde Period (664)

In the first month of the third year of Xianqing (658), the Emperor returned from the Eastern Capital Luoyang to the Western Capital Chang'an. The Master also returned with him.

In the seventh month in this autumn, an imperial order was issued asking the Master to move to the Ximing Monastery[1]. The construction of it commenced on the nineteenth day of the eighth month in the autumn of the first year of Xianqing (656); at the time, an imperial order was issued with the effect that the old estate of the Prince of Pu[2] at the Yankang Ward was to be given to the Crown Prince for the construction of one Buddhist monastery and one Daoist temple, and that the Master was to carry out a preliminary inspection of the site. After the inspection, the Master reported that the place was not spacious enough for two monasteries, so the whole place was allocated solely for the construction of a Buddhist monastery, and the site of the Daoist temple was changed to the Puning Ward. Then the construction of the Buddhist monastery was started and completed in the sixth month in the summer of the third year of Xianqing. The front of the monastery was three hundred fifty *bu* in width, and the perimeter of it was several *li*. On both sides of the monastery flanked thoroughfares, in the front and at the back of it distributed residential quarters; green locust trees were planted lavishly in rows outside the monastery and a brook of clear water was ceaselessly and solemnly flowing through the courtyard inside, which made the monastery the most distinguished one among others in the capital. Within the monastery, corridors, halls, storeyed houses and turrets were imposing high, with birds flying above; the door knocker-holders were gilded and the beams exquisitely decorated, dazzling enough to throw back the sunshine and outdo the rosy clouds. Totally, there were ten courtyards with more than 4,000 chambers. Neither the Tongtai Monastery of the Liang Dynasty[3] nor the Yongning Monastery of the Wei Dynasty[4] could rival with it in solemnity and adornment.

First an edict came and ordered the official in charge to select fifty eminent monks to reside in the monastery, each of whom could be accompanied by one attendant; then, another edict was issued to choose one hundred fifty young Buddhist practitioners by examination to receive ordination. On the thirteenth day of the same month, an almsgiving ceremony was held at the monastery to ordain new monks. The Master was invited to supervise the ordination ceremony. On the fourteenth day of the seventh month in the autumn, the newly-ordained monks were received into the monastery by a solemn procession that was decorated with banners and canopies, music being performed, with the same rituals as when the Master and the stele were escorted into the Ci'en monastery. Later, another imperial edict came ordering to lodge the Master in a best room of the monastery and assign him ten newly-ordained *Śramaṇeras* (including Haihui and others) as disciples.

Considering the Master had been esteemed by the late emperor, the reigning Emperor has showed even more veneration to the Master since his succession of the Throne, and very often dispatched palace messengers and officials to inquire after him. Besides, at different times, the Emperor offered the Master with gifts, including over ten thousand rolls of floss silk, damask and brocade, as well as several hundred religious robes, patchwork garments, Kāṣāya (cassocks), and so forth, which were all used by the Master to construct pagodas, transcribe scriptures and make Buddha images with the purpose to benefit the empire and the people. Besides, he also distributed some of them as alms to people in need or as gifts to the Brāhmaṇa visitors. Actually, the Master handed out whatever he had obtained without delay, not keeping anything for himself. He once vowed to have ten Koṭis of Buddha images molded, ten Koṭis being one million, and finally kept it.

In the eastern country, a great importance had always been attached to the *Mahāprajñāpāramitā Sūtra*; however, the previous Chinese versions of this Sūtra were all abridged ones[5], so the Master was always solicited by others to translate it anew. The Master was afraid that he was not able to fulfill the task because this Sūtra was a voluminous work and would take a lot of time to translate, but in the capital, he had to cope with numerous mundane affairs. In addition, the life was so impermanent and limited. Thus, he entreated the Emperor to permit him to move to the Yuhua Palace[6] to do the translation work. Fortunately, the Emperor gave consent to his request. In the tenth month in the winter of the fourth year of Xianqing Period (659), the Master left the capital for the Yuhua Palace, together with other monk translators and disciples. The sustenance and demands were supplied to the same standards as those when he was in the capital. Upon his arrival at the Yuhua Palace, the Master was lodged at the Sucheng Court.

On the first day of the first month in the spring of the fifth year (of Xianqing) (660), the Master began to translate the *Mahāprajñāpāramitā Sūtra.* As the original voluminous Sanskrit text comprises two hundred thousand stanzas, so the disciples often persuaded the Master to abridge it. However, when the Master planned to adopt their suggestion and cut off such trivial details as the repetitive and the overelaborate parts, just as what Kumārajīva had done before, he had a night dream that warned him with some frightening situations, such as sailing in a dangerous boat or walking on a precipitous cliff or struggling against ferocious animals, which he narrowly escaped but woke up in perspiration, shuddering all over. Feeling very fearful, he told the dream to his disciples and then resolved to translate the original text in full. At the very night he thought of it, he had another dream, in which he saw various buddhas and bodhisattvas emitting light from between the eyebrows. Bathing in the light, he felt very carefree and comfortable. He then offered flowers and lamps to buddhas, and ascended to a lofty seat to preach the Dharma. Also he was surrounded by people who were lauding his merits respectfully, with some of them presenting him with the best fruits. After he woke up, he was full of joy. From then on, he dared not to make any alteration or abridgment but kept his translation every bit faithful to the original Sanskrit text.

In the past, the Buddha preached this holy scripture to sixteen assemblies at four places namely: (1) the Vulture Peak near the city of Rājagṛha, (2) the Anāthapiṇḍika Garden of the Jetavana Park, (3) the Heavenly Palace of Paranirmita-vaśavartins[7], and (4) Veṇuvana Vihāra (Bamboo Forest Monastery) in the city of Rājagṛha, and the sermons were collected into one Sūtra. What the Master had obtained from the Western Regions were three different versions of this Sūtra. When he was undertaking the translation, if there were any ambiguities and uncertainties in the text, he would compare the three versions together to settle them; only after deliberating over the questions time and again did he start to translate. The prudence and carefulness he exercised in dealing with his translation was indeed unprecedented in history. Whenever he came by some intractable problems, such as the inscrutable wording or the abstruse meaning, he would be instructed by some deity in mysterious visions so that he was able to dispel his doubts, like catching sight of the sun after pushing aside clouds. He once told others, "How could [Xuan]Zang with a shallow mind have obtained such a profound understanding? It is all credited to the assistance of Buddhas and Bodhisattvas."

The first chapter of the *Sūtra* is *on the Purity and Adornment of Buddha lands,* which records that various Bodhisattvas and Mahābodhisattvas, due to their Prajñā Pāramitā, exercised their supernatural potency and power of vows to adorn the venue for the Dharma preaching by offering the rare treasures of a great chiliocosm, varied incenses and fragrant flowers, foods of variegated flavors, garments, music, and other wondrous items pleasant to the five senses created from their will. At one night, Huide, abbot of the Yuhua Monastery, and a monk translator named Jiashang, had the same dream as follows:

The Yuhua Monastery looked very spacious, solemn and clean, splendidly adorned with pennants, curtains, precious carriages, flowers and banners; melodious musical tunes were permeating in the air; numerous monks and laity, holding flowery canopies and other offering items, came to pay homage to the *Mahāprajñāpāramitā Sūtra;* the walls of alleyways within the monastery were all decorated with gorgeous brocades; the ground was carpeted with rare flowers for people to tread on. Approaching the translation court, they saw that it became wondrously beautiful, a treasures-adorned place as what was depicted in the scriptures. They also heard lectures being delivered in three separate halls there simultaneously, and in the middle hall it was the Master who was preaching.

After seeing all those sights, they woke up with a pleasant surprise. Then they paid a visit to the Master and told him what they had dreamed. The Master said, "Because we are translating this chapter at present, various bodhisattvas must have come to present offerings. Now that Your Reverences have seen the sight, you are confirmed in your belief, aren't you?" At the time there were two apple trees on both sides of the hall, unexpectedly and untimely they blossomed lavishly for several times, with six petals on each flower, freshly rosy and white, pleasing to eye, about which monks talked among themselves, saying that it must be an auspicious omen to indicate the re-propagation of Prajñā, and that six petals must represent six Pāramitā by which the yonder shore of the suffering ocean could be reached. When the Master was translating this Sūtra, he felt a sense of urgency for fear of the impermanence of his life. He once said to other monks, "I am sixty-five years old[8] this year. I'm afraid my life will come to an end at this monastery soon, but this Sūtra is so voluminous that I am really worried the translation would not be finished. Let us redouble our exertion and spare no toil."

On the twenty-third day of the tenth month in the winter of the third year of Longshuo (663), the translation work was finally completed. Consisting of six hundred fascicles in total, the scripture was entitled *Dabore jing* (the *Scripture of the Great Wisdom*) in Chinese. Joining his palms together in exhilaration, the Master said to his disciples, "This scripture has a karmic affiliation to this place. It is by the power of this Sūtra that I came to the Yuhua Monastery. If I had stayed in the capital and burdened with innumerable affairs of all sorts, how could I have completed the translation? Now owing to the blessings of numerous buddhas as well as the protection of heavenly beings and dragons, the translation has been finished at length. This Sūtra is not only the grand canon which is capable of giving protection and blessings to our country, but also a precious treasure greatly valued by both the celestial and human beings. You disciples should rejoice at its completion."

Then Jizhao, Director of Duties[9] of the Yuhua Monastery, organized a celebration party for the completion of the Sūtra's translation by offering a fasting assembly to monks. On that day, when he intended to take the Sūtra on *prajñā* from Sucheng Hall to Jiashou Hall for elucidation and recitation, no sooner had he touched it than the Sūtra gave off a light illumining the place near and far, and all at once, a special aroma pervaded the air. The Master said to his disciples, "According to the Sūtra, at this place there should be the kings, ministers, and the four divisions of disciples[10] to prefer Mahāyāna teachings, and to copy, hold, recite and circulate this Sūtra; and this would be the cause for them to be reborn in heavens, even to obtain the ultimate emancipation. Now that there is such a passage in the Sūtra, we must not keep silent about it."

On the twenty-second day of the eleventh month, the Master asked his disciple Kuiji[11] to write a petition inviting the Emperor to write a preface to the Sūtra. On the seventh day of the twelfth month, Fengyi, a court secretary, announced the imperial decree of consent.

After the translation of the *Mahāprajñāpāramitā Sūtra*, the Master felt physically exhausted, and acknowledging his final release was impending, he told his disciples, "Thanks to this Sūtra on *prajñā,* I came to the Yuhua Monastery. Now that the translation work has already been finished, my life is near its end. After my death you should manage my funeral in a frugal and simple way. You should wrap my corpse in a coarse bamboo or reed mat, and choose a secluded spot beside a mountain stream as my burial ground. Don't bury me close to the palace or a monastery, for it seems to be better to dispose my impure physical body in a remote place afar off." On hearing those words, the disciples began to sob in sadness. Wiping off the tears, they said, "Your Reverence is in normal health condition and your countenance looks fine as usual. For what reason did you suddenly say so?" The Master said, "I know it myself. How could you know?"

On the first day of the first month in the spring of the first year of Linde (664), the great virtuous translators and other monks of the monastery sincerely besought the Master to translate the *Mahāratnakūta Sūtra.* On seeing they were so earnest in their request, with a great effort, the Master managed to translate it but stopped after several lines. Putting away the Sanskrit text, he told his disciples, "This Sūtra is as voluminous as the *Mahāprajñāpāramitā Sūtra.* I know best that I have not got enough energy to translate it. My death time is approaching, and my life wanders the earth no longer. I wish to go to Lanzhi Valley and other places to pay homage and bid farewell to Koṭis of Buddha images." Then he went out of the room with his disciples. Monks looked at each other in tears. After the worship, he returned to the monastery. Afterwards, he began to engage himself exclusively in practicing the Way and did no more translation.

On the eighth day, one of his disciples named Xuanjue, a monk from Gaochang, told the Master about his dream, in which he saw a lofty stūpa suddenly collapsing. Roused with a start, he came over to report the dream to the Master. The Master said, "It has nothing to do with you. It is a portent for my death."

In the evening of the ninth day, when the Master was crossing a ditch behind his chamber, he tumbled over, getting some scratches on the shin. Then he was confined to bed and became gradually infirm.

On the sixteenth day, just like waking up from a dream, he said,

"There are white lotus flowers, dish-large, fresh and lovely, before my eyes." On the seventeenth day, he dreamed that hundreds of people, gigantic in stature, donning brocade garments, were using colorful silk textiles, wonderful flowers, and precious jewelry to decorate the chamber where he was lying as well as other rooms inside and outside the translation court. Also, he dreamed that on the mountain ridges and in the woods behind the monastery, banners and canopies were erected in various colors, and the ethereal music performed. Moreover, outside the door, there were numerous precious carts carrying delicious foods and tasty fruits of hundreds and thousands of different colors and kinds, none being earthly things, all of which were presented to the Master, but the Master refused to accept them by saying, "Only those who have obtained supernatural powers are qualified to have such great delicacies. I have not mounted such a stage; how dare I accept them?" Although he constantly declined, the foods were offered to him incessantly. Not until one of his attendants coughed beside his bed did the Master open his eyes and wake up from the dream. Then he told Huide, abbot of the monastery, about all the foregoing dreams. In addition, the Master said, "From the scene in my dreams, it seems that the merits and wisdom I have accumulated from my religious deeds in this life are not in vain. From it we can see the theories of Buddhism, such as causation, are not fallacies." Then he asked Jiashang to enlist all the scriptures and treatises translated by him. Totally there were seventy-four works, amounting to 1335 fascicles. Besides, the Master had already made a thousand pictures of Bhṛkuṭī and a thousand pictures of Maitreya, and ten Koṭis of print copies of Buddha image. Also, he had transcribed the *Vajracchedikāprajñāpāramitā Sūtra*, the *Bhaiṣajyaguru Sūtra*, the *Śaḍdvāradhāraṇī Sūtra*, and others, 1,000 copies for each. To cultivate his Field of Compassion, he had given alms to ten thousand people in need, and to till his Field of Reverence, he presented offerings to ten thousand monks. He had lighted hundreds of lamps and redeemed thousands of living creatures. When the list was made, Jiashang was ordered to read it aloud to him. Upon hearing it, the Master joined his palms together in joy. Then, the Master said to his disciples, "It is time for me to pass away and I wish to get rid of my avarice thoroughly. Please summon all monks to come here." Then he gave away all his garments and property as alms, again had more Buddha's images made and invited the monks to perform religious rituals.

On the twenty-third day, the fasting assembly was held and alms given. Song Fazhi, a sculptor, was also asked to erect a bone-structure of a Buddha statue at the Jiashou Hall. After that, the Master pleasantly bade farewell to the monk-translators, disciples, monks of the monastery and others. At last, he said, "The filthy physical body of me is what I have deeply loathed. It is of no significance for me to linger on the world any longer after I have done what I should do. I'd like to bestow my blessing and wisdom accumulated from my religious deeds on all sentient beings, and together with them, I would like to ascend to Tuṣita Heaven to join in the inner retinue of Maitreya, Holy One of Compassion, and attend on Him. When the Maitreya Buddha descends into the human world, I'd like to follow Him and perform the Buddha's deeds extensively until I attain the supreme Bodhi." After saying those words, the Master concentrated his mind rightly and fell into silence, after a while, he recited: "The aggregate of matter is void; the aggregates of perception, conception, volition, and the consciousness are also void. The realm of sight is void; (all sense realms) up to the realm of mind are also void. The realm of sight-perception is void; (all sense-perception realms) up to the realm of the mental faculty are also void. Ignorance is void; (all nidāna) up to old age and death are also void. Even enlightenment is void; emptiness itself is also void." Then he uttered a stanza and taught the people surrounding him to recite after him "Paying homage to Maitreya Tathāgata, Rightly and Fully Enlightened One, may I with all living beings be present speedily before your compassionate countenance. Paying homage to the inner retinue of Maitreya Tathāgata, may I be born among them after I forsake my present life!" Huide, abbot of the monastery, dreamed that there were one thousand golden statues descending from the eastern heaven to the translation court that was enveloped in fragrant smoke and celestial flowers.

At midnight of the fourth day of the second month, Chan (Dhyāna) Master Mingzang, who was looking after the Master, saw two persons coming, who were about one *zhang*[12] tall, holding together a white lotus flower as large as a small cartwheel, with pedals of three layers and a leaf of more than one-foot long in diameter. The flower was fresh, pure and lovely, which was to be presented to the Master. One of them who were holding the flower said to the Master, "Your Reverence, due to the paltry ailment you are suffering now, all of the troubles you formerly had brought to sentient beings have already been thoroughly eliminated, so does your unwholesome karma accumulated since the time immemorial. Now you should feel joyous and grateful." The Master looked at them and joined his palms together for a long time; then he supported his head with his right hand, stretched his left hand on the left thigh, and lay down on his right side with one foot resting on the other. He kept this posture, without moving and taking in any water or food.

At midnight of the fifth day, his disciple Puguang and others inquired of him, "Shall Your Reverence be reborn among the inner retinue of Maitreya?" The Master replied, "Yes, I shall." With those words, his breath faded away. After a short time, he passed away peacefully, which was unnoticed by his attendants until they put a piece of new floss on his nose to make sure whether he was breathing or not. His body began to get cold from his feet, and then gradually up to the top of his head which remained as the last warm spot. His complexion was pinkish white, and his countenance looked much more pleasant than ever. After seven days, the Master still looked the same, without giving off any unusual smell. If he had not practiced self-cultivation through meditation guided by wisdom, and if he had not practiced himself by observing commandments, how could he have achieved such a superb condition?

There was a monk at the Ci'en Monastery, named Minghui, who performed religious practices diligently by reciting scriptures and often walking in meditation during the first, the middle and the last parts of night, never slack off. At the very night when the Master passed away, Minghui was circumambulating at the Buddha Hall. He saw there were four beams of white light appearing in the western sky, very bright and clear, flying from the north to the south across the constellation Jingxiu[13] to reach the Ci'en Pagoda Court. This weird sight reminded him of a record that in the past, when the Tathāgata attained nirvāṇa, there were twelve beams of white light arising from the west and reaching the constellation Taiwei[14], which has been regarded as a symbol for the transformation of Great Holy One. "Now the sight appears again. Was it not a sign to show that the Master in the Yuhua Monastery perished?" he asked himself. At daybreak he told other monks what he had seen the night before, which made everyone amazed. On the morning of the ninth day, the grievous tidings of the Master' s demise came to the capital, exactly coinciding with the appearance of light seen by Minghui. Whoever had heard it marveled at the mysterious link between those two events.

The Master was over seven feet high in stature. With a pinkish white complexion, broad eyebrows and starry eyes, he was dignified and stately as a deity, handsome as a character in drawing. His voice was so clear and sonorous and his remarks so refined and well-turned that his listeners never felt bored when talking with him. Whenever sitting among his disciples or entertaining guests, he always could keep a straight posture without moving even for half a day. He preferred to wear Gandhāra garment[15] of fine cotton cambric, neither too tight nor too loose. When walking, he was graceful and poised, with eyes looking straight ahead and never glancing awry. He was as generous as a broad river flowing extensively over the earth, or as distinguished as a lotus flower growing gracefully out of the water. From the ordination to the end of life, he had consistently observed the disciplinary rules, showing even more prudence than what a man shows in protecting his floating bag when crossing a river, and adhering to Buddhist precepts even more strictly than Kuśa-bandhana

Bhikṣu[16]. Having a serene disposition, he did not like social life and relished simple things, so after entering the monastic order, he seldom came out the monastery unless he was summoned by an imperial decree.

After the demise of the Master, during the period of Qianfeng (666–668)[17], the Vinaya Master Daoxuan(596–667)[18], abbot of the Ximing Monastery, who was capable of seeing divine beings, saw a deity appearing before him and saying, "I am General Wei(tuo)[19], son of Heavenly Beings. I'm ruling over ghosts and deities. When Tathāgata was about to attain nirvāṇa, He ordered me to guide and maintain the bequeathed Dharma in Jambudvīpa. I see Your Reverence has observed commandments strictly and devoted ardently to the study of Vinaya Piṭaka, so those who have doubts often came to consult you, but your compilation of the major and minor precepts often went in vagueness and errors. Now Your Reverence is getting on in years, and if your compilation had incorrect points, you might mislead the later generations. In order to avoid it, I've come here to reveal you the Buddha's true teaching."

Then, having explicitly pointed out the mistakes and absurdities in Daoxuan's transcripts of Vinaya texts and his commentaries on the major and minor precepts, the deity urged him to correct them all. Under the instruction, Daoxuan shuddered in shamefulness and exhilaration. Then he inquired about the other doubts he met in reading scriptures, commandments and treatises, and got the answers from the deity. In addition, he asked the deity about the ranking of Master Xuanzang on merit among the Dharma-transmitting monks since ancient times.

The deity commended, "Since ancient times, every master has had weaknesses or strengths in comprehension and practice of the Dharma, so we lack a unitary measurement to judge them. Only Master Xuanzang has cultivated his blessedness and wisdom for many lives. In each of his previous lives, he was always erudite, perspicacious, and eloquently convincing, ranking first in Cina of Jambudvīpa, and it is true to his merits and virtues. His translation is faithful to the original Sanskrit texts both in content and form. Because of his wholesome karmic power, he was already born in the inner retinue of Maitreya's Tuṣita Heaven, where he is able to listen to the Dharma preaching, thereupon will gain complete comprehension of the Dharma and thus achieve enlightenment. In the future, he will not be reborn in the human world." After those words, the deity vanished. This event was recorded by Daoxuan in a book stored at the Ximing Monastery. If there had not been the deity who validated the enormous talents and the lofty virtues of the Master, how were we ordinary persons to fathom and assess?

When the Master was ill, Xu Xuanbei, an official sent to inspect the translation work, made a report to the Emperor on the third day of the second month of that year, saying that the Master had fallen ill because of the foot injury. On the seventh day, an imperial decree was issued ordering the Palace Service Department to dispatch physicians to treat the Master with medicines. Then the official in charge sent the imperial doctors, Zhang Dezhi and Cheng Tao, to go to see the Master post-haste with medicines. But when they arrived, the Master had already passed away. It was too late for the treatment. Then, Dou Shilun, Prefectural Magistrate of Fangzhou[20], reported the Master's demise to the Emperor. At the tidings, the Emperor fell into such a deep grief that he suspended his governmental affairs. "We have lost a national treasure", he said repeatedly. Hearing the words, the civil and military officials present began to shed tears in sadness, and the Emperor also could not refrain himself from sobbing. On the following day, again the Emperor said to his ministers, "What a pity it is that our country has lost His Reverence Xuanzang! The pillar of Śākyamuni Buddha's teachings was broken and the living creatures of Four Modes of Birth[21] were left alone without a guide. A boat suddenly sinks on the vastly expansive sea. A chamber remains in darkness when the lamps and torches have gone out! There is absolutely no difference!" With those words, the Emperor kept sighing mournfully.

On the twenty-sixth day of the month, an imperial decree was issued, which reads, "As in the report of Dou Shilun, His Reverence Xuanzang of the Yuhua Monastery, has already passed away. All funeral expenses will be covered by the government." On the sixth day of the third month, another decree was given, which reads, "Now that His Reverence Xuanzang of the Yuhua Monastery has passed away, the translation work might as well be stopped. What have already been translated should be transcribed by the government as usual, and the rest works which have not been translated should be handed over to the Ci'en Monastery for storage. Don't let them be lost or damaged. The disciples and translation colleagues of the Master who were not monks of the Yuhua Monastery should be dismissed back to their own monasteries." On the fifteenth day of the third month, there came the third imperial decree, saying, "On the funeral day of the late Reverend Xuanzang of the Yuhua Monastery, monks and nuns of the capital are to be permitted to make banners and canopies and escort his remains to cemetery."

As a man of lofty virtue, the Master was an excellent practitioner of the Buddha-truth, who had been adored by the reigning monarchs; even after his demise, the imperial favors were bestowed on him over and over again. None of the ancients could be compared with him in this respect.

Obeying the Master's testament, his disciples made a hearse out of the coarse bamboo mats. Then they escorted his holy coffin back to the capital and placed it in the translation hall at the Ci'en Monastery. The loud wailing from several hundred disciples was shaking the earth. Every day, hundreds of the capital people, both laity and monks, rushed there to weep at him. On the fourteenth day of the fourth month, when it was the time to bury him on the east bank of the Chan River[22], monks, nuns, intellectuals and ordinary people assembled to hold a funeral ceremony for him. There were undercoated canopies and white banners, carriages of nirvāṇa with curtains, golden inner and silver outer coffins, Śāla trees, etc, totally more than five hundred items lining all over the thoroughfares and lanes. Also resounding in the air, dismal and mournful tunes were performed by flutes. From the capital and its surrounding states within a radius of five hundred *li*, more than one million people attended the funeral procession. The funeral affairs were arranged in good order, looking solemn and grandiose; nevertheless, the coffin of the Master was still placed in the bamboo-mat hearse. Silk shops at the Eastern Market of the capital had made a hearse of nirvāṇa out of three thousand rolls of brocade in various colors, and also decorated it with flowery ornaments, extraordinarily exquisite and wondrous in looking, in which the holy coffin of the Master was intended to be placed, but the disciples refused to use it for they feared that the last will of the Master would be violated; as a substitute, only a set of three monastic robes of the Master and a religious patch-robe worth a hundred gold pieces given by Emperor Taizong were placed in the hearse. Then, the hearse was proceeding ahead in the procession with the bamboo-mat carriage behind. Onlookers were either shedding tears or chocked with sobs. On that night, monks and laity who stayed up to lament at the graveyard amounted to more than thirty thousand. On the morning of the fifteenth day, after the coffin pit was filled up, a fasting assembly was held at the graveyard; after that, the people were dispersed. In those days, even heaven and earth became gloomy and murky while birds and beasts blared grievously, which must be the responses from the animals and physical world to the Master's demise, let alone the grief of people that was not hard to be conceived of. Everybody was talking about it, saying that the river of desire was still extending vastly whereas the boat of compassion had suddenly sunk, that the endless night was black but the lamp of wisdom had died out, and that the torture of losing the Master was as painful as a man lost his eyes. All in all, it seems not enough to analogize the loss of the Master to the collapse of a mountain or the break of a beam. How piteous it is!

On the eighth day of the fourth month of the second year of Zongzhang (669), an imperial edict was issued to the effect that the tomb of the Master should be moved to the northern plateau of

Fanchuan[23], where a pagoda and a temple were to be built. It was because the tomb was originally located in the precinct of the capital and the sight of it often threw the Emperor in sorrow and grief at the palace. Thus, it was better to choose another site as the new graveyard. Alas! At the reburial ceremony, the disciples were as grievous and wayfarers as mournful as ever.

Comment by Shi Huili:

The stars and the moon continue the light after the sun sets; rivers and streams contribute to the vastness of the eastern sea, from which we know even the material objects follow the principle of mutual assistance and interdependence, why should human beings alone be ignorant of inheritance and renewal? After the Nirvāṇa of Dharma Lord, ever since the dharma congregations held by Ānanda, over one thousand years have elapsed. During this period, the saints cropped up from time to time and the worthy men arose one by one, each brewing some high aspiration and all endowed with intelligence. Inheriting the teachings bequeathed by Buddha, leading the celestial and mortal beings, they have spread the Way at a speed fast as the gale and exhibited their power enough to topple the mountains and overturn the seas. Displaying the supernatural power, some stretched their fingers to ooze the oil (to light a candle)[24] and others issued a wondrous light in dark chambers; some acted as mediums to subdue devils and others converted the monarchs to (Buddhism) even at a single audience; some vowed to spread the Dharma to outlying places and others risked their lives on perilous cruise into the sea; some treated people and handled things with disinterested motives, and others, enduring the torments of hunger, plunged ahead in dangerous places to seek truth for the sake of the sentient beings. Consequently, the dew of the ultimate truth has moistened the boundless land and the teachings have been passed down from generation to generation; thereby the expectations of Buddha have been fulfilled. All these facts could be verified by reviewing the historical literature, could not they? As the source is inexhaustible and the stream long, so at present we have the Master as a dharma heir.

A god of constellation descending to the world, the Master possesses the dignity as austere as a lofty mountain. With an extraordinary talent, he enjoys a highest reputation even among the bright people. He is a man of immaculate integrity, which makes him preeminent and distinguishable. In order to undertake the responsibility of sheltering and saving the living beings of four modes of birth, he was highly motivated by propagating the Right Dharma. He is as sublime as the Song[25] and Hua[26] mountains rising high to support the sky. His morality is also impeccably pure just like white carnelian shining brightly beneath the clear water of sea. Born perspicacious and handsome, he ignores the wealth and rank but is interested in pursuing the Way. As regards his erudition and broad horizon, he surpasses (Dao) heng (346–417)[27] and (Seng) zhao (384–414)[28] and even goes higher; in the exploration of the abstruse or in the comprehension of the subtleties, he exceeds (Dao) sheng (355–434)[29] and (Dao) rong (372–445)[30] and even advances farther. How great and magnificent he is! He is truly the most remarkable person available by far to boost the Buddha's teachings. It seems to be destined that the teachings of the Image Period would be revitalizes in this decadent age, so a wise and virtuous person like him was born.

In the opinion of the Master, when those great virtuous teachers, either in ancient times or in the contemporary era, were expounding the scriptures and treatises, they all based their convictions on holy teachings but quoted different passages, which often gave rise to controversies and debates. More than one hundred topics have long been debated, such as: whether Ālaya-vijñāna[31] (the basic consciousness) suffers retribution or not. whether a person, an illusorily emanation, has mind or not. whether the twenty-four non-associated compositional factors[32] are annihilated or non-annihilated after the seeds[33] are infused from hearing the correct Dharma. All these problems are complicated for they are involved in the Tripiṭaka, the Four Āgamas and the essential gist of the Greater and Lesser Vehicles. On them the preceding scholars had failed to show an explicit view, so the Master's contemporaries were left in doubts. What's more, the Master was often curious about the true meanings of some controversial passages and felt very depressed at the bewilderment caused by some specific doctrines. He once sighed with regret, "The scriptures and treaties available in our country are the branches and leaves rather than the root of the Dharma. Various teachers are holding varied views and there are many doubts yet to be settled. It is necessary for us to take reference to the comprehensive and inclusive texts at the Jetavana Grove so as to obtain the ability to discriminate right and wrong."

Thereafter, cherishing a lofty ideal, he made up his mind to travel to the distant land. In the eighth month in the autumn of the third year of the Zhenguan period (629), after making a great vow before the Buddha image, he packed up and set off on his journey resolutely.

At last, he arrived at Nālandā Mahāvihāra in Central India, where he met a great teacher named Śilabhadra (meaning "being eminent in virtue"), a scholar of an extraordinarily acute discernment, who was practicing both the Mahāyāna and Hīnayāna Buddhism. Well versed in the Tripiṭaka and conversant with the Four Vedas, Śilabhadra had acquired a particular proficiency in the *Saptadaśabhūmi Śāstra,* and often lectured on it, recognizing its leading position among all other scriptures. This Śāstra was composed by Bodhisattva Maitreya and taken as the very root of all Mahāyāna teachings, and to learn it was the preliminary aim the Master strove to pursue. At the time, all the sixteen kingdoms of India admired this Śāstra and over ten thousand students came to study it throughout the year. The Master went to Śilabhadra for it too. When they met, they were so delighted that they thought it is regrettable that they hadn't met earlier. Then, the Master wholeheartedly studied with Śilabhadra, inquiring of him about some dubious problems pressing on mind. No matter how difficult a theory might be, once the Master learned it, he was capable of absorbing the essence of it completely without leaving out any point, which is just like the big Mengsi River draining water from various streams, or the Mengzhu Lake taking in the waters of the Yunmeng swamp. Śilabhadra sighed amazingly for he had never come across a student like the Master. Once he told others, "I have rarely heard of anyone like him, much less could I expect to have a talk with such a person on the cryptic convictions at present." From that time on, the Master had become well renowned in the region west of the Pamir Ranges, and his reputation had widely spread in eight kingdoms of India. At the time, having heard the Master's name, some well-learned senior scholars in these kingdoms formulated many knotty questions and came together to challenge him. They proceeded either in cart or on foot, following one and another like wild geese flying in row or a school of fish swimming in file. They brought forth their arguments in tart remarks, with witty and well-turned phrases bursting out endlessly; as a response, the Master confuted and explained in an easy manner, either resorting to his opponents' own convictions to invalidate their arguments or pointing out their logical fallacies to attack their views. As a result, none of the opponents did not abandon his false views. Smiling satisfactorily in submission, they said, "This venerable teacher is a prodigy dispatched by Heaven. He is hard to refute." Upon hearing this, King Śilāditya and others could not help clapping in delight. They prostrated themselves before the Master with their elbows on the ground to kiss his feet, and offered him all the precious treasures they possessed.

After this debate congregation, the Master continued to study more Sanskrit books and various scriptures and treatises, ranging from all the Vaipulya teachings preached by the Tathāgata during his lifetime on the Gṛdhrakūṭa Mountain and the incomplete texts (Hīnayāna teachings) taught at the Deer Park to the works composed by later saints, including Aśvaghoṣa, Nāgārjuna, Asaṅga, and Vasubandhu; additionally, he also learned the knowledge of the eighteen schools[34] of Hīnayāna Buddhism, such as Gokulikas and others, as well as the essential gist of the five versions of the Vinaya[35]. He made an exhaustive research in all above works and carried out extensive study on them; thereupon, he not only grasped their tenets but was at home to their textual literature. What's more, he paid homage to all the traces left by Buddha when he was living, including the woods of evergreen Śāla tree where the Buddha attained His Nirvāṇa, the Bodhi tree under which the Tathāgata subjugated the Māras, the lofty stūpa built by Ajātaśatru, the mountain where the Buddha left his shadow, so on and so forth. Besides, he also had witnessed many other mysterious and wondrous phenomena.

After fulfilling all his wishes and making a thorough study of various kinds of knowledge, the Master finally intended to return to his homeland, then he had over six hundred texts of both Hīnayāna and Mahāyāna copied, and seven Buddha statues as well as more than one hundred grains of Śarīra relics collected. On the twenty-fifth day of the first month in the spring of the nineteenth year of the present reign (Zhenguan Period, 645), he arrived at Chang'an. Both clerics and laypeople rushed rejoicingly out of the capital city to welcome him, even leaving the marketplaces empty. At this juncture, the natural scenery was charmingly beautiful, with the sky entirely clear of cloud or fog and fresh breezes gently blowing. The decorated curtains crammed the roads, festoons and canopies obscured the sun, and the auspicious clouds gathered into a tender palette of various colors. The main roads were permeated with chanting and eulogies of the ordinary people and scholars, their voices shimmering loud and low. The erroneous views were eliminated immediately as the Sun of Wisdom comes to illumine brightly again. Although the people missed the scene when World-Honored One was descending from Trāyastriṃśa Heaven to Jambudvīpa, what they witnessed at that time was truly a happy and harmonious occasion that happened once in a thousand years.

The Master traveled tens of thousands of *li,* encountering numerous hardships and perils. On the road, braving the extreme cold to scale the mountains covered with thick ice, crossing the rivers surging with violent billows, narrowly escaping from the poisonous fog and fierce beasts[36], passing by the sites where the companions of Faxian[37] once lost their lives and where Zhiyan[38] was parted by death from his followers, stepping on the land where neither Ban Chao[39] had ever been to nor Zhang and Hai[40] traversed before, the Master was proceeding, resolutely and solitarily, breaking all hindrances dauntlessly. He had spread the moral ethos of the Tang Empire beyond her domain and propagated her edification among the five realms of India, so that the princes and dukes of distant lands aspired for witnessing our royal palace and the chieftains of remote areas longed for visiting our capitals. The influences exerted in the foreign land, on the one hand, have been attributed to the Master's unsurpassed merits, on the other hand, to the mighty imperial court.

Obeying the mandate of Heaven, fulfilling the destiny to be a sovereign, the Emperor Taizong of Tang ascended the Throne in yellow imperial robe. Since then, he ruled over the empire as a supreme monarch. The people were rescued from vicious warlords and the sky cleared of clouds so the sun and the moon illuminated once more. Ever since his enthronement, renewals as well as reforms have been carried out. The four basic Confucian ethical codes[41] nearly deserted were advocated once more; an obsolescence of law and order was checked as if the reverse turbulence of the sea was intercepted. In a word, he did better than Shun and Yu[42] in the activation of the Nine Functions[43]; his Seven Martial Virtues[44] outdid Cao and Liu of the

Han and Wei periods (208 BC–265 CE)[45]. Subsequently, seas became placid and rivers turned clear; weather was propitious and harvests abundant. In the places remote from him there was no disturbance, and near him, no unrest at all. To the deities and mortals' enduring pleasure, the nation spontaneously followed the law of nature, and thus would enjoy the harmony forever. The sun and the moon were illuminating once more, and the three principles of goodness[46] have been demonstrated explicitly within the domain. Officials and ministers were loyal, diligent, and competent, hence winning eulogies from the people; just as the earth is responsible to nurture all things, so the Emperor made exploits by taking up his great mission. Therefore, because of his lofty virtues and grand accomplishments, many mystical natural scenes were called forth. The purple ganoderma were blooming at the jade steps in the royal palace, while flowers and fruits were borne on trees amid crimson pavilions. The auspicious stone was discovered in Xizhou Prefecture and a piece of jade bearing the prophecy found in Song County, both of which predicted the eternity of the reign of our sagacious Emperor and the everlasting succession of the Crown Princes. What's more, for a long time had we neither beheld the excellent articles written by the talented scholars nor read the essays concerning the superior fruition of Buddhahood, but both of them turned up during the reign of the Emperor. Would it not be the assistance granted by divinities or the true blessings from heaven in response to the high virtues of the Emperor? Also, the Emperor put his mind on the true reality, thus the Five Vehicles were protected like a city strongly defended by its wall and moat. He was reminiscently conceiving of the Buddha's visage at the vulture peak and pondering over the teachings delivered at the bank of Ajitavatī River, so the Vaidurya-haired Buddha's images finally arrived here, along with them, the holy canon as well as prominent monks congregated in our country. The clouds of compassion thus were hovering over every corner of the land; the dharma drum sounded resonantly throughout the entire tri-chiliocosms. Celestial flowers were dancing in the pleasant and favorable wind while the emerald mist from the burning incense was expiring fragrance. Subsequently, some submerged in the turmoil stream were inspired to go ashore, and others pursuing spiritual gains by practicing the Way developed a firm conviction that the threefold emptiness[47] was attainable in their near future. That is why the popular saying goes: not until the compass indicates the direction could a stray man find his way, and only when the autumn wind is blowing into the trees are the varied natural sounds ringing at the same time spontaneously. The Master was born in an age like this and his great virtues are aforementioned in the book. However, he is totally different from Faya[48] and Buddhasiṁha[49] or Dao'an and Kumārajīva, for the former two cherished the Way but were very hapless for being confronted by the ferocity of two Shi rulers[50], and the latter unluckily transmitted the scriptures in the tyrannical reigns of usurpers Fu and Yao[51]. If we try to make a comparison between the Master and them in the personal fortune, what we are doing truly is to make a comparison between the amount of water in a river or a lake with that in a ditch. Similarly, to compare the virtue of the Emperor with that of others is to juxtapose the light of the rising sun and the gleam of glowworms.

In the past, when a good piece of penannular jade was presented,

King Wen (187–226) of the Wei Dynasty[52] eulogized it by composing a prose poem; when a magic bird of five colors appeared, Jia Kui (30–101)[53] submitted an ode to this wonder. As we see, insignificant and humble as the jade and bird were, they were complimented by the ancients in poems and verses. How could we keep silent about the prosperity of this age without relating and eulogizing the merits and accomplishments of the Master? Huili is inferior to the former scholars in learning and no match for ancient worthies in virtue, but fortunately enough I joined the monastic order in this Image Period to be an insignificant monk, so to bathe in the teachings of the Buddha. I am a man with an admiration hundred times stronger than that of an ordinary man, and after overcoming my mediocrity and stupidity with all efforts, I ventured to compose his biography. About his immaculate integrity, his high reputation, and his unprecedented and unrepeatable exploits, other great men of letters are supposed to relate separately in other books. I, however, am unable to give a more detailed narration here. I sincerely hope gentlemen with clear discernment would excuse me for my awkwardness and not sneer at me.

The encomium says:

Living beings were overwhelmed by grief,
For the greatest saint attained His Nirvāṇa.
To inherit His bequeathed teachings,
Who then, if not sages, can do?

Aśvaghoṣa took the lead in propagating the truth,
Then Āryadeva followed the line.
When Sun sets to its daily doom,

Moon displays its light in the sky.

The Master is solemn and venerable,
Certainly a man of integrity;
Extraordinary as a celestial being,
He annihilates the mundane defilements.

He delved into the abstruse theories of metaphysics,
And acquainted himself with the Confucian doctrines;
He got a pearl-like pure nature,
And his virtues were as fragrant as angelica and orchids.

He worried that the scriptures available had been incomplete,
And there were errors in elucidations;
So, ascending peaks and descending valleys,
He risked his life on the truth-seeking journey afield.

He was dauntless and magnanimous,
A man of enormous sincerity and prudence;
Winning a brilliant reputation in the Western land,
He attributed his exploits to the Eastern nation.

The Master was living in an age of sagacious governance,
That has been ushered by our emperors;
They have been ruling fairly and impartially,
To have the administration and jurisdiction better adjusted.

The theories of Three Vehicles have been propagated,
Together with the practices of Ten Stages of Bodhisattvahood;
So once again, the Sun of wisdom,
Is setting forth its light from obscurity.

Humble as I am,
I'm fortunate enough to be a monk.
I have grown up in a plaited hut,
Neither spacious nor ornamented.

A lofty mountain deserves admiration,
And a clear stream gratifies thirsty men.
I do hope to attach myself to the Master,
Like a vine to creep on a tree.

A Note by Shi Yancong:

As what I have observed, since the Buddhism was introduced into the Eastern Land, tens of thousands of the people of great intelligence and virtues have renounced their homes to live monastic lives to seek the Way; however, they may be good at merely one or two points of the teachings, and it is hard to come by someone who is perfect for an all-round way like the Tripiṭaka Master. Besides, the Master has fine countenance, with extraordinary faculties of sight, hearing and speech; his memory is remarkable, and he is erudite and broad in vision. Rallying his spirit of sacrifice for pursuing the Way, he solitarily took a long journey in the remote and perilous lands. His impeccable integrity is upright as pine trees and bamboos, and his lofty ideal is stronger than metal and stone. He had an ability to remove the doubts from the intellectuals' hearts and guide the sagacious monarchs back to the Buddhism. I also have heard that the Tripiṭaka Master never perspired in the hottest midsummer, nor did he shudder in the coldest winter; and that he never cowered, nor did he ever lazily stretch himself.; and that he never yawned, nor did he ever sneeze. I am not sure who could be compared with him as a way to fathom his spiritual plane. Moreover, when the Master was ill in Northern Palace[54], frequently the auspicious signs mysteriously appeared, and on the day when he passed away his complexion and countenance kept pleasantly amiable, which were hard for us to come by and imagine. Also, more than a month after the Master's demise, one day there came a man carrying some ground incense of sandalwood. He asked the monks to permit him to apply the incense on the body of the Tripiṭaka Master in an Indian manner, but was bluntly refused, which made the man displeased, so he angrily said, "I came here to do so to fulfill a special edict. If you are not to give me permission, you may write a report to the Emperor." Then, a consent had to be given. When the coffin was opened and the shroud was unbuttoned, the people standing around smelled a kind of fantastic fragrance, resembling the aroma of the lotus flower. With disbelief, each one asked his neighbor about the fragrance and got the confirmation in return. Then the man took off the outside shroud of the Master, only leaving the underclothes on the body. On seeing that the visage of the Tripitaka Master looked like he was alive, people could not help but wail bitterly. After rubbing the body all over with sandalwood powder, the man redressed it in the cerement and closed the coffin. All at once, he disappeared. People suspected that he was a celestial being.

Considering the aspirations harbored by the Tripitaka Master, and reviewing all the activities done in his life, I wonder if he were not a Mahāsattva, who else he could be. My fellow monks, now we are so fortunate that we have a chance to worship him, so let us go forth to encourage each other to follow his brilliant steps forever!

ANNOTATION

1 The site of Ximing Monastery is discovered in the modern Baimiaocun of Beilin District, Xi'an.

2 Li Tai李泰(620–652), Prince Gong of Pu 濮恭王, whose mother was Empress Wende. He was the fourth son of Emperor Taizong of Tang, Li Shimin.

3 The Tongtai Monastery was built in 521 during the reign of Emperor Wu of Liang梁武帝 (r.502–549), which is situated in modern Nanjing, Jiangsu Province.

4 The Yongning Monastery was built in 516 by Empress Dowager Hu 胡太后 (personal name unknown) (died in 528), formally Empress Ling 灵皇后 of Northern Wei Dynasty (386–534). It was located east to Luoyang and destroyed by the fire in 534.

5 *The Mahāprajñāpāramitā Sūtra* (*The Perfection of Great Wisdom Sutra*) didn't exist in its present voluminous form from the start. Rather, it underwent an extremely complicated process of textual formation, perhaps by accretion from one single primary text, or perhaps through expansion or rearrangement of two basic versions of the *Prajñāpāramitā Sūtra* (*The Perfection of Wisdom*

Sutra). As for its translation into Chinese, although it is not until Xuanzang's version that a complete translation of the *Mahāprajñāpāramitā Sūtra* saw the light of the day, different parts or different versions of this sutra had arrived in China much earlier and had been translated, even if only partially or in the form of extracts. The more famous ones were the *Daoxing Jing* 《道行经》, the *Fangguang Jing* 《放光经》 and the *Guangzan Jing* 《光赞经》. There were also a few that are no longer extant; there were heavily edited versions or collations of extracts in translation. When Kumārajīva came to China, he brought forth two versions which were based on different diversions of the source—*the Dapin Jing* 《大品经》 and the *Xiaopin jing* 小品经—to contribute to the growing understanding of some of the vital issues involved in Mahāyāna Buddhism. The complete translation of the *Mahāprajñāpāramitā Sūtra* which we now have in the tripiṭaka was the work of Xuanzang. The full-size text, comprising sixteen parts, comes to nearly six million Chinese characters (based on a word count of the *Mahāprajñāpāramitā Sūtra* collected in the *Chinese Tripiṭaka* (*Zhonghua dazangjing* 《中华大藏经》). The above note is quoted from the note 253 on page 164 of Martha P.Y. Cheung's *An Anthology of Chinese Discourse on Translation Volume1: From Earliest Times to the Buddhist Project,* published by *Shanghai Foreign Language Education Press,* 2010.

6 The Yuhua Palace is situated in modern Tongchuan, a prefecture-level city located in central Shaanxi Province.

7 The mythic realm in Buddhist cosmology inhabited by Devás.

8 It was the first year of Linde (664), so Master Xuanzang should be sixty-three years old.

9 See note 39 of Fascicle III.

10 Monks, nuns, male and female devotees.

11 Kuiji窥基 (632–682), an exponent of Yogācāra, was a Chinese monk and a prominent disciple of Xuanzang. His posthumous name was the Great

Teacher of the Cien Monastery慈恩大师. According to biographies, he was an orphan who became a monk as a teenager and was sent to the imperial translation bureau headed by Xuanzang, from whom he later would learn Sanskrit, Abhidharma, and Yogācāra. Kuiji collaborated closely with Xuanzang on the *Cheng Weishi Lun*《成唯识论》, a redacted translation of commentaries on Vasubandhu's Triṃśikā-vijñaptimātratā. Kuiji's commentaries on the former text, the *Cheng Weishi Lun Shuji*《成唯识论述记》, along with his original treatise on Yogācāra, the *Essays on the Forest of Meanings in the Mahāyāna Dharma Garden* (*Dasheng Fayuan Yilin Chang*《大乘法苑义林章》) became foundations of the Faxiang School 法相宗. Kuiji is also known for his commentaries on Dharmapāla's Yogācāra philosophy.

12 Ten feet in height.

13 Jingxiu井宿 (Chinese "Well" constellation) is one of the twenty-eight mansions of the Chinese constellations. It is one of the southern mansions of the Vermilion Bird 朱雀: Well 井, Ghost 鬼, Willow(柳, Star 星, Extended Net 张, Wings 翼, Chariot 轸.

14 Taiwei 太微(or Taiweiyuan, 太微垣the Supreme Palace Enclosure), is one of the Sanyuan 三垣 (Three enclosures): Purple Forbidden enclosure (*ziweiyuan* 紫微垣), Supreme Palace enclosure (*taiweiyuan* 太微垣), Heavenly Market enclosure (*tianshiyuan*天市垣) . Stars and constellations of this group are visible during spring in the Northern Hemisphere (autumn in the Southern).

15 The robes after a yellowish-brown dye of Gandhāra tree, refers to Kāṣāya of Buddhist monks and nuns.

16 In the *Brahmajāla Sūtra* (《梵网经》*Brahma Net Sūtra / Fanwang jing*) which lists the bodhisattva precepts, there is a story about monks who was caught by robbers and bound up by unpulled grass. Because the monks were strictly adhering to Buddhist precepts, they'd rather starve to death than harm the life of the grass by cutting it. They are called Kuśa-bandhana bhikṣu in

Sanskrit.

17 The reign title of Tang Emperor Gozong, Li Zhi (628–683).

18 Daoxuan道宣 (596–667) was the founder of the Nanshan branch of the Precepts school (南山宗) in China. In 20 he entered the priesthood and studied the vinaya, or rules of monastic discipline, under Zhishou 智首. In 624 he went to Mt. Zhongnan 终南山 to study and practice and eventually founded a school based on the precepts of *The Fourfold Rules of Discipline* (四分律), the vinaya text of the Dharmagupta school. From 645, he assisted Xuanzang with his translation work. Daoxuan also authored several books on precepts, as well as a number of historical works. His works include five essential works of "The Fourfold Rules of Discipline," which are the principal texts of the Nanshan school. His other works include *The Anthology of the Propagation of Light* (*Guanghongming Ji* 《广弘明集》), a thirty-volume anthology of essays on Buddhism by various Chinese Buddhists, *The Great T'ang Dynasty Catalog of Buddhist Scriptures* (*Datang Neidian Lu* 《大唐内典录》), a ten-volume catalog of the Buddhist canon, The *Continued Biographies of Eminent Monks* (*Xu Gaoseng Zhuan* 《续高僧传》), containing the biographies of five hundred priests active from 502 to 645, etc.

19 Also known as skanda, a devoted guardian of Buddnist monasteries who guards the teachings of Buddhism.

20 Today Huangling 黄陵 and Yijun 宜君 counties, Shaanxi Province.

21 The four types of birth by which the beings of six modes of existence can be reborn: (1) born alive; (2) egg-born; (3) moisten-or water-born; (4) born by metamorphosis, i.e. not by a "mother" but rather through the power of karma alone.

22 The Chan River 浐河 is located in the eastern surburbs of Xi'an, Shaanxi Province.

23 Modern Shaolingyuan 少陵原 in southern Xi'an, Shaanxi Province.

24 Or may refer to Fotucheng 佛图澄(ca. 232–348), who is said to be able to see

the shape of events a thousand miles away by applying oil to his hands.

25 See note 7 of Fascicle VII.

26 See note 6 of Fascicle VII.

27 Daoheng 道恒(346–417). See note 103 of Fascicle VI.

28 Sengzhao僧肇 (384–414) was a Chinese Buddhist philosopher from Later Qin around 384-417 at Chang'an. He was known as being among the ablest of the disciples of Kumārajīva. He was recognized as a both a scholar of high skill and someone of profound understanding relating to religious matters. He was involved in translating Indian treatises, which formed the only source of study for early Chinese Mādhyamika Buddhism. He also authored a small number of texts, but is famous for the book *Zhao Lun*《肇论》. Its chapters are as follows: *Things Do Not Shift*, *Non-Absolute Emptiness*, *Prajna Is Without Dichotomizing Knowledge*, and *nirvāṇa Is Without Conceptualization*.

29 Daosheng道生 (355–434), or Zhu Daosheng 竺道生, was an eminent Six Dynasties era Chinese Buddhist scholar. He is known for advocating the concepts of sudden enlightenment and the universality of the Buddha nature. He was known as being among the ablest of the disciples of Kumārajīva. Born in Pengcheng, Daosheng left home to become a monk at eleven. He studied in Jiankang from Zhu Fatai, and later at a Lushan (Mount Lu) monastery with Huiyuan, and from 405 or 406 from Kumarajiva in Chang'an, where he stayed for some two years perfecting his education. He became one of the foremost scholars of his time, counted among the "fifteen great disciples" of Kumarajiva. Sengzhao reports that Daosheng assisted Kumarajiva in his translation of the *Lotus Sutra*, Daosheng wrote commentaries on the *Lotus Sutra*, the *Vimalakīrti-nirdesa Sutra* and the *Astasahasrika-prajnaparamita Sutra* (the last of which has been lost).

30 Daorong道融(372–445) was among the ablest of the disciples of Kumārajīva.

31 Basic consciousness, in which is stored the seeds of all phenomena. The

Eight Consciousnesses (aṣṭa vijñānakāya) is a classification developed in the tradition of the Yogācāra school of Mahāyāna Buddhism. They enumerate the five sense consciousnesses, supplemented by the mental consciousness (manovijñāna), the defiled mental consciousness (kliṣṭamanovijñāna), and finally the fundamental store-house consciousness (ālayavijñāna), which is the basis of the other seven. This eighth consciousness is said to store the impressions or imprints (vāsanā) of previous experiences, which form the seeds (bīja) of future karma in this life and in the next after rebirth.

32 Those factors are not directly associated with a specific mental function.

33 Refers to the content of the ālayavijñāna as the seeds of all phenomena.

34 A Chinese list of the "eighteen" sects of the Hīnayāna, omitting Mahāsāṅghikāḥ, Sthavira, and Sarvāstivādaḥ as generic schools: I. 大众部 The Mahāsāṅghikāḥ is divided into eight schools as follows: (1) 一说部 Ekavyavahārikāḥ; (2) 说出世部 Lokottaravādinaḥ; (3) 鸡胤部 Kaukkuṭikāḥ (Gokulikā); (4) 多闻部 Bahuśrutīyāḥ; (5) 说假部 Prajñāptivadinaḥ; (6) 制多山部 Jetavaniyāḥ, or Caityaśailāḥ; (7) 西山住部 Aparaśailāḥ; (8) 北山住部 Uttaraśailāḥ. II. 上坐部 Āryasthavirāḥ, or Sthāviravādin, divided into eight schools: (1) 雪山部 Haimavatāḥ. The 说一切有部 Sarvāstivādaḥ gave rise to; (2) 犊子部 Vātsīputrīyāḥ, which gave rise to; (3) 法上部 Dharmottarīyāḥ; (4) 贤胄部 Bhadrayānīyāḥ; (5) 正量部 Saṃmatīyāḥ; and (6) 密林山 Saṇṇagarikāḥ; (7) 化地部 Mahīśāsakāḥ produced; (8) 法藏部 Dharmaguptāḥ. From the Sarvāstivādins arose also; (9) 饮光部 Kāśyaḥpīyā; (10) 经量部 Sautrāntikāḥ. The division of the two schools is ascribed to Mahādeva a century after the nirvāṇa. Under I the first five are stated as arising two centuries after the nirvāṇa, and the remaining three a century later, dates which are unreliable. Under II, the Haimavatāḥ and the Sarvāstivādaḥ are dated some 200 years after the nirvāṇa; from the Sarvāstivādins soon arose the Vātsīputrīyas, from whom soon sprang the third, fourth, fifth, and sixth; then from the Sarvāstivādins there arose the seventh which gave rise to the eighth, and again, nearing the 400th year, the

Sarvāstivādins gave rise to the ninth and soon after the tenth. In the list of eighteen the Sarvāstivādaḥ is not counted, as it split into all the rest; eighteen lesser vehicle schools.

35 The five versions of the Vinaya, namely: (1) the Dharmagupta; (2) the Mahīśāsaka; (3) the Kāśyapīya; (4) the Sarvāstivāda; (5) the Mahāsāṃghika.

36 In original Chinese text, Suan'ni狻猊 refers to one of the nine sons of the dragon, which looks like a lion. Chu貙 is a palm civet-like animal, and An豻, a black-mouth dog, looks like a fox. They are all legendary beasts in Chinese mythology.

37 See note 61 of Fascicle I.

38 See note 62 of Fascicle I.

39 See note 67 of Fascicle VI.

40 See note 65 of Fascicle VI.

41 Courtesy礼, Righteousness义, Integrity廉, Sense of Shame耻.

42 Yu 虞 refers to Youyu 有虞, Shun's clan name, while his ancestral name is Yao 姚, and his given name was Chonghua 重华. Shun is sometimes called as the Great Shun 大舜 or as Yu Shun 虞舜. The " Youyu " was also the name of the his fiefdom, which Shun received from Emperor Yao尧. Before his death, Shun is recorded as relinquishing his seat of power to Yu禹, the founder of the Xia Dynasty (2155–1767 BC).

43 The earliest appearance of the Nine Functions was in *Zuo Zhuan*《左传》, "*The Commentary of Zuo (Qiuming)*", comprised by the Six Essential Conditions for Survival, namely water, fire, metal, wood, earth, grain and the Three Principles, including rectification of virtues正德, munificence and manipulation利用, and public welfare厚生.

44 In the *Zuozhuan: in the 12th year of Duke Xuan* (597 BC), the Seven Martial Virtues was mentioned as seven effects of taking a military action, namely forbidding violence, stopping employing arms, remaining strong, consolidating exploits, pacifying the world, uniting the mass, and accumulating wealth and

property.

45 Mainly refers to Cao Cao (155–220), and Liu Bei. Cao Cao was a warlord and the penultimate Chancellor of the Eastern Han Dynasty who rose to great power in the final years of the dynasty. As one of the central figures of the Three Kingdoms Period, he laid the foundations for what was to become the state of Cao Wei and was posthumously honoured as "Emperor Wu of Wei." Liu Bei 刘备(161–223), courtesy name Xuande玄德, was a warlord in the late Eastern Han Dynasty who founded the state of Shu Han in the Three Kingdoms Period and became its first ruler. They are praised as brilliant rulers and military geniuses.

46 Refers to three basic moral principles of Confucianism, namely ministers obey rulers, sons obey fathers and the younger obeys the older.

47 See note 117 of Fascicle VI.

48 Zhu Faya 竺法雅 or Faya was a Chinese Jin Dynasty (265–420) Buddhist monk and teacher from Hejian (in modern Hebei Province), best known for developing the Geyi格义 method of explaining numbered categories of Sanskrit terms from the Buddhist canon with comparable lists from the Chinese classics. The dates of Zhu Faya's life are unknown, but he was a student of the Indian monk Fotucheng 佛图澄(ca. 232–348) and a contemporary of the translators Dao'an道安 (312–385) and Zhu Fatai 竺法汰(320–387).

49 See note 30 of Preface.

50 Shi Hu 石虎(295–349) and Shi Le石勒(274–333) of the later Zhao Period (319–351). Shi Hu, courtesy name Jilong 季龙, formally Emperor Wu of (Later) Zhao (后)赵武帝, was an emperor of the Chinese/Jie state Later Zhao. He was the founding emperor Shi Le's distant nephew, who took power in a coup after Shi Le's death from Shi Le's heir Shi Hong. Shi Le, courtesy name Shilong 石龙, the Emperor Ming of Zhao, was the founding emperor of the Later Zhao (319–351).

51 Yao Chang姚苌(330–394) was the founder of the former Qin Dynasty (351–394) and Fu Jian苻坚(338–385), the founder of the Later Qin Dynasty(384–417).

52 Refers to Cao Pi曹丕 (187–226).

53 Jia Kui 贾逵 (30-101), courtesy name Jingbo 景伯, was a Confucian philosopher who lived in the early Eastern Han Period. He was a descendant of the Western Han politician and writer Jia Yi 贾谊(200–168BC). He was born in was Pingling 平陵, Youfufeng Commandery 右扶风郡, which is located northeast of present-day Xingping兴平, Shaanxi. Upon Emperor Zhang's ascension to the throne, he ordered Jia to write of the *Zuo Zhuan*'s superiority to both the *Guliang Zhuan*《穀梁传》and the *Gongyang Zhuan*《公羊传》. Jia produced the work, arguing that only *Zuo Zhuan* agreed with the supposedly-prophetic chen, proclaiming that the House of Liu (the Han dynastic family) was destined to rule as successors of the legendary Emperor Yao. Impressed by the result, the emperor then commanded Jia to select twenty scholars then studying the *Gongyang Zhuan*, instruct them in the *Zuo Zhuan* and compile a new edition and commentary. Around 82 CE, he completed three more works in which he compared the "New Text" and "Old Text" versions (i.e. those saved from the Qin book burnings by Fu Sheng and those discovered in a wall of Confucius' estate and transcribed by Kong Anguo) of the *Book of Documents*, *Rites of Zhou* and the *Classic of Poetry*.

54 Refers to Yuhua Palace.

Chinese Units of Measurement in the Tang Dynasty

*bu*步 is about 5 *chi,* 150cm.

*chi*尺 is about ⅓ meter/one foot. Although it is often translated as the "Chinese foot", its length is originally derived from the distance measured by a human hand, from the tip of the thumb to the tip of the forefinger, similar to the ancient Span.

*cun*寸 is often glossed as the Chinese inch, representing one-tenth of a *chi* (Chinese foot).

*dou*斗 is a unit of volume, equal to 10 liters / a peck. One *dou* weighs about 12.5 pounds, which is about 6.25 kilograms. Also, it refers to a kind of container for grain.

*fen*分is one tenth of an inch.

*hu*斛 is a unit of volume equal to ten *dou*.

li 里is about 540 meters, approximately l/3 mile.

mu 亩is about 0.382 hectare, or 0.0326 acre.

shi 石is equal to ten *dou*.

zhang 丈is a customary Chinese unit of length, equal to 10 *chi* (Chinese feet). Its value varied over time and place with different values of the *chi,* although it is occasionally standardized. In the Tang dynasty, one *zhang* is equal to 3 meters.

*Zhong*钟is *equal to 64 dou.*

Selected Bibliography

Translated by Li Rongxi（Li Yung-hsi）：

Hui-Ii. *The Life of Hsuan-tsang, the Tripitaka-Master of the Great Tzu En Monastery.* Peking: Chinese Buddhist Association, 1959.

Sramana Huili and Shi Yancong. *A Biography of the Tripitaka Master of the Great Ci'en Monastery of the Great Tang Dynasty.* Berkeley, California: Numata Center for Buddhist Translation and Research, 1995.

Translated by Samuel Beal：

Hwui Li. *The Life of Hiuen-Tsiang*. London:Kegan Paul, Trubner and Co.Ltd., 1911.Reprint Munshiram Manoharlal, New Delhi. 1973.

Hui-Ii. *The Life of Hsuan-tsang.* London: Trubner, 1884; reprint, Delhi: Motilal Banarsidass, 1981.

Hiuen Tsiang. *Si-Yu-Ki.: Buddhist Records of the Western World.* London: Trubner, 1884; reprint, Delhi: Motilal Banarsidass, 1981.

Charles Hucker, *A Dictionary of Official Titles in Imperial China,* Stanford: Stanford University Press, 1985.

[唐]慧立本、彦悰笺，孙毓棠、谢方点校：《大慈恩寺三藏法师传》，北京：中华书局，2004年。

高永旺译注：《大慈恩寺三藏法师传》，北京：中华书局，2018年。

贾二强译注：《大慈恩寺三藏法师传选译》，南京：凤凰出版社，2011年。

刘汝霖：《唐玄奘法师年谱》，《现代佛教学术丛刊第8册》，台北：大乘文化出版社，1980年。

张力生：《玄奘法师年谱》（*The Chronological Life of the Master Xuan Zang*）[英汉对照]，北京：宗教文化出版社，2016。

杨廷福：《玄奘年谱》，上海：上海古籍出版社，2011年。

赵晓莺：《大唐慈恩寺：玄奘法师传》，北京：华文出版社，2011年。

周连宽：《大唐西域记史地研究丛稿》，北京：中华书局，1989年。

Network Resource:

CBETA 電子佛典：

https://cbetaonline.dila.edu.tw/

佛教藏经目录数位资料库：

https://jinglu.cbeta.org/index.htm

Chinese Text Project (ctext.org): Chinese Text Project (ctext.org)

Buddhist Terms:

http://www.sutrasmantras.info/glossary.html#faculty

NTI Buddhist Text Reader:

http://ntireader.org/index.html

Free Chinese & Japanese Online Dictionary:

https://www.orientaloutpost.com/dictionary.php?

佛学大辞典：

https://foxue.51240.com/

Dictionaries for the Study of Buddhist and East Asian Language and Thought:

http://www.buddhism-dict.net/

Martha P.Y. Cheung's *An Anthology of Chinese Discourse on Translation Volume1: From Earliest Times to the Buddhist Project. shanghai: Shanghai Foreign Language Education Press,* 2010.

附录

目　录

大唐大慈恩寺三藏法师传序

垂拱四年三月十五日仰上沙门释彦悰述

恭惟：释迦氏之临忍土也，始演八正、启三宝以黜群邪之典，由是佛教行焉。方等一乘，圆宗十地，谓之大法，言真筌也。化城垢服，济鹿驰羊，谓之小学，言权旨也。至于禅戒咒术，厥趣万途，而灭惑利生，其归一揆。是故历代英圣仰而宝之。八会之经谓之为本，根其义也；三转之法谓之为末，枝其义也。暨夫天雨四华，地现六动，解其髻宝，示以衣珠，借一以破三，摄末归本者也。

《付法藏传》曰：圣者阿难能诵持如来所有法藏，如瓶泻水，置之异器，即谓释尊一代四十九年应物逗机适时之教也。逮提河辍润，坚林晦景，邃旨冲宗，于焉殆绝。我先昆迦叶，属五棺已掩，千氎将焚。痛人、天眼灭，苍生莫救，故召诸圣众，结集微言。考绳墨以立定门，即贯华而开律部，据优波提舍以之为论，剖析空、有，显别断、常，示之以因修，明之以果证。足以贻范当代，轨训将来，归向之徒，并遵其义。

及王、秦奉使，考日光而求佛；腾、兰应请，策练影以通经。厥后易首抽肠之宾播美于天外，篆叶结鬘之典译粹于区中。然至赜至神，思虑者或迷其性相；唯恍唯惚，言谈者有昧其是非。况去圣既遥，来教多阙；殊涂竞轸，别路扬镳而已哉。

法师悬弭诞辰，室表空生之应；佩觿登岁，心符妙德之诚。以爱海无出要之津，觉地有栖神之宅。故削发矫翰，翔集二空，异县他山，载驰千里。每慨古贤之得本行本，鱼鲁致乖；痛先匠之闻疑传疑，豕亥斯惑。窃惟：音乐树下必存金石之响，五天竺内想具百篇之义。遂发愤忘食，履险若夷。轻万死以涉葱河，重一言而之奈苑。鹫山猿沼，仰胜迹以瞻奇；鹿野仙城，访遗编于蠹简。春秋寒暑一十七年，耳目见闻百三十国，扬我皇之盛烈，振彼后之权豪，偃异学之高轒，拔同师之巨帜。名王拜首，胜侣摩肩；万古风猷，一人而已。

法师于彼国所获大、小二乘三藏梵本等，总六百五十七部，并载以巨象，并诸邮骏，蒙霜犯雪，自天佑以元亨；阳苦阴淫，假皇威而利涉。粤以贞观十有九祀达于上京，道俗迓之，阗城溢郭，锵锵济济，亦一期之盛也。及谒见天子，劳问殷勤，爰命有司，诏令宣译，人皆敬奉，难以具言。至如氏族簪缨，捐亲入道；游践远迩，中外赞扬；示息化以归真，同薪尽而火灭。若斯之类则备乎兹传也。

《传》本五卷，魏国西寺前沙门慧立所述。立俗姓赵，豳国公刘人，隋起居郎司隶从事毅之子。博考儒释，雅善篇章，妙辩云飞，溢思泉涌。加以直词正色，不惮威严；赴水蹈火，无所屈挠。睹三藏之学行，瞩三藏之形仪，钻之仰之，弥坚弥远。因循撰其事，以贻终古。乃削藁云毕，虑遗诸美，遂藏之地府，代莫得闻。尔后役思缠痾，气悬钟漏，乃顾命门徒，掘以启之，将出而卒。门人等哀恸荒鲠，悲不自胜，而此《传》流离分散他所，后累载搜购，近乃获全。

因命余以序之，迫余以次之。余抚己缺然，拒而不应。因又谓余曰："佛法之事岂预俗徒，况乃当仁苦为辞让？"余再怀惭退，沉吟久之，执纸操翰，汍澜腷臆，方乃参犬羊以虎豹，糅瓦石以琳璆，错综本文，笺为十卷，庶后之览者，无或嗤焉。

卷第一

起载诞于缑氏终西届于高昌

法师讳玄奘，俗姓陈，陈留人也。汉太丘长仲弓之后。曾祖钦，后魏上党太守。祖康，以学优仕齐，任国子博士，食邑周南，子孙因家，又为缑氏人也。父慧，英洁有雅操，早通经术，形长八尺，美眉明目，褒衣博带，好儒者之容，时人方之郭有道。性恬简，无务荣进，加属隋政衰微，遂潜心坟典。州郡频贡孝廉及司隶辟命，并辞疾不就，识者嘉焉。有四男，法师即第四子也。

幼而圭璋特达，聪悟不群。年八岁，父坐于几侧口授《孝经》，至曾子避席，忽整襟而起。问其故，对曰："曾子闻师命避席，某今奉慈训，岂宜安坐？" 父甚悦，知其必成，召宗人语之，皆贺曰："此公之扬乌也！"其早慧如此。自后备通经典，而爱古尚贤，非雅正之籍不观，非圣哲之风不习；不交童幼之党，无涉阛阓之门；虽钟鼓嘈囋于通衢，百戏叫歌于闾巷，士女云萃，其未尝出也。又少知色养，温清淳谨。

其第二兄长捷先出家，住东都净土寺，察法师堪传法教，因将诣道场，教诵习经业。俄而有敕于洛阳度二七僧，时业优者数百，法师以幼少不预取限，立于公门之侧。时使人大理卿郑善果有知士之鉴，见而奇之，问曰："子为谁家？"答以氏族。

又问曰："求度耶？"答曰："然。但以习近业微，不蒙比预。"

又问："出家意何所为？"答曰："意欲远绍如来，近光遗法。"

果深嘉其志，又贤其器貌，故特而取之。因谓官僚曰："诵业易成，风骨难得。若度此子，必为释门伟器，但恐果与诸公不见其翔翥云霄，洒演甘露耳。又名家不可失。"以今观之，则郑卿之言为不虚也。

既得出家，与兄同止。时寺有景法师讲《涅槃经》，执卷伏膺，遂忘寝食。又学严法师《摄大乘论》，爱好逾剧。一闻将尽，再览之后，无复所遗。众咸惊异，乃令升座覆述，抑扬剖畅，备尽师宗。美闻芳声，从兹发矣，时年十三也。

其后隋氏失御，天下沸腾。帝城为桀、跖之窠；河、洛为豺狼之穴。衣冠殄丧，法众销亡，白骨交衢，烟火断绝。虽王、董僭逆之衅，刘、石乱华之灾，刳斮生灵，芟夷海内，未之有也。法师虽居童幼，而情达变通，乃启兄曰："此虽父母之邑，而丧乱若兹，岂可守而死也！今闻唐主驱晋阳之众，已据有长安，天下依归如适父母，愿与兄投也。”兄从之，即共俱来，时武德元年矣。

是时国基草创，兵甲尚兴，孙、吴之术斯为急务，孔、释之道有所未遑，以故京城未有讲席，法师深以慨然。初，炀帝于东都建四道场，召天下名僧居焉。其征来者，皆一艺之士，是故法将如林，景、脱、基、暹为其称首。末年国乱，供料停绝，多游绵、蜀，知法之众，又盛于彼。法师乃启兄曰："此无法事，不可虚度，愿游蜀受业焉。”兄从之。又与兄经子午谷入汉川，遂逢空、景二法师，皆道场之大德，相见悲喜。停月余，日从之受学，仍相与进向成都。

诸德既萃，大建法筵。于是更听基、暹《摄论》、《毗昙》及震法师《迦延》。敬惜寸阴，励精无怠，二三年间，究通诸部。时天下饥乱，唯蜀中丰静，故四方僧投之者众，讲座之下常数百人。法师理智宏才，皆出其右，吴、蜀、荆、楚，无不知闻，其想望风徽，亦犹古人之钦李、郭矣。

法师兄因住成都空慧寺，亦风神朗俊，体状魁杰，有类于父。好内、外学，凡讲《涅槃经》、《摄大乘论》、《阿毗昙》，兼通《书传》，尤善《老》、《庄》，为蜀人所慕，总管、酇公特所钦重。至于属词谈吐，蕴藉风流；接物诱凡，无愧于弟。若其亭亭独秀，不杂埃尘，游八纮，穷玄理，廓宇宙以为志，继圣达而为心，匡振隤网，苞挫殊俗，涉风波而意靡倦，对万乘而节逾高者，固兄所不能逮也。然昆季二人懿业清规，芳声雅质，虽庐山兄弟无得加焉。

法师年满二十，即以武德五年于成都受具，坐夏学律，五篇七聚之宗，一遍斯得。益部经论研综既穷，更思入京询问殊旨。条式有碍，又为兄所留，不能遂意。乃私与商人结侣，泛舟三峡，沿江而遁，到荆州天皇寺。彼之道俗承风斯久，既属来仪，咸请敷说。法师为讲《摄论》、《毗昙》，自夏及冬，各得三遍。时汉阳王以盛德懿亲，作镇于彼，闻法师至，甚欢，躬申礼谒。发题之日，王率群僚及道俗一艺之士，咸集荣观。于是征诘云发，关并峰起，法师酬对解释，靡不辞穷意服。其中有深悟者，悲不自胜。王亦称叹无极，嚫施如山，一无所取。

罢讲后，复北游，询求先德。至相州，造休法师，质难问疑。又到赵州，谒深法师学《成实论》。又入长安，止大觉寺。就岳法师学《俱舍论》。皆一遍而尽其旨，经目而记于心，虽宿学耆年不能出也。至于钩深致远，开微发伏，众所不至，独悟于幽奥者，固非一义焉。

时长安有常、辩二大德，解究二乘，行穷三学，为上京法匠，缁素所归，道振神州，声驰海外，负笈之侣从之如云。虽含综众经，而偏讲《摄大乘论》。法师既曾有功吴、蜀，自到长安，又随询采。然其所有深致，亦一拾斯尽。二德并深嗟赏，谓法师曰："汝可谓释门千里之驹，其再明慧日，当在尔躬，恨吾辈老朽恐不见也。"自是学徒改观，誉满京邑。

法师既遍谒众师，备餐其说，详考其义，各擅宗涂，验之圣典，亦隐显有异，莫知适从。乃誓游西方以问所惑，并取《十七地论》以释众疑，即今之《瑜伽师地论》也。又言："昔法显、智严亦一时之士，皆能求法导利群生，岂使高迹无追，清风绝后？大丈夫会当继之。”于是结侣陈表，有诏不许。诸人咸退，唯法师不屈。

既方事孤游，又承西路艰险，乃自试其心，以人间众苦种种调伏，堪任不退。然始入塔启请，申其意志，愿乞众圣冥加，使往还无梗。初法师之生也，母梦法师着白衣西去。母曰：“汝是我子，今欲何去？”答曰：“为求法故去。”此则游方之先兆也。

贞观三年秋八月，将欲首涂，又求祥瑞。乃夜梦见大海中有苏迷卢山，四宝所成，极为严丽。意欲登山，而洪涛汹涌，又无船檝，不以为惧，乃决意而入。忽见石莲华踊乎波外，应足而生，却而观之，随足而灭。须臾至山下，又峻峭不可上。试踊身自腾，有抟飙飒至，扶而上升，到山顶，四望廓然，无复拥碍。喜而寤焉，遂即行矣。时年二十六也。

时有秦州僧孝达，在京学《涅槃经》，功毕返乡，遂与俱去。至秦州，停一宿，逢兰州伴，又随去至兰州。一宿，遇凉州人送官马归，又随去至彼。停月余日，道俗请开《涅槃》、《摄论》及《般若经》，法师皆为开发。

凉州为河西都会，襟带西蕃、葱右诸国，商侣往来，无有停绝。时开讲日，盛有其人，皆施珍宝，稽颡赞叹，归还各向其君长称叹法师之美，云欲西来求法于婆罗门国，以是西域诸城无不预发欢心，严洒而待。散会之日，珍施丰厚，金钱、银钱，口马无数，法师受一半然灯，余外并施诸寺。

时国政尚新，疆埸未远，禁约百姓不许出蕃。时李大亮为凉州都督，既奉严敕，防禁特切。有人报亮云："有僧从长安来，欲向西国，不知何意。"亮惧，追法师问来由。法师报云："欲西求法。"亮闻之，逼还京。

彼有慧威法师，河西之领袖，神悟聪哲，既重法师辞理，复闻求法之志，深生随喜，密遣二弟子，一曰慧琳，二曰道整，窃送向西。自是不敢公出，乃昼伏夜行，遂至瓜州。时刺史独孤达闻法师至，甚欢喜，供事殷厚。法师因访西路。或有报云："从此北行五十余里有瓠芦河，下广上狭，洄波甚急，深不可渡。上置玉门关，路必由之，即西境之襟喉也。关外西北又有五烽，候望者居之，各相去百里，中无水草。五烽之外即莫贺延碛，伊吾国境。"闻之愁愦，所乘之马又死，不知计出，沉默经月余日。

未发之间，凉州访牒又至，云："有僧字玄奘，欲入西蕃，所在州县宜严候捉。"州吏李昌，崇信之士，心疑法师，遂密将牒来呈云："师不是此耶？"法师迟疑未报。昌曰："师须实语。必是，弟子为师图之。"法师乃具实而答。昌闻，深赞希有，曰："师实能尔者，为师毁却文书。"即于前裂坏之，仍云："师须早去。"

自是益增忧惘。所从二小僧，道整先向敦煌，唯慧琳在，知其不堪远涉，亦放还。遂贸易得马一匹，但苦无人相引。即于所停寺弥勒像前启请，愿得一人相引渡关。其夜，寺有胡僧达摩梦法师坐一莲华向西而去。达摩私怪，旦而来白。法师心喜为得行之征，然语达摩云："梦为虚妄，何足涉言。"

更入道场礼请，俄有一胡人来入礼佛，逐法师行二三匝。问其姓名，云姓石字槃陀。此胡即请受戒，乃为授五戒。胡甚喜，辞还。少时赍饼果更来。法师见其明健，貌又恭肃，遂告行意。胡人许诺，言送师过五烽。法师大喜，乃更贸衣资为买马而期焉。明日日欲下，遂入草间，须臾彼胡更与一胡老翁乘一瘦老赤马相逐而至，法师心不怿。

少胡曰："此翁极谙西路，来去伊吾三十余返，故共俱来，望有平章耳。"胡公因说西路险恶，沙河阻远，鬼魅热风，过无免者。徒侣众多，犹数迷失，况师单独，如何可行？愿自斟量，勿轻身命。法师报曰："贫道为求大法，发趣西方，若不至婆罗门国，终不东归。纵死中涂，非所悔也。"胡翁曰："师必去，可乘我马。此马往返伊吾已有十五度，健而知道。师马少，不堪远涉。"法师乃窃念在长安将发志西方日，有术人何弘达者，诵咒占观，多有所中。法师令占行事，达曰："师得去。去状似乘一老赤瘦马，漆鞍桥前有铁。"既睹胡人所乘马瘦赤，漆鞍有铁，与何言合，心以为当，遂即换马。胡翁欢喜，礼敬而别。

于是装束，与少胡夜发。三更许到河，遥见玉门关。去关上流十里许，两岸可阔丈余，傍有梧桐树丛。胡人乃斩木为桥，布草填沙，驱马而过。法师既渡而喜，因解驾停憩，与胡人相去可五十余步，各下褥而眠。少时胡人乃拔刀而起，徐向法师，未到十步许又回，不知何意，疑有异心。即起诵经，念观音菩萨。胡人见已，还卧遂睡。天欲明，法师唤令起取水盥漱，解斋讫欲发，胡人曰："弟子将前涂险远，又无水草，唯五烽下有水，必须夜到偷水而过，但一处被觉，即是死人。不如归还，用为安隐。”法师确然不回。乃俛仰而进，露刀张弓，命法师前行。法师不肯居前，胡人自行数里而住，曰：“弟子不能去。家累既大而王法不可忤也。”法师知其意，遂任还。胡人曰：“师必不达。如被擒捉，相引奈何？”法师报曰：“纵使切割此身如微尘者，终不相引。”为陈重誓，其意乃止。与马一匹，劳谢而别。

自是孑然孤游沙漠矣。唯望骨聚、马粪等渐进，顷间忽见有军众数百队满沙碛间，乍行乍息，皆裘褐驼马之像及旌旗矟纛之形，易貌移质，倏忽千变，遥瞻极着，渐近而微。法师初睹，谓为贼众；渐近见灭，乃知妖鬼。又闻空中声言“勿怖，勿怖”，由此稍安。

经八十余里，见第一烽。恐候者见，乃隐伏沙沟，至夜方发。到烽西见水，下饮盥手讫，欲取皮囊盛水，有一箭飒来，几中于膝。须臾更一箭来，知为他见，乃大言曰：“我是僧，从京师来。汝莫射我。”即牵马向烽。烽上人亦开门而出，相见知是僧，将入见校尉王祥。祥命爇火令看，曰：“非我河西僧，实似京师来也。”具问行意。法师报曰：“校尉颇闻凉州人说有僧玄奘欲向婆罗门国求法不？”答曰：“闻承奘师已东还，何因到此？”法师引示马上章疏及名字，彼乃信。仍言：“西路艰远，师终不达。今亦不与师罪，弟子敦煌人，欲送师向敦煌。彼有张皎法师，钦贤尚德，见师必喜，请就之。”法师对曰：“奘桑梓洛阳，少而慕道。两京知法之匠，吴、蜀一艺之僧，无不负笈从之，穷其所解。对扬谈说，亦忝为时宗，欲养己修名，岂劣檀越敦煌耶？然恨佛化，经有不周，义有所阙，故无贪性命，不惮艰危，誓往西方，遵求遗法。檀越不相励勉，专劝退还，岂谓同厌尘劳，共树涅槃之因也？必欲拘留，任即刑罚，玄奘终不东移一步以负先心。”祥闻之，愍然曰：“弟子多幸，得逢遇师，敢不随喜。师疲倦且卧，待明自送，指示涂路。” 遂拂筵安置。至晓，法师食讫，祥使人盛水及麨饼，自送至十余里，云：“师从此路径向第四烽，彼人亦有善心，又是弟子宗骨，姓王名伯陇，至彼可言弟子遣师来。”泣拜而别。

既去，夜到第四烽，恐为留难，欲默取水而过。至水未下间，飞箭已至，还如前报，即急向之，彼亦下来。入烽，烽官相问，答：“欲往天竺，路由于此，第一烽王祥校尉故遣相过。”彼闻欢喜留宿，更施大皮囊及马麦相送。云：“师不须向第五烽。彼人疏率，恐生异图。可于此去百里许，有野马泉，更取水。”

从此已去，即莫贺延碛，长八百余里，古曰“沙河”，上无飞鸟，下无走兽，复无水草。是时顾影唯一，心但念观音菩萨及《般若心经》。初，法师在蜀，见一病人，身疮臭秽，衣服破污，愍将向寺施与衣服饮食之直。病者惭愧，乃授法师此经，因常诵习。至沙河间，逢诸恶鬼，奇状异类，绕人前后，虽念观音不得全去，即诵此经，发声皆散。在危获济，实所凭焉。

时行百余里，失道，觅野马泉不得。下水欲饮，袋重，失手覆之，千里之资一朝斯罄。又路盘回，不知所趣，乃欲东归还第四烽。行十余里，自念：我先发愿，若不至天竺终不东归一步，今何故来？宁可就西而死，岂归东而生！于是旋辔，专念观音，西北而进。是时四顾茫然，人鸟俱绝。夜则妖魑举火，烂若繁星，昼则惊风拥沙，散如时雨。虽遇如是，心无所惧，但苦水尽，渴不能前。是时四夜五日无一滴沾喉，口腹干燋，几将殒绝，不复能进。遂卧沙中默念观音，虽困不舍。启菩萨曰："玄奘此行不求财利，无冀名誉，但为无上正法来耳。仰惟菩萨慈念群生，以救苦为务。此为苦矣，宁不知耶？"如是告时，心心无辍。至第五夜半，忽有凉风触身，冷快如沐寒水。遂得目明，马亦能起。体既苏息，得少睡眠。即于睡中梦一大神长数丈，执戟麾曰："何不强行，而更卧也！"法师惊寤进发，行可十里，马忽异路，制之不回。经数里，忽见青草数亩，下马恣食。去草十步欲回转，又到一池，水甘澄镜澈。下而就饮，身命重全，人马俱得苏息。计此应非旧水草，固是菩萨慈悲为生，其志诚通神，皆此类也。即就草池一日停息，后日盛水取草进发。更经两日，方出流沙到伊吾矣。此等危难百千，不能备叙。

既至伊吾，止一寺。寺有汉僧三人，中有一老者，衣不及带，跣足出迎，抱法师哭，哀嚎鲠咽，不能已已，言："岂期今日重见乡人！"法师亦对之伤泣。自外胡僧、王悉来参谒。王请届所居，备陈供养。

时高昌王麹文泰使人先在伊吾，是日欲还，适逢法师，归告其王。王闻，即日发使，敕伊吾王遣法师来，仍简上马数十匹，遣贵臣驰驱，设顿迎候。比停十余日，王使至，陈王意，拜请殷勤。法师意欲取可汗浮图过，既为高昌所请，辞不获免，于是遂行，涉南碛，经六日至高昌界白力城。时日已暮，法师欲停，城中官人及使者曰："王城在近请进。数换良马前去，法师先所乘赤马留使后来。"

即以其夜半时到王城。门司启王，王敕开门。法师入城，王与侍人前后列烛，自出宫迎法师入后院，坐一重阁宝帐中，拜问甚厚，云："弟子自闻师名，喜忘寝食，量准涂路，知师今夜必至，与妻子皆未眠，读经敬待。"须臾，王妃共数十侍女又来礼拜。是时渐欲将晓，言久疲勚欲眠，王始还宫，留数黄门侍宿。方旦，法师未起，王已至门，率妃已下俱来礼问。王云："弟子思量碛路艰阻，师能独来，甚为奇也。"流泪称叹，不能已已。遂设食，解斋讫，而宫侧别有道场，王自引法师居之，遣阉人侍卫。彼有彖法师曾学长安，善知法相，王珍之，命来与法师相见。少时出，又命国统王法师，年逾八十，共法师同处；仍遣劝住，勿往西方。法师不许。

停十余日，欲辞行，王曰："已令统师咨请，师意何如？"师报曰："留住实是王恩，但于来心不可。"王曰："泰与先王游大国，从隋帝历东、西二京及燕、岱、汾、晋之间，多见名僧，心无所慕。自承法师名，身心欢喜，手舞足蹈，拟师至止，受弟子供养以终一身。令一国人皆为师弟子，望师讲授；僧徒虽少，亦有数千，并使执经充师听众。伏愿察纳微心，不以西游为念。"

法师谢曰："王之厚意，岂贫道寡德所当。但此行不为供养而来，所悲本国法义未周，经教少阙，怀疑蕴惑，启访莫从，以是毕命西方，请未闻之旨，欲令方等甘露不但独洒于迦维，决择微言庶得尽沾于东国。波仑问道之志，善财求友之心，只可日日坚强，岂使中涂而止！愿王收意，勿以泛养为怀。"

王曰："弟子慕乐法师，必留供养，虽葱山可转，此意无移。乞信愚诚，勿疑不实。"法师报曰："王之深心，岂待屡言然后知也？但玄奘西来为法，法既未得，不可中停，以是敬辞，愿王相体。又大王曩修胜福，位为人主，非唯苍生恃仰，固亦释教依凭，理在助扬，岂宜为碍？"王曰："弟子亦不敢障碍，直以国无导师，故屈留法师以引愚迷耳。"

法师皆辞不许。王乃动色，攘袂大言曰："弟子有异涂处师，师安能自去。或定相留，或送师还国，请自思之，相顺犹胜。"法师报曰："玄奘来者为乎大法，今逢为障，只可骨被王留，识神未必留也！"因呜咽不复能言。王亦不纳，更使增加供养。每日进食，王躬捧盘。法师既被停留，违阻先志，遂誓不食以感其心。于是端坐，水浆不涉于口三日。至第四日，王觉法师气息渐惙，深生愧惧，乃稽首礼谢云："任师西行，乞垂早食。"

法师恐其不实，要王指日为言。王曰："若须尔者，请共对佛更结因缘。"遂共入道场礼佛，对母张太妃共法师约为兄弟，任师求法；还日请住此国三年，受弟子供养；若当来成佛，愿弟子如波斯匿王、频婆娑罗等与师作外护檀越；

仍屈停一月讲《仁王般若经》，中间为师营造行服。法师皆许。太妃甚欢，愿与师长为眷属，代代相度。于是方食。其节志贞坚如此。

后日，王别张大帐开讲，帐可坐三百余人，太妃已下王及统师大臣等各部别而听。每到讲时，王躬执香炉自来迎引。将升法座，王又低跪为蹬，令法师蹑上，日日如此。

讲讫，为法师度四沙弥以充给侍；制法服三十具；以西土多寒，又造面衣、手衣、靴、袜等各数事；黄金一百两，银钱三万，绫及绢等五百匹，充法师往还二十年所用之资；给马三十匹，手力二十五人。遣殿中侍御史欢信送至叶护可汗衙；又作二十四封书，通屈支等二十四国，每一封书附大绫一匹为信；又以绫绢五百匹，果味两车献叶护可汗，并书称："法师者是奴弟，欲求法于婆罗门国，愿可汗怜师如怜奴，仍请敕以西诸国给邬落马递送出境。"

法师见王送沙弥及国书绫绢等至，惭其优饯之厚，上启谢曰：

奘闻：江海遐深，济之者必凭舟楫；群生滞惑，导之者实假圣言。是以如来运一子之大悲，生兹秽土；镜三明之慧日，朗此幽昏。慈云荫有顶之天，法雨润三千之界。利安已讫，舍应归真。遗教东流，六百余祀。腾、会振辉于吴、洛，谶、什钟美于秦、凉；不坠玄风，咸匡胜业。但远人来译，音训不同；去圣时遥，义类差舛。遂使双林一味之旨，分成当、现二常；大乘不二之宗，析为南、北两道。纷纭诤论，凡数百年。率土怀疑，莫有匠决。

玄奘宿因有庆，早预缁门；负笈从师，年将二纪。名贤胜友，备悉咨询；大小乘宗，略得披览。未尝不执卷踌躇，捧经侘傺。望给园而翘足，想鹫岭而载怀。愿一拜临，启申宿惑。然知寸管不可窥天，小蠡难为酌海。但不能弃此微诚，是以束装取路，经涂荏苒，遂到伊吾。

伏惟大王，禀天地之淳和，资二仪之淑气。垂衣作王，子育苍生。东祇大国之风，西抚百戎之俗。楼兰、月氏之地，车师、狼望之乡，并被深仁，俱沾厚德。加以钦贤爱士，好善流慈；忧矜远来，曲令引接。既而至止，渥惠逾深；赐以话言，阐扬法义。又蒙降结娣季之缘，敦奖友于之念。并遗书西域二十余蕃，煦饰殷勤，令递饯送。又愍西游茕独，雪路凄寒，爰下明敕，度沙弥四人以为侍伴；法服、纶帽、裘毯、靴袜，五十余事，及绫绢、金银钱等，令充二十年往还之资。伏对惊惭，不知启处，决交河之水，比泽非多，举葱岭之山，方恩岂重？悬度陵溪之险，不复为忧；天梯道树之乡，瞻礼非晚。傥蒙允遂，则谁之力焉？王之恩也。

然后展谒众师，禀承正法；归还翻译，广布未闻。翦邪见之稠林，绝异端之穿凿；补像化之遗阙，定玄门之指南。庶此微功，用答殊泽。又前涂既远，不获久留；明日辞违，预增凄断。不任铭荷，谨启谢闻。

王报曰：“法师既许为兄弟，则国家所畜，共师同有，何因谢也？”

发日，王与诸僧、大臣、百姓等倾都送出城西。王抱法师恸哭，道俗皆悲，伤离之声振动郊邑。敕妃及百姓等还，自与大德已下各乘马送数十里而归。其所经诸国王侯礼重，皆此类也。

从是西行，度无半城、笃进城后，入阿耆尼国（旧曰乌耆讹也）。

卷第二

起阿耆尼国　终羯若鞠阇国

从此西行至阿耆尼国阿父师泉。泉在道南沙崖，崖高数丈，水自半而出。相传云：旧有商侣数百，在途水尽，至此困乏不知所为。时众中有一僧，不裹行资，依众乞活。众议曰：“是僧事佛，是故我曹供养，虽涉万里，无所赍携。今我等熬然，竟不忧念，宜共白之。”僧曰：“汝等欲得水者，宜各礼佛，受三归五戒，我为汝等登崖作水。”众既危困，咸从其命。受戒讫，僧教曰：“吾上崖后，汝等当唤‘阿父师为我下水’，任须多少言之。”其去少时，众人如教而请，须臾水下充足。大众无不欢荷，师竟不来。众人上观，已寂灭矣。大小悲号，依西域法焚之。于坐处聚砖石为塔。塔今犹在，水亦不绝。行旅往来，随众多少，下有细粗；若无人时，津液而已。法师与众宿于泉侧。

明发，又经银山。山甚高广，皆是银矿，西国银钱所从出也。山西又逢群贼，众与物而去。遂至王城所处川岸而宿。时同侣商胡数十，贪先贸易，夜中私发，前去十余里，遇贼劫杀，无一脱者。比法师等到，见其遗骸，无复财产，深伤叹焉。

渐去遥见王都，阿耆尼王与诸臣来迎，延入供养。其国先被高昌寇扰，有恨，不肯给马。法师停一宿而过。

前渡一大河，西履平川，行数百里，入屈支国界(旧云龟兹，讹也)。将近王都，王与群臣及大德僧木叉鞠多等来迎。自外诸僧数千，皆于城东门外，张浮幔，安行像，作乐而住。法师至，诸德起来相慰讫，各还就坐。使一僧擎鲜华一盘来授法师。法师受已，将至佛前散华，礼拜讫，就木叉鞠多下坐。坐已，复行华。行华已，行蒲桃浆。于初一寺受华、受浆已，次受余寺亦尔，如是展转日晏方讫，僧徒始散。

有高昌人数十于屈支出家，别居一寺，寺在城东南。以法师从家乡来，先请过宿，因就之，王共诸德各还。明日，王请过宫，备陈供养，而食有三净，法师不受，王深怪。法师报："此渐教所开，而玄奘所学者大乘不尔也。"受余别食。

食讫，过城西北阿奢理儿寺(此言奇特也)，是木叉鞠多所住寺也。鞠多理识闲敏，彼所宗归，游学印度二十余载，虽涉众经，而声明最善，王及国人咸所尊重，号称"独步"。见法师至，徒以客礼待之，未以知法为许。谓法师曰："此土《杂心》、《俱舍》、《毗婆沙》等一切皆有，学之足得，不烦西涉受艰辛也。"法师报曰："此有《瑜伽论》不？"鞠多曰："何用问是邪见书乎？真佛弟子者，不学是也。"法师初深敬之，及闻此言，视之犹土。报曰：“《婆沙》、《俱舍》本国已有，恨其理疏言浅，非究竟说，所以故来欲学大乘《瑜伽论》耳。又《瑜伽》者是后身菩萨弥勒所说，今谓邪书，岂不惧无底枉坑乎？”彼曰：“《婆沙》等汝所未解，何谓非深？”法师报曰：“师今解不？”曰：“我尽解。”法师即引《俱舍》初文问，发端即谬，因更穷之，色遂变动，云：“汝更问余处。”又示一文，亦不通，曰：“《论》无此语。”时王叔智月出家，亦解经、论，时在傍坐，即证言《论》有此语。乃取本对读之。鞠多极惭，云：“老忘耳。”又问余部，亦无好释。

时为凌山雪路未开，不得进发，淹停六十余日，观眺之外，时往就言，相见不复踞坐，或立或避。私谓人曰：“此支那僧非易酬对。若往印度，彼少年之俦，未必有也。”其畏叹如是。至发日，王给手力、驼马，与道俗等倾都送出。

从此西行二日，逢突厥寇贼二千余骑，其贼乃预共分张行众资财，悬诤不平，自斗而散。

又前行六百里，渡小碛，至跋禄迦国（旧曰姑墨），停一宿。又西北行三百里，渡一碛，至凌山，即葱岭北隅也。其山险峭，峻极于天。自开辟已来，冰雪所聚，积而为凌，春夏不解，凝冱汗漫，与云连属，仰之皑然，莫睹其际。其凌峰摧落横路侧者，或高百尺，或广数丈，由是蹊径崎岖，登涉艰阻。加以风雪杂飞，虽复屦重裘，不免寒战。将欲眠食，复无燥处可停，唯知悬釜而炊，席冰而寝。七日之后，方始出山，徒侣之中萎冻死者，十有三四，牛马逾甚。

出山后至一清池（清池，亦云热海，见其对凌山不冻故得此名，其水未必温也），周千四五百里，东西长，南北狭，望之淼然，无待激风而洪波数丈。循海西北行五百余里，至素叶城，逢突厥叶护可汗，方事畋游，戎马甚盛。可汗身着绿绫袍，露发，以一丈许帛练裹额后垂。达官二百余人皆锦袍编发，围绕左右。自余军众皆裘毼毳毛，矟纛端弓，驼马之骑，极目不知其表。既与相见，可汗欢喜，云："暂一处行，二三日当还，师且向衙所。"令达官答摩支引送安置至衙。

三日可汗方归，引法师入。可汗居一大帐，帐以金华装之，烂眩人目。诸达官于前列长筵两行侍坐，皆锦服赫然，余仗卫立于后。观之，虽穹庐之君亦为尊美矣。法师去帐三十余步，可汗出帐迎拜，传语慰问讫，入座。突厥事火不施床，以木含火，故敬而不居，但地敷重茵而已。仍为法师设一铁交床，敷蓐请坐。须臾，更引汉使及高昌使人入，通国书及信物，可汗自目之，甚悦，令使者坐。命陈酒设乐，可汗共诸臣使人饮，别索蒲桃浆奉法师。于是恣相酬劝，窣浑钟椀之器交错递倾，僸佅兜离之音铿锵互举，虽蕃俗之曲，亦甚娱耳目、乐心意也。少时，更有食至，皆烹鲜羔犊之质，盈积于前。别营净食进法师，具有饼饭、酥乳、石蜜、刺蜜、蒲桃等。食讫，更行蒲桃浆，仍请说法。法师因诲以十善，爱养物命，及波罗蜜多解脱之业。乃举手叩额，欢喜信受。

因留停数日。劝住曰："师不须往印特伽国（谓印度也），彼地多暑，十月当此五月，观师容貌，至彼恐销融也。其人露黑，类无威仪，不足观也。"法师报曰："今之彼，欲追寻圣迹，慕求法耳。"可汗乃令军中访解汉语及诸国音者，遂得年少，曾到长安数年，通解汉语，即封为摩咄达官，作诸国书，令摩咄送法师到迦毕试国。又施绯绫法服一袭，绢五十匹，与群臣送十余里。

自此西行四百余里，至屏聿，此曰“千泉”，地方数百里，既多池沼，又丰奇木，森沈凉润，即可汗避暑之处也。自屏聿西百五十里，至呾逻斯城。又西南二百里，至白水城。又西南二百里，至恭御城。又南五十里，至笯赤建国。又西二百里，至赭时国（此言石国），国西临叶河。又西千余里，至窣堵利瑟那国，国东临叶河。河出葱岭北源，西北流。又西北入大碛，无水草，望遗骨而进。

五百余里，至飒秣建国（此言康国）。王及百姓不信佛法，以事火为道。有寺两所，迥无僧居，客僧投者，诸胡以火烧逐，不许停住。法师初至，王接犹慢。经宿之后，为说人、天因果，赞佛功德，恭敬福利。王欢喜，请受斋戒，遂致殷重。所从二小师往寺礼拜，诸胡还以火烧逐。沙弥还以告王。王闻，令捕烧者，得已，集百姓，令截其手。法师将欲劝善，不忍毁其支体，救之。王乃重笞之，逐出都外。自是上下肃然，咸求信事，遂设大会，度人居寺。其革变邪心，诱开矇俗，所到如此。

又西三百余里，至屈霜你迦国。又西二百余里，至喝捍国（此言东安国）。又西四百里，至捕喝国（此言中安国）。又西百余里，至伐地国（此言西安国）。又西五百里，至货利习弥伽国，国东临缚刍河。又西南三百余里，至羯霜那国（此言史国）。又西南二百里入山，山路深险，才通人步，复无水草。

山行三百余里，入铁门，峰壁狭峭而崖石多铁矿，依之为门，扉又鍱铁，又铸铁为铃。多悬于上，故以为名，即突厥之关塞也。出铁门至睹货罗国（旧曰吐火罗，讹也）。

自此数百里渡缚刍河，至活国，即叶护可汗长子呾度设所居之地，又是高昌王妹婿。高昌王有书至其所。比法师到，公主可贺敦已死。呾度设又病，闻法师从高昌来，又得书，与男女等呜咽不能止。因请曰："弟子见师目明，愿少停息。若差，自送师到婆罗门国。"时更有一梵僧至，为诵咒，患得渐除。其后娶可贺敦，年少，受前儿嘱，因药以杀其夫。设既死，高昌公主男小，遂被前儿特勤纂立为设，仍妻后母。为逢丧故，淹留月余。

彼有沙门名达摩僧伽，游学印度，葱岭已西推为法匠，其疏勒、于阗之僧无敢对谈者。法师欲知其学深浅，使人问师解几部经、论。诸弟子等闻皆怒。达摩笑曰："我尽解，随意问。"法师知不学大乘，就小教《婆沙》等问数科，不是好通。因谢服，门人皆惭。从是相见欢喜，处处誉赞，言己不能及。

时新设既立，法师从求使人及邬落，欲南进向婆罗门国。设云："弟子所部有缚喝国，北临缚刍河，人谓小王舍城，极多圣迹，愿师暂往观礼，然后取乘南去。"时缚喝僧数十人闻旧设死，子又立，共来吊慰。法师与相见，言其意。彼曰："即当便去，彼有好路，若更来此，徒为迂会。"法师从其言，即与设辞，取乘随彼僧去。

既至，观其城邑，郊郭显敞，川野腴润，实为胜地。伽蓝百所，僧徒三千余人，皆小乘学。城外西南有纳缚伽蓝（此言新），装严甚丽。伽蓝内佛堂中有佛澡罐，量可斗余。又有佛齿长一寸，广八九分，色黄白，每有光瑞。又有佛扫帚，迦奢草作，长三尺余，围可七寸，其帚柄饰以杂宝。此三事，斋日每出，道俗观礼，至诚者感发神光。伽蓝北有窣堵波，高二百余尺。伽蓝西南有一精庐，建立多年，居中行道证四果者，世世无绝，涅槃后皆有塔记，基址接连数百余矣。大城西北五十里，至提谓城。城北四十里，有波利城。城中有二窣堵波，高三丈。昔佛初成道，受此二长者麨蜜，初闻五戒、十善，并请供养。如来当授发爪令造塔及造塔仪式。二长者将还本国，营建灵刹，即此也。城西七十余里有窣堵波，高逾二丈，过去迦叶佛时作也。

纳缚伽蓝有磔迦国小乘三藏名般若羯罗（此言慧性），闻缚喝国多有圣迹，故来礼敬。其人聪慧尚学，少而英爽，钻研九部，游泳四含，义解之声，周闻印度。其小乘阿毗达磨《迦延》、《俱舍》、《六足》、《阿毗昙》等无不晓达。既闻法师远来求法，相见甚欢。法师因申疑滞，约《俱舍》、《婆沙》等问之，其酬对甚精熟。遂停月余，就读《毗婆沙论》。伽蓝又有二小乘三藏，达摩毕利（此言法爱）、达摩羯罗（此言法性），皆彼所宗重。睹法师神彩明秀，极加敬仰。

时缚喝西南有锐末陀、胡实健国。其王闻法师从远国来，皆遣贵臣拜请过国受供养。辞不行。使人往来再三，不得已而赴。王甚喜，乃陈金宝饮食施法师，皆不受而返。

自缚喝南行，与慧性法师相随入揭职国。东南入大雪山，行六百余里，出睹货罗境，入梵衍那国。国东西二千余里，在雪山中，涂路艰危，倍于凌碛之地，凝云飞雪，曾不暂霁，或逢尤甚之处，则平涂数丈，故宋玉称西方之艰，层冰峨峨，飞雪千里，即此也。嗟乎，若不为众生求无上正法者，宁有禀父母遗体而游此哉！昔王尊登九折之坂，自云："我为汉室忠臣。"法师今涉雪岭求经，亦可谓如来真子矣！

如是渐到梵衍都城。有伽蓝十余所，僧徒数千人，学小乘说出世部。梵衍王出迎，延过宫供养，累日方出。彼有摩诃僧祇部学僧阿梨耶驮婆（此言圣使）、阿梨斯那（此言圣军），并深知法相，见法师，惊叹支那远国有如是僧，相引处处礼观，殷勤不已。王城东北山阿，有立石像，高百五十尺。像东有伽蓝，伽蓝东有鍮石释迦立像，高一百尺。伽蓝内有佛入涅槃卧像，长一千尺。并装严微妙。此东南行二百余里，度大雪山至小川，有伽蓝，中有佛齿及劫初时独觉齿，长五寸、广减四寸。复有金轮王齿，长三寸、广二寸。商诺迦缚娑（旧曰商那和修，讹也）所持铁钵，量可八九升，及僧伽胝衣，赤绛色。其人五百身中阴、生阴，恒服此衣，从胎俱出，后变为袈裟，因缘广如别传。

如是经十五日，出梵衍，二日逢雪，迷失道路，至一小沙岭，遇猎人示道，度黑山，至迦毕试境。国周四千余里，北背雪山。王则刹利种也，明略有威，统十余国。将至其都，王共诸僧并出城来迎。伽蓝百余所，诸僧相诤，各欲邀过所住。有一小乘寺名沙落迦，相传云是昔汉天子子质于此时作也。其寺僧言："我寺本汉天子儿作。今从彼来，先宜过我寺。"

法师见其殷重，又同侣慧性法师是小乘僧，意复不欲居大乘寺，遂即就停。

质子造寺时，又藏无量珍宝于佛院东门南大神王足下，拟后修补伽蓝。诸僧荷恩，处处屋壁图画质子之形。解安居日，复为讲诵树福。代代相传，于今未息。近有恶王贪暴，欲夺僧宝，使人掘神足下，地便大动。其神顶上有鹦鹉鸟像，见其发掘，振羽惊鸣。王及众军，皆悉闷倒，惧而还退。寺有窣堵波相轮摧毁，僧欲取宝修营，地还震吼，无敢近者。法师既至，众皆聚集，共请法师陈说先事。法师共到神所，焚香告曰："质子原藏此宝拟营功德，今开施用，诚是其时。愿鉴无妄之心，少戢威严之德。如蒙许者，奘自观开，称知斤数，以付所司，如法修造，不令虚费。唯神之灵，愿垂体察。"言讫，命人掘之，夷然无患，深七八尺得一大铜器，中有黄金数百斤、明珠数十颗。大众欢喜，无不嗟服。

法师即于寺夏坐。其王轻艺，唯信重大乘，乐观讲诵，乃屈法师及慧性三藏于一大乘寺法集。彼有大乘三藏名秣奴若瞿沙（此言如意声）、萨婆多阿黎耶伐摩（此言圣胄）、弥沙塞部僧求那跋陀（此言德贤），皆是彼之称首。然学不兼通，大小各别，虽精一理，终偏有所长。唯法师备谙众教，随其来问，各依部答，咸皆惬伏。如是五日方散。王甚喜，以纯锦五匹别施法师，以外各各有差。于沙落迦安居讫，其慧性法师重为睹货罗王请，却还，法师与别。

东进行六百余里，越黑岭，入北印度境，至滥波国。国周千余里。伽蓝十所，僧徒皆学大乘。停三日，南行至一小岭，岭有窣堵波，是佛昔从南步行到此住立，后人敬恋，故建兹塔。自斯以北境域，皆号蔑戾车（此言边地）。如来欲有教化，乘空往来，不复履地，若步行时，地便倾动。

从此南二十余里，下岭渡河，至那揭罗喝国（北印度境）。大城东南二里有窣堵波，高三百余尺，无忧王所造，是释迦菩萨于第二僧祇遇然灯佛敷鹿皮衣及布发掩泥得受记处。虽经劫坏，此迹恒存，天散众华，常为供养。法师至彼礼拜旋绕，傍有老僧为法师说建塔因缘。法师问曰："菩萨布发之时，既是第二僧祇，从第二僧祇至第三僧祇中间经无量劫，一一劫中世界有多成坏，如火灾起时，苏迷卢山尚为灰烬，如何此迹独得无亏？"

答曰："世界坏时，此亦随坏，世界成时，当其旧处迹现如本。且如苏迷卢山坏已还有，在乎圣迹，何得独无？以此校之，不烦疑也。"上为名答。次西南十余里有窣堵波，是佛买华处。

又东南度沙岭十余里，到佛顶骨城。城有重阁，第二阁中有七宝小塔，如来顶骨在中。骨周一尺二寸，发孔分明，其色黄白，盛以宝函。但欲知罪福相者，磨香末为埿，以帛练裹，隐于骨上，随其所得，以定吉凶。法师即得菩提树像，所将二沙弥，大者得佛像，小者得莲华像。其守骨婆罗门欢喜，向法师弹指散华，云："师所得甚为希有，足表有菩提之分。"

复有髑髅骨塔，状如荷叶。复有佛眼，睛大如柰，光明晖赫，彻烛函外。复有佛僧伽胝，上妙细氎所作。复有佛锡杖，白铁为环，栴檀为茎。法师皆得礼拜，尽其哀敬，因施金钱

五十、银钱一千、绮幡四口、锦两端、法服二具，散众杂华，辞拜而出。

又闻灯光城西南二十余里，有瞿波罗龙王所住之窟，如来昔日降伏此龙，因留影在中。法师欲往礼拜，承其道路荒阻，又多盗贼，二三年已来人往多不得见，以故去者稀疏。法师欲往礼拜，时迦毕试国所送使人贪其速还，不愿淹留，劝不令去。法师报曰："如来真身之影，亿劫难逢，宁有至此不往礼拜？汝等且渐进，奘暂到即来。"

于是独去。至灯光城，入一伽蓝问访涂路，觅人相引，无一肯者。后见一小儿，云："寺庄近彼，今送师到庄。"即与同去，到庄宿。得一老人知其处所，相引而发。行数里，有五贼人拔刀而至，法师即去帽，现其法服。贼云："师欲何去？"答："欲礼拜佛影。"贼云："师不闻此有贼耶？"答云："贼者，人也。今为礼佛，虽猛兽盈衢，奘犹不惧，况檀越之辈是人乎！"贼遂发心，随往礼拜。

既至窟所，窟在石涧东壁，门向西开，窥之窈冥，一无所睹。老人云："师直入，触东壁讫，却行五十步许，正东而观，影在其处。"法师入，信足而前，可五十步，果触东壁。依言却立，至诚而礼，百余拜一无所见。自责障累，悲号懊恼，更至心礼诵《胜鬘》等诸经、赞佛偈颂，随赞随礼，复百余拜，见东壁现如钵许大光，倏而还灭。悲喜更礼，复有槃许大光现，现已还灭。益增感慕，自誓若不见世尊影，终不移此地。如是更二百余拜，遂一窟大明，见如来影皎然在壁，如开云雾，忽睹金山，妙相熙融，神姿晃昱，瞻仰庆跃，不知所譬。佛身及袈裟并赤黄色，自膝已上相好极明，华座已下稍似微昧，左右及背后菩萨、圣僧等影亦皆具有。见已，遥命门外六人将火入烧香。比火至，欻然佛影还隐。急令绝火，更请方乃重现。六人中五人得见，一人竟无所睹。如是可半食顷，了了明见，得申礼赞，供散华香讫，光灭，尔乃辞出。所送婆罗门欢喜，叹未曾有，云："非法师志诚愿力之厚，无致此也。"窟门外更有众多圣迹，说如别传。相与归还，彼五贼皆毁刀杖，受戒而别。

从此复与伴合。东南山行五百余里，至健陀逻国（旧云健陀卫，讹也，北印度境也）。其国东临信度河，都城号"布路沙布罗"。国多贤圣，古来作论诸师那罗延天、无着菩萨、世亲菩萨、法救、如意、胁尊者等，皆此所出也。王城东北有置佛钵宝台。钵后流移诸国，今见在波剌拏斯国。

城外东南八九里有毕钵罗树，高百余尺，过去四佛并坐其下，现有四如来像，当来九百九十六佛，亦当坐焉。其侧又有窣堵波，是迦腻色迦王所造，高四百尺，基周一里半，高一百五十尺，其上起金刚相轮二十五层，中有如来舍利一斛。大窣堵波西南百余步有白石像，高一丈八尺，北面立，极多灵瑞，往往有人见像夜绕大塔经行。

迦腻色迦伽蓝东北百余里，渡大河至布色羯罗伐底城，城东有窣堵波，无忧王造，即过去四佛说法处也。城北四五里伽蓝内有窣堵波，高二百余尺，无忧王所立，即释迦佛昔行菩萨时，乐行惠施，于此国千生为王，即千生舍眼处。此等圣迹无量，法师皆得观礼。自高昌王所施金银、绫绢、衣服等，所至大塔、大伽蓝处，皆分留供养，申诚而去。

从此又到乌铎迦汉荼城。城北陟履山川，行六百余里，入乌仗那国(此言苑，昔阿轮迦王之苑也，旧称乌长，讹也)。夹苏婆萨堵河，昔有伽蓝一千四百所，僧徒一万八千，今并荒芜减少。其僧律仪传训有五部焉：一、法密部；二、化地部；三、饮光部；四、说一切有部；五、大众部。其王多居瞢揭釐城，人物丰盛。城东四五里有大窣堵波，多有奇瑞，是佛昔作忍辱仙人，为羯利王(此言斗诤，旧曰歌利讹也)割截身体处。城东北二百五十里入大山，至阿波逻罗龙泉，即苏婆河之上源也。西南流。其地寒冷，春夏恒冻，暮即雪飞，仍含五色，霏霏舞乱，如杂华焉。龙泉西南三十余里，水北岸磐石上有佛脚迹，随人福愿，量有修短，是佛昔伏阿波逻罗龙时，至此留迹而去。顺流下三十余里，有如来濯衣石，袈裟条叶文相宛然。城南四百余里至醯罗山，是如来昔闻半偈(旧曰偈，梵文略也。或曰偈他，梵文讹也。今从正，宜云伽他。伽他，唐言颂，颂有三十二言也)，报药叉之恩舍身下处。

瞢揭釐城西五十里渡大河，至卢醯呾迦(此言赤)窣堵波，高十余丈，无忧王造，是如来往昔作慈力王时，以刀刺身飤五药叉处(旧云夜叉，讹也)。城东北三十余里，至遏部多(此言奇特)石窣堵波，高三十尺，在昔佛于此为人、天说法，佛去后自然踊出此塔。塔西渡大河三四里至一精舍，有阿嚩卢枳多伊湿伐罗菩萨像(唐言观自在，合字连声，梵语如上；分文而言，即阿嚩卢枳多，译曰观，伊湿伐罗，译曰自在。旧云光世音，或观世音，或观世音自在，皆讹也)，威灵极著。

城东北闻说有人登越山谷，逆上徙多河，涂路危险，攀缘絙锁，践蹑飞梁，可行千余里，至达丽罗川，即乌杖那旧都也。其川中大伽蓝侧有刻木慈氏菩萨像，金色庄严，高百余尺。末田底加（旧曰末田地，讹也）阿罗汉所造。彼以神通力，将匠人升睹史多天（旧曰兜率陀，讹也），令亲观妙相，往来三返，尔乃功毕。

自乌铎迦汉荼城南渡信渡河。河广三四里，流极清急，毒龙恶兽多窟其中，有持印度奇宝名华及舍利渡者，船辄覆没。渡此河至呾叉始罗国（北印度境）。其城北十二三里有窣堵波，无忧王所建，每放神光，是如来昔行菩萨道为大国王，号“战达罗钵剌婆”（此言月光），志求菩提舍千头处。塔侧有伽蓝，昔经部师拘摩逻多（此言童寿），于此制造众论。从此东南七百余里，间有僧诃补罗国（北印度境）。又从呾叉始罗北界渡信度河，东南行二百余里，经大石门，是昔摩诃萨埵王子于此舍身飤饿乌择七子处。其地先为王子身血所染，今犹绛赤，草木亦然。

又从此东南山行五百余里，至乌剌尸国。又东南登危险，度铁桥，行千余里，至迦湿弥罗国（旧曰罽宾，讹也）。其都城西临大河，伽蓝百所，僧五千余人。有四窣堵波，崇高壮丽，无忧王所建，各有如来舍利升余。法师初入其境，至石门，彼国西门也，王遣母弟将车马来迎。入石门已，历诸伽蓝礼拜，到一寺宿，寺名护瑟迦罗。其夜众僧皆梦神人告曰：“此客僧从摩诃支那来，欲学经印度，观礼圣迹，师禀未闻。其人既为法来，有无量善神随逐，见在于此。师等宿福为远人所慕，宜勤诵习，令他赞仰，如何懈怠沉没睡眠！”诸僧闻已，各各惊寤，经行禅诵，至旦，并来说其因缘，礼敬逾肃。

如是数日，渐近王城，离可一由旬，到达摩舍罗（此言福舍，王教所立，使招延行旅，给赡贫乏）。王率群臣及都内僧诣福舍相迎，羽从千余人，幢盖盈涂，烟华满路。既至相见，礼赞殷厚，自手以无量华供养散讫，请乘大象相随而进。至都，止阇耶因陀罗寺（寺，王舅所立也）。明日，请入宫供养，并命大德僧称等数十人。食讫，王请开讲，令法师论难，观之甚喜。又承远来慕学，寻读无本，遂给书手二十人，令写经、论。别给五人供承驱使，资待所须，事事公给。

彼僧称法师者，高行之人，戒禁淳洁，思理淹深，多闻总持，才睿神茂，而性爱贤重士，既属上宾，盱衡延纳。法师亦倾心咨禀，晓夜无疲，因请讲授诸论。彼公是时年向七十，气力已衰，庆逢神器，乃励力敷扬，自午已前讲《俱舍论》，自午已后讲《顺正理论》，初夜后讲《因明》、《声明论》。由是境内学人无不悉集。法师随其所说，领悟无遗，研幽击节，尽其神秘。彼公欢喜，叹赏无极，谓众人曰：“此支那僧智力宏赡，顾此众中无能出者，以其明懿，足继世亲昆季之风，所恨生乎远国，不早接圣贤遗芳耳！”

时众中有大乘学僧毗戍陀僧诃（此言净师子也）、辰那饭茶（此言最胜亲）、萨婆多学僧苏伽蜜多罗（此言如来友）、婆苏蜜多罗（此言世友）、僧祇部学僧苏利耶提婆（此言日天）、辰那呾逻多（此言最胜救）。其国先来尚学，而此僧等皆道业坚贞，才解英富，比方僧称虽不及，比诸人足有余。既见法师为大匠褒扬，无不发愤难诘法师。法师亦明目酬酢，无所蹇滞，由是诸贤亦率惭服。

国先是龙池。佛涅槃后第五十年，阿难弟子末田底迦阿罗汉教化龙王舍池，立五百伽蓝，召诸贤圣于中住止，受龙供养。其后健陀罗国迦腻色迦王，如来灭后第四百年，因胁尊者请诸圣众，内穷三藏、外达五明者，得四百九十九人，及尊者世友，合五百贤圣于此结集三藏。先造十万颂《邬波第铄论》(旧曰《优波提舍》，讹也)释《素呾缆藏》(旧曰《修多罗》，讹也)。次造十万颂《毗柰耶毗婆沙论》，释《毗柰耶藏》(旧曰《毗那耶》，讹也)。次造十万颂《阿毗达磨毗婆沙论》，释《阿毗达磨藏》(或曰《阿毗昙》，讹也)。凡三十万颂，九十六万言。王以赤铜为鍱，镂写论文，石函封记，建大窣堵波而储其中，命药叉神守护。奥义重明，此之力也。如是停留首尾二年，学诸经、论，礼圣迹已，乃辞。

西南逾涉山涧，行七百里，至半笯嗟国。从此东南行四百余里，至遏逻阇补罗国(北印度境)。从此东南下山渡水行七百余里，至磔迦国(北印度境)。自滥波至于此土，其俗既住边荒，仪服语言稍殊印度，有鄙薄之风焉。自出曷逻阇补罗国，经二日，渡栴达罗婆伽河(此云月分)，到阇耶补罗城，宿于外道寺，寺在城西门外，是时徒侣二十余人。后日进到奢羯罗城，城中有伽蓝，僧徒百余人，昔世亲菩萨于中制《胜义谛论》，其侧有窣堵波，高二百尺，是过去四佛说法之处，见有经行遗迹。

从此出那罗僧诃城，东至波罗奢大林中，逢群贼五十余人。

法师及伴所将衣资劫夺都尽，仍挥刀驱就道南枯池，欲总屠害。其池多有蓬棘萝蔓，法师所将沙弥遂映刺林，见池南岸有水穴，堪容人过，私告法师，师即相与透出。东南疾走可二三里，遇一婆罗门耕地，告之被贼。彼闻惊愕，即解牛与法师，向村吹贝，声鼓相命，得八十余人，各将器仗，急往贼所。贼见众人，逃散各入林间，法师遂到池解众人缚，又从诸人施衣分与，相携投村宿。诸人悲泣，犹法师笑无忧戚。同侣问曰："行路衣资贼掠俱尽，唯余性命，仅而获存。困弊艰危，理极于此，所以却思林中之事，不觉悲伤。法师何因不共忧之，倒为欣笑？"答曰："居生之贵，唯乎性命。性命既在，余何所忧。故我土俗书云：'天地之大宝曰生。'生之既在，则大宝不亡。小小衣资，何足忧吝。"由是徒侣感悟。其澄波之量，浑之不浊如此。

明日到磔迦国东境，至一大城。城西道北有大庵罗林，林中有一七百岁婆罗门，及至观之，可三十许，形质魁梧，神理淹审，明《中》、《百》诸论，善《吠陀》等书。有二侍者，各百余岁。法师与相见，延纳甚欢。又承被贼，即遣一侍者，命城中信佛法者，令为法师造食。其城有数千户，信佛者盖少，宗事外道者极多。法师在迦湿弥罗时，声誉已远，诸国皆知，其使乃遍城中告唱云："支那国僧来，近处被贼，衣服总尽，诸人宜共知时。"福力所感，遂使邪党革心，有豪杰等三百余人，闻已各将斑氎布一端，并奉饮食，恭敬而至，俱积于前，拜跪问讯。法师为咒愿，并说报应因果，令诸人等皆发道意，弃邪归正，相对笑语，舞跃而还。长年叹未曾有。于是以氎布分给诸人，各得数具衣直，犹用之不尽，以五端布奉施长年。仍就停一月，学《经百论》、《广百论》。其人是龙猛弟子，亲得师承，说甚明净。

从此东行五百余里，到至那仆底国。诣突舍萨那寺，有大德毗腻多钵腊婆（此云调伏光，即北印度王子）。好风仪，善三藏，自造《五蕴论释》、《唯识三十论释》，因住十四月，学《对法论》、《显宗论》、《理门论》等。

大城东南行五十余里，至答秣苏伐那僧伽蓝（此言闇林），僧徒三百余人，学说一切有部。贤劫千佛皆当于此地集人、天说法。释迦如来涅槃后第三百年中，有迦多衍那（旧曰迦旃延，讹也）论师，于此制《发智论》。

从此东北行百四五十里，至阇烂达那国（北印度境）。入其国，诣那伽罗驮那寺，有大德旃达罗伐摩（此云月胄），善究三藏。因就停四月，学《众事分毗婆沙》。

从此东北行登履危险，行七百余里，至屈露多国（北印度境）。自屈露多国南行七百余里，越山渡河，至设多图卢国（北印度境）。从此西南行八百余里，至波理夜呾罗国（中印度境）。从此东行五百余里，至秣兔罗国（中印度境）。释迦如来诸圣弟子舍利子等遗身窣堵波，谓舍利子（旧曰舍梨子，又曰舍利弗，皆讹也）、没特伽罗子（旧曰目乾连，讹也）等塔皆见在。呾丽衍尼弗呾罗（此言满慈子，旧曰弥多罗尼子，讹略也）、优婆釐、阿难陀、罗怙罗（旧曰罗睺罗，又曰罗云，皆讹也）及曼殊室利（此言妙吉祥，旧曰濡首，又曰文殊师利，又言曼殊尸利，曰妙德，讹也），如是等诸窣堵波，每岁修福之日，僧徒相率随所宗事而修供养。阿毗达磨众供养舍利子；习定之徒供养没特伽罗子；诵持经者供养满慈子；学毗柰耶众供养优婆釐；诸比丘尼供养阿难；未受具戒者供养罗怙罗；学大乘者供养诸菩萨。城东五六里，至一山伽蓝，尊者乌波鞠多（此言近护）之所建也。其中爪、发舍利。伽蓝北岩有石室，高二十余尺，广三十余尺，四寸细筹，填积其内。尊者近护说法导夫妻俱证阿罗汉果者，乃下一筹；单己及别族者，虽证不记。

从此东北行五百余里，至萨他泥湿伐罗国（中印度境）。又东行四百余里，至禄勒那国（中印度境）。东临殑伽河，北背大山，阎牟那河中境而流。又河东行八百余里，至殑伽河源，广三四里，东南流入海处广十余里。其味甘美，细沙随流。彼俗书记谓之“福水”，就中沐浴，罪舋销除；啜波漱流，则殃灾殄灭；没而死者，即生天受福。愚夫愚妇常集河滨，皆外道邪言，无其实也。后提婆菩萨示其正理，方始停绝。国有大德名阇耶鞠多，善闲三藏。法师遂住一冬半春，就听《经部毗婆沙》讫。

渡河东岸至秣底补罗国。其王戍陀罗种也。伽蓝十余所，僧徒八百余人，皆学小乘一切有部。大城南四五里有小伽蓝，僧徒五十余人。昔瞿拏钵剌婆（此言德光）论师于此作《辩真》等论，凡百余部。论师是钵伐多国人，本习大乘，后退学小乘。时提婆犀那（此言天军）阿罗汉往来睹史多天，德光愿见慈氏，决诸疑滞，请天军以神力接上天宫。既见慈氏，揖而不礼。言：“我出家具戒，慈氏处天同俗，礼敬非宜。”如是往来三返，皆不致礼。既我慢自高，疑亦不决。

德光伽蓝南三四里有伽蓝，僧二百余人，并小乘学。是众贤论师寿终处。论师本迦湿弥罗国人，博学高才，明一切有部《毗婆沙》。时世亲菩萨亦以睿智多闻，先作《阿毗达磨俱舍论》，破毗婆沙师所执。理奥文华，西域学徒莫不赞仰，爰至鬼神亦皆讲习。众贤览而心愤，又十二年，覃思作《俱舍雹论》二万五千颂，八十万言。造讫，欲与世亲面定是非，未果而终。世亲后见其论，叹有知解，言："其思力不减《毗婆沙》之众也。虽然甚顺我义，宜名《顺正理论》。"遂依行焉。众贤死后，于庵没罗林中起窣堵波，今犹见在。

林侧又有窣堵波，是毗末罗蜜多罗（此言无垢称）论师遗身处。论师迦湿弥罗国人，于说一切有部出家，游五印度，学穷三藏，将归本国，涂次众贤之塔，悲其著述未及显扬，奄便逝殁。因自誓更造诸论，破大乘义，灭世亲名，使论师之旨永传遐代。说此语已，心智狂乱，五舌重出，遍体血流，自知此苦原由恶见，裁书忏悔，劝诸同侣，勿谤大乘，言终气绝。当死之处，地陷为坑。

其国有大德名蜜多斯那，年九十，即德光论师弟子，善闲三藏。法师又半春一夏就学萨婆多部《怛埵三弟铄论》（此言《辩真论》，二万五千颂，德光所造也）、《随发智论》等。

又从此北行三百余里，至婆罗吸摩补罗国（中印度境）。又此东南行四百余里，至醯掣怛罗国（中印度境）。又南行二百余里，渡殑伽河，西南至毗罗那拏国（中印度境）。又东行二百余里，至劫比他国（中印度境）。城东二十余里有大伽蓝，院内有三宝阶，南北列，面东西下，是佛昔于忉利天为摩耶夫人说法讫，归赡部洲下处。中是黄金，左是水精，右是白银。如来起善法堂，将诸天众蹑中阶而下，大梵天王执白拂，履银阶，处右，天帝释持宝盖，蹈水精阶，居左。是时百千天众、诸大菩萨陪随而下。自数百年前犹有阶级，今并沦没，后王恋慕，垒砖石拟其状，饰以杂宝，见高七十余尺。上起精舍，中有石佛像，左右有释、梵之像，并仿先仪，式彰如在。傍有石柱高七丈，无忧王所立。傍有石基，长五十余步，高七尺，是佛昔经行处。

从此西北行二百里，至羯若鞠阇国（此言曲女城，中印度）。国周四千里。都城西临殑伽河，长二十余里，广五六里。伽蓝一百余所，僧万余人，大小俱学。其王吠奢种也，字曷利沙伐弹那（此言喜增），父字波罗羯逻伐弹那（此言作增），兄字遏罗阇伐弹那（此言王增）。喜增在位仁慈，国人称咏。时东印度羯罗拏苏伐剌那（此言金耳）国设赏迦王（此言日），恶其明略而为邻患，乃诱而害之。大臣婆尼（此言明了）及群僚等，悲苍生之无主，共立其弟尸罗阿迭多（此言戒日）统承宗庙。王雄姿秀杰，算略宏远，德动天地，义感人神，遂能雪报兄仇，牢笼印度，威风所及，礼教所沾，无不归德。天下既定，黎庶斯安，于是戢武韬戈，营树福业，敕其境内无得杀生，凡厥元元，普令断肉。随其圣迹，皆建伽蓝，岁三七日遍供众僧。五年一陈无遮大会，府库所积并充檀舍，详其所行，须达拏之流矣。

城西北有窣堵波，高二百余尺；东南六七里殑伽河南有窣堵波，高二百余尺，并无忧王所造，皆是佛昔说法处。法师入其国，到跋达逻毗诃罗寺住三月，依毗离耶犀那三藏读佛使《毗婆沙》、日胄《毗婆沙》讫。

卷第三

起阿逾陀国　终伊烂拏国

自此东南行六百余里，渡殑伽河，南至阿逾陀国（中印度境）。寺百余所，僧徒数千人，大小乘兼学。大城中有故伽蓝，是伐苏盘度菩萨（此言世亲，旧曰婆薮盘豆，译为天亲，讹也）于此制大、小乘论及为众讲处。城西北四五里，临殑伽河岸大伽蓝中，有窣堵波，高二百余尺，无忧王所建，佛昔三月说法处。其傍又有过去四佛经行处。

城西南五六里有故伽蓝，是阿僧伽菩萨说法处。菩萨夜升睹史多天，于慈氏菩萨所受《瑜伽论》、《庄严大乘论》、《中边分别论》，昼则下天为众说法。阿僧伽亦名无著，即健陀逻国人也。佛灭度后一千年中出现于世，从弥沙塞部出家，后信大乘。弟世亲菩萨于说一切有部出家，后信大乘。兄弟皆禀明圣之器，含著述之才，广造诸论，解释大乘，为印度宗匠。如《摄大乘论》、《显扬圣教》、《对法》、《唯识》、《俱舍论》等，皆其笔也。

法师自阿逾陀国礼圣迹，顺殑伽河与八十余人同船东下，欲向阿耶穆佉国。行可百余里，其河两岸皆是阿输迦林，非常深茂。于林中两岸各有十余船贼，鼓棹迎流，一时而出。船中惊扰，投河者数人，贼遂拥船向岸，令诸人解脱衣服，搜求珍宝。然彼群贼素事突伽天神，每于秋中觅一人质状端美，杀取肉血用以祠之，以祈嘉福。见法师仪容伟丽，体骨当之，相顾而喜曰："我等祭神时欲将过，不能得人，今此沙门形貌淑美，杀用祠之，岂非吉也！"法师报："以奘秽陋之身，得充祠祭，实非敢惜。但以远来，意者欲礼菩提像、耆阇崛山，并请问经法。此心未遂，檀越杀之，恐非吉也。"船上诸人皆共同请，亦有愿以身代，贼皆不许。

于是贼帅遣人取水，于华林中治地设坛，和泥涂扫，令两人拔刀牵法师上坛，欲即挥刃。法师颜无有惧，贼皆惊异。既知不免，语贼："愿赐少时，莫相逼恼，使我安心欢喜取灭。"法师乃专心睹史多宫念慈氏菩萨，愿得生彼恭敬供养，受《瑜伽师地论》，听闻妙法，成就通慧，还来下生，教化此人，令修胜行，舍诸恶业，及广宣诸法，利安一切。于是礼十方佛，正念而坐，注心慈氏，无复异缘。于心想中，若似登苏迷卢山，越一二三天，见睹史多宫慈氏菩萨处妙宝台，天众围绕。此时身心欢喜，亦不知在坛，不忆有贼。同伴诸人发声号哭。须臾之间黑风四起，折树飞沙，河流涌浪，船舫漂覆。贼徒大骇，问同伴曰:“沙门从何处来?名字何等?”报曰:“从支那国来,求法者此也。诸君若杀,得无量罪。且观风波之状,天神已嗔,宜急忏悔。”贼惧,相率忏谢,稽首归依。时亦不觉,贼以手触,尔乃开目,谓贼曰:“时至耶?”贼曰:“不敢害师,愿受忏悔。”法师受其礼谢,为说杀盗邪祠诸不善业,未来当受无间之苦。何为电光朝露少时之身,作阿僧企耶长时苦种!

贼等叩头谢曰:“某等妄想颠倒,为所不应为,事所不应事。若不逢师福德,感动冥祇,何以得闻启诲。请从今日已去,即断此业,愿师证明。”于是递相劝告,收诸劫具总投河流,所夺衣资各还本主,并受五戒,风波还静。贼众欢喜,顶礼辞别。同伴敬叹,转异于常。远近闻者,莫不嗟怪。非求法殷重,何以致兹!

从此东行三百余里,渡殑伽河,北至阿耶穆佉国(中印度境)。从此东南行七百余里,渡殑伽河南、阎牟那河北,至钵罗耶伽国(中印度境)。城西南瞻博迦华林中有窣堵波,无忧王所造,是佛昔降外道处。其侧有伽蓝,是提婆菩萨作《广百论》,挫小乘外道处。

大城东两河交处,其西有墠,周十四五里,土地平正,自古已来诸王豪族仁慈惠施,皆至于此,因号其处为“大施场”。今戒日王亦继斯轨,五年积财,七十五日散施,上从三宝,下至孤穷,无不悉施。

从此西南入大林,多逢恶兽、野象。经五百余里,至憍赏弥国(旧曰俱睒弥,讹。中印度境)。伽蓝十余所,僧徒三百余人。城内故宫中有大精舍,高六十余尺,有刻檀佛像,上悬石盖，邬陀衍那王（此言出爱，旧云优填王，讹）之所造也。昔如来在忉利天经夏为母说法，王思慕，乃请目连将巧工升天，观佛尊颜容止，还以紫檀雕刻以像真容。世尊下来时，像迎佛，即此也。

城南有故宅，是瞿史罗（旧曰瞿师罗，讹）长者故居也。城南不远有故伽蓝，即长者之园地。中有窣堵波，高二百余尺，无忧王所造。次东南重阁是世亲造《唯识论》处。次东庵没罗林有故基，是无著菩萨作《显扬论》处。

从此东行五百余里，至鞞索迦国。伽蓝二十余所，僧三千许人，学小乘正量部。东南道左有大伽蓝，是昔提婆设摩阿罗汉造《识身足论》，说“无我人”；瞿波阿罗汉作《圣教要实论》，说“有我人”。因此法执，遂深诤论。又是护法菩萨七日中摧伏小乘一百论师处。其侧又有如来六年说法处。有一树高七十余尺，昔佛因净齿，木弃其余枝，遂植根繁茂至今。邪见之徒数来残伐，随伐随生，荣茂如本。

从此东北行五百余里，至室罗伐悉底国（旧曰舍卫，讹也）。周六千余里，伽蓝数百，僧徒数千，并学正量部。佛在时，钵罗斯那恃多（此言胜军，旧曰波斯匿，讹）王所居都也。城内有王殿故基，次东不远有故基，上建窣堵波，胜军王为佛造大讲堂处。次复有塔，是佛姨母钵罗阇钵底（此言生主，旧曰波阇波提，讹也）比丘尼精舍。次东有塔，是苏达多（此言乐施，旧曰须达，讹也）故宅。宅侧有大窣堵波，是鸯窭利摩罗（旧曰央崛摩罗，讹也）舍邪之处。

城南五六里有逝多林（此曰言胜林，旧曰祇陀，讹也），即给孤独园也。昔为伽蓝，今已颓毁。东门左、右各建石柱，高七十余尺，无忧王所立。诸屋并尽，独一砖室在，中有金像。昔佛升天为母说法，胜军王心生恋慕，闻出爱王刻檀为像，因造此也。伽蓝后不远是外道梵志杀妇谤佛处。伽蓝东百余步有大深坑，是提婆达多以毒药害佛，生身入地狱处。其南复有大坑，瞿伽梨比丘谤佛，生身入地狱处。坑南八百余步，是战遮婆罗门女谤佛，生身入地狱处。凡此三坑，窥不见底。

伽蓝东七十余步，有精舍，伽蓝高大，中有佛像东面坐，如来昔共外道论议处。次东有天祠，量等精舍，日光移转，天祠影不及精舍，精舍影常覆天祠。次东三四里有窣堵波，是舍利子与外道论议处。大城西北六十余里有故城，是贤劫中人寿二万岁时，迦叶波佛父城也。城南是佛成正觉已，初见父处。城北有塔，塔有迦叶波佛全身舍利。并无忧王所立。

从此东南行八百余里，至劫比罗伐窣堵国（旧曰迦毗罗卫国）。国周四千余里，都城十余里，并皆颓毁。宫城周十五里，垒砖而成，极牢固。内有故基，净饭王之正殿，上建精舍，中作王像。次北有故基，是摩耶夫人之寝殿，上建精舍，中作夫人之像。其侧有精舍，是释迦菩萨降神母胎处，中作菩萨降生之像。上座部云，菩萨以嗢怛罗頞娑荼月三十日夜降神母胎，当此五月十五日。诸部则以此二十三日，当此五月八日。东北有窣堵波，阿私陀仙相太子处。于城左右有太子共诸释种捔力处。又有太子乘马逾城处，及先于四门见老、病、死及沙门，厌离世间回驾处。

从此东行荒林五百余里，至蓝摩国（中印度境）。居人稀少。故城东有砖窣堵波，高百余尺。如来涅槃后，此国先王分得舍利，还而造也。每放光明。其侧有龙池，龙数变身为人，绕塔行道。野象衔华，常来供养。其侧不远有伽蓝，以沙弥知寺任。相传昔有苾刍招命同学，远来礼拜，见野象衔华，安置塔前，复以牙芟草，以鼻洒水，众见无不感叹。有一苾刍便舍大戒，愿留供养，谓众人曰："象是畜生，犹知敬塔献华洒扫，我居人类，依佛出家，岂可目睹荒残，不供事也！"即辞众住，结宇疏地，种华植果，虽涉寒暑，不以劳惓。邻国闻之，各舍财宝，共建伽蓝，仍即屈知僧务。自此相承，遂为故事矣。

沙弥伽蓝东大林中行百余里，有窣堵波，无忧王所建，是太子逾城至此，解宝衣、天冠、髻珠付阐铎迦（旧曰车匿，讹也）还处也。及剃发，皆有塔记。

出此林已，至拘尸那揭罗国。处极荒梗。城内东北隅有窣堵波，无忧王所建，准陀（旧曰纯陀，讹）故宅。宅中有井，将营献供时凿也，水犹澄映。

城西北三四里，渡阿恃多伐底河（此言无胜，旧曰阿利跋提河，讹也），河侧不远至娑罗林，其树似槲而皮青叶白，甚光润，四双齐高，即如来涅槃处也。有大砖精舍，内有如来涅槃之像，北首而卧。傍有大窣堵波，高二百余尺，无忧王所造。又立石柱记佛涅槃事，不书年月。相传云：佛处世八十年，以吠舍佉月后半十五日入涅槃，当此二月十五日。说一切有部复云：佛以迦剌底迦月后半入涅槃，当此九月八日。自涅槃已来，或云千二百岁、或千五百、或云过九百未满千年。

又如来坐金棺为母说法，出臂问阿难，现足示迦叶，香木焚身，八王分骨，皆有塔记。

从此复大林中经五百余里，至婆罗痆斯国。国周四千余里，都城西临殑伽河，长十余里，广五六里。伽蓝三十余所，僧二千余人，学小乘一切有部。

渡婆罗痆斯河，东北行十余里，至鹿野伽蓝。台观连云，长廊四合。僧徒一千五百人，学小乘正量部。大院内有精舍，高百余尺，石阶砖龛，层级百数，皆隐起黄金佛像。室中有鍮石佛像，量等如来身，作转法轮状。精舍东南有石窣堵波，无忧王所建，高百余尺。前有石柱，高七十余尺，是佛初转法轮处。其侧有梅怛丽（此言慈氏，旧曰弥勒，讹也）菩萨受记处。次西有窣堵波，是佛昔为护明菩萨，于贤劫中人寿二万岁时，迦叶波佛所受记处。

释迦受记南，有过去四佛经行处，长五十余步，高七尺，以青石积成，上有四佛经行之像。

伽蓝西有如来澡浴池，又有涤器池，又有浣衣池，并神龙守护，无人秽触。池侧有窣堵波，佛修菩萨行时，为六牙白象施猎师牙处。又为鸟时，与猕猴、白象约尼拘律树，定长幼巡行化人处。又作鹿王，又度憍陈如等五人处。

从此顺殑伽河流东行三百余里，至战主国。从此东北渡殑伽河行百四五十里，至吠舍釐国（旧曰毗舍离，讹也）。国周五千余里，土壤良沃，多庵没罗果、茂遮果。都城荒毁。故基周六七十里，居人甚少。宫城西北五六里有一伽蓝，旁有窣堵波，是佛昔说《毗摩罗诘经》处。次东北三四里，有窣堵波，是毗摩罗诘故宅，其宅尚多灵异。去此不远有一室，积石所作，是无垢称现疾说法处。其侧亦有宝积故宅、庵摩罗女故宅。次北三四里，有窣堵波，是佛将往拘尸那国般涅槃，天、人、随从伫立处。次西复有佛最后观吠舍釐处，次南又有庵摩罗女持园施佛处，又有佛许魔王涅槃处。

从吠舍釐南境，去殑伽河百余里，到吠多补罗城，得《菩萨藏经》。又南渡殑伽河，至摩揭陀国（旧曰摩伽陀，讹也），周五千余里。俗崇学重贤。伽蓝五十余所，僧万余人，多大乘学。河南有故城，周七十余里，虽复荒颓，犹有雉堞。昔人寿无量岁时，号“拘苏摩补罗城”（此言香华宫城）。王宫多华，故致此号。后至人寿数千岁时，更名波咤釐子城（旧曰熙连弗邑，讹也），复约波咤釐树为名。

至佛涅槃后第一百年，有阿输迦王（此言无忧王，旧曰阿育王，讹也），即频毗娑罗王（此言影坚）之曾孙也，自王舍城迁都来此。年代浸远，今唯故基。伽蓝数百，存者二三。故宫北临殑伽河为小城，城有千余家。宫北有石柱，高数十尺，无忧王作地狱处。法师在小城停七日，巡礼圣迹。地狱南有窣堵波，即八万四千之一也。王以人功建立，中有如来舍利一斗，每放神光。次有精舍，中有如来所履石，石上有佛双迹，长一尺八寸，广六寸，两足下有千辐轮相，十指端有万字华文及瓶鱼等，皎然明著，是如来将入涅槃，发吠舍釐至此，于河南岸大方石上立，顾谓阿难：“此是吾最后望金刚座及王舍城所留之迹也！”

精舍北有石柱，高三十余尺，书记无忧王三以赡部洲施佛、法、僧，三以珍宝赎嗣也。故城东南有屈屈咤阿滥摩（此言鸡园）僧伽蓝故基，无忧王所造，是召千僧四事供养处。是等圣迹，凡停七日，礼拜方遍。

又西南行六七由旬，至低罗磔迦寺。寺有三藏数十人，闻法师至，皆出迎引。从此又南行百余里，到菩提树。树垣垒砖，高峻极固。东西长，南北稍狭。正门东对尼连禅河，南门接大华池，西带险固，北门通大伽蓝，其内圣迹连接，或精舍，或窣堵波，并诸王、大臣、豪富、长者，慕圣营造，用为旌记。正中有金刚座。贤劫初成，与大地俱起，据三千大千之中，下极金轮，上齐地际，金刚所成，周百余步。言金刚者，取其坚固难坏，能沮万物。若不依本际则地不能停，若不以金刚为座，则无地堪发金刚定。今欲降魔成道，必居于此，若于余地，地便倾戾。故贤劫千佛皆就此焉。又成道之处亦曰“道场”，世界倾摇，独此不动。

一二百年来众生薄福，往菩提树不见金刚座。佛涅槃后，诸国王以两躯观自在菩萨像南北标界，东向而坐。相传此菩萨身没不现，佛法当尽，今南边菩萨已没至胸。其菩提树即毕钵罗树也，佛在时高数百尺，比频为恶王诛伐，今可五丈余，佛坐其下，成无上等觉，因谓菩提树。树茎黄白，枝叶青润，秋冬不凋，唯至如来涅槃日，其叶顿落，经宿还生如本。每至是日，诸国王与臣僚共集树下，以乳灌洗，然灯散华，收叶而去。

法师至，礼菩提树及慈氏菩萨所作成道时像，至诚瞻仰讫，五体投地，悲哀懊恼，自伤叹言："佛成道时，不知漂沦何趣。今于像季，方乃至斯；缅惟业障，一何深重。"悲泪盈目。时逢众僧解夏，远近辐凑数千人，观者无不呜噎。其处一逾缮那圣迹充满，停八九日，礼拜方遍。

至第十日，那烂陀寺众差四大德来迎，即与同去。行可七逾缮那至寺庄。庄是尊者目连本生之村。至庄食，须臾，更有二百余僧与千余檀越将幢盖、华、香复来迎引，赞叹围绕入那烂陀。既至，合众都集。法师共相见讫，于上座头别安床，命法师坐，徒众亦坐。坐讫，遣维那击犍稚唱。法师住寺，寺中一切僧所畜用法物道具咸皆共同。仍差二十人非老非少、闲解经律、威仪齐整者，将法师参正法藏，即戒贤法师也（传云年百六岁，状云年百六十），众共尊重，不斥其名，号为正法藏。于是随众入谒。既见，方事师资，务尽其敬，依彼仪式，膝行肘步，呜足顶礼。问讯赞叹讫，法藏令广敷床座，命法师及诸僧坐。

坐讫，问："法师从何处来？"报曰："从支那国来，欲依师学《瑜伽论》。"闻已啼泣，唤弟子佛陀跋陀罗（此言觉贤），即法藏之侄也，年七十余，博通经、论，善于言谈。法藏语曰："汝可为众说我三年前病恼因缘。"觉贤闻已，啼泣扪泪而说昔缘，云："和上昔患风病，每发，手足拘急，如火烧刀刺之痛，乍发乍息，凡二十余载。去三年前，苦痛尤甚，厌恶此身，欲不食取尽。于夜中梦三天人（传状但梦一金色人），一黄金色，二琉璃色，三白银色，形貌端正，仪服轻明，来问和尚曰：'汝欲弃此身耶？经云："说身有苦，不说厌离于身。”汝于过去曾作国王，多恼众生，故招此报。今宜观省宿愆，至诚忏悔，于苦安忍，勤宣经、论，自当销灭。直尔厌身，苦终不尽。’和尚闻已，至诚礼拜。其金色人指碧色者语和尚曰：‘汝识不？此是观自在菩萨。’又指银色曰：‘此是慈氏菩萨。’和上即礼拜慈氏，问曰：‘戒贤常愿生于尊宫，不知得不？’报曰：‘汝广传正法，后当得生。’金色者自言：‘我是曼殊室利菩萨。我等见汝空欲舍身，不为利益，故来劝汝。当依我语，显扬正法《瑜伽论》等，遍及未闻，汝身即渐安隐，勿忧不差。有支那国僧乐通大法，欲就汝学，汝可待教之。’法藏闻已，礼拜报曰：‘敬依尊教。’言已不见。自尔已来，和尚所苦瘳除。”僧众闻者莫不称叹希有。

法师得亲承斯记，悲喜不能自胜，更礼谢曰：“若如所说，玄奘当尽力听习，愿尊慈悲摄受诲教。”法藏又问曰：“法师汝在路几年？”答：“三年。”既与昔梦符同，种种诲喻令法师欢喜，以申师弟之情。

言讫辞出，向幼日王院安置于觉贤房第四重阁。七日供养已，更安置上房在护法菩萨房北，加诸供给。日得赡步罗果一百二十枚，槟榔子二十颗，豆蔻二十颗，龙脑香一两，供大人米一升。其米大于乌豆，作饭香鲜，余米不及，唯摩揭陀国有此粳米，余处更无，独供国王及多闻大德，故号为“供大人米”。月给油三斗，酥乳等随日取足。净人一人（传作四）、婆罗门一人，免诸僧事，行乘象舆。那烂陀寺主客僧万，预此供给添法师合有十人（传寺素立法，通三藏者，员额十人，由来缺一，以奘风问，便处其位）。其游践殊方，见礼如此。

那烂陀寺者，此云“施无厌寺”。耆旧相传，此伽蓝南庵没罗园中有池，池有龙名那烂陀，傍建伽蓝，故以为号。又云，是如来昔行菩萨道时，为大国王，建都此地，怜愍孤穷，常行惠舍，物念其恩，故号其处为“施无厌”也。地本庵没罗长者园，五百商人以十亿金钱买以施佛，佛于此处三月说法，商人多有证果。佛涅槃后，此国先王铄伽罗阿迭多（此言帝日）敬恋佛故，造此伽蓝。王崩后，其子佛陀鞠多王（此言觉密）纂承鸿业，次南又造伽蓝。至子怛他揭多王（此言如来）次东又造伽蓝。至子婆罗阿迭多（此言幼日）王，次东北又建伽蓝。后见圣僧从此支那国往赴其供，心生欢喜，舍位出家。其子伐阇罗（此言金刚）嗣位，次北又建伽蓝。其后中印度王于侧又造伽蓝。

如是六帝相承，各加营造，又以砖垒其外，合为一寺，都建一门。庭序别开，中分八院。宝台星列，琼楼岳峙；观竦烟中，殿飞霞上；生风云于户牖，交日月于轩檐；加以渌水逶迤，青莲菡萏，羯尼华树晖焕其间，庵没罗林森竦其外。诸院僧室皆有四重重阁，虬栋虹梁，绿栌朱柱，雕楹镂槛，玉础文薨；甍接瑶晖，榱连绳彩。印度伽蓝数乃千万，壮丽崇高，此为其极。

僧徒主客常有万人，并学大乘，兼十八部，爰至俗典、《吠陀》等书，因明、声明、医方、术数，亦俱研习。凡解经、论二十部者一千余人，三十部者五百余人，五十部者并法师十人。唯戒贤法师一切穷览，德秀年耆，为众宗匠。寺内讲座日百余所，学徒修习，无弃寸阴。德众所居，自然严肃。建立已来七百余载，未有一人犯讥过者。国王钦重，舍百余邑充其供养，邑二百户，日进粳米、酥乳数百石。由是学人端拱无求而四事自足，艺业成就，斯其力焉。

法师于那烂陀寺安置已，向王舍城观礼圣迹。王舍旧城彼云“矩奢揭罗补罗城”（此言上茅宫城），城处摩揭陀国之中，古昔君王多住其内。其地又生好香茅，故取为称。四面皆山，峻峭如削，西通小径，北有大门，东西长，南北狭，周一百五十余里。其内更有小城，基周三十余里，羯尼迦树处处成林，发萼开荣，四时无间，叶如金色。

宫城北门外有窣堵波，是提婆达多与未生怨王放护财醉象欲害佛处。此东北有窣堵波，是舍利子闻阿湿婆恃苾刍说法证果处。次北不远有大深坑，是室利鞠多（此言胜密）受外道邪言，以火坑、毒饭欲害佛处。次大坑东北山城之曲有窣堵波，是时缚迦大医（旧曰耆婆，讹也）于此为佛造说法堂处。其侧现有时缚迦故宅。

宫城东北行十四五里，至姞栗陀罗矩吒山（此言鹫峰，亦云鹫台，旧曰耆阇崛山，讹也），其山连岗北岭，隆崛特高，形如鹫鸟，又状高台，故取为称。泉石清奇，林树森郁，如来在世多居此山说《法华》、《大般若》等无量众经。

山城北门行一里余，至迦兰陀竹园。今现有砖室，如来在昔多居其中，制诸戒律。园主名迦兰陀，先以此园施诸外道。后见佛，又闻深法，恨不以园得施如来。时地神知其意，为现灾怪怖诸外道，逐之令出，告曰：“长者欲以园施佛，汝宜速去。”外道含怒而出，长者欢喜，建立精舍讫，躬往请佛，佛为受之。竹园东有窣堵波，阿阇多设咄路王(此言未生怨，旧曰阿阇世，讹也)之所建。如来涅槃后，诸王共分舍利，未生怨王得已将归，立塔供养。无忧王发心欲遍造诸塔，开取舍利，尚留少许，今每放光明。

竹园西南行五六里，山侧有别竹林，中有大石室，是尊者摩诃迦叶波于此与九百九十九大阿罗汉，如来涅槃后结集三藏处。当结集时，无量圣众云集，迦叶告曰：“众中自知具三明、六通，总持如来一切法藏无错谬者住，余各随所安。”时简得九百九十九人。阿难在于学地，迦叶语阿难：“汝漏未尽，勿污清众。”阿难惭愧而出。一夜勤修，断三界结，成阿罗汉，还来叩门。迦叶问曰：“汝结尽耶？”答曰：“然！”复曰：“若结尽者，不劳开门，随意所入。”阿难乃从户隙而入，礼拜僧足。迦叶执其手曰：“我欲汝除断诸漏证圣果，故驱逐汝出，汝当知之，勿以为恨。”阿难曰：“若怀恨者，岂名结尽。”于是礼谢而坐。即初安居十五日时也。迦叶语阿难曰：“如来常于众中称汝多闻，总持诸法，汝可升座为众诵素呾缆藏，即一切经也。”阿难承命而起，向佛般涅槃山方作礼讫，升坐诵经，诸众随口而录。录讫，又命优波离诵毗柰耶藏，即一切戒律也。诵讫，迦叶波自诵阿毗达磨藏，即一切论议。经两三月安居中，集三藏讫，书之贝叶，方遍流通。诸圣相谓曰：“我等集此，名报佛恩，今日得闻，斯其力也。”以大迦叶僧中上座，因名“上座部”。

又此西二十里有窣堵波，无忧王所建，即大众部共集之处。诸学、无学数千人，大迦叶结集时不预者，共集此中，更相谓曰："如来在日，同一师学。世尊灭度，驱简我等，我等岂不能结集法藏报佛恩耶？"复集素怛缆藏、毗柰耶藏、阿毗达磨藏、杂集藏、禁咒藏，别为五藏，此中凡、圣同会，因谓之"大众部"。

次东北三四里至曷罗阇姞利呬多城（此言王舍）。外郭已坏，内城犹峻，周二十余里，面有一门。初频毗娑罗王居上茅宫时，百姓殷稠，居家鳞接，数遭火灾，乃立严制，有不谨慎，先失火者，徙之寒林。寒林即彼国弃尸恶处也。顷之，王宫忽复失火。王曰："我为人王，自犯不行，无以惩下。"命太子留抚，王徙居寒林。时吠舍釐王闻频婆娑罗野居于外，欲简兵袭之。候望者知而奏，王乃筑邑。以王先舍于此，故名"王舍城"，即新城也。后阇王嗣位，因都之。至无忧王迁都波咤釐，以城施婆罗门。今城中无杂人，唯婆罗门千余家耳。宫城内西南隅有窣堵波，是殊底色迦长者（此言星历，旧云树提伽，讹也）故宅，傍又有度罗怙罗处（即佛子也）。

那烂陀寺西北有大精舍，高三百余尺，婆罗阿迭多王之所建也。庄严甚丽，其中佛像同菩提树像。精舍东北有窣堵波，如来昔于此七日说法处。西北又有过去四佛坐处。其南鍮石精舍，戒日王之所建，功虽未毕，详其图量，限高十余丈。城次东二百余步有铜立佛像，高八十余尺，重阁六层方得覆及，昔满胄王之所作也。又东行数里有窣堵波，佛初成道向王舍城至此，频毗娑罗王与国人百千万众迎见佛处。

又东行三十余里，至因陀罗势罗窭诃山。东峰伽蓝前有窣堵波，谓僧娑（此言雁也）。昔此伽蓝依小乘渐教，食三净肉。于一时中贯赎不得，其检校人傍徨无措，乃见群雁翔飞，仰而戏言曰："今日僧供有阙，摩诃萨埵宜知是时。"言讫，其引前者应声而回，铩翮高云，投身自坠。苾刍见已惭惧，遍告众僧，闻者惊嗟，无不对之叹泣。各相谓曰："此菩萨也。我曹何人，敢欲啖食。又如来设教，渐次而防，我等执彼初诱之言，便为究竟之说，守愚无改，致此损伤。自今已后，宜依大乘，不得更食三净。"仍建灵塔，以死雁埋中，题表其心，使永传芳烈，以故有兹塔也。

如是等圣迹，法师皆周遍观礼讫。还归那烂陀寺，方请戒贤法师讲《瑜伽论》，同听者数千人。开题讫，少时，有一婆罗门于众外悲嚎而复言笑。遣人问其所以。答言："我是东印度人，曾于布磔迦山观自在菩萨像所发愿为王，菩萨为我现身，诃责我言：'汝勿作此愿！后某年月日那烂陀寺戒贤法师为脂那国僧讲《瑜伽论》，汝当往听。因此闻法后得见佛，何用王为！'今见支那僧来，师复为讲，与昔言同，所以悲喜。戒贤法师因令住听经。十五月讲彻，遣人将婆罗门送与戒日王，王封以三邑。

法师在寺听《瑜伽》三遍，《顺正理》一遍，《显扬》、《对法》各一遍，《因明》、《声明》、《集量》等论各二遍，《中》、《百》二论各三遍。其《俱舍》、《婆沙》、《六足》、《阿毗昙》等，已曾于迦湿弥罗诸国听讫，至此寻读决疑而已。

兼学婆罗门书。

印度梵书名为“记论”，其源无始，莫知作者。每于劫初，梵王先说，传授天人，以是梵王所说，故曰“梵书”。其言极广，有百万颂，即旧译云《毗伽罗论》者是也。然其音不正，若正应云《毗耶羯剌諵》，此翻名为《声明记论》，以其广记，诸法能诠，故名《声明记论》。昔成劫之初，梵王先说具百万颂。后至住劫之初，帝释又略为十万颂。其后北印度健驮罗国婆罗门睹罗邑波腻尼仙又略为八千颂，即今印度现行者是。近又南印度婆罗门为南印度王复略为二千五百颂，边鄙诸国多盛流行，印度博学之人所不遵习。此并西域音字之本。其支分明相助者，复有《记论略经》，有一千颂。又有字体三百颂，又有字缘两种，一名《间择迦》三千颂；二名《温那地》二千五百颂，此辩字缘、字体。又有《八界论》八百颂，此中略合字之缘、体。

此诸记论，辩能诠所诠，有其两例：一名底彦多声，有十八啭；二名苏漫多声，有二十四啭。其底彦多声于文章壮丽处用，于诸泛文亦少用。其二十四啭者于一切诸文同用。其底彦多声十八啭者，有两：一般罗飒迷，二阿答末埿，各有九啭，故合有十八。初九啭者，如泛论一事有三。说他有三，自说有三：一一三中，说一、说二、说多，故有三也。两句皆然，但其声别，故分二九耳。

依般罗飒迷声说，有无等诸法。且如说“有”，“有”即三名：一名婆啵（换人字旁）底，二名婆啵（换人字旁）破，三名婆饭底。说他三者，一名婆啵（换人字旁）斯，二名婆啵（换人字旁）破，三名婆啵（换人字旁）他。自说三者，一婆啵（换人字旁）弥，二婆啵（换人字旁）靴（去声），三婆啵（换人字旁）摩（此第三依《四吠陀论》中说多言婆啵（换人字旁）末斯）。依阿答末埿九啭者，于前九啭下各置毗耶底言，余同上。安此者令文巧妙无别义，亦表极美义也。

苏漫多声二十四啭者，谓言总有八啭，于八啭中一一各三。谓说一、说二、说多，故开为二十四。于二十四中一一皆三：谓男声、女声、非男非女声。言八啭者：一诠诸法体，二诠所作业，三诠作具及能作者，四诠所为事，五诠所因事，六诠所属事，七诠所依事，八诠呼召事。且以男声寄“丈夫”上作八啭者，“丈夫”印度语名“布路沙”。体三啭者，一布路杀，二布路筲，三布路沙（去声）。所作业三者，一布路芆，二布路筲，三布路霜。作具作者三者，一布路铩拏，二布路[言★(穴/之)]，三布路铩鞞，或言布铩呬。所为事三者，一布路厦邪，二布路沙[言★(穴/之)]，三布路铩韵。所因三者，一布路沙哆，二布路铩[言★(穴/之)]，三布路铩韵。所属三者，一布路铩[言★罝]，二布路铩[言★(穴/之)]。三布路铩諵。所依三者，一布路膳，二布路杀谕，三布路铩绉（换金字旁）。呼召三者，一系布路杀，二系布路稍，三系布路沙。

略举一二如此，余例可知，难为具述。法师皆洞达其词，与彼人言，清典逾妙。如是钻研诸部，及学梵书，凡经五岁。

从此复往伊烂拏钵伐多国。在路至迦布德迦伽蓝。伽蓝南二三里有孤山，岩巘崇崪，灌木萧森，泉沼清澄，鲜华芬馥。

既为胜地，灵庙实繁，感变之奇，神异多种。最中精舍有刻檀观自在菩萨像，威神特尊，常有数十人，或七日、二七日绝粒断浆，请祈诸愿，心殷至者，即见菩萨具相庄严，威光朗曜，从檀像中出，慰喻其人，与其所愿。

如是感见数数有人，以故归者逾众。其供养人恐诸来者坌污尊仪，去像四面各七步许，竖木构阑，人来礼拜，皆于阑外，不得近像。所奉香华，亦并遥散。其得华住菩萨手及挂臂者，以为吉祥，以为得愿。

法师欲往求请，乃买种种华，穿之为鬘，将到像所，至诚礼赞讫，向菩萨跪发三愿："一者，于此学已还归本国，得平安无难者，愿华住尊手；二者，所修福慧，愿生睹史多宫事慈氏菩萨，若如意者，愿华贯挂尊两臂；三者，圣教称众生界中有一分无佛性者，玄奘今自疑不知有不，若有佛性，修行可成佛者，愿华贯挂尊颈项。"语讫，以华遥散，咸得如言。既满所求，欢喜无量。其傍同礼及守精舍人见已，弹指鸣足，言："未曾有也！当来若成道者，愿忆今日因缘先相度耳。"

自此渐去至伊烂拏国。伽蓝十所，僧徒四千余人，多学小乘说一切有部义。近有邻王废其国君，以都城施僧，于中并建二寺，各有千僧。有二大德，一名怛他揭多毱多(唐云如来密)，二名羼底僧诃(唐云师子忍)，俱善萨婆多部。又停一年，就读《毗婆沙》、《顺正理》等。

大城南有窣堵波，佛昔于此三月为天、人说法，其傍又有过去四佛遗迹。国西界殑伽河，南至小孤山，佛昔于此三月安居，降薄句罗药叉。山东南岩下大石上有佛坐迹，入石寸余，长五尺二寸，广四尺一寸。又有佛置裙稚迦(即澡罐也，旧曰军持，讹也)迹，深寸余，作八出华文。国南界荒林，多有大象，壮而高大焉。

卷第四

起瞻波国　终迦摩缕波国王请

自此顺殑伽河南岸东行三百余里，至瞻波国（中印度境）。伽蓝十所，僧徒二百余人，习小乘教。城垒砖高数丈，基隍深阔，极为崇固。昔者劫初，人皆穴处，后有天女下降人中，游殑伽河浴，水灵触身，生四子，分王赡部洲，别疆界，筑闾邑，此则一子之都。国南界数十由旬有大山林，幽茂连绵，二百余里，其间多有野象，数百为群，故伊烂拏、瞻波二国象军最多，每于此林令象师调捕充国乘用。又丰豺、兕、黑豹，人无敢行。

相传云，先佛未出之时，有一放牛人牧数百头牛，驱至林中，有一牛离群独去，常失，不知所在，至暮欲归，还到群内，而光色姝悦，鸣吼异常，诸牛咸畏，无敢处其前者。

如是多日，牧牛人怪其所以，私候目之，须臾还去，遂逐观之。见牛入一石孔，人亦随入，可行四五里，豁然大明，林野光华，多异华果，烂然溢目，并非俗内所有。见牛于一处食草，草色香润，亦人间所无。其人见诸果树黄赤如金，香而且大，乃摘取一颗，心虽贪爱，仍惧不敢食。少时牛出，人亦随归，至石孔未出之间，有一恶鬼夺其果留。牧牛人以此问一大医，并说果状，医言不可即食，宜方便将一出来。后日复随牛入，还摘一颗，怀欲将归，鬼复遮夺，其人以果内于口中，鬼复撮其喉，人即咽之。果既入腹，身遂洪大，头虽得出，身犹在孔，竟不得归。后家人寻访，见其形变，无不惊惧，然尚能语，说其所由。家人归还，多命手力欲共出之，竟无移动。国王闻之自观，虑为后患，遣人掘挽，亦不能动。年月既久，渐变为石，犹有人状。后更有王知其为仙果所变，谓侍臣曰："彼既因药身变，即身是药，观虽是石，其体终是神灵，宜遣人将锤钻斫，取少许将来。"臣奉王命，与工匠往，尽力镌凿，凡经一旬，不得一片。今犹现在。

自此东行四百余里，至羯末嗢只罗国（中印度境）。寻礼圣迹，伽蓝六七所，僧徒三百余人。自此东度殑伽河，行六百余里，至奔那伐弹那国（南印度境）。寻礼圣迹，伽蓝二十余所，僧三千余人，大小乘兼学。城西二十余里有跋姑婆伽蓝，台阁壮峻，僧徒七百人。其侧有窣堵波，无忧王所建，昔如来在此三月说法处，数放光明。又有四佛经行之迹。傍有精舍，中有观自在菩萨像。至诚祈请，无愿不遂。

自此东南行九百余里，至羯罗拏苏伐剌那国（东印度境）。

伽蓝十余所，僧徒三百余人，学小乘正量部法。别有三伽蓝，不食奶酪，此承提婆达多遗教也。大城侧有络多末知僧伽蓝（唐言赤泥），即往昔此国未有佛法时，南印度沙门客游此国，降挫鍱腹外道邪论已，国王为立。其侧又有窣堵波，无忧王所建，是佛昔于此七日说法处。

从此东南出至三摩怛咤国（东印度境）。滨近大海，气序和畅。伽蓝三十余所，僧徒二千余人，习上座部义。天祠外道其徒亦众，去城不远有窣堵波，无忧王所建，昔佛为诸人、天于此七日说法处。去此不远又有伽蓝，中有青玉佛像，高八尺，相好端严，常有自然妙香，芬馨满院。五色光瑞，往往烛天。凡预见闻，无不深发道意。

从此东北，海滨山谷间有室利差怛罗国，次东南海隅有迦摩浪迦国，次东有堕罗钵底国，次东有伊赏那补罗国，次东有摩诃瞻波国（此云林邑），次西有阎摩那洲国。凡此六国，山海深远，虽不入其境，而风俗可知。

自此三摩怛咤国西行九百余里，至耽摩栗底国（东印度境）。居近海隅，伽蓝十余所，僧徒千余人。城侧有窣堵波，高二百余尺，无忧王所建，傍有过去四佛经行遗迹。

是时，闻海中有僧伽罗国（此云执师子也），有明上座部三藏及解《瑜伽论》者，涉海路七百由旬方可达彼。未去间，逢南印度僧，相劝云："往师子国者不须水路，海中多有恶风、药叉、涛波之难，可从南印度东南角，水路三日行即到。虽复跋履山川，然用为安稳，并得观乌荼等诸国圣迹。"

法师即西南向乌荼国（东印度境），伽蓝百余所，僧徒万余人，学大乘法，亦有天祠外道，邪正杂居。窣堵波十余所，皆无忧王所建，灵相间起。国东南境临大海有折利怛罗城，(唐言发行)，即入海商人及远方客旅往来停止之路，南去僧伽罗国二万余里。每夜静无云之时，遥望见彼佛牙窣堵波上宝珠，光明莹然，状似空中星烛。

自此西南大林中行千二百余里，至恭御陀国(东印度境)。从此西南行大荒林一千四五百里至羯[饥－几＋麦]伽国(南印度境)，伽蓝十余所，僧五百余人，学上座部法。往昔人极殷稠，为扰触一五通仙人，仙人嗔忿，以恶咒残害，国人少长俱死，后余处稍渐迁居，犹未充实。

自此西北行千八百余里，至南憍萨罗国(中印度境)。王，刹帝力也。崇敬佛法，爱尚学艺。伽蓝百所，僧徒万人。天祠外道，颇亦殷杂。城南不远有故伽蓝，傍有窣堵波，无忧王所立。昔者如来于此处现大神变，降挫外道，后龙猛菩萨止此伽蓝。时此国王号“娑多婆诃(唐言引正)”，珍敬龙猛，供卫甚厚。时提婆菩萨自执师子国来求论难，造门请通，门司为白。龙猛素知其名，遂满钵盛水，令弟子持出示之。提婆见水，默而投针。弟子将还，龙猛见已，深加喜叹，曰：“水之澄满，以方我德；彼来投针，遂穷其底。若斯人者，可与论玄议道，嘱以传灯。”即令引入。坐讫，发言往复，彼此俱欢，犹鱼水相得。龙猛曰：“吾衰迈矣，朗辉慧日，其在子乎。”提婆避席礼龙猛足曰：“某虽不敏，敢承慈诲。”其国有婆罗门善解因明，法师就停月余日，读《集量论》。

从此南大林中东南行九百余里，至案达罗国(南印度境)。

城侧有大伽蓝,雕构宏壮,尊容丽肃。前有石窣堵波,高数百尺,阿折罗(唐言所行)阿罗汉所造。罗汉伽蓝西南二十余里有孤山,上有石窣堵波,是陈那(唐言授)菩萨于此作《因明论》处。

从此南行千余里,至驮那羯磔加国(南印度境)。城东据山有弗婆势罗(唐言东山)僧伽蓝,城西据山有阿伐罗势罗(唐言西山)僧伽蓝,此国先王为佛造立,穷大厦之规式,尽林泉之秀丽,天神保护,贤圣游居。佛涅槃千年之内,每有千凡夫僧同来安居,竟安居已,皆证罗汉,陵虚而去。千年之后,凡圣同居,自百余年来,山神易质,扰恼行人,皆生怖惧,无复敢往,由是今悉空荒,寂无僧侣。城南不远有一大石山,是婆毗吠迦(唐言清辩)论师住阿素洛宫,待慈氏菩萨成佛拟决疑处。

法师在其国逢二僧,一名苏部底,二名苏利耶,善解大众部三藏,法师因就停数月,学大众部《根本阿毗达摩》等论,彼亦依法师学大乘诸论。遂结志同行,巡礼圣迹。

自此西行千余里,至珠利耶国(南印度境)。城东南有窣堵波,无忧王所建,是佛昔于此地现大神通,摧伏外道,说法度人、天处。城西有故伽蓝,是提婆菩萨与此寺嗢怛啰(唐言上)阿罗汉论议,至第七转已去,罗汉无答,乃窃运神通,往都史多宫问慈氏菩萨,菩萨为释,因告言“彼提婆者,植功曩久,当于贤劫成等正觉,汝勿轻也。”既还,复解前难。提婆曰:“此慈氏菩萨义,非仁者自智所得也。”罗汉惭服,避席礼谢之处。

从此南经大林,行千五六百里,至达罗毗荼国(南印度境)。

国大都城号“建志补罗”，建志城即达磨波罗（唐言护法）菩萨本生之处。菩萨此国大臣之子，少而爽慧，弱冠之后，王爱其才，欲妻以公主。菩萨久修离欲，无心爱染，将成之夕，特起忧烦，乃于佛像前请祈加护，愿脱兹难。而至诚所感，有大神王携负而出，送离此城数百里，置一山寺佛堂中。僧徒来见，谓之为盗，菩萨自陈由委，闻者惊嗟，无不重其高志，因即出家。尔后专精正法，随能究通诸部。乃造《声明杂论》二万五千颂，又《释广百论》、《唯识论》及《因明》数十部，并盛宣行。其茂德高才，别自有传。

建志城即印度南海之口，向僧伽罗国水路三日行到。未去之间而彼王死，国内饥乱。有大德名“菩提迷祇湿伐罗”（此云自在觉云）、“阿跋耶邓瑟［念－今＋折］239罗”（此云无畏牙），如是等三百余僧，来投印度，到建志城。法师与相见讫，问彼僧曰：“承彼国大德等解上座部三藏及《瑜伽论》，今欲往彼参学，师等何因而来？”报曰：“我国王死，人庶饥荒，无可依仗。闻赡部洲丰乐安隐，是佛生处，多诸圣迹，是故来耳。又知法之辈无越我曹，长老有疑，随意相问。”法师引《瑜伽》要文大节征之，亦不能出戒贤之解。

自此国界三千余里，闻有秣罗矩吒国（南印度境），既居海侧，极丰异宝。其城东有窣堵波，无忧王所建，昔如来于此说法，现大神变，度无量众处。国南滨海有秣剌耶山，崖谷崇深，中有白檀香树，栴檀你婆树，树类白檀，其质凉冷，蛇多附之，至冬方蛰，用以别檀也。又有羯布罗香树，松身异叶，华果亦殊，湿时无香，采干之后，折之中有香，状类云母，色如冰雪，此所谓龙脑香也。

又闻东北海畔有城，自城东南三千余里至僧伽罗国（唐言执师子，非印度境也）。国周七千余里，都城周四十余里，人户殷稠，谷稼滋实，黑小急暴，此其俗也。国本宝渚，多有珍奇。其后南印度有女娉邻国，路逢师子王，侍送之人怖畏逃散，唯女独在车中，师子来见，负女而去，远入深山，采果逐禽以用资给。岁月既淹，生育男女，形虽类人，而性暴恶。男渐长大，白其母曰："我为何类？父兽母人。"母乃为陈昔事。子曰："人畜既殊，何不舍去而相守耶？"母曰："非不有心，但无由免脱。"子后逐父登履山谷，察其经涉。他日伺父去远，即担携母妹，下投人里，至母本国，访问舅氏，宗嗣已绝，寄止村闾。其师子王还，不见妻子，愤恚出山，哮吼人里，男女往来多被其害。百姓以事启王，王率四兵，简募猛士，将欲围射。师子见已，发声嗔吼，人马倾坠，无敢赴者。如是多日，竟无其功。王复标赏告令，有能杀师子者赏赐亿金。子语母曰："饥寒难处，欲赴王募，如何？"母曰："不可。彼虽是兽，仍为尔父，若其杀者，岂复名人？"子曰："若不如是，彼终不去，或当寻逐我等来入村闾。一旦王知，我等还死，亦不相留。何者？师子为暴，缘娘及我，岂有为一而恼多人？二三思之，不如应募。"于是遂行。师子见已，驯伏欢喜，都无害心，子遂以利刀开喉破腹，虽加此苦，而慈爱情深，含忍不动，因即命绝。王闻欢喜，怪而问之："何因尔也？"竟不实言。种种穷迫，方乃具述。王曰："嗟乎！非畜种者，谁办此心。虽然，我先许赏，终不违言。但汝杀父，勃逆之人，不得更居我国。”敕有司多与金宝，逐之荒外，即装两船，多置黄金及资粮等，送著海中，任随流逝。男船泛海至此宝渚，见丰奇玩，即便止住。后商人将家属采宝，复至其间，乃杀商人，留其妇女。如是产育子孙，经无量代，人众渐多，乃立君臣。以其远祖执杀师子，因为国称。女船泛海至波剌斯西，为鬼魅所得，生育群女，今西大女国是也。又言僧伽罗是商人子名，以其多智，免罗刹鬼害，后得为王，至此宝渚，杀除罗刹，建立国都，因之为名，语在《西域记》。

其国先无佛法，如来涅槃后一百年中，无忧王弟摩酰因陀罗厌舍欲爱，获四沙门果，乘空往来，游化此国，显赞佛教，发示神通，国人信慕，建立伽蓝。见百余所，僧徒万人，遵行大乘及上座部教。缁徒肃穆，戒节贞明，相勖无怠。王宫侧有佛牙精舍，高数百尺，以众宝庄严，上建表柱，以钵昙摩罗伽大宝置之刹端，光曜映空，静夜无云，虽万里同睹。

其侧又有精舍，亦以杂宝庄严。中有金像，此国先王所造，髻有宝珠，无知其价。后有人欲盗此珠，守卫坚牢，无由得入，乃潜穴地中入室欲取，而像形渐高，贼不能及。却而言曰：“如来昔修菩萨道，为诸众生不惜躯命，无吝国城，何于今日反悭固也？以此思之，恐往言无实。”像乃伛身授珠。其人得已，将出货卖，人有识者，擒之送王。王问所得。贼曰：“佛自与我。”乃具说所由。王自观之，像首尚低。王睹灵圣，更发深心，以诸珍宝于贼处赎珠，还施像髻。今犹现在。

国东南隅有駿迦山，多神鬼依住。如来昔于此山说駿迦经（旧曰楞伽，讹）。国南浮海数千里至那罗稽罗洲，洲人短小，长余三尺，人身鸟喙，无稼穑，食椰子。其国海浪辽长，身不能至，访诸人口，梗概如是。

自达罗毗荼与师子国僧七十余人，西北归，观礼圣迹，行二千余里，至建那补罗国（南印度境）。伽蓝百余所，僧徒万余人，大小乘兼习。天祠外道亦甚众多。王宫城侧有大伽蓝，僧徒三百余人，并博赡文才。其精舍中有一切义成太子（旧曰悉达太子，讹也）宝冠，高减二尺，盛以宝函，每到斋日，出置高台，其至诚观礼者，多感异光。城侧伽蓝有精舍，中有刻檀慈氏菩萨像，高十余尺，亦数有光瑞，是闻二百亿罗汉所造也。城北有多罗树林，周三十余里，叶长色润，诸国抄写，最以为贵。

从此西北经大林暴兽之野，行二千四五百里，至摩诃剌侘国（南印度境）。其俗轻死重节。王，刹帝种也。好武尚戎，故其国士、兵马齐整，法令严明，每使将与敌战，虽丧军失利，不加刑罚，但赐女服，使其羞惭，彼人耻愧，多至自死。常养勇士数千人，暴象数百，临将对阵又多饮酒，量其欲醉，然后麾旗，以此奋冲，未有不溃。恃兹慢傲，莫顾邻敌。戒日王自谓智略宏远，军师强盛，每亲征罚，亦不能摧制。伽蓝百余所，僧徒五千余人，大小乘兼习。亦有天祠、涂灰之道。大城内外有五窣堵波，皆数百尺，是过去四佛所游之迹，无忧王建也。

自此西北行千余里，渡耐秣陀河，至跋禄羯咕婆国（南印度境）。从此西北二千余里，至摩腊婆国（南罗罗国也，南印度境）。风俗调柔，崇爱艺业，五印度中唯西南摩腊婆、东北摩揭陀二国称为好学尚贤，善言谈，有风韵。此国伽蓝百余所，僧徒二万余人，习小乘正量部教。亦有涂灰外道、事天之众。

相传云，自六十年前有王名“戒日”，高才博学，仁慈惠和，爱育黎元，崇敬三宝。始自为王，至于崩逝，口绝粗言，颜无愠色，不伤臣庶之意，无损蚊蚁之形。每象、马饮水，漉而后饮，恐害水居之命也。爰至国人，亦令断杀。由是野兽依人，豺狼息毒，境内夷静，祥瑞日兴。营构精庐，穷极轮奂，造七佛之仪，设无遮之会。如是胜业，在位五十余年，无时暂辍，黎庶思慕，于今不止。大城西北二十余里，婆罗门邑傍有陷坑，是大慢婆罗门谤毁大乘，生身入地狱处，语在《西域记》。

自此西北行二千四五百里，至阿咤釐国（南印度境）。土出胡椒树，树叶似蜀椒；出熏陆香树，树叶类此棠梨也。

自此西北行三日，至契咤国（南印度境）。自此北行千余里，至伐腊毗国（南印度境）。伽蓝百余所，僧徒六千余人，学小乘正量部法。如来在日，屡游此国，无忧王随佛至处皆有表记。今王，刹帝力种也。即羯若鞠阇国尸罗阿迭多王之女婿，号“杜鲁婆跋咤”（唐言帝胄）。性躁急，容止疏率，然贵德尚学，信爱三宝，岁设大会七日，延诸国僧，施以上味奇珍，床座、衣服，爰至药饵之资，无不悉备。

自此西北行七百余里，至阿难陀补罗国（西印度境）。又西北行五百余里，至苏剌侘国（西印度境）。自此东北行千八百里至瞿折罗国。又东南行二千八百余里，至乌阇衍那国（南印度境）。去城不远有窣堵波，是无忧王作地狱处。从此东北行千余里，至掷枳陀国（南印度境）。从此东北行九百余里，至摩醯湿伐罗补罗国（中印度境）。从此又西还苏刺侘国。自此复西行，至阿点婆翅罗国（西印度境）。昔如来在日，频游其地，无忧王随有圣迹之处皆起窣堵波，今皆具在。

从此西行二千余里，至狼揭罗国（西印度境）。临近大海，向西女国之路。自此西北至波刺斯国（非印度境），闻说之，其地多珠宝、大锦、细褐、善马、驼驼其所出也。伽蓝二三，僧徒数百，学小乘教说一切有部，释迦佛钵在此王宫。国东境有鹤秣城，西北接拂懔国，西南海岛有西女国，皆是女人，无男子，多珍货，附属拂懔。拂懔王岁遣丈夫配焉，其俗产男，例皆不举。

又从狼揭罗国东北行七百余里，至臂多势罗国（西印度境）。中有窣堵波，高数百尺，无忧王所建，中有舍利，数放光明。是如来昔作仙人，为国王害处也。

从此东北行三百余里，至阿奆荼国（西印度境）。城东北大林中有伽蓝故基，是佛昔于此处听诸苾刍著亟缚屣（此言靴）。有窣堵波，无忧王所建。傍有精舍，中有青石立佛像，数放光明。次南八百余步大林中，有窣堵波，无忧王所建，是如来昔日止此，夜寒，乃以三衣重覆，至明旦开诸苾刍著纳衣处。

从此又东行七百余里，至信度国（西印度境）。土出金、银、鍮石、牛、羊、骆驼、赤盐、白盐、黑盐等，余处取以为药。如来在日，数游此国，所有圣迹，无忧王皆建窣堵波以为表记。又有乌波毱多大阿罗汉游化之迹。

从此东行九百余里，渡河东岸，至茂罗三部卢国（西印度境)。俗事天神，祠宇华峻，其日天像铸以黄金，饰诸杂宝，诸国之人多来求请。华林池沼，接砌萦阶。凡预瞻观，无不爱赏。

从此东北行七百余里，至钵伐多国(北印度境)。城侧有大伽蓝，百余僧皆学大乘，是昔慎那弗怛罗(唐言最胜子)论师于此制《瑜伽师地论释》，亦是贤爱论师、德光论师本出家处。又其国有二三大德，并学业可遵。法师因停二年，就学正量部《根本阿毗达摩》及《摄正法论》、《教实论》等。

从此复东南，还摩揭陀施无厌寺，参礼正法藏讫。闻寺西三逾缮那有低罗择迦寺，有出家大德名般若跋陀罗，本缚罗钵底国人，于萨婆多部出家，善自宗三藏及《声明》、《因明》等。法师就停两月，咨决所疑。

从此复往杖林山居士胜军论师所。军本苏剌佗国人，刹帝力种也。幼而好学，先于贤爱论师所学《因明》，又从安慧菩萨学《声明》、大小乘论，又从戒贤法师学《瑜伽论》，爰至外籍群言，四《吠陀》典、天文、地理、医方、术数，无不究览根源，穷尽枝叶，既学该内外，德为时尊。摩揭陀主满胄王钦贤重士，闻风而悦，发使邀请，立为国师，封二十大邑，论师不受。满胄崩后，戒日王又请为师，封乌茶国八十大邑，论师亦辞不受。王再三固请，亦皆固辞。谓王曰："胜军闻受人之禄，忧人之事。今方救生死萦缠之急，岂有暇而知王务哉？"言罢揖而出，王不能留。自是每依杖林山养徒教授，恒讲佛经，道俗宗归，常逾数百。法师就之，首末二年，学《唯识决择论》、《意义理论》、《成无畏论》、《不住涅槃》、《十二因缘论》、《庄严经论》、及问《瑜伽》、

《因明》等疑已。

于夜中忽梦见那烂陀寺房院荒秽，并系水牛，无复僧侣。法师从幼日王院西门入，见第四重阁上有一金人，色貌端严，光明满室，内心欢喜，欲登上无由，乃请垂引接。彼曰：“我曼殊室利菩萨也。以汝缘业未可来也。”乃指寺外曰：“汝看是。”法师寻指而望，见寺外火焚烧村邑，都为灰烬。彼金人曰：“汝可早归。此处十年后，戒日王当崩，印度荒乱，恶人相害，汝可知之。”言讫不见。法师觉已怪叹，向胜军说之。胜军曰：“三界无安，或当如是。既有斯告，任仁者自图焉。”是知大士所行，皆为菩萨护念。将往印度，告戒贤而驻待；淹留未返，示无常以劝归。若所为不契圣心，谁能感此？及永徽之末，戒日果崩，印度饥荒，并如所告。国家使人王玄策备见其事。

当此正月初时也，西国法以此月菩提寺出佛舍利，诸国道俗咸来观礼，法师即共胜军同往。见舍利骨或大或小，大者如圆珠，光色红白，又肉舍利如豌豆大，其状润赤。无量徒众献奉香华赞礼讫，还置塔中。至夜过一更许，胜军共法师论舍利大小不同。云：“弟子见余处舍利大如米粒，而此所见何其太大？师意有疑不？”法师报曰：“玄奘亦有此疑。”更经少时，忽不见室中灯，内外大明，怪而出望。乃见舍利塔光晖上发，飞焰属天，色含五彩，天地洞朗，无复星月，兼闻异香，氛氲溢院。于是递相告报，言舍利有大神变，诸众乃知，重集礼拜，称叹希有。经食顷，光乃渐收，至于欲尽，绕覆钵数匝，然始总入，天地还暗，辰象复出。众睹此已，咸除疑网。礼菩提树及诸圣迹，经八日，复还那烂陀寺。

时戒贤论师遣法师为众讲《摄大乘论》、《唯识决择论》。时大德师子光先已为众讲《中》、《百》论，述其旨，破《瑜伽》义。法师妙闲《中》、《百》，又善《瑜伽》，以为圣人立教，各随一意，不相违妨，惑者不能会通，谓为乖反，此乃失在传人，岂关于法也。愍其局狭，数往征诘，复不能酬答，由是学徒渐散，而宗附法师。

法师又以《中》、《百》论旨唯破遍计所执，不言依他起性及圆成实性，师子光不能善悟，见《论》称："一切无所得，"谓《瑜伽》所立圆成实等亦皆须遣，所以每形于言。法师为和会二宗言不相违背，乃着《会宗论》三千颂。《论》成，呈戒贤及大众，无不称善，并共宣行。师子光惭赧，遂出往菩提寺，别命东印度一同学名旃陀罗僧诃来相论难，冀解前耻。其人既至，惮威而默，不敢致言，法师声誉益甚。

初师子光未去前，戒日王于那烂陀寺侧造鍮石精舍，高逾十丈，诸国咸知。王后自征恭御陀，行次乌荼国，其国僧皆小乘学，不信大乘，谓为空华外道，非佛所说。既见王来，讥曰："闻王于那烂陀侧作鍮石精舍，功甚壮伟，何不于迦波釐外道寺造，而独于彼也？"王曰："斯言何甚？"答曰："那烂陀寺空华外道，与迦波釐不殊故也。"

先是，南印度王灌顶师老婆罗门，名般若毱多，明正量部义，造《破大乘论》七百颂，诸小乘师咸皆叹重。因取示王曰："我宗如是，岂有大乘人能难破一字者？"王曰："弟子闻狐行鼷鼠之群，自谓雄于师子。及其见也，则魂亡魄散。师等未见大乘诸德，所以固守愚宗。若一见时，恐还同彼。"

彼曰："王若疑者，何不集而对决是非？"王曰："此亦何难。"

即于是日发使修书与那烂陀寺正法藏戒贤法师，曰："弟子行次乌荼，见小乘师恃凭小见，制论诽谤大乘，词理切害，不近人情，仍欲张鳞，共师等一论。弟子知寺中大德并才慧有余，学无不悉，辄以许之，谨令奉报。愿差大德四人，善自他宗兼内外者，赴乌荼国行从所。"正法藏得书，集众量择，乃差海慧、智光、师子光及法师为四人，以应王之命。

其海惠等咸忧，法师谓曰："小乘诸部三藏，玄奘在本国及入迦湿弥罗已来遍皆学讫，具悉其宗。若欲将其教旨能破大乘义，终无此理。奘虽学浅智微，当之必了。愿诸德不烦忧也。若其有负，自是支那国僧，无关此事。"诸人咸喜。后戒日王复有书来，云："前请大德未须即发，待后进止。"

时复有顺世外道来求论难，乃书四十条义，悬于寺门，曰："若有难破一条者，我则斩首相谢。"经数日，无人出应。法师遣房内净人出，取其义毁破，以足蹉蹑。婆罗门大怒，问曰："汝是何人？"答曰："我是摩诃耶那提婆奴。"婆罗门亦素闻法师名，惭耻更不与论。法师令唤入，将对戒贤法师及命诸德为证，与之共论，征其宗本历外道诸家所立。

其词曰：

"如餔多外道、离系外道、髅鬘外道、殊征伽外道，四种形服不同；数论外道（旧曰僧佉）、胜论外道（旧曰卫世师也），二家立义有别。餔多之辈以灰涂体，用为修道，遍身艾白，犹寝灶之猫狸。离系之徒则露质标奇，拔发为德，皮裂足皴，状临河之朽树。髅鬘之类，以髅骨为鬘，装头挂颈，陷枯魂磊，若冢侧之药叉。征伽之流披服粪衣，饮啖便秽，腥臊臭恶，譬溷中之狂豕。尔等以此为道，岂不愚哉！

至如数论外道，立二十五谛义，从自性生大，从大生我执，次生五唯量，次生五大，次生十一根，此二十四并供奉于我，我所受用；除离此已则我得清净。胜论师立六句义，谓实、德、业有同异性、和合性，此六是我所受具，未解脱已来受用前六；若得解脱，与六相离，称为"涅槃"。

今破数论所立，如汝二十五谛中，我之一种是别性，余二十四展转同为一体，而自性一种以三法为体，为萨埵、剌阇、答摩。此三展转合成大等二十三谛，二十三谛一一皆以三法为体。若使大等一一皆揽三成，如众如林，即是其假，如何得言一切是实？又此大等各以三成，即一是一切。若一则一切，则应一一皆有一切作用。既不许然，何因执三为一切体性？又若一则一切，应口、眼等根，即是大小便路。又一一根有一切作用。应口、耳等根闻香见色。若不尔者，何得执三为一切法体？岂有智人而立此义？又自性既常，应如我体，何能转变作大等法？又所计我其性若常，应如自性，不应是我。若如自性，其体非我，不应受用二十四谛。是则我非能受，二十四谛非是所受，既能所俱无，则谛义不立。"

如是往复数番，婆罗门默无所说，起而谢曰："我今负矣，任依先约。"法师曰："我曹释子，终不害人，今役汝为奴，随我教命。"婆罗门欢喜敬从，即将向房。闻者无不称庆。

时法师欲往乌荼，乃访得小乘所制《破大乘义》七百颂者。法师寻省有数处疑，谓所伏婆罗门曰："汝曾听此《义》不？"

答曰："曾听五遍。"法师欲令其讲。彼曰："我今为奴，岂合为尊讲？"法师曰："此是他宗，我未曾见，汝但说无苦。"彼曰："若然，请至夜中，恐外闻引从奴学，污尊名称。"于是至夜，屏去诸人，令讲一遍，备得其旨。遂寻其谬节，申大乘义而破之，为一千六百颂，名《破恶见论》。将呈戒贤法师及宣示徒众，无不嗟赏，曰："以此穷覈，何敌不亡。"其论如别。因谓婆罗门曰："仁者论屈为奴，于耻已足，今放仁者去，随意所之。"婆罗门欢喜辞出，往东印度迦摩缕波国，向鸠摩罗王谈法师德义。王闻甚悦，即发使来请焉。

卷第五

起尼乾占归国　终至帝城之西漕

鸠摩罗使未至间，有一露形尼乾子名伐阇罗，忽入房来。法师旧闻尼乾善于占卜，即请坐，问所疑。曰："玄奘支那国僧，来此学问，岁月已久。今欲归还，不知达不？又去住二宜，何最为吉？及寿命长短，愿仁者占看。"尼乾乃索一白石，画地而筮，报法师曰："师住时最好，五印度及道俗无不敬重；去时得达，于敬重亦好，但不如住。师之寿命，自今已去，更可十年。若凭余福转续，非所知也。"法师又问："意欲思归，经、像既多，不知若为胜致？"尼乾曰："勿忧，戒日王、鸠摩罗王自遣人送师，必达无苦。"法师报曰："彼二王者从来未面，如何得降此恩？"尼乾曰："鸠摩罗王已发使来请，二三日当到，既见鸠摩罗，亦便见戒日。"如是言讫而去。

法师即作还意，庄严经、像。诸德闻之，咸来劝住，曰：“印度者，佛生之处。大圣虽迁，遗踪具在，巡游礼赞，足豫平生，何为至斯而更舍也？又支那国者，蔑戾车地，轻人贱法，诸佛所以不生；志狭垢深，圣贤由兹弗往。气寒土险，亦焉足念哉！”

法师报曰：“法王立教，义尚流通，岂有自得沾心而遗未悟。且彼国衣冠济济，法度可遵，君圣臣忠，父慈子孝，贵仁贵义，尚齿尚贤。加以识洞幽微，智与神契。体天作则，七耀无以隐其文；设器分时，六律不能韬其管。故能驱役飞走，感致鬼神，消息阴阳，利安万物。自佛遗法东被，咸重大乘，定水澄明，戒香芬馥。发心造行，愿与十地齐功；敛掌熏修，以至三身为极。向蒙大圣降灵，亲麾法化；耳承妙说，目击金容，并辔长涂，未可知也！岂得称佛不往，遂可轻哉！”

彼曰：“经言：‘诸天随其福德，共食有异。’今与法师同居赡部，而佛生于此，不往于彼，以是将为边恶地也。地既无福，所以劝仁勿归。”法师报曰：“无垢称言：‘夫日何故行赡部洲？’答曰：‘为之除冥。’今所思归，意遵此耳。”

诸德既见不从，乃相呼往戒贤法师所，具陈其意。戒贤谓法师曰：“仁意定何如？”报曰：“此国是佛生处，非不爱乐。但玄奘来意者，为求大法，广利群生。自到已来，蒙师为说《瑜伽师地论》，决诸疑网，礼见圣迹，及闻诸部甚深之旨，私心慰庆，诚不虚行。愿以所闻，归还翻译，使有缘之徒同得闻见，用报师恩，由是不暇停住。”戒贤喜曰：“此菩萨意也！吾心望尔亦如是。任为装束，诸人不须苦留。”言讫还房。

经二日，东印度鸠摩罗王遣使奉书与戒贤法师，曰：“弟子愿见支那国大德，愿师发遣，慰此钦思。”戒贤得书，告众曰：“鸠摩罗王欲请玄奘，但此人众差拟往戒日王所，与小乘对论，今若赴彼，戒日傥须，如何可得？不宜遣去。”乃谓使曰：“支那僧意欲还国，不及得赴王命。”使到，王更遣来请，曰：“师纵欲归，暂过弟子，去亦非难。必愿垂顾，勿复致违。”

戒贤既不与遣，彼王大怒，更发别使赍书与戒贤法师，曰：“弟子凡夫，染习世乐，于佛法中未知回向。今闻外国僧名，身心欢喜，似开道芽之分，师复不许其来，此乃欲令众生长沦永夜，岂是大德绍隆遗法，汲引物哉？不胜渴仰，谨遣重咨。若也不来，弟子则分是恶人，近者设赏迦王犹能坏法毁菩提树，师谓弟子无此力耶？必当整理象军，云萃于彼，踏那烂陀寺，使碎如尘。此言如日，师好试看。”

戒贤得书，谓法师曰：“彼王者善心素薄，境内佛法，不甚流行。自闻仁名，似发深意。仁或是其宿世善友，努力为去，出家以利物为本，今正其时。譬如伐树，但断其根，枝条自殄。到彼令王发心，则百姓从化。若违不赴，或有魔事。勿惮小劳。”

法师辞，与使俱去。至彼，王见甚喜，率群臣迎拜赞叹，延入宫，日陈音乐，饮食华香，尽诸供养，请受斋戒。如是经月余。

戒日王讨恭御陀还，闻法师在鸠摩罗处，惊曰：“我先频请不来，今何因在彼？”发使语鸠摩罗王：“急送支那僧来！”王曰：“我头可得，法师未可即来。”使还报，戒日王大怒，谓侍臣曰：“鸠摩罗王轻我也，如何为一僧发是粗语！”

更遣使责曰：“汝言头可得者，即付使将来。”鸠摩罗深惧言失，即命严象军二万，乘船三万艘，共法师同发，溯殑伽河以赴王所，至羯朱嗢祇罗国，遂即参及。鸠摩罗王将欲发引，先令人于殑伽河北营行宫。是日渡河至宫，安置法师讫，自与诸臣参戒日王于河南。戒日见来甚喜，知其敬爱于法师，亦不责其前语，但问：“支那僧何在？”报曰：“在某行宫。”王曰：“何不来？”报曰：“大王钦贤爱道，岂可遣师就此参王。”王曰：“善。且去，某明日自来。”鸠摩罗还，谓法师曰：“王虽言明日来，恐今夜即至，仍须候待。若来，师不须动。”法师曰：“玄奘佛法，理自如是。”至夜一更许，王果来。有人报曰：“河中有数千炬烛，并步鼓声。”王曰：“此戒日王来。”即敕擎烛，自与诸臣远迎。其戒日王行时，每将金鼓数百，行一步一击，号为“节步鼓”。独戒日王有此，余王不得同也。

既至，顶礼法师足，散华瞻仰，以无量颂赞叹讫，谓法师曰：“弟子先时请师，何为不来？”报曰：“玄奘远寻佛法，为闻《瑜伽师地论》。当奉命时，听论未了，以是不遂参王。”王又问曰：“师从支那来，弟子闻彼国有《秦王破阵乐》歌舞之曲，未知秦王是何人？复有何功德，致此称扬？”

法师曰：“玄奘本土见人怀圣贤之德，能为百姓除凶剪暴、覆润群生者，则歌而咏之，上备宗庙之乐，下入闾里之讴。

秦王者，即支那国今之天子也。未登皇极之前，封为秦王。是时天地版荡，苍生乏主，原野积人之肉，川谷流人之血，妖星夜聚，沴气朝凝，三河苦封豕之贪，四海困长蛇之毒。王以帝子之亲，应天策之命，奋威振旅，扑剪鲸鲵，仗钺麾戈，肃清海县，重安宇宙，再耀三光。六合怀恩，故有兹咏。”王曰：“如此之人，乃天所以遣为物主也。”又谓法师曰：“弟子且还。明日迎师，愿不惮劳。”于是辞去。

诘旦使来，法师共鸠摩罗同去。至戒日宫侧，王与门师二十余人出迎。入坐，备陈珍膳，作乐散华，供养讫。王曰：“闻师作《制恶见论》，何在？”法师报：“在此。”因取观。观讫，王甚悦，谓其门师等曰：“弟子闻日光既出则萤烛夺明，天雷震音而锤凿绝响。师等所守之宗，他皆破讫，试可救看？”诸德无敢言者。王曰：“师等上座提婆犀那，自云解冠群英，学该众哲，首兴异见，常毁大乘。及闻客大德来，即往吠舍釐礼观圣迹，托以逃潜，故知师等无能也。”王有妹聪慧利根，善正量部义，坐于王后。闻法师序大乘，宗涂奥旷，小教局浅，夷然欢喜，称赞不能已。

王曰：“师《论》大好，弟子及此诸师普皆信伏，但恐余国小乘外道尚守愚迷，望于曲女城为师作一会，命五印度沙门、婆罗门、外道等，示大乘微妙，绝其毁谤之心；显师盛德之高，摧其我慢之意。”是日发敕，告诸国及义解之徒，集曲女城，观支那国法师之《论》焉。

法师自冬初共王逆河而进，至腊月方到会场。五印度中有十八国王到，谙知大、小乘僧三千余人到，婆罗门及尼乾外道二千余人到，那烂陀寺千余僧到。是等诸贤，并博蕴文义，富赡辩才，思听法音，皆来会所。兼有侍从，或象或舆，或幢或幡，各自围绕，峨峨岌岌，若云兴雾涌，充塞数十里间。虽六齐之举袂成帷，三吴之挥汗为雨，未足方其盛也。

王先敕会所营二草殿，拟安像及徒众，比到并成。其殿峻广，各堪坐千余人。王行宫在会场西五里。日于宫中铸金像一躯，装一大象，上施宝帐，安佛在其中。戒日王作帝释形，手执白拂侍右，鸠摩罗王作梵王形，执宝盖侍左，皆着天冠华鬘，垂璎佩玉。又装二大象，载宝华逐佛后，随行随散。令法师及门师等各乘大象，次列王后。又以三百大象，使诸国王、大臣、大德等乘象，鱼丽于道侧，称赞而行。从旦装束，自行宫引向会所，至院门各令下乘，捧佛入殿，置于宝座。王共法师以次供养。然后命十八国王入；诸国僧名称最高、文义赡博者，使千余人入；婆罗门、外道有名行者，五百余人入；诸国大臣等二百余人入。自外道俗，各令于院门外部伍安置。王遣内外并设食。

食讫，施佛金槃一、金椀七、金澡灌一、金锡杖一枚、金钱三千、上氎衣三千。法师及诸僧等施各有差。施讫，别设宝床，请法师坐，为论主，称扬大乘，序作《论》意，仍遣那烂陀寺沙门明贤法师读示大众。别令写一本悬会场门外示一切人，若其间有一字无理能难破者，请斩首相谢。如是至晚，无一人致言，戒日王欢喜，罢会还宫，诸王及僧各归所止，次法师共鸠摩罗王亦还自宫。明旦复来，迎像送引，聚集如初。

经五日，小乘、外道见毁其宗，结恨，欲为谋害。王知，宣令曰：

“邪党乱真，其来自久。埋隐正教，误惑群生，不有上贤，何以鉴伪。支那法师者，神宇冲旷，解行渊深，为伏群邪，来游此国，显扬大法，汲引愚迷，妖妄之徒，不知惭悔，谋为不轨，翻起害心，此而可容，孰不可恕！众有一人伤触法师者斩其首，毁骂者截其舌。其欲申辞救义，不拘此限。”

自是邪徒戢翼，竟十八日无一人发论。将散之夕，法师更称扬大乘，赞佛功德，令无量人返邪入正，弃小归大。

戒日王益增崇重，施法师金钱一万、银钱三万、上氎衣一百领；十八国王亦各施珍宝，法师一皆不受。王命侍臣庄严一大象，施幢请法师乘，令贵臣陪卫，巡众告唱，表立义无屈。西国法，凡论得胜如此。法师让不行。王曰：“古来法尔，事不可违。”乃将法师袈裟遍唱曰：“支那国法师立大乘义，破诸异见，自十八日来无敢论者，普宜知之。”诸众欢喜，为法师竞立美名，大乘众号曰“摩诃耶那提婆”，此云“大乘天”；小乘众号曰“木叉提婆”，此云“解脱天”。烧香散华，礼敬而去。自是德音弥远矣。

王行宫西有一伽蓝，王所供养，中有佛牙，长可寸半，其色黄白，每放光明。昔迦湿弥罗国讫利多种灭坏佛法，僧徒解散。有一苾刍远游印度。其后睹货罗国雪山下王忿诸贱种毁灭佛法，乃诈为商旅，率三千勇士，多赍珍宝，伪言献奉。其王素贪，闻之甚喜，遣使迎接。但雪山王禀质雄猛，威肃如神，既至其座，去帽而叱之，讫利多王睹便惊慑，颠仆于地。

雪山王按其首而斩之，谓其群臣曰："我雪山下王。念尔诸奴毁坏佛法，故来罚汝。然则过在一人，非关汝辈，各宜自安，唯扇惑其王首为恶者逐之他国，余无所问。"既歼丑孽，建立伽蓝，召集僧徒，奉施而返。

前投印度苾刍闻国平定，杖锡旋归，路逢群象鸣吼而来。苾刍见已，升树藏避，象乃吸水灌树，以牙排掘，须臾树倒。象以鼻卷苾刍，置背上负载而去。至一大林，中有病象，患疮而卧。象引苾刍手触其苦处，见疮有竹刺，为拔刺引去脓血，裂衣为裹，象得渐安。明日诸象竞求果味，奉施苾刍，苾刍食已，有一象将金函授于病者，病象得已，授与苾刍，苾刍受已，诸象载送出林，到旧处，置于地，跪拜而去。苾刍开函，乃佛牙也，将归供养。

近戒日王闻迦湿弥罗有佛牙，亲至界首，请看礼拜。诸众吝惜，不听将出，乃别藏之。但其王惧戒日之威，处处掘觅，得已将呈，戒日见之，深生敬重，倚恃强力，遂夺归供养，即此牙也。散会后，王以所铸金像、衣、钱等付嘱伽蓝，令僧守护。

法师先以辞那烂陀诸德，及取经、像讫，罢论竟，至十九日辞王欲还。王曰："弟子嗣承宗庙，为天下主，三十余年，常虑福德不增广，往因不相续，以故积集财宝，于钵罗耶伽国两河间立大会场，五年一请五印度沙门、婆罗门及贫穷孤独，为七十五日无遮大施。已成五会，今欲作第六会，师何不暂看随喜。"

法师报曰："菩萨为行，福慧双修，智人得果，不忘其本。

王尚不吝珍财，玄奘岂可辞少停住，请随王去。”王甚喜。

至二十一日，发引向钵罗耶伽国就大施场。殑伽河在北，阎牟那河在南，俱从西北东流至此国而会。其二河合处，西有大墠，周围十四五里，平坦如镜，自昔诸王皆就其地行施，因号“施场”焉。相传云，若于此地施一钱，胜余处施百千钱，由是古来共重。王敕于墠上建施场，竖芦为篱，面各千步，中作草堂数十间，安贮众宝，皆金、银、真珠、红玻璃宝、帝青珠、大青珠等，其傍又作长舍数百间，贮憍奢耶衣、斑氎衣、金银钱等。篱外别作造食处，于宝库前更造长屋百余行，似此京邑肆行，一一长屋可坐千余人。

先是王敕告五印度沙门、外道尼乾、贫穷孤独，集施场受施。有因法师曲女城会不归便往施所者，十八国王亦便逐王行。比至会场，道俗到者五十余万人。戒日王营殑伽河北岸，南印度王杜鲁婆跋吒营合河西，鸠摩罗王营阎牟那河南华林侧，诸受施人营跋吒王西。

辰旦，其戒日王与鸠摩罗王乘船军，跋吒王从象军，各整仪卫，集会场所，十八国诸王以次陪列。初一日，于施场草殿内安佛像，布施上宝、上衣及美馔，作乐散华，至日晚归营。第二日，安日天像，施宝及衣半于初日。第三日，安自在天像，施如日天。第四日，施僧万余人，百行俱坐，人施金钱百、文珠一枚、氎衣一具，及饮食香华，供养讫而出。第五番施婆罗门，二十余日方遍。第六番施外道，十日方遍。第七番遍施远方求者，十日方遍。第八番施诸贫穷孤独者，一月方遍。至是，五年所积府库俱尽，唯留象、马、兵器，拟征暴乱，守护宗庙。自余宝货及在身衣服、璎珞、耳珰、臂钏、宝鬘、颈珠、髻中明珠，总施无复孑遗。一切尽已，从其妹索粗弊衣著，礼十方佛，踊跃欢喜，合掌言曰："某比来积集财宝，常惧不入坚牢之藏。今得贮福田中，可谓入藏矣。愿某生生常具财法，等施众生，成十自在，满二庄严。"

会讫，诸王各持诸宝钱物，于诸众边赎王所施璎珞、髻珠、御服等还将献王。经数日，王衣服及上宝等服用如故。

法师辞欲归，王曰："弟子方欲共法师阐扬遗法，何遽即归？"如是留连复十余日，鸠摩罗王殷勤亦如是，谓法师曰："师能住弟子处受供养者，当为师造一百寺。"法师见诸王意不解，乃告以苦言，曰："支那国去此遐远，晚闻佛法，虽沾梗概，不能委具，为此故来访殊异耳。今果愿者，皆由本土诸贤思渴诚深之所致也，以是不敢须臾而忘。经言'障人法者，当代代无眼'。若留玄奘，则令彼无量行人失知法之利，无眼之报宁不惧哉！"

王曰："弟子慕重师德，愿常瞻奉，既损他人之益，实惧于怀，任师去住。虽然，不知师欲从何道而归？师取南海去者，当发使相送。"法师报曰："玄奘从支那来，至国西界，有国名高昌，其王明睿乐法，见玄奘来此访道，深生随喜，资给丰厚，愿法师还日相过，情不能违，今者还须北路而去。"

王曰："师须几许资粮？"法师报："无所须。"王曰："何得尔？"于是命施金钱等物，鸠摩罗王亦施众珍，法师并皆不纳。唯受鸠摩罗王曷刺釐帔（即粗毛下细者所作），拟在涂防雨。于是告别，王及诸众相饯数十里而归。将分之际，呜噎各不能已。

法师以经、像等附北印度王乌地多军，鞍乘渐进。后戒日王更附乌地王大象一头、金钱三千、银钱一万，供法师行费。别三日，王更与鸠摩罗王、跋吒王等各将轻骑数百复来送别，其殷勤如是。仍遣达官四人名“摩诃怛罗”(类此散官也)。王以素氎作书，红泥封印，使达官奉书送法师，所经诸国，令发乘递送，终至汉境。

自发钵罗耶伽国西南大林野中，行七日，到憍赏弥国。城南劬师罗长者施佛园处。礼圣迹讫，复与乌地多王西北行。一月余日，历数国，重礼天梯圣迹。复西北行三逾缮那，至毗罗那拏国都城。停两月日，逢师子光、师子月同学二人，讲《俱舍》、《摄论》、《唯识论》等，皆来迎接甚欢。法师至，又开《瑜伽决择》及《对法论》等，两月讫，辞归。

复西北行一月余日，经数国，至阇兰达国，即北印度王都，复停一月。乌地王遣人引送，西行二十余日，至僧诃补罗国，时有百余僧，皆北人，赍经、像等，依法师而还。如此复二十余日，山涧中行，其处多贼，法师恐相劫掠，常遣一僧预前行，若逢贼时，教说：“远来求法，今所赍持并经、像、舍利，愿檀越拥护，无起异心。”法师率徒侣后进。时亦屡逢，然卒无害。

如是二十余日行，至呾叉尸罗国，重礼月光王舍千头处。国东北五十逾缮那，即迦湿弥罗国，其王遣使迎请，法师为象行辎重不果去。停七日，又西北行三日至信度大河，河广五六里，经、像及同侣人并坐船而进，法师乘象涉渡。时遣一人在船看守经及印度诸异华种，将至中流，忽然风波乱起，摇动船舫，数将覆没，守经者惶惧堕水，众人共救得出，遂失五十夹经本及华种等，自余仅得保全。

时迦毕试王先在乌铎迦汉荼城，闻法师至，躬到河侧奉迎，问曰："承师河中失经，师不将印度华果种来？"答曰："将来。"王曰："鼓浪倾船，事由于此。自昔以来，欲将华种渡者，并然。"因共法师还城，寄一寺，停五十余日，为失经本，更遣人往乌长那国抄写迦叶臂耶部三藏。迦湿弥王闻法师渐近，亦忘远，躬来参拜，累日方归。

法师与迦毕试王相随西北行，一月余日，至蓝波国境。王遣太子先去，敕都人及众僧装办幢幡，出城迎候。王与法师渐发。比至，道俗数千人，幢幡甚盛，众见法师，欢喜礼拜讫，前后围绕赞咏而进。至都，停一大乘寺，时王亦为七十五日无遮大施。

自此复正南行十五日，往伐刺拏国，礼圣迹。又西北，往阿薄健国。又西北，往漕矩咤国。又北行五百余里，至佛栗氏萨傥那国。从此东出，至迦毕试国境。王又为七日大施。讫，法师辞发。东北行一逾缮那，至瞿卢萨谤城，与王别，北行。

王遣一大臣将百余人，送法师度雪山，负刍草粮食资给。行七日，至大山顶。其山叠嶂危峰，参差多状，或平或耸，势非一仪，登陟艰辛，难为备叙。自是不得乘马，策杖而前。复经七日，至一高岭，岭下有村，可百余家，养羊畜，羊大如驴。其日宿于此村，至夜半发，仍令村人乘山驼引路。其地多雪涧凌溪，若不凭乡人引导，交恐沦坠。至明昼日，方渡凌险，时唯七僧并雇人等有二十余，象一头、骡十头、马四匹。明日到岭底，寻盘道复登一岭，望之如雪，及至，皆白石也。此岭最高，虽云结雪飞，莫至其表。是日将昏，方到山顶，而寒风凄凛，徒侣之中无能正立者。又山无卉木，唯积石攒峰，岌岌然如林笋矣。其处既山高风急，鸟将度者皆不得飞，自岭南岭北各行数百步外，方得舒其六翮矣。寻赡部洲中岭岳之高，亦无过此者。

法师从西北下数里，有少平地，施帐宿，旦而进，经五六日下山，至安怛罗缚婆国，即睹货罗之故地。伽蓝三所，僧徒数十，习大众部法。有一窣堵波，无忧王建也。法师停五日。西北下山行四百余里，至阔悉多国，亦睹货罗之故地。从此西北复山行三百余里，至活国，居缚刍河侧，即睹货罗东界，都城在河南岸。因见叶护可汗孙王睹货罗，自称“叶护”。至衙停一月，叶护遣卫送，共商侣东行。

二日，至瞢健国。其傍又有阿利尼国、曷逻胡国、讫栗瑟摩国、钵利曷国，皆睹货罗故地也。自瞢健复东行入山三百余里，至呬摩怛罗国，亦睹货罗故地。风俗大同突厥，而尤异者，妇人首冠木角，高三尺余，前有两岐，表夫父母，上岐表父，下岐表母，随先丧亡，除去一岐，若舅姑俱殁，则举冠全弃。自此复东行二百余里，至钵创那国，亦睹货罗故地也。为寒雪，停月余日。

从此又东南山行二百余里，至淫薄健国。又东南履危蹑险，行三百余里，至屈浪拏国。从此又东北山行五百余里，至达摩悉铁帝国（亦名护密也）。国在两山间，临缚刍河，出善马，形小而健。俗无礼义，性暴形陋，眼多碧绿，异于诸国。伽蓝十余所。昏驮多城，国之都也，中有伽蓝，此国先王所立。伽蓝中石佛像上有金铜圆盖，杂宝装莹，自然住空，当于佛顶，人有礼旋，盖亦随转，人停盖止，莫测其灵。（寺立因缘广如别传）

从此国大山北至尸弃尼国。又越达摩悉铁帝国至商弥国。从此复东山行七百余里，至波谜罗川。川东西千余里，南北百余里，在两雪山间，又当葱岭之中，风雪飘飞，春夏不止，以其地寒冽，卉木稀少，稼穑不滋，境域萧条，无复人迹。川中有大池，东西三百里，南北五十余里，处赡部洲中，地势高隆，瞻之漭漭，目所不能极。水族之类千品万种，喧声交聒，若百工之肆焉。复有诸鸟，形高丈余，鸟卵如瓮。旧称条支巨觳，或当此也。池西分出一河，西至达摩悉铁帝国东界，与缚刍河合而西流赴海，以右诸水亦皆同会。池东分一大河，东至佉沙国西界，与徙多河合而东流赴海，以左诸水亦并同会。川南山外有钵露罗国，多金、银，金色如火。又此池南北与阿耨池相当。

从此川东出，登危履雪，行五百余里，至朅盘陀国。城依峻岭，北背徙多河，其河东入盐泽，潜流地下，出积石山，为此国河源也。又其王聪慧，建国相承多历年所，自云本是脂那提婆瞿怛罗（唐言汉日天种）。王故宫有故尊者童寿论师伽蓝。尊者，怛叉始罗国人也。神悟英秀，日诵三万二千言，兼书亦尔，游戏众法，雅闲著述，凡制论数十部，并盛宣行，即经部本师也。是时，东有马鸣，南有提婆，西有龙猛，北有童寿，号为“四日”，能照有情之惑。童寿声誉既高，先王躬伐其国，迎而供养。

城东南三百余里，至大石壁，有二石室，各一罗汉于中入灭尽定，端坐不动，视若羸人，而竟无倾朽，已经七百余岁矣。法师在其国停二十余日。

复东北行五日，逢群贼，商侣惊怖登山，象被逐，溺水而死。贼过后，与商人渐进东下，冒寒履险，行八百余里，出葱岭至乌铩国。

城西二百里有大山，峰崿甚峻，上有窣堵波。旧说曰：数百年前，雷震山崩，中有苾刍，身量枯伟，冥目而坐，鬓发鬖鬖，垂覆肩面。有樵者见而白王，王躬观礼，士庶传闻，远近同集，咸申供养，积华成篑。王曰：“此何人也？”有苾刍对曰：“此出家罗汉，入灭尽定者，岁月滋淹，故发长耳。”王曰：“若何警寤令其起也？”对曰：“段食之身，出定便坏，宜先以酥乳灌洒，使润沾腠理，然后击揵槌，感而悟之，或可起也。”王曰：“善哉！”遂依僧语，灌乳击槌。罗汉举目而视，曰：“尔辈何人，形被法服？”对曰：“我辈苾刍也。”彼曰：“我师迦叶波如来，今何所在？”对曰：“久入涅槃。”闻之愀然。重曰：“释迦文佛成无上等觉未？”答曰：“已成。利物斯周，亦从寂灭。”闻已低眉良久，以手举发，起升虚空，作大神变，化火焚身，遗骸堕地。王与大众收骨，起窣堵波，即此塔也。

从此北行五百余里，至佉沙国(旧曰疏勒，乃称其城号也。正音宣云室利讫栗利多底也。疏勒之言，尚讹也)。又从此东南行五百余里，渡徙多河，逾大岭，至斫句迦国（旧曰沮渠）。国南有大山，山多龛室，印度证果人多运神通，就之栖止，因入寂灭者众矣。今犹有三罗汉住岩穴，入灭心定，鬓发渐长，诸僧时往为剃。又此国多大乘经典，十万颂为部者，凡有数十。

从此东行八百余里，至瞿萨旦那国（唐曰地乳，即其俗之雅言也。俗谓“涣那国”，匈奴谓之“于遁”，诸胡谓之“豁旦”，印度谓之“屈丹”。旧曰于阗，讹也）。沙碛大半，宜谷丰果。出氍毹、细毡、氎，工绩絁紬。又土多白玉、瑿玉。气序和调，俗知礼义，尚学好音，风仪详整，异诸胡俗。文字远遵印度，微有改耳。重佛法，伽蓝百所，僧五千余人，多学大乘。其王雄智勇武，尊爱有德，自云毗沙门天之胤也。

王之先祖即无忧王之太子，在怛叉始罗国，后被谴出雪山北，养牧逐水草，至此建都，久而无子，因祷毗沙门天庙，庙神额上剖出一男，复于庙前地生奇味，甘香如乳，取而养子，遂至成长。王崩后，嗣立，威德遐被，力并诸国，今王即其后也。先祖本因地乳资成，故于阗正音称“地乳国”焉。

法师入其境，至勃伽夷城，城中有坐佛像，高七尺余，首戴宝冠，威颜圆满。闻诸旧说：像本在迦湿弥罗国，请来到此。昔有罗汉，有一沙弥身婴疹疾，临将舍寿，索酢米饼，师以天眼观见瞿萨旦那有，潜运神足，乞而与之。沙弥食已欢喜，乐生其国，愿力无违，命终即生王家。嗣立之后，才略骁雄，志思吞摄，乃逾雪山伐其旧国。时迦湿弥王亦简将练兵，欲事攘拒。罗汉曰：“不劳举刃，我自遣之。”即往瞿萨旦那王所，为说顶生贪暴之失，及示先身沙弥衣服。王见已得宿命智，深生愧恧，与迦湿弥王结好而罢，仍迎先所供像，随军还国。像至此城住而不进，王与众军尽力移转，卒不能动，即于像上营构精庐，招延僧侣，舍所爱冠庄严佛顶。其冠见在，极多贵宝，睹者叹焉。

法师停七日。于阗王闻法师到其境，躬来迎谒。后日发引，王先还都，留儿侍奉。行二日，王又遣达官来迎，离城四十里宿。明日，王与道俗将音乐香华接于路左。既至，延入城，安置于小乘萨婆多寺。

王城南十余里有大伽蓝，此国先王为毗卢折那（唐言遍照）阿罗汉造也。昔此国法教未沾，而罗汉自迦湿弥罗至此，宴坐林中。时有见者，怪其形服，以状白王。王闻亲往观其容止，问曰："尔何人，独栖林野？"曰："我如来弟子，法尔闲居。"王曰："称如来者，复何义也？"答曰："如来者即佛陀之德号。昔净饭王太子一切义成，愍诸众生沉没苦海，无救无归，乃弃七宝千子之资，四洲轮王之位，闲林进道，六年果成，获金色之身，证无师之法，洒甘露于鹿苑，耀摩尼于鹫峰，八十年中，示教利喜，化缘既尽，息应归真，遗像遗典，传通犹在。王以宿福，位为人主，当法轮之付嘱，作有识之依归，冥而不闻，是何理也？"王曰："某罪累淹积，不闻佛名。今蒙圣人降德，犹是余福。既有遗像、遗典，请奉修行。"罗汉报曰："必愿乐者，当先建立伽蓝，则灵像自至。"王于是旋驾，与群臣详择胜地，命选匠人，问罗汉造立之式，因而建焉。寺成，王重请曰："伽蓝已就，佛像何在？"报曰："王但至诚，像至非远。"王共大臣及士庶等，各烧香捧华，一心而立。须臾间有佛像自空而来，降于宝座，光晖晃朗，容颜肃然。王见欢喜，称庆无极，并请罗汉为众说法，因与国人广兴供养。故此伽蓝即最初之立也。

法师前为渡河失经，到此更使人往屈支、疏勒访本，及为于阗王留连，未获即还，因修表使高昌小儿逐商伴入朝，陈已昔往婆罗门国求法，今得还归到于阗。其表曰：

沙门玄奘言：奘闻马融该赡，郑玄就扶风之师；伏生明敏，晁错躬济南之学。是知儒林近术，古人犹且远求，况诸佛利物之玄踪，三藏解缠之妙说，敢惮涂遥而无寻慕者也。玄奘往以佛兴西域，遗教东传，然则胜典虽来，而圆宗尚阙，常思访学，无顾身命。遂以贞观三年四月，冒越宪章，私往天竺。践流沙之浩浩，陟雪岭之巍巍；铁门巉险之涂，热海波涛之路。始自长安神邑，终于王舍新城，中间所经五万余里。虽风俗千别，艰危万重，而凭恃天威，所至无鲠。仍蒙厚礼；身不辛苦，心愿获从，遂得观耆阇崛山，礼菩提之树；见不见迹，闻未闻经；穷宇宙之灵奇，尽阴阳之化育；宣皇风之德泽，发殊俗之钦思，历览周游一十七载。今已从钵罗耶伽国经迦毕试境，越葱岭，渡波谜罗川归还，达于于阗。为所将大象溺死，经本众多，未得鞍乘，以是少停，不获奔驰早谒轩陛，无任延仰之至。谨遣高昌俗人马玄智随商侣奉表先闻。

是后为于阗诸僧讲《瑜伽》、《对法》、《俱舍》、《摄大乘论》，一日一夜，四论递宣，王与道俗归依听受，日有千数。时间经七八月，使还，蒙恩敕降使迎劳，曰："闻师访道殊域，今得归还，欢喜无量，可即速来与朕相见。其国僧解梵语及经义者，亦任将来。朕已敕于阗等道，使诸国送师，人力鞍乘应不少乏，令敦煌官司于流沙迎接，鄯善于沮沫迎接。”法师奉敕已，即进发，于阗王资饯甚厚。

自发都三百余里，东至媲摩城。城有雕檀立佛像，高三丈余，姿状端严，甚多灵应。人有疾病，随其苦处以金簿帖像，病即瘳愈；凡有愿求，多蒙果遂。相传云：昔佛在世，憍赏弥国邬陀衍那王所作，佛灭度后，自彼飞来，至此国北曷劳落迦城，后复自移到此（因缘如别传）。又相传有记云：释迦法灭，像入龙宫。

从媲摩城东入沙碛，行二百余里，至泥壤城。又从此东入大流沙，风动沙流，地无水草，多热毒魑魅之患。无迳路，行人往返，望人畜遗骸以为幖帜，硗确难涉，委如前序。又行四百余里，至睹货罗故国。又行六百余里，至折摩驮那故国，即沮沫地。又东北行千余里，至纳缚波故国，即楼兰地，展转达于自境。得鞍乘已，放于阗使人及驮马还。有敕酬其劳，皆不受而去。

既至沙州，又附表。时帝在洛阳宫，表至，知法师渐近，敕西京留守左仆射梁国公房玄龄使有司迎待。法师承上欲问罪辽滨，恐稽缓不及，乃倍涂而进，奄至漕上。官司不知迎接，威仪莫暇陈设，而闻者自然奔凑。观礼盈衢，更相登践，欲进不得，因宿于漕上矣。

卷第六

起十九年春正月入西京
终二十二年夏六月谢御制经序并答

贞观十九年春正月景子，京城留守左仆射梁国公房玄龄等承法师赍经、像至，乃遣右武侯大将军侯莫陈实、雍州司马李叔昚、长安县令李乾佑等奉迎。自漕而入，舍于都亭驿（传云在朱雀街），其从若云。

是日，有司颁诸寺，具帐舆、华幡等，拟送经、像于弘福寺，人皆欣踊，各竞庄严。翌日，大会于朱雀街之南，凡数百件，部伍陈列。即以安置法师于西域所得如来肉舍利一百五十粒；拟摩揭陀国前正觉山龙窟留影金佛像一躯，通光座高三尺三寸；拟婆罗痆斯国鹿野苑初转法轮像刻檀佛像一躯，通光座高三尺五寸；拟憍赏弥国出爱王思慕如来刻檀写真像刻檀佛像一躯，通光座高二尺九寸；拟劫比他国如来自天宫下降宝阶像银佛像一躯，通光座高四尺；拟摩揭陀国鹫峰山说《法华》等经像金佛像一躯，通光座高三尺五寸；拟那揭罗曷国伏毒龙所留影像刻檀佛像一躯，通光座高尺有三寸；拟吠舍釐国巡城行化，刻檀像等。又安置法师于西域所得大乘经二百二十四部，大乘论一百九十二部，上座部经、律、论一十五部，大众部经、律、论一十五部，三弥底部经、律、论一十五部，弥沙塞部经、律、论二十二部，迦叶臂耶部经、律、论一十七部，法密部经、律、论四十二部，说一切有部经、律、论六十七部，因明论三十六部，声论一十三部，凡五百二十夹，六百五十七部，以二十匹马负而至。

其日所司普颁诸寺，俱有宝帐、幢、幡供养之具，限明二十八日旦并集朱雀街，拟迎新至经、像于弘福寺。于是人增勇锐，各竞庄严，穷诸丽好。幢帐、幡盖、宝案、宝舆，寺别将出分布讫，僧尼等整服随之，雅梵居前，熏炉列后，至是并到朱雀街内，凡数百事。布经、像而行，珠佩流音，金华散彩，预送之俦莫不歌咏希有，忘尘遣累，叹其希遇。始自朱雀街内，终届弘福寺门，数十里间，都人士子、内外官僚，迾道两傍，瞻仰而立，人物阗噎。所司恐相腾践，各令当处烧香散华，无得移动，而烟云赞响，处处连合。昔如来创降迦毗，弥勒初升睹史，龙神供养，天众围绕，虽不及彼时，亦遗法之盛也。其日众人同见天有五色绮云现于日北，宛转当经、像之上，纷纷郁郁，周圆数里，若迎若送，至寺而微。

释彦悰笺述曰："余考寻图史，此盖谓天之喜气，识者嘉焉。昔如来创降迦维，慈氏将升睹史，龙神供养，天众奉迎，虽不及往时，而遗法东流，未有若兹之盛也。”

壬辰，法师谒文武圣皇帝于洛阳宫。二月己亥，见于仪鸾殿，帝迎慰甚厚。既而坐讫，帝曰：“师去何不相报？”法师谢曰：“玄奘当去之时，以再三表奏，但诚愿微浅，不蒙允许。无任慕道之至，乃辄私行，专擅之罪，唯深惭惧。”

帝曰：“师出家与俗殊隔，然能委命求法，惠利苍生。朕甚嘉焉，亦不烦为愧。但念彼山川阻远，方俗异心，怪师能达也。”

法师对曰：“奘闻乘疾风者，造天池而非远；御龙舟者，涉江波而不难。自陛下握乾符，清四海，德笼九域，仁被八区。淳风扇炎景之南，圣威镇葱山之外，所以戎夷君长，每见云翔之鸟自东来者，犹疑发于上国，敛躬而敬之，况玄奘圆首方足，亲承育化者也。既赖天威，故得往还无难。”

帝曰：“此自是师长者之言，朕何敢当也。”

因广问彼事。自雪岭已西，印度之境，玉烛和气，物产风俗，八王故迹，四佛遗踪，并博望之所不传，班、马无得而载。法师既亲游其地，观觌疆邑，耳闻目览，记忆无遗，随问酬对，皆有条理。帝大悦。谓侍臣曰：“昔符坚称释道安为神器，举朝尊之。朕今观法师词论典雅，风节贞峻，非惟不愧古人，亦乃出之更远。”

时赵国公长孙无忌对曰：“诚如圣旨。臣尝读《三十国春秋》，见叙安事，实是高行博物之僧。但彼时佛法来近，经、论未多，虽有钻研，盖其条叶，非如法师躬窥净域，讨众妙之源，究泥洹之迹者矣。”

帝曰：“公言是也。”帝又谓法师曰：“佛国遐远，灵迹法教，前史不能委详，师既亲睹，宜修一传，以示未闻。”

帝又察法师堪公辅之寄，因劝罢道，助秉俗务。法师谢曰：“玄奘少践缁门，服膺佛道，玄宗是习，孔教未闻。今遣从俗，无异乘流之舟使弃水而就陆，不唯无功，亦徒令腐败也。愿得毕身行道，以报国恩，即玄奘之幸甚。”如是固辞乃止。

时帝将问罪辽滨，天下兵马已会于洛，军事忙迫，闻法师至，命引入朝，期暂相见，而清言既交，遂不知日昃。赵国公长孙无忌奏称法师停在鸿胪，日暮恐不及。帝曰：“匆匆言犹未尽意，欲共师东行，省方观俗，指麾之外，别更谈叙，师意如何？”

法师谢曰：“玄奘远来，兼有疾疹，恐不堪陪驾。”

帝曰：“师尚能孤游绝域，今此行盖同跬步，安足辞焉？”

法师对曰：“陛下东征，六军奉卫。罚乱国，诛贼臣，必有牧野之功，昆阳之捷。玄奘自度，终无裨助行阵之效，虚负涂路费损之惭。加以兵戎战斗，律制不得观看。既佛有此言，不敢不奉。伏愿天慈哀矜，即玄奘幸甚。”帝信纳而止。

法师又奏云：“玄奘从西域所得梵本六百余部，一言未译。今知此嵩岳之南，少室山北有少林寺，远离鄽落，泉石清闲，是后魏孝文皇帝所造，即菩提留支三藏翻译经处。玄奘望为国就彼翻译，伏听敕旨。”帝曰：“不须在山，师西方去后，朕奉为穆太后于西京造弘福寺，寺有禅院甚虚静，法师可就翻译。”

法师又奏曰：“百姓无知，见玄奘从西方来，妄相观看，遂成阛阓，非直违触宪纲，亦为妨废法事，望得守门，以防诸过。”帝大悦，曰：“师此意可谓保身之言也，当为处分。师可三五日停憩，还京就弘福安置。诸有所须，一共玄龄平章。”自是辞还矣。

三月己巳，法师自洛阳还至长安，即居弘福寺。将事翻译，乃条疏所须证义、缀文、笔受、书手等数，以申留守司空梁国公房玄龄，玄龄遣所司具状发使定州启奏。令旨依所须供给，务使周备。

夏六月戊戌，证义大德谙解大小乘经、论，为时辈所推者，一十二人至，即京弘福寺沙门灵润，沙门文备，罗汉寺沙门慧贵、实际寺沙门明琰、宝昌寺沙门法祥、静法寺沙门普贤、法海寺沙门神昉、廓州法讲寺沙门道琛、汴州演觉寺沙门玄忠、蒲州普救寺沙门神泰。绵州振音寺沙门敬明、益州多宝寺沙门道因等。又有缀文大德九人至，即京师普光寺沙门栖玄、弘福寺沙门明濬、会昌寺沙门辩机、终南山丰德寺沙门道宣、简州福聚寺沙门静迈、蒲州普救寺沙门行友、栖岩寺沙门道卓、豳州昭仁寺沙门慧立、洛州天宫寺沙门玄则等。又有字学大德一人至，即京大总持寺沙门玄应。又有证梵语、梵文大德一人至，即京大兴善寺沙门玄谟。自余笔受、书手，所司供料等并至。

丁卯，法师方操贝叶开演梵文，创译《菩萨藏经》、《佛地经》、《六门陀罗尼经》、《显扬圣教论》等四部。其翻《六门经》当日了，《佛地经》至辛巳了，《菩萨藏经》、《显扬论》等岁暮方讫。二十年春正月甲子，又译《大乘阿毗达磨杂集论》，至二月讫。又译《瑜伽师地论》。

秋七月辛卯，法师进新译经、论现了者，表曰：

沙门玄奘言：窃闻八正之旨，实出苦海之津梁；一乘之宗，诚升涅槃之梯蹬。但以物机未熟，致蕴葱山之西，经胥庭而莫闻，历周、秦而靡至。暨乎摩腾入洛，方被三川；僧会游吴，始沾荆、楚。从是以来，遂得人修解脱之因，家树菩提之业，固知传法之益，其利博哉。次复严、显求经，澄、什继译，虽则玄风日扇，而并处伪朝。唯玄奘轻生，独逢明圣，所将经、论咸得奏闻。蒙陛下崇重圣言，赐使翻译，比与义学诸僧等专精夙夜，无堕寸阴，虽握管淹时，未遂终讫。已绝笔者，见得五部五十八卷，名曰《大菩萨藏经》二十卷、《佛地经》一卷、《六门陀罗尼经》一卷、《显扬圣教论》二十卷、《大乘阿毗达磨杂集论》一十六卷、勒成八帙，缮写如别，谨诣阙奉进。玄奘又窃见弘福寺尊像初成，陛下亲降銮舆，开青莲之目。今经、论初译，为圣代新文，敢缘前义，亦望曲垂神翰，题制一序，赞扬宗极。冀冲言奥旨与日月齐明，玉字银钩将乾坤等固，使百代之下诵咏不穷，千载之外瞻仰无绝。

前又洛阳奉见日，敕令法师修《西域记》，至是而成。乙未，又进表曰：

沙门玄奘言：窃寻蟠木、幽陵，云官记轩皇之壤；流沙沧海，夏载著伊尧之域。西母白环，荐垂衣之主；东夷楛矢，奉刑措之君。固已飞英曩代，式徽前典。伏惟陛下，握纪乘时，提衡范物。刳舟弦木，威天下而济群生；鳌足芦灰，堙方舆而补圆盖。耀武经于七德，阐文教于十伦。泽遍泉源，化沾萧苇；芝房发秀，浪并开华。乐囿驯班，巢阿响律；浮紫膏于贝阙，霏白云于玉检。遂苑弱水而池蒙汜，圃炎火而照积冰，梯赤阪而承朔，泛沧津而委贶。史旷前良，事绝故府。岂如汉开张掖，近接金城；秦戍桂林，裁通珠浦而已。玄奘幸属天地贞观，华夷静谧；冥心梵境，敢符好事。命均朝露，力譬秋螽。徒以凭假皇灵，飘身进影；展转膜拜之乡，流离重驿之外。条支巨鷇，方验前闻；罽宾孤鸾，还稽曩实。时移岁积，人愿天从，遂得下雪岫而泛提河，窥鹤林而观鹫岭。祇园之路，仿像犹存；王城之基，坡陀尚在。寻求历览，时序推迁；言返帝京，淹逾一纪。所闻所履，百有二十八国。

窃以章、亥之所践藉，空陈广袤；夸父之所陵厉，无述土风。班超侯而未远，张骞望而非博。今所记述，有异前闻。虽未极大千之疆，颇穷葱外之境，皆存实录，匪敢雕华。谨具编裁，称为《大唐西域记》，凡一十二卷，缮写如别。望班之右笔，饰以左言；掩博物于晋臣，广《九丘》于皇代。但玄奘资识浅短，遗漏实多；兼拙于笔语，恐无足观览。

丙申，神笔自答书曰："省书具悉来意。法师夙摽高行，早出尘表，泛宝舟而登彼岸，搜妙道而辟法门。弘阐大猷，荡涤众罪。是故慈云欲卷，舒之荫四空；慧日将昏，朗之照八极。舒朗之者，其唯法师乎！朕学浅心拙，在物犹迷，况佛教幽微，岂能仰测？请为经题，非己所闻。又云新撰《西域记》者，当自披览。敕奘尚。

丁酉，法师重表曰：

沙门玄奘言：伏奉墨敕，猥垂奖喻，祇奉纶言，精守振越。玄奘业行空疏，谬忝缁侣。幸属九瀛有截，四表无虞。凭皇灵以远征，恃国威而访道。穷遐冒险，虽励愚诚；纂异怀荒，实资朝化。所获经、论，蒙遣翻译，见成卷轴，未有诠序。伏惟陛下睿思云敷，天华景烂。理包《繫》、《象》，调逸《咸》、《英》；跨千古以飞声，掩百王而腾实。窃以神力无方，非神思不足铨其理；圣教玄远，非圣藻何以序其源？

故乃冒犯威严，敢希题目。宸眷冲邈，不垂矜许，抚躬累息，相顾失图。

玄奘闻日月丽天，既分晖于户牖；江河纪地，亦流润于岩崖。云和广乐，不秘响于聋昧；金壁奇珍，岂韬彩于愚瞽？敢缘斯理，重以千祈。伏乞雷雨曲垂，天文俯照，配两仪而同久。与二曜而俱悬。然则鹫岭微言，假神笔而弘远；鸡园奥典，托英词而宣畅。岂止区区梵众，独荷恩荣；蠢蠢迷生，方超尘累而已。

自此方许。

二十二年春，驾幸玉华宫。夏五月甲午，翻《瑜伽师地论》讫，凡一百卷。

六月庚辰，敕追法师赴宫。比发在途，屡有使至，令缓进，无得劳损。既至，见于玉华殿，甚欢。帝曰："朕在京苦暑，故就此山宫，泉石既凉，气力稍好，能省览机务。然忆法师，故遣相屈，涉途当大劳也。”

法师谢曰：“四海黎庶依陛下而生，圣躬不安则率土惶灼。伏闻銮舆至此，御膳顺宜，凡预含灵，孰不蹈舞。愿陛下永保崇高，与天无极。玄奘庸薄，猥蒙齿召，衔荷不觉为劳。”

帝以法师学业该赡，仪韵淹深，每思逼劝归俗，致之左右，共谋朝政。往于洛阳宫奉见之际，已亲论之，至是又言曰：“昔尧、舜、禹、汤之君，隆周、炎汉之主，莫不以为六合务广，万机事殷，两目不能遍鉴，一心难为独察，是以周凭十乱，舜托五臣，翼亮朝猷，弼谐邦国。彼明王圣主犹仗群贤，况朕寡闇而不寄众哲者也？意欲法师脱须菩提之染服，挂维摩诘之素衣，升铉路以陈谟，坐槐庭而论道，于意何如？”

法师对曰：“陛下言：六合务广，三五之君不能独守，寄诸贤哲共而成之。仲尼亦云：君失臣得，故君为元首，臣为股肱。玄奘谓，此言将诫中庸，非为上智。若使有臣皆得，桀、纣岂无臣耶？以此而推，不必由也。仰惟陛下上智之君，一人纪纲，万事自得其绪，况抚运以来，天地休平，中外宁晏，皆是陛下不荒、不淫、不丽、不侈，兢兢业业，虽休勿休，居安思危，为善承天之所致也，余何预哉！请辨二三以明其事。

陛下经纬八纮之略，驱驾英豪之才，克定祸乱之功，崇阐雍熙之业，聪明文思之德，体元合极之姿，皆天之所授，无假于人，其义一也。

敦本弃末，尚仁尚礼，移浇风于季俗，反淳政于上皇，赋遵薄制，刑用轻典，九州四海禀识怀生，俱沐恩波，咸遂安乐。此又圣心至化，无假于人，其义二也。

至道旁通，深仁远洽，东逾日域，西迈昆丘，南尽炎洲，北穷玄塞。雕蹄鼻饮之俗，卉服左衽之人，莫不候雨瞻风，稽颡屈膝，献珍贡宝，充委夷邸，此又天威所感，无假于人，其义三也。

猃狁为患，其来自久，五帝所不臣，三王所不制，遂使河、洛为被发之野，酆、鄗为鸣镝之场，中国陵迟，匈奴得志，殷周已来不能攘弭。至汉武穷兵，卫、霍尽力，虽毁枝叶，根本犹存。自后以来，无闻良策。及陛下御图，一征斯殄，倾巢倒穴，无复孑遗，瀚海、燕然之域并入堤封，单于弓骑之人俱充臣妾。若言由臣，则虞、夏已来贤辅多矣，何因不获？故知有道斯得，无假于人，其义四也。

高丽小蕃，失礼上国，隋帝总天下之师，三自征罚，攻城无伤半堞，掠卒不获一人，虚丧六军，狼狈而反。陛下暂行，将数万骑，摧驻跸之强阵，破辽、盖之坚城，振旅凯旋，俘馘三十万众。用兵御将，其道不殊，隋以之亡，唐以之得，故知由主，无假于人，其义五也。

又如天地交泰，日月光华，和气氤氲，庆云纷郁，四灵见质，一角呈奇，白狼、白狐、朱鸾、朱草，昭彰杂沓，无量亿千，不能遍举，皆是应德而至，无假于人。乃欲比喻前王，寄功十乱，窃为陛下不取。纵复须人，今亦伊、吕多矣。玄奘庸陋，何足以预之？至于守戒缁门，阐扬遗法，此其愿也。伏乞天慈，终而不夺。”

帝甚悦，谓法师曰：“师向所陈，并上玄垂佑，及宗庙之灵，卿士之力，朕安能致也。既欲敷扬妙道，亦不违高志，可努力，今日已后，亦当助师弘道。”

释彦悰笺曰：法师才兼内外，临机酬答，其辩洽如是，难哉！昔道安陈谏，符坚之驾不停；恒、标奋辞，姚兴之心莫止。终致败军之辱，逃遁之劳。岂如法师雅论才申，皇情允塞，清风转洁，美志逾贞。以此而言，可不烦月旦而优劣见矣。

时中书令褚遂良奏曰：“今四海廓清，九域宁晏，皆陛下圣德，实如师言，臣等备位而已。日月之下，萤爝何功？”帝笑曰：“不如此。夫珍裘非一狐之腋，大厦必众材共成。何有君能独济？师欲自全雅操，故滥相光饰耳。”

帝又问：“法师此翻何经、论？”

答：“近翻《瑜伽师地论》讫，凡一百卷。”

帝曰：“此论甚大，何圣所说？复明何义？”

答曰：“论是弥勒菩萨说，明十七地义。”

又问：“何名十七地？”。

答：“谓五识相应地、意识相应地、有寻有伺地、无寻唯伺地、无寻无伺地、三摩呬多地、非三摩呬多地、有心地、无心地、闻所成地、思所成地、修所成地、声闻地、独觉地、菩萨地、有余依地、无余依地。”

及举纲提目，陈列大义。帝深爱焉。遣使向京取《瑜伽论》。《论》至，帝自详览，睹其词义宏远，非从来所闻，叹谓侍臣曰：

“朕观佛经，譬犹瞻天俯海，莫测高深。法师能于异域得是深法。朕比以军国务殷，不及委寻佛教。而今观之，宗源杳旷，靡知涯际，其儒道九流之典，犹汀滢之池方溟渤耳。而世云三教齐致，此妄谈也！”

因敕所司简秘书省书手写新翻经、论为九本，与雍、洛、并、兖、相、荆、杨、凉、益等九州展转流通，使率土之人同禀未闻之义。

时司徒赵国公长孙无忌、中书令褚遂良等奏曰：“臣闻佛教冲玄，天人莫测，言本则甚深，语门则难入。伏惟陛下至道昭明，飞光昱日；泽沾遐界，化溢中区；拥护五乘，建立三宝。故得法师当菽叶而秀质，间千载而挺生；陟重阻以求经，履危途而访道；见珍殊俗，具获真文。归国翻宣，若庵园之始说；精文奥义，如金口之新开。皆是陛下圣德所感。臣等愚瞽，预此见闻。苦海波澜，舟航有寄。又天慈广远，使布之九州；蠢蠢黔黎，俱餐妙法。臣等亿劫希逢，不胜幸甚！”

帝曰：“此是法师大慈愿力，又卿等宿福所逢，非朕独所致也。”

帝先许作新经序，机务繁剧，未及措意。至此法师重启，方为染翰。少顷而成，名《大唐三藏圣教序》，凡七百八十一字，神笔自写，敕贯众经之首。

帝居庆福殿，百官侍卫，命法师坐，使弘文馆学士上官仪以所制《序》对群寮宣读，霞焕锦舒，极褒扬之致。其词曰：

盖闻二仪有像，显覆载以含生；四时无形，潜寒暑以化物。是以窥天鉴地，庸愚皆识其端；明阴洞阳，贤哲罕穷其数。

然而天地苞乎阴阳而易识者，以其有像也；阴阳处乎天地而难穷者，以其无形也。故知像显可征，虽愚不惑；形潜莫睹，在智犹迷。况乎佛道崇虚，乘幽控寂；弘济万品，典御十方。举威灵而无上，抑神力而无下；大之则弥于宇宙，细之则摄于毫釐。无灭无生，历千劫而不古；若隐若显，运百福而长今。妙道凝玄，遵之莫知其际；法流湛寂，挹之莫测其源。故知蠢蠢凡愚，区区庸鄙，投其旨趣，能无疑惑者哉！

然则大教之兴，基乎西土，腾汉庭而皎梦，照东域而流慈。昔者，分形分迹之时，言未驰而成化；当常、现常之世，民仰德而知遵。及乎晦影归真，迁仪越世。金容掩色，不镜三千之光；丽象开图，空端四八之相。

于是微言广被，拯含类于三涂；遗训遐宣，导群生于十地。然而真教难仰，莫能一其旨归；曲学易遵，邪正于焉纷纠。所以空有之论，或习俗而是非；大、小之乘，乍沿时而隆替。

有玄奘法师者，法门之领袖也。幼怀贞敏，早悟三空之心；长契神情，先苞四忍之行。松风水月，未足比其清华；仙露明珠，讵能方其朗润！故以智通无累，神测未形；超六尘而迥出，只千古而无对。凝心内境，悲正法之陵迟；栖虑玄门，慨深文之讹谬。思欲分条析理，广彼前闻；截伪续真，开兹后学。是以翘心净土，往游西域；乘危远迈，杖策孤征。积雪晨飞，涂间失地；惊砂夕起，空外迷天。万里山川，拨烟霞而进影；百重寒暑，蹑霜雨而前踪。诚重劳轻，求深愿达。周游西宇，十有七年；穷历道邦，询求正教。双林、八水，味道餐风；鹿苑、鹫峰，瞻奇仰异。承至言于先圣，受真教于上贤；探赜妙门，精穷奥业。一乘五律之道，驰骤于心田；八藏三箧之文，波涛于口海。爰自所历之国，总将三藏要文，凡六百五十七部，译布中夏，宣扬胜业。引慈云于西极，注法雨于东垂；圣教缺而复全，苍生罪而还福。湿火宅之干焰，共拔迷涂；朗爱水之昏波，同臻彼岸。

是知恶因业坠，善以缘升；升坠之端，惟人所托。譬夫桂生高岭，零露方得泫其华；莲出渌波，飞尘不能污其叶。非莲性自洁，而桂质本贞，良由所附者高，则微物不能累；所凭者净，则浊类不能沾。夫以卉木无知，犹资善而成善，况乎人伦有识，不缘庆而成庆？方冀兹经流施，将日月而无穷；斯福遐敷，与乾坤而永大。

时法师既奉《序》，表谢曰：

沙门玄奘言：窃闻六爻探赜，局于生灭之场；百物正名，未涉真如之境。犹且远征羲册，睹奥不测其神；遐想轩图，历选并归其美。伏惟皇帝陛下玉毫降质，金轮御天。廓先王之九州，掩百千之日月；广列代之区域，纳恒沙之法界。遂使给园精舍并入提封，贝叶灵文咸归册府。玄奘往因振锡，聊谒崛山。经涂万里，恃天威如咫步；匪乘千叶，诣双林如食顷。搜扬三藏，尽龙宫之所储；研究一乘，穷鹫岭之遗旨。并已载于白马，还献紫震。寻蒙下诏，赐使翻译。玄奘识乖龙树，谬忝传灯之荣；才异马鸣，深愧泻瓶之敏。所译经、论，纰舛尤多。遂荷天恩，留神构序。文超《象》、《繫》之表，理括众妙之门。忽以微生亲承梵响，踊跃欢喜，如闻受记，无任欣荷之极。谨奉表诣阙陈谢以闻。

帝看表后，手报书曰：

朕才谢圭璋，言惭博达。至于内典，尤所未闲。昨制序文，深为鄙拙；唯恐秽翰墨于金简，标瓦砾于珠林。忽得来书，谬承褒赞；循躬省虑，弥益厚颜。盖不足称，空劳致谢。

卷第七

起二十二年夏六月天皇太子制《述圣记》终永徽五年春二月法师答书

二十二年夏六月，天皇大帝居春宫，奉睹圣文，又制《述圣记》，其词曰：

夫显扬正教，非智无以广其文；崇阐微言，非贤莫能定其旨。盖真如圣教者，诸法之玄宗，众经之轨躅也。综括宏远，奥旨遐深，极空有之精微，体生灭之机要。词茂道旷，寻之者不究其源；文显义幽，履之者莫测其际。故知圣慈所被，业无善而不臻；妙化所敷，缘无恶而不剪。开法网之纲纪，弘六度之正教；拯群有之涂炭，启三藏之秘局。是以名无翼而长飞，道无根而永固。道名流庆，历遂古而镇常；赴感应身，经尘劫而不朽。晨钟夕梵，交二音于鹫峰；慧日法流，转双轮于鹿苑。排空宝盖，接翔云而共飞；庄野春林，与天华而合彩。

伏惟皇帝陛下，上玄资福，垂拱而治八荒；德被黔黎，敛衽而朝万国。恩加朽骨，石室归贝叶之文；泽及昆虫，金匮流梵说之偈。遂使阿耨达水通神甸之八川，耆阇崛山接嵩、华之翠岭。窃以法性凝寂，靡归心而不通；智地玄奥，感恳诚而遂显。岂谓重昏之夜，烛慧炬之光；火宅之朝，降法雨之泽。于是百川异流，同会于海；万区分义，总成乎实。岂与汤、武校其优劣，尧、舜比其圣德者哉！

玄奘法师者，夙怀聪令，立志夷简；神清龆龀之年，体拔浮华之世。凝情定室，匿迹幽岩；栖息三禅，巡游十地。超六尘之境，独步迦维；会一乘之旨，随机化物。以中华之无质，寻印度之真文。远涉恒河，终期满字；频登雪岭，更获半珠。问道往还，十有七载；备通释典，利物为心。以贞观十九年二月六日，奉敕于弘福寺翻译圣教要文，凡六百五十七部。引大海之法流，洗尘劳而不竭；传智灯之长焰，皎幽闇而恒明。自非久植胜缘，何以显扬斯旨？所谓法性常住，齐三光之明；我皇福臻，同二仪之固。伏见御制众经、论序，照古腾今，理含金石之声，文抱风云之润。治辄以轻尘足岳，坠露添流；略举大纲，以为斯记。

法师进启谢曰：

玄奘闻七耀摛光，凭高天而散景；九河洒润，因厚地而通流。是知相资之美，处物既然；演法依人，理在无惑。伏惟皇太子殿下，发挥睿藻，再述天文；赞美大乘，庄严实相。

珠回玉转，霞烂锦舒；将日月而联华，与《咸》、《韶》而合韵。玄奘轻生多幸，沐浴殊私；不任铭佩，奉启陈谢。

时降令答法师书曰："治素无才学，性不聪敏；内典诸文，殊未观览。所作序记，鄙拙尤繁。忽得来书，褒扬赞述；抚躬自省，惭悚交并。劳师等远臻，深以为愧。"

释彦悰笺述曰："自二圣序文出后，王公、百辟、法、俗、黎庶手舞足蹈，欢咏德音，内外揄扬，未浃辰而周六合；慈云再荫，慧日重明，归依之徒波回雾委。所谓上之化下，犹风靡草，其斯之谓乎！如来所以法付国王，良为此也。"

时弘福寺寺主圆定及京城僧等，请镌二序文于金石，藏之寺宇。帝可之。后寺僧怀仁等乃鸠集晋右军将军王羲之书，勒于碑石焉。

庚辰，皇太子以文德圣皇后早弃万方，思报昊天，追崇福业，使中大夫守右庶子臣高季辅宣令曰：

"寡人不造，咎谴所钟；年在未识，慈颜弃背。终身之忧，贯心滋甚；风树之切，刻骨冥深。每以龙忌之辰，岁时兴感。空怀陟屺之望，益疚寒泉之心。既而笙歌遂远，瞻奉无逮；徒思昊天之报，罔寄乌鸟之情。窃以觉道洪慈，实资冥福；冀申孺慕，是用归依。宜令所司，于京城内旧废寺，妙选一所，奉为文德圣皇后，即营僧寺。寺成之日，当别度僧。仍令挟带林泉，务尽形胜。仰规忉利之果，副此罔极之怀。"

于是有司详择胜地，遂于宫城南晋昌里，面曲池，依净觉故伽蓝而营建焉。瞻星揆地，像天阙，仿给园，穷班、倕巧艺，尽衡霍良木，文石、梓桂、橡樟、栟榈充其林，珠玉、丹青、赭垩、金翠备其饰。而重楼复殿，云阁洞房，凡十余院，总一千八百九十七间，床褥器物，备皆盈满。

文武圣皇帝又读法师所进《菩萨藏经》，美之，因敕春宫作其经后序。其词曰：

盖闻羲皇至赜，精粹止于龟文；轩后通幽，雅奥穷于鸟篆。考丹书而索隐，殊昧实际之源；征绿错以研几，盖非常乐之道。犹且事光图史，振熏风于八埏；德洽生灵，激尧波于万代。

伏惟皇帝陛下，转轮垂拱而化渐鸡园；胜殿凝旒而神交鹫岭。总调御于徽号，匪文思之所窥；综波若于纶言，岂《系》、《象》之能拟。由是教覃溟表，咸传八解之音；训浃寰中，皆践四禅之轨。遂使三千法界，尽怀生而可期；百亿须弥，入堤封而作镇。尼连德水，迩帝里之沧池；舍卫庵园，接上林之茂苑。虽复法性空寂，随感必通；真乘深妙，无幽不阐。所谓大权御极，导法流而靡穷；能仁抚运，拂石劫而无尽。体均具相，不可思议；校美前王，焉可同年而语矣！

爰自开辟，地限流沙，震旦未融，灵文尚隐。汉王精感，托梦想于玄霄；晋后翘诚，降修多于白马。有同蠡酌，岂达四海之涯；取譬管窥，宁穷七曜之隩。洎乎皇灵遐畅，威加铁围之表；至圣发明，德被金刚之际。恒沙国土，普袭衣冠；开解脱门，践真实路。龙宫梵说之偈，必萃清台；猊吼贝叶之文，咸归册府。洒兹甘露，普润芽茎；垂此慧云，遍沾翾走。岂非归依之胜业，圣政之灵感者乎！

夫《菩萨藏经》者，大觉义宗之要旨也。佛修此道，以证无生；菩萨受持，咸登不退。六波罗蜜，关键所资；四无量心，根力斯备。盖彼岸之津涉，正觉之梯航者焉。

贞观中年，身毒归化，越热阪而颁朔，跨悬度以输赈。文轨既同，道路无拥。沙门玄奘，振锡寻真，出自玉关，长驱奈苑，至于天竺，力士生处，访获此经，归而奏上，降诏翻译，于是毕功。

余以问安之暇，澄心妙法之宝，奉述天旨，微表赞扬，式命有司，缀于终卷。

自是帝既情信日隆，平章法义，福田功德，无辍于口，与法师无暂相离。敕加供给，及时服卧具数令换易。秋七月景申，夏罢，又施法师纳袈裟一领，价直百金。观其作制，都不知针线出入所从。帝库内多有前代诸纳，咸无好者，故自教后宫造此，将为称意，营之数岁方成，乘舆四巡，恒将随逐。二十二年，驾幸洛阳宫，时苏州道恭法师、常州慧宣法师并有高行，学该内外，为朝野所称。帝召之。既至，引入坐，言讫。时二僧各披一纳，是梁武帝施其先师，相承共宝。既来谒龙颜，故取披服。帝哂其不工，取纳令示，仍遣赋诗以咏。

恭公诗曰：

福田资象德，
圣种理幽熏。
不持金作缕，
还用彩成文。
朱青自掩映，
翠绮相氤氲。

独有离离叶，

恒向稻畦分。

宣公诗末云：

如蒙一披服，

方堪称福田。

意欲之。帝并不与，各施绢五十匹，即此纳也。传其丽绝，岂常人所宜服用，唯法师盛德当之矣。时并赐法师剃刀一口。法师表谢曰：

沙门玄奘，伏奉敕赐衲袈裟一领、剃刀一口。殊命荐臻，宠灵隆赫；恭对惶悸，如履春冰。玄奘幸遭邕穆之化，早预息心之侣。三业无纪，四恩靡答；谬回天眷，滥叨云泽。忍辱之服，彩合流霞；智慧之刀，铦逾切玉。谨当衣以降烦恼之魔，佩以断尘劳之网。起余讥于彼己，惧空疏于冒荣。惭恧屏营，趍承俯偻，鞠心局蹐，精爽飞越，不任悚荷之至。谨奉表谢闻。尘黩圣鉴，伏深战栗。

帝少劳兵事，纂历之后又心存兆庶，及辽东征罚，栉沐风霜，旋旆已来，气力颇不如平昔，有忧生之虑。既遇法师，遂留心八正，墙堑五乘，遂将息平复。帝因问曰："欲树功德，何最饶益？"法师对曰："众生寝惑，非慧莫启。慧芽抽殖，法为其资。弘法由人，即度僧为最。"帝甚欢。

秋九月己卯，诏曰："昔隋季失御，天下分崩，四海涂炭，八埏鼎沸。朕属当戡乱，躬履兵锋；亟犯风霜，宿于马上。比加药饵，犹未痊除；近日已来，方就平复。岂非福善所感，而致此休征耶？京城及天下诸州寺宜各度五人，弘福寺宜度五十人。”

计海内寺三千七百一十六所，计度僧尼一万八千五百余人。未此已前，天下寺庙遭隋季凋残，缁侣将绝，蒙兹一度，并成徒众。美哉君子！所以重正言也。

帝又问：“《金刚般若经》一切诸佛之所从生，闻而不谤，功逾身命之施，非恒沙珍宝所及。加以理微言约，故贤达君子多爱受持，未知先代所翻，文义具不？”

法师对曰：“此经功德实如圣旨。西方之人咸同爱敬。今观旧经，亦微有遗漏。据梵本具云‘能断金刚般若’，旧经直云‘金刚般若’。欲明菩萨以分别为烦恼，而分别之惑，坚类金刚，唯此经所诠无分别慧，乃能除断，故曰‘能断金刚般若’，故知旧经失上二字。又如下文，三问阙一，二颂阙一，九喻阙三，如是等。什法师所翻舍卫国也，留支所翻婆伽婆者，少可。”

帝曰：“师既有梵本，可更委翻，使众生闻之具足。”然经本贵理，不必须饰文而乖义也。故今新翻《能断金刚般若》，委依梵本。奏之，帝甚悦。

冬十月，车驾还京，法师亦从还。先是敕所司于北阙紫微殿西别营一所，号“弘法院”。既到，居之。昼则帝留谈说，夜乃还院翻经。更译无性菩萨所释《摄大乘论》十卷、世亲所释《摄大乘论》十卷、《缘起圣道经》一卷、《百法明门论》一卷。

戊申，皇太子又宣令曰：

“营慈恩寺，渐向毕功，轮奂将成，僧徒尚阙，伏奉敕旨度三百僧，别请五十大德，同奉神居，降临行道。其新营道场，宜名大慈恩寺，别造翻经院。虹梁藻井，丹青云气；琼础铜锴，金环华铺，并加殊丽。令法师移就翻译，仍纲维寺任。”

法师既奉令旨，令充上座，进启让曰：

沙门玄奘启：伏奉令旨，以玄奘为慈恩寺上座。恭闻嘉令，心灵靡措，屏营累息，深增战悚。玄奘学艺无纪，行业空疏，敢誓捐礬，方期光赞。凭恃皇灵，穷遐访道；所获经、论，奉敕翻译。诚冀法流渐润，克滋鼎祚，圣教绍宣，光华史册。玄奘昔冒危涂，久婴痾疹；驽蹇力弊，恐不卒业；孤负国恩，有罚无赦。命知僧务，更贻重谴；鱼鸟易性，飞沈失途。伏惟皇太子殿下，仁孝天纵，爱敬因心；感风树之悲，结寒泉之痛。式建伽蓝，将弘景福；匡理法众，任在能人；用非其器，必有踬仆。伏愿睿情远鉴，照弘法之福因；慈造曲垂，察愚诚之忠款。则法僧无悔吝之咎，鱼鸟得飞沈之趣。不任诚恳之至，谨奉启陈情，伏用惭惶，追增悚悸。

十二月戊辰，又敕太常卿江夏王道宗将九部乐，万年令宋行质、长安令裴方彦各率县内音声，及诸寺幢帐，并使务极庄严，己巳旦，集安福门街，迎像送僧入大慈恩寺。至是陈列于通衢，其锦彩轩槛，鱼龙幢戏，凡千五百余乘，帐盖三百余事。先是内出绣画等像二百余躯，金银像两躯，金缕绫罗幡五百口，宿于弘福寺；并法师西国所将经、像、舍利等。爰自弘福引出，安置于帐座及诸车上，处中而进。又于像前两边各丽大车，车上竖长竿悬幡，幡后布师子神王等为前引仪。

又庄宝车五十乘，坐诸大德；次京城僧众执持香华，呗赞随后；次文武百官各将侍卫部列陪从，太常九部乐挟两边，二县音声继其后。而幢幡钟鼓，訇磕缤纷，眩日浮空，震曜都邑，望之极目，不知其前后。皇太子遣率尉迟绍宗、副率王文训，领东宫兵千余人充手力，敕遣御史大夫李乾祐为大使，与武侯相知检校。帝将皇太子、后宫等，于安福门楼，执香炉目而送之，甚悦。衢路观者数亿万人。经像至寺门，敕赵公、英公、中书褚令执香炉引入，安置殿内，奏九部乐、破阵舞及诸戏于庭，讫而还。

壬申，将欲度僧。辛未，皇太子与仗卫出宿故宅。后日旦，从寺南列羽仪而来，至门，下乘步入，百僚陪从。礼佛已，引五十大德相见，陈造寺所为意，发言呜噎，酸感傍人，侍臣及僧无不哽泣，观烝烝之情，亦今之舜也。言讫，升殿东阁，令少詹事张行成宣恩宥降京畿见禁囚徒，然后剃发观斋，及赐王公已下束帛讫。屏人下阁礼佛，与妃等巡历廊宇。至法师房，制五言诗帖于户，曰：

停轩观福殿，游目眺皇畿。
法轮含日转，华盖接云飞。
翠烟香绮阁，丹霞光宝衣。
幡虹遥合彩，空外迥分晖。
萧然登十地，自得会三归。

观讫还宫。是时缁素欢欣，更相庆慰，莫不歌玄风重盛，遗法再隆，近古已来，未曾有也。其日，敕追法师还北阙。

二十三年夏四月，驾幸翠微宫，皇太子及法师并陪从。

既至，处分之外，唯谈玄论道，问因果报应，及西域先圣遗芳故迹，皆引经酬对。帝深信纳，数攘袂叹曰：："朕共师相逢晚，不得广兴佛事。"

帝发京时，虽少违和，而神威睿虑，无减平昔。至五月己巳，微加头痛，留法师宿宫中。庚午，帝崩于含风殿。时秘不言，还京发丧，殡太极殿。其日皇太子即皇帝位于梓宫之侧。逾年改元曰永徽。万方号恸，如丧考妣。

法师还慈恩寺。自此之后，专务翻译，无弃寸阴。每日自立程课，若昼日有事不充，必兼夜以续之。遇乙之后，方乃停笔。摄经已，复礼佛行道，至三更暂眠。五更复起，读诵梵本，朱点次第，拟明旦所翻。每日斋讫，黄昏二时，讲新经、论，及诸州听学僧等恒来决疑请义。既知上座之任，僧事复来咨禀。复有内使遣营功德，前后造一切经十部，夹纻宝装像二百余躯，亦令取法师进止。日夕已去，寺内弟子百余人咸请教诫，盈廊溢庑，皆酬答处分，无遗漏者。虽众务辐凑，而神气绰然，无所拥滞。犹与诸德说西方圣贤立义，诸部异端，及少年在此周游讲肆之事，高论剧谈，竟无疲怠，其精敏强力，过人若斯。复数有诸王卿相来过礼忏，逢迎诱导，并皆发心，莫不舍其骄华，肃敬称叹。

二年春正月壬寅，瀛州刺史贾敦颐、蒲州刺史李道裕、谷州刺史杜正伦、恒州刺史萧锐因朝集在京，公事之暇，相命参法师请受菩萨戒。法师即授之，并为广说菩萨行法，劝其事君尽忠，临下慈爱。群公欢喜，辞去。各舍净财，共修书遣使参法师，谢闻戒法。其书曰：

窃闻身非欲食，如来受纯陀之供；法无所求，净名遂善德之请。皆为显至理之常恒，示凡圣之无二。又是因机以接物，假相而弘道，为之者表重法之诚，受之者为行檀之福，岂曰心缘于彼此，情染于名利者哉！

仰惟宿殖德本，非于三四五佛；深达法相，善识十二部经。独悟真宗，远寻圣迹；游崛山之净土，浴恒水之清流。入深法界，求善知识；收至文于百代之后，探玄旨于千载之前。津梁庶品，不皦不昧；等施一切，无先无后。

颐等识蔽二空，业沦三界；犹蚕丝之自缠，如井轮之不息。虽复顺教生信，随缘悟解，顶礼归依，受持四句，隐身而为宴坐，厌苦而求常乐；而远滞无明，近昏至理；未能悟佛性之在身，知境界之唯识；心非去取，义涉有无；不能即八邪而入八正，行非道而通佛道。譬涉海而无津，犹面墙而靡见。昨因事隙，遂得参奉，曲蒙接引，授菩萨戒。施以未曾有法，发其无上道心。一念破于无边，四心尽于来际。菩提之种起自尘劳，火中生莲曷足为喻！始知如来之性即是世间，涅槃之际不殊生死，行于波若便是不行，得彼菩提翻为无得。忽以小机预闻大教，顶受寻思，无量欢喜。然夫檀义摄六，法施为优；尊位有三，师居其一。弘慈利物，虽类日月之无心；仰照怀恩，窃同葵藿之知感。大士闻法捐躯，非所企及；童子见佛奉土，辄敢庶几。谨送片物表心，具如别疏。所愿照其诚恳，生其福田，受兹微施，随意所与，使夫坠露添海，将渤澥而俱深；飞尘集岳，与须弥而永固。可久可大，幸甚幸甚！春寒尚重，愿动止休宜。谨遣白书，诸无所具。贾敦颐等和南。

其为朝贤所慕如是。

三年春三月，法师欲于寺端门之阳造石浮图，安置西域所将经、像，其意恐人代不常，经本散失，兼防火难。浮图量高三十丈，拟显大国之崇基，为释迦之故迹。将欲营筑，附表闻奏。敕使中书舍人李义府报法师云："所营塔功大，恐难卒成，宜用砖造。亦不愿师辛苦，今已敕大内、东宫、掖庭等七宫亡人衣物助师，足得成办。"

于是用砖，仍改就西院。其塔基面各一百四十尺，仿西域制度，不循此旧式也。塔有五级，并相轮、露盘，凡高一百八十尺。层层中心皆有舍利，或一千、二千，凡一万余粒。上层以石为室。南面有两碑，载二圣《三藏圣教序》、《记》，其书即尚书右仆射河南公褚遂良之笔也。

初基塔之日，三藏自述诚愿，略曰：

玄奘自惟薄祜，生不遇佛；复乘微善，预闻像教。傥生末法，何所归依？又庆少得出家，目睹灵相。幼知慕法，耳属遗筌。闻说菩萨所修行，思齐如不及；闻说如来所证法，仰止于身心。所以历尊师授，博问先达。信夫！汉梦西感，正教东传；道阻且长，未能委悉。故有专门竞执，多滞二常之宗；党同嫉异，致乖一味之旨。遂令后学相顾，靡识所归。是以面鹫山以增哀，慕常啼而假寐，潜祈灵佑，显恃国威，决志出一生之域，投身入万死之地。经是圣迹之处，备谒遗灵，但有弘法之人，遍寻正说。经一所，悲见于所未见；遇一字，庆闻于所未闻。故以身命余资，缮写遗阙。既遂诚愿，言归本朝，幸属休明，诏许翻译。

先皇道跨金轮，声振玉鼓；绍隆象季，允膺付属。又降发神衷，亲裁《三藏》之序，今上春宫讲道，复为《述圣》之记，可谓重光合璧，振彩联华，涣汗垂七耀之文，铿鍧韵九成之奏。自东都白马，西明草堂，传译之盛，讵可同日而言者也！但以生灵薄运，共失所天。唯恐三藏梵本，零落忽诸，二圣天文，寂寥无纪，所以敬崇此塔，拟安梵本，又树丰碑，镌斯《序》、《记》，庶使巍峨永劫，愿千佛同观；氤氲圣迹，与二仪齐固。

时三藏亲负篑畚，担运砖石，首尾二周，功业斯毕。

夏五月乙卯，中印度国摩诃菩提寺大德智光、慧天等致书于法师。光于大、小乘及彼外书、四《韦陀》、五明论等莫不洞达，即戒贤法师门人之上首，五印度学者咸共宗焉。慧天于小乘十八部该综明练，匠诱之德亦彼所推重，法师游西域日常共切磋。彼虽半教有功，然未措心于《方等》，为其执守偏见，法师恒诋诃。曲女城法集之时，又深折挫，彼亦愧伏。自别之后，钦伫不忘，乃使同寺沙门法长将书，并赍赞颂及氎两端，揄扬之心甚厚。其书曰：

微妙吉祥世尊金刚座所、摩诃菩提寺、诸多闻众所共围绕、上座慧天，致书摩诃支那国于无量经律论妙尽精微木叉阿遮利耶：敬问无量，少病少恼。我慧天苾刍，今造《佛大神变赞颂》，及诸经、论比量智等，今附苾刍法长，将往此无量多闻老大德阿遮利耶。智光亦同前致问，邬波索迦日授稽首和南。今共寄白氎一双，示不空心，路远莫怪其少，愿领。彼须经、论，录名附来，当为抄送木叉阿遮利耶，愿知。

其为远贤所慕如此。

五年春二月，法长辞还，又索报书。法师答，并信物。其书写文录奏，然后将付使人。其词曰：

大唐国苾刍玄奘，谨修书中印度摩揭陀国三藏智光法师座前：目一辞违，俄十余载。境域遐远，音徽莫闻。思恋之情，每增延结。彼苾刍法长至，蒙问，并承起居康豫，豁然目朗，若睹尊颜。踊跃之怀，笔墨难述。节候渐暖，不审信后何如？又往年使还，承正法藏大法师无常，奉问摧割，不能已已。呜呼！可谓苦海舟沈，天人眼灭；迁夺之痛，何期速欤！惟正法藏，植庆曩晨，树功长劫，故得挺冲和之茂质，标懿杰之宏才。嗣德圣天，继辉龙猛；重然智炬，再立法幢。扑炎火于邪山，塞洪流于倒海；策疲徒于宝所，示迷众于大方。荡荡焉！巍巍焉！实法门之栋干也。又如三乘半满之教，异道断常之书，莫不韫综胸怀，贯练心腑。文盘节而克畅，理隐昧而必彰，故使内外归依，为印度之宗袖。加以恂恂善诱，晓夜不疲，罇樽自盈，酌而不竭。玄奘昔因问道，得预参承，并荷指诲，虽曰庸愚，颇亦蓬依麻直。及辞还本邑，嘱累尤深，殷勤之言，今犹在耳。方冀保安眉寿，式赞玄风，岂谓一朝奄归万古，追惟永往，弥不可任。

伏惟法师，夙承雅训，早升堂室，攀恋之情，当难可处，奈何奈何？有为法尔，当可奈何？愿自裁抑。昔大觉潜晖，迦叶绍宣洪业；商那迁化，毱多阐其嘉猷。今法将归真，法师次任其事，唯愿清词妙辩，共四海而恒流；福智庄严，与五山而永久。

玄奘所将经、论，已翻《瑜伽师地论》等大小三十余部，其《俱舍》、《顺正理》，见译未周，今年必了。即日大唐天子圣躬万福，率土安宁，以轮王之慈，敷法王之化，所出经、论，并蒙神笔制序，令所司抄写，国内流行。爰至邻邦亦俱遵习。虽居像运之末，而法教光华，雍雍穆穆，亦不异室罗筏誓多林之化也，伏愿照知。又前渡信渡河失经一驮，今录名如后，有信请为附来。并有片物供养，愿垂纳受。路远不得多，莫嫌鲜薄。玄奘和南。

又答慧天法师，书曰：

大唐国苾刍玄奘谨致书摩诃菩提寺三藏慧天法师足下：乖别稍久，企仰唯深；音寄不通，莫慰倾渴。彼苾刍法长至，辱书敬承休豫，用增欣悦。又领细白氎两端、赞颂一夹，来意既厚，寡德愧无以当，悚息悚息！节气渐和，不知信后体何如也？想融心百家之论，栖虑九部之经。建正法幢，引归宗之客；击克胜鼓，挫鍱腹之宾。颉颃王侯之前，抑扬英俊之上，故多欢适也。玄奘庸弊，气力已衰，又加念德钦仁，唯丰劳积。昔因游方在彼，遇瞩光仪。曲女城会，又亲交论。当对诸王及百千徒众，定其深浅。此立大乘之旨，彼竖半教之宗，往复之间，词气不无高下。务存正理，靡护人情，以此辄生凌触。罢席之后，寻已豁然。今来使犹传法师，寄申谢悔，何怀固之甚也！法师学富词清，志坚操远。阿耨达水，无以比其波澜；净末尼珠，不足方其皦洁。后进仪表，属在高人。愿勖良规，阐扬正法。至如理周言极，无越大乘，意恨法师未为深信。所谓耽玩羊鹿，弃彼白牛；赏爱水精，舍颇胝宝。

明明大德，何此惑之滞欤？又坏器之身，浮促难守，宜早发大心，庄严正见。勿使临终，方致嗟悔。今使还国，谨此代诚，并附片物，盖欲示酬来意，未是尽其深心也。愿知。前还日渡信渡河，失经一驮，今录名如别，请为附来。余不能委述。苾刍玄奘谨呈。

卷第八

起永徽六年夏五月译《理门论》终显庆元年春三月百官谢示御制寺碑文

六年夏五月庚午，法师以正译之余，又译《理门论》。又先于弘福寺译《因明论》。此二论各一卷，大明立、破方轨、现、比量门，译寮僧伍竟造文疏。时译经僧栖玄将其论示尚药奉御吕才，才遂更张衢术，指其长短，作《因明注解立破义图》，序曰：

“盖闻一消一息，范围天地之仪；大哉！至哉！变通爻画之纪。理则未弘于方外，事乃犹拘于域中。推浑元而莫知，穷阴阳而不测。岂闻《象》、《系》之表，犹开八正之门；形器之先，更弘二智之教者也。故能运空有而双照，冥真俗而两夷；泛六度于爱河，驾三车于火宅。是知法王法力，超群生而自在；自觉觉人，摧众魔而独悟。业运将启，乃雷震而电耀；化缘斯极，亦火灭而薪尽。观其应迹，若有去来；察此真常，本无生住。但以宏济之道，有缘斯应；天祚明德，无远不臻。是以萌蔕畴昔，神光聊见于曩时；祥瑞有归，净土咸欢于兹日。

伏惟皇唐之有天下也，运金轮而临四有，握璇极而抚万方。耀慧日于六天，蒸法云于十地。西越流沙，遂荒妙乐之域；东渐于海，掩有欢喜之都。振声教于无边，通车书于有顶。遂使百亿须弥，既咸颁于望袟；三千法界，亦共沐于皇风。故令五方印度，改荒服于藁街；十八韦陀，译梵文于秘府。

乃有三藏玄奘法师者，所谓当今之能仁也。聪慧夙成，该览宏赡，德业纯粹，律业翘勤，实三宝之栋梁，四众之纲纪者也。每以释教东迁，为日已久，或恐邪正杂扰，水乳不分，若不稽实相于迦维，验真文于摩揭，何以成决定之藏，为毕竟之宗者乎？幸逢二仪交泰，四海无尘，遂得拂衣玄漠，振锡葱岭。不由味于蒟酱，直路夷通；岂藉佩于杜衡，遥途近易。于是穷河源于西域，涉恒水于东维；采贝叶于鹫山，窥金文于鹤树。所历诸国，百有余都；所获经、论，向七百部。并传以藩驲，聿归上京，因得面奉圣颜，对扬宗极。

此《因明论》者，即是三藏所获梵本之内之一部也。理则包括于三乘，事乃牢笼于百法；研机空有之际，发挥内外之宗。虽词约而理弘，实文微而义显。学之者当生不能窥其奥，游之者数载未足测其源。以其众妙之门，是以先事翻译。其有神泰法师、靖迈法师、明觉法师等，并以神机昭晰，志业兼该，精习群经，多所通悟，皆蒙别敕，追赴法筵，遂得函丈请益，执卷承旨。三藏即善宣法要，妙尽幽深，泰法师等，是以各录所闻，为之义疏。诠表既定，方拟流通，无缘之徒，多未闻见。

复有栖玄法师者，乃是才之幼少之旧也。昔栖遁于嵩岳，尝枉步于山门；既筮仕于上京，犹曲睠于穷巷。自蒙修摄，三十余年，忉怛之诚，二难俱尽。然法师节操精洁，戒行冰霜，学既照达于一乘，身乃拘局于《十诵》。才既睹其清苦，时以开遮折之。但以内外不同，行已各异，言戏之间，是非蜂起。师乃从容谓才曰：'檀越复研味于六经，探赜于百氏，推阴阳之愆伏，察律吕之忽微。又闻生平未见《太玄》，诏问须臾即解，由来不窥象戏，试造旬日复成。以此有限之心，逢事即欲穿凿，但以佛法玄妙，量谓未与彼同。虽复强学推寻，恐非措心之所。何因今将内论，翻用见讥者乎？'法师后逢《因明》创行，义趣幽隐，是以先写一通，故将见遗。仍附书云：'此论极难，深究玄妙，比有聪明博识，听之多不能解，今若复能通之，可谓内外俱悉矣。'

其论既近至中夏，才实未之前闻，耻于被试不知，为复强加披阅。于是，依极成而探深义，凭比量而求微旨，反复再三，薄识宗趣。后复借得诸法师等三家义疏，更加究习。然以诸法师等，虽复序致泉富，文理会通，既以执见参差，所说自相矛盾。义既同禀三藏，岂合更开二门，但由衅发萧墙，故容外侮窥测。然佛以一音演说，亦许随类各解，何必独简白衣，不为众生之例？

才以公务之余，辄为斯注，至于三法师等所说，善者因而成之，其有疑者，立而破之，分为上、中、下三卷，号曰《立破注解》。其间墨书者，即是论之本文；朱书注者，以存师等旧说；其下墨书注者，是才今之新撰，用决师等前义，凡有四十余条；自郐已下，犹未具录。至于文理隐伏，稍难见者，仍画为‘义图’，共相比校，仍更别撰一方丈大图，独存才之近注。论既外无人解，无处道听途说。若言生而知之，固非才之望也。然以学无再请，尚曰‘传灯’；闻一知十，方称‘殆庶’。况乎生平不见，率尔辄事含毫；今既不由师资，注解能无纰紊？

窃闻雪山夜叉，说生灭法；丘井野兽，叹未曾有。苟令所言合理，尚得天仙归敬。才之所注，庶几于兹。法师等若能忘狐鬼之微陋，思句味之可尊，择善而从，不简真俗，此则如来之道，不坠于地。弘之者众，何常之有？必以心未忘于人我，义不察于是非，才亦扣其两端，犹拟质之三藏。”

秋七月己巳，译经沙门慧立闻而愍之，因致书于左仆射燕国于公，论其利害，曰：

立闻诸佛之立教也，文言奥远，旨义幽深；等圆穹之廓寥，类沧波之浩汗。谈真如之性相，居十地而尚迷；说小草之因缘，处无生其犹昧。况有萦缠八邪之网，沉沦四倒之流，而欲窥究宗因，辩彰其同异者，无乃妄哉！

窃见大慈恩寺翻译法师，慧基早树，智力夙成；行洁圭璋，操逾松杞；遂能躬游圣域，询禀微言。总三藏于胸怀，包四含于掌握；嗣清徽于曩哲，扇遗范于当今，实季俗之舟航，信缁林之龟镜者也。所翻圣教已三百余轴，中有小论，题曰《因明》，诠论难之旨归，序折邪之轨式，虽未为玄门之要妙，然亦非造次之所知也。

近闻尚药吕奉御以常人之资，窃众师之说，造《因明图》，释宗因义。不能精悟，好起异端；苟觅声誉，妄为穿凿。诽众德之正说，任我慢之褊心；媒炫公卿之前，嚣喧闾巷之侧，不惭颜厚，靡倦神劳；颇历炎凉，情犹未已。然奉御于俗事少闲，遂谓真宗可了。何异鼷鼠见釜窖之堪陟，乃言昆、阆之非难；蛛蝥睹棘林之易罗，亦谓扶桑之可网。不量涯分，何殊此焉！抑又闻之，大音希声，大辩若讷。所以净名会理，杜口毗城；尼父德高，恂恂乡党。又叔度汪洋之称，元礼摸揩之誉，亦未闻夸竞自媒而获搢绅之推仰也云。

立致书，其事遂寝。

冬十月丁酉，太常博士柳宣闻其事寝，乃作《归敬书偈》以檄译经僧众曰：

稽首诸佛，愿护神威；当陈诚请，罔或尤讥。

沉晦未悟，圆觉所归；久沦爱海，舟楫攸稀。

异执乖竞，和合是依；玄离取有，理绝过违。

慢乖八正，戏入百非；取舍同辩，染净混微。

简金去砾，琢玉禅辉；能仁普鉴，凝虑研几。

契诚大道，孰敢毁诽；谔谔崇德，唯唯浸衰。

惟愿留听，庶有发挥；望矜悃悃，垂诲斐斐。

《归敬》曰：

昔能仁示现王宫，假殁双树；微言既畅，至理亦弘。刹土蒙摄受之恩，怀生沾昭苏之惠。自佛树西荫，塔影东临，汉、魏实为滥觞，符、姚盛其风彩。自是名僧间出，贤达连镳；慧日长悬，法轮恒驭。开凿之功，始自腾、显；弘阐之力，仍资什、安。别有单开远适罗浮，图澄近现赵、魏；麤言圭角，未可缕陈。莫不谈空有于一乘，论苦集于四谛。假铨明有，终未离于有为；息言明道，方契证于凝寂。犹执玄以求玄，是玄非玄；理因玄以忘玄，玄或是玄。义虽冥会幽涂，事理绝于言象，然摄生归寂，终藉筌蹄。亦既立言，是非锋起；如彼战争，干戈竞发；负者屏气，胜者先鸣。故尚降魔，制诸外道，自非辩才无畏，答难有方，则物辈喧张，我等耻辱。是故专心适道，一意总持，建立法幢，祇植法鼓。旗鼓既正，则敌者残摧；法轮既转，能威不伏。若使望风旗靡，对难含胶，而能阐弘三宝，无有是处。

尚药吕奉御入空有之门，驰正见之路；闻持拟于昔贤，洞微侔于往哲。其词辩，其义明，其德真，其行著。已沐八解之流，又悟七觉之分。影响成教，若净名之诣庵园；闻道必求，犹波仑之归无竭。意在弘宣佛教，立破《因明》之疏。若其是也，必须然其所长；如其非也，理合指其所短。今见僧徒云集，并是采石他山。朝野俱闻吕君请益，莫不侧听泻瓶，皆望荡涤掉悔之源，销屏疑忿之聚。

有太史令李淳风者，闻而进曰：

‘仆心怀正路，行属归依，以实际为大觉玄躯，无为是调御法体。然皎日丽天，实助上玄运用；贤僧阐法，实裨天师妙道。是所信受，是所安心。但不敢以黄叶为金，山鸡成凤，

南郭滥吹，淄渑混流耳。或有异议，岂仆心哉！岂仆心哉！’

然鹤林已后，岁将二千，正法既萎，末法初践，玄理郁而不彰，觉道寖将湮落。玄奘法师头陀法界，远达迦维，目击道树金流，仍睹七处八会，毗城、鹫岭，身入彼邦，娑罗宝阶仍验虚实。至于历览王舍、檀特、恒河，如斯等辈，未易具言也。加之西域名僧，莫不面论般若；东国疑义，悉皆质之彼师。毗尼之藏，既奉持而不舍；毗昙明义，亦洞观而为常。苏妒路既得之于声明，耨多罗亦剖断于疑滞。法无大小，莫不韫之胸怀；理无深浅，悉能决之敏虑。故三藏之名，振旦之所推定；摩诃之号，乃罗卫之所共称。名实之际，何可称道？

然吕君学识该博，义理精通，言行枢机，是所详悉。至于陀罗佛法，禀自生知；无碍辩才，宁由伏习。但以《因明》义隐，所说不同，触象各得其形，共器饭有异色。吕君既已执情，道俗企望指定。秋霜已降，侧听钟鸣；法云既敷，雷震希发。但龙象蹴蹋，非驴所堪，缁服壶奥，白衣不践。脱如龙种抗说，无垢释疑，则苾刍悉昙，亦优婆能尽。辄附微志，请不为烦。若有滞疑，望咨三藏裁决。以所承禀，传示四众，则正道克昌，覆障永绝。绍隆三宝，其在兹乎！’过此已往，非复所悉。弟子柳宣白。”

庚子，译经僧明濬答柳博士宣，以《还述颂》言其得失曰：

于赫大圣，种觉圆明；无幽不察，如响酬声。

弗资延庆，孰语归诚；良导可仰，实引迷生。

百川邪浪，一味吞并；物有取舍，正匪亏盈。

八邪驰锐，四句争名；饰非滥是，抑重为轻。

照日冰散，投珠水清；显允上德，体道居贞。

纵加誉毁，未动遗荣；昂昂令哲，郁郁含情。

俟诸达观，定此权衡；聊申悱悱，用简英英。

《还述》曰：

顷于望表预瞻《归敬》之词，览其雄文，焕乎何伟丽也！详其雅致，诚哉！岂不然欤！悲夫！爱海滔天，邪山概日。封人我者，颠坠其何已？恃慢结者，沉沦而不穷。故六十二见争翳荟而自处，九十五道竞扶伏以忘归。如来以本愿大悲，亡缘俯应，内圆四智，外显六通，运十力以伏天魔，飞七辩而摧外道。竭兹爱海，济稟识于三空；殄彼邪山，驱肖形于八正。指因示果，返本还源。大矣哉！悲智妙用，无得而言焉。昔道树登庸，被声教于百亿；双林寝迹，振遗烈于三千。自佛日西倾，余光东照；周感夜明之瑞，汉通宵梦之征。腾、兰爇慧炬于前，澄、什嗣传灯于后。其于译经弘法，神异济时，高论摧邪，安禅肃物。缉颓网者接武，维绝纽者肩随，莫不夷夏钦风，幽明翼化，联华靡替。可略而详。

惟今三藏法师，蕴灵秀出，含章而体一味，瓶泻以瞻五乘。悲去圣之逾远，悯来教之多阙。缅思圆义，许道以身；心口自谋，形影相吊。振衣擎锡，讨本寻源；出玉关而远游，指金河而一息。稽疑梵宇，探幽洞微；旋化神州，扬真殄谬。遗诠阙典，大备兹辰；方等圆宗，弥广前烈。所明胜义，妙绝环中之中；真性真空，极逾方外之外。以有取也，有取丧其真；就无求之，无求蠹其实。拂二边之迹，忘中道之相，则累遣未易洎其深，重空何以臻其极？要矣！妙矣！至哉！大哉！契之于心，然后以之为法。在心为法，形言为教；法有自相、共相，教乃遮诠、表诠。粹旨冲宗，岂造次所能覼缕。法师凝神役智，详本正末，缉熙玄籍，大启幽关。秘希声，应扣击之大小；廓义海，纳朝宗之巨细。于是殊方硕德，异域高僧，伏膺问道，蓄疑请益。固已饮河满腹，莫测其浅深；聆音骇听，孰知其远近。至于因明小道，现比盖微，斯乃指初学之方隅，举立论之幖帜，至若灵枢秘键，妙本成功，备诸奥册，非此所云也。

而吕奉御以风神爽拔，早擅多能，器宇该通，夙彰博物。戈猎开坟之典，钩深坏壁之书，触类而长，穷诸数术。振风飙于辩囿，摛光华于翰林，骧首云中，先鸣日下。五行资其笔削，六位伫其高谈，一览《太玄》，应问便释；再寻象戏，立试即成。实晋代茂先、汉朝曼倩，方今蔑如也。既而翱翔群略，绰有余功，而散慕大乘，夙敦诚信，比因友生戏尔，忽复属想《因明》，不以师资，率己穿凿，比决诸疏，指斥求非。諠议于朝廷，形言于造次。考其志也，固已难加；核其知也，诚为可惑。

此论以一卷成部，五纸成卷，研机三疏，向已一周。举非四十，自无一是。自既无是而能言是；疏本无非而能言非。言非不非，言是不是。言是不是，是而恒非；言非不非，非而恒是。非非恒是，不为是所是；是是恒非，不为非所非。以兹贬失，致或病诸。且据生因了因，执一体而亡二义；能了所了，封一名而惑二体。又以宗依宗体，留依去体以为宗；喻体喻依，去体留依而为喻。缘斯两系，妄起多疑；迷一极成，谬生七难。但以钻穷二论，师已一心，滞文句于上下，误字音于平去。复以“数论”为“声论”，举“生城”为“灭城”。岂唯差离合之宗因，盖亦违倒顺之前后。又探鄙俚讹韵，以拟梵本啭音，虽复广援七种，而只当彼一啭。然非彼七所目，乃是第八呼声。舛杂乖讹，何从而至？

又案：《胜论》立常极微，数乃无穷，体唯极小；后渐和合，生诸子微。数则倍减于常微，体又倍增于父母。迄乎终已，体遍大千；究其所穷，数唯是一。吕公所引《易·系辞》云：‘太极生两仪，两仪生四象，四象生八卦，八卦生万物，’云此与彼，言异义同。今案太极无形，肇生有象；元资一气，终成万物。岂得以多生一，而例一生多？引类欲显博闻，义乖复何所托？设引大例，生义似同，若释同于邪见，深累如何自免？岂得苟要时誉，混正同邪，非身之雠，奚至于此！凡所纰紊，胡可胜言！特由率己，致斯狼狈。根既不正，枝叶自倾，逐误生疑，随疑设难，曲形直影，其可得乎？试举二三，冀详大意，深疵繁绪，委答如别。寻夫吕公达鉴，岂孟浪而至此哉！示显真俗，云泥难易，楚越因彰。佛教弘远，正法凝深，譬洪炉非掬雪所投，渤澥岂胶舟能越也？

太史令李君者，灵府沈秘，襟期邈远；专精九数，综涉六爻。博考坟图，瞻观云物；鄙卫宏之失度，陋裨灶之未工。神无滞用，望实斯在。既属吕公余论，复致问言。以实际为大觉玄躯，无为是调御法体。此乃信熏修容有分证，禀自然终不可成。良恐言似而意违，词近而旨远。天师妙道，幸以再思。且寇氏天师，崔君特荐；共贻伊咎，夫复何言？虽谓不混于淄、渑，盖已自滥金鍮耳。

惟公逸宇寥廓，学殚坟索，庇身以仁义，应物以枢机。肃肃焉！汪汪焉！擢劲节以干云，淡清润而镇地。腾芳文苑，职处儒林，捃摭九畴之宗，研详二戴之说。至于《经礼》三百，《曲礼》三千，莫不义符指掌，事如俯拾。樽俎咸推其准的，法度必待其雌黄，遂令《相鼠》之诗绝闻于野，《鱼丽》之咏盈耳于朝。惟名与实尽善尽美。而诚敬之重，禀自夙成，弘护之心，实惟素蓄。属斯諠议，同耻疚怀。故能投刺含胶，允光大义。非夫才兼内外，照实邻几，岂能激扬清浊，济俗匡真者耶！

昔什公门下，服道者三千；今此会中，同德者如市。贫道猥以庸陋，叨厕末筵，虽庆朝闻，终惭夕惕。详以造疏三德，并是贯达五乘，墙仞罕窥，词峰难仰。既属商羊鼓舞，而霈泽必沾；疾雷迅发，恐无暇掩耳。佥议，古人曰：‘一枝可以戢羽，何繁乎邓林；潢洿足以沉鳞，岂俟于沧海。’故不以愚愞，垂逼课虚。辞弗获免，粗陈梗概。虽文不足取，而义或可观。顾己庸疏，弥增悚恧，指述还答，余无所申。释明濬白。

癸卯，宣得书，又激吕奉御因奏其事，敕遣群公学士等往慈恩寺，请三藏与吕公对定。吕公词屈，谢而退焉。

显庆元年春正月景寅，皇太子忠自以非嫡，不敢久处元良，乃慕太伯之规，陈表累让。大帝从之，封忠为梁王，赐物一万段、甲第一区，即以其月册代王弘为皇太子。

戊子，就大慈恩寺为皇太子设五千僧斋，人施布帛三段，敕遣朝臣行香。时黄门侍郎薛元超、中书侍郎李义府因参法师，遂问曰："翻经固法门之美，未审更有何事可以光扬？又不知古来翻译仪式如何？"

法师报曰："法藏冲奥，通演实难，然则内阐住持由乎释种，外护建立属在帝王。所以泛海之舟能驰千里，依松之葛遂竦万寻，附托胜缘，方能广益。今汉、魏遥远，未可详论。且陈符、姚已来翻宣经、论。除僧之外，君臣赞助者，符坚时昙摩难提译经，黄门侍郎赵政执笔；姚兴时鸠摩罗什译经，姚王及安城侯姚嵩执笔；后魏菩提留支译经，侍中崔光执笔及制经序。齐、梁、周、隋皆如是。贞观初波颇罗那译经，敕左仆射房玄龄、赵郡王李孝恭、太子詹事杜正伦、太府卿萧璟等监阅详缉。今独无此。又慈恩寺，圣上为文德圣皇后营建，壮丽轮奂，今古莫俦，未得建碑传芳示后，显扬之极莫过于此。公等能为致言，则斯美可至。"

二公许诺而去。明日因朝，遂为法师陈奏，天皇皆可之。

壬辰，光禄大夫中书令兼检校太子詹事监修国史柱国固安县开国公崔敦礼宣敕曰：

"大慈恩寺僧玄奘所翻经、论，既新翻译，文义须精，宜令太子太傅尚书左仆射燕国公于志宁、中书令兼检校吏部尚书南阳县开国男来济、礼部尚书高阳县开国男许敬宗、守黄门侍郎兼检校太子左庶子汾阴县开国男薛元超、守中书侍郎兼检校右庶子广平县开国男李义府、中书侍郎杜正伦等，时为看阅，有不稳便处，即随事润色。若须学士，任量追三两人。"

罢朝后，敕遣内给事王君德来报法师云："师须官人助翻经者，已处分于志宁等令往，其碑文朕望自作，不知称师意不？且令相报。”

法师既奉纶旨，允慰宿心，当对使人悲喜，不觉泪流襟袖。翌日，法师自率徒众等诣朝堂奉表陈谢。(表文失)

二月，有尼宝乘者，高祖神尧皇帝之婕妤，隋襄州总管临河公薛道衡之女也。德芬彤管，美擅椒闱。父既学业见称，女亦不亏家训。妙通经史，兼善文才。大帝幼时，从其受学，嗣位之后，以师傅旧恩，封河东郡夫人，礼敬甚重。夫人情慕出家，帝从其志，为禁中别造鹤林寺而处之，并建碑述德。又度侍者数十人，并四事公给，将进具戒。至二月十日，敕迎法师并将大德九人，各一侍者，赴鹤林寺为河东郡夫人薛尼受戒。又敕庄校宝车十乘、音声车十乘，待于景曜门内。先将马就寺接入城门已，方乃登车发引，大德居前，音声从后。是时春之仲月，景物妍华，柳翠桃红，松青雾碧，锦轩紫盖，交映其间，飘飘然犹给园之众适王城矣。既到，安置别馆，设坛席，为宝乘等五十余人受戒。唯法师一人为阇梨，诸德为证而已。三日方了。受戒已，复命巧工吴智敏图十师形，留之供养。鹤林寺侧先有德业寺，尼众数百人，又奏请法师受菩萨戒，于是复往德业寺，事讫辞还。嚫施隆重，敕遣内给事王君德将手力执华盖引送，衢路观者极生善焉。鹤林后改为隆国寺焉。

无几，御制碑文成，敕遣太尉公长孙无忌，以碑宣示群公。其词曰：

朕闻乾坤缔构之初，品物权舆之始，莫不载形后土，藉覆穹苍。然则二曜辉天，靡测盈虚之象；四溟纪地，岂究波澜之极。况乎法门冲寂，现生不灭之前；圣教牢笼，示有无形之外。故以道光尘劫，化洽含灵者矣。缅惟王宫发迹，莲披起步之华；神沼腾光，树曲空低之干。演德音于鹿苑，会多士于龙宫；福已罪之群生，兴将灭之人代。能使下愚挹道，骨碎寒林之野；上哲钦风，魂沈雪山之偈。丝流法雨，清火宅而辞炎；轮升慧日，皎重昏而归昼。朕逖览缃史，详观道艺，福崇永劫者，其唯释教欤！

文德皇太后，凭柯琼树，疏派璇源，德照涂山，道光妫汭。流芬彤管，彰懿则于八纮；垂训紫宫，扇徽猷于万古。遽而阴精掩月，永戢贞辉；坤维绝纽，长沦茂迹。抚奁镜而增感，望陟屺而何追？昔仲由兴叹于千钟，虞丘致哀于三失。朕之罔极，实有切于终身，故载怀兴葺，创兹金地。却背邠郊，点千庄之树锦；前临终岳，吐百仞之峰莲。左面八川，水皎池而分镜；右邻九达，羽飞盖而连云。抑天府之奥区，信上京之胜地。示其雕轩架迥，绮阁凌虚。丹空晓乌，焕日宫而泛彩；素天初兔，鉴月殿而澄辉。熏径秋兰，疏庭佩紫；芳岩冬桂，密户丛丹。灯皎繁华，焰转烟心之鹤；幡标迥刹，彩萦天外之虹。飞陛参差，含文露而栖玉；轻帘舒卷，网靥宿而编珠。霞班低岫之红，池泛漠烟之翠；鸣佩与宵钟合韵，和风共晨梵分音。岂直香积天宫，远惭轮奂；阆风仙阙，遥愧雕华而已哉！

有玄奘法师者，实真如之冠冕也。器宇凝邃，若清风之肃长松；缛思繁蔚，如绮霞之辉迥汉。腾今照古之智，挺自生知；蕴寂怀真之诚，发乎龆龀。孤标一代，迈生、远以照前；迥秀千龄，架澄、什而光后。以为淳风替古，浇俗移今；悲巨夜之长昏，痛微言之永翳。遂乃投迹异域，广餐秘教；乘杯云汉之外，振锡烟霞之表。滔天巨海，侵惊浪而羁游；亘地严霜，犯凄氛而独逝。平郊散绪，衣单雪岭之风；旷野低轮，肌弊流沙之日。遐征月路，影对宵而暂双；远迈危峰，形临朝而永只。

研穷智境，探赜至真；心罄玄津，研几秘术。通昔贤之所不逮，悟先典之所未闻。遂得金牒东流，续将断之教；宝偈西徙，补已缺之文。于时眷彼灵基，栖心此地。弘宣奥旨，叶方翠于祇林；远辟幽关，波再清于定水。

朕所以虔诚八正，肃志双林，将延景福，式资冥助。奉愿皇太后逍遥六度，神游丹阙之前；偃息四禅，魂升紫极之境。悲夫！玉烛易往，促四序于炎凉；金箭难留，驰六龙于晷漏。恐波迁树在，夷溟海于桑田；地是势非，沦高峰为幽谷，于是敬刊贞石，式旌真境。

其铭曰：

三光照象，万品流形；人涂超忽，时代虚盈。

淳风久谢，浇俗潜生；爱波滔识，业雾昏情。

猗欤调御，迦维腾迹；妙道乘幽，玄源控寂。

鹫峰遐峙，龙宫广辟；慧日舒光，慈云吐液。

眷言圣教，载想德音；义崇往劫，道冠来今。

腾神九域，晦迹双林；汉梦如在，周星遽沈。

悲缠奁镜，哀深栋宇；濯龙潜润，椒风韬绪。

霜露朝侵，风枝夕举；云车一驾，悠哉万古。

乃兴轮奂，寔构雕华；紫栋留月，红梁藻霞。

云窗散叶，风沼翻华；盖低凤偃，桥侧虹斜。

爰有慧命，英器虚冲；孤标千载，独步三空。

给园味道，雪岭餐风；智灯再朗，真筌重崇。

四运流速，六龙驰骛；巨夜销氛，幽关启曙。

茂德垂范，微尘表誉；勒美披文，遐年永着。

三月（二十三日）庚申，群公等奉圣制，咸诣朝堂上表陈谢曰：

跪发天华，观河宗之奇宝；虔开秘篆，聆《云》、《英》之丽曲。包万叶之鸿规，笼千祀之殊观；相趋庆抃，莫知所限。

窃以慧日西照，朗巨夜而开冥；法流东徙，洽陈荄而挺秀。无方之化不一，应物之理同归；历代迨兹，咸崇斯典。伏惟陛下垂衣截海，作镜中区。锡类之道弥光，出要之津尤重。开给园于胜境，延称首以闲居。地穷轮奂，人标龙象。重兹濬发冲旨，爰制丰碑。妙思难涯，玄襟独王；义超系表，理邃环中。臣等夙蔽真宗，幸窥天藻。以坳堂之量，揣灵鳌之峻壑；蜉蝣之情，议仙骥之遐寿。式歌且舞，咸诵在心，循览周遑，不胜欣跃。

卷第九

起显庆元年三月谢慈恩寺碑成终二年十一月法师谢敕问病表

显庆元年春三月癸亥，御制大慈恩寺碑文讫。时礼部尚书许敬宗遣使送碑文与法师，鸿胪寺又有符下寺。甲子，法师率寺众诣阙陈谢，曰：

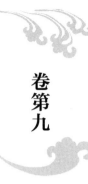

沙门玄奘言：被鸿胪寺符，伏奉敕旨，亲纡圣笔，为大慈恩寺所制碑文已成。睿泽傍临，宸词曲照；玄门益峻，梵侣增荣。局厚地而怀惭，负层穹而寡力。玄奘闻造化之功，既播物而成教；圣人之道，亦因辞以见情。然则画卦垂文，空谈于形器；设爻分象，未逾于寰域。羲皇之德，尚见称于前古；姬后之风，亦独高于后代。岂若开物成务，阐八政以摛章；诠道立言，证三明而导俗。理穷天地之表，情该日月之外，较其优劣，斯为盛矣。

伏惟皇帝陛下金轮在运，玉历乘时；化溢四洲，仁覃九有。道包将圣，功茂乃神，纵多能于生知，资率由于天至。始悲奁镜，即创招提；俄树胜幢，更敷文律。若乃天华颖发，睿藻波腾。吞笔海而孕龙宫，掩词林而包鹤树。内该八藏，外聂六经，奥而能典，宏而且密。固使给园遗迹，托宝思而弥高；奈苑余芬，假琼章而不昧。岂直抑扬梦境，照晢迷涂，谅以镕范四天，牢笼三界者矣！

玄奘言行无取，猥预缁徒；亟叨恩顾，每谓多幸。重忝曲城之造，欣逢像法之盛，且惭且跃，实用交怀。无任竦戴之诚，谨诣朝堂，奉表陈谢。

乙丑，法师又惟主上文明天纵，圣而多能，非直文丽魏君，亦乃书迈汉主。法师以见碑是圣文，其书亦望神笔，因诣阙请皇帝自书。表曰：

沙门玄奘等言：窃以应物垂象，神用溥该；随时设教，圣功毕尽。是知日月双朗，始极经天之运；卉木俱秀，方穷丽地之德。伏惟皇帝陛下，智周万物，仁沾三界；既隆景化，复阐玄风。鄙姬穆之好道，空赏瑶池之咏；蔑汉明之崇法，徒开白马之祠。遂乃俯降天文，远扬幽旨；用雕丰琬，长垂茂则。同《六英》之发音，若五纬之摛曜；敷至怀而感俗，弘大誓以匡时。岂独幽赞真如，显扬玄赜者也！虽玉藻斯畅，翠版将刊，而银钩未书，丹字犹韫。

然则夔乐已箕，匪里曲之堪预；龙乡既昼，何爝火之能明？非夫牙、旷抚律，羲和总驭，焉得扬法鼓之大音，褌慧日之冲彩。

设二千僧斋，陈九部乐等于佛殿前，日晚方散。至十六日，法师又与徒众诣朝堂陈谢碑至寺。表曰：

沙门玄奘等言：今月十四日，伏奉敕旨，送御书大慈恩寺碑。并设九部乐供养。尧日分照，先增慧炬之晖；舜海通波，更足法流之广。丰碣岩峙，天文景烛；状彩霞之映灵山，疑缛宿之临仙峤。凡在缁素，电激云奔，瞻奉惊跃，得未曾有。窃以八卦垂文，六爻发《系》，观鸟制法，泣麟敷典；圣人能事，毕见于兹。将以轨物垂范，随时立训；陶铸生灵，抑扬风烈。然则秦皇刻石，独昭美于封禅；魏后刊碑，徒纪功于《大飨》。犹称题目，高视百王。岂若亲纡睿藻，俯开仙翰，金奏发韶，银钩绚迹。探龙宫而架三玄，轶凤篆而穷八体；扬春波而骋思，滴秋露以标奇。弘一乘之妙理，赞六度之幽赜；化总三千之域，声腾百亿之外。奈苑微言，假天词而更显；竹林开士，托神笔而弥尊。因使梵志归心，截疑网而祇训；波旬革虑，偃邪山而徇道。岂止尘门之士，始悟迷方；滞梦之宾，行超苦际。像教东渐，年垂六百，弘阐之盛，未若于兹。至如汉明通感，尚咨谋于傅毅；吴主归宗，犹考疑于阚泽。自斯已降，无足称者。随缘化物，独推昭运；为善必应，克峻昌基。若金轮之王，神功不测；同宝冠之帝，休祚方永。

玄奘等谬忝朝恩，幸登玄肆，属慈云重布，法鼓再扬。三明之化既隆，八正之门长辟，而顾非贞恳，虚蒙奖导。仰层旻而荷泽，俯浚谷以怀惭。无任竦戴之诚，谨诣阙陈谢以闻。

碑至，有司于佛殿前东北角别造碑屋安之。其舍复拱重栌，云楣绮栋，金华下照，宝铎上晖，仙掌露盘，一同灵塔。

帝善楷、隶、草、行、尤精飞白。其碑作行书，又用飞白势作‘显庆元年’四字，并穷神妙。观者日数千人。文武三品以上表乞模打，许之。自结绳息用，文字代兴，二篆形殊，楷、草势异，悬针垂露，云气偃波，铭石章程，八分行隶，古人互有短长，不能兼美。至如汉元称善史书，魏武工于草、行；钟繇闲于三体，王仲妙于八分；刘邵、张弘发誉于飞白，伯英、子玉流名于“草圣”。唯中郎、右军稍兼众美，亦不能尽也。故韦文休见二王书曰：“二王自可称能，未是知书也。”若其天锋秀拔，颓郁遒健，该古贤之众体，尽先哲之多能，为毫翰之阳春，文字之寡和者，信归之于我皇矣。

法师少因听习，及往西方，涉凌山、雪岭，遂得冷病，发即封心，屡经困苦。数年已来，凭药防御得定。今夏五月，因热追凉，遂动旧疾，几将不济。道俗忧惧，中书闻奏，敕遣供奉上医尚药奉御蒋孝璋、针医上官琮专看，所须药皆令内送。北门使者日有数般遣伺气候，递报消息。乃至眠寝处所，皆遣内局上手安置。其珍惜如是，虽慈父之于一子，所不过也。孝璋等给侍医药，昼夜不离，经五日方损，内外情安。

法师既荷圣恩，翌日进表谢曰：

沙门玄奘言：玄奘拙自营卫，冷疹增动，几至绵笃，殆辞昭运。天恩矜悯，降以良医，针药才加，即蒙瘳愈。驻颓龄于欲尽，反营魄于将消，重睹昌时，复遵明导，岂止膏肓永绝，腠理恒调而已。顾循庸菲，屡荷殊泽，施厚命轻，罔知输报。唯凭慧力，庶酬冥祉。玄奘犹自虚惙，未堪诣阙陈谢，无任悚戴之至，谨遣弟子大乘光先奉表以闻。

帝览表，遣给事王君德慰问法师曰：“既初服药后，气力固当虚劣，请法师善自摄卫，未宜即用心力。”法师又蒙圣问，不胜喜惧之至，又表谢曰：

沙门玄奘言：玄奘业累所婴，致招疾苦，呼吸之顷，几隔明时。忽蒙皇帝、皇后降慈悲之念，垂性命之忧。天使频临，有逾十慰；神药俯救，若遇一丸。饮沐圣慈，已祛沉痛；蒙荷医疗，遂得痊除。岂期已逝之魂，见招于上帝；将夭之寿，重禀于洪炉。退省庸微，何以当此！抚膺愧越，言不足宣。荷殊泽而讵胜，粉微躯而靡谢。方冀勖兹礼诵，罄此身心，以答不次之恩，少塞无穷之责。无任感戴之极，谨附表谢闻。喜惧兼并，罔知攸措；尘黩听览，伏增惶悚。

贞观十一年中，有敕曰：“老子是朕祖宗，名位称号宜在佛先。”时普光寺大德法常、总持寺大德普应等数百人于朝堂陈诤，未蒙改正。法师还国来已频内奏，许有商量，未果而文帝升遐。永徽六年，有敕：“道士、僧等犯罪，情难知者，可同俗法推勘。”边远官人不闲敕意，事无大小动行枷杖，亏辱为甚。法师每忧之，因疾委顿，虑更不见天颜，乃附人陈前二事于国非便：“玄奘命垂日夕，恐不获后言，谨附启闻，伏枕惶惧。”

敕遣报云：“所陈之事闻之。但佛道名位，先朝处分，事须平章。其同俗敕，即遣停废。师宜安意，强进汤药。”

至二十三日，降敕曰：

“道教清虚，释典微妙，庶物藉其津梁，三界之所遵仰。比为法末人浇，多违制律，且权依俗法，以申惩诫，冀在止恶劝善，非是以人轻法。但出家人等具有制条，更别推科，恐为劳扰。前令道士、女道士、僧、尼有犯依俗法者，宜停。必有违犯，宜依条制。”

法师既荷兹圣泽，奉表诣阙陈谢曰：

沙门玄奘言：伏见敕旨，僧、尼等有过，停依俗法之条，还依旧格。非分之泽，忽委缁徒；不訾之恩，复沾玄肆。晞旸沐道，实用光华；跼地循躬，唯增震惕。窃以法王既没，像化空传；宗绍之规，寄诸明后。伏惟皇帝陛下，宝图御极，金轮乘正；眷兹释教，载怀宣阐。以为落饰玄门，外异流俗，虽情牵五浊，律行多亏，而体被三衣，福田斯在。削玉条之密网，布以宽仁；信金口之直词，允兹回向。斯固天祇载悦，应之以休征；岂止梵侣怀恩，加之以贞确。若有背兹宽贷，自贻伊咎，则违大师之严旨，亏圣主之深慈。凡在明灵，自宜谴谪。岂待平章之律，方科奸妄之罪？玄奘庸昧，猥厕法流，每忝鸿恩，忌怀惭惕，重祇殊奖，弥复兢惶。但以近婴疾疹，不获随例诣阙。无任悚戴之至，谨遣弟子大乘光先奉表陈谢以闻。

自是僧徒得安禅诵矣。法师悲喜交集，不觉泪沾襟袖，不胜抃跃之至，又重进表谢曰：

沙门玄奘言：伏奉恩敕，除僧等依俗法推勘条章。喜戴之心，莫知准譬。窃寻正法隆替，随君上所抑扬；彝伦厚薄，俪玄风以兴缺。自圣运在璇，明皇执粹；甄崇道艺，区别玄儒。开不二之键，广唯一之辙；写龙宫于蓬阁，接鹫壤于神皋。俾夫钟梵之声，洋溢区宇；福善之业，濯沐黎氓。寔法门之嘉会，率土之幸甚。顷为僧徒不整，诲驭乖方，致使内亏佛教，外犯王法；一人获罪，举众蒙尘。遂触天威，令依俗法；所期清肃，志在惩诫。僧等震惧，夙夜惭惶，而圣鉴天临，仁泽昭被。笃深期于玄妙，掩纤垢于含弘，爰降殊恩，释兹严罚。非其人之足惜，顾斯法之可尊。遂令入网之鱼复游江汉，触笼之鸟还飏杳冥，法水混而更清，福田卤而还沃。僧等各深荷戴，人知自勉，庶当励情去恶，以副天心；专精礼念，用答鸿造。伏惟皇帝、皇后以绍隆之功，永凝百福；乘慈悲之业，端拱万春。震域缔祥，维城具美。不胜舞跃感荷之至，谨重附表陈谢以闻。轻黩冕旒，伏增惶恐。

帝览表，知法师病愈，遣使迎法师入，安置于凝阴殿院之西阁供养。仍彼翻译，或经二旬、三旬方乃一出。

冬十月，中宫在难，归依三宝，请垂加祐。法师启曰：“圣体必安和无苦，然所怀者是男，平安之后愿听出家。”当蒙敕许。至十一月五日，皇后施法师衲袈裟一领，并杂物等数十件。法师启谢曰：

沙门玄奘启：垂赍衲并杂物等，捧对惊惭，不知比喻。且金缕上服，传自先贤，或无价衣，闻诸圣典，未有穷神尽妙，目击当如今之赐者也。观其均彩浓淡，敬君不能逾其巧；裁缝婉密，离娄无以窥其际。便觉烟霞入室，兰囿在身，旋俯自瞻，顿增荣价。昔道安言珍秦代，未遇此恩；支遁称礼晋朝，罕闻斯泽。唯玄奘庸薄，独窃洪私，顾宠循躬，弥深战汗。伏愿皇帝、皇后富众多之子孙，享无疆之福祚，长临玉镜，永御宝图，覆育群生，与天无极。不任惭佩之至。谨启谢闻。

施重词轻，不能宣尽。

五日申后，忽有一赤雀飞来止于御帐，玄奘不胜喜庆，陈表贺曰：

沙门玄奘言：玄奘闻白鸠彰瑞，表殷帝之兴；赤雀呈符，示周王之庆。是知穹昊降祥以明人事，其来久矣。玄奘今日申后酉前，于显庆殿庭帷内见有一雀，背羽俱丹，腹足咸赤，从南飞来，入帐止于御座，徘徊踊跃，貌甚从容。见是异禽，乃谓之曰："皇后在孕未遂分诞，玄奘深怀忧惧，愿乞平安；若如所祈，为陈喜相。"雀乃回旋蹀足，示平安之仪，了然解人意。玄奘深心欢喜，举手唤之，又徐徐相向，乃至逼之不惧，抚之不惊，左右之人咸悉共见。玄奘因为受三归，报其雅意。未及执捉，从其徘徊，遂复飞去。

伏惟皇帝、皇后德通神明，恩加兆庶，礼和乐洽，仁深义远，故使羽族呈祥，神禽效质，显子孙之盛，彰八百之隆，既为曩代之休符，亦是当今之灵贶。玄奘轻生有幸，肇属嘉祥，喜抃之深，不敢缄默，略疏梗概，谨以奏闻。若其羽翼之威仪，阳精之淳伟，历代之稽古，出见之方表，所不知也。谨言。

表进已，顷间有敕令使报法师："皇后分娩已讫，果生男，端正奇特，神光满院，自庭烛天。朕欢喜无已，内外舞跃，必不违所许，愿法师护念，号为'佛光王'。"

法师进贺曰：

沙门玄奘言：窃闻至道攸敷，启天人于载算；深期所感，诞玄圣于克岐。伏惟皇帝、皇后，情镜三空，化孚九有，故能辟垂旒于二谛，却走马于一乘。兰殿初歆，爰发俱胝之愿；

琎柯在孕，便结逾城之征。俾夫十号降灵，弘兹摄受；百神翼善，肃此宫闱。所以灾厉克清，安和载诞。七华俨以承步，九龙低而濯质。玄门伫迹，道树灵阴，虽昔之履帝呈祥，扪天表异，宁足以方斯感贶，匹此英猷？率土咏歌，喜皇階之纳佑；缁林勇锐，欣绀马之来游。伏愿无替前思，特令法服，靡局常恋，迴构良因。且帝子之崇，出处斯在；法王之任，高尚弥隆。加以功德无边，津梁载远，傥圣泽无舛，弘誓不移。窃谓殚四海之资，不足比斯檀行；倾十地之业，无以譬此福基。当愿皇帝、皇后百福凝华，齐辉北极；万春表寿，等固南山。罄娱乐于延龄，践萨云于遐劫。储君允茂，绥绍帝猷。宠蕃惟宜，翊亮王室。禋祳英胤，休祉日繁，标峻节于本枝，嗣芳尘于草座。玄奘滥偶丕运，局影禁门；贵匪德升，宠缘恩积。幸属国庆惟始，净业开基，踊跃之怀，尘粉无恨。不胜喜贺之至，谨奉表以闻。轻触威严，伏增战越。

佛光王生满三日，法师又进表曰：

沙门玄奘言：奘闻《易》嘉日新之义，《诗》美无疆子孙，所以周祚过期，汉历遐绪者，应斯道也。又闻龙门洄激，资源长而流远；桂树丛生，藉根深而芳蔼。伏惟皇运累圣相承，重规叠矩，积植仁义，浸润黎元，其来久也。由是二后光膺大宝，为子孙基，可谓根深源长矣。逮陛下受图，功业逾盛。还淳反素，迈三五之踪；制礼作乐，逸殷、周之轨。不恃黄屋为贵，以济兆庶为心。未明求衣，日昃忘食；一人端拱，万里廓清。虽成、康之隆，未至于此。是故卿云纷郁，江海无波；日域遵风，龙乡沐化。荡荡乎，巍巍乎，难得而备言矣！既而道格穹苍，明神降福；令月嘉辰，皇子载诞。天枝广茂，琼萼增敷；率土怀生，莫不庆赖。在于玄奘，特百恒情，岂直喜圣后之平安，实亦欣如来之有嗣。伏愿不违前敕，即听出家。移人王之胤，为法王之子，披着法服，制立法名，授以三皈，列于僧数。绍隆像化，阐播玄风，再秀禅林，重晖觉苑。追净眼之茂迹，践月盖之高踪。断二种缠，成无等觉。色身微妙，譬彼山王；焰网庄严，过于日月。然后荫慈云于大千之境，扬慧炬于百亿之洲，振法鼓而挫天魔，麾胜幡而摧外道，接沈流于倒海，扑燎火于邪山，竭烦恼之深河，碎无明之巨轂，为天人师，作调御士。唯愿：先庙、先灵，藉孙祉而升彼岸；皇帝、皇后，因子福而享万春；永握灵图，常临九域。子能如此，方名大孝，始曰荣亲。所以释迦弃国而务菩提，盖为此也。岂得以东平琐琐之善，陈思庸庸之才，并日而论优劣，同年而议深浅矣！谨即严衣棒钵，以望善来之宾；拂座清涂，用伫逾城之驾。不胜庆慰颙颙之至。谨奉表以闻。轻触宸威，追深战越。

当即受三归服袈裟，虽保傅养育，所居常近于法师。十二月五日，满月，敕为佛光王度七人，仍请法师为王剃发。法师进表谢曰：

沙门玄奘言：昨奉恩旨，令玄奘为佛光王剃发，并敕度七人。所剃之发，则王之烦恼落也；所度之僧，则王之侍卫具也。是用震动波旬之殿，踊跃净居之怀；弘愿既宣，景福弥盛。岂谓庸贱之手，得效伎于天肤；凡庶之人，蒙入道于嘉会。上下欣抃，悲喜交集。窃寻覆护之重，在褓所先；解脱之因，落饰为始。伏惟皇帝、皇后，道凝象外，福洽区中，所以光启妙门，聿修德本。所愿皇阶纳佑，玉扆延和；临百亿天下，毕千万岁期。佛光高子，乳哺惟宜；善神卫质，诸佛摩顶；增华睿哲之姿，允穆绍隆之寄。新度之僧荷泽既深，亦当翘勤道业，专精戒行；允嗣僧伦，伫当取草。不胜感荷之至，谨奉表以闻。

其日，法师又重庆佛光王满月，并进法服等。奏曰：

沙门玄奘言：窃闻抟风迅羽，累日而冲空；泻月明玑，逾旬而就满。是知禀灵物表，亮彩天中者，固以后发其姝，惟新厥美者矣。惟佛光王，资上善以缔祥，阐中和而育德。自微园降诞，天祠动瞻，睿气清襟，寝兴纳佑，玉颜秀表，晨夕增华。自非皇帝、皇后，慧日在躬，法流濯想，寄绍隆于盘石，启落饰于天人，其孰能福此褓衣，安兹乳哺，无灾无害，克岐克嶷者哉！今魄照初环，满月之姿盛矣；蓂枝再长，如莲之目倩兮。所以紫殿慰怀，黔首胥悦；七众归怙，四门伫鉴。岂唯日索后言，鹤駼待驭而已。玄奘幸蒙恩宠，许垂荫庇。师弟之望，非所庶几，同梵之情，实切怀抱。辄敢进金字《般若心经》一卷并函，《报恩经变》一部，袈裟法服一具，香炉宝子、香案、澡瓶、经架、数珠、锡杖、澡豆合各一，以充道具，以表私欢。所冀簉载弄于半璋，代辟邪于蓬矢。俾夫善神见而踊跃，弘誓因以坚固，轻用干奉，寔深悚惕。伏愿皇帝、皇后，尊迈拱辰，明兼合耀，结欢心于兆庶，享延龄于万春。少海澄辉，掩丕钊而取俊；宠蕃振美，轥间平以载驰。所愿佛光王，千佛摩顶，百福凝躯，德音日茂，善规丕相。不胜感荷，奉表以闻。

二年春二月，驾幸洛阳宫，法师亦陪从，并翻经僧五人、弟子各一人，事事公给。佛光王驾前而发，法师与王子同去，余僧居后。既到，安置积翠宫。

夏四月，车驾避暑于明德宫，法师又亦陪从，安置飞华殿。其宫南接皂涧，北跨洛滨，则隋之显仁宫也。

五月，敕法师还于积翠宫翻译。法师既奉帝旨，进表辞曰：

沙门玄奘言：伏蒙恩旨许令积翠宫翻经。仰佩优渥，情深喜戴；伏念违离，旋增悯然。玄奘功微勋府，道谢德科，而久紊荣章，镇荷曾覆；循涯知惧，临谷匪危。伏惟皇帝、皇后，圣哲含弘，仁慈亭育，故使万类取足，一物获安。而近隔兰除，听扬銮而悲结；甫瞻茨岭，想多豫而欣然。伏愿玉宇延和，仙桃荐寿；迈甘泉之清暑，等瑶水之佳游。所冀温树迎秋，凉飙造夏；候归轩于砥陌，俨幽锡于乔林。称庆万春，甘从九逝。不胜感恋之极。谨附表奉辞以闻，荒越在颜，冰火交虑。

法师在京之日，先翻《发智论》三十卷及《大毗婆沙》未了。至是有敕报法师曰：“其所欲翻经、论，无者先翻，有者在后。”

法师进表曰：

窃闻冕旒庸俗，咸竞前修；述作穷神，必归睿后。皇帝造物，玄猷远畅；掩王城于侯甸，光贝叶于羽陵。傍启译寮，降缉鸿序；腾照千古，流辉万叶。陛下纂承丕业，光敷远韵；神用日新，赏鉴无怠。玄奘滥沐天造，肃承明诏；每抚庸躬，恒深悚息。去月日奉敕，所翻经、论，在此无者宜先翻，旧有者在后翻。但《发智》、《毗婆沙论》有二百卷，此土先唯有半，但有百余卷，而文多舛杂，今更整顿翻之。去秋以来，已翻得七十余卷，尚有百三十卷未翻。此《论》于学者甚要，望听翻了。余经、论有详略不同，及尤舛误者，亦望随翻，以副圣述。

帝许焉。

法师少离京洛，因兹扈从，暂得还乡，游览旧廛，问访亲故，沦丧将尽。唯有姊一人，适瀛州张氏，遣迎，相见悲喜。问姊父母坟陇所在，躬自扫谒。为岁久荒颓，乃更详胜地，欲具棺椁而改葬。虽有此心，未敢专志。法师乃进表请曰：

沙门玄奘言：玄奘不天，夙钟荼蓼。兼复时逢隋乱，殡掩仓卒。日月不居，已经四十余载，坟垄颓毁，殆将湮灭。追惟平昔，情不自宁。谨与老姊一人，收捧遗柩，去彼狭陋，改葬西原。用答昊天，微申罔极。昨日蒙敕，放玄奘出三两日检校。但玄奘更无兄弟，唯老姊一人。卜远有期，用此月二十一日安厝。今观葬事，尚寥落未办，所赐三两日，恐不周匝。望乞天恩，听玄奘葬事了还。又婆罗门上客，今相随逐，过为率略，恐将嗤笑。不任缠迫忧惵之至，谨附表以闻。伏乞天覆云回，曲怜孤请。

帝览表，允其所请。仍敕所司，其法师营葬所须，并宜公给。法师既荷殊泽，又进启谢曰：

沙门玄奘启：玄奘殃深舋积，降罚明灵，不能殒亡，偷存今日。但灰律骤改，盈缺匪居，坟垄沦颓，草棘荒蔓，思易宅兆，弥历岁年，直为远隔关山，不能果遂。幸因陪从銮驾，得届故乡；允会宿心，遂兹改厝。陈设所须，复蒙皇帝、皇后曲降天慈，赐遣营佐。不谓日月之光，在瓦砾而犹照；云雨之泽，虽蓬艾而必沾。感戴屏营，喜鲠兼集，不任存亡衔佩之至，谨附启谢闻。事重人微，不能宣尽。

法师既蒙敕许，遂改葬焉。其营送威仪，并公家资给。时洛下道俗赴者万余人。

后魏孝文皇帝自代徙都洛阳，于少室山北造少林伽蓝，因地势之高卑，有上方、下方之称，都一十二院。东据嵩岳，南面少峰，北依高岭，兼带三川。耸石巉岩，飞泉萦映，松萝共筼筜交葛，桂柏与杞梓萧森，壮婉清虚，实域中之佳所。其西台最为秀丽，即菩提流支译经处，又是跋陀禅师宴坐之所，见有遗身定塔。大业之末，群贼以火焚之，不然，远近珍异。寺西北岭下缑氏县之东南凤凰谷陈村，亦名“陈堡谷”，即法师之生地也。

秋九月二十日，法师请入少林寺翻译。表曰：

沙门玄奘言：玄奘闻菩提路远，趣之者必假资粮；生死河深，渡之者须凭船筏。资粮者，三学三智之妙行，非宿舂之类也；船筏者，八忍八观之净业，非方舟之徒也。是以诸佛具而升彼岸，凡夫阙而沉生死。由是茫茫三界，俱漂七漏之河；浩浩四生，咸溺十缠之浪。莫不波转烟回，心迷意醉；穷劫石而靡殆，尽芥城而弥固。曾不知驾三车而出火宅，乘八正而适宝坊，实可悲哉！岂直秋之为气，良增叹矣！宁惟孔父之情，所以未尝不临食辍餐，当寐而惊者也。玄奘每惟此身众缘假合，念念无常，虽岸树井藤不足以俦危脆，干城水沫无以譬其不坚，所以朝夕是期，无望长久。而岁月如流，六十之年，飒焉已至。念兹遄速，则生涯可知。加复少因求法，寻访师友，自他邦国，无处不经，途路遐遥，身力疲竭。顷年已来，更增衰弱。顾阴视景，能复几何？既资粮未充，前途渐促，无日不以此伤嗟，笔墨陈之不能尽也。

然轻生多幸，属逢明圣，蒙先朝不次之泽，荷陛下非分之恩，沐浴隆慈，岁月久矣。至于增名益价，发誉腾声；无翼而飞，坐凌霄汉；受四事之供，超伦辈之华；求之古人，所未有也！玄奘何德何功，以至于此！皆是天波广润，日月曲临，遂使燕石为珍，驽骀取贵。抚躬内省，唯深惭恧！且害盈恶满，乃前哲之雅旨；少欲知足，亦诸佛之诚言。玄奘自揆艺业空虚，名行无取；天慈圣泽，无宜久冒。望乞骸骨，毕命山林；礼诵经行，以答提奖。又蒙陛下以轮王之尊，布法王之化；西域所得经本，并令翻译。玄奘猥承人乏，滥当斯任。既奉天旨，夙夜匪宁。今已翻出六百余卷，皆三藏、四含之宗要，大、小二乘之枢轴；凡圣行位之林薮，八万法门之海泽。西域称咏，以为镇国镇方之典。所须文义，无披不得。譬犹择木邓林，随求小大；收珍海浦，任取方圆。学者之宗，斯为仿佛。玄奘用此奉报国恩，诚不能尽，虽然，亦冀万分之一也。

但断伏烦恼，必定慧相资，如车二轮，阙一不可。至如研味经、论，慧学也；依林宴坐，定学也。玄奘少来，颇得专精教义，唯于四禅九定未暇安心。今愿托虑禅门，澄心定水，制情猿之逸躁，絷意象之奔驰，若不敛迹山中，不可成就。

窃承此州嵩高少室，岭嶂重叠，峰涧多奇，含孕风云，包蕴仁智，果药丰茂，萝薜清虚，实海内之名山，域中之神岳。其间复有少林伽蓝、闲居寺等，皆跨枕岩壑，萦带林泉，佛事尊严，房宇闲邃。即后魏三藏菩提留支译经之处也，实可依归，以修禅观。又两疏朝士，尚解归海辞荣；巢、许俗人，犹知栖真蕴素。况玄奘出家为法，翻滞阛中，清风激人，念之增愧者也！

伏惟陛下明逾七曜，照极九幽。伏乞亮此愚诚，特垂听许，使得绝嚣尘于众俗，卷影迹于人间；陪麋鹿之群，随凫鹤之侣。栖身片石之上，庇影一树之阴；守察心猿，观法实相。令四魔九结之贼，无所穿窬；五忍十行之心，相从引发。作菩提之由渐，为彼岸之良因。外不累于皇风，内有增于行业。以此送终，天之恩也。傥蒙矜许，则庐山慧远，雅操庶追；剡岫道林，清徽望续。仍冀禅观之余，时间翻译。无任乐愿之至，谨诣阙奉表以闻。轻触宸威，追深战越。

帝览表不许。

其月二十一日，神笔自报书曰：

省表知欲晦迹岩泉，追林、远而驾往；讬虑禅寂，轨澄、什以标今。仰挹风徽，实所钦尚！朕业空学寡，靡究高深。然以浅识薄闻，未见其可。法师津梁三界，汲引四生，智皎心灯，定凝意水。非情尘之所翳，岂识浪之能惊！道德可居，何必太华叠岭？空寂可舍，岂独少室重峦？幸戢来言，勿复陈请。则市朝大隐，不独贵于昔贤；见闻弘益，更可珍于即代。

敕既令断表，不敢更言。法师既奉敕书，进启谢曰：

沙门玄奘言：使人李君信至，垂赐手诏。银钩丽于丹字，睿藻蔚彼河图；磊落带峰岳之形，郁润挹风云之气。不谓白藏之暮，更睹春葩之文；身居伊、洛之涧，忽瞩昆、荆之宝。捧对欢欣，手舞足蹈。昔季重蒙魏君之札，唯叙睽离；慧远辱晋帝之书，才令给米。未睹词兼空寂可舍之旨，诲示大隐朝市之情。固知圣主之怀，穷真罄俗，综有该无，超羲、轩而更高，驾曹、马而逾远者矣。但玄奘素丝之质，尤畏朱蓝，葛虆之身，实希松杞。思愿媲烟霞于少室，偶泉石于嵩阿；允避溺之情，终防火之志。所以敢竭愚瞽，昧死陈闻，庶陶甄之慈，无遗凫鹥；云雨之泽，不弃蛛蝥。而明诏霈临，不垂亮许。仍降恩奖，曲存辉贲。五情战惧，不知所守。既戢来言，不敢更请。谨附表谢闻，唯增悚越。

冬十一月五日，佛光王晬日，法师又进法衣一具上佛光王。表曰：

沙门玄奘言：玄奘闻兰荣紫畹，过之者必观；桂茂青溪，逢之者斯悦。卉木犹尔，况人伦乎，况圣胤乎？伏惟皇帝、皇后，挹神睿之姿，怀天地之德，抚宁区夏，子育群生。兼复大建伽蓝，广兴福聚。益宝图常恒不变之业，助鼎命金刚坚固之因。既妙善熏修，故使皇太子机神日茂，潞王懿杰逾明。佛光王岐嶷增朗，可谓超周越商，与黄帝比崇，子子孙孙，万年之庆者也。玄奘猥以庸微，时得参见王等，私心踊悦，诚欢诚喜。今是佛光王诞晬之日，礼有献贺，辄率愚怀，谨上法服一具。伏愿王子，万神拥卫，百福扶持，寤寐安和，乳哺调适。绍隆三宝，摧伏四魔，行菩萨行，继如来事。不胜琼萼天枝，英华美茂，欢喜之至。谨附表并衣以闻。轻触宸严，追深战越。

法师时在积翠宫翻译，无时暂辍，积气成疾。奏帝，帝闻之不悦，即遣供奉内医吕弘哲宣敕慰问法师。法师悲喜不已，进表谢曰：

沙门玄奘言：使人吕弘哲等至，宣敕慰问玄奘所患，并许出外将息。慈旨忽临，尪骸用起，若对旒冕，如置冰泉。玄奘摄慎乖方，疾瘵仍集。自违离銮跸，倍觉婴缠，心痛背闷，骨酸肉楚，食眠顿绝，气息渐微，恐有不图，点秽宫宇。思欲出外，自屏沟壑，仍恐惊动圣听，不敢即事奏闻。遂依门籍出至寺所，病既困劳转笃，心亦分隔明时。乃有尚药司医张德志为针疗，因渐瘳降，得存首领。还顾专辄之罪，自期粉墨之诛。伏惟日月之明，久谅愚拙；江海之泽，特肆含容。岂可移幸于至微，屈法于常典。望申公道，以穆宪司，枉狱为轻，伏鈇是俟。而残魂朽质，仍被恩光，抚臆言怀，用铭肌骨。自惟偃顿，非复寻常，纵微下里之忧，亦尽生涯之冀，但恨隆恩未答，末命先亏。

仰惟帝勤，亲劳薄狩，期于阅武，情在训戎。既昭仁于放麟，又策勋于献凤，遐迩庆集，上下欢并。风伯清尘，山祇护野；敬惟动止，固极休祯。申炯诫于十旬，浃辰而返；鄙宣游于八骏，密迩而旋。玉乘可伫，冰怀以慰；抚事恛惶，终期殒越。不胜荷惧之至，谨奉表待罪以闻。荒惴失图，伏听敕旨。

帝览表甚欢。经三日后，遣使迎法师入，四事供养，留连累日，敕送法师还积翠宫仍旧宣译焉。

冬十二月，改洛阳宫为东都。嫌封畿之褊隘，乃东分郑州之汜水、怀州之河阳，西废谷州，取宜阳、永宁、新安、渑池等县皆隶属焉。法师以乡邑增贵，修表贺曰：

沙门玄奘言：窃闻鹑首锡秦，上帝兆金城之据；龟图荐夏，中畿启玉泉之窥。是知灵贶所基，皇猷显属。吕诵由其卜远，高光所以阐期。允迪厥猷，率遵斯在。

伏惟皇帝、皇后，揆物裁务，悬衡抚俗。即土中之重隩，匝虞巡而驻跸；因旧制之瓌伟，仪镐京而建郛。仍以卑宫载怀，改作劳于曩役；驭奔在念，轸居逸于晨兴。自非折中华夷，均一傜输，岂能留连圣眷，焕汗纶言。是以令下之初，山川郁其改观；柘制爰始，烟云霏而动色。飞甍日丽，驰道风清，神期肸响，彝伦郁穆。若赋武昌之鱼，乐迁王里；争企云亭之鹤，愿奉属车。既小晋、郑之依，更褊刘、张之策。前王龌龊，丰、洛递开；我后牢笼，伊、咸并建。麟宗克茂，鼎祚惟远，自可东宴平乐，西临建章。伫吹笙而驻寿，秉在藻而流咏。荡荡至公，巍巍罕述。奘散材莫效，贻惧增深。但三川之郊，猥沾故里；千载之幸，郁为新邑。荜门虽翳，刍命犹存；喜编毂下，匪惭关外。况光宅之庆，遐迩所同欢；圣上允安，庸微所特荷。不胜喜抃之极，谨奉表陈谢以闻。

三年春正月，驾还西京，法师亦随归。

卷第十

起显庆三年正月随车驾自洛还西京
终至麟德元年二月玉华宫舍化

显庆三年正月，驾自东都还西京，法师亦随还。

秋七月，敕法师徙居西明寺。寺以元年秋八月戊子十九日造，时有敕曰："以延康坊濮王故宅为皇太子分造观、寺各一。"命法师案行其处，还奏地窄，不容两所，于是总用营寺，其观改就普宁坊。仍先造寺，以其年夏六月营造功毕。其寺面三百五十步，周围数里，左右通衢，腹背廛落。青槐列其外，渌水亘其间，亹亹耽耽，都邑仁祠，此为最也。而廊殿楼台，飞惊接汉，金铺藻栋，眩日晖霞。凡有十院，屋四千余间。庄严之盛，虽梁之同泰，魏之永宁，所不能及也。

敕先委所司简大德五十人、侍者各一人，后更令诠试业行童子一百五十人拟度。至其月十三日，于寺建斋度僧，命法师看度。至秋七月十四日，迎僧入寺，其威仪、幢盖、音乐等一如入慈恩及迎碑之则。敕遣西明寺给法师上房一口，新度沙弥（海会等）十人充弟子。

帝以法师先朝所重，嗣位之后礼敬逾隆，中使朝臣问慰无绝，嚫施绵帛、绫绵前后万余段，法服、纳、袈裟等数百事。法师受已，皆为国造塔及营经像，给施贫穷并外国婆罗门客等，随得随散，无所贮畜。发愿造十俱胝像，百万为十俱胝，并造成矣。

东国重于《般若》，前代虽翻，不能周备，众人更请委翻。然《般若》部大，京师多务，又人命无常，恐难得了，乃请就于玉华宫翻译。帝许焉。即以四年冬十月，法师从京发向玉华宫，并翻经大德及门徒等同去，其供给诸事一如京下，到彼安置肃诚院焉。

至五年春正月一日，起首翻《大般若经》。梵本总有二十万颂，文既广大，学徒每请删略。法师将顺众意，如罗什所翻，除繁去重。作此念已，于夜梦中即有极怖畏事以相警诫，或见乘危履险，或见猛兽搏人，流汗战栗，方得免脱。觉已惊惧，向诸众说，还依广翻。夜中乃见诸佛菩萨眉间放光，照触己身，心意怡适；法师又自见手执华灯供养诸佛；或升高座为众说法，多人围绕，赞叹恭敬；或梦见有人奉己名果。觉而喜庆，不敢更删，一如梵本。

佛说此经凡在四处：一，王舍城鹫峰山；二，给孤独园；三，他化自在天王宫；四，王舍城竹林精舍。总一十六会，合为一部。然法师于西域得三本，到此翻译之日，文有疑错，即校三本以定之，殷勤省覆，方乃著文，审慎之心，古来无比。或文乖旨奥，意有踌蹰，必觉异境，似若有人授以明决，情即豁然，若披云睹日。自云：“如此悟处，岂奘浅怀所通，并是诸佛菩萨所冥加耳。”

经之初会有《严净佛土品》，中说诸菩萨摩诃萨众为般若波罗蜜故，以神通愿力，盛大千界上妙珍宝、诸妙香华、百味饮食、衣服、音乐、随意所生五尘妙境种种供养，严说法处。时玉华寺主慧德及翻经僧嘉尚，其夜同梦见玉华寺内广博严净，绮饰庄严，幢帐、宝舆、华幡、伎乐盈满寺中，又见无量僧众手执华盖，如前供具，共来供养《大般若经》。寺内衢巷墙壁皆庄绮饰，地积名华，众共履践。至翻经院，其院倍加胜妙，如经所载，宝庄严土。又闻院内三堂讲说，法师在中堂敷演。既睹此已，欢喜惊觉，俱参法师说所梦事。法师云：“今正翻此品，诸菩萨等必有供养。诸师等见信有是乎？”时殿侧有双柰树，忽于非时数数开华，华皆六出，鲜荣红白，非常可爱。时众详议，云是《般若》再阐之征。又六出者，表六到彼岸。然法师翻此经时，汲汲然恒虑无常，谓诸僧曰：“玄奘今年六十有五，必当卒命于此伽蓝，经部甚大，每惧不终，人人努力加勤，勿辞劳苦。”

至龙朔三年冬十月二十三日，方乃绝笔，合成六百卷，称为《大般若经》焉。合掌欢喜，告徒众曰：“此经于此地有缘，玄奘来此玉华寺者，经之力也。向在京师，诸缘牵乱，岂有了时。今得终讫，并是诸佛冥加，龙天拥祐。此乃镇国之典，人天大宝，徒众宜各踊跃欣庆。”

时玉华寺都维那寂照，庆贺功毕，设斋供养。是日请经从肃诚殿往嘉寿殿斋所讲读。当迎经时，《般若》放光，照烛远迩，兼有非常香气。法师谓门人曰：“经自记此方当有乐大乘者国王、大臣、四部徒众，书写受持，读诵流布，皆得生天，究竟解脱。既有此文，不可缄默。”

至十一月二十二日，令弟子窥基奉表闻，请御制经序。至十二月七日，通事舍人冯义宣敕垂许。

法师翻《般若》后，自觉身力衰竭，知无常将至，谓门人曰：“吾来玉华，本缘《般若》。今经事既终，吾生涯亦尽。若无常后，汝等遣吾宜从俭省，可以蘧蒢裹送，仍择山涧僻处安置，勿近宫寺。不净之身宜须屏远。”门徒等闻之哀哽，各抆泪启曰：“和尚气力尚可，尊颜不殊于旧，何因忽出此言？”法师曰：“吾自知之，汝何由得解。”

麟德元年春正月朔一日，翻经大德及彼寺众殷勤启请翻《大宝积经》。法师见众情专至，俛仰翻数行讫，便收梵本停住，告众曰：“此经部轴与《大般若》同，玄奘自量气力不复办此，死期已至，势非赊远。今欲往兰芝等谷礼拜辞俱胝佛像。”于是与门人同出，僧众相顾莫不潸然。礼讫还寺，专精行道，遂绝翻译。

至八日，有弟子高昌僧玄觉，因向法师自陈所梦，见有一浮图端严高大，忽然崩倒，见已惊起，告法师。法师曰：“非汝身事，此是吾灭谢之征。”

至九日暮间，于房后度渠，脚跌倒，胫上有少许皮破，因即寝疾，气候渐微。

至十六日，如从梦觉，口云：“吾眼前有白莲华，大于盘，鲜净可爱。”十七日，又梦见百千人，形容伟大，俱着锦衣，将诸绮绣及妙华珍宝，从法师所卧房室以次庄严，遍翻经院内外，爰至院后山岭林木，悉竖幡幢，众彩间错，并奏音乐；门外又见无数宝舆，舆中香食美果色类百千，并非人中之物，各各擎来供养于法师。法师辞曰：“如此珍味，证神通者方堪得食。玄奘未阶此位，何敢辄受。”虽此推辞，而进食不止。侍人謦欬，遂尔开目，因向寺主慧德具说前事。

法师又云：“玄奘一生以来所修福慧，准斯相貌，欲似功不唐捐，信如佛教因果并不虚也。”

遂命嘉尚法师，具录所翻经、论，合七十四部，总一千三百三十五卷。又录造俱胝画像、弥勒像，各一千帧，又造素像十俱胝，又写《能断般若》、《药师》、《六门陀罗尼》等经各一千部，供养悲、敬二田各万余人，烧百千灯，赎数万生。录讫，令嘉尚宣读，闻已合掌喜庆。又告门人曰：“吾无常期至，意欲舍堕，宜命有缘总集。”于是罄舍衣资，更令造像，并请僧行道。

至二十三日，设斋嚫施。其日又命塑工宋法智于嘉寿殿竖菩提像骨已，因从寺众及翻经大德并门徒等乞欢喜辞别，云：“玄奘此毒身深可厌患，所作事毕，无宜久住，愿以所修福慧回施有情，共诸有情同生睹史多天弥勒内眷属中，奉事慈尊，佛下生时，亦愿随下广作佛事，乃至无上菩提。”辞讫，因默正念，时复口中诵：“色蕴不可得，受想行识亦不可得；

眼界不可得，乃至意界亦不可得；眼识界不可得，乃至意识界亦不可得；无明不可得，乃至老死亦不可得；乃至菩提不可得，不可得亦不可得。”复口说偈，教傍人云：“南无弥勒、如来应正等觉，愿与含识速奉慈颜，南无弥勒、如来所居内众，愿舍命已，必生其中。”时寺主慧德又梦见有千躯金像从东方来，下入翻经院，香华满空。

至二月四日夜半，瞻病僧明藏禅师见有二人各长一丈许，共捧一白莲华如小车轮，华有三重，叶长尺余，光净可爱，将至法师前。擎华人云：“师从无始已来所有损恼有情，诸有恶业，因今小疾并得消殄，应生欣庆。”法师顾视，合掌良久，遂以右手而自搘颐，次以左手申左髀上，舒足重累右胁而卧，暨乎属纩竟不回转，不饮不食。

至五日夜半，弟子光等问云：“和尚决定得生弥勒内众不？”法师报云：“得生。”言讫，气息渐微。少间神游，侍人不觉。属纩方委，从足渐冷，最后顶暖，颜色赤白，怡悦胜常，过七日竟无改变，亦无异气。自非定慧庄严，戒香资被，孰能致此。

又慈恩寺僧明慧业行精苦，初中后夜念诵经行，无时懈废，于法师亡夜夜半后，旋绕佛堂行道，见北方有白虹四道从北亘南贯井宿，直至慈恩塔院，皎洁分明，心怪所以。即念昔如来灭度，有白虹十二道从西方直贯太微，于是大圣迁化。今有此相，将非玉华法师有无常事耶？天晓向众说其所见，众咸怪之。至九日旦，凶问至京，正符虹现之象，闻者嗟其感异。

法师形长七尺余，身赤白色，眉目疏朗，端严若神，美丽如画；音词清远，言谈雅亮，听者无厌；或处徒众，或对嘉宾，一坐半朝，身不倾动；服尚乾陀，裁唯细氎，修广适中；行步雍容，直前而视，辄不顾眄。滔滔焉若大江之纪地，灼灼焉类芙蕖之在水。加以戒范端凝，始终如一，爱惜之意过护浮囊，持戒之坚超逾草系。性爱怡简，不好交游，一入道场，非朝命不出。

法师亡后，西明寺上座道宣律师有感神之德，至乾封年中见有神现，自云："弟子是韦将军，诸天之子，主领鬼神。如来欲入涅槃，敕弟子护持赡部遗法，比见师戒行清严，留心律部，四方有疑皆来咨决，所制轻重仪，时有乖错。师年寿渐促，文记不正，便误后人，以是故来示师佛意。"

因指宣所出律抄及轻重仪僻谬之处，并令改正。宣闻之悚栗悲喜，因问经、律、论等心所不决者，神并为决之。又问古来传法之僧德位高下，并问法师。

神答云："自古诸师解行互有短长而不一准。且如奘师一人，九生已来备修福慧，生生之中多闻博洽，聪慧辩才，于赡部洲支那国常为第一，福德亦然。其所翻译，文质相兼，无违梵本。由善业力，今见生睹史多天慈氏内众，闻法悟解，更不来人间受生。"神授语已，辞别而还。宣因录入别记，见西明寺藏矣。据此而言，自非法师高才懿德，乃神明知之，岂凡情所测度。

法师病时，检校翻经使人许玄备以其年二月三日奏云："法师因损足得病。"至其月七日，敕中御府宜遣医人将药往看。

所司即差供奉医人张德志、程桃捧将药急赴。比至，法师已终，医药不及。时坊州刺史窦师伦奏法师已亡，帝闻之哀恸伤感，为之罢朝，数曰“朕失国宝矣！”时文武百寮莫不悲哽流涕，帝言已呜噎，悲不能胜。翌日，又谓群臣曰：“惜哉！朕国内失奘法师一人，可谓释众梁摧矣，四生无导矣。亦何异苦海方阔，舟楫遽沈；暗室犹昏，灯炬斯掩！”帝言已，嗟惋不止。

至其月二十六日，下敕曰：“窦师伦所奏玉华寺僧玄奘法师已亡，葬事所须并令官给。”至三月六日，又敕曰：“玉华寺奘法师既亡，其翻经之事且停。已翻成者，准旧例官为抄写；自余未翻者，总付慈恩寺守掌，勿令损失。其奘师弟子及同翻经先非玉华寺僧者，宜放还本寺。”至三月十五日，又有敕：“玉华寺故大德玄奘法师葬日，宜听京城僧尼造幡、盖，送至墓所。”法师道茂德高，为明时痛惜，故于亡后重叠降恩，求之古人无比此也。

于是门人遵其遗命，以籧篨为舆，奉神柩还京，安置慈恩寺翻经堂内。弟子数百哀号动地，京城道俗奔赴哭泣，日数百千。以四月十四日将葬浐东，都内僧尼及诸士庶，共造殡送之仪，素盖、幡幢、泥洹、帐舆、金棺、银椁、娑罗树等五百余事，布之街衢，连云接汉，悲笳凄挽，响匝穹宇，而京邑及诸州五百里内送者百万余人。虽复丧事华整，而法师神柩仍在籧篨本舆。东市绢行用缯彩三千匹结作泥洹舆，兼以华佩庄严，极为殊妙，请安法师神柩。门徒等恐亏师素志，因止之。乃以法师三衣及国家所施百金之纳置以前行，籧篨舆次其后，观者莫不流泪哽塞。是日缁素宿于墓所者三万余人。

十五日旦，掩坎讫，即于墓所设无遮会而散。是时天地变色，鸟兽鸣哀，物感既然，则人悲可悉。皆言爱河尚淼，慈舟遽沈，永夜犹昏，慧灯先灭。攀恋之痛如亡眼目，不直比之山颓木坏而已。惜哉！

至总章二年四月八日，有敕徙葬法师于樊川北原，营建塔宇。盖以旧所密迩京郊，禁中多见，时伤圣虑，故改卜焉。至于迁殡之仪，门徒哀感，行侣悲恸，切彼如初。呜呼！

释慧立论曰：

观夫夜星霄月继西日之明，三江九河助东溟之大；相资之道在物既然，传袭之风于人岂异。自法王潜耀之后，阿难结集已来，岁越千年，时逾十代。圣贤间出，英睿递生，各韫雄图，俱包上智，负荷遗法，控御天人，道制风飙，神倾海岳。或舒指而流膏液，或异室而朗奇光，或连尸以伏天魔，或一对而回时主。或愿通法于边刹，冒浪波于险涂；或虚己以应物，求裹粮而行死地。终令玄津溢漾，惠济无疆，既益传灯，实符付嘱，考之前册，可不然哉！而清源不穷，今复遇法师嗣承之矣。

惟法师星像降灵，山岳腾气，才过东箭，誉美南金，雅操不群，坚芳独拔。以四生为己任，建正法为身事；巍巍乎似嵩、华之负穹苍，皎皎焉若琅玕之映澄海。而聪机俊骨，发于自然；味道轻荣，率由天性。至夫多识洽闻之奥，冠恒、肇而逾高；详玄造微之功，跨生、融而更远。滔滔乎，荡荡乎，实绍隆之器也。神之将使像化重光于颓季之期，故诞兹明德者矣。法师以今古大德，阐扬经、论，虽复俱依圣教，而引据不同，诤论纷然，其来自久。至如黎耶是报非报，化人有心无心，和合怖数之徒闻熏灭不灭等，百有余科，并三藏四含之檠根，大小两宗之钳键，先贤之所不决，今哲之所共疑。法师亦踌躕此文，怏怏斯旨，慨然叹曰："此地经、论，盖法门枝叶，未是根源。诸师虽各起异端，而情疑莫遣，终须括囊大本，取定于祇洹耳。"

由是壮志发怀，驰心遐外。以贞观三年秋八月立誓束装，拂衣而去。到中天竺那烂陀寺，逢大法师名"尸罗跋陀"，此曰"戒贤"。其人体二居宗，神鉴奥远，博闲三藏，善四《韦陀》。于《十七地论》最为精熟，以此论该冠众经，亦偏常宣讲，元是弥勒菩萨所造，即摄大乘之根系，是法师发轫之所祈者。十六大国靡不归宗，禀义学徒恒有万许。法师既往修造，一面尽欢，以为相遇之晚。于是伏膺听受，兼咨决所疑，一遍便覆，无所遗忘。譬蒙汜之纳群流，若孟诸之吞云梦。彼师嗟怪，叹未曾有，云："若斯人者，闻名尚难，岂谓此时共谈玄耳。"法师从是声振葱岭，名流八国。彼诸先达英杰闻之，皆宿构重关，共来难诘，雁行鱼累，毂驾肩随，其并论之词，云屯雨至。法师从容辩释，皆入其室、操其戈，取其矛、击其盾，莫不人人丧辙，解颐虔伏，称为此公天纵之才，难酬对也。戒日王等见之抃喜，皆肘步呜足，倾珍供养。

罢席之后，更学梵书，并余经、论。自如来一代所说，耆山方等之教，鹿苑半字之文，爰至后圣马鸣、龙树、无着、天亲诸所制作，及灰山住等十八异执之宗，五部殊涂之致，并收罗研究，达其旨、得其文。并佛处世之迹，如泥洹坚固之林，降魔菩提之树，迦路崇高之塔，那揭留影之山，皆躬伸礼敬，备睹灵奇，亦无遗矣。

法师心期既满，学览复周，将旋本土，遂缮写大小乘法教六百余部，请像七躯，舍利百有余粒，以今十九年春正月二十五日还至长安。道俗奔迎，倾都罢市。是时也，烟收雾卷，景丽风清，宝帐盈衢，华幢掩日。庆云垂彩于天表，郁郁纷纷；庶士咏赞于通庄，轰轰隐隐。邪风于焉顿戢，慧日赫以重明。虽不逢世尊从忉利之下阎浮，此亦足为千载之休美也。

法师此行经涂数万，备历艰危。至如涸阴冱寒之山，飞涛激浪之壑，厉毒黑风之气，狻猊貙豻之群，并法显失侣之乡，智严遗伴之地，班超之所不践，章、亥之所未游。法师孑尔孤征，坦然无梗，扇唐风于八河之外，扬国化于五竺之间，使乎遐域侯王驰心辇毂，远方酋长系仰天衢，虽法师不世之功，抑亦圣朝运昌感通之力也。

皇帝握龙图而纂历，应赤服以君临，戮鲸豕以济群生，荡云霓而光日月。正四维之绝柱，息沧海之横流，重立乾坤，再施镕造。九功包于虞、夏，七德冠于曹、刘。海晏河清，时和岁阜；远无不顺，迩无不安；天成地平，人庆神悦。加以重明丽正，三善之义克隆；宰辅忠勤，良哉之歌斯允。既而功穷厚载，德感上玄；紫芝含秀于玉阶，华果结英于朱阁，又如西州石瑞，松县琨符，纪圣主千年之期，显储君嗣承之业。凤毛才子之句，上果佛日之文，历万古而不闻，当我皇而始出。岂非明灵辅德，玄天福眷者焉。加复游心真际，城堑五乘，追思鹫岭之容，伫想提河之说。故使遗形绀发，焕彩来仪；胜典高僧，相辉而至。慈云布于六合，法鼓振于三千，天华将景风共飞，翠雾与香烟同馥，于是溺俗沈流之士，望涯岸而有期；清虚蹈玄之宾，顾三空而非远。所谓司南启路，而众惑知方；商飙袭林，而群籁自响。法师盛德也如彼，逢时也如此，岂同雅、澄怀道，遇二石之凶残；安、什传经，值符、姚之伪历。校之深浅，即行潦之类江湖；比之明闇，乃朝阳之与萤曜矣。

昔钟玦既至，魏文奉赋以赞扬；神雀斯呈，贾逵献颂而论异。在禽物之微贱，古人犹且咏歌，况法师不朽之神功，栋梁之大业，岂可缄默于明时而无称述者也。立学愧往贤，德非先达，直以同沾像化，叨厕末尘，欣慕之怀，百于恒品，所以力课庸愚，辄申斯传。其清徽令望之美，绝后光前之踪，别当分诸鸿笔，非此所能觑缕也。冀明鉴君子收意而不哂焉。

赞曰：

生灵感绝，大圣迁神；其能绍继，唯乎哲人。

马鸣先唱，提婆后申；如日斯隐，朗月方陈。

穆矣法师，谅为贞士；迥秀天人，不羁尘滓。

穷玄之奥，究儒之理；洁若明珠，芬同蕙芷。

悼经之阙，疑义之错；委命询求，陵危践壑。

恢恢器宇，赳赳诚恪；振美西州，归功东阁。

属逢有道，时唯我皇；重悬玉镜，再理珠囊。

三乘既阐，十地兼扬；俾夫慧日，幽而更光。

粤余庸眇，幸参尘末；长自蓬门，靡雕靡括。

高山斯仰，清流是渴；愿得攀依，比之藤葛。

释彦悰笺述曰：

余观佛教东土已来，英俊贤明，舍家入道者万计，其中罕能兼善，一二美者有焉。至若视听貌言，洽闻强识；轻生重道，绝域遐征，贞操劲松筠，雅志陵金石；群雄革虑，圣主回光者，于三藏备之矣。抑又闻之，三藏当盛暑之辰，体无沾液；祁寒之际，貌不惨凄；不夭不申，不欠不嚏，斯盖未详其地位，何贤圣之可格哉！又北宫现疾之时，征庆繁缛；将终之日，色貌敷愉，亦难得而测也！及终后月余日，有人赍栴檀末香至，请依西国法以涂三藏身，众咸莫之许。其人作色曰："弟子别奉进止，师等若不许，请录状以闻。"众从之。及开棺发殓已，人觉异香等莲华之气，互相惊问，皆云若兹。向人除并殓衣，唯留衬服，众睹三藏貌如生人，百姓号绝共视。向人涂香服殓盖棺已，俄失所在，众疑天人焉。余考三藏夙心，稽其近迹，自非摩诃萨埵其孰若之乎？曰我同俦，幸希景仰，勖哉！

图书代号　SK24N0556

图书在版编目(CIP)数据

大唐大慈恩寺三藏法师传：汉英对照 / （唐）慧立，（唐）彦悰撰、笺；王欣译. — 西安：陕西师范大学出版总社有限公司，2024.7
（玄奘法师经典译丛）
ISBN 978-7-5695-3924-0

Ⅰ. ①大… Ⅱ. 。①慧… ②彦… ③王… Ⅲ. ①玄奘（602-664）—传记—汉、英 Ⅳ. ①B949.92

中国国家版本馆CIP数据核字（2023）第187383号

大唐大慈恩寺三藏法师传（汉英对照）

DA TANG DA CIENSI SANZANG FASHI ZHUAN (HAN-YING)

[唐]慧立　撰　彦悰　笺　王欣　译

出 版 人　刘东风
责任编辑　陈柳冬雪
责任校对　王红凯
特约审稿　龙达瑞
封面设计　观止堂
出版发行　陕西师范大学出版总社
（西安市长安南路199号　邮编 710062）
网　　址　http://www.snupg.com
印　　刷　山东临沂新华印刷物流集团有限责任公司
开　　本　880 mm×1240 mm　1/32
印　　张　26.125
插　　页　4
字　　数　260千
版　　次　2024年7月第1版
印　　次　2024年7月第1次印刷
书　　号　ISBN 978-7-5695-3924-0
定　　价　98.00元

读者购书、书店添货或发现印刷装订问题，请与本公司营销部联系、调换。
电话：（029）85307864　85303629　传真：（029）85303879